Directors' Duties

Third Edition

Directors' Duties

Andrew Keay LLB, M Div, LLM, PhD

Professor of Corporate and Commercial Law
Centre for Business Law and Practice
School of Law
University of Leeds

Professorial Research Fellow
Deakin Law School
Deakin University
Melbourne
Barrister, Kings Chambers (Manchester, Leeds and Birmingham)
Legal Practitioner (Aust)

Published by LexisNexis

LexisNexis
Regus
Terrace Floor
Castlemead
Lower Castle Street
Bristol BS1 3AG

British Library Cataloguing-in-Publication Data

A catalogue record for this book is available from the British Library.

ISBN 978 1 78473 221 9

Typeset by Letterpart Limited, Caterham on the Hill, Surrey CR3 5XL

Printed in Great Britain by Hobbs the Printers Limited, Totton, Hampshire SO40 3WX

PREFACE TO THE THIRD EDITION

Since the first edition was published, not long after all the provisions in the Companies Act 2006 dealing with the general duties had been put into force, there was little case-law that was available on the provisions that facilitated interpretation of the provisions, although we did have, of course, existing case-law that had been decided on the previous common law rules and equitable principles. Notwithstanding the fact that some of the codified duties have been in operation for in excess of nine years we still do not have a huge corpus of case-law on any provisions, and little on some provisions. Nevertheless, we have seen since the publication of the second edition of this book several important cases and some interesting debate and discussion concerning the interpretation and application of the provisions. This edition seeks to address those cases and the discussion that has been forthcoming as well including some discussion or mention of, where relevant, recent academic scholarship.

Most chapters of the book have been expanded or revised in some way, and some, such as Chapters 2, 4, 5, 6, 8, 9, 11, 13, 14 and 15, have, to varying degrees, been significantly revised and/or expanded. This has been due to the advent of cases that have been decided in the areas covered by these chapters and my reflection on what I wrote in the earlier editions. In some places, such as in Chapter 4 with the issue of the limitation of actions, I felt that while I did not want to engage in sustained examination of the area, further elaboration of what I included in the earlier editions was warranted.

As indicated above, consideration has been given to, or mention of, cases decided since the last edition, and which I have deemed relevant, and these *include* the UK Supreme Court decisions in *Williams v Central Nigeria Bank, Eclairs Group Ltd v JKX Oil & Gas plc, AIB Group (GB) v Redler* and *FHR European Ventures LLP v Cedar Capital Partners LLC*, the Privy Council decision in *Central Bank of Ecuador v Conticorp SA*, the decisions of the Court of Appeal in *Burnden Holdings (UK) Ltd v Fielding, Goldtrail Travel Ltd v Aydin, Novoship (UK) Ltd v Nikitin* and *Smithton Ltd (formerly Hobart Capital Markets Ltd) v Naggar*, and decisions at first instance, such as *Bhullar v Bhullar, BTI 2014 LLC v Sequana SA, Re Cosy Seal Insulation Ltd, Re Finch plc, Wey Education plc v Atkins* and *Hook v Sumner*. Also included are the decisions of other superior common law courts, such as that of the Hong Kong Court of Final Appeal in *Chen Wai Too v Poon Ka Man Jason*, the Australian Federal Court in *ASIC v Mariner* and the New Zealand Court of

Appeal in *Morgenstern v Jeffreys*. I have also taken into account relevant recent academic and practitioner commentaries on aspects of the law.

I am again particularly thankful to my very supportive and insightful colleague, Joan Loughrey, for the fact that many of our discussions on directors have probably helped to shape some of the pages of this volume. Also I am thankful to other colleagues in the Centre for Business Law and Practice in the School of Law at the University of Leeds for their willingness to discuss issues and stimulate my thinking, and in this regard I thank Jingchen Zhao in particular. Outside of the School I would like to thank Daniel Attenborough, Chris Riley and Charlotte Villiers for some interesting discussions on directors from time to time that have probably indirectly informed my writing in this book.

I thank Mary Kenny from the publisher who was the initiating force behind the edition. Also, I thank Kate Hather for managing the production side of things. As usual, Kate was her normal efficient, helpful, supportive and pleasant self. I thank Cheryl Prophett for editorial assistance.

I have sought to state the law as at 1 August 2016.

Andrew Keay
Leeds

PREFACE TO THE SECOND EDITION

When the first edition was published, the Companies Act 2006 was in its infancy and the provisions of it that codified the duties of directors had not been put in force much before publication of the book. Since then while we have not had much in the way of case-law on some provisions, what case-law we have got indicates clearly that the courts will apply, where possible, the law extant at the time at which the codified provisions came into operation. Certainly the courts have followed section 170(5) and interpreted and applied the duties in the same way as common law rules and equitable principles and regard has been had to the corresponding common law rules and equitable principles in the interpretation and application of the codified duties.

Most chapters of the book have been expanded and some, such as chapters 5, 13, 14 and 15 and parts of Chapters 6, 8, and 9, significantly so. This has been due to the cases that have been decided in the areas covered by these Chapters. I have considered or mentioned all relevant cases decided since the publication of the last edition, including the English cases of *O'Donnell v Shanahan*, *Sinclair Investments v Versailles Trade Finance*, *Paycheck Services*, *Re UKLI Ltd*, *McKillen v Misland* and *GHLM Trading Ltd v Maroo*. Also, I have dealt with some of the more relevant and important Commonwealth cases such as the litigation in *Bell Group v Westpac Banking* in Western Australia, *ASIC v Healey* (the Centro litigation) and *Buzzle Operations*.

I am thankful to my very supportive colleague, Joan Loughrey, for permitting me to draw on a couple of papers that we wrote together, namely 'Derivative Proceedings in a Brave New World for Company Management and Shareholders' [2010] JBL 151 and 'An assessment of the present state of statutory derivative proceedings' in J Loughrey (ed) *Directors' Duties and Shareholder Litigation in the Wake of the Financial Crisis* (Cheltenham, Edward Elgar, 2013), Chapter 7. I am also thankful to her for the fact that many of our discussions on directors have probably helped to shape some of the pages of this volume.

I thank Mary Kenny and Kate Hather from the publisher for their work relating to this book, and for the editing assistance of Claire Banyard.

I have sought to state the law as at 30 August 2013, but at the proof stage I have been able to include some reference to cases decided after that date.

Andrew Keay
Leeds

PREFACE TO THE FIRST EDITION

I think that it is generally accepted that one of the most important and interesting aspects of company law is the law on directors' duties. Over the years it has certainly attracted a great deal of litigation and a significant number of cases have been reported, allowing for a sophisticated jurisprudence to develop. The enactment of the Companies Act 2006 sees a new development in directors' duties. After reliance on common law rules and equitable principles, the UK has finally decided to codify the law on the subject. It is rather ironic that the UK, which gave its company law to a significant portion of the world, mostly countries that are part of the Commonwealth, has lagged far behind many Commonwealth nations in taking this step. This is partly because a number of commentators and advisory committees to government have opposed the codification of duties.

This book deals solely with the general duties of directors that are set out in Chapter 2 of Part 10 of the Companies Act 2006. Essentially the book is a doctrinal exposition of the law with, because the law is in its early stages, some discussion of the way in which I think that the law will develop. In a few places I have made, without being too self-indulgent (I hope), submissions on the way that I think that the law ought to develop. Generally speaking I have refrained, save in Chapter 3 where I felt that the topic warranted it, from including theoretical considerations of the law.

Company law has been in something of a confusing state ever since the enactment of the Companies Act 2006 as the legislation is being implemented in stages. At the time of writing a large proportion of the Act is now in operation, and, critically, the sections that are most relevant to this book apply. However, a few sections that pertain to issues discussed in the book are not yet in force and, where this is the case, I have sought to note that either in the text or in footnotes.

The Part of the Companies Act that is the focus of the book is young, with some sections commencing operation as late as 1 October 2008. Obviously, there will be events with which practitioner and director readers, in particular, will be concerned, that pre-date the commencement of sections. In such a case 'the old law' (the common law rules and equitable principles) will apply to those events. Consequently, I do deal with many aspects of the pre-codified law. I do this also because clearly the codified provisions are heavily founded on the common law rules and equitable principles that have been developed for many years, and which operated prior to the advent of the codified regime. In addition, s 170(4) of the Act provides that the duties in the Act are to be interpreted and applied in the same way as the common law rules and equitable principles, and regard is to be had to the rules and principles in interpreting and applying the codified duties.

I have not cited all cases that have touched upon the issue of directors' duties. I have avoided citing a long list of authorities save where that is helpful. I have generally limited myself to citing the main cases that stand for particular propositions. Of course, I have mentioned most appellate cases as these have either laid down important statements of law or have interpreted existing law helpfully and are, naturally, binding on lower courts.

A number of people have kindly assisted me along the way in the production of this book. First, I express my sincere thanks to Leslie Kosmin QC for being kind enough to read and comment (graciously) on several draft chapters of the book, notwithstanding a busy life in practice, as well as providing me with encouragement. Of course, any errors are my responsibility.

Second, I would like to thank my colleague, Joan Loughrey, for permitting me to draw on our joint article, 'Something Old, Something New, Something Borrowed: An Analysis of the New Derivative Action Under the Companies Act 2006' (2008) 124 Law Quarterly Review 469-500 in a couple of chapters. Again, I am thankful to Joan and also to our former colleague, Dr Luca Cerioni (now of Brunel University), for permitting me to draw on our joint article, 'Legal Practitioners, Enlightened Shareholder Value and the Shaping of Corporate Governance' (2008) 8 Journal of Corporate Law Studies 79-111.

I am most thankful to several publishers for allowing me to draw upon material that I have had published by them in articles and books. I acknowledge that I use, with the permission of the named publishers, material from the following:

- Company Directors' Responsibilities to Creditors (Routledge-Cavendish, 2007).

- 'Something Old, Something New, Something Borrowed: An Analysis of the New Derivative Action Under the Companies Act 2006' (2008) 124 Law Quarterly Review 469-500 (Sweet and Maxwell).

- 'Legal Practitioners, Enlightened Shareholder Value and the Shaping of Corporate Governance' (2008) 8 Journal of Corporate Law Studies 79-111 (Hart Publishing).

- 'Tackling the Issue of the Corporate Objective: An Analysis of the United Kingdom's 'Enlightened Shareholder Value Approach' (2007) 29 Sydney Law Review 577-612 (Sydney University Law School).

- 'Section 172(1): An Interpretation and Assessment' (2007) 28 Company Lawyer 106-110 (Sweet and Maxwell).

- 'The Duty of Directors to Exercise Independent Judgment' (2008) 29 Company Lawyer 290-296 (Sweet and Maxwell).

- 'Enlightened shareholder value, the reform of the duties of company directors and the corporate objective' [2006] Lloyds Maritime and Commercial Law Quarterly 335-361 (Informa Publishing).

During the course of the book I have included some quotations from reports prepared by professional organisations and I am thankful for their kind permission in permitting me do so. I acknowledge the following organisations and the relevant publications:

- Institute of Chartered Secretaries and Administrators (*ICSA Guidance on Directors' General Duties* (February 2007));

- Association of Chartered Certified Accountants (and particularly John Davies *A Guide to Directors' Responsibilities Under the Companies Act 2006* (August 2007)).

- GC100 (the Association of General Counsel and Company Secretaries of the FTSE 100 companies) (*Companies Act 2006 – Directors' conflicts of interest* (Association of General Counsel and Company Secretaries of the FTSE 100, 18 January 2008)).

I am very grateful to Sarah Maddock who acted as the publisher's commissioning editor when this project was commissioned. I also wish to thank both Mary Kenny for liaising, on behalf of the publisher, with me, and Kate Hather for overseeing the editorial and production stage. Others at Jordan Publishing who have been of assistance in one form or another, and deserve thanks, are Sally Drever and Deborah Saunders.

Last, and by no means least, I thank my wife Rhonda for her unswerving support and for her understanding my need to research and write.

I have endeavoured to state the law as it was available to me as at 1 October 2008.

Andrew Keay
Leeds, October 2008

CONTENTS

TABLE OF CASES

References are to paragraph numbers.

TABLE OF STATUTES

References are to paragraph numbers.

TABLE OF STATUTORY INSTRUMENTS

References are to paragraph numbers.

CHAPTER 1

INTRODUCTION

1.1   The directors of companies play critical roles in the affairs of their companies and in relation to commercial life generally. Middleton J of the Federal Court of Australia said, in a very influential case, that:[1]

> 'A director is an essential component of corporate governance. Each director is placed at the apex of the structure of direction and management of a company. The higher the office that is held by a person, the greater the responsibility that falls upon him or her. The role of a director is significant as their actions may have a profound effect on the community, and not just shareholders, employees and creditors.'

1.2   As members of the board (of directors), directors direct the decision-making of a company and will oversee the management of companies. Companies, being legal but not human entities, need human agents to deal with the outside world. The number of directors around the world is large, and it was estimated a few years ago that there are about 2 million persons alone in the United Kingdom who are acting as directors.[2] Given growth since that time, there is likely to be more now. What directors do or do not do can have a significant effect on their companies' fortunes, and ultimately on those of shareholders and others who have an interest or a stake in companies. The law regards directors as fiduciaries because of their highly responsible and critical position in companies. The designation of fiduciary is only given to those in life who are in positions of control in relation to others and the affairs of others. The significance of the role of a director was summed up by Lord Goldsmith during debate on the Company Law Reform Bill 2005, when he said: 'But it is a position of great responsibility which involves running the affairs of a company for the benefit of other people. It is a heavy responsibility we should not water down.'[3]

1.3   The law imposes many responsibilities and obligations on directors to ensure that they deal fairly with their companies' affairs, although directors do not guarantee the profitability or eventual success of the business actions of the company. Within the broad range of responsibilities and obligations that the

---

[1]   *ASIC v Healey* [2011] FCA 717 at [14].
[2]   J De Lacy 'The Concept of a Company Director: Time for a New Expanded and Unified Concept?' [2006] JBL 276 at 276.
[3]   Lords Grand Committee, 6 February 2006, col 291. Also, see *Re Westmid Packing Services Ltd* [1998] 2 All ER 124 at 130; [1998] 2 BCLC 646 at 653.

law imposes on directors, the law requires directors to adhere to what it calls 'duties', and this book focuses on such duties. The word 'duty' is, as Professor Len Sealy pointed out, a slippery word,[4] and can have a wide ambit, so the book only deals with obligations placed on directors that the relevant companies legislation, the Companies Act 2006 (CA 2006), characterises as general duties. Obviously directors have other obligations but they are not classified as duties.

1.4   Notwithstanding the fact that the law imposes duties on directors as well as other responsibilities, the law does not lay down any qualifications[5] or require a particular kind of experience for persons who are to become directors. Of course, companies themselves may require certain qualifications, skills or experience. Also, the Institute of Directors provides courses that lead to qualifications, such as the Certificate in Company Direction,[6] and directors can seek to qualify as a Chartered Director.[7]

1.5   Traditionally, in UK law, two kinds of duties have been imposed on directors, namely fiduciary duties and duties of care and skill. UK law, unlike American law,[8] does not regard the duty of care as a fiduciary duty,[9] although it takes it very seriously, and arguably more so in recent years. In UK law fiduciary duties involve a requirement to act honestly and loyally, while duties of care are all about competence and, so, the duties are often of different quality.[10] The aforementioned dichotomy with respect to duties remains broadly the case today under the latest companies legislation as it was at common law and in equity. These duties have been said to be owed by directors to their companies as a whole. Fiduciary duties are duties of loyalty, honesty and good faith,[11] and they are not generally owed to any individual members of the company, or other persons, and this includes creditors.[12] They are owed to

---

[4]   L S Sealy 'Director's Wider Responsibilities – Problems Conceptual Practical and Procedural' (1987) 13 *Monash University Law Review* 164 at 175.

[5]   Notwithstanding the fact that there have been calls for it. For example, see A McKenzie 'A Company Director's Obligations of Care and Skill' [1982] JBL 460 at 475.

[6]   See details on the Institute of Directors' website, at: www.iod.com/developing/chartered-director-qualifications/certificate-in-company-direction.

[7]   See details on the Institute of Directors' website, at: www.iod.com/developing/chartered-director-qualifications.

[8]   American law provides that the duty of care is not a common law rule, but a fiduciary duty. American law divides fiduciary duties into two, namely duties of loyalty and duties of care: Tamar Frankel 'Fiduciary Duties as Default Rules' (1995) 74 *Oregon Law Review* 1209 at 1210.

[9]   *Extrasure Travel Insurances Ltd v Scattergood* [2003] 1 BCLC 598. Nor does Australian law: *Permanent Building Society (in liq) v Wheeler* (1994) 14 ACSR 109; (1994) 12 ACLC 674.

[10]   See *Extrasure Travel Insurances Ltd v Scattergood* [2003] 1 BCLC 598 at 617–618.

[11]   *Bristol and West Building Society v Mothew* [1998] 1 Ch 1; [1996] 4 All ER 698 (CA).

[12]   *Percival v Wright* [1902] 2 Ch 421; *Multinational Gas and Petrochemical Co v Multinational Gas and Petrochemical Services Ltd* [1983] Ch 258; *Peskin v Anderson* [2000] BCC 1110 (and affirmed on appeal by the Court of Appeal [2001] BCC 874). This is the case in many common law jurisdictions. For the United States, see, for example, *Nuclear Corp of America v Hale* 355 F Supp 193 (1973) (ND); *Revlon Inc v MacAndrews and Forbes Holdings Inc* 506 A 2d 173 at 179 (1986) (Delaware).

the company[13] and imposed on directors in order to deter them from acting against the company's interests.[14] Such duties are derived from equitable principles. Much more is said about fiduciary duties in **Chapter 4**. The second type of duty, the duties of care and skill, is based on common law rules and equitable principles, and these duties, as indicated in **Chapter 8**, have become more important over the past 20 years or so, with the development of a stricter approach to the rules. The CA 2006 embraces this stricter approach.

1.6 Duties have been imposed on directors over the years in order to deal with the fact that directors are usually granted unlimited management powers by the articles. However, 'some critics would argue that there is no need for such strict rules as the markets for management and control will effectively constrain managerial discretion within reasonable limits and in a more cost-effective way than the legal rules'.[15] But, others would take the view that there is theoretical argument[16] and some empirical research[17] that denies the efficacious nature of the market for corporate control.

1.7 Until the advent of the CA 2006, the duties owed by directors were merely owed under the common law and in equity. Now the duties have been codified, and no longer are those duties owed under common law and in equity,[18] although, as will be discussed later, it would appear that the courts are not prohibited from declaring other duties are owed under the common law or in equity. This book will focus on the provisions in the CA 2006. Nevertheless, as we will see, the common law and equitable heritage in relation to duties, and developed over the past 150 or so years, will be of significant relevance to any examination of the present law. Clearly the UK courts continue to rely on the law as it existed before codification.

1.8 In setting out the duties imposed on directors, the CA 2006 does not distinguish between large and small companies. Yet, obviously, the manner in which directors of companies operate will differ according to size, as well as because of other factors, such as the field of commerce in which the company functions. It is not uncommon for most, if not all, of the members of a small private company to act as directors of the company. But this is, of course, not possible for large private companies and most, if not all, public limited

---

[13] What is meant by 'the company' is considered later in the book. See **3.45–3.51**.

[14] *Murad v Ali-Saraj* [2005] EWCA Civ 959.

[15] B Hannigan *Company Law* (London, LexisNexis, 2003) at 190.

[16] M Lipton and S Rosenblum 'A New System of Corporate Governance: The Quinquennial Election of Directors' (1991) 58 U Chi L Rev 187 at 188; Richard Booth 'Stockholders, Stakeholders and Bagholders (or How Investor Diversification Affects Fiduciary Duty)' (1998) 53 *The Business Lawyer* 429 at 440. For a more recent view, see L Bebchuk 'The Myth of the Shareholder Franchise' (2007) 93 *Virginia Law Review* 275.

[17] J Franks and C Mayer 'Hostile Takeovers in the UK and the Correction of Managerial Failure' (1996) 40 *Journal of Financial Economics* 163.

[18] It might be said that directors do owe a duty to their company at common law to consider the interests of creditors when their company is in some form of financial difficulty. See **Chapter 13**. In contrast to the UK approach, Australia retained duties at common law and in equity after codifying its duties, so there is a dual scheme.

companies. The directors of such companies may not have any shares in their company. This leads to the concept of separation of ownership and control, a concept that is discussed in **Chapter 3**, in particular. Briefly this concept involves the situation where one has people, who do not own the company through shareholding,[19] managing the company. While in the small private company the shareholder/directors will often be directly involved in the daily operations of the company's business, in larger companies there will be a pyramid-type arrangement with various levels of management. Although private companies are only required to have one director, public companies must have two directors.[20] With larger companies, of course, there are far more than two. Besides the size of the company, the role of a particular director might be of relevance. For instance, when it comes to exercising care and skill in relation to financial issues, more might be expected of, say, the finance director than the other directors. This aspect is discussed in **Chapter 8**.

1.9 The CA 2006 contemplates that the board of directors will manage the company. How that is done, provided the relevant provisions of both the CA 2006 and some leftover from the Companies Act 1985 (CA 1985),[21] as well as the articles, are fulfilled is a matter of discretion. The manner in which directors discharge their functions varies widely, depending upon the nature of the issues in question and the company concerned.[22] Of course, in medium to large companies the board of directors cannot manage all aspects of the company's business. Hence, companies operate through company executives and managers. The board's role includes:

- selecting and setting the remuneration of the chief executive officer of the company;
- determining objectives for the company's business, including strategic planning and risk management;
- formulating strategy and approving business plans;
- reviewing at intervals the company's progress in achieving its goals;
- determining the extent of the company's investment in new ventures;

---

[19] It is highly debatable whether the shareholders can be said to own the company. See M Lipton and S Rosenblum 'A New System of Corporate Governance: The Quinquennial Election of Directors' (1991) 58 U Chi L Rev 187 at 195; P Ireland 'Capitalism Without the Capitalist: The Joint Stock Company Share and the Emergence of the Modern Doctrine of Separate Corporate Personality' (1996) 17 *Legal History* 40; M Eisenberg 'The Conception that the Corporation is a Nexus of Contracts, and the Dual Nature of the Firm' (1999) 24 J Corp L 819; S Worthington 'Shares and Shareholders: Property, Power and Entitlement (Part 1)' (2001) 22 Co Law 258 and '(Part 2)' (2001) 22 Co Law 307; A Keay *The Corporate Objective* (Cheltenham, Edward Elgar, 2011) at 100–104. Also, see *Short v Treasury Commissioners* [1948] 1 KB 116 at 122 where Evershed LJ denied the fact that shareholders were the owners of a company; Committee on the Financial Aspects of Corporate Governance (Cadbury Report) (London, Gee, 1992) at para 6.1; Confederation of British Industries *Boards Without Tiers: A CBI Contribution to the Debate* (London, CBI, 1996) at 8.

[20] Section 154.

[21] The vast majority of the provisions of this legislation have been repealed.

[22] Association of General Counsel and Company Secretaries of the FTSE 100 ('GC100'), 'Companies Act (2006) – Directors' Duties' February 2007 at para 3.1.

- approving revenue and capital expenditure budgets;

- considering and approving important management decisions;

- ensuring that the company has accounting and information systems that are adequate to monitor company performance;

- monitoring the performance of the managers and how the company is performing overall;

- providing direction to the company;

- reporting, and being accountable, to the shareholders at appropriate points.[23]

1.10   It has been asserted that 'Much of a board's role is a function of the corporation's needs at any given point in time, which is, in turn, dependent on such characteristics as age, size and type of business.'[24]

1.11   Directors are granted the wide powers referred to above because it tends to enhance efficiency. But the downside might be seen in the fact that because directors are granted such wide discretionary powers in the carrying on of the company's business, it is not easy to control them. Directors are those to whom the duty of managing the affairs of their company is delegated,[25] and this involves directors making the majority of decisions in the life of a company.[26] As a result the company has relatively little control over the directors and the manner in which they exercise their powers.[27] For instance, while shareholders are sometimes said to be the owners of the company[28] (although many would take issue with this description,[29] including the courts in some UK decisions[30]), and they are the ones who have ultimate control, this is not, in practice, correct, certainly for large companies. Shareholders do have legal rights that might seemingly permit them a good degree of control, but this is not in reality the

---

[23]   Based on: *AWA Ltd v Daniels* (1992) 10 ACLC 933 at 1013; *Dairy Containers Ltd v NZI Bank Ltd* [1995] 2 NZLR 30 at 79; R P Austin, H A J Ford and I M Ramsay *Company Directors* (Sydney, LexisNexis Butterworths, 2005) at 60; A E Onetto 'Agency Problems and the Board of Directors' (2007) 22(7) *Journal of International Banking and Financial Law* 414.

[24]   Onetto, ibid at 414.

[25]   *Aberdeen Rly Co v Blaikie Bros* [1854] 2 Eq Rep 1281; [1854] 1 Macq 461; [1843–1860] All ER Rep 249 (HL).

[26]   This is also the case in the United States: S Bainbridge 'Director Primacy in Corporate Takeovers: Preliminary Reflections' (2002) 55 Stanford L R 791 at 801.

[27]   See A Keay 'Company Directors Behaving Poorly: Disciplinary Options for Shareholders' [2007] JBL 656.

[28]   M Eisenberg 'The Conception that the Corporation is a Nexus of Contracts, and the Dual Nature of the Firm' (1999) 24 J Corp L 819. Also, see Committee on the Financial Aspects of Corporate Governance (Cadbury Report) (Gee, 1992) at para 6.1; Confederation of British Industries *Boards Without Tiers: A CBI Contribution to the Debate* (London, CBI, 1996) at 8.

[29]   For example, M Lipton and S Rosenblum 'A New System of Corporate Governance: The Quinquennial Election of Directors' (1991) 58 U Chi L Rev 187 at 195; P Ireland, 'Capitalism Without the Capitalist: The Joint Stock Company Share and the Emergence of the Modern Doctrine of Separate Corporate Personality' (1996) 17 *Legal History* 40; S Worthington 'Shares and Shareholders: Property, Power and Entitlement (Part 1)' (2001) 22 Co Law 258 and '(Part 2)' (2001) 22 Co Law 307.

[30]   For instance, see *Short v Treasury Commissioners* [1948] 1 KB 116 at 122, where Evershed LJ denied the fact that shareholders were the owners of a company.

situation. Their rights and powers to control the directors are very limited.[31] Also, as we will examine in **Chapter 3**, the granting of broad discretionary powers means that there is a risk that directors will exercise them in favour of themselves or associates. Because of this, and the lack of control, the law places substantial duties on directors and the manner in which they exercise their powers. The White Paper in July 2002 that set out many of the matters that the Government wished to include in reforms to the CA 1985, observed, taking into account a 1999 survey of members of the Institute of Directors, that directors are not sure about the general duties which they owe.[32] There are probably a number of reasons for this. Perhaps foremost is the fact that the duties are based on case-law that is generally inaccessible to non-lawyers and even difficult for many lawyers to synthesise. The duties are, legally speaking, quite complex.

1.12 What the law on duties has to do is to strike a balance between ensuring directors are accountable to the company, on the one hand, and, on the other hand, permitting them to have a significant amount of discretion; the latter naturally involves an element of risk.[33] An important aspect of imposing duties is to make directors, to a reasonable extent, accountable for what they do and how they do it.[34] Duties are part of trying to ensure that the law has a process, amongst others, to prevent unauthorised overreaching or inadequate exercise of powers in the decision-making system.[35] What is crucial is the fact that the courts have said that anyone who accepts the office of director is required to understand the nature of the duty that he or she is asked to perform.[36] What is also critical is that the company, as far as possible, must ensure that their directors are aware of their duties under the companies legislation.[37]

1.13 Many parts of the CA 2006, and particularly Chapter 2 of Part 10, the chapter that houses the general duties, are based on recommendations both from the Law Commission contained in its report in 1999 and titled, 'Company Directors: Regulating Conflicts of Interest and Formulating a Statement of Duties'[38] and the Company Law Review Steering Group ('CLRSG') whose Final Report on the reform of company law in the UK was delivered to the Government in July 2001. From time to time I will advert to some of these recommendations. The CLRSG was appointed in 1998 by the Department of

---

[31]   For a discussion of the rights that shareholders have, together with some of the problems which they face when seeking to exercise control, see A Keay 'Company Directors Behaving Poorly: Disciplinary Options for Shareholders' [2007] JBL 656.

[32]   'Modernising Company Law' Cm 5553-1, HMSO, 2002 at para 3.2.

[33]   R P Austin, H A J Ford and I M Ramsay *Company Directors* (Sydney, LexisNexis Butterworths, 2005) at 212.

[34]   For a broad discussion of the accountability of directors, see A Keay *Board Accountability in Corporate Governance* (Abingdon, Routledge, 2015).

[35]   S Bottomley *The Constitutional Corporation* (Aldershot, Ashgate, 2007) at 81.

[36]   See *Re Barings (No 5)* [2000] BCLC 523.

[37]   Association of General Counsel and Company Secretaries of the FTSE 100 ('GC100'), 'Companies Act (2006) – Directors' Duties' February 2007 at paras 6.1(i), 6.2.

[38]   Report 261, 1999. This was a joint report with the Scottish Law Commission (SLC Report 173).

Trade and Industry (one of the precursors of the Department of Business Innovation and Skills) to undertake a comprehensive review of company law in the UK, the most wide-ranging since the middle of the nineteenth century, and to formulate a framework of company law which 'facilitates enterprise and promotes transparency and fair-dealing'.[39] The CLRSG compiled a number of consultation reports between 1998 and 2000 and, as indicated above, in July 2001 delivered a final report to the Government.

1.14 This book is concerned with an examination of the duties found in Chapter 2 of Part 10 of the CA 2006, and known as the general duties of directors. It seeks to interpret the relevant provisions as well as identifying and applying the existing case-law in light of these duties, as well as noting and analysing any shortcomings in the law. The book also considers aspects that relate directly to the duties, namely the consequences of a breach of duties and what relief courts can and might order, the legislative excusing of directors for breach, and the statutory derivative proceedings provisions as far as they might apply to the case of a breach of duty.

1.15 The book seeks to articulate the law at present. But, of course, any alleged breaches of duties that occurred before these provisions began to operate are covered by the common law and equity, because the legislative provisions are not retrospective. The book does not purport to deal with the 'old law' per se, although many aspects of it are discussed as it has been and will continue to be highly relevant in interpreting and applying significant parts of the new law.

1.16 The book is essentially a doctrinal study of the law, which includes, besides ascertaining, analysing and synthesising UK law, drawing on the experience in other common law jurisdictions, but occasionally it also seeks to identify any need for reform and to address some theoretical issues.

1.17 The book does not purport to deal with everything that could be regarded as a duty owed by directors. Many duties are imposed on directors[40] in the companies legislation, such as the duty to file accounts and reports with the registrar of companies[41] and the duty to prepare a directors' report.[42] But the emphasis is on general duties of directors as specified by the CA 2006. These duties can be seen as the core duties of a director. Those obligations that are imposed on directors by Chapters 3 and 4 of Part 10 are not addressed, save

---

[39] Company Law Review *Modern Company Law for a Competitive Economy* (London, DTI, 1998), Foreword.

[40] For a readable and useful general guide to the responsibilities imposed on directors by the CA 2006, see J Davies 'A Guide to Directors Obligations Under the Companies Act 2006' Association of Chartered Certified Accountants, August 2007, and accessible at www.accaglobal.com/content/dam/acca/global/PDF-technical/business-law/tech-tp-cdd.pdf (accessed 4 October 2016).

[41] CA 2006, s 441.

[42] CA 2006, s 415.

in passing. The same can be said for other obligations imposed by other legislation, such as s 214 of the Insolvency Act 1986 (IA 1986), the provision that deals with wrongful trading.[43]

1.18   Chapters 2, 3 and 4 of the book are to be seen as introductory in that, inter alia, they consider who directors are, their role and their position in the corporate governance process, with **Chapter 4** setting the scene for a consideration of the whole range of duties owed, as well as discussing the issue of codification. The following Chapters, from **Chapter 5** to, and including, **Chapter 12**, individually discuss the duties laid down in the CA 2006. **Chapter 5** focuses on the duty of directors to act within the company's constitution and to use their powers for the purposes for which they were conferred. **Chapter 6** examines the duty to act in such a way as to promote the success of the company. **Chapter 7** discusses the duty of directors to exercise an independent judgment. **Chapter 8** considers the duty of care, skill and diligence. **Chapters 9** and **10** analyse the duty of directors to avoid placing themselves in positions where they have a conflict of interests. **Chapter 11** examines the duty that forbids directors from accepting benefits from third parties. **Chapter 12** considers the duty to declare any interests in a proposed transaction.

1.19   **Chapter 13** discusses a duty that is not comprehensively provided for in CA 2006, as it refers to a duty that has developed at common law and through a line of cases dating back to the mid-1970s, namely the duty that requires directors to take into account the interests of creditors in certain circumstances.[44] While this was a duty provided for under common law, it is sanctioned indirectly by s 172(3) of the CA 2006. The last four chapters of the book examine issues and topics that are highly relevant to any consideration of the duties of directors. **Chapter 14** examines the fact that the CA 2006 permits shareholders to initiate derivative claims against directors and others for breach of duties. Hitherto, shareholders had to rely on common law developments to enable them to bring such actions. **Chapter 15** provides an exposition of the consequences of breach of the duties, including relief. **Chapter 16** discusses the relevance and ramifications of authorisation and ratification of breaches of duty by the members. Finally, **Chapter 17** examines s 1157 of the CA 2006 which permits courts, in certain circumstances, to excuse directorial breaches of duty.

---

[43]   This is considered in some depth in A Keay *Company Directors' Responsibilities to Creditors* (Abingdon, Routledge-Cavendish, 2007) at 71–150.

[44]   Under the present law it is not strictly correct to talk about it being a duty to creditors. It is more correctly to be referred to as a duty to the company to take into account the interests of creditors, but the literature tends to abbreviate this to a duty to creditors.

CHAPTER 2

DIRECTORS: BACKGROUND AND ROLE

I INTRODUCTION

2.1　This chapter introduces the position of the director and what his or her role is in the company. Of importance is the fact that the chapter considers the definition of 'director' in the CA 2006 as well as discussing the various types of directors that exist. Finally, the chapter examines the director as a fiduciary.

2.2　What is surprising, especially taking into account the critical position of directors, is that the CA 2006 fails to set out the role of directors in any detail. This is a task that is largely left to the articles of association to fulfil, although soft corporate governance law such as the UK's Corporate Governance Code,[1] formulated by the Financial Reporting Council, also provides assistance in this regard as far as directors of large companies are concerned. The Act also fails to provide an exhaustive definition of a director.

II TYPES OF DIRECTOR

A General

2.3　Although it is not intended, nor appropriate, to engage in a long discussion of the various kinds of director there can be, it is worthwhile identifying and explaining the main types, for some discussion later in the book presupposes an understanding of the types and this can form a basis for understanding some of the issues that pertain to directors other than those regularly appointed according to law and the company's articles.

2.4　While all companies are required by law to have at least one director,[2] what they actually do will depend on the constitution of the company. The company's articles of association will vest the board of directors, elected by the shareholders at a general meeting, with very broad general management powers,[3] many of which are then delegated to company managers and officers.[4]

---

[1]　September 2014, and accessible at: www.frc.org.uk/Our-Work/Publications/Corporate-Governance/UK-Corporate-Governance-Code-2014.pdf (accessed 31 July 2016).

[2]　CA 2006, s 154(1). Public companies must have at least two directors (s 154(2)). At least one director of a company must be a person (s 155(1)).

[3]　See Companies (Tables A–F) Regulations 1985, Table A, reg 70; Companies (Model Articles) Regulations 2008, SI 2008/3229, reg 2, Sch 1, art 5 (private companies); reg 4, Sch 3, art 5 (public companies). Many companies that were registered before CA 2006 came into force will

The directors only have to follow any directions given by the members at a general meeting if the articles provide accordingly. Article 4 of Schedule 1 (for private companies) and article 4 of Schedule 3 (for public companies) of the UK's model articles, which apply to all companies by default where they do not exclude it, provides that the shareholders may, by special resolution, direct the directors to do something or refrain from doing something. Obtaining a special resolution is not easy to achieve,[5] but it does potentially place some curb on board power.[6] In any event common law, the CA 2006, subordinate companies legislation and even some non-companies legislation, dictate that directors fulfil certain duties and functions.

2.5   The Act does not provide a detailed definition of who directors are, rather it provides, in CA 2006, s 250, that 'director' includes any person occupying the position of director, by whatever name called. So, it is not necessarily critical before a person is to be regarded as a director for the purposes of company law, that he or she is called 'a director'; what is critical is whether a person occupies the position of director. Unfortunately, there is no legislative interpretation of 'occupying the position of a director'.

2.6   In becoming directors, persons should realise the important duties that they owe, the extensive powers they wield and the substantial obligations and responsibilities with which they must comply.[7] A critical point is that notwithstanding the extent of a director's obligations, a director is not usually personally liable for the liabilities of his or her company because of the fact that a director's company is a separate legal entity.[8]

B Executive and non-executive

2.7   In practice directors can be divided into either executive directors (sometimes known simply as 'managers' in places such as the United States) or non-executive directors (known as 'independent directors' or 'outside directors' in the US), although one does not find these designations mentioned in the CA 2006. Mention of them is made, however, in self-regulatory documentation, corporate governance proposals and Codes of Practice, and importantly in the UK Corporate Governance Code, and courts clearly accept the terms and the difference between the two posts. Executive directors are employed full-time by

---

be subject to the Companies (Tables A–F) Regulations 1985, Table A, reg 70. Under CA 2006, s 20(2) the model articles that were in existence at the time of the registration of a company will apply.

4   Susan Watson argues that no significance should be suggested where the powers are provided for in the articles as opposed to a statute: 'The Significance of the Source of the Powers of Boards of Directors in UK Company Law' [2011] *Journal of Business Law* 597 at 599. For a legislative delegation, see s 130 of the Companies Act 1993 (NZ).

5   In the UK it requires the vote by a 75 per cent of those votes able to be cast at a meeting: CA 2006, s 283.

6   The Companies (Model Articles) Regulations 2008, SI 2008/3229, reg 2 and Sch 1, art 4 (private companies); reg 4 and Sch 3, art 4 (public companies).

7   *Re Westmid Packing Service Ltd* [1998] 2 All ER 124 at 130–131.

8   If authority is needed, see *Salomon v Salomon and Co Ltd* [1897] AC 22.

the company, and, in some companies, they might be appointed to specific posts, such as finance director or sales director, and they are given specific tasks related to the day-to-day conduct of the company's business. They will often have service contracts and be granted significant management powers. One of the executives is the chief executive officer who has overall responsibility for the management of the company's affairs. In contrast, the non-executive directors are not engaged on a full-time basis and are not commissioned with the task of overseeing the daily operations of the company. They are often appointed to attract customers and/or lenders or add prestige to the company's business.[9] Often former executive directors of the company or other companies, as well existing executive directors of other companies, will be appointed as non-executives. With larger companies they are appointed to provide expertise and experience for the board and to act as monitors of the executives to protect the shareholders. Companies are entitled to look to them for independence of judgment[10] and supervision of the executives.[11] Whether non-executives achieve all of this is debatable. It has been argued that directors are inhibited in their independence and their ability to supervise due to various things such as the fact that directors: are often chosen for their passivity; lack incentives to be active; have the information to which they have reference controlled by executives; lack time; and are often regarded as being obsequious to the chief executive officer.[12] Often in the past non-executives have been appointed because of business connections, friendships or reputation and standing in the community, but nevertheless Romer J in *Re City Equitable Fire Insurance Co Ltd*[13] said that they were not to regard themselves merely as 'window dressing'. In companies that are not defined as 'small companies' by the UK Corporate Governance Code, namely those which are not below those which are listed on the FTSE 350 throughout the year immediately preceding the reporting year, the Code requires at least half of the board to be constituted by non-executive directors.[14]

2.8   A major difficulty for non-executives in medium-large companies is to attain a balance in relation to their primary tasks, namely monitoring the managers and contributing to the development of strategy for the company. It can be argued that there is a conflict with these two tasks in that if the non-executives are involved in the latter they may be less active in relation to the former and may be rather reluctant to examine what the executives are

---

9   *Daniels v Anderson* (1995) 13 ACLC 614 at 662 (NSWCA).
10   For a study of the issue of independence, see A Palmiter 'Reshaping the Corporate Fiduciary Model: A Director's Duty of Independence' (1989) 67 *Texas Law Review* 1351.
11   *Equitable Life Assurance Society v Bowley* [2003] EWHC 2263 (Comm); [2004] 1 BCLC 180 at [41].
12   L Lin 'The Effectiveness of Outside Directors as a Corporate Governance Mechanism: Theories and Evidence' (1996) 90 *Northwestern University Law Review* 898 at 898–903 and 914–917. It is interesting to note that the Enron board was dominated by independent directors, but that did not stop the excesses for which that company is famed.
13   [1925] Ch 407 at 444.
14   September 2014, at para B.1.2, and accessible at: www.frc.org.uk/Our-Work/Publications/Corporate-Governance/UK-Corporate-Governance-Code-2014.pdf (accessed 31 July 2016).

doing in carrying out a strategy the devising of which was due to contributions from the non-executives. This can create internal tensions between the two roles.[15]

2.9   Non-executives are usually paid annual retainers and expenses for giving their advice and attending board meetings. While non-executive directors are not required to engage in as much work as executives, the companies legislation does not, as indicated earlier, distinguish between executive and non-executive directors when imposing duties and obligations on directors.[16] However, in application of the duties there may be different levels expected and generally more will usually be expected of executive directors because of the nature of their full-time role. As indicated above, the courts in more recent times have acknowledged the different roles that are played by individual directors, and they have taken that into account.[17] To date it would appear that both the role of, and the law relating to, non-executive directors is very unclear.[18] In his influential report, 'Review of the Role and Effectiveness of Non-Executive Directors'[19] in 2003, Derek Higgs referred to the role of the non-executive as 'largely invisible and poorly understood', although it is arguable that the role has developed since the Higgs Report was delivered, and the UK Corporate Governance Code has specific parts of it devoted to consideration of non-executive directors.

III DIRECTORS RECOGNISED AT LAW[20]

2.10   Effectively, there are three main kinds of director at which the law is aimed: de jure, de facto and shadow.

2.11   Before discussing these kinds of directors, it should be pointed out that there are other kinds of directors that might well be mentioned in the articles. First, companies might have nominee directors (discussed in detail in **Chapter 7**),[21] who are de jure directors owing their appointment to some third person, often a member or members of the company who hold(s) a strong position in relation to company affairs. Such directors owe the same duties as

---

[15]   See M Essamel and R Watson 'Wearing Two Hats: The Conflicting Control and Management Roles of Non-Executive Directors' in K Keasey et al (eds) *Corporate Governance: Economic, Management and Financial Issues* (OUP, 1997).

[16]   *Equitable Life Assurance Society v Bowley* [2003] EWHC 2263 (Comm) at [35]; [2004] 1 BCLC 180.

[17]   For example, see *Dorchester Finance Co Ltd v Stebbings* [1989] BCLC 498; *Daniels v AWA Ltd* (1995) 37 NSWLR 438; (1995) 16 ACSR 607; (1995) 13 ACLC 614 (NSWCA).

[18]   L Roach 'Equitable Life and Director Liability' (2006) 17 Co Law 225 at 227.

[19]   DTI, London at 3.

[20]   For further discussion, see J De Lacy 'The Concept of a Company Director: Time for a New Expanded and Unified Concept?' [2006] JBL 276.

[21]   For further consideration of this topic, see E Thomas 'The Role of Nominee Directors and the Liability of their Appointors' in F Patfield (ed) *Perspectives on Company Law* (London, Kluwer, 1997), vol 2 at 235; J De Lacy 'The Concept of a Company Director: Time for a New Expanded and Unified Concept?' [2006] JBL 276 at 284–287.

other directors, and to the company as a whole.[22] Second, an alternate director is a person who only acts temporarily on behalf of a director who has nominated the alternate to act for him or her on the board when the director is absent, perhaps because of illness or other pressing commitments. The articles of association must, and often they will, permit the nomination of an alternate. Generally speaking, an alternate director is in the same legal position as other directors when acting as a director.[23] But, an alternate is only liable when called upon to act, namely to fulfil the role empowered by the appointment.[24]

A De jure directors

2.12 These directors are those who have been formally appointed by their consent, and according to the company's articles.[25] Such appointments will appear on the company records held by the registrar of companies.

B De facto directors[26]

2.13 Notwithstanding the fact that there is no legislative provision that defines the term, 'de facto director', it is a term that has a reasonably long lineage, being referred to as far back as in *Re Canadian Land Reclaiming and Colonizing Co*[27] by Jessel MR, and as recently in the Supreme Court judgment in *Revenue and Customs Commissioners v Holland; Re Paycheck Services 3 Ltd*.[28] Lord Collins, in the latter case, referred back to the decision of *Mangles v Grand Collier Dock Co*[29] where persons were said to be 'directors de facto'.[30] A de facto director is a person who assumes the functions and status of a director, while never being appointed according to law.[31] This might be as a result of some defect in the appointment of a person as a de jure director,[32] but more often than not it covers someone who is not appointed, but is involved in directorial roles. If a person had assumed responsibility to act as a director then the court would have to determine in what capacity the person was acting.[33] The Supreme Court in *Revenue and Customs Commissioners v Holland; Re Paycheck Services 3 Ltd*[34] held (by a majority judgment of 3-2) that being a

---

[22] *Credit Suisse v Waltham Forest London Borough Council* [1997] QB 362.

[23] *Markwell Bros Pty Ltd v CPN Diesels (Qld) Pty Ltd* [1983] Qd R 508; (1982) 7 ACLR 425.

[24] *Playcorp Pty Ltd v Shaw* (1993) 10 ACSR 212 (Vic S Ct).

[25] For instance, see Companies (Tables A–F) Regulations 1985, Table A, reg 78.

[26] For a detailed discussion of de facto directors, see C Noonan and S Watson 'Examining Company Directors through the Lens of the De Facto Directorship' [2008] JBL 587.

[27] (1880) 14 Ch D 660 at 664 (CA). Also, see *Re Kaytech International plc* [1999] 2 BCLC 351.

[28] [2010] UKSC 51; [2011] BCC 1.

[29] (1840) 10 Sim 519.

[30] [2010] UKSC 51; [2011] BCC 1at [58].

[31] *Re Hydrodan (Corby) Ltd* [1994] BCC 161; [1994] 2 BCLC 180 at 183; *Re Kaytech International* [1999] 2 BCLC 351; *Re Mea Corp Ltd* [2006] EWHC 1846 (Ch) at [83]; [2007] BCC 288 at 305.

[32] This occurred in *Re Canadian Land Reclaiming and Colonizing Co* (1880) 14 Ch D 660 (CA). Also, see *Corporate Affairs Commission (NSW) v Drysdale* (1978) 141 CLR 236 (Aust HC).

[33] *Smithton Ltd (formerly Hobart Capital Markets Ltd) v Naggar* [2014] EWCA Civ 939; [2015] 1 WLR 189; [2014] BCC 482 at [36].

[34] [2010] UKSC 51; [2011] BCC 1.

member of a corporate director will not, of itself, mean that one is a de facto of any company of which the corporate director is a director.[35]

2.14   A person will only be held to be a de facto director if it can be established that he or she carried out director-like functions, and they are functions that could only be discharged by a director.[36] According to Millett J (as he then was):[37]

> 'It is not sufficient to show that he [the alleged de facto director] was concerned in the management of the company's affairs or undertook tasks in relation to its business which can properly be performed by a manager below board level.'

2.15   The variety in commercial life generally, and the many different types of companies that exist means that it is not helpful to provide a general statement concerning who might be regarded as a director.[38] It has been said that it covers a person who is held out as a director by the company,[39] although subsequent cases seem to indicate that this is only one element to consider when deciding whether someone is a de facto director or not.[40] The critical issue appears to be that the person, to be a de facto, has to have been part of the corporate governance structure.[41] A person who is alleged to have acted as a de facto director must be shown to have assumed the status and functions of a company director and to have exercised 'real influence' in the corporate governance of the company.[42] It is likely that the nature of the functions or powers which are exercised and the extent of their exercise will be of great importance.[43] The role of a de facto director need not extend over the whole range of a company's activities.[44]

2.16   There is not one decisive test that establishes that a person is or is not a de facto director.[45] Courts have to take into account all relevant factors[46] including whether:

---

[35]   When s 156A is put in force it will not be permissible to have corporate directors save in limited cases (see s 156B).

[36]   *Re Hydrodan (Corby) Ltd* [1994] BCC 161; [1994] 2 BCLC 180; *Secretary of State for Trade and Industry v Becker* [2003] 1 BCLC 555.

[37]   *Re Hydrodan (Corby) Ltd* [1994] BCC 161 at 163; [1994] 2 BCLC 180 at 183.

[38]   *Deputy Commissioner of Taxation v Austin* (1998) 16 ACLC 1555 at 1559 (Aust Fed Ct).

[39]   *Re Hydrodan (Corby) Ltd* [1994] BCC 161 at 163; [1994] 2 BCLC 180 at 183.

[40]   *Secretary of State for Trade and Industry v Tjolle* [1998] BCC 282; [1998] 1 BCLC 333.

[41]   *Secretary of State for Trade and Industry v Tjolle* [1998] BCC 282; [1998] 1 BCLC 333 at 344; *Re Mumtaz Properties Ltd* [2011] EWCA Civ 610; [2012] 2 BCLC 109.

[42]   *Re Kaytech International Plc* [1999] 2 BCLC 351 at 423; *Gemma v Davies* [2008] EWHC 546 (Ch); [2008] BCC 812 at [40].

[43]   *Deputy Commissioner of Taxation v Austin* (1998) 16 ACLC 1555 at 1559.

[44]   *Smithton Ltd (formerly Hobart Capital Markets Ltd) v Naggar* [2014] EWCA Civ 939; [2015] 1 WLR 189; [2014] BCC 482 at [32].

[45]   *Revenue and Customs Commissioners v Holland; Re Paycheck Services 3 Ltd* [2010] UKSC 51; [2011] BCC 1; *Re Mumtaz Properties Ltd* [2011] EWCA Civ 610; [2012] 2 BCLC 109; *Smithton Ltd (formerly Hobart Capital Markets Ltd) v Naggar* [2014] EWCA Civ 939; [2015] 1 WLR 189; [2014] BCC 482 at [33].

[46]   *Re Mumtaz Properties Ltd* [2011] EWCA Civ 610; [2012] 2 BCLC 109.

- there was a holding out of the person as a director;[47]
- the person used the title;[48]
- the person had proper information on which to base decisions; and
- the person had to make major decisions.[49]

2.17 But none of these factors are necessarily decisive on their own, and even where a person uses the title of 'director' a court might not hold that the person is a de facto director.[50] Furthermore, in *Forkserve Pty Ltd v Jack and Aussie Forklift Repairs*[51] it was stated that the fact that a person had a business card with the title of 'Director' does not necessarily mean he or she is a de facto director. But, in *Re Sykes (Butchers) Ltd*[52] the fact that a person signed bank mandates and letters as a director of the company led to the court concluding that the person was a de facto director.

2.18 In *Elsworth Ethanol Co Ltd v Hartley*[53] HHJ Hacon said that a court could take into account all relevant factors in determining whether a person was a de facto director or not and this included whether the person concerned was acting on an equal footing with one or more of the persons who were true directors. In the Australian case of *Deputy Commissioner of Taxation v Solomon*[54] two persons who had resigned as directors of a company were held to be de facto directors because they were involved in the main activity of the company, performed top level management functions, acted for the company in important matters, and outsiders perceived that they were directors. Specifically, one of the persons had daily contact with directors, had the right to approve an asset sale, and was actively involved in the preparation of projections of cash flows. The other person was involved in negotiations with directors and third parties in relation to possible capital injections into the company, sought professional advice for the company and also was actively involved in the preparation of projections of cash flows. But it has been argued that the performance of top level management functions is not of itself sufficient to say that a person is a de facto director for in large diversified companies very important matters may be delegated to employees.[55]

2.19 A person does not have to intend or believe that he or she is a director, before being regarded as a de facto director,[56] nor arguably does the company have to intend to hold out someone as a director for that person to be

---

[47] Ibid.
[48] Ibid; *Smithton Ltd (formerly Hobart Capital Markets Ltd) v Naggar* [2014] EWCA Civ 939; [2015] 1 WLR 189; [2014] BCC 482.
[49] *Secretary of State for Trade and Industry v Tjolle* [1998] 1 BCLC 333.
[50] *Secretary of State for Trade and Industry v Tjolle* [1998] 1 BCLC 333.
[51] (2001) 19 ACLC 299 (NSWSC).
[52] [1998] 1 BCLC 110.
[53] [2014] EWHC 99 (IPEC).
[54] (2003) 199 ALR 325.
[55] *Deputy Commissioner of Taxation v Austin* (1998) 16 ACLC 1555 at 1559.
[56] *Mistmorn Pty Ltd v Yasseen* (1996) 14 ACLC 1387 (Aust Fed Ct); *Forkserve Pty Ltd v Jack and Aussie Forklift Repairs* (2001) 19 ACLC 299 (NSWSC); *Re Kaytech International* [1999] 2 BCLC 351.

designated a de facto director,[57] although such holding out could be important evidence in support of the conclusion that a person acted as a director in fact.[58] Also, a person does not have to be actually referred to as a director, for it is not what a person calls himself or herself or what the person is referred to that is critical, but what he or she did in relation to the company.[59] According to s 250(1) a director includes anyone occupying the position of director 'by whatever name called'. Consequently, the law is concerned with the substantive nature of what the person does in the life of the company, rather than to how he or she is referred.[60] Interestingly, a person was not held to be a de facto director despite the fact that the titles of 'Deputy Managing Director' and 'Chief Executive' were used to describe her,[61] but it has been said that the use of 'director' to refer to a person is significant in moving towards a view that a person is a de facto director.[62] In *Deputy Commissioner of Taxation v Austin*,[63] Madgwick J of the Australian Federal Court said that how a person is perceived by others dealing with the company can be of relevance.[64]

2.20 For a court to find a person to be a de facto director it was necessary for it to ascertain that the person participated in directing the affairs of the company on an equal footing with the other director(s) and not in a subordinate role.[65] But, simply because the other directors sometimes act without reference to the person who is alleged to be a de facto director does not mean that he or she is not a director of the company.[66] Furthermore, merely because the person alleged to be a director (but not appointed as such) resisted a suggestion that he or she be formally appointed does not mean that that person is not to be regarded as a director for he or she might just have been seeking to avoid responsibility.[67] In *Smithton Ltd v Naggar*,[68] Rose J said that in deciding whether a person is a de facto director 'hat identification' was important. What her Ladyship meant was that it is necessary to identify the hat that a person was wearing when he or she dealt with the company.[69] The judge went on to say that this issue of hat identification was 'an important legal qualification to the general principle that one must look at what the putative

---

[57]   See *Gemma v Davies* [2008] EWHC 546 (Ch); [2008] BCC 812 at [40]; *Deputy Commissioner of Taxation v Austin* (1998) 16 ACLC 1555; M Markovic 'When You Are a Director when You're Not a Director: The Law of De Facto Directors' (2007) 25 *Company and Securities Law Journal* 101 at 103.

[58]   *Secretary of State for Trade and Industry v Hollier* [2007] BCC 11; *Gemma v Davies* [2008] EWHC 546 (Ch); [2008] BCC 812 at [40].

[59]   *Re Mea Corp Ltd* [2006] EWHC 1846 (Ch); [2007] BCC 288 at [82], [83]; *Gemma v Davies* [2008] EWHC 546 (Ch); [2008] BCC 812 at [42].

[60]   *Deputy Commissioner of Taxation v Austin* (1998) 16 ACLC 1555 at 1559 (Aust Fed Ct).

[61]   *Secretary of State for Trade and Industry v Tjolle* [1998] 1 BCLC 333.

[62]   *Secretary of State for Trade and Industry v Jones* [1999] BCC 336 at 349.

[63]   (1998) 16 ACLC 1555.

[64]   Ibid at 1560.

[65]   *Secretary of State for Trade and Industry v Hollier* [2007] BCC 11; *Gemma v Davies* [2008] EWHC 546 (Ch); [2008] BCC 812 at [40].

[66]   *International Cat Manufacturing Pty Ltd v Rodrick* [2013] QSC 91.

[67]   Ibid.

[68]   [2013] EWHC 1961 (Ch); [2014] 1 BCLC 602.

[69]   Ibid at [61].

director actually does rather than how he is described when deciding whether to impose fiduciary duties upon him'.[70] On appeal, the judge's decision was upheld by the Court of Appeal, and Rose J's hat identification approach was not criticised. In the Court of Appeal Arden LJ, with whom the other judges agreed, gave a judgment that clarified the approach that courts should adopt in determining whether someone is a de facto director or not. Her Ladyship provided some helpful practical applications of the law. She said that it was relevant to note whether he was part of the corporate governance system of the company and whether he assumed the status and function of a director so as to make himself responsible as if he were a director.[71] Arden LJ said that the court would normally have to determine the corporate governance structure of the company to decide whether the actions of a person who is alleged to be a de facto director were directorial in nature.[72] Her Ladyship went on to say that the court was required to look at what the director actually did and not his or her job title,[73] and whether or not persons acted as directors was to be determined objectively and irrespective of their motivation or belief, so that they would not avoid liability if they showed that in good faith they thought they were not acting as directors.[74] The judge opined that the court had not only to assess the cumulative effect of a person's activities but also the acts in their context, as a single act could lead to liability in an exceptional case.[75] She said that relevant factors that a court would consider included: (i) whether the company considered the person to be a director and held him or her out as such; (ii) whether third parties considered that the person was a director. The fact that a person was asked about directorial decisions, or for his or her approval, did not in general make the person a director because he or she was not making a decision.[76] Arden LJ said that acts that occurred outside of the period when a person is said to have been a de facto director may throw light on whether he or she was a de facto director in the relevant period.[77]

2.21 Clearly a de facto director owes the same duties owed by a de jure director.[78]

---

[70] Ibid at [67].
[71] *Smithton Ltd (formerly Hobart Capital Markets Ltd) v Naggar* [2014] EWCA Civ 939; [2015] 1 WLR 189; [2014] BCC 482 at [33].
[72] Ibid at [37].
[73] Ibid at [38].
[74] Ibid at [39].
[75] Ibid at [40], [41].
[76] Ibid at [42], [43].
[77] Ibid at [44].
[78] *Re Canadian Land Reclaiming and Colonizing Co* (1880) 14 Ch D 660 at 670 (CA); *Mistmorn Pty Ltd (in liq) v Yasseen* (1996) 21 ACSR 173; (1996) 14 ACLC 1387; *Ultraframe UK Ltd v Fielding* [2004] RPC 24 at [39]; *Ultraframe UK Ltd v Fielding* [2005] EWHC 1638 (Ch); [2006] FSR 17 at [1257]; *Primlake Ltd v Matthews Associates* [2006] EWHC 1227 (Ch); [2007] 1 BCLC 686 at [284].

C Shadow directors

2.22 While the definition in CA 2006, s 250 only encompasses de jure and de facto directors, there is one other kind of director who is recognised by the law – the shadow director. The recognition is to be found in s 251 and s 22(5) of the Company Directors Disqualification Act 1986. It is provided in s 251(1) of the CA 2006 that a shadow director means 'a person in accordance with whose directions or instructions the directors of the company are accustomed to act'. Then s 251(2) states that persons are not deemed to be shadow directors just because the directors act on their advice, in situations where the advice is given in a person's professional capacity. Ordinarily, this will exclude as shadow directors people such as lawyers, accountants and auditors. But, while professional advisers are not considered to be shadow directors, they might act in such a way that they cross the line and move from advising to instructing. A company, say Y Ltd, could be held to be a shadow director of another company,[79] say X Ltd,[80] but if Y Ltd is deemed to be a shadow director, it does not mean that the directors of Y Ltd will be regarded as shadows themselves simply because they are members of the board of the shadow.[81] It might be different though, in our example, if the director of the shadow gave direct instructions to the board of X Ltd.[82]

2.23 The purpose behind the legislation referring to shadow directors is to identify those, other than professional advisers, who have real influence over the affairs of companies.[83] But, it should be added, that just as with consideration of whether someone was a de facto director or not, it is not a requirement that the person exercises influence over the whole field of activities of the company.[84] In *McKillen v Misland (Cyprus) Investments Ltd*[85] the Court indicated that someone might be a shadow director if he or she exercised influence over a narrow range of matters and might owe duties to the company in relation to those matters where instructions had been given or influence exerted.[86] In *Ultraframe (UK) Ltd v Fielding*[87] Lewison J (as he then was) said that the legislative policy was to subject those who effectively control the company's affairs to the duties that apply to a director.[88]

2.24 In *Ultraframe (UK) Ltd v Fielding*[89] Lewison J adverted to the problem in construing the phrase 'the directors of the company' in relation to the former

---

[79] *Re a Company No 005009 of 1987* (1988) 4 BCC 424; *Akai Pty Ltd v Ho* [2006] FCA 511 (Aust Fed Ct).

[80] This will still be possible when s 156A comes into force (see s 156A(4)).

[81] *Re Hydrodan (Corby) Ltd* [1994] BCC 161 at 164; [1994] 2 BCLC 180 at 183.

[82] *Akai Pty Ltd v Ho* [2006] FCA 511.

[83] *Secretary of State for Trade and Industry v Deverell* [2001] Ch 340; [2000] 2 WLR 907; [2000] 2 BCLC 133 (CA) at [35].

[84] Ibid; *Smithton Ltd (formerly Hobart Capital Markets Ltd) v Naggar* [2014] EWCA Civ 939; [2015] 1 WLR 189; [2014] BCC 482 at [32].

[85] [2012] EWHC 521 (Ch).

[86] Ibid.

[87] [2005] EWHC 1638 (Ch); [2006] FSR 17.

[88] Ibid at [1272].

[89] [2005] EWHC 1638 (Ch); [2006] FSR 17.

CA 1985, s 741(2) (now CA 2006, s 251(2)). Could the fact that a majority of directors acted in accordance with directions from a person mean that that person was able to be classified as a shadow director? His Lordship seemed to think that it could.[90] This appears to be supported by the view of Harman J in *Re Unisoft Group Ltd (No 3)*[91] when he said that where there is a multi-member board, a person cannot be said to be a shadow unless the whole of the board, or at the very least a governing majority of it are accustomed to act on the directions of the alleged shadow.[92] Also the opinion of Hart J in *Lord v Sinai Securities Ltd*[93] is supportive of this approach, for the judge said that it must be demonstrated that all the directors, or at least a consistent majority of them, had been accustomed to act on the directions of the person alleged to be a shadow director. The Australian case of *Buzzle Operations Pty Ltd v Apple Computer (Australia Pty Ltd*[94] lends further support as in that case White J of the New South Wales Supreme Court said that control of the governing majority is sufficient to constitute one as a shadow director.[95]

2.25 In determining whether a person is a shadow director, courts will look at the communications between the alleged shadow and the board, and ascertain, from an objective perspective, whether those communications might be able to be regarded as directions or instructions.[96] In this regard the outcome of the communication is the important element on which to focus.[97] There is no need to establish the fact that the giver of instructions expected them to be followed.[98] If the board is able to be characterised as subservient to a particular person, that indicates shadow directorship on the part of that person, but it is not necessary to establish subservience before one can deem a person to be a shadow director.[99] It is necessary to establish that the directors acted on more than one occasion on the instructions or directions of a person for him or her to be regarded as a shadow, but there is no need to prove that the directors either constantly took instructions during the life of the company or even for a significant period of time,[100] provided, that it can be said that they were accustomed to acting on instructions.[101] According to *Re Unisoft Group Ltd (No 3)*[102] this means that the directors act on the directions or instructions of

---

[90] Ibid at [1272].
[91] [1994] 1 BCLC 609.
[92] Ibid at 620.
[93] [2004] EWHC 1764 (Ch).
[94] [2010] NSWSC 233.
[95] Ibid. The case went on appeal to the NSW Court of Appeal, but the appeal was dismissed ([2011] NSWCA 109).
[96] *Secretary of State for Trade and Industry v Deverell* [2001] Ch 340; [2000] 2 WLR 907; [2000] 2 BCLC 133 (CA) at [35].
[97] Ibid.
[98] Ibid.
[99] Ibid.
[100] *Secretary of State for Trade and Industry v Becker* [2003] 1 BCLC 555.
[101] *Secretary of State for Trade and Industry v Deverell* [2001] Ch 340; [2000] 2 WLR 907; [2000] 2 BCLC 133 (CA).
[102] [1994] 1 BCLC 609 at 620.

the alleged shadow as a matter of regular practice. Lewison J in his mammoth judgment in *Ultraframe (UK) Ltd v Fielding*[103] referred to *Unisoft Group* with apparent approval.[104]

2.26 But it must be noted, as was mentioned earlier when dealing with de facto directors,[105] that in *Smithton Ltd v Naggar*,[106] Rose J said that in deciding whether a person is a shadow director 'hat identification' was important. This means that it is necessary to identify the hat that a person was wearing when he or she had dealings with the company.[107] The judge went on to say that this issue of hat identification was 'an important legal qualification to the general principle that one must look at what the putative director actually does rather than how he is described when deciding whether to impose fiduciary duties upon him'.[108] So, for instance, it would seem that a person that had lent money to a company was entitled to closely monitor what was being done with his or her money and in doing that he or she is likely to be seen as wearing a lender's hat and not the hat of a director.[109] On appeal, the judge's decision was upheld by the Court of Appeal, and Rose J's hat identification approach was not criticised.

2.27 While a bank will not usually be regarded as a shadow director, the possibility of this being proven has been raised.[110] But banks will not be categorised as shadow directors when they merely lay down terms for continuing to provide credit for the business of a company, as these cannot be taken as instructions, for the company is at liberty to take or leave the terms.[111] In *Ultraframe (UK) Ltd v Fielding*[112] Lewison J said that in circumstances where a person who is an alleged shadow director of the company, he or she is entitled to protect his or her own creditor interests without necessarily being regarded as a shadow director.[113] In the Australian case of *Buzzle Operations Pty Ltd v Apple Computer Australia Pty Ltd*[114] a relatively high hurdle was established before a lender or other creditor could be held to be a shadow director. This, together with the comments of Rose J in *Smithton Ltd v Naggar*,[115] might provide some comfort to banks which have been concerned about the possibility of liability being imposed on them on the basis that they have been acting as shadow directors.

---

[103] [2005] EWHC 1638 (Ch); [2006] FSR 17.
[104] Ibid at [1273].
[105] At 2.20.
[106] [2013] EWHC 1961 (Ch).
[107] Ibid at [61].
[108] Ibid at [67].
[109] See *Ultraframe (UK) Ltd v Fielding* [2005] EWHC 1638 (Ch).
[110] *Re a Company (No 005009 of 1987)* (1988) 4 BCC 424.
[111] *Re PFTZM Ltd* [1995] BCC 280 at 292.
[112] [2005] EWHC 1638 (Ch).
[113] Ibid at [1267].
[114] [2010] NSWSC 233 and on appeal at [2011] NSWCA 109.
[115] [2013] EWHC 1961 (Ch).

2.28 As mentioned earlier,[116] the interpretation by the courts of the legislation covering shadow directors has made it plain that it is not sufficient to establish that a person had control of a single or even several directors; he or she must control a governing majority of the board.[117] While the legislation focuses on the concepts of 'direction' and 'instruction', this is not meant to exclude the concept of 'advice' for, according to the Court of Appeal in *Secretary of State for Trade and Industry v Deverell*,[118] all three share the common feature of 'guidance'.

2.29 Section 170(5) originally provided that 'the general duties apply to shadow directors where, and to the extent that, the corresponding common law rules or equitable principles so apply'. There was significant uncertainty for several years as to whether shadow directors owed the fiduciary duties that are owed by directors in general. In *Yukong Line Ltd of Korea v Rendsburg Investments Corp of Liberia (No2)*[119] Toulson J (as he then was) was strongly of the view that they did. His Lordship said: 'Mr Yamvrias undoubtedly owed a fiduciary duty to Rendsburg. Although he was not formally a director, he was a "shadow director" and controlled the company's activities.'[120] Yet later, in *Ultraframe (UK) Ltd v Fielding*,[121] Lewison J was not so persuaded. His Lordship went on to say that the indirect influence that is provided by the paradigm shadow director, who is not directly involved with or claims the right to deal directly with the company's assets, will not usually be sufficient to impose fiduciary duties upon the shadow,[122] although his Lordship did think that the company might be able to take action against the shadow if he or she could be said to have knowingly assisted the breaching of duties by the directors of the company.[123] More recently what was said in obiter by Hildyard J in *Secretary of State for Business Innovation and Skills; Re UKLI Ltd*[124] seemed to suggest that a shadow director might owe such duties. His Lordship, after referring to what Lewison J had stated, said that the defendant before him plainly was in a fiduciary position whether he was to be regarded as acting as a de facto or as a shadow director. Hence, to his Lordship it did not matter whether the defendant was a de facto or a shadow, he had to be considered a fiduciary, and, therefore, he would be subject to fiduciary duties. This view was supported even more recently by Newey J in *Viviendi SA v Richards*.[125] His Lordship provided a helpful examination of the issue in his judgment. The judge came to the conclusion that there were a number of reasons for taking the view that shadow directors do commonly owe fiduciary duties to at least some

---

[116] At 2.24.
[117] P Witney 'Duties Owed by Shadow Directors: Closing in on the Puppet Masters?' [2016] JBL 311 at 313 and referring to *Re Unisoft Group Ltd (No 3)* [1994] 1 BCLC 609 at 620; *Lord v Sinai Securities Ltd* [2004] EWHC 1764, [2004] BCC 986.
[118] [2001] Ch 340; [2000] 2 WLR 907; [2000] 2 BCLC 133 (CA).
[119] [1998] BCC 870.
[120] [1998] BCC 870 at 884.
[121] [2005] EWHC 1638 (Ch) at [1284].
[122] [2005] EWHC 1638 (Ch) at [1289].
[123] [2005] EWHC 1638 (Ch) at [1280].
[124] [2013] EWHC 680 (Ch) at [48].
[125] [2013] EWHC 3006 (Ch).

degree.[126] His Lordship felt that *Ultraframe (UK) Ltd v Fielding* understated the extent to which shadow directors owe fiduciary duties, and opined: 'It seems to me that shadow directors will typically owe such [fiduciary] duties in relation to at least the directions or instructions that he gives to the de jure directors.'[127] With respect, this approach certainly appears to be a stronger and preferable one, with the result that the approach of Newey J is likely to meet with the approval of several academic commentators who disagreed with Lewison J.[128] Also, White J in the Australian case of *Buzzle Operations Pty Ltd v Apple Computer Australia Pty Ltd*[129] said that a shadow director does owe a duty to act in good faith in the best interests of the company,[130] and this is the leading fiduciary duty to which directors have been subject for many years.

2.30 The view that shadows should be subject to fiduciary duties is further backed up by the fact that it seems strange if the persons who are accustomed to following the directions and instructions of the shadow do owe fiduciary duties, yet the one giving the directions does not. It could be argued that it is up to the directors who are under duties to be careful and not to fall 'under the spell' of anyone who neither has any right to direct company business nor has any obligation of loyalty to the company. Perhaps even more importantly the 'company does not look to him [a shadow] to promote its interests'.[131] It is up to the directors to be discerning. Section 89(1) of the Small Business, Enterprise and Employment Act 2015, which came into force on 26 May 2015,[132] seems to address the foregoing debate by amending s 170(5). Section 170(5) now provides: 'The general duties apply to a shadow director of a company where and to the extent that they are capable of so applying.' The provision appears to sidestep the case-law as any reference to the common law rules is removed, and while that might render the uncertainty emanating from the debate discussed above otiose, it does not state the position clearly. It could indeed be argued that the Parliament was intending to make shadow directors as responsible as de jure directors as far as duties are concerned, but as indicated, I am not sure that it is providing as much clarity as one might have hoped for.[133]

2.31 Finally, Professor Riz Mokal has made the point that if a director delegates his or her decision-making power to a person (X) lower in the chain of command and the director is accustomed to acting on the instructions of X then X may be regarded as a shadow director and liable under certain provisions.[134]

---

[126] Ibid at [142].

[127] Ibid at [143].

[128] For example, see D D Prentice and J Payne 'Directors' Fiduciary Duties' (2006) 122 LQR 558 at 562; D Kershaw *Company Law in Context* (OUP, 2nd edn, 2012) at 330.

[129] [2010] NSWSC 233.

[130] Ibid at [247].

[131] [2005] EWHC 1638 (Ch) at [1280].

[132] Small Business, Enterprise and Employment Act 2015, s 164(3)(g)(iii).

[133] But see C Moore 'Obligations in the Shade: The Application of Fiduciary Duties to Shadow Directors' (2016) 36 *Legal Studies* 326 at 327.

[134] *Corporate Insolvency: Theory and Application* (OUP, 2005) at 266.

D Distinguishing between de facto and shadow directors

2.32   While it was the prevailing position at one time in English law that one had to distinguish between a shadow and a de facto director, as the terms did not overlap,[135] this has been overturned. In *Re Kaytech International plc*[136] Robert Walker LJ tentatively said that the two different designations were not necessarily mutually exclusive.[137] Subsequently, in *Re Mea Corp Ltd*,[138] Lewison J saw no conceptual difficulty in saying that a person might be both a shadow and a de facto director simultaneously. The judge did add in the later case that a person might be both a shadow and a de facto in succession.[139] The Court of Appeal in *Smithton Ltd (formerly Hobart Capital Markets td) v Naggar* has affirmed that a person may be both a shadow director and a de facto director at the same time.[140] Also, the Supreme Court in *Revenue and Customs Commissioners v Holland; Re Paycheck Services 3 Ltd* has acknowledged that the tests for de facto and shadow directors are overlapping and not mutually exclusive.[141] This can only be a good thing as it makes the law far more clear and able to be applied sensibly.

2.33   After saying all of that, what are the distinguishing features? A de facto director claims, and purports, to act for the company as a director and is held out as such by the company even though he or she has never been appointed properly. To prove that a person was a de facto director, it is necessary 'to plead and prove that he undertook functions in relation to the company which could properly be discharged only by a director',[142] and it is not sufficient that it is proved that the person was involved in the company's management. In contrast, a shadow does not make a claim to act for the company as a director; on the contrary he or she usually maintains that he or she is not a director. Shadows tend to act behind the scenes (although this is not necessary) and hide behind the de jure directors of the company, perhaps 'pulling the strings',[143] while the activity of de facto directors may well be more obvious.[144]

IV THE DIRECTOR'S POSITION AS A FIDUCIARY

2.34   In the early company cases directors were described as trustees.[145] Trustees and directors have a lot in common, such as the fact that they both must avoid conflicts of interest situations and neither must profit from their

---

[135] *Re Hydrodan (Corby) Ltd* [1994] BCC 161 at 163; [1994] 2 BCLC 180.
[136] [1999] 2 BCLC 351.
[137] Ibid at 423.
[138] [2006] EWHC 1846 (Ch) at [89]; [2007] BCC 288 at 307.
[139] Ibid.
[140] [2014] EWCA Civ 939; [2015] 1 WLR 189; [2014] BCC 482 at [32].
[141] [2010] UKSC 51; [2011] BCC 1.
[142] *Re Hydrodan (Corby) Ltd* [1994] BCC 161 at 163; [1994] 2 BCLC 180.
[143] *Re PFTZM Ltd* [1995] BCC 280 at 292 per HHJ Paul Baker QC.
[144] *Re Hydrodan (Corby) Ltd* [1994] BCC 161 at 163; [1994] 2 BCLC 180.
[145] For instance, see *Re Cameron's Coalbrook Railway Co* (1854) 18 Beav 339; 52 ER 134; *Ferguson v Wilson* (1866) LR 2 Ch App 77; *Overend Gurney & Co v Gurney* (1869) LR 4 Ch App 701.

positions of trust. Historically, the fact that directors were described as trustees is related to the fact that in early company law, when companies were unincorporated, the property of the company was vested in trustees. But after the time when companies could incorporate under the Joint Stock Companies Act 1844, directors still tended to be referred to as trustees,[146] with Lindley LJ in *Re Lands Allotment Co*[147] saying that the law has always treated directors as trustees of money that is received by the company or which is under their control. Sir George Jessel expressed a similar view in *Re Forest of Dean, Coal Mining Co*[148] when he said: 'directors are called trustees. They are no doubt trustees of assets which have come into their hands, or which are under their control.'[149] This appears still to be the case.[150]

2.35 Sir George Jessel had said earlier:[151]

> 'Directors have sometimes been called trustees, or commercial trustees, and sometimes they have been called managing partners, it does not matter what you call them so long as you understand what their true position is, which is that they are really commercial men managing a trading concern for the benefit of themselves and all other shareholders in it.'

Continuing the idea that directors were trustees was not appropriate as the property of the company was held by the company (as a separate legal entity) and did not need to vest in any persons acting as trustees.

2.36 Nevertheless, while James LJ in *Smith v Anderson*[152] adverted to the fact that trustees and directors were clearly distinguishable, some subsequent cases referred to directors as 'quasi-trustees'.[153] The fact that directors were trustees was finally dismissed in *Re City Equitable Fire Insurance Co*[154] in 1925 when Romer J accepted that directors were, like trustees, fiduciaries but he said that the duties of directors were not analogous to those of trustees.[155] It has been made plain more recently that directors are not trustees, but they are

---

[146] For instance, see *A-G v Belfast Corporation* (1844) Ir Ch 119. For a classic discussion of the area, see L S Sealy 'The Director as Trustee' [1967] CLJ 83.

[147] [1894] 1 Ch 616 (CA).

[148] (1878) 10 Ch D 450. Also, see *Great Eastern Ry Co v Turner* (1872) LR 8 Ch 149.

[149] *Re Forest of Dean, Coal Mining Co* (1878) 10 Ch D 450 at 453. Also, see *Re Duckwari plc (No 2), Duckwari plc v Offerventure Ltd (No 2)* [1999] Ch 253 at 262; [1998] 2 BCLC 315 at 321.

[150] *Re Duckwari plc (No 2), Duckwari plc v Offerventure Ltd (No 2)* [1999] Ch 253 at 262; [1998] 2 BCLC 315 at 321.

[151] (1878) 10 Ch D 450 at 451–452.

[152] (1880) 15 Ch D 247 at 275.

[153] For instance, *Re Exchange Banking Co (Flitcroft's Case)* (1882) 21 Ch D 519 at 534; *Leeds Estate, Building and Investment Co v Shepherd* (1887) 36 Ch D 787 at 798.

[154] [1925] Ch 407 at 426. More recently, see *Ultraframe (UK) Ltd v Fielding* [2005] EWHC 1638 (Ch); [2006] FSR 17 at [1252], [1295].

[155] Also, see the comments of the Law Commission in its inquiry in *Company Directors: Regulating Conflicts of Interests and Formulating a Statement of Duties*, Law Com No 153, Scots Law Com No 105, 1998 at para 11.2.

fiduciaries.[156] For, unlike trustees, who are to exercise a degree of restraint, directors are entitled to take greater risks with company property and embrace investments never able to be considered by trustees; taking such action is perhaps consistent with the director's entrepreneurial role. So, directors have different discretions and expectations to fulfil.[157] And, of course, at the heart of the fiduciary relationship is the matter of trust.[158] Perhaps the best we can say is that directors have trustee-like duties in some circumstances and they are in a closely analogous position.[159] After all is said and done, directors are fiduciaries[160] and fiduciary principles are trust principles.[161]

2.37   We can also say that directors are agents of the company,[162] and are, on that interpretation alone to be regarded as fiduciaries and to owe fiduciary duties to their principal. Also, courts have regularly applied trustee duties to directors by way of analogy, and the duties of good faith imposed by the fiduciary relationship 'are virtually identical with those imposed on trustees'.[163] In the Australian High Court decision of *Mills v Mills*[164] Dixon J referred to directors as 'fiduciary agents'.

2.38   So, directors are fiduciaries, but we cannot go further than that. While we can categorise a director as a fiduciary, that does not solve everything because there is some uncertainty about the role of a fiduciary. This is not helped by the fact that the judiciary has failed to define the fiduciary concept.[165] What the courts have said about fiduciaries is that loyalty is the distinguishing obligation of such persons.[166] The fundamental aspect of loyalty is that the director acts for proper purposes and without self-interest[167] (concepts dealt

---

[156] For example, see *Bairstow v Queen's Moat Houses plc* [2001] EWCA Civ 712; [2001] 2 BCLC 531 at [50]; *Westpac Banking Corp v Bell Group Ltd (No 3) [2012] WASCA 157*; (2012) 89 ACSR 1 at [848].

[157] See L S Sealy 'The Director as Trustee' [1967] CLJ 83.

[158] *Youyang Pty Ltd v Minter Ellison Morris Fletcher* [2003] HCA 15; (2003) 212 CLR 484; *Westpac Banking Corp v Bell Group Ltd (No 3) [2012] WASCA 157*; (2012) 89 ACSR 1.

[159] *Bairstow v Queens Moat Houses plc* [2001] EWCA Civ 712 at [49]–[52], [2001] 2 BCLC 531 at [49]–[52]; *Sinclair Investments (UK) Ltd Versailles Trade Finance Ltd* [2011] EWCA Civ 347; [2011] 3 WLR 1153; [2011] 2 BCLC 501 at [34].

[160] See *Regal (Hastings) Ltd v Gulliver* [1967] 2 AC 134 at 159; *Eclairs Group Ltd v JKX Oil & Gas Plc* [2015] UKSC 71; [2015] Bus L R 1395; [2016] BCC 79; [2016] 1 BCLC 1. Also, see R Parsons 'The Director's Duty of Good Faith' (1967) 5 MULR 395 at 397.

[161] L S Sealy 'The Director as Trustee' [1967] CLJ 83 at 86.

[162] *Aberdeen Rly Co v Blaikie Bros* [1854] 2 Eq Rep 1281; [1854] 1 Macq 461; [1843–1860] All ER Rep 249 (HL). Some, particularly those holding to a neo-classical economics perspective, will argue that directors are agents of the shareholders (the shareholders often being referred to as 'the owners' of the company). This is discussed later in the next chapter.

[163] P Davies *Gower and Davies' Principles of Modern Company Law* (London, Sweet and Maxwell, 7th edn, 2003) at 380.

[164] (1938) 60 CLR 150 at 185.

[165] For example, *Lloyds Bank v Bundy* [1975] QB 326; *Hospital Products Ltd v United States Surgical Corp* (1985) 156 CLR 41 and referred to in M Conaglen 'The Nature and Function of Fiduciary Loyalty' (2005) 121 LQR 452 at 452. Also, see S Worthington 'Fiduciaries: When is Self-Denial Obligatory?' (1999) 58 CLJ 500 at 501.

[166] *Bristol and West Building Society v Mothew* [1998] 1 Ch 1 at 18 (CA).

[167] S Worthington 'Reforming Directors' Duties' (2001) 64 MLR 439 at 448.

within the scope of Chapter 2 of Part 10 of CA 2006), and a fiduciary, is someone who agrees to act for another person's interests.[168] According to Millett LJ in *Bristol and West Building Society v Mothew*:[169] 'The principal is entitled to the single-minded loyalty of his fiduciary ... he may not act ... for the benefit of a third person without the informed consent of his principal.'[170] Millett LJ said in this case that 'fiduciary duty' is restricted to duties that are peculiar to fiduciaries and if it is breached it leads to different consequences from the breach of other duties.[171] The House of Lords in *Hilton v Barker Booth and Eastwood*[172] has said that not every breach committed by a fiduciary is a breach of fiduciary duty. For example, as we noted in **Chapter 1**, the duty of care is not a fiduciary duty; this is because it is a duty that is not peculiar to fiduciaries.[173]

2.39 The original notion of fiduciary duty is a product of the law of equity concerning the duty of a person in a discretionary position of trust to serve the interests of another person.[174] Despite the fact that the fiduciary relationship has been an element in English law for over 250 years,[175] it is based on what still remains an elusive concept,[176] and is difficult to define.[177] This is probably exacerbated by the fact that one should not think of fiduciary duties that are owed to companies as something that is fixed.[178] The critical aspect of the relationship is that the fiduciary agrees to act on behalf of another in exercising powers or a discretion, and the fiduciary is given a special opportunity to use powers or the discretion to the prejudice of the other person, who is vulnerable, and, in effect, at the mercy of the fiduciary.[179] The fiduciary is obliged to act in the interests of the vulnerable person to the exclusion of his or her own interests.[180] It is accepted that directors of companies are fiduciaries for the assets of their companies which come under their control.[181] As indicated above, loyalty is very much at the heart of the relationship and is reflected in the duties that are imposed on directors. As mentioned previously, directors

---

[168] A Scott 'The Fiduciary Principle' (1949) 37 *California Law Review* 539 at 540.
[169] [1998] 1 Ch 1.
[170] Ibid at 18.
[171] Ibid at 16.
[172] [2005] UKHL 8; [2005] 1 WLR 567 at [29].
[173] M Conaglen 'The Nature and Function of Fiduciary Loyalty' (2005) 121 LQR 452 at 456.
[174] See *Re Smith & Fawcett Ltd* [1942] Ch 304 at 306, 308. Also, see D DeMott 'Beyond Metaphor: An Analysis of Fiduciary Obligation' (1988) Duke L J 879 at 880–881.
[175] The roots of fiduciary duties are explained in *Bishop of Woodhouse v Meredith* (1820) 1 Jac & W 204 at 213. See R Cooter and B Freedman 'The Fiduciary Relationship: Its Economic Character and Legal Consequences' (1991) 66 NYU L Rev 1045 at 1045–1046.
[176] D DeMott 'Beyond Metaphor: An Analysis of Fiduciary Obligation' (1988) Duke LJ 879 at 879; P Finn 'Fiduciary Law and the Modern Commercial World' in E McKendrick (ed) *Commercial Aspects of Trusts and Fiduciary Obligations* (Oxford, Clarendon Press, 1992) at 8.
[177] *Hospital Products Ltd v United States Surgical Corporation* (1984) 156 CLR 41 (Aust HC).
[178] Ibid. See E Thomas 'The Role of Nominee Directors and the Liability of their Appointors' in F Padfield (ed) *Perspectives on Company Law* (London, Kluwer, 1997), vol 2 at 248.
[179] *Hospital Products Ltd v United States Surgical Corporation* (1984) 156 CLR 41 at 96–97.
[180] P Finn 'Fiduciary Law and the Modern Commercial World' in E McKendrick (ed) *Commercial Aspects of Trusts and Fiduciary Obligations* (Oxford, Clarendon Press, 1992) at 9.
[181] See *J J Harrison (Properties) Ltd v Harrison* [2002] 1 BCLC 162.

have always, in addition, owed duties of care, which have evolved out of the equitable fiduciary relationship between director and company.[182]

2.40 It is worth mentioning at this point that directors are members of a board of directors and they will act collectively and owe duties collectively.[183] Yet, all directors individually owe fiduciary duties to the company.[184]

2.41 The above addresses the purely legal issue of fiduciary duties. The economic function of such duties has become of importance in later years. In the view of perhaps the leading school of thinking in corporate law, the law and economics scholars, 'the economic function of fiduciary duties is to regulate the complex web of agency relationships which comprise the structure of the corporate enterprise'.[185] Put another way, fiduciary duties, according to the law and economics school, are a contractual 'device uniquely crafted to fill in the massive gap in this open-ended bargain between shareholders and corporate officers and directors'.[186] We will come back to this in the next chapter when considering some of the theory behind corporate governance that involves directors.

V GROUPS OF COMPANIES

2.42 It is frequently the case in today's world to find companies are part of a group. This presents all sorts of problems, such as identifying which company might be liable for a particular action. The law is that each company is a separate legal personality and, in the context of this work, we must note that directors owe duties to the individual company to which they have been appointed, and not to a group.[187]

VI DURATION OF DUTIES

2.43 Obviously a person is not subject to the duties under consideration here until he or she is appointed as a director, unless previously regarded as a shadow or de facto director. But the duties do not necessarily come to an end when the director's post is terminated, whether by dismissal or resignation. At common law a director is not generally under the general duties after he or she

---

[182] R P Austin, H A J Ford and I M Ramsay *Company Directors* (Sydney, LexisNexis Butterworths, 2005) at 53.

[183] *Re Barings plc (No 5)* [1999] 1 BCLC 433 at 486.

[184] *Re Westmid Packing Service Ltd (No 3)* [1998] 2 All ER 124; [1998] BCC 836 at 842; [1998] 2 BCLC 646 at 653; *Re Barings plc (No 5)* [1999] 1 BCLC 433 at 486.

[185] R Sappideen 'Fiduciary Obligations to Corporate Creditors' [1991] JBL 365 at 382 and referring to F Easterbrook and D Fischel 'Corporate Control Transactions' (1982) 92 Yale L J 698 at 700. In fact the correct volume number is '91'.

[186] J Macey 'An Economic Analysis of the Various Rationales for Making Shareholders the Exclusive Beneficiaries of Corporate Fiduciary Duties' (1991) 21 *Stetson Law Review* 23 at 41.

[187] *Secretary of State for Trade and Industry v Goldberg* [2003] EWHC 2843 (Ch); [2004] 1 BCLC 597 at [29].

has left the company.[188] Section 170 of CA 2006 provides that a person who ceases to be a director continues to be subject to the duties covered by ss 175 and 176,[189] duties that deal, in general terms, with conflict of interests and profiting from one's position. More will be said on this issue in **Chapter 4**. A director who has been involved in a breach but resigns before the breach is complete, is not able to avoid liability by simply resigning.[190]

2.44 If an administrative receiver is appointed the directors still owe duties of loyalty and obligations in relation to conflict of duties.[191] This might not be the case where an administrator is appointed as his or her appointment means that the directors virtually lose their management powers, for those powers are vested in the administrator.[192] However, there might be situations in administration where the obligation to ensure that there is no conflict might be retained.[193] Where a liquidator is appointed to a company the general duties of the directors discussed in this book end; some duties are imposed by legislation for the period of the liquidation. Finally, a director does not owe duties if he or she is effectively excluded from any involvement in company affairs.[194]

---

[188] *Hunter Kane Ltd v Watkins* [2002] EWHC 186 (Ch) and referred to with apparent approbation in *Plus Group Ltd v Pyke* [2002] EWCA Civ 370; [2002] 2 BCLC 201 at [71]; *Foster Bryant Surveying Ltd v Bryant* [2007] EWCA Civ 200; [2007] 2 BCLC 239 at [8].

[189] In *Wilkinson v West Coast Capital* [2005] EWHC 3009 (Ch); [2007] BCC 717 at [251] the same position was articulated in relation to the common law rules.

[190] *Addstead Pty Ltd v Liddan Pty Ltd* (1997) 15 ACLC 1687.

[191] *Ultraframe (UK) Ltd v Fielding* [2005] EWHC 1638 (Ch); [2006] FSR 17 at [1329].

[192] Insolvency Act 1986, Sch B1, paras 59–64.

[193] D D Prentice and J Payne 'Directors' Fiduciary Duties' (2006) 122 LQR 558 at 559. The learned commentators give, as an example, the requirement of the directors under s 235 of the Insolvency Act 1986 to cooperate with the administrator.

[194] *Plus Group Ltd v Pyke* [2002] EWCA Civ 370; [2002] 2 BCLC 201.

CHAPTER 3

DIRECTORS IN THE CORPORATE GOVERNANCE PROCESS

I INTRODUCTION

3.1   While this book focuses on directors' duties, this topic cannot be addressed adequately without considering the position of directors in relation to the corporate governance process, because directors' duties are regarded as a critical corporate governance mechanism.[1] The way that directors act and make decisions is central to corporate governance. The board of directors is responsible for the governance of their companies.[2] It is appropriate that a consideration of corporate governance issues relating to directors and how they fulfill their duties is included in this work. However, it must be emphasised that this chapter does not purport to engage in a substantial consideration of the whole topic of corporate governance, which is voluminous. It merely seeks to set out the context and act as a form of introduction to what follows in relation to duties of directors. First, the Chapter explains the meaning of 'corporate governance.' Then the Chapter proceeds to discuss the problem that exists in large companies, namely the separation of ownership and control. This is followed by an examination of the issue that has been debated for many years: to whom are duties of directors owed? In this regard the focus is on the two primary theories that have addressed this issue, namely the shareholder value theory and the stakeholder theory. Next, the Chapter provides a brief discussion of the agency theory as this theory is often used as the basis for arguing for the existence of duties. The Chapter ends with a discussion of the need for directors, as part of the corporate governance process, to ensure that they record actions and decisions.

II DEFINING CORPORATE GOVERNANCE

3.2   While concerns over corporate governance have been with us since the emergence of the joint stock company many years ago,[3] it is over the past 25

---

[1]   I M Ramsay 'The Corporate Governance Debate and the Role of Directors' Duties' in I M Ramsay (ed) *Corporate Governance and the Duties of Company Directors* (Centre for Corporate Law and Securities Regulation, University of Melbourne, 1997) at 10.

[2]   *Report on the Financial Aspects of Corporate Governance* (London, Gee, 1992) at para 2.5 ('Cadbury Report').

[3]   D Prentice 'Some Aspects of the Corporate Governance Debate' in D Prentice and P Holland (eds) *Contemporary Issues in Corporate Governance* (Oxford, Clarendon Press, 1993) at 26.

years or so that the topic of corporate governance has become a critical aspect of company law, and it has spawned a huge amount of literature. Notwithstanding all of this, it is not an easy expression to define. It has been variously defined. Some commentators emphasise that it is about the understanding of, and institutional arrangements for, relationships among the many actors who may have direct or indirect interests in the company.[4] There are a myriad of explanations of corporate governance. Here are some of them.

3.3   It has been said that it is 'concerned with the relationship between the structure of rules, laws and conventional practices within which companies operate and their style of management and the decisions that they make'.[5]

3.4   Professor John Farrar has said that corporate governance is a subject that involves considerations of 'the legitimacy of corporate power, corporate accountability and standards by which the corporation is to be governed and by whom'.[6] Professors Simon Deakin and Alan Hughes have defined corporate governance at a fundamental level as being 'concerned with the relationship between the internal governance mechanisms of corporations, and society's conception of the scope of corporate accountability'.[7]

3.5   Perhaps the broadest (and briefest) explanation is the statement of Thomas Clarke in his introduction to the excellent inter-disciplinary book on corporate governance, *Theories of Corporate Governance*: 'It concerns the exercise of power in corporate entities.'[8]

3.6   Of importance for this book is the definition contained in the *Report on the Financial Aspects of Corporate Governance* (commonly referred to as 'the Cadbury Report'), namely, 'the system by which companies are directed and controlled'.[9] This is a definition that has been frequently cited all around the world. The Department for Business Enterprise and Regulatory Reform took the Cadbury definition and added to it. It stated:[10]

---

[4]   S Letza, X Sun and J Kirkbride 'Shareholding and Stakeholding: A Critical Review of Corporate Governance' (2004) 12 *Corporate Governance: An International Review* 242 at 242.

[5]   C Villiers and G Boyle 'Corporate Governance and the Approach to Regulation' in L Macgregor, T Prosser and C Villiers (eds) *Regulation and Markets Beyond 2000* (Dartmouth, Ashgate, 2000) at 221 and referring to J Kay and K Silberston 'Corporate Governance' (1995) 153 *National Institute Economic Review* at 85.

[6]   J Farrar 'Corporate Governance, Business Judgment and the Professionalism of Directors' (1993) 5 *Corporate and Business Law Journal* 1.

[7]   'Comparative Corporate Governance: An Interdisciplinary Agenda' (1997) 24 *Journal of Law and Society* 1 at 2.

[8]   New York, Routledge, 2004 at 1.

[9]   London, Gee, 1992 at para 2.5.

[10]   The definition originally appeared at www.berr.gov.uk/bbf/corp-governance/page15267.html and now this has been superseded by the following address: http://webarchive.nationalarchives. gov.uk/20090902193559/berr.gov.uk/whatwedo/businesslaw/corp-governance/page15267.html (accessed 4 October 2016).

'Corporate governance is the system by which companies are directed and controlled. It deals largely with the relationship between the constituent parts of a company – the directors, the board (and its sub-committees) and the shareholders.'

3.7　There is much to be said for the view that corporate governance is concerned with: who controls the company, for whom is the company governed and the ways in which control is exerted.[11]

3.8　According to the financial economists, agency theorists and law and economics scholars, corporate governance is a matter of how shareholders address directorial opportunism and shirking.

3.9　Certainly, corporate governance is of concern because of the potential (if not actual) conflict of interest that exists for those persons who are involved in the company. For instance, the directors who effectively control the company, the managers, have a conflict of interest, namely between benefitting themselves through their position or benefitting the company (and ultimately the shareholders). Dealing with the conflicts concerned cannot be left entirely to contract, because, inter alia, it is difficult, if not impossible, to draft contracts that cover all possible eventualities. The result is that all contracts are incomplete (due to cognitive limitations).[12]

3.10　The duties owed by directors are clearly seen as an integral part of the corporate governance system, and operate to address, to a degree, the conflicts that directors have in their role.[13] But, one of the major debates that has haunted company law for many years is: to whom do directors owe their duties in the governance process? This is an issue that is considered in **Chapters 4** and **6**, but we need to deal with it in the context of corporate governance at this point as it is a critical aspect of company law and really involves issues that go well beyond the topic of duties. We will consider the area once we have examined some critical theories that are relevant to dealing with the issue of: to whom are duties owed?[14]

III SEPARATION OF OWNERSHIP AND CONTROL AND DIRECTORIAL DISCIPLINE

3.11　There are two principal organs of the company: the members in general meeting and the board of directors.[15] During the nineteenth century the board

---

[11]　H Gospel and A Pendleton 'Finance, Corporate Governance and the Management of Labour: A Conceptual and Comparative Analysis' (2003) 41 *British Journal of Industrial Relations* 557 at 560.

[12]　See A Keay and H Zhang 'Incomplete Contracts, Contingent Fiduciaries and a Director's Duty to Creditors' (2008) 32 *Melbourne University Law Review* 141.

[13]　There are, of course, other mechanisms that are employed, such as contracts and members' powers to vote and remove directors.

[14]　For a discussion of this issue, see A Keay *The Corporate Objective* (Cheltenham, Edward Elgar, 2011).

[15]　See *John Shaw & Sons (Salford) Ltd v Shaw* [1935] 2 KB 113 at 134.

was seen as the delegate of the general meeting and the meeting could direct the board.[16] But since the decisions in *Automatic Self-Cleansing Filter Syndicate Co Ltd v Cunninghame*[17] and *Quin & Arxtens Ltd v Salmon*,[18] where the powers of the board are given by provisions in the articles, the members have not been able to interfere in the actions taken by the directors, and the members cannot direct how the board operates. Barwick CJ of the Australian High Court said in *Ashburton Oil NL v Alpha Minerals NL*[19] that:

> 'Directors who are minded to do something which in their honest view is for the benefit of the company are not to be restrained because a majority shareholder or shareholders holding a majority of shares in the company do not want the directors so to act.'[20]

3.12 There is little said in the CA 2006 concerning the division of power between members and directors. Typically, today the company's articles of association will vest in the board of directors' broad general management powers[21] concerning the affairs of the company, and this will determine the power distribution in a company. Where directors have been given wide-ranging powers, then they alone can exercise them, and the only thing that the members can do is to pass a special resolution to amend the articles.[22] The directors must report to the members in general meeting, but a major issue in corporate governance is whether the directors are sufficiently accountable to the members.[23] Undoubtedly, 'the requirement of accountability in financial and managerial decision-making is a mainstay of the regulatory system of modern corporate law'.[24] If there was not accountability then directors could well engage in furthering self-interests (referred to usually as 'opportunism') or failing to do all that they could for shareholders (referred to as 'shirking') and members could become mistrustful of the directors. But the fact of the matter is that without accountability then no matter whether directors acted properly or

---

[16]   For instance, see *Isle of Wight Rly Co v Tahourdin* (1883) and noted in A Dignam and J Lowry *Company Law* (OUP, 5th edn, 2008) at 264.

[17]   [1906] 2 Ch 34.

[18]   [1909] AC 442. This is the position also in Australia. For instance, see *Howard Smith Ltd v Ampol Petroleum Ltd* [1974] AC 821 at 837 (a Privy Council decision on appeal from Australian courts); *NRMA Ltd v Parker* (1986) 6 NSWLR 517; (1986) 11 ACLR 1; (1986) 4 ACLC 609.

[19]   (1971) 123 CLR 614.

[20]   Ibid at 620.

[21]   The Companies (Model Articles) Regulations 2008, SI 2008/3229, reg 2, Sch 1, art 5 (private companies); reg 4, Sch 3, art 5 (public companies); the Companies (Tables A–F) Regulations 1985, art 70 of Table A.

[22]   *John Shaw & Sons (Salford) Ltd v Shaw* [1935] 2 KB 113.

[23]   R P Austin, H A J Ford and I M Ramsay *Company Directors* (Sydney, LexisNexis Butterworths, 2005) at 62. See A Keay *Board Accountability in Corporate Governance* (Abingdon, Routledge, 2015).

[24]   S Bottomley *The Constitutional Corporation* (Aldershot, Ashgate, 2007) at 58.

not, the element of suspicion would exist.[25] Accountability of boards is required to balance the fact that boards are given such broad power and authority.[26]

3.13   In the larger Anglo-American company, a critical element of corporate governance is, traditionally, that as the shareholding is so dispersed no one shareholder or group of shareholders have effective control over the management of the company. Besides running and overseeing the running of the company, the board of directors has the ability to control the processes of meetings of shareholders, being able to rely on proxy voting and the conduct of meetings to enhance their control. The movement of power from those who 'own' the company, namely the shareholders,[27] to those who control it, the managers, and with it the idea of separation of control and ownership, was first identified by American academics, Adolf Berle and Gardiner Means in the early 1930s,[28] and it has generally been accepted today as explaining the situation that exists in larger companies.[29] However, it must be said that there is not so much of a dispersed ownership in listed UK companies now compared with previous years.[30] A large portion of UK shares in listed companies are owned either by institutional shareholders or foreign shareholders.

3.14   As directors are in control of a company, and key to the whole corporate governance process, it is necessary to ensure that they are subject to some disciplinary measures if they fail to perform or act improperly. It has been asserted that the concept of separation of ownership and control 'leads inexorably to the conclusion that the central goal of corporate governance is to

---

[25]   Ibid at 73. For a discussion of the importance of accountability in corporate governance, see M Moore *Corporate Governance in the Shadow of the State* (Hart Publishing, 2013); A Keay *Board Accountability in Corporate Governance* (Abingdon, Routledge, 2015).

[26]   A Keay *Board Accountability in Corporate Governance* (Abingdon, Routledge, 2015).

[27]   It is debatable whether the shareholders can be said to own the company. See M Lipton and S Rosenblum 'A New System of Corporate Governance: The Quinquennial Election of Directors' (1991) 58 U Chi L Rev 187 at 195; P Ireland 'Capitalism Without the Capitalist: The Joint Stock Company Share and the Emergence of the Modern Doctrine of Separate Corporate Personality' (1996) 17 *Legal History* 40; M Eisenberg 'The Conception that the Corporation is a Nexus of Contracts, and the Dual Nature of the Firm' (1999) 24 J Corp L 819; S Worthington 'Shares and Shareholders: Property, Power and Entitlement' (Part 1) (2001) 22 Co Law 258 and Part 2 (2001) 22 Co Law 307. Also, see *Short v Treasury Commissioners* [1948] 1 KB 116 at 122 where Evershed LJ denied the fact that shareholders were the owners of a company; Committee on the Financial Aspects of Corporate Governance (Cadbury Report) (London, Gee, 1992) at para 6.1; Confederation of British Industries, *Boards Without Tiers: A CBI Contribution to the Debate* (London, CBI, 1996) at 8.

[28]   See A A Berle and G Means *The Modern Corporation and Private Property* (New York, MacMillan, 1932).

[29]   In small companies the shareholders and the directors are often one and the same, so there is no real separation between ownership and control.

[30]   See the latest available report from the Office for National Statistics on *Ownership of UK Quoted Shares 2014* and accessible at: www.ons.gov.uk/economy/ investmentspensionsandtrusts/bulletins/ownershipofukquotedshares/2015-09-02 (accessed 4 October 2016).

discipline managers ...'.[31] Professors Julian Franks, Colin Mayer and Luc Renneboog identify[32] five ways in which managers can be disciplined for poor performance. These are:

- replacement following the acquisition of a large block of shares;
- bidders may take action after acquiring a company;
- non-executive directors might replace directors;
- financial crises might lead to interventions by shareholders when new equity is issued; and
- shareholders might intervene and remove directors or request the board to replace directors.[33]

3.15 The effectiveness of these avenues for discipline vary. The mechanism that has attracted a lot of support over the years is the takeover. The theory provides that if directors are not performing, then they risk the company being taken over by another company that sees the potential of the former company, and subsequently, after completion of the takeover, the directors in post before that will be dismissed. But there has been theoretical argument[34] and some empirical research[35] that denies the efficacious nature of the takeover in this regard. The general use of the market for corporate control has also been questioned as an adequate device for disciplining directors.[36] Much is often made of the fact that the shareholders have ultimate power in a company, because they can vote to remove directors or refrain from re-electing them, but it has been argued that there are significant hurdles put in front of shareholders if they wish to take disciplinary action against directors.[37]

3.16 One of the major concerns is to ensure that directors do not engage in opportunistic and self-serving activity or shirking (failing to do their jobs properly). Various strategies can be put in place to prevent this. One of those is

---

[31] M Lipton and S Rosenblum 'A New System of Corporate Governance: The Quinquennial Election of Directors' (1991) 58 U Chi L Rev 187 at 187.

[32] 'Who Disciplines Management in Poorly Performing Companies?' (2001) 10 *Journal of Financial Intermediation* 209 at 210.

[33] Perhaps we can add liquidation and administration to the list. These insolvency regimes will see the control of the company being taken from the directors and given to an independent office-holder. Generally, see A Keay 'Company Directors Behaving Poorly: Disciplinary Options for Shareholders' [2007] JBL 656.

[34] M Lipton and S Rosenblum 'A New System of Corporate Governance: The Quinquennial Election of Directors' (1991) 58 U Chi L Rev 187 at 188; R Booth 'Stockholders, Stakeholders and Bagholders (or How Investor Diversification Affects Fiduciary Duty)' (1998) 53 *The Business Lawyer* 429 at 440. For a more recent view, see L Bebchuk 'The Myth of the Shareholder Franchise' (October 2005) and accessible at http://papers.ssrn.com/sol3/papers.cfm?abstract_id=829804.

[35] J Franks and C Mayer 'Hostile Takeovers in the UK and the Correction of Managerial Failure' (1996) 40 *Journal of Financial Economics* 163.

[36] See I Anabtawi 'Some Skepticism About Increasing Shareholder Power' (2006) 53 UCLA L Rev 561 at 568.

[37] A Keay 'Company Directors Behaving Poorly: Disciplinary Options for Shareholders' [2007] JBL 656.

the imposition of duties on directors. Duties imposed on directors are attempts to lay down standards of behaviour, whatever the circumstances.

3.17 A large proportion of companies that are incorporated in the UK are small companies. In such companies ownership and control are often not separated. If individual directors do shirk or act opportunistically in such companies then they might be subject to action from the board. Where all directors shirk or act opportunistically it might precipitate the presentation of a petition under CA 2006, s 994 where the petitioner claims that the company's affairs are being conducted in a manner that is unfairly prejudicial to the interests of the members, or the bringing of a derivative action against the directors.[38]

IV TO WHOM ARE DUTIES OWED?

3.18 As indicated earlier in the Chapter, this has been a hotly debated question for many years, and continues to be so. It is not possible to do justice to the question in this book,[39] given the focus on duties, but we do need to discuss it to some extent. In this section of the Chapter the major arguments, and some of the primary counter-arguments, are set out.

3.19 Notwithstanding which of the major views is adopted concerning the correct subjects of duties, all are agreed that the duties of directors are a significant aspect of company law. As indicated earlier, this book, while touching on policy and some theoretical issues at times, is focused on providing an examination of the law and seeking to undertake an analysis of it.

3.20 There are two primary views as to whom directors owe duties,[40] known as the shareholder value theory[41] (also known as 'shareholder primacy' and 'shareholder wealth maximisation'[42]), and stakeholder theory.

---

[38] See **Chapter 14**.

[39] For a detailed discussion, see A Keay *The Corporate Objective* (Cheltenham, Edward Elgar, 2011).

[40] Another recently devised approach, based on entity theory, is the entity maximisation and sustainability model. See A Keay 'Ascertaining the Corporate Objective: An Entity Maximisation and Sustainability Model' (2008) 71 MLR 663; A Keay *The Corporate Objective* (Cheltenham, Edward Elgar, 2011).

[41] For a discussion of the theory, see, for example, D Gordon Smith 'The Shareholder Primacy Norm' (1998) 23 *Journal of Corporate Law* 277; L Stout 'Bad and Not-so-Bad Arguments for Shareholder Primacy' (2002) 75 *Southern California Law Review* 1189; A Keay 'Shareholder Primacy in Corporate Law: Can it Survive? Should it Survive?' (2010) 7 *European Company and Financial Law Review* 369.

[42] S Bainbridge 'In Defense of the Shareholder Wealth Maximization Norm: A Reply to Professor Green' (1993) 50 *Washington and Lee Law Review* 1423; M Roe 'The Shareholder Wealth Maximization Norm and Industrial Organization' (2001) U Pa L Rev 2063; S Bainbridge 'Director Primacy: The Means and Ends of Corporate Governance' (2003) 97 *Northwestern University Law Review* 547 at 549, 552, 565. The UK's Company Law Review Steering Group did in fact refer to the principle simply as 'shareholder value' (Company Law Review, *Modern Company Law for a Competitive Economy*: 'The Strategic Framework' (London, DTI, 1999) at paras 5.1.12ff).

A Shareholder value principle

1 From a theoretical viewpoint

3.21 The shareholder value theory has been largely fostered as a leading principle of corporate law by the contractarian school of thought in the United States.[43] It was in the US in the early 1930s that we find the genesis of the debate concerning the objective of a company. It all really started in earnest with the debates between Professors Adolf Berle of Columbia University and E Merrick Dodd of Harvard University, and carried out in the literature published at the time.[44] Berle maintained, inter alia, that while there was merit in directors, as managers of companies, having responsibilities to stakeholders in general he could not see that approach being able to be enforced so he accepted a form of shareholder primacy for companies.[45] On the other hand, Dodd resolutely held that the public saw companies as economic institutions that have a social service role to play as well as making profits for shareholders, and that companies had responsibilities to the company's shareholders, employees, customers, and to the general public.[46] While the former conceded defeat eventually, the last three decades of the twentieth century has arguably been characterised as a time when many of Berle's views held sway, especially in the US. It has been said that there has been an ever-increasing focus on shareholder value since the early-1980s.[47] As we will see, Dodd's approach has effectively been championed by the second theory we will consider.

3.22 In a nutshell the shareholder value approach is that the directors are to aim to run the company for the ultimate benefit of the shareholders, that is all decisions should be directed to providing benefits for shareholders, and so directors' duties are owed to the shareholders.

---

[43]   This is not to say that those who do not see themselves as contractarians do not agree with shareholder primacy. For some of the leading works on the principle, see J Macey 'An Economic Analysis of the Various Rationales for Making Shareholders the Exclusive Beneficiaries of Corporate Fiduciary Duties' (1991) 21 *Stetson Law Review* 23; S Bainbridge 'In Defense of the Shareholder Maximization Norm: A Reply to Professor Green' (1993) 50 *Washington and Lee Law Review* 1423; B Black and R Kraakman 'A Self-Enforcing Model of Corporate Law' (1996) 109 *Harvard Law Review* 1911; D Gordon Smith 'The Shareholder Primacy Norm' (1998) 23 J Corp L Rev 277. It must be noted that some contractarians do not accept shareholder primacy: D D Prentice 'The Contractual Theory of the Company and the Protection of Non-Shareholder Interests' in D Feldman and F Meisel (eds) *Corporate and Commercial Law: Modern Developments* (London, Lloyds of London Press, 1996) at 121.

[44]   See A A Berle 'Corporate Powers as Powers in Trust' (1931) 44 Harv L R 1049; E M Dodd 'For Whom are Corporate Managers Trustees?' (1932) 45 Harv L R 1145; A A Berle 'For Whom Managers are Trustees: A Note' (1932) 45 Harv L R 1365. Also, see A A Berle and G Means *The Modern Corporation and Private Property* (New York, MacMillan, 1932); E M Dodd 'Is Effective Enforcement of the Fiduciary Duties of Corporate Managers Practicable?' (1935) 2 U Chi L R 194.

[45]   A A Berle 'Corporate Powers as Powers in Trust' (1931) 44 Harv L R 1049 at 1049. The view was put forward, in effect, in the earlier decision of *Dodge v Ford Motor Co* (1919) 170 NW 668 (Michigan).

[46]   E M Dodd 'For Whom are Corporate Managers Trustees?' (1932) 45 Harv L R 1145 at 1148.

[47]   M Omran, P Atrill and J Pointon 'Shareholders Versus Stakeholders: Corporate Mission Statements and Investor Returns' (2002) 11 *Business Ethics: A European Review* 318 at 319.

3.23 The contractarian theorists, many of whom advocate a law and economics approach to law, focus on the contractual relationships that exist between persons involved in the affairs of the company, and, accordingly, hold to the principle of the sanctity of contract. Many contractarians[48] regard the company as nothing more than a number of complex, private consensual contract-based relations,[49] either express or implied, and they consist of many different kinds of relations that are worked out by those voluntarily associating in a company.[50] The parties involved in these contracts are regarded as rational economic actors, and includes shareholders, managers, creditors and employees, and it is accepted that each of these constituencies endeavour in their contracting to maximise their own positions, with the intention of producing concomitant benefits for themselves.[51] This scheme is usually known by the shorthand expression of 'a nexus of contracts'.[52] The nexus of contracts theory in relation to the firm was devised by economists[53] and embraced by economically inclined law academics.[54] The contractarians generally[55] regard shareholder value as the focal point of their view of the public company.[56] The principle fills gaps in the corporate contract;[57] it establishes 'the substance of the corporate fiduciary duty'.[58]

---

[48] For example, Eugene Fama 'Agency Problems and the Theory of the Firm' (1990) 99 *Journal of Political Economics* 288 at 290.

[49] Referring to the relations as contracts is probably incorrect from a legal perspective. Some authors refer to the relations as bargains as some of the relations do not constitute contracts in a technical sense. See M Klausner 'Corporations, Corporate Law and Networks of Contracts' (1995) 81 *Virginia Law Review* 757, 759.

[50] F Easterbrook and D Fischel 'The Corporate Contract' (1989) 89 Colum L Rev 1416 at 1426. At 1428 the learned commentators give examples of some of the arrangements.

[51] See H Butler 'The Contractual Theory of the Corporation' (1989) 11 *George Mason University Law Review* 99; C A Riley 'Understanding and Regulating the Corporation' (1995) 58 MLR 595 at 598.

[52] The literature considering the nexus of contracts is too voluminous to cite. But see, for example, E E Fama 'Agency Problems and the Theory of the Firm' (1980) 88 *Journal of Political Economy* 228, 290; F Easterbrook and D Fischel 'The Corporate Contract' (1989) 89 Colum L Rev 1416, 1426–1427. The nexus of contracts approach is critiqued by William W Bratton Jr in 'The "Nexus of Contracts Corporation": A Critical Appraisal' (1989) 74 Cornell L Rev 407 at 412, 446–465.

[53] See R Coase 'The Nature of the Firm' (1937) 4 *Economica* 386 at 390–392; A Alchian and H Demsetz 'Production, Information Costs, and Economic Organization' (1972) 62 Am Econ Rev 777 at 794; M Jensen and W Meckling 'Theory of the Firm: Managerial Behaviour, Agency Costs, and Ownership Structure' (1976) 3 *Journal of Financial Economics* 305.

[54] See F Easterbrook and D Fischel 'The Corporate Contract' (1989) 89 Colum L Rev 1416; Easterbrook and Fischel *The Economic Structure of Company Law* (Cambridge, Mass, Harvard University Press, 1991) at 37–39; W Bratton Jr 'The "Nexus of Contracts" Corporation: A Critical Appraisal' (1989) 74 Cornell L Rev 407.

[55] Not all contractarians might agree with this.

[56] M Bradley, C Schipani, A Sundaram and J Walsh 'The Purposes and Accountability of the Corporation in Contemporary Society: Corporate Governance at a Crossroads' (1999) 62 *Law and Contemporary Problems* 9 at 38.

[57] F Easterbrook and D Fischel *The Economic Structure of Company Law* (Cambridge, Mass, Harvard University Press, 1991) at 90–93; J Macey and G Miller 'Corporate Stakeholders: A Contractual Perspective' (1993) 43 *University of Toronto Law Review* 401 at 404.

[58] T Smith 'The Efficient Norm for Corporate Law: A Neotraditional Interpretation of Fiduciary Duty' (1999) 98 *Michigan Law Review* 214 at 217. A view with which Professor Smith disagrees (ibid).

3.24 The preference for shareholder value is not a consequence of a 'philosophical predilection'[59] towards shareholders, but a concern that the business should be run for the benefit of the residual claimants, namely, the shareholders, while the company is solvent.[60] That is, putting it simply, the shareholders get the residue of the company's earnings, after paying off all obligations. This is probably regarded as the primary argument in favour of the shareholder value approach. The residual claimants have the greatest stake in the outcome of the company,[61] as they will benefit if the company's fortunes increase, but they will lose out if the company hits hard times (with their claims being last in line if the company is liquidated), and they will value the right to control above any other stakeholders,[62] as they have an interest in every decision that is taken by a solvent firm.[63] It has been said by some that as shareholders are the owners of the company,[64] those who manage the company should do so for the benefit of the shareholders.[65]

3.25 There are other arguments[66] that are propounded in favour of shareholder value.[67] First, according to the prevailing agency theory,[68] which is discussed a little later in the Chapter, directors are the agents of the

---

[59] M Bradley, C Schipani, A Sundaram and J Walsh 'The Purposes and Accountability of the Corporation in Contemporary Society: Corporate Governance at a Crossroads' (1999) 62 *Law and Contemporary Problems* 9 at 37.

[60] F Easterbrook and D Fischel *The Economic Structure of Company Law* (Cambridge, Mass, Harvard University Press, 1991) at 36–39.

[61] J Macey 'Fiduciary Duties as Residual Claims: Obligations to Nonshareholder Constituencies from a Theory of the Firm Perspective' (1999) 84 *Cornell Law Review* 1266 at 1267. This has been queried by several commentators, such as Professor Margaret Blair (*Ownership and Control* (Washington DC, The Brookings Institute, 1995) at 229).

[62] M Van der Weide 'Against Fiduciary Duties to Corporate Stakeholders' (1996) 21 *Delaware Journal of Corporate Law* 27 at 57; M Bradley, C Schipani, A Sundaram and J Walsh 'The Purposes and Accountability of the Corporation in Contemporary Society: Corporate Governance at a Crossroads' (1999) 62 *Law and Contemporary Problems* 9 at 38.

[63] J Macey and G Miller 'Corporate Stakeholders: A Contractual Perspective' (1993) 43 *University of Toronto Law Review* 401 at 408.

[64] For example, see Committee on the Financial Aspects of Corporate Governance (Cadbury Report) (London, Gee, 1992) at para 6.1; Confederation of British Industries *Boards Without Tiers: A CBI Contribution to the Debate* (London, CBI, 1996) at 8.

[65] This view has been criticised by many. See E Sternberg 'The Defects of Stakeholder Theory' (1997) 5 *Corporate Governance: An International Review* 3.

[66] For a detailed discussion, see, for example, D Gordon Smith 'The Shareholder Primacy Norm' (1998) 23 *Journal of Corporate Law* 277; L Stout 'Bad and Not-so-Bad Arguments for Shareholder Primacy' (2002) 75 *Southern California Law Review* 1189; A Keay 'Shareholder Primacy in Corporate Law: Can it Survive? Should it Survive?' (2010) 7 *European Company and Financial Law Review* 369.

[67] Parts of the following arguments are taken from A Keay 'Enlightened Shareholder Value, the Reform of the Duties of Company Directors and the Corporate Objective' [2006] LMCLQ 335 at 339–340; A Keay 'Ascertaining the Corporate Objective: An Entity Maximisation and Sustainability Model' (2008) 71 MLR 663 at 668–669.

[68] This is based on a large number of works, but arguably the most influential are: M Jensen and W Meckling 'Theory of the Firm: Managerial Behavior, Agency Costs and Ownership Structure' (1976) 3 *Journal of Financial Economics* 305; E Fama 'Agency Problems and the Theory of the Firm' (1980) 88 J Pol Econ 288; E Fama and M Jensen 'Separation of Ownership and Control' (1983) 26 *Journal of Law and Economics* 301; F Easterbrook and D Fischel *The Economic Structure of the Corporate Law* (Cambridge, MA, Harvard University Press, 1991).

shareholders and are employed to run the company's business for the shareholders who do not have the time or ability to do so, and it is the shareholders who are best suited to guide and discipline directors in the carrying out of their powers and duties.[69] It is said that if we do not have shareholder value as the guiding principle, the directors are able to engage in opportunistic behaviour and to shirk. Costs, known as 'agency costs',[70] will be incurred in monitoring the work of the directors, and so as to reduce the incidence of shirking and engaging in opportunistic activity the existence of duties owed to shareholders reduces those costs and, at the same time, protects the shareholders. The upshot is that shareholder value means that directors are fully accountable for what they do in running the company's business.

3.26 Second, it is argued that the principle is based on efficiency (the great concern of economists and those favouring a law and economics approach to legal analysis). Shareholders have incentives to maximise profits and so they are likely to foster economic efficiency. It is more efficient if directors operate on the basis of maximising shareholder wealth, because the least cost is expended in doing this;[71] the directors can work more efficiently if they are focused only on one objective, rather than worrying about a range of objectives.

3.27 Third, and allied to the previous argument, if directors owe duties to various constituencies, then it would be impossible for directors to balance all of the divergent interests, with the result that directors will make poor decisions.[72] It is said that the principle is certain and easy to administer, especially when compared with the stakeholder theory,[73] under which directors are to act with all stakeholder interests in view. With shareholder value there is just one main aim and that is to foster the interests of the shareholders. Shareholder value allows, so the argument goes, courts to review managerial conduct with some rationality,[74] because directors are to focus on only one goal.

3.28 Fourth, it is argued that constituencies other than the shareholders are able to protect themselves by the terms of the contracts that they make (eg a creditor lends money subject to a loan agreement), while shareholders do not have this kind of protection. The assertion is made that the shareholders are

---

[69] J Matheson and B Olson 'Corporate Law and the Long-term Shareholder Model of Corporate Governance' (1992) 76 *Minnesota Law Review* 1313 at 1328.

[70] These costs are those resulting from managers failing to act appropriately and the costs expended in monitoring and disciplining the managers in order to prevent them abusing their positions.

[71] M van der Weide 'Against Fiduciary Duties to Corporate Stakeholders' (1996) 21 *Delaware Journal of Corporate Law* 27 at 56–57.

[72] The Committee on Corporate Law 'Other Constituency Statutes: Potential for Confusion' (1990) 45 *The Business Lawyer* 2253 at 2269. It is generally felt that life would be made somewhat easier for directors if shareholder value did not exist as they could more easily justify decisions that they make.

[73] M van der Weide 'Against Fiduciary Duties to Corporate Stakeholders' (1996) 21 *Delaware Journal of Corporate Law* 27 at 68.

[74] Ibid at 69.

vulnerable[75] in that they are not, unlike say creditors, able to negotiate special terms by way of contract, and they are, in many ways, at the mercy of the directors, for they have difficulty in monitoring the work of directors. Fifth, unlike some groups, such as creditors, shareholders are not always able to diversify their exposure to losses sustained by their investments. Finally, shareholders are not, except in listed companies, always able to exit easily a company with which they are not happy, and, therefore, they warrant some special treatment.

3.29 It has been asserted in recent times that corporate governance debates have now been resolved in favour of the shareholder value model.[76] Professor Ronald Gilson has even said that corporate law's only distinctive feature is as a means to increase shareholder value.[77] But, while this theory is hugely popular, it has not been without significant opposition. Many who oppose it have adopted a progressive (formerly known as communitarian) or pluralist approach to corporate law[78] and have argued that directors should be required to consider the interests of others besides shareholders, namely those whom we can call stakeholders. It is said that directors should be obliged to run companies for the benefit of all potential stakeholders or constituencies in companies, such as creditors, employees, suppliers, customers and the communities in which the company operates. It is asserted by many that the interests of shareholders are not the only interests to be considered by directors when carrying out their functions, for there are other important constituencies that warrant consideration from directors.[79] The effect of invoking a shareholder value approach is, arguably, to damage the incentives of non-shareholder stakeholders to make firm-specific investments in companies as they are aware that their investments will be subordinated to shareholder interests at all times,[80] and Professor Lyman Johnson has said that 'a radically

---

[75] See L Zingales 'Corporate Governance' in *The New Palgrave Dictionary of Economics and Law* (Basingstoke, MacMillan, 1997) at 501.

[76] H Hansmann and R Kraakman 'The End of History for Corporate Law' (2001) 89 *Georgetown Law Journal* 439.

[77] 'Separation and the Function of Corporation Law' (January 2005) Stanford Law and Economics Olin Working Paper No 307 and available at: http://ssrn.com/abstract=732832.

[78] For discussions of this approach to corporate law, see, for example, L Mitchell (ed) *Progressive Corporate Law* (Westview Press, 1995); W Bratton Jr 'The "Nexus of Contracts Corporation": A Critical Appraisal' (1989) 74 Cornell L Rev 407; L Mitchell 'The Fairness Rights of Bondholders' (1990) 65 *New York University Law Review* 1165; D Millon 'Theories of the Corporation' [1990] Duke LJ 201; L Johnson 'The Delaware Judiciary and the Meaning of Corporate Life and Corporate Law' (1990) 68 *Texas Law Review* 865. Also, see W Leung 'The Inadequacy of Shareholder Primacy: A Proposed Corporate Regime that Recognizes Non-Shareholder Interests' (1997) 30 *Columbia Journal of Law and Social Problems* 589; G Crespi 'Rethinking Corporate Fiduciary Duties: The Inefficiency of the Shareholder Primacy Norm' (2002) 55 SMU Law Rev 141; L Talbot *Progressive Corporate Governance for the 21st Century* (Abingdon, Routledge, 2014).

[79] For example, Professor Lawrence Mitchell criticises the whole notion of shareholder maximisation in corporate law ('A Theoretical and Practical Framework for Enforcing Corporate Constituency Statutes' (1992) 70 *Texas Law Review* 579 at 640).

[80] G Kelly and J Parkinson 'The Conceptual Foundations of the Company: A Pluralist Approach' in J Parkinson, A Gamble and G Kelly (eds) *The Political Economy of the Company* (Oxford, Hart Publishing, 2000) at 131.

proshareholder vision of corporate endeavour [is] substantially out of line with prevailing social norms',[81] and that courts must acknowledge this and define 'the meaning of corporate endeavour'[82] by embracing norms 'wider than the thin thread of shareholder primacy'.[83]

3.30 Others, besides progressives (communitarians) and pluralists, have criticised the shareholder value theory on a number of varied grounds. First, it can be argued that shareholders do not have effective control of managers[84] and so directors cannot be seen as being accountable to them. This means that the theory is not workable because directors are not always going to be held responsible if they shirk and fail to foster shareholder maximisation. Even if it can be said that there is some shareholder control of directors, it will usually be vested in those with the largest shareholdings and the control, therefore, may not bring benefits to those with small holdings. The fact is that to be in real control the shareholders would have to be able to make decisions that affect the benefits of other contributors to the company.[85] Arguably they cannot.

3.31 Second, it has been argued that shareholder value does not really increase social wealth.[86] It merely benefits shareholders, and only, perhaps, some of the shareholders. For in seeking to pursue shareholder value, the company might fail to be able to meet its obligations and all stakeholders will suffer. Also, in achieving shareholder value, a company might find that it is appropriate to engage in externalising, that is, transferring value away from one or more stakeholders, eg closing down a factory and making some employees redundant. Finally on this point, while promoting shareholder value might lead indirectly to benefits for other stakeholders, the promotion of this approach might lead to financial difficulty and that will adversely affect all other investors.

3.32 Third, if one accepts the concept of a nexus of contracts, there are surely many persons who constitute the nexus that can be said to be residual claimants. The shareholders are not necessarily the ones most affected by a

---

[81] 'The Delaware Judiciary and the Meaning of Corporate Life and Corporate Law' (1990) 68 *Texas Law Review* 865 at 934.

[82] Ibid.

[83] Ibid.

[84] See A Keay 'Company Directors Behaving Poorly: Disciplinary Options for Shareholders' [2007] JBL 656.

[85] L Zingales 'In Search of New Foundations' (2000) 55 *Journal of Finance* 1623 at 1632.

[86] P Joerg, C Loderer, L Roth and U Waelchli 'The Purpose of the Corporation: Shareholder-value Maximization?' European Corporate governance Institute Finance Working Paper No 95/2005, February 2006 and available at http://ssrn.com/abstract=690044.

company's decisions.[87] For example, employees invest firm-specific human capital in the company and this places them in a position where they are vulnerable to management caprice.[88]

3.33 Fourth, it has been argued that the shareholder value principle is not relevant to business decisions today and that it was introduced originally to resolve disputes among majority and minority shareholders in closely-held companies and courts tended not to distinguish between closely-held and public companies until the middle of the last century.[89]

3.34 Fifth, the shareholder value theory does not allow for the fact that many investors are diversified and will be both shareholders and creditors (often bondholders) in companies.[90] Those in this situation are not going to have the same goals as those who are purely shareholders. Shareholders who have diversified interests will be looking for a more balanced approach to the making of investment and other decisions that directors have to make.

3.35 One of the main criticisms that are espoused by advocates of shareholder value when it comes to a consideration of stakeholder theory (to which we come shortly) is that the latter does not provide managers with any guidance as to how they should manage, with no aim being set, and in fact it could provide an opportunity for managers to shirk or self-deal. Yet the shareholder value paradigm is itself able to be criticised on the basis that the goal is ill-defined to start with.[91] The reason is that different shareholders will have different aims and so it is not clear what managers should actually be doing. There is the problem of whether short-term or long-term horizons should be set.[92] Professor Eric Orts has said that 'shareholders have different time and risk preferences that managers must somehow factor together, if they are to represent fairly the artificially unified interest of "the shareholders" in general'.[93] Clearly short-term and long-term strategies differ. Orts gives the example of drastic

---

[87]   L Zingales 'In Search of New Foundations' (2000) 55 *Journal of Finance* 1623 at 1632; M Blair and L Stout 'Specific Investments and Corporate Law' presented by Lynn Stout at the Corporate Law Teachers' Conference on 6 February 2006 at the University of Queensland, Brisbane, Australia at 15.

[88]   See M O'Connor 'The Human Capital Era' (1993) 78 Cornell L Rev 899 at 905–917.

[89]   D Gordon Smith 'The Shareholder Primacy Norm' (1998) 23 *Journal of Corporation Law* 277 at 279.

[90]   T Smith 'The Efficient Norm for Corporate Law: A Neotraditional Interpretation of Fiduciary Duty' (1999) 98 *Michigan Law Review* 214 at 217.

[91]   P Joerg, C Loderer, L Roth and U Waelchli 'The Purpose of the Corporation: Shareholder-value Maximization?' European Corporate governance Institute Finance Working Paper No 95/2005, February 2006 and available at http://ssrn.com/abstract=690044. See A Keay 'Getting to Grips with the Shareholder Value Theory in Corporate Law' (2010) 39 *Common Law World Review* 358.

[92]   See H Hu 'Risk, Time and Fiduciary Principles in Corporate Investment' (1990) 38 UCLA L Rev 277.

[93]   'The Complexity and Legitimacy of Corporate Law' (1993) 50 *Washington and Lee Law Review* 1565 at 1591.

cost-cutting that might achieve short-term results by improving the bottom line for a short while, but in the long-run this might deleteriously affect the company's business.[94]

3.36 Sixth, while some have acknowledged the fact that shareholder value provides a convenient common metric, it is too glib to reduce everything to a matter of profit, as, it is argued, the theory does.[95] Many see the theory as cold and uncaring and totally omitting the human dimension that is critical to all facets of life, including business.

3.37 Finally, there have been indications from time to time that in practice directors do not solely focus on shareholder value as their aim. An empirical study of 50 FTSE 100 companies seems to support that view to some degree.[96] Before completing this section it would be remiss of me not to mention the fact that many, if not the vast majority, take the view that shareholder primacy does not mean ignoring the interests of other stakeholders. It is often argued that it is necessary for the directors to take into account the interests of various stakeholders, although the ultimate benefit must be for the shareholders.

2 From a positive perspective: What do the cases say?[97]

3.38 Notwithstanding that there are many assertions that the historical position of the courts in the UK is to favour the shareholder value approach, a study of UK case-law does not show an unequivocal acceptance of this approach. More often than not the courts have been content to say that the duties of the directors are owed to the company, something that s 170 of the CA 2006 states, as we will consider in **Chapter 4**. What does it mean to say that duties are owed to the company? As pointed out by Nourse LJ in *Brady v Brady*,[98] this is an expression that is often used, but is rarely defined, and it is probably one of the most problematical expressions in company law. His Lordship opined that it was sometimes misunderstood. Professor Dan Prentice has referred to the phrase as being 'indeterminate',[99] and another commentator has said that it was 'unclear'.[100] Does the expression mean that the directors are to act in the best interests of the shareholders, or do broader interests have to be considered? Notwithstanding the comments about the lack of clarity with the expression, the Company Law Review Steering Group stated that the

---

[94] Ibid at 1592.

[95] D Wood 'Whom Should Business Serve?' (2002) 14 *Australian Journal of Corporate Law* 1 at 13.

[96] A Keay and R Adamopoulou 'Shareholder Value and UK Companies: A Positivist Inquiry' (2012) 13 *European Business Organization Law Review* 1.

[97] Parts of the discussion under this heading are taken from A Keay 'Enlightened Shareholder Value, the Reform of the Duties of Company Directors and the Corporate Objective' [2006] LMCLQ 335 at 341–345.

[98] (1987) 3 BCC 535 at 552.

[99] D D Prentice 'Creditor's Interests and Director's Duties' (1990) 10 OJLS 265 at 273.

[100] J Heydon 'Directors' Duties and the Company's Interests' in P Finn (ed) *Equity and Commercial Relationships* (Sydney, Law Book Co, 1987) at 122.

directors are to manage the company's business for the benefit of the company, and this normally means that it is managed for the benefit of the shareholders as a whole.[101]

3.39 The phrase has been employed by judges in several corporate law areas and not only when hearing cases involving the exercise of directors' duties.[102] For instance, it is part of the test that is used when assessing whether an alteration to the articles of association of a company is permissible,[103] and some of those cases will be referred to below.

3.40 One of the first indications that shareholder value was to be the focus of directors of companies in UK law came with the comments of Jessel MR in *Re Wincham Shipbuilding*[104] in 1878. His Lordship (with the concurrence of James and Bramwell LJJ), after asking the question, for whom are the directors trustee, said that 'the directors are trustees for the shareholders, that is, for the company'.[105] Shortly after that case, *Hutton v West Cork Railway Co*[106] was decided (by a differently constituted Court of Appeal) and it is often cited as supporting shareholder value. It is also well known for the classic statement by Bowen LJ that: 'The law does not say that there shall be no cake and ale, but there are to be no cakes and ale except such as are required for the benefit of the company.'[107] The fact is that the court did not make a specific statement concerning the identity of the beneficiaries of the directors' management efforts. The court was concerned that any action was taken for the benefit of the company, and the court did not, it appears, notwithstanding the assertions of a number of writers,[108] state that this meant benefitting the shareholders' interests. The case does not stand unequivocally for shareholder value.

3.41 As mentioned above, there are many cases that have considered the meaning of the expression in the context of dealing with whether an alteration to the articles of association was in the best interests of the company as a whole.[109] In one of the strongest cases supporting a shareholder value

---

[101] Company Law Review, *Modernising Company Law: The Strategic Framework* (London, DTI, 1999) at para 5.1.5; B Hannigan *Company Law* (London, LexisNexis Butterworths, 2003) at 203.

[102] For instance, see *Re Smith & Fawcett Ltd* [1942] Ch 304 at 306, 308 (CA).

[103] For instance, see *Allen v Gold Reefs of West Africa Ltd* [1900] 1 Ch 656 at 671.

[104] (1878) LR 9 Ch D 322.

[105] Ibid at 328. Such a view was posited in New Zealand in *Re H Linney & Co Ltd* [1925] NZLR 907 at 922. In more recent times the idea that directors are trustees has been exploded. For instance, see L S Sealy 'The Director as Trustee' [1967] CLJ 83. However, even more recently reference has still been made to directors acting as trustees. For instance, see Lord Cullen in *Dawson International plc v Coats Paton plc (No 1)* 1988 SLT 854 at 858; [1989] BCLC 233 at 237.

[106] (1883) 23 Ch D 654.

[107] Ibid at 673.

[108] For instance, J MacIntosh 'Designing an Efficient Fiduciary Law' (1993) 43 *University of Toronto Law Journal* 425 at 452.

[109] For example, see *Allen v Gold Reefs of West Africa Ltd* [1900] 1 Ch 656; *Sidebottom v Kershaw Leese and Co Ltd* [1921] 1 Ch 154; *Shuttleworth v Cox Bros and Co (Maidenhead) Ltd* [1927] 2 KB 9.

interpretation, *Greenhalgh v Arderne Cinemas*,[110] Lord Evershed MR, with whose judgment the other members of the Court of Appeal agreed, said that the phrase 'interests of the company as a whole' did not mean the company as a commercial entity, but rather it meant the corporators as a general body.[111] It is interesting to note that his Lordship had said something quite different only a few years earlier, in *Short v Treasury Commissioners*:[112] 'Shareholders are not in the eyes of the law, part owners of the undertaking. The undertaking is something different from the totality of its shareholding.' The approach espoused in *Greenhalgh* might be said to be consistent with what Dixon J said in the Australian High Court case of *Peters American Delicacy v Heath*,[113] where his Honour said that the company as a whole is a corporate entity consisting of all of the shareholders.[114] Yet, it must not be forgotten that these cases, and all the cases dealing with an alteration to the articles are referring to how the members of the company are to act, and not the directors. Only directors are subjected under UK law to fiduciary duties. Furthermore, the cases dealing with the articles are not addressing the issue of: to whom are duties owed. But, there is authority involving consideration of directors' duties, such as *Parke v Daily News Ltd*,[115] where it has been said that the benefit of the company meant the benefit of the shareholders as a general body.[116] Then in *Gaiman v National Association for Mental Health*,[117] Megarry J said that 'it is not very easy to determine what is in the best interests of the [company] without paying due regard to the members of the [company]'.[118] His Lordship went on to say that he regarded the expression to mean the interests of present and future shareholders as a whole.

3.42 Perhaps one of the clearest statements to favour shareholder value was emitted by Nourse LJ in *Brady v Brady*.[119] His Lordship said:[120]

> 'The interests of a company, an artificial person, cannot be distinguished from the interests of the persons who are interested in it. Who are those persons? Where a company is both going and solvent, *first and foremost* come the shareholders, present and no doubt future as well.' (my emphasis)

---

[110] [1951] Ch 286.
[111] Ibid at 291.
[112] [1948] 1 KB 116 at 122.
[113] (1939) 61 CLR 457.
[114] The difficulties with the 'benefit of the company as a whole' test caused the Australian High Court in *Gambotto v WCP Ltd* (1995) 182 CLR 432, to say that it was time that the test was dispensed with. But the Company Law Review Steering Group felt that that the test was too well-established in English law, and should be retained (*Modern Company Law for a Competitive Economy: Completing the Structure* (London, DTI, 2000) at paras 5.94–5.99; Company Law Review, *Modern Company Law for a Competitive Economy: Final Report* (London, DTI, 2001) vol 1, at paras 7.52–7.62).
[115] [1962] Ch 927.
[116] Ibid at 963.
[117] [1971] Ch 317.
[118] Ibid at 330.
[119] (1987) 3 BCC 535.
[120] Ibid at 552.

3.43 However, the case was essentially dealing with whether there had been a breach of CA 1985, s 151 (now CA 2006, s 678), the provision that prohibited the giving of financial assistance by a company in the purchase of its shares, and not directors' duties, so while it is of some assistance it is not directly on point.

3.44 Notwithstanding the comments supporting shareholder value, there are cases in which judges have played down the pre-eminence of shareholders' interests. The shareholder value paradigm was indirectly questioned by Lord Diplock in *Lonrho Ltd v Shell Petroleum Co Ltd*,[121] where he stated, by way of obiter, that:[122]

> '[I]t is the duty of the board to consider whether to accede to the request [for inspection of documents] would be in the best interests of the company. These are not exclusively those of its shareholders but may include those of its creditors.'

The other four Law Lords concurred with his Lordship's speech.

3.45 More recently the Court of Appeal in *Fulham Football Club Ltd v Cabra Estates plc*[123] appeared to adopt a similar approach when it stated that 'the duties owed by the directors are to the company and the company is more than just the sum total of its members'.[124]

3.46 Many of the cases[125] that have been regarded as holding that directors must act for shareholders, do not in fact support that proposition. The courts in these cases have said that directors might owe fiduciary duties to the shareholders where special circumstances exist, such as when the company is the subject of a takeover offer.[126] Absent special circumstances, directors clearly do not owe such duties to shareholders,[127] save perhaps in small family companies.[128] Take the judgment in the Scottish case of *Dawson International plc v Coats Paton plc (No 1)*[129] for example. It was stated in that case that the directors were, in conducting the affairs of the company and discharging their duties, to consider the interests of the company.[130] The court said that directors owed no general fiduciary duty to shareholders, although directors might become subject to a duty to shareholders if they were to make recommendations to the shareholders in light of a takeover offer, for if directors

---

[121] [1980] 1 WLR 627.

[122] Ibid at 634.

[123] [1994] 1 BCLC 363.

[124] Ibid at 379.

[125] For instance, see *Heron International Ltd v Lord Grade* [1983] BCLC 244; *Peskin v Anderson* [2000] BCC 1110; [2000] 2 BCLC 1 (and affirmed on appeal by the Court of Appeal [2001] BCC 874).

[126] For instance, see *Gething v Kilner* [1972] 1 WLR 337; [1972] 1 All ER 1166; *Re a Company* [1986] BCLC 382; *Brunninghausen v Glavanics* [1999] NSWCA 199; (1999) 17 ACLC 1247.

[127] For example, see *Dawson International plc v Coats Paton plc (No 1)* 1988 SLT 854; [1989] BCLC 233. Also, see *Platt v Platt* [1999] 2 BCLC 745.

[128] See *Coleman v Myers* [1977] 2 NZLR 225.

[129] 1988 SLT 854; [1989] BCLC 233.

[130] Ibid at 860; 241.

took the decision to recommend the acceptance of that offer they had a duty (which might be called a secondary fiduciary duty) to the shareholders.[131]

3.47 The equivocal position that appears to exist in the UK, seems to reflect the experience in other parts of the Commonwealth. In the New Zealand Court of Appeal in *Nicholson v Permakraft (NZ) Ltd*[132] Cooke J indicated that the duties of creditors are owed to the company, and he went on to say unequivocally that directors had to act in the best interests of the company as a whole.[133] There are comments by Latham CJ and Dixon J in the Australian High Court case of *Richard Brady Franks Ltd v Price*[134] that support the notion that we are talking about the shareholders when we say that directors are to act in the best interests of the company. In *Kinsela v Russell Kinsela Pty Ltd,*[135] Street CJ of the New South Wales Court of Appeal stated that when a company is solvent, 'the proprietary interests of the shareholders entitle them as a general body to be regarded as the company when questions of the duty of directors arise'.[136] But, other courts have been more precise. In a post-*Kinsela* New South Wales Court of Appeal case, *Brunninghausen v Glavanics,*[137] Handley JA said that: 'The general principle that a director's fiduciary duties are owed to the company and not to shareholders is undoubtedly correct ....' The British Columbia Court of Appeal in *Canadian Metals Exploration Ltd v Wiese*[138] said that duties are owed to the company and not the shareholders.

3.48 In *Peoples' Department Stores v Wise*[139] Canada's highest court, the Supreme Court of Canada, said that directors had a duty to act in the best interests of the corporation and that 'the best interests of the corporation' meant acting to maximise the value of the corporation. Major and Deschamps JJ, in delivering the judgment of the court, specifically stated that the expression acting in the 'best interests of the corporation' does not mean acting in the best interests of the shareholders or any one stakeholder's interests.[140] The judges went on to say that:[141]

> 'But if they [the directors] observe a decent respect for other interests lying beyond those of the company's shareholders in the strict sense, that will not ... leave directors open to the charge that they have failed in their fiduciary duty to the company ... We accept as an accurate statement of law that in determining whether they are acting with a view to the best interests of the corporation it may be legitimate, given all the circumstances of a given case, for the board of directors

---

[131] Ibid at 859; 240. This was acknowledged in *Prudential Assurance Co Ltd v Newman Industries Ltd (No 2)* [1982] Ch 204; *Gething v Kilner* [1972] 1 WLR 337; [1972] 1 All ER 1166.
[132] (1985) 3 ACLC 453 at 459.
[133] Ibid at 462.
[134] [1937] HCA 42; (1937) 58 CLR 112.
[135] (1986) 4 ACLC 215; (1986) 10 ACLR 395.
[136] Ibid at 221; 395.
[137] [1999] NSWCA 199; (1999) 17 ACLC 1247 at [43].
[138] [2007] BCCA 318 (CanLII) at [28].
[139] [2004] SCC 68; (2004) 244 DLR (4th) 564.
[140] Ibid at [42].
[141] Ibid at [42]–[43].

to consider, inter alia, the interests of the shareholders, employees, suppliers, creditors, consumers, governments and the environment ... At all time, directors and officers owe their fiduciary duties to the corporation. The interests of the corporation are not to be confused with the interests of the creditors or those of any other stakeholders.'

3.49 Subsequently, in *BCE Inc v 1976 Debentureholders*[142] the Canadian Supreme Court followed the approach taken in *Peoples' Department Stores* and said that: 'There is no principle that one set of interests – for example the interests of shareholders – should prevail over another set of interests.'[143]

3.50 In the Australian case of *Darvall v North Sydney Brick and Tile Company Ltd*,[144] the judge, Hodgson J, tried to cover all bases and said that it is proper for directors to have regard for the interests of the shareholders as well as having regard for the company as a commercial entity. He also felt that creditors' interests should be taken into account.[145]

3.51 In sum, there is not a clear strain of authority running through UK or Commonwealth case-law supporting the shareholder value principle. Undoubtedly some cases suggest that the focus should be on shareholders, while others either merely blandly state that the directors are to act in the interests of the company, or indicate that the interests of the company involves something more than the interests of shareholders.

B Stakeholder theory

3.52 This is the second major theory that exists. Under this theory it is advocated that the duties of directors of companies are owed to a range of people. Directors have a responsibility to create optimal value for all parties affected by a company's decisions,[146] consequently they owe duties to all stakeholders.[147]

3.53 There clearly was some incipient form of stakeholder theory in company law evident throughout much of the twentieth century. It can be seen in the work of Harvard University law professor, E Merrick Dodd in the early 1930s,[148] the approach of successful American companies (who referred to

---

[142] [2008] SCC 69.

[143] Ibid at [84].

[144] (1988) 6 ACLC 154.

[145] Ibid at 176.

[146] R E Freeman *Strategic Management: A Stakeholder Approach* (Boston, Pitman/Ballinger, 1984).

[147] M Clarkson 'A Stakeholder Framework for Analyzing and Evaluating Corporate Social Performance' (1995) 20 *Academy Management Review* 92 at 112. For a detailed discussion, see A Keay 'Stakeholder Theory in Corporate Law: Has it Got What it Takes?' (2010) 9 *Richmond Journal of Global Law & Business* 249.

[148] Dodd said that the advancing of the interests of stakeholder groups such as employees and customers as well as the general community seemed to be less abnormal than shareholder value ('Is Effective Enforcement of the Fiduciary Duties of Corporate Managers Practicable?' (1934) 2 U Chi LR 194 at 199).

stakeholder management) in the 1920s to the 1950s,[149] many of the directors of which employed managerial theory, and the work of the reformer, Ralph Nader, in the 1960s and 1970s. However, the development of the theory is usually traced to Professor Edward Freeman, an organisational behaviour academic, and particularly to his book, *Strategic Management: a stakeholder approach,* published in 1984.[150] Of course, stakeholder theory in broader social terms has been invoked by several theorists for a great number of years, and one can trace it back to the work of a German social theorist, Johannes Althusius, in the seventeenth century.[151]

3.54 In his book Freeman called for a re-think about business organisations, arguing that economic theories that had been pre-eminent were outdated. His view was that there are more than just shareholders who contribute to a company, and they can be referred to as stakeholders[152] or constituencies. Some of these stakeholders do not have contractual protection and it was argued that their interests deserve consideration by directors in how they manage the company, in what decisions they make and how their duties are to be exercised. So, stakeholder theory rejects the idea of maximising a single objective, as one gets with shareholder value.

3.55 As a normative thesis stakeholder theory holds to the legitimacy of the claims on the company that many different groups and people have and this justifies its implementation.[153] In other words, this theory is premised on the idea that in addition to shareholders other groups have claims on the property of companies as they contribute to its capital (in broad terms).[154] This is often referred to as firm-specific capital.

3.56 Under the stakeholder theory it is advocated that the duty of directors of companies is to create optimal value for all social actors who might be regarded as parties affected by a company's decisions.[155] The argument is that all stakeholders have a right to be regarded as an end and not a means to an end.[156] So, the company should be managed for the benefit of all of its stakeholders: its customers, suppliers, creditors, shareholders, employees, the

---

[149] See L Preston and H Sapienza 'Stakeholder Management and Corporate Performance' (1990) 19 *Journal of Behavioral Economics* 361 at 362.

[150] Boston, Pitman/Ballinger, 1984.

[151] E Orts 'A North American Legal Perspective on Stakeholder Management Theory' in F Patfield (ed) *Perspectives on Company Law* (Kluwer, 1997) vol 2, at 170.

[152] The term 'stakeholder' is said to have its genesis in a 1963 Stanford Research Institute memorandum where it was used to refer to 'those groups without whose support the organization would cease to exist': R E Freeman and D Reed 'Stockholders and Stakeholders: A New Perspective on Corporate Governance' (1983) 25 *California Management Review* 88 at 89.

[153] See T Donaldson and L Preston 'The Stakeholder Theory for the corporation: Concepts, Evidence, Implications' (1995) 20 *Academy Management Review* 65 at 66–67.

[154] R Karmel 'Implications of the Stakeholder Model' (1993) 61 *George Washington Law Review* 1156 at 1171.

[155] R E Freeman *Strategic Management: A Stakeholder Approach* (Boston, Pitman/Ballinger, 1984).

[156] Ibid at 97.

tax authorities, the natural environment and local communities in which the company operates. The rights of these groups must be ensured, and, further, the groups must participate, in some sense, in decisions that substantially affect their welfare.[157] Stakeholding has been said to be a matter or 'taming' the 'harsher aspects of capitalism'.[158]

3.57 The theory is embraced by many who hold to a managerialist approach to companies. They believe that managers are at the centre of companies and they advocate wide powers being given to managers who can be trusted to act as stewards of the company and its affairs.[159]

3.58 The adherents to this theory have advocated concepts of individual autonomy and fairness to all members of society.[160] The theory holds to equality of stakeholders in that they are entitled morally to be considered in the management of the company's affairs and to be considered simultaneously.[161] It has been asserted that: 'The economic and social purpose of the corporation is to create and distribute wealth and value to all its primary stakeholder groups, without favoring one group at the expense of others.'[162] In comparison with shareholder value, no grouping has automatic priority over another.[163]

3.59 Those who would advocate stakeholder theory vary in thinking, so what is considered here are only what can be regarded as the views held by the majority of scholars and practitioners of the theory. As far back as the 1920s Owen Young, the President of General Electric said that he acknowledged that he had an obligation to the stockholders to pay a fair rate of return, but he said that he also had an obligation to labour, customers and the public.[164] The chairman of the US company, Standard Oil, stated, in 1946, that the business of companies should be carried on 'in such a way as to maintain an equitable and working balance among the claims of the various directly interested groups – stockholders, employees, customers and the public at large'.[165] More recently, a corporate reputation survey of *Fortune 500* companies (the largest listed

---

[157] W Evans and R E Freeman 'A Stakeholder Theory of the Modern Corporation: Kantian Capitalism' in T Beauchamp and N Bowie (eds) *Ethical Theory and Business* (Englewood Cliffs, NJ, Prentice-Hall, 1988) at 103.

[158] J Plender *The Stakeholding Solution* (London, Nicholas Brealey, 1997) referred to in J Dean *Directing Public Companies* (London, Cavendish, 2001) at 117.

[159] Unlike many communitarians who eschew economics and focus solely on ethics and fairness, stakeholder theory as advocated by managerialists seeks to combine economics and ethics.

[160] For example, J Boatright 'Fiduciary Duties and the Shareholder-Management Relation: Or, What's So Special about Shareholders?' (1994) 4 *Business Ethics Quarterly* 393.

[161] R Mitchell 'Toward a Theory of Stakeholder Identification and Salience: Defining the Principle of Who and What Really Counts' (1997) 22 *Academy Management Review* 853 at 862.

[162] M Clarkson 'A Stakeholder Framework for Analyzing and Evaluating Corporate Social Performance' (1995) 20 *Academy Management Review* 92 at 112.

[163] T Donaldson and L Preston 'The Stakeholder Theory for the Corporation: Concepts, Evidence, Implications' (1995) 20 *Academy Management Review* 65.

[164] E Merrick Dodd 'For Whom are Corporate Managers Trustees?' (1932) 45 Harv LR 1145 at 1154.

[165] Quoted in M Blair *Ownership and Control* (Washington DC, The Brookings Institute, 1995) at 212.

companies in the US) found that satisfying the interests of one stakeholder does not automatically mean that this is at the expense of other stakeholders.[166] This is supported by empirical evidence, obtained in a study by the *Financial Times of Europe*'s most respected companies, which found that chief executive officers were of the view that one of the features of a good company was the ability to ensure that there was a balancing of the interests of stakeholder groups.[167] Chancellor William Allen of the Delaware Chancery Court in the US has said extra-judicially that the dominant view among leaders for the past 50 years has been that no single constituency's interests should exclude the interests of other constituencies from the fair consideration of the board.[168] As mentioned earlier, a recent empirical study of 50 FTSE 100 companies in the UK suggests that a good percentage of listed companies do take into account stakeholder interests in the decisions that they make, and shareholder primacy might not be as prominent as is often thought.[169]

3.60   One of the major problems that the theory faces is that it is not always clearly articulated and has been a difficult concept to define.[170] It has been said that stakeholding is 'a slippery creature ... used by different people to mean widely different things which happen to suit their arguments'.[171]

3.61   Freeman et al say that the best deal for everyone is if the company is run in such a manner that as much value for stakeholders as possible is created.[172] Shareholder value advocates say similar things, but get there via a different route.

3.62   Some suggest that if stakeholding were employed it would enhance the company's reputation and lead others to feel that their company operates on principle and can be trusted. All of this would benefit everyone involved.[173] So for a company to thrive it must: produce competitive returns for shareholders; satisfy customers in order to produce profits; recruit and motivate excellent employees; build successful relationships with suppliers.[174] It has been asserted that stakeholding is the instrument through which efficiency, profitability,

---

[166] L Preston and H Sapienza 'Stakeholder Management and Corporate Performance' (1990) 19 *Journal of Behavioral Economics* 361.

[167] Referred to in E Scholes and D Clutterbuck 'Communication with Stakeholders: An Integrated Approach' (1998) 31 *Long Range Planning* 227 at 230.

[168] 'Our Schizophrenic Conception of the Business Corporation' (1992) 14 Cardozo LR 261 at 271.

[169] A Keay and R Adamopoulou 'Shareholder Value and UK Companies: A Positivist Inquiry' (2012) 13 *European Business Organization Law Review* 1.

[170] M Omran, P Atrill and J Pointon 'Shareholders Versus Stakeholders: Corporate Mission Statements and Investor Returns' (2002) 11 *Business Ethics: A European Review* 318 at 318.

[171] M V Weyer 'Ideal World' (1996) *Management Today*, September, 35 at 35.

[172] R E Freeman, A C Wicks and B Parmar 'Stakeholder Theory and the Corporate Objective Revisited' (2004) 15 *Organization Science* 364 at 365.

[173] J Dean *Directing Public Companies* (London, Cavendish, 2001) at 108.

[174] Ibid at 251.

competition and economic success can be promoted on the basis that if one removed cohesion among stakeholders it would not be possible for companies to be competitive.[175]

3.63 Probably more can be learned about the theory from the criticisms that have been aimed at it. Some critical comments are very broad, such as those of Elaine Sternberg, a shareholder value theorist. She argues that the theory is 'deeply dangerous and wholly unjustified'[176] on the basis that it 'undermines private property, denies agents' duties to principals, and destroys wealth'.[177]

3.64 As mentioned above, the theory has not been clearly defined, and notwithstanding the fact that many years have now passed since Freeman introduced the theory, we have yet to see a robust and workable theory formulated. Many proposals have been propounded but they have tended to rely on 'a serious mismatch of variables which are mixed and correlated almost indiscriminately with a set of stakeholder-related performance variables that are not theoretically linked'.[178]

3.65 One of the main difficulties has been in identifying and defining who are in fact stakeholders.[179] Definitions have varied from the narrow to the very broad. Probably the first articulation of the concept was provided in an internal memorandum at the Stanford Research Institute in 1963,[180] which said that stakeholders were: 'Those groups without whose support the organisation would cease to exist.' Freeman built on this and in 1984 defined them as 'any group or individual who can affect or is affected by the achievement of the organisation's objectives'.[181] This broadens the category of stakeholders to include governments, customers, the environment, while in the past employees had tended to be the focus of those wanting a broader perspective in management.[182] The criticism is that managers are given no basis for identifying who are stakeholders. Furthermore, some stakeholders are more important than others, but there is no guidance to determine who is the more important.[183] And as Leung has said: 'there is no easy way to delineate the

---

[175] A Campbell 'Stakeholders, the Case in Favour' (1997) 30 *Long Range Planning* 446 at 446.

[176] 'The Defects of Stakeholder Theory' (1997) 5 *Corporate Governance: An International Review* 3 at 6.

[177] Ibid at 9.

[178] D J Wood and R E Jones 'Stakeholder Mismatching: A Theoretical Problem in Empirical Research on Corporate Social Performance' (1995) 3(3) *The International Journal of Organizational Analysis* 229 at 231.

[179] Mitchell and his co-authors in 'Toward a Theory of Stakeholder Identification and Salience: Defining the Principle of Who and What Really Counts' (1997) 22 *Academy Management Review* 853 at 858 identify 27 definitions of stakeholders.

[180] Referred to by Freeman in his book, *Strategic Management: A Stakeholder Approach* (Boston, Pitman/Ballinger, 1984) at 31.

[181] Ibid at 246.

[182] Often advocating some forms of industrial democracy or even advocating the embracing of something similar to German co-determinism.

[183] A Sundaram and A Inkpen 'The Corporate Objective Revisited' (2004) 15 *Organization Science* 350 at 352.

stakeholder class'.[184] There are a huge number of potential stakeholders and the problem for a board is to determine how they are to address the needs of groups with divergent interests.[185] The stakeholder case has probably been harmed by the fact that Freeman included terrorist groups as stakeholders in some companies (on the basis that they can affect how companies are run).[186] Many have sought to distance the theory from this approach. Some commentators have said that one must distinguish between those who influence the company and those who are true stakeholders. Some groups are in both categories. But the media, for instance, is in the first category only.[187] Other commentators have distinguished between primary and secondary stakeholders, with the former being the focus of directors. Primary stakeholders are seen as those who have a formal, official or contractual relationship with the company.[188]

3.66 Perhaps the primary argument that is mounted against stakeholder approach is that in discharging their duties the directors have to balance the interests of all stakeholders and that is an impossible task. Even stakeholder theorists accept that stakeholder management involves 'a never-ending task of balancing and integrating multiple relations and multiple objectives'.[189] Sternberg agrees with this comment (although coming to a different conclusion) and she has said that the 'essential principle of stakeholder theory that corporations are accountable to *all* their stakeholders' is something that is 'unworkable'.[190]

3.67 Another leading argument against the theory, and based on the notion that directors have to consider many interests, is that it is likely to lead directors to opportunistic activities and shirking, because directors end up being accountable to no one (known as the 'too many masters' problem):[191]

> 'A manager who is told to serve two masters (a little for the equity holders, a little for the community) has been freed of both and is answerable to neither ... Agency costs rise and social wealth falls.'

3.68 The concern for many is that directors can play off one group against another; they can say that after balancing interests they made a decision to

---

[184] W Leung 'The Inadequacy of Shareholder Primacy: A Proposed Corporate Regime that Recognizes Non-Shareholder Interests' (1997) 30 *Columbia Journal of Law and Social Problems* 589 at 622.

[185] Ibid at 621.

[186] R E Freeman *Strategic Management: A Stakeholder Approach* (Boston, Pitman/Ballinger, 1984) at 53.

[187] T Donaldson and L Preston 'The Stakeholder Theory for the Corporation: Concepts, Evidence, Implications' (1995) 20 *Academy Management Review* 65 at 86.

[188] A Carroll *Business and Society* (Cincinnati, South-Western Publishing, 1993) at 62.

[189] R E Freeman and J McVea 'A Stakeholder Approach to Strategic Management' in M Hitt et al (eds) *Handbook of Strategic Management* (Wiley-Blackwell, 2001) at 194.

[190] E Sternberg 'The Defects of Stakeholder Theory' (1997) 5 *Corporate Governance: An International Review* 3 at 6.

[191] F Easterbrook and D Fischel *The Economic Structure of Company Law* (Cambridge, Mass, Harvard University Press, 1991) at 38.

benefit stakeholders X and Y, and this decision just happened to benefit or protect the directors themselves. It is difficult to impugn such a decision. Putting it another way, many commentators say that requiring managers to consider the interests of all constituencies 'is essentially vacuous, because it allows management to justify almost any action on the grounds that it benefits some group'.[192] In such a system the directors are arguably given too much of an unfettered discretion that cannot be monitored. Goyder says that in adopting stakeholderism in lieu of shareholder value one is sacrificing clarity for blancmange,[193] presumably because blancmange is difficult to get hold of and can be moulded to anything one wishes. The riposte from the stakeholder adherents is that you have to rely upon the professionalism and trustworthiness of the directors. This really then comes down to a philosophical debate. Many in the shareholder value school says that you cannot trust directors because human nature is such that it will want to seek benefits at every possible turn (and you must have tight monitoring measures in place), whereas most in the stakeholder theory school states that while there will be some improper actions by directors, generally they will be fair and can be trusted.

3.69 Another major problem with stakeholder theory is enforcing any breach by directors. Do you give the power to anyone to bring proceedings or do you limit it to specific constituencies? We will see later in the book that the law has grappled with the whole idea of allowing a party, other than the company itself, to bring proceedings where directors have not done their jobs properly or have acted in an improper way. Legislation now permits shareholders to bring what are known as 'derivative claims' for the company in such circumstances (discussed in **Chapter 14**), but the Government has not countenanced the possibility of any other stakeholders being given that right. And it is highly unlikely that it will, certainly in the short-medium term.

3.70 The approach of stakeholder theory is to incorporate important values as a critical aspect of the strategic management process, but the riposte from shareholder value advocates is: how do managers identify these values and in what way are they to inform decision-making?[194] They argue that arriving at a set of values that accounts for the concerns across a heterogeneous group of stakeholders requires managers to fulfil unrealistic expectations.[195]

3.71 Another difficulty that is identified because of the large number of constituencies that a company might have is that they will usually have conflicting claims, and each constituency will be subject to the opportunistic actions of other constituencies.[196] This complicates any decisions that the directors are to make in balancing interests.

---

[192] O Hart 'An Economist's View of Fiduciary Duty' (1993) 43 *University of Toronto Law Journal* 299 at 303.

[193] M Goyder *Living Tomorrow's Company* (London, Gower, 1998) at 3.

[194] A Sundaram and A Inkpen 'The Corporate Objective Revisited' (2004) 15 *Organization Science* 350 at 352 at 353.

[195] Ibid at 352.

[196] M Blair and L Stout 'A Team Production Theory of Corporate Law' (1999) 85 *Virginia Law*

3.72 Finally, shareholder value scholars argue that non-shareholder stakeholders, such as creditors and employees are adequately protected, for the most part, by contract and/or statutory provisions and so if you require directors to take the interests of such constituencies into account they are receiving very special preferential treatment.[197]

C Summary

3.73 How duties are seen depends largely as to which corporate law theory one adheres to. Those taking a progressive or managerialist approach want to grant directors wide discretion, but also seek to have duties imposed on them to ensure there is significant regulation of what directors do. Conversely, those who advocate contractarian theories tend to use an economic analysis approach and duties are perceived as a contractual 'device uniquely crafted to fill in the massive gap in this open-ended bargain between shareholders and corporate officers and directors'.[198] It is said that 'the fiduciary principle is fundamentally a standard term in a contract'.[199] Providing a fiduciary duty is 'an alternative to elaborate promises and extra monitoring'.[200] All of this is to overcome the fact that contracts are seen as incomplete.[201]

3.74 Historically in Anglo-American law and much of the law of the Commonwealth, shareholder value has held sway and directors have been seen as owing their duties to the shareholders. In practice, though, there are indications that directors have adopted a broader approach and embraced aspects of stakeholder theory.[202] Certainly many who adhere to shareholder value openly accept that directors must not ignore the interests of stakeholders as it is necessary to consider them in order for shareholders to be benefited ultimately.

3.75 Some of the issues discussed above were addressed by the Company Law Review Steering Group in its review of UK company law, and it plumped for what it saw as a different approach, namely enlightened shareholder value. This is discussed in detail in **Chapter 6**.

Review 247 at 276–287. The answer according to the learned commentators (pursuant to what they call 'the team production theory') is that the board must make the ultimate decisions in reconciling competing interests and disputes (at 276–277).

[197] See A Keay 'Directors' Duties to Creditors: Contractarian Concerns Relating to Efficiency and Over-Protection of Creditors' (2003) 66 MLR 665.

[198] J Macey 'An Economic Analysis of the Various Rationales for Making Shareholders the Exclusive Beneficiaries of Corporate Fiduciary Duties' (1991) 21 *Stetson Law Review* 23 at 41.

[199] F Easterbrook and D Fischel 'Corporate Control Transactions' (1982) 92 Yale L J 698 at 702.

[200] F Easterbrook and D Fischel *The Economic Structure of Corporate Law* (Harvard University Press, 1991) at 92.

[201] For a useful discussion of the concept, see I MacNeil 'Company Law Rules: An Assessment from the Perspective of Incomplete Contract Theory' (2001) 1 *Journal of Corporate Law Studies* 107. Also, see A Keay and H Zhang 'Incomplete Contracts, Contingent Fiduciaries and a Director's Duty to Creditors' (2008) 32 *Melbourne University Law Review* 141.

[202] South Africa is a good example.

D Duties to individual shareholders?

3.76 No matter what approach one takes concerning to whom directors' duties are owed, clearly directors do not owe duties to the shareholders individually[203] except in special circumstances.[204] In *Peskin v Anderson*,[205] while the Court of Appeal said that there was no duty owed to the shareholders in the case before it, it acknowledged the fact that there may be circumstances where there was a relationship between directors and shareholders that would lead to a fiduciary obligation existing.[206] Many of the cases in this area have related to share disposal transactions. It is also true to say that a fiduciary obligation might be owed to shareholders where a special relationship between the directors and the shareholders exists.[207] An example of this occurred in *Coleman v Myers*,[208] a decision of the Court of Appeal in New Zealand, and one regularly cited by English courts, and approved of by Browne-Wilkinson V-C in *Re Chez Nico (Restaurants) Ltd*.[209] In the latter case it was held that a duty existed in the situation where the directors were acquiring shares in the company from shareholders. In the recent decision of *Sharp v Blank*[210] Nugee J applied the above approach to reject a claim by shareholders of Lloyds Bank that the directors of the Bank owed, and had breached, fiduciary duties to the shareholders. His Lordship acknowledged that duties are only owed to shareholders in special factual relationship.[211] The judge went on to say:[212]

> '[T]his special relationship must be something over and above the usual relationship that any director of a company has with its shareholders. It is not enough that the director, as a director, has more knowledge of the company's affairs than the shareholders have: since they direct and control the company's affairs this will almost inevitably be the case. Nor is it enough that the actions of the directors will have the potential to affect the shareholders – again this will always, or almost always, be the case.'

E Duties to creditors?

3.77 Some have argued that UK and Commonwealth case-law can be read as supporting the fact that when a company is in financial difficulties, the directors owe fiduciary duties to the creditors of the company. While certain

---

[203] *Percival v Wright* [1902] 2 Ch 421; *Peskin v Anderson* [2001] 1 BCLC 372 (CA).

[204] For instance, see *Gething v Kilner* [1972] 1 WLR 337; [1972] 1 All ER 1166; *Re a Company* [1986] BCLC 382; *Glandon Pty Ltd v Strata Consolidated Pty Ltd* (1993) 11 ACSR 543 (NSWCA); *Brunninghausen v Glavanics* [1999] NSWCA 199; (1999) 17 ACLC 1247.

[205] [2001] 1 BCLC 372 (CA).

[206] Ibid at 379.

[207] Robert Valentine has asserted that the courts should tread carefully in this area: 'The Director-Shareholder Fiduciary Relationship: Issues and Implications' (2001) 19 *Company and Securities Law Journal* 92 at 93.

[208] [1977] 2 NZLR 225.

[209] [1992] BCLC 192 at 208. Also, see *Platt v Platt* [1999] 2 BCLC 745.

[210] [2015] EWHC 3220 (Ch).

[211] Ibid at [10], [12].

[212] Ibid at [12].

cases may be read in such a way, it is submitted that from a doctrinal point of view it would seem that this case-law does not represent the law. There is a significant amount of case-law in the UK, as well as in many Commonwealth countries and Ireland, to the effect that in certain circumstances, namely when the company is in financial straits, directors have to take into account the interests of creditors, but this obligation can only be seen as part of their duties to the company. The stronger view is that directors only owe an indirect duty to creditors, and not a direct independent duty. Nothing more will be said at this point as **Chapter 13** is devoted to this whole matter, and it is better left until we reach that Chapter.

V AGENCY THEORY

3.78   In a book dealing with directors, it behoves us to consider the agency theory, albeit briefly. It is a theory that is allied to the concept of separation of control and ownership, and adhered to by many corporate law academics and practitioners. The theory[213] seeks to examine the role of managers/directors inside the firm, as the company is often referred to, particularly by economists. The managers or directors are, pursuant to the agency theory, regarded as the agents of the shareholders in the running of the company's business,[214] with the latter being the principals. This relationship causes what are known as 'agency problems.' These result potentially from the fact that the shareholders and the managers have divergent interests. The theory suggests that mechanisms are required to ensure that the managers/directors, who are self-interest seeking parties, do not use their positions opportunistically to benefit themselves, or shirk their responsibilities to the detriment of shareholders. To resolve this problem there must be some co-alignment of incentives, and this co-alignment seeks to resolve a series of conflicting interests.[215] The mechanisms proposed by agency theory to mitigate director opportunism are, invariably, market based. The mechanisms include performance/profit based compensation, critical composition of independent directors on the board, the market of corporate control, the labour market for directors, as well as sufficient managerial ownership of the firm. The emphasis of agency analysis is on engendering incentive compatibility between directors and shareholders through market forces.[216]

3.79   A further problem facing the principals in the above relationship is that of information asymmetry, namely the principals and the agent do not have, or access to, the same information. The agents will have far more information than the principals because they are in control of the company. Agents can

---

[213]   M Jensen and W Meckling 'Theory of the Firm: Managerial Behaviour, Agency Costs, and Capital Structure.' (1976) 3 *Journal of Financial Economics* 305.

[214]   Case-law does not support this. For example, see *Pascoe Ltd (in liq) v Lucas* (1998) 16 ACLC 1247 at 1273.

[215]   Ways of effecting a co-alignment include providing incentive payments to managers and the market for corporate control.

[216]   See A Keay and H Zhang 'Incomplete Contracts, Contingent Fiduciaries and a Director's Duty to Creditors' (2008) 32 *Melbourne University Law Review* 141.

effectively choose what they will disclose to principals, and principals do have difficulty obtaining information and often knowing what information to try and obtain, and whether certain kinds of information actually exist. One of the ways of rectifying this is to have non-executive directors who are independent, sitting on boards to protect shareholders' interests, but that does not always work, witness the US company, Enron,[217] where all but one of the members of the board were non-executive directors.

3.80 The problems highlighted above, as well as other problems, produce agency costs, that is, the cost of overcoming agency problems. For instance, one way of resolving the problems mentioned is to ensure that there is adequate monitoring and disciplining of directors. However, that is costly and creates transactions costs.

3.81 The agency problem is, in effect, an incomplete contracting problem as it is not possible to lay down a contract that covers every conceivable contingency. The notion of one kind of duty owed by directors, the fiduciary duty, can be construed as a legal provision (along with other provisions) to 'complete' an incomplete contract between the principal and agent to a degree that the contract remains viable. Duties also can address the agency problem as they impose obligations on directors and give the company rights against the directors for breach.

VI PROCESS

3.82 As one would expect, the way in which each company operates is likely to differ in some way. How a company operates is likely to depend on many factors, such as size of the company, size of the board, area of commerce and industry in which the company operates, business goals.

3.83 Obviously various procedures and processes will be (or should be) formulated to enhance good corporate governance. As far as matters which require a formal decision of the board the process may typically involve,[218] initially, the distribution of a briefing paper which commonly addresses all of those issues which the directors are likely to consider in making their decision, including, for instance: the strategic rationale for the proposal, the financial effects, a summary of legal and regulatory issues, issues relating to employees and factors that might affect the company's reputation. Naturally, how the paper is constructed will depend on the type of proposal that is involved. Before the relevant board meeting the paper will be disseminated amongst board members, except where the situation is exceptional. It might be argued that this paper represents the most important written support for the decision process.

---

[217] The company, which had grown to be the seventh largest company in the US, collapsed later in 2001. The collapse of the company is seen as one of the greatest scandals in American corporate history. The losses of investors alone exceeded $70 billion.

[218] The following is based on Association of General Counsel and Company Secretaries of the FTSE 100 ('GC100') 'Companies Act (2006) – Directors' Duties' February 2007 at para 3.2(a).

At the board meeting a presentation, in order to supplement the briefing paper, may be made. This will be followed by a discussion by the board members. After due deliberation the board will come to a decision.

3.84 A minute will be taken and it will usually summarise the main points of the board's discussion, as well as recording any decision that is made. It is possible that the minutes may include some sort of statement to the effect that, having taken into account all factors, the directors are of the view that the proposal is in the company's interests. However, it has been suggested that this approach only operates in situations where formal board minutes have to be disclosed to external third parties.

VII RECORDING ACTIONS AND DECISIONS

3.85 From a corporate governance perspective it is proper that directors keep appropriate and accurate records of the actions and decisions that they take from time to time. A large part of corporate governance, particularly as far as public companies and large private companies are concerned, is involved with the decisions that are made by directors in board meetings.[219] Besides perhaps enhancing corporate governance, there is another reason for making and retaining records. Directors must realise that they may well be called to account, at any time, for their actions and decisions whilst a director of the company, but particularly if the company: enters some form of insolvency regime, the company is sold and another set of directors are appointed, or after their term of office ends. Not only must directors ensure that they discharge their duties properly and competently, they must ensure that this is recorded objectively so that they are able to resist any claims made against them, and to support their contention that they acted according to law. This is something that the board as a collective has to take into account. It is imperative that it ensures that there are records made and retained indicating why and how it made decisions and what actions it felt were appropriate in any given situation. Particularly it is critical that accurate and thorough minutes are taken at board meetings and meetings of committees of the board, such as the audit committee. The minutes should not only record the decisions made, but also the background discussions and rationales for any decisions taken.

3.86 Also, it is important that directors have the opportunity to deliberate on issues and so processes should exist before the board meeting takes place that permits this to occur.[220]

3.87 At various points during the book, and especially in **Chapters 6** and **8**, comments will be made about record-keeping and other actions that ought to be taken by boards and individual directors.

---

[219] S Bottomley *The Constitutional Corporation* (Aldershot, Ashgate, 2007) at 68.
[220] Ibid at 112.

3.88   Given the fact that it is not totally clear what is required of directors in discharging their duties under some provisions of the CA 2006, it is prudent that directors take every step they can to ensure that there is a record of what they have done and reasons provided for the actions taken (possibly with references to supporting evidence). Directors should carefully examine minutes of meetings and ensure that they are an accurate and faithful account of the meetings to which they relate, and that they record what was said and done.

CHAPTER 4

CODIFICATION AND AN INTRODUCTION TO THE GENERAL DUTIES

I INTRODUCTION

4.1 Following introductory matters we now move on to begin our consideration of the particular duties of directors provided in some detail. But before doing so we need to examine the fact that the passing of the CA 2006 saw a change in direction of the law regarding the general duties of directors. For, until this legislation was enacted, directors' duties were only provided for at common law and in equity, but now the duties are contained in statute. Therefore, the first aim of this chapter is to consider the background to, and the rationale for, the codification of duties. Then, as an introduction to the general duties which we examine in the following Chapters, we will study s 170 of the CA 2006, which serves as an introduction to Chapter 2 of Part 10 of the Act.

II CODIFICATION

4.2 Directors' duties in common law and equity have been provided ever since the development of company law in the mid-nineteenth century. It has been said that to get a picture of the duties of directors one had to digest 'a confusing and compendious mass of case-law and the occasional statutory measure.'[1] Now the general duties are found in Chapter 2 of Part 10. The journey to get to this point has been a long one. The inclusion of duties in statutory form was rejected by the Greene Committee in the mid-1920s on the basis that it would be a hopeless task.[2] Later the Jenkins Committee in the early 1960s also rejected the notion of a codification on the basis that it was not possible to provide specific definitions of the duties of directors in legislation,[3] but it did recommend a non-exhaustive statement of the basic principles underlying the fiduciary duties which a director owed to his or her company. But nothing eventuated from this. In the meantime several Commonwealth jurisdictions, who received their law from England, and including Australia, Ghana, Canada, New Zealand and Malaysia, codified the duties of directors. The issue of codification was again considered in the UK in the late 1990s by the Law Commission and the Scottish Law Commission in their joint inquiry,

---

[1] L Roach 'The Legal Model of the Company and the Company Law Review' (2005) 26 Co Law 98.

[2] Report of the Company Law Amendment Committee (1925-26) (Cmd 2657) at para 46, p 20.

[3] Ibid at para 87.

Company Directors: Regulating Conflicts of Interests and Formulating a Statement of Duties.[4] Initially the Law Commissions were against the idea of codification, taking the view that it would be too restrictive and it would hinder the evolution of the law.[5] However, following consultation they proposed, in their subsequent report, partial codification.[6] Shortly after the Law Commissions reported, the Company Law Review Steering Group (CLRSG), which had been established to undertake a comprehensive review of UK company law, proposed an exhaustive statement of duties, and to address the concerns of the Law Commissions it indicated that the drafting should provide a restatement that involved a high level of generality, and would not prevent the courts inventing new principles outside the field, including wholly new bases for the liability of directors.[7]

4.3   Traditionally, lawyers in common law jurisdictions have seen statutes as essentially providing an imposition on the common law,[8] with the pre-existing common law not being easily eliminated or modified. Nevertheless, it has been asserted that a more modern approach is to regard statutes as the dominant source of law,[9] or at least to view the legal landscape as being constituted by an amalgam of the two. Certainly Chapter 2 of Part 10 of the CA 2006 drew heavily on the existing common law, even where the statute lays down a duty that is framed in a different way to the existing duties. A prime example is s 172, discussed in **Chapter 6**. The result is that there is a rather awkward relationship between the statutory duties and the existing corpus of common law rules and equitable principles. While the former supplants the latter to a large extent, the legislation indicates that the latter should be drawn on by the judiciary in developing the law. As the judges can do this the legislature has been able to refrain from setting out in detail aspects of the respective duties. To be fair, hitherto, there do not appear to have been any appreciable problems in practice with the approach that was adopted. Although, as indicated in **Chapter 6**, the courts have tended to rely heavily on the pre-existing case-law and the principles that they emit, to the detriment of providing an interpretation and exposition of the new provisions, which are, to some degree, different even if they are based on the existing common law rules and equitable principles.

4.4   The purpose of codification was, according to the Law Commissions' report, to restate the law on directors' duties in order to clarify it and make it

---

[4]   Law Com No 153, Scot Law Com No 105.
[5]   Ibid at para 4.27.
[6]   Law Com No 261, Scot Law Com No 173 at para 4.31.
[7]   Company Law Review *Modern Company Law for a Competitive Economy: Developing the Framework* (London, HMSO, 2000) at para 3.15 and 3.82.
[8]   H Stone 'The Common Law in the United States' (1936) 50 *Harvard Law Review* 15 and referred to in G Gunasekara and A Sims 'Statutory Trends and the "Genetic Modification" of the Common Law: Company Law as a Paradigm' (2005) *Statutory Law Review* 82 at 83.
[9]   G Calabresi *A Common Law for the Age of Statutes* (Cambridge, Mass, Harvard University Press, 1982) and referred to in G Gunasekara and A Sims, ibid.

more accessible,[10] with the aim of bringing about a change in directors' behaviour by educating directors and providing them with greater certainty regarding what the law required of them.[11] The Law Commissions were concerned that from an international perspective, businesses that were founded overseas would expect to see a set of statements about directors' duties in the relevant corporate legislation.[12] The CLRSG agreed with the accessibility[13] and clarity points, but it would appear that it also envisaged the statute would not merely restate the existing law but it would also both modernise, and overcome defects in, the existing law.[14] The intention behind the CLRSG's recommendations was that the provisions would be drafted at a sufficiently high level of generality so as to permit judicial development within the terms of the legislation.[15] In the debates on the Company Law Reform Bill 2005, subsequently re-named as the Companies Bill 2006, the Government, through the statements of Lord Goldsmith, indicated that clarifying and making accessible the duties was the primary reason for codification.[16] However, it would appear that the provisions in the CA 2006 that purport to codify directors' duties only do so partially. This was recognised by the Court of Appeal in *Ranson v Computer Systems plc*.[17] It is also implicitly acknowledged by s 178(2) for it refers to 'any other fiduciary duty owed to a company by its directors,' besides those in Chapter 2 of Part 10.

4.5   The codified statement of duties that the CLRSG proposed was regarded by it as accessible and containing a modern, inclusive view of the range of decision-making and standards of skill that are moulded to the function of individual directors.[18]

4.6   The problem is that the codified duties are not self-standing in that there will be a need to refer to the common law rules and equitable principles that have developed over many years. This is not a problem for lawyers in a common law system, generally speaking, but it will mean limitations

---

[10]   For a discussion of this issue, see D Ahern 'Directors' Duties, Dry Ink and the Accessibility Agenda' (2012) 128 LQR 114.

[11]   Law Com No 261, Scot Law Com No 173 at paras 4.40–4.41. The Law Commission and the Institute of Directors have expressed concerns in the past that directors have a generally low level of understanding of their duties: Company Law Review *Modern Company Law for a Competitive Economy: Developing the Framework*, (London, HMSO, 2000) at para 3.37; Law Com No 261, Scot Law Com No 173 at para 4.25–4.26 and Appendix B.

[12]   Ibid at para 4.43.

[13]   It felt that accessibility was particularly important for small companies which are not able to have, or afford, regular contact with legal advisers: Company Law Review *Modern Company Law for a Competitive Economy: The Strategic Framework* (London, HMSO, 2001) at para 2.25.

[14]   Company Law Review *Modern Company Law for a Competitive Economy: Final Report* (London, HMSO, 2001) at para 3.7.

[15]   Company Law Review *Modern Company Law for a Competitive Economy: Completing the Structure* (London, HMSO, 2000) at para 3.12.

[16]   Lords Grand Committee, 6 February 2006, col 254.

[17]   [2012] EWCA Civ 841 at [20].

[18]   Company Law Review *Modern Company Law for a Competitive Economy: Final Report* (London, HMSO, 2001) at para 1.56.

concerning the extent of the actual assistance that will be given to directors and others. On the positive side, it will give them, in one place, a statement of their duties, and much of Chapter 2 of Part 10 of the CA 2006 is able to be followed by a director. However, there are parts that are not clear as far as the language used, and a full understanding cannot be obtained without some knowledge of the case-law. In addition, codification seeks to do what Romer J in *Re City Equitable Fire Insurance Co*[19] said was impossible, namely describing the duties of directors in general terms.[20] The reason for questioning whether it is possible to codify duties is that companies differ in size, nature of business and how they are organised, as well as the fact that there are different kinds of directors undertaking different roles.[21]

4.7 It is interesting to note that research commissioned by the Law Commissions found that a codified statement of directors' duties was likely to be of most use, and have the most impact, in smaller, non-listed and closely-held companies,[22] and while in the early days of the legislation most discussion had been in relation to public companies, and this was especially the case in relation to s 172 of the CA 2006, we have seen most cases relating to SMEs. The statement of duties does not discriminate between large public companies and small private companies, notwithstanding the fact that they are totally different types of bodies with different agenda and modus operandi. However, it is likely that the case-law that develops in relation to the CA 2006 will make distinctions. Before its advent, this has been particularly the situation in relation to the duty of care, and arguably this is implicit in the provision that codifies the duty of care, skill and diligence, s 174. This section is discussed in detail in **Chapter 8**.

4.8 As indicated above, a primary intention behind the codification is educational, namely to instruct directors as to their duties and to enable them to have easy access to them, and this certainly seems to be the case with s 172 as we will see in **Chapter 6**. The problem remains that many aspects of the duties are not clear to a layperson and directors will need legal advice to understand them,[23] something which is overt when one considers s 172. Furthermore, it is acknowledged in s 170 of the CA 2006 that the codified duties (known as general duties) are based on certain common law rules and equitable principles, and the legislation goes on to provide that the general duties will be interpreted and applied in the same way as the aforementioned rules and principles, and regard is to be had to the corresponding rules and principles in the process of interpreting and applying the general duties.[24] The upshot, therefore, is that the law that has developed until now will be most

---

[19]   [1925] Ch 407.

[20]   Ibid at 426.

[21]   G Santow 'Codification of Directors' Duties' (1999) 73 *Australian Law Journal* 336 at 340.

[22]   S Deakin and A Hughes 'Directors' Duties: Empirical Findings' (ESRC Centre for Business Research, University of Cambridge, August 1999).

[23]   Something pointed out as far back as November 1998 by the Law Society (Company Law Committee, No 366 at p 2) in its response to the Law Commission's Consultation Paper on 'Company Directors: Regulating Conflicts of Interest and Formulating a Statement of Duties'.

[24]   CA 2006, s 170(3)(4).

important. Naturally, lawyers will have to advise directors what these rules and principles are, and how they might be used in the interpretation and application of the general duties. The fact of the matter is that it might be argued that the code as we presently have it is not readily intelligible to a great many directors for it is not drafted in a user-friendly manner. The expression of this and other concerns necessitated the Government publishing a statement,[25] to act as a form of guidance for directors, in more intelligible language about the duties. With the greatest respect, the statement was not very expansive and primarily consisted of excerpts from speeches made by ministers in the Parliament.

4.9 According to the Government in its post-enactment statement about the duties, the duties in Chapter 2 of the CA 2006 can be looked at in one of two ways. On the one the hand Chapter 2 can be regarded as merely codifying the existing common law obligations of directors; on the other hand it 'marks a radical departure in articulating the connection between what is good for a company and what is good for society at large'.[26] Section 172 is pin-pointed as a good example of the latter interpretation. Following the first view of the duties, the Government has said that there is continuity with the existing law for the statute lays down duties that are essentially the same as the existing duties established by case-law, the only major exception being the new procedures for dealing with conflicts of interest. In the House of Commons, David Howarth of the Company Law Review panel said that part of the intention was to place in statutory form that which already existed in some form at common law because that would clarify, rather than make more confusing, what was being done.[27]

4.10 The guidance to directors from the Government, as a result of the codification of duties, is as follows:[28]

'1   Act in the company's best interests, taking everything you think relevant into account.
2   Obey the company's constitution and decisions taken under it.
3   Be honest, and remember that the company's property belongs to it and not to you or to its shareholders.
4   Be diligent, careful and well informed about the company's affairs. If you have any special skills or experience, use them.
5   Make sure the company keeps records of your decisions.
6   Remember that you remain responsible for the work you give to others.
7   Avoid situations where your interests conflict with those of the company. When in doubt disclose potential conflicts quickly.

---

[25]   Duties of Company Directors, DTI, June 2007, Introduction and Statement of Rt Hon Margaret Hodge, and available at http://webarchive.nationalarchives.gov.uk/20070603164510/http://www.dti.gov.uk/files/file40139.pdf (accessed 5 October 2016).
[26]   Ibid at p 1.
[27]   HC Comm D cols 531–537 (6 July 2006).
[28]   Duties of Company Directors, DTI, June 2007, Introduction and Statement of Rt Hon Margaret Hodge, at p 2 and available at http://webarchive.nationalarchives.gov.uk/20070603164510/http://www.dti.gov.uk/files/file40139.pdf.

8   Seek external advice where necessary, particularly if the company is in
       financial difficulty.'

4.11 Guidance can also be obtained from the Association of Chartered
Certified Accountants' Guide to Directors' Responsibilities under the
CA 2006.[29]

4.12 Obviously how things transpire over time will allow us to assess whether
codification is a good thing or not. Even though we are entering the tenth year
since many of the duties were put in force, it is still too early to pass any
definitive view. One of the arguments for codification is that it brings certainty
because one cannot rely on the courts to find a correct balance. This assumes
that the courts are not to be depended on to deal with the actions against
directors without statutory guidance. The danger, according to a former justice
of appeal of the New South Wales Court of Appeal, Kim Santow, when writing
extra-judicially,[30] is that codification provides a broad brush approach with the
use of general statements, such as the use of 'reasonable', to the extent that it
does not produce certainty or it is so precise that it operates with unpredictable
harshness. It is also possible to say that codification will inhibit flexibility,
which can be fostered by the common law; courts are able to adjust and
develop principles at common law in ways that they cannot do when faced with
the words of a statute. So, the code means that flexibility is a trade-off for
certainty and accessibility.

4.13 As alluded to earlier, it is worth noting that that Chapter 2 might not
encompass all duties owed, an issue discussed at the end of the Chapter.
Section 178(2) of the CA 2006 recognises the fact that there might be other
fiduciary duties owed by directors (see, the use of 'other' in reference to
fiduciary duties in s 178(2)). Also, s 172(3) indicates that the duty of directors
to promote the success of the company, as required by s 172(1), is subject to
any rule requiring directors, in certain circumstances, to consider the interests
of creditors. In **Chapter 13** we will consider this obligation in some detail. So,
any duties that are not covered by ss 171–177 and that existed at common law
or in equity apparently still operate and may be developed.

4.14 The Association of General Counsel and Company Secretaries of the
FTSE 100 ('GC100') did not disapprove of the codification and the
introduction of new duties, but it did express concerns that this innovation
together with the new statutory derivative claim provisions, making it easier, it
was thought,[31] for shareholders to bring derivative actions, could have the
effect of increasing bureaucracy in companies, making the decision-making
process more cumbersome and potentially increasing the liability of directors.[32]

---

[29] July 2007. The guide is written by John Davies, Head of Business Law at the Association. It is
      accessible at www.accaglobal.com/content/dam/acca/global/PDF-technical/business-law/tech-
      tp-cdd.pdf.
[30] G Santow 'Codification of Directors' Duties' (1999) 73 *Australian Law Journal* 336 at 347.
[31] As we will see in Chapter 14, this might not be the case.
[32] 'Companies Act (2006) – Directors' Duties' (February 2007) at para 1.1.

4.15 While many opposed the codification of duties, it might be said that provided that it is able to be interpreted broadly and there can be development of duties, then it is not likely to cause untold problems.[33] All sections in Chapter 2 of Part 10 became operative on 1 October 2007 through Companies Act 2006 (Commencement No 3, Consequential Amendments, Transitional Provisions and Savings) Order 2007,[34] save for ss 175–177, which became operative on 1 October 2008 through Companies Act 2006 (Commencement No 5, Transitional Provisions and Savings) Order 2007.[35] Relatively speaking, there still has not been a large corpus of cases dealing with the duties, notwithstanding that we are in either the ninth and tenth year of operation of the provisions, and so we are forced to engage in the examination of many pre-codification cases to enable us to ascertain how the sections will be interpreted and applied. This is certainly the approach adopted by the courts.

III INTERPRETATION

4.16 The first thing to note is that many of the duties contained in Chapter 2 of Part 10 of the CA 2006 do not accord with the way that their counterparts under the common law and in equity were articulated. So how have they been interpreted?

4.17 The normal rules of statutory interpretation dictate that case-law dealing with the previous legal position would not be relevant and the courts would have to interpret the new provisions 'from scratch'.[36] Lord Herschell said in *Bank of England v Vagliano Brothers*[37] that:

> 'I think the proper course is in the first instance to examine the language of the statute and to ask what is its natural meaning, uninfluenced by any considerations derived from the previous state of the law, and not to start with inquiring how the law previously stood, and then, assuming that it was probably intended to leave it unaltered, to see if the words of the enactment will bear an interpretation in conformity with this view.'

4.18 In *Re MC Bacon Ltd (No 1)*,[38] Millett J, in hearing a case on preferences under the then new insolvency legislation (Insolvency Act 1986, s 239), refused to consider cases on the previous preference provisions in the Bankruptcy Act. However, to the point where the provisions enact what were the extant common law rules and equitable principles, the existing case-law is able to be

---

[33] J Birds 'The Reform of Directors' Duties' in J de Lacy (ed) *The Reform of United Kingdom Company Law* (London, Cavendish, 2003) at 156.
[34] SI 2007/2194.
[35] SI 2007/3495.
[36] *Bank of England v Vagliano Brothers* [1891] AC 107 at 144–145. Also, see D Ahern 'Directors' Duties, Dry Ink and the Accessibility Agenda' (2012) 128 LQR 114 at 127–128.
[37] [1891] AC 107 at 144–145.
[38] [1990] BCLC 324.

applied to explain the nature of the duties which they codify.[39] The Government in the parliamentary debates felt that it was advantageous for the law on the duties to develop in line with recent developments in the law.[40] The courts have certainly followed this approach and they have referred to pre-codified cases on many occasions in dealing with claims brought under one or more of ss 171–177. This is clearly demonstrated in Chapters 6–13 of the book.

4.19 The legislation has sought to be precise. In s 170(3) it acknowledges the fact that the duties in Chapter 2 are based on certain common law rules and equitable principles, but indicates that the codified duties have application in lieu of the said rules and principles. Nevertheless, these rules and principles, developed over years of decision-making by the courts, are not being dispatched to the rubbish bin, for in the next subsection the legislation provides that the codified duties should be interpreted and applied in the same way as the common law rules and equitable principles, and regard is to be had to the corresponding rules and principles in the process of interpreting and applying the general duties. The rules and principles that have been replaced by the statement of general duties will not apply directly, but the approaches and views of the courts in defining directors' duties over many years have been very influential in the manner in which the courts have decided to interpret the new statutory provisions. So, in cases where the statute adopts wording and terminology that is similar to the pronouncements of common law rules and equitable principles, case-law has been followed faithfully. Now when it comes to statements that adopt new wording and terminology one might have thought that there would be a different approach, witness the views of Millett J in *Re MC Bacon Ltd (No 1)*[41] mentioned above. The way that the new scheme has been put together suggests that the codified law should not merely be seen as re-stating the common law rules and equitable principles, but adding to them. Nevertheless, as we will see in the forthcoming Chapters, most cases that have been decided thus far have not entered into an analysis of the new provisions to ascertain their meaning, but have simply 'equated the provisions with the pre-existing law and decided the case by reference to pre-existing case-law principles'.[42] Deidre Ahern expresses the problem with adopting this, perhaps slavish, approach well when she states:[43]

> 'While the appeal of familiar principles is understandable and is endorsed by s 170(4), an overly expansive embracement of the pre-existing law is detrimental to establishing the legislative framework as the central and overriding source of law in relation to the general duties of directors. That is not to deny the relevance of pre-existing case-law but it would be preferable if the courts first looked at the

---

[39] Company Law Review *Modern Company Law for a Competitive Economy: Completing the Structure* (London, HMSO, 2000) at para 3.12.

[40] Lord Goldsmith, *Hansard*, House of Lords, GC Day 3, vol 678, cols 243–245 (6 February 2006).

[41] [1990] BCLC 324.

[42] D Ahern 'Directors' Duties, Dry Ink and the Accessibility Agenda' (2012) 128 LQR 114 at 130.

[43] Ibid.

natural meaning of the provision and then used case-law to help understand the application of the provision in practice where necessary.'

4.20 Section 172 is a case in point. While this provision is certainly a successor to the duty to act bona fide in the best interests of the company, it clearly is somewhat different and warrants a judicial analysis of the text. But, the courts have generally been content merely to say it follows on from the duty to act bona fide in the best interests of the company,[44] and they have applied the pre-existing law on that duty without adding anything.

4.21 It would seem that the pre-existing law has supplemented the duties and the law that has been developed to interpret them, so as to fill in the gaps.[45]

4.22 Clearly the statement of duties is merely a code of conduct and it does not purport to tell directors what to do.[46]

4.23 Finally, on the question of interpretation, the point should be made that the Explanatory Notes to the CA 2006 should only be considered where there are real doubts concerning the effect of the legislation discussed in this book. The same goes for ministerial statements, such as the statement of the Honourable Margaret Hodge, concerning how directors should regard the sections in Chapter 2 of Part 10 of the CA 2006.[47] In relation to this kind of statement, the court in *Melluish (Inspector of Taxes) v BMI (No 3) Ltd*[48] said that ministerial statements made after enactment provide no assistance to courts.[49] In this book a number of references are made to statements by the ministers who promoted the Bill in the respective chambers of Parliament, and there is some case authority for holding that such statements are to be disregarded as it cannot be assumed that Parliament agreed with the ministers' reasoning.[50] Clearly Explanatory Notes and the statements of ministers are to be treated cautiously and not relied on as a matter of course. In *Pepper v Hart*[51] the House of Lords stated that parliamentary materials should only be relied on where: the legislation is ambiguous, obscure or leads to absurdity; one seeks to rely on material that consists of one or more statements by a minister or other person promoting the Bill 'together with other parliamentary material as is

---

[44] For instance, see *Re West Coast Capital (LIOS) Ltd* [2008] CSOH 72; 2008 Scot (D) 16/5 (Outer House, Court of Sessions, Lord Glennie); *Cobden Investments Ltd v RWM Langport Ltd* [2008] EWHC 2810 (Ch).

[45] D Ahern 'Directors' Duties, Dry Ink and the Accessibility Agenda' (2012) 128 LQR 114 at 132–133; P Hood 'Directors' Duties Under the Companies Act 2006: Clarity or Confusion?' (2013) 13 JCLS 1 at 6.

[46] Explanatory Notes to the CA 2006 at para 280.

[47] See Duties of Company Directors, DTI, June 2007, Introduction and Statement of Rt Hon Margaret Hodge, at p 2 and available at http://webarchive.nationalarchives.gov.uk/20070603164510/http://www.dti.gov.uk/files/file40139.pdf.

[48] [1996] AC 454 (HL).

[49] Ibid at 480.

[50] See *McDonnell v Congregation of Christian Brothers* [2003] 1 AC 1101 at 1117; *Wilson v First Country Trust Ltd (No 2)* [2004] 1 AC 816 at [58]–[59].

[51] [1993] AC 593.

necessary to understand such statements and their effect';[52] the statements are clear.[53] Later cases have emphasised the restrictions on the use of non-legislative material in interpreting sections. But Lord Steyn in *McDonnell v Congregation of Christian Brothers*[54] stated that: 'it is, therefore, unobjectionable to use ministerial and other promoters' statements to identify the objective background to the legislation.'[55] This approach followed what Lord Browne-Wilkinson had to say on the matter in *Pepper v Hart*.[56]

IV FIDUCIARY DUTIES

4.24   It is not within the scope of the book to provide an analysis of fiduciary duties and to examine in detail which duties are fiduciary and which are not.[57] Interestingly there is no mention of any duties in the sections being of a 'fiduciary' nature, and that includes s 170 of the CA 2006, but s 178(2) does mention the term in the context of consequences of a breach. The effect of s 178(2) is that all duties mentioned in Chapter 2 of Part 10 are fiduciary save for that covered by s 174, which provides a duty of care.[58] As a result judges will undoubtedly continue to refer to some duties as fiduciary.[59] And while predominantly this chapter is concerned about s 170, it is appropriate to consider the fiduciary duties of directors in general terms, because, as foreshadowed above, the duties contained in all but s 174 effectively represent fiduciary duties. We will consider aspects of fiduciary duties throughout the book, and the following section of the Chapter merely discusses them in outline and notes some of the theory that underlies them.

4.25   The original notion of fiduciary duty is a product of the law of equity concerning the duty of a person in a discretionary position of trust to serve the interests of another person.[60] Despite the fact that the fiduciary relationship has been an element in English law for over 250 years,[61] it is based on what still

---

[52]   Ibid at 640.

[53]   Ibid.

[54]   [2003] 1 AC 1101.

[55]   Ibid at 1116.

[56]   [1993] AC 593 at 635. Also, see *Wilson v First Country Trust Ltd (No 2)* [2004] 1 AC 816 at [58].

[57]   For a discussion, see, for example, A Stafford and S Ritchie *Fiduciary Duties: Directors and Employees* (Bristol, Jordan Publishing, 2nd edn, 2015).

[58]   This is confirmed by Arden LJ in *Re Tobian Properties Ltd; Maidment v Attwood* [2012] EWCA Civ 998; [2012] BCC 98 at [22].

[59]   J Birds 'The Reform of Directors' Duties' in J de Lacy (ed) *The Reform of United Kingdom Company Law* (London, Cavendish, 2003) at 158.

[60]   See *Re Smith & Fawcett Ltd* [1942] Ch 304 at 306, 308. Also, see D DeMott 'Beyond Metaphor: An Analysis of Fiduciary Obligation' (1988) Duke LJ 879 at 880–881.

[61]   The roots of fiduciary duties are explained in *Bishop of Woodhouse v Meredith* (1820) 1 Jac & W 204 at 213. See R Cooter and B Freedman 'The Fiduciary Relationship: Its Economic Character and Legal Consequences' (1991) 66 NYU L Rev 1045 at 1045–1046.

remains an elusive concept.[62] Professor Len Sealy has said that it is used in an indefinite sense.[63] It has been said to be a slippery notion.[64]

4.26   Clearly the principles on which these duties are based are trust principles, although the director is not a trustee.[65] We considered the fact that the director was a fiduciary in **Chapter 2**.

4.27   Newbury J (with whom the other judges concurred) of the British Columbia Court of Appeal in *Canadian Metals Exploration Ltd v Wiese*[66] put it well when she said that:[67]

> 'The essence of the fiduciary relationship is the right of the beneficiary (in this case the company) to the impartial and bona fide exercise of decision-making powers by the fiduciary, free of any suggestion of personal interest.'

4.28   In a similar vein in another Canadian case, *Canadian Aero Service Ltd v O'Malley*,[68] Laskin J stated, in relation to the fiduciary relationship, that:[69]

> 'It is a necessary supplement, in the public interest, of statutory regulation and accountability which themselves are, at one and the same time, an acknowledgment of the importance of the corporation in the life of the community and of the need to compel obedience by it and by its promoters, directors and managers to norms of exemplary behaviour.'

In his oft-cited judgment in *Bristol & West Building Society v Mothew*,[70] Millet LJ (as he then was) said (and approved of by the House of Lords[71]):[72]

> 'The expression "fiduciary duty" is properly confined to those duties which are peculiar to fiduciaries and the breach of which attracts legal consequences differing from those consequent upon the breach of other duties. Unless the expression is so limited, it is lacking practical utility. In this sense it is obvious that not every breach of duty by a fiduciary is a breach of fiduciary duty.'

---

[62]   D DeMott 'Beyond Metaphor: An Analysis of Fiduciary Obligation' (1988) Duke LJ 879 at 879.

[63]   'Fiduciary Relationships' [1962] CLJ 69 at 72.

[64]   W Heath 'The Director's Fiduciary Duty of Care and Skill: A Misnomer' (2007) 25 *Company and Securities Law Journal* 370 at 370.

[65]   For instance, see *Re City Equitable Fire Insurance Co* [1925] Ch 407 at 426. Also, see L S Sealy 'The Director as Trustee' [1967] CLJ 83 at 86.

[66]   [2007] BCCA 318 (CanLII).

[67]   Ibid at [19]. It has been argued that the fiduciary model in corporate law derives largely from the separation of ownership and control evident in large public companies and discussed in **Chapter 3** (A Palmiter 'Reshaping the Corporate Fiduciary Model: A Director's Duty of Independence' (1989) 67 *Texas Law Review* 1351 at 1367). But this overlooks the fact that fiduciary duties in company law existed before the advent of the public company that is marked by separation of ownership and control.

[68]   [1974] SCR 592.

[69]   Ibid at 610.

[70]   [1998] 1 Ch 1.

[71]   *Hilton v Barker Booth & Eastwood* [2005] 1 WLR 567 at [28].

[72]   [1998] 1 Ch 1 at 17.

An instance of a breach by a fiduciary not being a fiduciary duty is a breach of the duty of care, and found in s 174.

4.29   There is no need for a claimant to establish culpability of the respondent director when it comes to a claim for a breach of fiduciary duty,[73] for fiduciary duties involve honesty and loyalty, and it is duties of care and skill that are concerned with the issue of competence.[74]

4.30   Fiduciary duties are regarded by the majority of contractarian scholars as operating as gap fillers in the incomplete contract between shareholders and directors. As Judge Frank Easterbrook and Professor Daniel Fischel have stated:[75]

> 'Corporate law – and in particular the fiduciary principle enforced by the courts – fills in the blanks and oversights with the terms that people have bargained for had they anticipated the problems and been able to contract costlessly in advance.'

4.31   As we noted in the previous Chapter, the contract between shareholders and directors is incomplete as it is not possible to lay down all of the terms that should operate in a contract and particularly one cannot specify how the directors are to exercise their discretion as they manage the company. What directors have to do is to exercise their discretion in conformity with their fiduciary duties. This tends to be predicated on the basis of economic analysis of law which provides that the directors owe their duties to the shareholders and not to the company, but, again as we saw in the last chapter, this is not clear.

4.32   Rather, traditionally in legal circles the thinking is that the duties are part of the protection provided for the company whose interests can be diminished by the directors. The law imposes the duties because if it did not then directors might act opportunistically, benefiting themselves at the expense of the company, and using their privileged and powerful position unfairly. The concept of fiduciary duties is to ensure there is protection. It has been argued that the function of fiduciary duties is to regulate cases where there is a temptation for a fiduciary to breach his or her non-fiduciary duties.[76] In this approach the company is seen as a separate entity.

4.33   The fiduciary duty of loyalty is designed to deter directors from conducting themselves in a manner which might injure the interests of their company, and we can see the thread of loyalty running through all of the duties in Chapter 2 of Part 10 that are regarded as fiduciary.

---

[73]   J Heydon 'Are the Duties of Company Directors to Exercise Care and Skill Fiduciary?' in S Degeling and J Edleman (eds) *Equity in Commercial Law* (Law Book Co, 2005) at 226.

[74]   *Extrasure Travel Insurances Ltd v Scattergood* [2003] 1 BCLC 598.

[75]   *The Economic Structure of Corporate Law* (1991) at 34. For a different view, see Deborah DeMott 'Beyond Metaphor: An Analysis of Fiduciary Obligation' (1988) Duke LJ 879.

[76]   M Conaglen 'The Nature and Function of Fiduciary Loyalty' (2005) 121 LQR 452 at 462.

V SCOPE AND NATURE OF THE DUTIES

4.34   Section 170 introduces the Chapter of the CA 2006 that deals with the general duties. What is notable is that the duties are said to be owed to the company. This embodies the principle provided for in the decision of *Percival v Wright*.[77] The principle is that the directors owed their fiduciary duties to the company and not the shareholders. The problem with saying this is that it is imprecise, as we saw in **Chapter 3**. While at common law, it was said that duties were owed to the company, some judgments had talked about the duties being owed to the shareholders. This might well have influenced the way that the duties have been drafted. For, notwithstanding the fact that the duty is owed to the company, s 172 makes it plain that the duty to promote the success of the company is mentioned in terms that indicate that the interests of the shareholders are in view. Pre-codification a duty was owed to the shareholders in general only in special circumstances,[78] such as when the directors are considering a takeover offer.[79] The argument accepted by many has always been that the shareholders deserve having the duty owed to them, effectively, as they are the residual owners of the company, that is the residual claimants have the greatest stake in the outcome of the company,[80] because they will benefit if the company's fortunes increase, but they will lose out if the company strikes financial difficulties (with their claims being last in line if the company is liquidated).[81] Notwithstanding s 170, in s 172(1) we find that the primary role of the directors is ultimately to benefit the members. This provides an apparent contradiction between s 170 and s 172(1). Interestingly, Proudman J in *City of London Group plc v Lothbury Financial Services Ltd*[82] said, without any qualification whatsoever, that one of the defendants, a Mr Padley, was a director and thus owed duties to both the company and its shareholders.

4.35   The contradiction would only appear to cause any problems if the interests of the company and the interests of the shareholders were different. As Parker Hood points out,[83] in practice this might not be as problematic as it first appears to be as the shareholders do have the power to remove directors, under s 168 of the CA 2006, provided that they can get a simple majority to support such action. Nevertheless, while this might well be possible in private

---

[77]   [1902] 2 Ch 421.
[78]   *Coleman v Myers* [1977] 2 NZLR 225. This New Zealand case has often been cited with approval in England.
[79]   See *Heron International Ltd v Grade* [1983] BCLC 244 at 265.
[80]   J Macey 'Fiduciary Duties as Residual Claims: Obligations to Nonshareholder Constituencies from a Theory of the Firm Perspective' (1999) 84 Cornell L Rev 1266 at 1267. This has been queried by several commentators, such as Margaret Blair (*Ownership and Control* (Washington DC, The Brookings Institute, 1995) at 229).
[81]   M van der Weide 'Against Fiduciary Duties to Corporate Stakeholders' (1996) 21 Del J Corp L 27 at 57.
[82]   [2012] EWHC 3148 (Ch) at [54].
[83]   P Hood 'Directors' Duties Under the Companies Act 2006: Clarity or Confusion?' (2013) 13 JCLS 1 at 15.

companies, obtaining a majority in public companies is not so easy to achieve, and the fact of the matter is that directors are rarely removed from public companies.[84]

4.36 **Chapter 3** covered the theory that has developed in relation to this whole issue of for whom are directors to act, and there will be more on it in **Chapter 6** when that duty is considered in depth. The statement in s 170 that the duty is owed to the company affirms earlier case-law that no duty is owed to parent[85] or subsidiary[86] companies.

4.37 It is interesting to note that when the Australian states codified their law on directors' duties in the various Companies Acts of the late 1950s and early 1960s,[87] they retained common law duties so that the legislative and common law duties applied side-by-side.[88] This remains the case under the present situation where the Corporations Act 2001 (which applies Australia-wide) provides for codified duties, and it does not appear to have caused any major problems. The UK approach, as we have already seen, has been different with s 170 providing that the duties are based on the common law rules and equitable principles and they shall be interpreted and applied in the same way as the common law rules and equitable principles and regard shall be had to these rules and principles,[89] but the duties under the common law as represented or reflected in the codified sections no longer apply.

4.38 It should be noted in this context that while at common law there are some special circumstances, such as when the company is the subject of a takeover offer,[90] where the directors could be said to be owed to members directly, there is no mention of this in the legislation. Nevertheless, there is nothing to suggest that Parliament wanted to abolish this rule.

4.39 It follows from the fact that the duties are said to be owed to the company, that, as with the law as it has been in the past, only the company can enforce them. However, Part 11 of the CA 2006 permits members, through the derivative claim procedure, to enforce the duties, in certain cases, on behalf of the company.[91]

4.40 The effect of the provisions in the CA 2006 is cumulative so more than one duty may apply to a particular state of affairs.[92] Where this occurs, a

---

[84] See A Keay 'Company Directors Behaving Poorly: Disciplinary Options for Shareholders' [2007] JBL 656.

[85] *Bell v Lever Bros Ltd* [1932] AC 161 at 228 (HL).

[86] *Lindgren v L & P Estates Ltd* [1968] Ch 572 (CA).

[87] For example, Companies Act 1961 (NSW). Actually the first legislation to codify a duty in the whole of the Commonwealth was the Victorian Companies Act 1958 (s 107).

[88] See *Daniels v Anderson* (1995) 13 ACLC 614 at 652 (NSWCA).

[89] CA 2006, s 170(3)(4).

[90] For instance, see *Gething v Kilner* [1972] 1 WLR 337; [1972] 1 All ER 1166; *Re a Company* [1986] BCLC 382; *Brunninghausen v Glavanics* [1999] NSWCA 199; (1999) 17 ACLC 1247.

[91] See **Chapter 14**.

[92] CA 2006, s 179. See Explanatory Notes to the CA 2006 at paras 311, 312.

director must comply with each applicable duty. The Explanatory Notes to the CA 2006 provides the following example:[93]

> 'Taking a bribe from a third party would, for example, clearly fall within the duty not to accept benefits from third parties (section 176) but could also, depending on the facts, be characterised as a failure to promote the success of the company for the benefit of its members (section 172) or as an aspect of failing to exercise independent judgment (section 173).'

4.41 The result is that a director cannot claim immunity if, for example, he or she was fulfilling the duty to promote the success of the company but the director fails to exercise the duty to act within directors' powers. This is the case even if the director considers that what he or she did would be most likely to promote the success of the company.[94] Likewise, directors cannot defend a claim that they have breached some other duty or obligation, that is, not one of the general duties, but some obligation required by other parts of the CA, by asserting that they fulfilled one of the general duties.[95] All of this is consistent with the position that has been often put, that the fiduciary duties owed by directors overlap. A general case example of the overlap can be found in the Australian decision of *Minlabs Pty Ltd v Assaycorp Pty Ltd.*[96] In that case a director was held liable for a breach of the duty of care for being party to several payments made by his company (X) to other companies in which he was a director, where X received no benefit and where the payments were not approved of by the directors of X. The court indicated that the director could have been liable for breaches of several duties, besides the duty of care.[97]

4.42 An exception to the point about the cumulative effect of duties is in relation to conflicts of interest that arise from a transaction with the company; they are not within the conflicts section, namely s 175 of the CA 2006;[98] they are only covered by s 177 or s 182.

4.43 The general duties are operative except where any rule of law enables the company to provide authority for anything to be done, or omitted, by the directors that would otherwise be a breach, and where the articles contain provisions for dealing with conflicts of interest are not contravened by anything done by the directors in accordance with those provisions of the articles.[99]

VI FORMER AND SHADOW DIRECTORS

4.44 Both former and shadow directors are specifically mentioned in s 170. Former directors (see s 170(2)) are subject both to the duty to avoid conflicts of

---

[93] Explanatory Notes at para 311.
[94] Explanatory Notes at para 313.
[95] Ibid at para 314.
[96] [2001] WASC 88; (2001) 37 ACSR 509.
[97] For a similar situation, see *Gamble v Hoffman* (1997) 24 ACSR 369; (1997) 15 ACLC 1314.
[98] CA 2006, s 175(3).
[99] CA 2006, s 180(4)(5).

interest as regards the exploitation of any property, information or opportunity of which they became aware whilst directors, and to the duty not to accept benefits from third parties as regards things done or omitted to be done by them before ceasing to be directors.[100] To the extent mentioned, the duties apply to former directors as to directors, but subject to any necessary adaptations. This does provide some degree of flexibility. Does this provision reflect the common law? It was stated in *Ultraframe (UK) Ltd v Fielding*[101] by Lewison J that the no-conflict rule ceased to apply to a director in relation to future activities after leaving his or her post. But s 170 does not seem to be so limited. This area is explored in **Chapter 10**.

4.45 It is notable that the provision makes the general duties applicable to shadow directors (see CA 2006, s 170(5)), but only to the extent that the relevant common law rules and equitable principles apply to shadow directors. It is clear that the duty of care dealt with in s 174 will apply. But it is not clear that shadow directors are subject to fiduciary duties. This was a matter that was raised and discussed in some detail in **Chapter 2**.[102] It will be recalled that in *Yukong Line Ltd of Korea v Rendsburg Investments Corp of Liberia (No 2)*,[103] Toulson J (as he then was) was strongly of the view that fiduciary duties did apply to shadow directors. However, in *Ultraframe (UK) Ltd v Fielding*[104] Lewison J (as he then was) took the view that generally speaking shadow directors do not owe fiduciary duties to the company.[105] This latter judgment has appeared to have had greater exposure over subsequent years and has often been referred to without any concomitant reference to the differing opinion of Toulson J. Those oversights were righted recently by Hildyard J in *Secretary of State for Business Innovation and Skills; Re UKLI Ltd*[106] and by Newey J in *Viviendi SA v Richards*.[107] Both of these judges preferred the view that shadow directors are subject to fiduciary duties.

4.46 As a de facto director clearly owes the same duties owed by a *de jure* director,[108] it is arguable that such a director is also covered by the provision. But it would appear that the common law position is that a person only owes duties once he or she commences as a director, and not when he or she is a director-elect.[109]

---

[100] For a decision where a former director was found liable for breach of duties, see *Safetynet Security v Coppage* [2012] All ER (D) 57 (Dec) (HHJ Brown, QBD).

[101] [2005] EWHC 1638 (Ch) at [1309].

[102] See **2.29–2.31**.

[103] [1998] 2 BCLC 485.

[104] [2005] EWHC 1638 (Ch).

[105] Ibid at [1284].

[106] [2013] EWHC 680 (Ch) at [48].

[107] [2013] EWHC 3006 (Ch).

[108] *Re Canadian Land Reclaiming and Colonizing Co* (1880) 14 Ch D 660 at 670 (CA); *Ultraframe UK Ltd v Fielding* [2005] EWHC 1638 (Ch) at [1257]; *Primlake Ltd v Matthews Associates* [2006] EWHC 1227 (Ch); [2007] 1 BCLC 686 at [284].

[109] *Lindgren v L & P Estates Ltd* [1968] Ch 572 (CA).

VII OTHER DUTIES

4.47 Whilst the focus of this book is on the general duties of directors found in the CA 2006, earlier we noted that Chapter 2 of Part 10 of the CA 2006 does not necessarily encompass all duties owed. In other words, the statutory code is not exhaustive. This appears to be recognised by s 178(2) for it refers to 'any other fiduciary duty owed to a company by its directors,' besides those in Chapter 2 of Part 10.

4.48 Prima facie this would seem to give permission to the courts to develop other duties that they have identified and which have not been codified. The advantage of this might be that it would overcome the fact that modern texts provide an exposition of duties which involves categorising cases under particular duties (sometimes uncomfortably) and this might, according to one commentator, lead to 'shoe-horning new cases into the narrow confines of previously decided ones'.[110] Of course, in codifying the duties of directors Parliament might be regarded as contributing to that trend. It must be said that one commentator adopts a rather conservative view in saying that the introduction of the general duties 'prevents or at least discourages the courts from developing new general duties at common law, except where the legislation specifically contemplates such judicial creativity'.[111]

4.49 There are possibly a couple of instances of duties that have been recognised at common law and are not mentioned in the CA 2006. First, it was established, at first instance in *Item Software (UK) Ltd v Fassihi*,[112] that besides their normal obligations under the duties to the company, directors have a separate and independent duty to inform the company if they have been engaged in misconduct.[113] In giving his judgment in *Item Software*, the learned deputy judge distinguished *Bell v Lever Bros Ltd* where Lord Atkin said that he did not think that a servant should have to disclose his or her theft from the employer, on the basis that an employee/director was in a different position from a director.[114] The duty is related to the American duty of candour that applies in relation to directors.[115] While the Court of Appeal in *Item Software (UK) Ltd v Fassihi*[116] dismissed the resultant appeal by the director, it did not agree with the judge at first instance when it came to the issue of the director owing a separate duty of confessing misconduct. The Court took the view that

---

[110] A Cloherty 'Directors' Duties of Disclosure' [2005] JBL 252 at 254.

[111] P Davies *Gower and Davies' Principles of Company Law* (London, Sweet and Maxwell, 8th edn, 2008) at 478. Perhaps one area of judicial creativity contemplated is in duties to consider creditor interests. See CA 2006, s 172(3).

[112] [2003] EWHC 3116 (Ch); [2003] BCC 858 at [52].

[113] For a discussion of this duty, see L Ho and P Lee 'A Director's Duty to Confess: A Matter of Good Faith' (2007) 66 CLJ 346.

[114] In the Court of Appeal in this case, the view was put that *Bell v Lever Bros* did not decide that an employee could never owe a duty to disclose misconduct ([2004] EWCA Civ 1244; (2004) BCC 994; (2005) 2 BCLC 91 (CA) at [56]).

[115] See S German 'What They Don't Know Can Hurt Them: Corporate Officers' Duty of Candor to Directors' (2009) 34 Del J Corp L 221. The commentator argues that the duty also ought to apply to officers as well as directors.

[116] [2004] EWCA Civ 1244; (2004) BCC 994; (2005) 2 BCLC 91 (CA).

the obligation to report one's own misconduct was part of the general duty to act in good faith for the best interests of one's company.[117] Simply, the director could not have reasonably believed that it was not in the company's best interests that it was made aware of the director's breach. Arden LJ, with whose judgment the other judges concurred, was concerned that to hold that the duty to disclose misconduct was a separate duty could lead to a proliferation of duties. But her Ladyship's comments pre-dated the codification of the general duties. There is no express duty in the legislation to act in good faith for the best interests of the company. However, the obligation to disclose misconduct has been held to fall under s 172 and the duty to promote the success of the company,[118] for as Arden LJ stated in *Item Software*,[119] the consequence of a non-disclosure might mean that the company makes erroneous business decisions. This is discussed further in Chapter 6. Also, Alan Berg makes an excellent point when he states that:[120]

> 'Although Arden LJ maintained that the duty of disclosure was not an independent duty separate from the fiduciary duty of good faith, it functioned in precisely that way. It operated as a separate and additional source of liability, a distinct cause of action. It rendered the defendant liable for substantial damages in circumstances where he had no liability, either for damages or an account of profits, in respect of his basic breach of duty in attempting to divert the contract to himself.'

4.50 In Australia the law, on the issue under consideration, appears to be uncertain at the moment as there is a difference of opinion extant amongst courts of different jurisdictions. While the Full Court of the South Australian Supreme Court (an appeal court) in *Southern Real Estate Pty Ltd v Dellow and Arnold*[121] held that a director owed, as part of her duty of good faith, a duty to advise her fellow directors of her intention to leave the company and set up a competing business (misconduct), a single judge of the Victorian Supreme Court, Hollingworth J, in *P & V Industries Pty Ltd v Porto*,[122] who did not make reference in her judgment to the South Australian decision, said that directors are not obliged to disclose wrongdoing to their companies.[123] Hollingworth J based her view on the fact that, in her opinion, directors' duties were proscriptive and do not prescribe any positive duties. The former decision is only binding on South Australian courts, but it will be persuasive authority in other states and territories, and courts will only follow the Victorian approach

---

[117] Ibid at [41].
[118] *Brandeaux Advisers (UK) Ltd v Chadwick* [2010] EWHC 3241 at [47]; *GHLM Trading Ltd v Maroo* [2012] EWHC 61 (Ch); [2012] 2 BCLC 369 at [195]; *Electrosteel Castings (UK) Ltd v Metapol* [2014] EWHC 2017 (Ch) at [34]; *GHLM Trading Ltd v Maroo* [2012] EWHC 61 (Ch); [2012] 2 BCLC 369 at [194]; *First Subsea Ltd v Balltec Ltd* [2014] EWHC 866 (Ch) at [187]; *IT Human Resources plc v Land* [2014] EWHC 3812 (Ch) at [121], [125]; *Haysport Properties Ltd v Ackerman* [2016] EWHC 393 (Ch).
[119] Ibid at [66].
[120] 'Fiduciary Duties: A Director's Duty to Disclose His Own Misconduct' (2005) 121 LQR 213 at 220.
[121] [2003] SASC 318; (2003) 87 SASR 1 at [29].
[122] [2006] VSC 131; (2006) 24 ACLC 573 (Vic S Ct).
[123] The court relied on *Breen v Williams* (1996) 186 CLR 71 (Aust HC).

if they feel that the decision in *Southern Real Estate Pty Ltd v Dellow* is clearly wrong. The English decision in *Item Software* could well come into the mix.

4.51 In *Item Software* Arden LJ[124] does identify the director's obligation to disclose as a 'fiduciary' obligation and this might suggest acceptance of the general North American approach, whereby all the equitable duties of a director are classified as 'fiduciary'. Certainly if the obligation is fiduciary then it might be regarded as one of the duties referred to in s 178(2) of the CA 2006. Nevertheless, one commentator is of the view that as there is no explicit discussion of the point in the judgment the use of the relevant terminology may simply reflect the traditional usage of the term in English company law.[125]

4.52 A second duty not addressed in the CA 2006 but raised in the courts is that directors are required to disclose to their companies attempts that are made by a potential competitor to poach them or their colleagues from the company.[126] Again, this might fall under s 172 of the CA 2006 for the same reason as mentioned above. Arguably, it does fit under s 172 more snugly than does the duty to disclose misconduct. Another duty that exists outside of the codified provisions, although there might well be an argument that it could be brought under one of them, possibly s 172, is the duty not to misapply the company's property.[127] The decision of the Supreme Court in *Re Paycheck Services 3 Ltd, HMRC v Holland*,[128] a case that concerned the specific duty of a director not to pay a dividend when the company does not have sufficient distributable profits.

4.53 It will be interesting to see if any further developments occur in later cases, especially in light of the codified general duties, for after all is said and done, *Item Software* was delivered pre-codification.

VIII PROCEEDINGS FOR BREACH OF DUTIES

A Who takes proceedings?

4.54 If there is a breach of duty by a director the company is the appropriate claimant. This has long been the position according to case-law,[129] but it is now able to be based on legislation. Section 170(5) states that the directors owe their duties to the company. The power to initiate litigation on behalf of the company is ordinarily bestowed on the board, as part of its broad management powers. But the initiation of proceedings by the board is not such a frequent occurrence for several reasons, absent the case where there has been a takeover

---

124 [2004] EWCA Civ 1244; (2004) BCC 994; (2005) 2 BCLC 91 (CA) at [41]–[44], [62].
125 A Cloherty 'Directors' Duties of Disclosure' [2005] JBL 252 at 256.
126 *British Midland Tool Ltd v Midland International Tooling Ltd* [2003] EWHC 466 (Ch); [2003] 2 BCLC 523 at [89].
127 See S Mortimore (ed) *Company Directors, Duties Liabilities and Remedies* (OUP, 2nd edn, 2013) at para 10.05.
128 [2010] UKSC 51; [2011] 1 BCLC 141; [2010] 1 WLR 2793.
129 *Foss v Harbottle* (1843) 2 Hare 461; 67 ER 189.

of the company and a replacement of the board. The board may, for a number of reasons, not take proceedings against a director(s) who has committed breaches of duty. First, the board may be under the influence, or even the control, of the miscreant director, or there are enough directors who are allies of the director in order to block the taking of any action. Of course, if the whole board has breached duties then self-interest will usually mean that it will not proceed. The board is not going to sue itself. Second, there is the cost of legal proceedings. Like any prospective litigant the board has to consider the likely costs that will be incurred. It will take into account that many successful parties are unable to reclaim all of their costs from the other party. Third, again like anyone considering taking legal action, the board has to be convinced that the company would have a good chance of succeeding. The shareholders are not going to thank the board for spending money in taking action that was not supported by cogent evidence. Fourth, the miscreant director might well be impecunious and any action that is successful might not produce any benefit. Fifth, the board might be embarrassed by the breach. Board members might feel that they were, or could be perceived as, 'asleep on the job,' or that they put too much faith in the miscreant director. Sixth, the board might feel that it is better for business that the breach is not publicised on the basis that it might bring either or both of the board and the company into disrepute. Seventh, boards are groups and are clearly affected by group dynamics. Directors may decide not to take action because they are influenced by: the fact that they have become friendly with the miscreant; other members of the board, and especially senior executives like the CEO,[130] support the miscreant; or issues of collegiality which might mean that directors find it difficult to question actions of colleagues.[131]

4.55   In their empirical study for the Law Commission in 1999,[132] Professors Simon Deakin and Alan Hughes reported that only two per cent of all of the directors in their study stated that their company had entered into litigation, within the past three years, against a director concerning a breach of his or her duties.[133]

4.56   Shareholders might seek permission to commence an action or leave to continue an action, known as a derivative claim, against directors if the board

---

[130] M O'Connor 'The Enron Board: The Perils of Groupthink' (2003) 71 *University of Cincinnati Law Review* 1233.

[131] J Macey *Corporate Governance: Promises Kept, Promises Broken* (Princeton University Press, 2008) at 61.

[132] 'Directors' Duties: Empirical Findings', Report to the Law Commission (ESRC Centre for Business Research, University of Cambridge, August 1999) at para 5.2. The findings formed an annex to the report of the Law Commission and the Scottish Law Commission joint report, *Company Directors: Regulating Conflicts of Interests and Formulating a Statement of Duties*, Law Com No 153, Scots Law Com No 105. The learned authors of the study sent out questionnaires to, and conducted interviews of, 5,500 directors who were members of the Institute of Directors (at para 3.2).

[133] For further discussion of the reason for directors not taking action, see A Keay 'An Assessment of Private Enforcement Actions for Directors' Breaches of Duty' (2014) 33 *Civil Justice Quarterly* 76.

fails to take action. This is discussed in detail in **Chapter 14**, and the statutory scheme that was introduced by the CA 2006 is considered in some detail. As indicated in Chapter 14 we have not seen more derivative actions instituted under this statutory scheme when compared with the situation that existed at common law.

4.57 Many actions that will lead to a court looking at a breach of duty are brought by liquidators, who will bring the action on behalf of the company, hoping to recover property or money in order to swell the amount that is paid out to creditors. Often the proceedings are brought under the so-called misfeasance proceedings provision, s 212 of the Insolvency Act 1986.[134] Administrators of companies may also bring proceedings against directors on behalf of the company.[135] No public regulator has power in the UK to bring proceedings against directors for breach of duty. This has been the subject of criticism,[136] and is beyond the scope of this book. It is notable that many cases have been brought against Australian directors for breach of duty by the Australian regulator, the Australian Securities and Investments Commission, a number of which are discussed, or at least mentioned, in succeeding pages.

4.58 It is appropriate in the context of this section of the Chapter to say a few words about limitations on actions.[137] The issue of limitation can be of considerable importance particularly where actions are sought to be instituted by liquidators of insolvent companies where the directors who committed breaches have been in control of a company for a substantial period following the breaches. Directors who might have been in breach might fail to assist the liquidator who comes to a company with little or no knowledge of its affairs, and so it could take a liquidator some time to discover whether breaches have occurred and even longer to gather evidence to support a claim. The limitation position for breaches of duties of directors is a complex matter. This is partly because there is no mention of breaches of duty in the Limitation Act 1980.

4.59 With breaches of ss 171–177 of CA 2006, discussed in subsequent chapters, the time limit applicable will depend on the nature of the breaches and the kind of relief that is sought. Generally these breaches are breaches of fiduciary duties, and the director might be regarded in the same way as a trustee.[138] That is, the directors are treated as if they were trustees of the funds

---

[134] For a discussion of the provision, see A Keay *McPherson's Law of Company Liquidation* (London, Sweet and Maxwell, 3rd edn, 2013) at 1006–1023.

[135] For an example, see *Lexi Holdings Ltd (in administration) v Luqman* [2008] EWHC 1639 (Ch).

[136] See A Keay 'The Public Enforcement of Directors' Duties: A Normative Inquiry' (2014) 43 *Common Law World Review* 89.

[137] For a discussion of limitation periods for actions in relation to fiduciaries in general, see J Mather 'Fiduciaries and the Law of Limitation' [2008] JBL 344, and in relation to directors and employees, see A Stafford and S Ritchie *Fiduciary Duties* (Bristol, Jordan Publishing, 2nd edn, 2015) at 505–528.

[138] *Re Lands Allotment Company* [1894] 1 Ch 616 at 631–632, 638–639 and 643; *J J Harrison v Harrison* [2002] BCLC 162 at 173 (CA); *Gwembe Valley Development Co Ltd v Koshy* [2003] EWCA Civ 1048; [2004] 1 BCLC 131 at [83].

and other property of the company that were in their control and that were the subject of any misapplication. So the starting point is to ascertain whether a particular claim is to be treated as one that constitutes a breach of trust. At one time there was no limitation period that operated against trustees, and, while that has changed, for the most part there are a couple of instances where the old position effectively applies. A specific provision of the Limitation Act 1980, namely s 21 that deals with claims by beneficiaries against trustees, is applied to claims by companies against directors where there is a breach of fiduciary duty involved.

4.60 It is probably helpful to set out s 21(1) of the Limitation Act 1980. It provides as follows:

> '(1) No period of limitation prescribed by this Act shall apply to an action by a beneficiary under a trust, being an action –
>
> (a)   in respect of any fraud or fraudulent breach of trust to which the trustee was a party or privy; or
> (b)   to recover from the trustee trust property or the proceeds of trust property in the possession of the trustee, or previously received by the trustee and converted to his use ....'

4.61 Generally speaking s 21 of the Limitation Act 1980 applies a limitation period of six years unless another provision in the Act applies or there is a provision in some other legislation that indicates a different period. Section 21(3) provides that subject to the preceding provisions of the section, an action by a beneficiary to recover trust property or in respect of any breach of trust, not being an action for which a period of limitation is prescribed by any other provision of this Act, shall not be brought after the expiration of six years from the date on which the right of action accrued. Section 21(1) quoted above constitutes an exception to the approach found in s 21(3) (s 21(2) is not really relevant for our discussion). We will come to the exception shortly.

4.62 Sometimes a company might favour taking proceedings against some third party (see **Chapter 15**), either alone or in addition to proceedings against the miscreant director, where that third party was allegedly involved in the breach in some way. Just as there are no references to breaches of duty in the Limitation Act, there are no references to actions against third parties who might be accessories to breaches. Where an action is against a third party for assisting in the breach, it would seem that the general limitation period of six years would apply, just as it would if action were brought against the trustee.[139]

4.63 If a claim against a director is for breach of duty of care, skill and diligence (see **Chapter 8**) then (as with any personal claim against a director in contract or tort) the general limitation period of six years applies, with the time beginning in relation to tortious claims from the date of the sustaining of

---

[139]   *Paragon Finance plc v D B Thackerar* [1999] 1 All ER 400 at 414 (CA).

damage. It is only in relation to a breach of fiduciary duties that the limitation period may be set aside, as we will now consider.

4.64 Section s 21(1) operates to exclude the six-year period mentioned in s 21(3) of the Limitation Act 1980 in relation to directors, in two circumstances. First, under s 21(1)(a) where the basis of the claim against directors is fraud and the director can be implicated in dishonest conduct,[140] and second, under s 21(1)(b), where the action seeks to recover trust property or proceeds of trust property held by the director as trustee for the company[141] or which he or she previously received, and converted to his or her own use, and this continues to apply notwithstanding the fact that the director no longer holds the property.[142] The Supreme Court has held in *Williams v Central Bank of Nigeria*[143] that s 21(1)(a) will only be available in respect of true or orthodox trustees. Directors were recognised as trustees of their company's property for the purposes of the provision by the Supreme Court,[144] even though, as was discussed earlier in this book (**2.34–2.37**), directors are not trustees notwithstanding the fact that in some old cases they were referred to as such. 'Party or privy' to a fraud or fraudulent breach of trust within s 21(1)(a) are to be narrowly construed and applied only to claims brought against trustees and not to claims brought against anyone else who was involved in the fraud or fraudulent breach of trust[145] and so while s 21(1)(a) could cover breaches by directors, as they are regarded as trustees, it would not cover the liability of third parties who assisted in a breach of trust, or, for our purposes, a breach of duty. The situation covered by s 21(1)(b) is often referred to as the situation where a class 1 trust exists.[146] This is derived from Millett LJ's judgment in *Paragon Finance plc v D B Thackerar*.[147] In that case Millett LJ distinguished two types of cases where a person is often referred to as a constructive trustee. In the first case a person is a constructive trustee where he or she, 'though not expressly appointed as trustee, has assumed the duties of a trustee by a lawful transaction which was independent of and preceded the breach of trust and is not impeached by the plaintiff'.[148] The Supreme Court in *Williams v Central*

---

[140] *Viviendi SA v Richards* [2013] EWHC 3006 (Ch); [2013] BCC 771 at [187].

[141] *Re Broadside Colours and Chemicals Ltd* [2011] EWHC 1034 (Ch).

[142] *J J Harrison v Harrison* [2002] 1 BCLC 162 (CA); *Gwembe Valley Development Co Ltd v Koshy* [2003] EWCA Civ 1048; [2004] 1 BCLC 131 at [111].

[143] [2014] UKSC 10; [2014] AC 1189.

[144] Although George Bompas QC (sitting as a deputy judge of the High Court) in *Gresport Finance Ltd v Battaglia* [2016] EWHC 964 (Ch) at [153] was not sure whether the Supreme Court accepted the fact that directors would always be regarded as trustees for the purposes of s 21(1)(a). In the recent Court of Appeal decision in *Burnden Holdings (UK) Ltd v Fielding* [2016] EWCA Civ 557 the Court accepted that s 21(1) did apply to claims against directors (at [31]). But some commentators have suggested that this is not logical and a director should not be seen as a trustee for the purposes of s 21: E Talbot Rice and A Holden 'A Trustee by Any Other Name: Who is "Trustee" for Limitation Purposes?' (2014) 29 *Journal of Banking and Finance Law* 438 at 439.

[145] Ibid at [28].

[146] This is considered in Chapter 15.

[147] [1999] 1 All ER 400.

[148] Ibid at 408–409.

Bank of Nigeria[149] approved of this approach. It has been indicated that
s 21(1)(b) also applies as an exception to the six-year limit where directors who
have breached their duties transfer property to a company controlled by the
directors.[150] It should be added that not all claims against directors will involve
directors being regarded as trustees for the purposes of s 21(1). In *Gwembe
Valley Development Co Ltd v Koshy*[151] the Court of Appeal distinguished
between two situations that are based on the classes of trust that Millett LJ
identified in *Paragon*. First, where a director transfers to himself or herself
property which previously belonged to the company, and in relation to which
he or she had 'trustee-like responsibilities' before the impugned transaction.
This is known as a class 1 trust and is within Millett LJ's first type of situation.
Second, where a director is liable to account for undisclosed profits, and any
constructive trust imposed on those profits where this does not depend on any
pre-existing responsibility for any property of the company, but where the
profits came to him or her as a result of a breach of duty. This is known as a
class 2 trust. In the former case a director would be regarded as a trustee for
s 21(1) purposes, but not in the latter case.

4.65 *J J Harrison (Properties) Ltd v Harrison*[152] is an example of a case (an
instance of a class 1 trust situation) where the director could not plead the
Limitation Act in response to a claim against him as he was regarded as being
the subject of an action to recover trust property or the proceeds of trust
property previously received by the trustee and converted to his use.[153] In that
case X was the director of a family property company. X had purchased
property from the company and failed to disclose information relating to its
value, which he uncovered while acting as a director. X had sold the property
for much more than he paid the company, and the company brought the action
to recover the proceeds flowing from the sale of the land.

4.66 A different time period might apply if the terms of s 32 of the Limitation
Act apply. Claimants might look to s 32 where their claim is barred by the
six-year rule in s 21 and elsewhere in the Act. Section 32(1)(b) provides that if
a fact that is relevant to the cause of action of a claimant has been deliberately
concealed from the claimant by the defendant then the time period (six years)
does not begin to run until the point when the claimant discovers the
concealment. Section 32(2) expands the meaning of s 32(1)(b) by providing that
the deliberate commission of a breach of duty in circumstances in which it is
unlikely to be discovered for some time amounts to deliberate concealment of
the facts involved in that breach of duty. In *Cave v Robinson Jarvis & Rolf*[154]
the House of Lords said that for the purposes of s 32 a deliberate breach of

---

[149] [2014] UKSC 10; [2014] AC 1189.
[150] *Re Pantone 485 Ltd* [2002] 1 BCLC 266 at [43], [44]. This was accepted as a correct
construction of s 21(1)(b) by the Court of Appeal in *Burnden Holdings (UK) Ltd v Fielding*
[2016] EWCA Civ 557 at [37].
[151] [2003] EWCA Civ 1048; [2004] 1 BCLC 131 at [119].
[152] [2002] 1 BCLC 162 (CA).
[153] Ibid at [40].
[154] [2002] UKHL 18.

duty requires the defendant to have known that he or she was committing a breach of duty. According to *Sheldon v RHM Outhwaite (Underwriting Agencies) Ltd*[155] the concealment does not have to have occurred at the same time as the wrong complained of; it can occur after the accrual of the cause of action. In the Court of Appeal in *Williams v Fanshaw Porter & Hazlehurst*[156] Park J mentioned four points about the paragraph in the legislation. These are:[157]

'(1) It does not say that the right of action must have been concealed from the claimant as the provision is only talking about a fact relevant to the cause of action;

(2) It does not require the defendant to have known that the fact was relevant to the right of action;

(3) It requires only that *any* fact, and not all facts, relevant to the right of action is concealed;

(4) For it to be said that a fact has been deliberately concealed the defendant must have considered whether to inform the claimant of the fact and decided not to, and the fact which the defendant decides not to disclose 'either must be one which it was his duty to disclose, or must at least be one which he would ordinarily have disclosed in the normal course of his relationship with the claimant, but in the case of which he consciously decided to depart from what he would normally have done and to keep quiet about it.'

4.67 Similarly, Mance LJ in the same case said that s 32(1)(b) applied where a defendant deliberately concealed facts knowing that they were relevant to an actual or potential breach of duty.[158] Later his Lordship said that where there was a duty to say something then intentionally suppressing information which it is known should be communicated was part of that duty, it can readily be regarded as concealment of the information.[159] Section 32(2) applies where the concealment was deliberate.[160] *Haysport Properties Ltd v Ackerman*[161] is a recent instance of a case where the judge permitted the claimants to rely on s 32 where a director had not disclosed his breaches of duty to the company.

4.68 In determining when time starts running against a claimant it is necessary to ascertain the persons who, on behalf of the company, might discover the director's wrongdoing. According to the Court of Appeal in *Burnden Holdings (UK) Ltd v Fielding*[162] it cannot be the wrongdoers themselves. It could be any director who was not alleged to be a wrongdoer.[163]

---

[155] [1996] AC 102. For a recent application, see *IT Human Resources plc v Land* [2014] EWHC 3812 (Ch) at [134].

[156] [2004] EWCA Civ 157; [2004] 1 WLR 3185.

[157] Ibid at [14].

[158] Ibid at [34].

[159] Ibid at [36].

[160] *IT Human Resources plc v Land* [2014] EWHC 3812 (Ch) at [135]; *Gresport Finance Ltd v Battaglia* [2016] EWHC 964 (Ch) at [134].

[161] [2016] EWHC 393 (Ch) at [116].

[162] [2016] EWCA Civ 557 at [49].

[163] Ibid.

4.69 Section 32 might be of particular importance to liquidators who seek to institute proceedings against directors for breach, for directors might well seek to conceal the breach, and, as stated earlier, liquidators might have some difficulty uncovering the truth concerning the affairs of the company. In companies where all of the directors are alleged to be wrongdoers the time would not start running, one would think, until the liquidator is appointed.

4.70 We have been focusing on breaches of directors' duties here; with other personal claims against directors that are based on other causes of action the limitation period will be covered by other provisions of the Limitation Act 1980 and will not be discussed here.

4.71 In sum, the starting point in any case, according to the Court of Appeal in *Gwembe Valley Development Co Ltd v Koshy*[164] is that a six-year limitation period will apply unless it is specifically excluded by the Limitation Act or established case-law. Claims for breach of fiduciary duty will normally be covered by s 21 of the Limitation Act 1980, and in certain circumstances no time limit will apply at all, or if it does (under s 32) it will not necessarily be at the time of the impugned action that led to a breach. It could be somewhat later.

IX SUMMARY

4.72 Chapter 2 of Part 10 of the CA 2006 provides a codification of the general duties of the directors, so long covered only by the common law and equity. In this regard the UK is a latecomer as many Commonwealth jurisdictions enacted codified duties well before the UK. Section 170, the provision that explains how Chapter 2 of Part 10 is to operate, provides that duties are owed to the company by directors. Later it goes on, in s 170(3), to state that the duties are based on certain common law rules and equitable principles, but indicates that the codified duties have application in lieu of the said rules and principles. Notwithstanding this, the rules and principles, developed over years of decision-making by the courts, are highly relevant for the codified duties are to be interpreted and applied in the same way as the common law rules and equitable principles, and regard is to be had to the corresponding rules and principles in the process of interpreting and applying the general duties. Much of the following discussion of the duties is informed by the common law rules and equitable principles that have been developed over many years.

---

[164] [2003] EWCA Civ 1048; [2004] 1 BCLC 131 at [111].

CHAPTER 5

DUTY TO ACT WITHIN POWERS

I INTRODUCTION

5.1   Section 171 of the CA 2006 sets out two duties that are encompassed by the broad title to the Chapter, a title based on the section's heading in the Act. The first duty is that directors must act in accordance with the company's constitution. Second, they must only exercise their powers for the purposes for which they were conferred. We will deal with these separately, with the major emphasis of the Chapter being on the second part of the section. It is to be noted that the two requirements mentioned in s 171 are mentioned together, probably because they both relate to the company's constitution. The way that the first relates to the constitution is obvious. The second is less obvious. It would seem to be related in the sense that the primary place where the powers of the directors will be set out is the constitution. Also, the High Court in *Hogg v Cramphorn*[1] and the Privy Council in *Howard Smith Ltd v Ampol Petroleum Ltd*[2] both said that if the directors were to use their powers for improper purposes, this would be an interference with the company's constitution. One commentator has even argued that, inter alia, a close analysis of the authorities that are generally referred to and discussed in relation to the proper purposes duty indicates that while they were purportedly decided on the basis of not using powers for a proper purpose, the courts' primary reason for impugning the use of the relevant powers was that the implied terms of the company's constitution were breached.[3]

5.2   Clearly s 171 is an important provision as the Company Law Review Steering Group said that compliance with the duties contained in the section is overriding.[4] The Steering Group went on to say that it is only if compliance with s 171 occurs are directors bound to promote the success of the company[5] as required by s 172 (discussed in Chapter 6).The first part of the Chapter deals with the requirement that directors must act in accordance with the company's constitution. This is followed by the second duty mentioned above, and a consideration of this duty occupies most of the Chapter.

---

[1]   [1967] Ch 254 at 268.
[2]   [1974] AC 821 at 837.
[3]   E Lim 'Directors' Duties: Improper Purposes or Implied Terms' (2014) 34 *Legal Studies* 395.
[4]   Company Law Review *Modern Company Law for a Competitive Economy: Completing the Structure* (London, DTI, 2000) at para 3.15.
[5]   Ibid.

II THE DUTY TO ACT IN ACCORDANCE WITH THE COMPANY'S CONSTITUTION

5.3   The company's constitution, which was not defined in the Companies Act 1985, means, according to s 17 of the CA 2006, the company's articles and the resolutions and agreements to which Chapter 3 of Part 3 of CA 2006 applies,[6] unless the context otherwise requires. The constitution is actually defined for the purpose of the general duties in s 257, and this section applies to Part 10 of the CA 2006. It includes, in addition to the company's articles of association, decisions taken in accordance with the company's constitution and other decisions of the members, or a class of them, if they are to be treated by virtue of any enactment or rule of law as equivalent to decisions of the company. The Explanatory Notes to the CA 2006 give the example of 'other decision of the members' as a decision taken by informal unanimous consent of all the members.[7]

5.4   There was no significant emphasis on this issue at common law. Professor Brenda Hannigan asserted in the first edition of her text on company law that while it is difficult to find express authority for a duty to act in accordance with the constitution, it is implicit in the obligation that directors are to exercise their powers for a proper purpose,[8] and, certainly, this duty has been asserted with little debate as to its existence.[9] Professors Paul Davies and Sarah Worthington submit that the duty was recognised through several cases during the early years of what we might refer to as modern company law.[10] The duty to act in accordance with the constitution probably can be seen as related to the duty to act for proper purposes (why else would it be contained in the same section?), for it is in the constitution where we will find most of the powers that directors will exercise and it is these powers that have to be used for carrying out the proper purpose. But it can be seen as a separate aspect of the duty to exercise powers properly. Brenda Hannigan suggests that what is now Chapter 2 of Part 10 provides a hierarchy of duties and, as s 171 of the CA 2006 is first, the duty to act in accordance with the constitution is pre-eminent.[11] But the section is drafted differently from the clause in the White Paper to which Hannigan was referring in her 2003 text, so that point may no longer carry the weight that it might have originally. In the Explanatory Notes to the Corporate Law Reform Bill 2005 it was stated that 'this duty [s 171(a)] codifies the director's duty to comply with the company's constitution', lending support for the assertion that a duty pre-existed the CA 2006. In *Clark v Cutland*,[12] Arden LJ said that directors had a duty to follow the appropriate procedures in the company's constitution. Section 35(3) of the Companies Act 1985 did provide that the directors had a duty to observe limits on their

---

6   This will be those referred to in s 29 of the Companies Act 2006.
7   Paragraph 324.
8   B Hannigan *Company Law* (London, LexisNexis Butterworths, 2003) at 218.
9   Ibid at 241.
10   P Davies and S Worthington *Gower and Davies' Principles of Company Law* (London, Sweet and Maxwell, 10th edn, 2016) at 487.
11   B Hannigan *Company Law* (London, LexisNexis Butterworths, 2003) at 218.
12   [2003] EWCA Civ 810; [2003] 2 BCLC 393 at [21].

powers under the company's memorandum. This provision was part of the legislation's attempt to abolish the ultra vires rule. The replacement for s 35, s 40 of the CA 2006, does not include a similar provision, but s 171 fills the void and effectively provides for the same duty. It is to be noted that s 40(5) states that an action might still exist against directors for exceeding their powers. This is often going to be the only action that the company can take if a contract is entered into by a director in excess of his or her powers and the third party has acted in good faith.[13]

5.5   It follows from the enactment of s 171(a) of the CA 2006 that companies can, through their articles, place more onerous demands on directors, than those provided under the statutory duties. Of course, that might mean that companies will find it more difficult to hire and retain the people that they want. Conversely, the company is not able to dilute the duties by using the articles to do so except to the extent that this is permitted by the following sections:[14]

- s 173 states that directors are not in breach of the duty to exercise independent judgment if they have acted in a way that is authorised by the constitution;
- s 175 permits authorisation of some conflicts of interest, subject to the constitution;
- s 180 preserves any rule of law enabling the company to give authority for anything that would otherwise be a breach of duty;
- s 180 also states that directors are not in breach of duty if they act in accordance with any provisions in the company's articles for dealing with conflicts of interest;
- s 232 places restrictions on the provisions that may be included in the company's articles. But nothing in that section prevents companies from including in their articles any such provisions that were previously lawful for dealing with conflicts of interest.

5.6   The Explanatory Notes to the CA 2006 point out that the company's constitution may include the goals of the company, especially in the case of an altruistic company which has goals other than the benefit of the company's members, and it is critical that directors understand the goals of the company, so that they are able to comply with their duty to promote the success of the company in s 172.[15] It would seem that meeting the specific goals of the company will go some way to determining whether directors have fulfilled their duty to promote the success of the company.

5.7   Davies suggested, prior to the advent of s 171, directors might be able to escape liability if the provisions of the constitution that it appears they have

---

[13]   See s 40(1) of CA 2006.
[14]   Explanatory Notes at para 316.
[15]   Explanatory Notes at para 317.

contravened were not clearly expressed.[16] The courts might, in such a situation, employ s 1157 of the CA 2006 to excuse liability.[17] Whether this is the case now that s 171 is in effect, is somewhat debatable, for if the directors breach this duty unwittingly or what they do is in the best interests of the company, but outside of the constitution, they remain liable.[18] This is in line with s 177(5) when directors are treated as being aware of matters of which they ought reasonably to be aware when it comes to making disclosures of interests. Certainly there is authority that provides that provisions in the constitution that confer power on directors should be viewed as widely as possible and that courts should not readily find that the constitution provides procedural restrictions on the exercise of powers.[19]

5.8   If directors do act in breach of s 171(a), then it would seem that the board could ratify what has been done. As Lord Hodge explained in *Eastford v Gillespie*,[20] it is well established at common law that, except where a company's constitution provides to the contrary, a board of directors can, within a reasonable time, ratify the acts of a director or directors who had no authority to bind the company when they took action that is impugned.[21] His Lordship went on to say that:[22]

> 'it is clear on examining the statutory statement of the general duties of directors that that statement does not prevent a company by a resolution of its board from ratifying the acts of a director which were unauthorised but were within the power of the board. One must look to the purpose of the statutory statement which is revealed in the 2006 Act. ... Parliament has directed the courts not only to treat the general duties in the same way as the pre-existing rules and principles but also to have regard to the continued development of the non-statutory law in relation to the duties of other fiduciaries when interpreting and applying the statutory statements. The interpretation of the statements will therefore be able to evolve. The statutory statement of the general duties of directors is intended to make those duties more accessible to commercial people. I see nothing in the statutory provisions, including section 180(5) (which provides that, subject to specified exceptions, the general duties have effect notwithstanding any rule of law), which suggests that Parliament intended to alter the pre-existing rules on ratification by a board of a director's unauthorised acts.'

5.9   Interestingly, while the New Zealand legislature has included this duty in its codified duties,[23] the Australian legislature has not. However, it has been argued in Australia that acting in accordance with the constitution is a duty of

---

[16]   P Davies *Gower and Davies' Principles of Company Law* (London, Sweet and Maxwell, 7th edn, 2003) at 383.

[17]   This provision is considered in detail in **Chapter 17**.

[18]   *J J Harrison v Harrison* [2002] 1 BCLC 162 (CA).

[19]   *Dome Resources NL v Silver* [2008] NSWCA 322.

[20]   [2009] CSOH 119 and referring to *Re Portuguese Consolidated Copper Mines Ltd* (1890) 45 Ch D 16; *Breckland Group Holdings Ltd v London & Suffolk Properties Ltd* (1988) 4 BCC 542; [1989] BCLC 100; *Municipal Mutual Insurance Ltd v Harrop* [1998] 2 BCLC 540.

[21]   [2009] CSOH 119 at [7].

[22]   Ibid at [8]–[9].

[23]   Companies Act 1993, s 134.

the directors, and it is an aspect of the duty to act in good faith in the interests of the company (which is a codified duty – see s 181(1) of the Corporations Act 2001) on the basis that the constitution is able to define and set parameters concerning the company's interests.[24]

III THE DUTY TO EXERCISE POWERS FOR THE PURPOSES FOR WHICH THEY WERE CONFERRED

A Introduction

5.10 While the first part of s 171 of the CA 2006 has not received much attention, the second aspect to the duty has, in the form of some academic commentary and a not insignificant amount of case-law, received substantial consideration, even though it has been suggested that the duty, in its non-codified form, was the least well discussed and understood of all the fiduciary duties to which a director is subject.[25] I should say that at this point that there has been some debate as to whether this duty is a fiduciary duty,[26] but high authority appears to come down firmly on the side of it being one.[27] But, it is not common that the decision concerning an issue that concerns breaches of directors' duties can be traced back to whether a duty is classified as fiduciary or not.[28]

5.11 It has been said that as a general rule all powers vested in directors under the company's articles are fiduciary powers to be exercised in the interests of the company.[29] The case-law provides that directors should use the powers granted to them for proper purposes and not for ulterior purposes,[30] and if the directors use powers for purposes other than for which they were given, then this is an abuse of powers.[31] The fact that this has been regarded as an abuse of powers led Professor Len Sealy, over 25 years ago, to query whether we should be talking about a duty in this context. He felt that we were simply dealing with

---

[24] R P Austin, H A J Ford and I M Ramsay *Company Directors* (Sydney, LexisNexis Butterworths, 2005) at 288.

[25] R C Nolan 'The Proper Purpose Doctrine and Company Directors' in B A K Rider (ed) *The Realm of Company Law* (London, Kluwer, 1998) at 1.

[26] Some commentators argue that to describe the duty of loyalty as a fiduciary obligation is a mistake: R Flannigan 'Fiduciary Duties of Shareholders and Directors' [2004] JBL 277 at 281; M Conaglen 'The Nature and Function of Fiduciary Loyalty' (2005) 121 LQR 452; E Waitzer and J Jaswal 'Peoples, BCE, and the Good Corporate "Citizen"' (2009) 47 *Osgoode Hall Law Journal* 439 at 444; M Conaglen 'Interaction Between Statutory and General Law Duties Concerning Company Director Conflicts' (2013) 31 *Company and Securities Law Journal* 403.

[27] For instance, see *Howard Smith Ltd v Ampol Petroleum Ltd* [1974] AC 821; *Eclairs Group Ltd v JKX Oil & Gas Plc* [2015] UKSC 71; [2016] BCC 79; [2016] 1 BCLC 1.

[28] A Stafford and S Ritchie *Fiduciary Duties: Directors and Employees* (Bristol, Jordan Publishing, 2nd edn, 2015) at 29.

[29] *Westpac Banking Corp v Bell Group Ltd (No 3)* [2012] WASCA 157; (2012) 89 ACSR 1 at [1949].

[30] *Re Smith & Fawcett Ltd* [1942] Ch 304 at 306; *Ngurli v McCann* (1953) 90 CLR 425 at 428 (Aust HC).

[31] *Re Cameron's Coalbrook Steam Coal* (1854) 3 De G M & G 284 at 298.

grounds upon which corporate decisions are made.[32] But, s 171(b) makes it clear that the obligation to use powers for the purpose they are conferred is now a duty, if it were not one before. After saying that, one might question whether it makes a whole lot of difference to the way that the law will administer the obligation. The duty encompasses the rule that fiduciary powers of directors may be exercised only for the purposes for which they were conferred. It is fundamental to the constitutional distinction between the respective bailiwicks of the board and the shareholders.[33] The rule has its foundations in the equitable doctrine which has been referred to as the doctrine of 'fraud on a power', even though it really relates to abuse of a power and not fraud.[34]

5.12 Section 171(b) of the CA 2006 does not clarify features of the duty. It does not explain how the proper purposes of the company are ascertained or the degree to which a decision based on an improper purpose stigmatises that decision. But the cases that have dealt with the provision, such as *Re West Coast Capital (LIOS) Ltd*[35] and *Eclairs Group Ltd v JKX Oil and Gas plc*,[36] have stated that the provision sets out the pre-existing law on the subject.

5.13 The duty owes its genesis to Chancery judges applying strict norms of conduct. And equity prevents the donee of a power from exercising that power either beyond the scope of the instrument creating the power, or in such a manner that the exercise is not justified by the instrument.[37] In using a power improperly directors were committing a fraud on the power.[38] The doctrine of proper purposes applies in other areas and notably in relation to public authorities under administrative law.[39] The proper purposes doctrine does not prescribe any responsibilities as far as directors are concerned, but imposes a criterion by which the actions of directors can be reviewed, and, where appropriate, made invalid.[40] The proper purpose doctrine effectively involves a way of providing for judicial control of the exercise of a discretionary power.[41]

5.14 The considerations relevant to both the requirement to use powers for proper purposes and the duty to act bona fide in the best interests of the

---

[32]   L S Sealy '"Bona Fides" and "Proper Purposes" in Corporate Decisions' (1989) 15 Mon U L R 265 at 268.

[33]   *Eclairs Group Ltd v JKX Oil and Gas plc* [2015] UKSC 71; [2016] 1 BCLC 1; [2016] BCC 79.

[34]   Ibid at [15].

[35]   [2008] CSOH 72; 2008 Scot (D) 16/5 (Outer House, Court of Sessions, Lord Glennie) at [21].

[36]   [2015] UKSC 71; [2016] 1 BCLC 1; [2016] BCC 79 at [14].

[37]   S Fridman 'An Analysis of the Proper Purpose Rule' (1998) 10 *Bond Law Review* 164.

[38]   *Mills v Mills* (1938) 60 CLR 150. See R Grantham 'The Powers of Company Directors and the Proper Purpose Doctrine' (1994–95) 5 Kings College LJ 16.

[39]   R P Austin, H A J Ford and I M Ramsay *Company Directors* (Sydney, LexisNexis Butterworths, 2005) at 288. Although as Austin et al note the doctrine in administrative law appears to be derived from the common law while in relation to directors it has equitable origins.

[40]   R C Nolan 'The Proper Purpose Doctrine and Company Directors' in B A K Rider (ed) *The Realm of Company Law* (London, Kluwer, 1998) at 15.

[41]   S Fridman 'An Analysis of the Proper Purpose Rule' (1998) 10 *Bond Law Review* 164.

company can be difficult to separate,[42] and arguably they have historically been a combined duty,[43] although, in more recent times, many have seen them as separate duties.[44] This is even the case in Australia where the two are found in the same section of the Corporations Act 2001 (s 181). But where the duty to use powers for proper purposes has been regarded as separate it has often been recognised as overlapping with the duty to act bona fide in the best interests of the company.[45] This is expected as there is a close connection between the two duties.[46] Nevertheless, there is recent authority that has said that the duties are separate and one must not conflate the two duties into one.[47] This certainly seems to have been implied by Mann J at first instance in *Eclairs Group Ltd v Glengary Overseas Ltd*.[48] The fact that they are separate duties is indicated by the fact that the duty to act for proper purposes and the duty to promote the success of the company (the successor to the duty to act bona fide in the best interests of the company) are housed in separate sections.[49] In *Eclairs Group Ltd v Glengary Overseas Ltd*[50] Mann J said that the duty in s 172 does not trump the provisions of s 171. His Lordship has said that considering whether a director has used powers for proper purposes has to be undertaken

---

[42] For example, see *Re Smith & Fawcett Ltd* [1942] Ch 304; [1942] 1 All ER 542; *Harlowe's Nominees Pty Ltd v Woodside (Lakes Entrance) Oil Co* [1968] HCA 37; (1968) 121 CLR 483.

[43] For example, see L C B Gower *Principles of Modern Company Law* (London, Stevens, 1954); L S Sealy 'Company – Directors' Powers – Proper Motive but Improper Purpose' [1967] CLJ 33 at 35; R Parsons 'The Director's Duty of Good Faith' (1967) 5 MULR 395 at 422; B Cheffins *Company Law: Theory, Structure and Operation* (OUP, 1997) at 313; S Fridman 'An Analysis of the Proper Purpose Rule' (1998) 10 *Bond Law Review* 164. Also, see *Re Smith & Fawcett Ltd* [1942] Ch 304; [1942] 1 All ER 542 and *Harlowe's Nominees Pty Ltd v Woodside (Lakes Entrance) Oil Co* [1968] HCA 37; (1968) 121 CLR 483. In the latter case it was claimed that the directors' decision to make an allotment of shares was wrongful in that the directors exercised fiduciary powers otherwise than bona fide in the interests of that company as a whole.

[44] For example, see A Dignam and J Lowry *Company Law* (OUP, 4th edn, 2006) at 301; J Birds et al *Boyle and Birds' Company Law* (Bristol, Jordan Publishing, 5th edn, 2003) at 144; B Hannigan *Company Law* (London, LexisNexis Butterworths, 2003) at 226; R C Nolan 'The Proper Purpose Doctrine and Company Directors' in B A K Rider (ed) *The Realm of Company Law* (London, Kluwer, 1998) at 1; E Klein and J du Plessis 'Corporate Donations, The Best Interest of the Company and the Proper Purpose Doctrine' (2005) 28 UNSWLJ 69 at 80.

[45] B Hannigan *Company Law* (London, LexisNexis Butterworths, 2003) at 226.

[46] *Bell Group Ltd (in liq) v Westpac Banking Corporation [No 9]* [2008] WASC 239; (2008) ACSR 1 at [4456]. In this case the judge, Owen J of the Supreme Court of Western Australia, was talking about the duty to use powers for proper purposes and the duty to act in the best interests of the company, but the latter is clearly the precursor to the duty in s 172 and, in general terms, can be seen in the same light.

[47] *Westpac Banking Corp v Bell Group Ltd (No 3)* [2012] WASCA 157; (2012) 89 ACSR 1 at [2002]. But note the fact that in *Colin Gwyer v London Wharf (Limehouse) Ltd* [2002] EWHC 2748 (Ch); [2003] 2 BCLC 153 at [83], Leslie Kosmin QC (sitting as a deputy High Court judge) did appear to refer to them as one, although the judge did not refer to the fact that he saw them as forming one duty.

[48] [2013] EWHC 2631 (Ch).

[49] In Australia the equivalent duties are contained in the one section (Corporations Act 2001, s 181), but given the judgment of the majority in *Westpac Banking Corp v Bell Group Ltd (No 3)* [2012] WASCA 157; (2012) 89 ACSR 1 at [2002] the duties are regarded as separate. It might be notable that the duties are in separate paragraphs within the section.

[50] [2013] EWHC 2631 (Ch).

before examining whether s 172 has been complied with.[51] This all means that it can be said that the former duty has greater prominence now, given that the legislation expressly makes it a duty in its own right, rather than subsuming it under another duty.

5.15 In determining whether directors have exercised a power for the purpose for which it was conferred, the provision in the articles or in another document that makes up the constitution that confers the power will have to be analysed and its function ascertained to determine its purpose(s).[52] The constitution might clearly set out the purpose or it might easily be identified from the analysis undertaken. In other cases more examination will be required. In the situation where the constitution does not provide an indication as to the purpose of a power the courts will need to make inferences founded on such things like the type, size and activities of the company.[53] The case-law tends to draw a distinction between powers the exercise of which is part of general management of a company in relation to which the courts traditionally take a broad view, and those powers which are non-managerial in nature.[54]

5.16 The courts have to adopt an objective approach in determining the purposes for which the power was conferred, which is a question of law as it depends on a construction of the company's constitution. Once this is established it is then necessary to determine whether the directors' purpose was in line with the purposes for which the power was conferred. This latter consideration is a subjective one. The problem for courts is that there might be nothing in the constitution that assists them in construing the purpose for which the power was granted and so, as a default position, courts have tended to interpret the purpose subject to the general limitation of the powers being exercised so as to benefit the company's interests.[55]

5.17 The constitution might authorise the use of a power in such a way that would otherwise constitute an improper purpose. An example is found in the decision of the Australian High Court in *Whitehouse v Carlton Hotel Pty Ltd*,[56] where the court accepted the fact that the articles of a private company might be so formulated that they conferred on a governing director the right to exercise a power to allot shares so as to diminish the voting power of other shareholders.

5.18 In order to establish that directors have breached the proper purposes duty it has not been necessary to prove dishonesty.[57] Historically, directors have tended to use powers other than for proper purposes either to enable them to

---

[51] Ibid at [210].
[52] For instance, see the judgment of Dixon J in *Mills v Mills* (1938) 60 CLR 150 (Aust HC).
[53] R P Austin, H A J Ford and I M Ramsay *Company Directors* (Sydney, LexisNexis Butterworths, 2005) at 294.
[54] *Mills v Mills* (1938) 60 CLR 150 at 185–186; *Howard Smith Ltd v Ampol Ltd* [1974] AC 821.
[55] S Fridman 'An Analysis of the Proper Purpose Rule' (1998) 10 *Bond Law Review* 164.
[56] [1987] HCA 11; (1987) 162 CLR 285 at 292.
[57] *Extrasure Travel Insurances Ltd v Scattergood* [2003] 1 BCLC 598 at [92].

retain control of the company or to benefit themselves in some way. Such conduct would constitute a breach of the duty to act bona fide in the best interests of the company at common law (and a likely breach of s 172 of the CA 2006 under the codified law), but on occasions directors have used powers improperly, but in doing so they have acted, in good faith, and believed that what they were doing was in the best interests of the company. It is in the latter set of circumstances where problems have arisen. Essentially the English cases have provided that it is not sufficient that the directors believed that the action was in the best interests of the company, for the exercise of power must have been for one of the purposes for which the power is permitted to be exercised under the company's constitution.[58] The same conclusion can be reached where directors have acted altruistically.[59]

5.19 As we have noted already, ascertaining the purpose of a power and its scope is achieved by consulting and interpreting the articles (and, possibly, resolutions) and determining the intention disclosed by the articles. In the typical set of articles there is either a grant of general managerial power or a grant of power, without express limitation, to the board.[60] Regulation 70 of the Table A articles for both public and private companies provides that directors 'may exercise all of the powers of the company'.[61] This is repeated in the model articles that now apply to companies registered under CA 2006, and may apply to companies that were registered under preceding legislation.[62] An example of an article which grants the power to issue shares without limitation was found in articles of the company in the case of *Hogg v Cramphorn*,[63] and it stated that 'the shares shall be under the control of the directors, who may allot or otherwise dispose of the same to such persons, on such terms and conditions, and at such times as the directors think fit'.

5.20 Section 171(b) of the CA 2006 merely states that directors have a duty to exercise powers only for the purposes for which they were conferred. The legislation does not specify what are to be regarded as the proper purposes of a director's powers. This will obviously be a matter left to the courts to decide as they develop the jurisprudence. As one might expect, the provision does not pick up on those aspects of the duty that have developed from the decisions of the courts. As a result there is little doubt that the courts will have recourse to existing case-law to interpret the provision. Undoubtedly, this is one of a number of areas where the existing case-law will be critical for it is probable that it will be applied with little, or no adaptation. Hence, we will now analyse the common law on the subject, but bearing in mind the advent of s 171(b).

---

[58] *Howard Smith Ltd v Ampol Ltd* [1974] AC 821 at 834. The Australian High Court in *Whitehouse v Carlton Hotel Pty Ltd* [1987] HCA 11; (1987) 162 CLR 285, expressed the same view (at [10] of the joint judgment of Mason, Deane and Dawson JJ; 294).

[59] *Permanent Building Society v Wheeler* (1994) 14 ACSR 109 at 137.

[60] S Fridman 'An Analysis of the Proper Purpose Rule' (1998) 10 *Bond Law Review* 164. See the comments in *Mills v Mills* (1938) 60 CLR 150 (Aust HC).

[61] Companies (Tables A-F) Regulations as amended by SI 2007/2541 and SI 2007/2826.

[62] The Companies (Model Articles) Regulations 2008, SI 2008/3229, reg 2, Sch 1, art 5 (private companies); reg 4, Sch 3, art 5 (public companies).

[63] [1967] Ch 254 at 268.

One problem is that there are clear differences in the decided cases, and this has caused confusion. Arguably this had been caused by the courts use of value judgment, which produces flexibility, but at the price of certainty.[64]

5.21 It is important to acknowledge that the effect of an exercise of power is not the critical issue, rather, it is the purpose of the directors in exercising the power. As one might expect the burden is on the person who alleges that the power has been used improperly by the directors,[65] but if a claimant can establish a prima facie improper use of power, it is for the director to show the propriety of his or her actions.[66] The person who wishes to impugn the use of the power might wish to consider obtaining an interim injunction if one of the following situations exists: the complainant is aware of the impending exercise of the power;[67] the use of the power is intended to be continuous; it is clear that the directors intend to employ it again.

5.22 As an improper use of power can be categorised as an abuse of power, it would enable a shareholder to bring proceedings for a breach of s 994 of the CA 2006, namely the unfair prejudice provision, provided that the shareholder can establish the elements of a successful action.[68] This would obviate the need for a disgruntled shareholder having to obtain permission from the courts under s 261 in order to continue derivative proceedings if he or she believed the directors had breached their duty. *Re West Coast Capital (LIOS) Ltd*[69] is a Scottish case where a petitioner under s 994 relied, inter alia, on a breach of s 171 to substantiate his claim for relief.[70]

B Complications

5.23 The enforcement of this duty can be subject to a number of complications and this might well be the reason for the fact that the case-law is not consistent. The first complication is with the meaning of 'purpose.' It has been defined as 'the reason for which something is done.'[71] But, as Sealy points out, in dealing with people we are more likely to be concerned with the goal or object which

---

[64] See S Fridman 'An Analysis of the Proper Purpose Rule' (1998) 10 *Bond Law Review* 164; J Farrar 'Abuse of Power by Directors' [1974] CLJ 221 at 223.

[65] *Mills v Mills* [1938] HCA 4; (1938) 60 CLR 150 (Aust HC); *Harlowe's Nominees Pty Ltd v Woodside (Lakes Entrance) Oil Co* [1968] HCA 37; (1968) 121 CLR 423 (Aust HC); *Ascot Investments Pty Ltd v Harper* (1981) 148 CLR 337 at 348 (Aust HC); *Lyford v Commonwealth Bank of Australia* (1995) 17 ACSR 211 (Aust Fed Ct).

[66] *Bishopsgate Investment Management Ltd v Maxwell* [1994] 1 All ER 261 at 265 per Hoffmann LJ.

[67] As occurred in *Pennell, Sutton and Moraybell Securities Ltd v Venida Investments Ltd* (July 1974, Chancery Div, Templeman J) (unreported, but discussed in detail in S Burridge 'Wrongful Rights Issues' (1981) 44 MLR 40).

[68] *CAS (Nominees) Ltd v Nottingham Forest FC plc* [2002] 1 BCLC 613; [2002] BCC 145.

[69] [2008] CSOH 72; 2008 Scot (D) 16/5 (Outer House, Court of Sessions, Lord Glennie).

[70] The judgment delivered involved an application by the petitioner for an interim interdict, and it was unsuccessful.

[71] J Pearsall (ed) *The New Oxford Dictionary of English* (OUP, 2001) at 1506.

they have in view.[72] In this context, it is so easy to focus on motive of directors and that might be different from purpose.

5.24   Second, a court has to ascertain the proper purpose behind the exercise of a power, usually found in the articles. The problem is how does one do this where the instrument creating the power is silent? According to the Supreme Court in *Eclairs Group Ltd v JKX Oil and Gas plc*[73] in such circumstances one determines the purpose of the power by inferring from the provision conferring the power what mischief it is seeking to address, and this itself is deduced from: the express terms of the provision; an analysis of the effect of the terms; the court's understanding of the business context.[74] In this case Lord Sumption accepted that the purpose of a power set out in the articles is rarely expressed, but it is usually obvious, from the context and the effect of the employment of the power, what is the reason for the bestowal of the power.[75] Third, the court needs to establish the directors' purpose in exercising the power. At the outset we need to note that it is never easy ascertaining what a person's purpose is. The comments of Bowen LJ in *ex p Hill*[76] are apposite. His Lordship said, rather colourfully:

> 'If we are to consider whether amongst all of the shadows which pass across a man's mind, some view as well as the dominant view influenced him to do the act, we shall be embarking on a dark and unknown voyage across an exceedingly misty sea.'

5.25   Things are made more difficult because usually with most exercise of powers there is a decision by the board or at least a group of directors, rather than the decision of one person. Determining the purpose of a group is, of course, harder than determining that of an individual, for in some cases one is likely to be faced with a multitude of purposes.[77] Naturally, in making a decision to exercise a power there might be dissenters on the board. If that is the case then the courts will consider the purposes of the majority that agreed to the exercise.[78] However, it is quite possible to have a situation where each director constituting the majority of the board in favour of the power being exercised had a different reason.[79] In *Re Southern Resources Ltd*[80] Perry J of the Supreme Court of South Australia took the view that each director's perspective on the use of the power must be considered separately. The decision

---

[72]   L S Sealy '"Bona Fides" and "Proper Purposes" in Corporate Decisions' (1989) 15 Mon U L R 265 at 274.

[73]   [2015] UKSC 71; [2016] 1 BCLC 1; [2016] BCC 79 at [30].

[74]   Ibid.

[75]   Ibid at [31].

[76]   (1883) 23 Ch D 695.

[77]   See *Darvall v North Sydney Brick & Tile Co Ltd* (1989) 7 ACLC 659 at 676 per Kirby P.

[78]   *Harlowe's Nominees Pty Ltd v Woodside (Lakes Entrance) Oil Co* [1968] HCA 37; (1968) 121 CLR 483; *Gwyer v London Wharf (Limehouse) Ltd* [2003] BCLC 153; [2002] EWHC 2748 at [92].

[79]   R P Austin, H A J Ford and I M Ramsay *Company Directors* (Sydney, LexisNexis Butterworths, 2005) at 300.

[80]   (1989) 15 ACLR 770.

in *Harlowe's Nominees Pty Ltd v Woodside (Lakes Entrance) Oil Co*[81] seems to suggest that where there might not be a consistent purpose amongst the majority, the job of the court is to discover the substantial purpose of the majority of the majority group even if that 'majority' constitutes a minority of the board overall.

5.26 The courts focus on the subjective purpose of the directors, but it has been held that the courts may take into account the circumstances that existed when the decision to exercise the power was made, so as to ascertain the state of mind of the directors.[82] This is illustrated in the decision at first instance in the case of *Howard Smith Ltd v Ampol Petroleum Ltd*.[83] Street J rejected the testimony of the directors who formed the majority of the board that decided to allot shares, the power that was under view in that case, that the purpose of the action they had taken was to raise capital. His Honour believed that the evidence given was a reconstruction.[84] The learned judge took this view because of the events that occurred before the board meeting at which the decision to issue was made, and these demonstrated that the directors were concerned about the strength of a company, Ampol, which held the majority shareholding and which was seeking to take over the company, and that the directors preferred that another company, Howard Smith, take over the company. Also, the judge took into account, inter alia: the urgency of both the board meeting and the subsequent issue of shares; the little information given at the board meeting concerning the financial needs of the company; and the fact that the board failed to consider the consequences of a share issue rather than a loan as a way of raising capital.[85] We shall return to the issue of a director's purpose later.

5.27 A third problem with the case-law is that it is impossible in many cases to arrive at an exhaustive statement of the legitimate purposes to which particular powers can be put.[86] Some purposes might be proper while others are not. Powers may be used for more than one legitimate purpose. In *Howard Smith Ltd v Ampol Petroleum Ltd*,[87] the Privy Council, on appeal from the New South Wales Supreme Court, made the point that it is impossible to define in advance the exact limits beyond which the directors of a company must not ordinarily go in exercising a fiduciary power to allot shares, because the variety of situations which directors encounter in different companies cannot be anticipated.[88] Lord Wilberforce said:[89]

---

[81]   [1968] HCA 37; (1968) 121 CLR 483.
[82]   *Hindle v John Craven Ltd* (1919) 56 SLR 625 at 630–631 and approved in *Howard Smith Ltd v Ampol Ltd* [1974] AC 821 at 835.
[83]   [1972] 2 NSWLR 850.
[84]   *Howard Smith Ltd v Ampol Ltd* [1974] AC 821 at 874.
[85]   Ibid.
[86]   P D Finn *Fiduciary Obligations* (Sydney, Law Book Company, 1977) at 40.
[87]   [1974] AC 821 at 837.
[88]   Ibid at 835. Also, see *Whitehouse v Carlton Hotel Pty Ltd* [1987] HCA 11; (1987) 162 CLR 285 at 289–290. It is noted that in *Howard Smith Ltd v Ampol Ltd* [1974] AC 821 the Privy Council rejected the contention that the power to allot shares could only be exercised in order for the company to raise new capital when it was necessary (at 835–836).

'The discretion is not in terms limited in this way: the law should not impose such a limitation on directors' powers. To define in advance exact limits beyond which directors must not pass is, in their Lordships' view, impossible. This clearly cannot be done by enumeration, since the variety of situations facing directors of different types of company in different situations cannot be anticipated.'

5.28 Legitimate purposes must be determined in light of the particular circumstances that are being considered. This approach has been sanctioned in the Explanatory Notes to the CA 2006 for they state that what constitutes a proper purpose must be ascertained in the context of the specific situation under consideration.[90]

5.29 Fourth, what is the case where directors have mixed purposes in taking action? As we will see, the leading cases adopt a substantial or dominant purpose approach which involves the courts having to determine: what is the substantial or dominant purpose of the directors in carrying out the action that is impugned? However, the cases demonstrate that ascertaining the purpose is not always easy.

C Background

5.30 The duty to exercise powers for proper purposes has operated in relation to directors' exercise of a variety of discretionary powers, such as the power: to forfeit shares;[91] to refuse to register share transfers;[92] to make calls;[93] to transfer assets;[94] to purchase property;[95] to enter into contracts generally;[96] and to allot shares.[97] But it is the last power mentioned, the power of allotment of shares that has caused particular problems, and tends to dominate the case-law. In fact most of the modern cases have related to a battle for the control of a company and this is certainly the situation as far as the cases with the greatest authority, such as the decision of the UK Supreme Court in *Eclairs Group Ltd v JKX Oil and Gas plc.*[98]

5.31 A good portion of the case-law has involved directors using the power to allot shares as part of a defensive strategy at a time when a party has been seeking to take over the company. Hence, it is worthwhile providing some background to this power and its use so that the case-law can be appreciated.

---

[89] Ibid.
[90] At para 323.
[91] For example, *Spackman v Evans* (1868) LR 3 HL 171 at 186.
[92] For example, *Re Smith & Fawcett Ltd* [1942] Ch 304; [1942] 1 All ER 542; *Charles Forte Investments Ltd v Amanda* [1964] Ch 240.
[93] For example, *Alexander v Automatic Telephone Co* [1890] 2 Ch 233; *Galloway v Halle Concert Society* [1915] 2 Ch 233.
[94] For example, *Bishopsgate Investment Management Ltd v Maxwell (No 2)* [1993] BCLC 1282 and affirmed on appeal at [1994] 1 All ER 261; [1993] BCLC 1282; *Pine Vale Investments Ltd v McDonnell & East Ltd* (1983) 1 ACLC 1294.
[95] For example, *Permanent Building Society v Wheeler* (1994) 14 ACSR 109.
[96] For example, see *Lee Panavision Ltd v Lee Lighting Ltd* [1991] BCC 620 (CA).
[97] For example, *Howard Smith Ltd v Ampol Ltd* [1974] AC 821.
[98] *Eclairs Group Ltd v JKX Oil and Gas plc* [2015] UKSC 71; [2016] 1 BCLC 1; [2016] BCC 79.

The allegation that is generally made is that the directors have used the power to allot wrongly – seeking to achieve improper purposes, such as entrenching their position in the company or thwarting a majority shareholder's attempt to gain control of the company.

5.32 The judicial roots of the state of the law on the issue of shares can be traced to *Punt v Symons & Co Ltd*[99] and *Piercy v S Mills & Co Ltd*[100] In the former case the directors issued shares with the purpose and object of enabling a minority to control the majority, and first and foremost to obtain the necessary statutory majority for passing a special resolution to permit the articles to be altered. In the latter case, followed on many occasions by other courts,[101] Peterson J invalidated an allotment of shares and said:[102]

> '[D]irectors are not entitled to use their powers of issuing shares merely for the purpose of maintaining their control or the control of themselves and their friends over the affairs of the company, or merely for the purpose of defeating the wishes of the existing majority of shareholders ... it was not ... open to the directors for the purpose of converting a minority into a majority, and solely for the purpose of defeating the wishes of the existing majority, to issue the shares which are in dispute in the present action.'

5.33 So if the directors acted in self-interest or in such a way as to preserve their control of the company, the exercise of the power would be improper.[103] An allotment of shares with the intention of ensuring that an existing majority is retained or a shareholder has its shareholding power diluted is improper.[104] It has been stated that it is simply no part of the function of the directors to prefer one shareholder or a group of shareholders by exercising a fiduciary power to allot shares for the purpose of diluting the voting power attaching to the issued shares held by some other shareholder or group of shareholders.[105] While an allotment of shares might lead to the dilution of the overall shareholding of a shareholder in a listed public company, it might not affect the value of the shareholding and cannot be attacked on that basis, but an allotment in a private company might render a shareholder's interest valueless, in which case the allotment would be improper.[106]

5.34 The power to allot shares is to be used generally to raise capital for the company and not to block the takeover of the company by someone acting legitimately. But, the power might be used legitimately for other purposes, such as providing employees with shares as part of a profit-sharing scheme, raising

---

[99]   [1903] 2 Ch 506.
[100] [1920] 1 Ch 77. In Canada a similar position was taken. For example, see *Madden v Dimond* (1905) BCR 80; *Smith v Hanson Tire & Supply Co Ltd* [1925] 3 DLR 786.
[101] For example, see *Mills v Mills* (1938) 60 CLR 150 (Aust HC); *Hogg v Cramphorn* [1967] Ch 254; *Lee Panavision Ltd v Lee Lighting Ltd* [1991] BCC 620 (CA).
[102] [1920] 1 Ch 77 at 84–85.
[103] *Punt v Symons & Co Ltd* [1903] 2 Ch 506; *Ngurli v McCann* [1953] HCA 39; (1953) 90 CLR 425; *Howard Smith Ltd v Ampol Ltd* [1974] AC 821.
[104] *Piercy v S Mills & Co Ltd* [1920] 1 Ch 77; *Howard Smith Ltd v Ampol Ltd* [1974] AC 821.
[105] *Kirwan v Cresvale Far East Ltd* [2002] NSWCA 395 at [125].
[106] *Kokotovich Constructions Pty Ltd v Wallington* (1995) 17 ACSR 478; (1995) 13 ACLC 1113.

capital so as to permit the company to carry on legal proceedings against the company's majority shareholder,[107] or to ensure the company has the requisite number of shareholders to enable it to be able to exercise its statutory functions.[108] The Judicial Committee of the Privy Council in *Howard Smith Ltd v Ampol Petroleum Ltd*[109] rejected an argument that because the allotment of shares in that case was not to raise capital it was improper on that basis alone, because, the Committee said that that would be too narrow an approach.[110] Much earlier in *Punt v Symons & Co Ltd*[111] the judge had said that while primarily given for the purpose of enabling the directors to raise capital when required for the purposes of the company, there may be times when the directors may quite properly issue shares for other reasons.[112] On the same theme, the Australian High Court said in *Harlowe's Nominees Pty Ltd v Woodside (Lakes Entrance) Oil Co*[113] that there may be occasions when the directors might fairly and properly issue shares for reasons other than to raise capital, provided those reasons relate to a purpose of benefiting the company as a whole, as distinguished from a purpose, for example, of maintaining control of the company in the hands of the directors themselves or their associates. This is rather a broad view that has not attracted similar views in other courts. However, the statement in the case that the power can be validly used to enhance links with other businesses, provided that the intention is to benefit the company as a whole,[114] might not be wide of the mark. Some purposes for the issue of shares are not proper and before there is a share issue that is based on such purposes there should be authorisation in the constitution of the company permitting such action.

5.35 While the Australian High Court in *Whitehouse v Carlton Hotel Pty Ltd*[115] said that in special circumstances the dilution of the voting power of an existing shareholder or group of shareholders, or the creation of new voting power, may constitute a legitimate purpose to be pursued by directors in the exercise of a fiduciary power to allot shares, that does not have the support of other authority,[116] and in any event that case was concerned with a closely-held company.

5.36 While the power to issue has precipitated the most litigation, this is not to say that the use of other powers has not led to litigation. In four cases the use

---

[107] *Abraham v Tunalex Pty Ltd* (1987) 5 ACLC 888.
[108] See *Punt v Symons & Co Ltd* [1903] 2 Ch 506 at 516.
[109] [1974] AC 821.
[110] Ibid at 835. Also, see *Harlowe's Nominees Pty Ltd v Woodside (Lakes Entrance) Oil Co* [1968] HCA 37; (1968) 121 CLR 423 at [6].
[111] [1903] 2 Ch 506.
[112] Ibid at 515–516. Also, see *Harlowe's Nominees Pty Ltd v Woodside (Lakes Entrance) Oil Co* [1968] HCA 37; (1968) 121 CLR 423 at [6].
[113] [1968] HCA 37; (1968) 121 CLR 483 at 493.
[114] *Harlowe's Nominees Pty Ltd v Woodside (Lakes Entrance) Oil Co* [1968] HCA 37; (1968) 121 CLR 423.
[115] [1987] HCA 11; (1987) 162 CLR 285 at 292.
[116] But see the case of *Kirwan v Cresvale Far East Ltd* [2002] NSWCA 395; (2002) 44 ACSR 21 where the share issue was allowed to stand.

of other powers has been the subject of consideration. The first is the case of *Ex parte Glossop*.[117] This case involved a petition brought against the directors of a company under a precursor of s 994 of the CA 2006, claiming unfair prejudice. The petition was based on the fact, inter alia, that the directors of a company had changed its dividend policy so as to favour certain members who drew remuneration from the company at the expense of the deceased estate of a shareholder which the petitioner represented. The case involved consideration of the directors' power to declare or not to declare dividends. In the course of his judgment Harman J said that:[118]

> 'It is, in my judgment, vital to remember that actions of boards of directors cannot simply be justified by invoking the incantation "a decision taken bona fide in the interests of the company". The decision of the Privy Council in *Howard Smith Ltd v Ampol Petroleum Ltd* [1974] AC 821 clearly establishes that a decision can be attacked in the courts and upset notwithstanding (a) that directors were not influenced by any "corrupt" motive, by which I mean any motive of personal gain as by obtaining increased remuneration or retaining office, and (b) that directors honestly believed that their decision was in the best interests of the company as they saw its interests. Lord Wilberforce's observations delivering the advice of the board at p. 831E acquits the directors of corrupt motive; at p. 832 he asserts the primacy of the board's judgment; but he goes on, at p. 835, to assert that there remains a test, applicable to all exercises of power given for fiduciary purposes, that the power was not to be exercised for any "bye-motives". If it were to be proved that directors resolved to exercise their powers to recommend dividends to a general meeting, and thereby prevent the company in general meeting declaring any dividend greater than recommended, with intent to keep moneys in the company so as to build a larger company in the future and without regard to the right of members to have profits distributed so far as was commercially possible, I am of opinion that the directors' decision would be open to challenge.'

5.37   The second case, *CAS (Nominees) Ltd v Nottingham Forest FC plc*,[119] involved the directors' use of the power to dispose of company property. In this case a company (C) acting for a consortium of investors was established in order to acquire control of a company (N) that ran a football club. As the club was experiencing problems on and off the pitch, an injection of funds was needed by someone respected in the city where the club was situated. D was willing to inject funds, but sought control of the club, as well as placing other conditions on his involvement in the club. It was envisaged that C would procure the issue of fresh shares to be issued to D who would gain control of N in exchange for putting more money into the club. A couple of routes were proposed to achieve this, but they did not appear to be able to be implemented successfully. So another route was sought. This involved C procuring N to issue shares to D in return for cash, the upshot being that C would be left with a 49 per cent minority shareholding in N, and D obtaining a controlling 51 per cent shareholding in N. This was subsequently approved of by an extraordinary meeting of C's shareholders. But dissenting shareholders of C

---

[117]   [1988] 1 WLR 1068; (1988) 4 BCC 506.
[118]   Ibid at 1077; 512.
[119]   [2002] BCC 145.

brought unfair prejudice proceedings on the basis that the effect of the transaction was substantially to reduce the value of their shares. They asserted that and in implementing the proposals the board had acted for an improper purpose and not in the interests of C. The shareholders argued that what was wrong with the transaction was that the directors had adopted a mechanism that avoided the need for a special resolution, knowing that it would not be able to be secured, and it was wrong to regard the abuse as being curable by an ordinary resolution. It was said that the transaction was not entered into on the basis that there was a genuine and primary purpose to secure capital for the club, but on the basis that it was done to secure D acquiring control of N without having to jump through the obstacles laid down by statute in order to gain control. Hart J ended up rejecting the claim of the shareholders on the basis that the directors' actions in ceding control to D in return for his investment, involving the disposition of assets, was quite proper.

5.38 In the third case, *Criterion Properties plc v Stratford UK Properties LLC*,[120] Hart J was faced with having to decide whether the entering into of a poison-pill agreement (regularly used in the US and Canada to ward off corporate raiders), an agreement that involved the divesting of company assets if a takeover succeeded was entered into with the express purpose of defeating attempts by a specific third party to gain control of the relevant company, was an improper exercise by the company's directors of their powers. His Lordship said that it was. He stated that the agreement was not in the best interests of the company. The case went on appeal[121] and the Court of Appeal upheld Hart J's view on the abuse of power point, agreeing that the agreement went beyond reasonable attempts to prevent the success of a party seeking to take control of the company, although it allowed the appeal on other grounds. When the matter went to the House of Lords[122] the appeal was dismissed, but their Lordships decided the matter on principles of agency. However, importantly for our purposes while Lord Scott, who gave the leading speech, did not commit himself as to whether it is open to a board of directors of a public company to approve the signing of a poison-pill agreement intended to deter outsiders from offering to buy shares where the deterrence involved a contingent divesting of company assets,[123] he did say that the agreement in this case went beyond deterring unwanted predators to the point of deterring desirable predators and entrenching the positions of the managing director and chairman.

5.39 The final case, and the most authoritative, is *Eclairs Group Ltd v JKX Oil and Gas plc*.[124] In this case the power that was the subject of challenge was the power of the directors to place restrictions on the voting power of shareholders. The facts will be sketched out rather than set out in full. The directors of J envisaged that two companies, E and G, which held a total of 39 per cent of the shares of J, would launch an attempt to gain control of J

---

[120] [2002] EWHC 496 (Ch); [2002] 2 BCLC 151.
[121] [2002] EWCA Civ 1783; [2003] 1 WLR 2108; [2003] 2 BCLC 129.
[122] [2004] UKHL 28; [2004] 1 WLR 1846.
[123] Ibid at [29].
[124] [2015] UKSC 71; [2016] 1 BCLC 1; [2016] BCC 79.

without paying what might be seen as a proper price for the shares acquired. So the directors of J sent out disclosure notices under s 793 of CA 2006 requesting information about the number of shares held, who held the beneficial ownership and any agreements between the various persons who held interests in the shares. E and G provided responses but the directors of J determined that the responses of E and G were not adequate. By a resolution the board of J issued restriction notices under the articles which enabled the directors preventing E and G voting their shares at a general meeting. E and G instituted proceedings against J in which they challenged the restriction notices. They pleaded s 171(1)(b) and argued that the board of J had acted for a collateral purpose that was improper. They said that the real purpose behind the actions of the directors of J was to ensure that resolutions needing to be passed as special resolutions would be passed. The directors could not guarantee this if E and G could vote as their votes could stymie any effort to obtain a special resolution.

5.40 When the matter came before Mann J his Lordship found in favour of the claimants on the basis that the predominant purpose of the board in imposing the restrictions was to increase the prospects of the special resolutions being passed. The judge held that this was an improper purpose and so the restrictions and the decision of the board to impose them were set aside even though he accepted that on the evidence the directors had acted in what they believed was in the best interests of J. The directors appealed to the Court of Appeal which allowed the appeal. The foundation for this reversal was that the judge had been wrong in his view that the restrictions imposed on the shareholders were defective because they were intended to prevent the shareholders from voting. The Court ruled that the purpose had been to enforce a demand that all shareholders were to provide certain information, and this was a proper purpose. The claimants could not complain as they were the victims of their own failure to respond or not to do so properly to the notices, and they were not the victims of the board's improper use of a power.

5.41 The claimants appealed to the Supreme Court which reinstated the trial judge's decision. Lord Sumption (with whose judgment Lord Hodge agreed in full and the other judges agreed with much of what Lord Sumption said) indicated in his judgment that one of the most common applications of the principle to prevent the improper use of directorial power is to stop the use of power, as here, in influencing the outcome of a general meeting.[125] The judge said that 'the inescapable inference [drawn from the mischief of the provision conferring the power (the articles)] is that the power to restrict the rights attaching to shares is wholly ancillary to the statutory power to call for information under section 793'.[126] As Mann J had said, and approved of by Lord Sumption, the failure to provide information pursuant to the disclosure notices is not to be regarded as justification for opening up a new assault on the

---

[125] Ibid at [16].
[126] Ibid at [31].

potential raider with the benefit of a fresh weapon.[127] Lord Sumption emphasised the fact that it would be expected that the power that was the subject of this case would be limited by something more than the directors' duty to act in the best interests of the company as it could interfere significantly in a shareholder's employment of his, her or its rights.[128]

D The purpose

5.42 In many cases there has been no dispute about what was the purpose behind the exercise of a power by the directors. In others the only purpose that could be ascribed to the directors was an improper one.[129] The law has generally developed in light of the use by directors of the power to allot shares. It has been argued in such cases that the directors have used the power to ensure that shares were allotted in such a way as to stymie the voting control of a shareholder.[130] In the recent case of *Eclairs Group Ltd v JKX Oil and Gas plc*[131] the power to prevent the use of shareholders' right to vote was used to stop shareholders gaining control. Where directors are acting in self-interest then the action is improper and will be invalidated.[132] However, as we will see, the absence of self-interest is not sufficient to ensure that an action is necessarily valid.

5.43 Where only one purpose behind an action can be discerned the application of the duty is not too difficult. First, it has to be decided what power has been exercised. Second, what was the purpose behind the action and is that purpose a proper one?

5.44 While the purpose behind an action of the directors is often going to be clear, there have been, and will be, cases where there are multiple purposes. This is where it becomes far more difficult to deal with a dispute. If there are multiple purposes identified then the courts have focused on what can be seen as the primary or substantial purpose of the directors.

5.45 Two classic examples in this area that have dealt with this issue are *Hogg v Cramphorn*[133] and *Howard Smith Ltd v Ampol Petroleum Ltd*.[134] These and other cases have laid down the general rule that when faced with directors who had mixed purposes in allotting shares, the courts have to ascertain what was the primary or substantial purpose and, if it was improper, then the allotment is not valid.

---

[127] Ibid at [32].
[128] Ibid at [36].
[129] Ibid at [17].
[130] For example, see *Piercy v S Mills & Co Ltd* [1903] 2 Ch 506.
[131] [2015] UKSC 71; [2016] 1 BCLC 1; [2016] BCC 79.
[132] *Fraser v Whalley* (1864) 2 H & M 10; (1864) 11 LT 175; *Hogg v Cramphorn* [1967] Ch 254.
[133] [1967] Ch 254.
[134] [1974] AC 821.

5.46 In the former case, a company was threatened with a takeover by X. To prevent this occurring, the directors established a trust for the company's employees and lent money to the trust to permit it to take up unissued shares at par value. The allotment precipitated a dilution of the shareholding of X, with the directors being able to rely on the support of more than half of the total votes of shareholders. The allotment to the trust was challenged on the basis that the directors had used the power to issue shares for purposes other than was intended by the conferral of those powers. The improper purpose alleged was the prevention of X gaining control of the company and ousting the existing board of directors. It was common ground that the action of the directors was designed to meet the threat of a takeover by X. The directors were of the view that if the takeover were successful there would be a detrimental change in the nature of the company's trading activities, and that would be bad for the company. The fact is, however, that the trust deed would not have come into existence, nor would the shares have been issued as they were, but for X's takeover moves. But, it was also common ground that the directors were not motivated by improper intentions relating to any personal advantage, but they acted in an honest belief that they were doing what was for the good of the company.[135] The board believed that providing a sizeable, though indirect, voice in the affairs of the company would benefit both the staff and the company. Nevertheless, it was held that the exercise of the power was improper. Buckley J said that the primary purpose behind the issue of the shares was to defeat the takeover.[136]

5.47 In *Howard Smith Ltd v Ampol Petroleum Ltd*[137] A and B held jointly 55 per cent of the issued share capital in X, and A unsuccessfully submitted a bid for the remaining shares. H, another corporate shareholder, submitted a rival bid. While it was rejected, X's directors preferred H's bid to that of A. X's board then allotted unissued shares to H and this had the effect of diluting the strength of A and B's shareholding to 36.6 per cent. The directors of X maintained throughout that they made the issue to bring in much-needed capital for the company as well as to reduce the shareholding of A and B, and the purpose of obtaining capital was the dominant purpose.[138] A challenged the share issue.

5.48 The case ultimately ended up before the Privy Council, on appeal by H from the decision of the New South Wales Supreme Court. The Judicial Committee rejected the argument that, once it was shown that the directors had acted in good faith in what they considered to be the company's interests, that

---

[135] [1967] Ch 254 at 265.

[136] Ibid at 266–267.

[137] David Bennett QC in 'The Ascertainment of Purpose When Bona Fides are in Issue – Some Logical Problems' (1989) 5 Syd L R 5 at 11 said that it is difficult to regard the case as making a useful contribution to the area, but, with respect, that is rather a harsh assessment. As noted later, there are some statements concerning judicial approach that do make a contribution. Having said that, it is submitted that the advice of the Judicial Committee is a little bewildering in places.

[138] This kind of argument was in fact upheld in *McGuire v Ralph McKay Ltd* (1987) 5 ACLC 891 (Vic S Ct (Full Ct)).

was the end of the matter. Before it could be said that a fiduciary power had been properly exercised, the purpose for which it might be exercised had first to be investigated. Their Lordships went on to say that courts will not interfere in the decisions of management to exercise powers when those decisions are made honestly.[139] But where there is more than one purpose evident for the exercise of a power a court has to determine the substantial or primary purpose and to this end it is entitled to look at the situation objectively so as to assess how substantial or insubstantial a requirement to act might have been.[140] Accordingly, if a court finds that a particular requirement to act was not real then the court may have reason to discount the statements of individuals and to take the view that the directors acted solely to address the requirement. Their Lordships found that the directors had acted honestly, and not in self-interest, but nevertheless they held in favour of A on the basis that the directors used the power improperly, namely intending to lead to a reduction in A and B's interest, and, as a result, destroy their majority position. The Judicial Committee said that the directors were not empowered either to destroy existing majority shareholdings or make new majority interests in the company, even where they are not acting in self-interest.[141] It was said that the action of the directors in this case was 'simply and solely to dilute the majority voting power … so as to enable a then minority of shareholders to sell their shares more advantageously'.[142] The issue of shares was set aside.

5.49 It should be noted that while the judicial pronouncements of the Privy Council on the issue of the duty at hand are still relevant to UK law, the relevance of the case on the facts is somewhat diminished because UK law requires a company proposing to allot shares to make an offer to each existing shareholder to allot to him or her the same, or on more favourable, terms a rateable proportion of those securities that is as nearly as practicable equal to the proportion in nominal value held by him or her of the ordinary share capital of the company.[143] Powers, such as the power to allot shares, might be limited by other articles or provisions in the CA 2006, eg s 549 places limits on directors allotting shares. Directors are not to exercise any power of the company to allot shares except in accordance with s 550 (for private) or s 551 (for public). The latter provision does permit directors to allot shares if the articles or a company resolution authorises them to do so. Nevertheless, in *Re West Coast Capital (LIOS) Ltd*[144] Lord Glennie, sitting in the Outer House of the Court of Session, and considering s 171(b), was happy to rely on *Ampol* and said that if it could be demonstrated in evidence that the decision to allot shares made no commercial sense, the court would be entitled to infer that the

---

[139] [1974] AC 821 at 835.
[140] Ibid at 832.
[141] Ibid at 834, 837.
[142] Ibid at 837.
[143] CA 2006, s 561(1). This is known as the right to pre-emption. The requirement provided under s 561 may be excluded by private companies (s 567). Also, private and public companies can disapply the pre-emption requirement in particular circumstances. For example, see s 571.
[144] [2008] CSOH 72; 2008 Scot (D) 16/5 (Outer House, Court of Sessions, Lord Glennie).

directors in so acting were not exercising their powers for the purpose for which they were conferred.[145] His Lordship went on to say that the test:[146]

> 'is essentially one of looking at the purpose or purposes for which the directors were exercising their powers, ie their motivation. If an improper motivation can be shown, if only by inference from an objective assessment of all the surrounding circumstances, the basis of a case of unfairly prejudicial conduct might be established.'

5.50 In *Ampol* Lord Wilberforce laid out the process, consisting of two broad steps, that a court had to follow in order to determine whether directors have failed to use powers for proper purposes. First, according to his Lordship (and as mentioned earlier in the Chapter), it is necessary to examine the power that has been exercised. This involves determining the nature of the power and its parameters.[147] One would think that this will usually involve interpreting the articles (and possibly resolutions), and ascertaining the functions of the power for the company, and in doing this an objective approach will be employed. Where the power is not limited the court will need to consider whether it has been used in order to foster the interests of the company. Second, the court is to ascertain the substantial purpose for which the power was exercised.[148] The test involves ascertaining and considering the purposes of the directors and then establishing which is the substantial one. In doing this the court must look, as mentioned earlier, at the situation objectively.[149] The courts will give credence to the evidence of the directors and accept it unless the background to the action or fair inferences can be drawn[150] to suggest that the directors' evidence is not credible. As part of the second step of the court's analysis, the court has to decide whether the substantial purpose was proper. Arguably this is the most critical issue. The courts do this by considering the directors' subjective reasons for exercising the power.[151] But, it is clear that the courts will not just accept what the director(s) asserts was the purpose(s).[152] Courts are entitled to examine the situation in which the exercise occurred objectively in order to determine purpose. If the substantial purpose behind the action is proper there is no breach even if there is some less substantial purpose that is improper, ie some incidental purpose.[153] So that even if a director benefits indirectly from an exercise of power, the power has not been improperly exercised if the substantial purpose was proper.

---

[145] Ibid at [21].

[146] Ibid.

[147] [1974] AC 821 at 835.

[148] This is an approach that had been invoked for many years and was mentioned in *Mills v Mills* (1938) 60 CLR 150 (Aust HC) at 186.

[149] *Howard Smith Ltd v Ampol Ltd* [1974] AC 821 at 832.

[150] See *Permanent Building Society v Wheeler* (1994) 14 ACSR 109 at 137–148.

[151] [1974] AC 821 at 837.

[152] This is similar to the view taken in *Charterbridge Corp Ltd v Lloyds Bank Ltd* [1970] Ch 62; [1969] 3 All ER 1185 and *Regentcrest plc v Cohen* [2002] 2 BCLC 80, in relation to the duty to act in good faith for the benefit of the company. See the discussion in **Chapter 6**, below at **6.54**.

[153] *Hirsche v Sims* (1894) AC 654; *Ngurli v McCann* [1953] HCA 39 at [24]; (1953) 90 CLR 425 (Aust HC).

5.51 More recently, Jonathan Crow (sitting as a deputy judge of the High Court) in *Extrasure Travel Insurances Ltd v Scattergood*,[154] a case which did not consider the allotment of shares, identified four steps a court should take in determining whether directors have breached the proper purposes duty. In some ways these reflect what the Privy Council said earlier. These steps are:[155]

- identify the power the exercise of which is subject to challenge;
- identify the proper purpose for which the relevant power was delegated to the directors;[156]
- identify the substantial purpose for which the power was in fact exercised; and
- determine if the purpose was proper.[157]

5.52 In this case a company paid a sum, which amounted to most of its funds, to its holding company in a corporate group. Subsequently it became insolvent and ultimately its business was sold off and the purchaser, together with the company, brought proceedings against two former directors who orchestrated the payment to the holding company. It was argued, inter alia, that the directors had breached their duty to use their powers for the purpose for which they were conferred. The directors stated that they acted in good faith and that the sum represented money owed to the holding company. The learned deputy judge rejected the defence that the defendants used the powers appropriately. In addressing the four steps mentioned above he said that:

- the power used was the directors' ability to deal with Extrasure's assets in the course of trading;
- the power's purpose was generally to ensure that Extrasure survived and to foster its business interests pursuant to its constitution;
- the substantial purpose of the directors was to enable another company in the corporate group to discharge its liabilities and not to ensure Extrasure's survival;
- the purpose was not proper.[158]

5.53 The judgment indicates that a significant emphasis was placed on the evidence of the witnesses in ascertaining the purpose of the exercise of power.[159]

---

[154] [2003] 1 BCLC 598.

[155] Ibid at [92]. These were applied in the recent decision in *Madoff Securities International Ltd (in liq) v Raven* [2013] EWHC 3147 (Comm) at [268].

[156] One assumes that this would entail a construction of the articles or other constitutional documents providing the power.

[157] [2003] 1 BCLC 598 at [92].

[158] Ibid at [140].

[159] In a similar vein, see *Southern Resources Ltd v Residues Treatment & Trading Co Ltd* (1991) 3 ACSR 207 (SA S Ct (Full Ct)).

5.54   How is a judge to determine what the directors' primary, dominant or substantial purpose is? It has been argued that the characterisation of a purpose as substantial is a value judgment and allows for flexibility,[160] but at the expense of certainty, and it permits the courts to intervene in company management, something that they have said, on many occasions, they will not do.[161] It is fair to say that the primary or substantial purpose idea is not easy to put into practice. It has been criticised as impracticable, for it is meaningless to require a court to choose between purposes in ascertaining the dominant one.[162] It might well be that where a person has more than one purpose in doing something, it is not possible to separate them. As Brennan J stated in *Whitehouse v Carlton Hotel Pty Ltd:*[163]

> 'When an issue of shares has the double effect of raising needed capital and buttressing shareholder support for the directors, it may be a nice question whether the directors made the issue honestly in the interests of the company albeit with the realization that the result would be agreeable to them or whether in making the issue they had an actual purpose of creating an advantage for themselves otherwise than as members of the general body of shareholders.'[164]

5.55   The problem with the use of qualifiers such as 'dominant' or 'substantial' is evident in the jurisprudence relating to s 423 of the Insolvency Act 1986. This provision states, in broad terms, that, effectively, creditors, amongst others, are able to impugn transactions entered into by their debtors at an undervalue, and courts are empowered to restore the position to what it would have been if there had been no transaction entered into.[165] The creditor must be able to establish that the purpose of the debtor in entering into the transaction was to put assets beyond the reach of those who are or may at some time make a claim against the debtor or to prejudice the interests of present or prospective claimants in relation to any claim that they have or might have. In *Chohan v Saggar*,[166] Mr Edward Evans-Lombe QC (sitting as a deputy judge of the High Court) said that a claimant does not have to establish that the debtor's sole purpose for the transaction was the purpose contained in s 423. The deputy judge took the view that a claimant must prove that the s 423 purpose was the debtor's 'dominant purpose.' In the Court of Appeal in *Royscott Spa Leasing Ltd v Lovett*[167] Sir Christopher Slade (with whom Beldam and Nourse LJJ agreed), opined, for the purposes of the appeal, that a judge had to be satisfied that it was the debtor's substantial purpose to injure claimants,

---

[160]   L S Sealy '"Bona Fides" and "Proper Purposes" in Corporate Decisions' (1989) 15 Mon U L R 265 at 276.

[161]   But see the comments of Drummond AJA in *Westpac Banking Corp v Bell Group Ltd (No 3)* *[2012] WASCA 157*; (2012) 89 ACSR 1 at [2019]–[2030].

[162]   D Bennett 'The Ascertainment of Purpose When Bona Fides are in Issue – Some Logical Problems' (1989) 5 Syd LR 5 at 6. Also, see J Birds 'Proper Purposes as a Head of Directors' Duties' (1974) 37 MLR 580; S Burridge 'Wrongful Rights Issues' (1981) 44 MLR 40.

[163]   (1987) 162 CLR 285 at 292.

[164]   [1987] HCA 11 at [12] of his judgment.

[165]   Insolvency Act 1986, s 423(2). Examples of the kind of orders that might be made by a court are set out in s 425.

[166]   [1992] BCC 306.

[167]   [1995] BCC 502.

rather than the dominant purpose.[168] Subsequently, in *IRC v Hashmi*,[169] Arden LJ expressed agreement with the view of the judge at first instance that often there will be the situation where the debtor will have two motives in defeating creditors and even the debtor may well not be able to say which was uppermost in his mind.[170] Laws LJ in the same case said that it was easy to contemplate cases where a debtor had more than one purpose and it would be impossible to distinguish the weight or influence of the purposes on what he actually did act.[171] This problem of determining primary purposes has been acknowledged as problematic and it has been suggested that if it can be established that directors have intended to interfere with the control of the company, it matters not if the purpose was secondary – the action is improper.[172] Certainly where a claim is made that directors have improperly used their powers, it is likely that the issue is only going to be clear-cut where the directors have patently sought to act in self-interest or dishonestly.[173] In many cases it is likely that it will be difficult to determine which of more than one purpose was the substantial one.

5.56 Paul Davies has said that as the Privy Council in *Ampol* construed the power in light of the whole of the company's constitutional arrangements, in the situation where one has a company that is not characterised by the principle of the separation of ownership and control (usually a large company and often listed, like the company in *Ampol*), a wider interpretation might be given by courts to the directors' powers set out in the articles.[174] For instance, in most private companies the constitution provides that directors are to be vigilant concerning the make-up of the membership, and the articles provide, in contrast to listed companies, an authority for directors to refuse registration of shares in certain situations. So, the directors might be entitled in such a company to refuse to register the registration of the transfer of shares of a competitor.[175]

5.57 In *Eclairs Group Ltd v JKX Oil and Gas plc*[176] Lord Sumption said that there are two possible ways of identifying the primary purpose, and they are, first, to ascertain what is the 'weightiest' purpose and that is the 'one about which the directors felt most strongly',[177] and second, to determine what is the purpose that has caused the decision taken by the directors.[178] His Lordship indicated that the two are connected. In his judgment he said that the weightiest test is one that is difficult to justify both from a practical and principles

---

[168] Ibid at 507.
[169] [2002] 2 BCLC 489.
[170] Ibid at 504.
[171] Ibid at 508.
[172] J Birds 'Proper Purposes as a Head of Directors' Duties' (1974) 37 MLR 580 at 584.
[173] E Klein and J du Plessis 'Corporate Donations, The Best Interest of the Company and the Proper Purpose Doctrine' (2005) 28 UNSWLJ 69 at 79.
[174] [1974] AC 821 at 386.
[175] For example, see *Charles Forte Investments Ltd v Amanda* [1964] Ch 240.
[176] [2015] UKSC 71; [2016] 1 BCLC 1; [2016] BCC 79.
[177] Ibid at [19].
[178] Ibid.

perspective.[179] The practical problem is that the application of the test involves 'a forensic enquiry into the relative intensity of the directors' feelings about the various considerations that influenced them'.[180] The principles problem is that the duty requires directors 'only' to exercise them for the purposes for which they were conferred. Yet if an improper purpose is discerned then equity ends up condoning the exercise of the power when a purpose, even though only minor, existed. Yet Lord Sumption felt that[181]

> 'if there were proper reasons for exercising the power and it would still have been exercised for those reasons even in the absence of improper ones, it is difficult to see why justice should require the decision to be set aside.'

His Lordship said that he favoured a causative approach. He said:[182]

> 'One has to focus on the improper purpose and ask whether the decision would have been made if the directors had not been moved by it. If the answer is that without the improper purpose(s) the decision impugned would never have been made, then it would be irrational to allow it to stand simply because the directors had other proper considerations in mind as well, to which they attached greater importance.'

5.58 In the course of his judgment Lord Sumption concurred[183] with the majority view in the High Court of Australia decision in *Whitehouse v Carlton House Pty Ltd*[184] when it was said:

> 'As a matter of logic and principle, the preferable view would seem to be that, regardless of whether the impermissible purpose was the dominant one or but one of a number of significantly contributing causes, the allotment will be invalidated if the impermissible purpose was causative in the sense that, but for its presence, "the power would not have been exercised".'

Lord Sumption stated that when Lord Wilberforce in *Howard Smith Ltd v Ampol Petroleum Ltd* said that one had to ascertain the substantial or primary purpose he meant the purpose which accounted for the board's decision to act.[185] While Lord Hodge agreed with Lord Sumption on this point, Lords Mance and Neuberger doubted whether his Lordship had interpreted Lord Wilberforce correctly.

5.59 In the context of the case before him, the facts of which were dealt with earlier,[186] Lord Sumption said that the same result was likely whether one

---

[179] Ibid at [20].
[180] Ibid.
[181] Ibid at [21].
[182] Ibid.
[183] Ibid at [22].
[184] (1987) 162 CLR 285 at 294.
[185] [2015] UKSC 71; [2016] 1 BCLC 1; [2016] BCC 79 at [24].
[186] Above at 5.39–5.41.

applied 'a but for test' or the identification of the primary purpose test, and that this is likely to be the case in most situations.[187]

5.60 In completing this section of the Chapter one other case is worth mentioning. It is the Australian decision of *Kirwan v Cresvale Far East Ltd*,[188] where the New South Wales Court of Appeal heard an appeal in relation to a deed of company arrangement[189] (similar to where a company voluntary arrangement follows administration in the UK) under which the company, X, was operating. The arrangement provided that shares were to be issued to K who was a director of X. Such an issue would result in the shareholding of X's parent company being reduced to a minority interest. The issue was sought to be impugned by the parent company on the basis that when issuing the shares the directors were acting improperly to enable K to get control of X. In a majority decision,[190] the court held that there was not a breach of duty notwithstanding the fact that it was found that the substantial or dominant purpose of the issue was to obtain control for K. The court did indicate that it was a rare situation where this would be permitted. In this case the court was greatly influenced by two factors. First, the company was in desperate need of more capital in order for it to survive, and no one but K was in a position to provide it. Second, the creditors, save for the parent company (which was a creditor as well as a shareholder), approved of it after they had a chance to consider the arrangement. The decision might be laudable, but it seems to fly in the face of other decisions, notably *Ampol*, where the Privy Council said that even if directors are acting in good faith for the benefit of the company, where the substantial purpose of the board was to place control in the hands of friendly parties the action is invalid.

5.61 Finally, as far as s 171(b) itself is concerned Professor Richard Nolan has argued that the provision means that if, on balance, it is held that the director exercised a power for proper purposes then the exercise of the power as a whole is regarded as a proper exercise of the power and compliance with s 171(b) has occurred.[191] Nolan takes the view that, inter alia, it would place an intolerable burden on directors if the law was such that a director who acts for mixed purposes is in breach of s 171(b), because that would mean that only acting exclusively for proper purposes would lead to fulfilment of the duty.[192]

E The 'but for' test

5.62 There is a line of Australian case-law that provides that where the directors have a number of purposes, the plaintiff (claimant in England and

---

[187] [2015] UKSC 71; [2016] 1 BCLC 1; [2016] BCC 79 at [19].
[188] [2002] NSWCA 395; (2002) 44 ACSR 21.
[189] Under Part 5.3A of the Corporations Act 2001.
[190] The dissenting judge, Meagher JA, was of the view that the use of the deed of company arrangement procedure was used to gain control for K when earlier attempts were thwarted. Meagher JA in effect agreed with the judge at first instance.
[191] 'Proper Purposes in the Supreme Court' (2016) 132 LQR 369 at 372.
[192] Ibid.

Wales) must establish that the purpose that is alleged to be improper is causative. That is, *but for* this improper purpose the directors would not have exercised their power in the way in which they did.[193] This approach is manifested in the case of *Whitehouse v Carlton Hotel Pty Ltd*[194] where the Australian High Court said, after referring to the substantive or dominant purpose approach, that:[195]

> 'As a matter of logic and principle, the preferable view would seem to be that, regardless of whether the impermissible purpose was the dominant one or but one of a number of significantly contributing causes, the allotment will be invalidated if the impermissible purpose was causative in the sense that but for its presence "the power would not have been exercised".'

5.63 It must be noted that the above comment only constituted dicta as their Honours thought that it was 'unnecessary to express a concluded view on the question of precise formulation of the relevant test in such cases since the present case does not raise any problem of competing permissible and impermissible purposes'.[196] However, subsequently, both the Full Court of the Supreme Court of Victoria in *McGuire v Ralph McKay Ltd*[197] and the Full Court of the Western Australian Supreme Court in *Permanent Building Society v Wheeler*[198] applied the approach, the latter in conjunction with the substantial purpose test. The dissenting judge in the appeal in *Westpac Banking Corporation v Bell Group Ltd (in liq) [No3]*,[199] Carr AJA took the view that the judge at first instance erred in not applying the but for test. However, the majority judges did not refer to the test in their respective judgments.

5.64 More importantly for the purposes of this book is the fact that, as discussed in the previous section of the Chapter, in *Eclairs Group Ltd v JKX Oil and Gas plc*[200] Lords Sumption and Hodge appeared to favour a causative approach and this leads to a form of 'but for test'. They approved of the approach adopted in *Whitehouse v Carlton House Pty Ltd*[201] and encapsulated in the quotation from that case above.[202] Nevertheless, it cannot be said that the application of a 'but for test' is the only approach to be applied in relation to the proper purposes issue, because while Lords Mance and Neuberger had sympathy with the view of Lords Sumption and Hodge that the 'but for test' offers a single, simple test which might be able to be substituted beneficially for the principal or primary purpose approach, Lords Mance and Neuberger felt that they needed to hear argument on the point before it could be said that this

---

[193] See *Ngurli v McCann* (1953) 90 CLR 425 at 445; *Haselhurst v Wright* (1991) 4 ACSR 527; *Kokotovich Constructions Pty Ltd v Wallington* (1995) 17 ACSR 478 at 492; *Permanent Building Society v Wheeler* (1994) 14 ACSR 109 at 137.
[194] [1987] HCA 11; (1987) 162 CLR 285.
[195] At [10] of the judgment of Mason, Deane and Dawson JJ; 294.
[196] [1987] HCA 11; (1987) 162 CLR 285.
[197] (1987) 5 ACLC 891 at 895.
[198] (1994) 14 ACSR 109 at 137.
[199] [2012] WASCA 157; (2012) 89 ACSR 1 at [2867].
[200] [2015] UKSC 71; [2016] 1 BCLC 1; [2016] BCC 79.
[201] (1987) 162 CLR 285 at 294.
[202] See **5.62**.

was a new development in company law.[203] Lord Clarke agreed with this reservation although he indicated some support for the acceptance of the approach of the Australian High Court.[204]

5.65 As one commentator has noted, the approach favoured by Lords Sumption and Hodge permitted some objectivity to be kept, without which the test would be mainly subjective, involving the evaluation of motives or reasons as against purposes that were allowed.[205] We await to see if a later case which reaches the Supreme Court will find a majority of the Court ready to hear argument on this issue and hold that it represents the law in the UK.

F Focus on the best interests of the company

5.66 While there has been significant acceptance of the substantial purpose approach in England and elsewhere, including, in many cases, Australia, another approach has found support. The best articulation of the approach is to be found in the Canadian case of *Teck Corp Ltd v Millar*,[206] where Berger J took a different approach than that which is exemplified in the English cases, although the Privy Council in *Ampol* did refer to the case and said that it was in line with the English and Australian decisions in the area. With respect, that does not appear to be the case. In *Teck Corp Ltd v Millar* T, the majority shareholder of A, a mining company, made it clear that it intended to replace the board of A and then to make an agreement with A for T to exploit the mining rights which A held. In order to stop this A's board entered into an agreement to exploit the rights with C and allotted shares to C. T took proceedings against A's board alleging that the purpose of A's board in issuing the shares was to frustrate T's attempt to gain control of A. Berger J held that the purpose of the directors was to obtain the best deal that they could for A and the realisation of its property, and hence T failed in its claim. His Honour was of the view that directors were at liberty to take the view that a particular takeover should be stopped provided that such action was in the best interests of the company. His Honour said that the directors would have to have acted in good faith and must have reasonable grounds for their belief that the thwarting of the takeover would be for the company's benefit.[207] The judge elected to see the issue as being whether the directors were acting bona fide in the best interests of the company rather than being concerned about a separate duty to use powers for proper purposes. His Honour indicated that the court in *Hogg v Cramphorn*[208] reasoned in a way that was inconsistent with the general principle laid down in *Re Smith & Fawcett Ltd*[209] that directors are obliged to

---

[203] [2015] UKSC 71; [2016] 1 BCLC 1; [2016] BCC 79 at [53].
[204] Ibid at [46].
[205] H Tjio 'The Proper Purposes Rule' [2016] 176 LMCLQ at 184.
[206] (1973) 33 DLR (3d) 288.
[207] Dixon J in *Mills v Mills* (1938) 60 CLR 150 (Aust HC) took a similar position when he said that all the circumstances surrounding the issue have to be examined so as to ascertain the substantial object of those taking the action (at 185–186). Also, see *Hindle v John Cotton Ltd* (1919) 56 ScLR 625 at 630–631.
[208] [1967] Ch 254.
[209] [1942] Ch 304.

act in good faith in the interests of the company.[210] The learned judge saw *Hogg v Cramphorn*[211] as purporting to lay down an exception to the principle of acting in good faith, namely if directors aim, by issuing shares, to thwart an attempt to gain control of the company then they are in breach even though they are acting in good faith.[212] Berger J took the view that acting for an improper purpose entailed failing to act in the best interests of the company.[213] He did not think that the exercise of powers should be limited to the extent stated in *Hogg v Cramphorn*,[214] with the result that if directors were of the opinion that a takeover were not in the best interests of the company, they could seek to take appropriate action to block it.[215] The judge said[216] that:

> 'I think that directors are entitled to consider the reputation, experience and policies of anyone seeking to take over the company. If they decide, on reasonable grounds, that a takeover will cause substantial damage to the company's interests, they are entitled to use their powers to protect the company. That is the test that ought to be applied in this case.'

5.67 Berger J essentially felt that one had to leave the use of the power to the honesty of the directors, and that they should be able to take into account the reputation, experience and policies of any party who endeavours to take over the company. If they decide, and this is based on reasonable grounds, that a takeover will substantially damage the company's interests, they are entitled to use their powers to protect the company.[217] *Teck Corp Ltd v Millar* has been followed on many occasions by Canadian courts.[218]

5.68 Arguably, the *Teck* decision is consistent with some case-law: *Re Smith & Fawcett Ltd*[219] and *Harlowe's Nominees Pty Ltd v Woodside (Lakes Entrance) Oil Co*[220] in particular. In the former case the Court of Appeal said that it is not permissible for directors to exercise their powers for improper collateral purposes, because that would not be acting in good faith for the benefit of the company as a whole.[221] In the latter case it was claimed that the directors' decision to make an allotment of shares was wrongful in that the directors

---

[210] (1973) 33 DLR (3d) 288 at 312.
[211] [1967] Ch 254.
[212] (1973) 33 DLR (3d) 288 at 312.
[213] Ibid.
[214] [1967] Ch 254 at 313.
[215] (1973) 33 DLR (3d) 288 at 312.
[216] Ibid at 317.
[217] (1973) 33 DLR (3d) 288.
[218] For example, see *Shield Development Co Ltd v Snyder* [1976] 3 WWR 44 (Alta S Ct); *Olsen v Phoenix Industrial Supply Ltd* [1984] 4 WWR 498. But note that the decision has not fared so well under the scrutiny of academics. For example, see J Ziegel 'Directors' Powers and the Proper Purposes' [1974] JBL 85 at 89.
[219] [1942] Ch 304.
[220] [1968] HCA 37; (1968) 121 CLR 483.
[221] [1942] Ch 304 at 306.

exercised fiduciary powers otherwise than bona fide in the interests of that company as a whole. The Australian High Court said:[222]

> 'An inquiry as to whether additional capital was presently required is often most relevant to the ultimate question upon which the validity or invalidity of the issue depends; but that the ultimate question must always be whether in truth the issue was made honestly in the interests of the company.'

5.69   *Teck* also seems to be in line with several comments in Australian High Court decisions as well as the decision in the unreported English case of *Cayne v Global Natural Resources plc*.[223] In *Mills v Mills*[224] Starke J appeared to link exercising powers for proper purposes and acting bona fide in the interests of the company and in *Ngurli v McCann*[225] the Court also seemed to do so when it said that 'powers conferred on directors by the articles of association of companies must be used bona fide for the benefit of the company as a whole.' In *Cayne v Global Natural Resources plc* the Court allowed the action of the directors, designed to hinder the takeover action of a bidder, because the bidder was a competitor of the company. Sir Robert Megarry VC, part of whose judgment was cited by Hart J at first instance in *Criterion Properties plc v Stratford UK Properties LLC*,[226] said:

> 'If Company A and Company B are in business competition and Company A acquires a large holding of shares in Company B with the object of running Company B down so as to lessen its competition, I would have thought that the directors of Company B might well come to the honest conclusion that it was contrary to Company B's best interests to allow Company A to effect its purpose [and that they should issue further shares to maintain their control]. I cannot see why that should not be a perfectly proper exercise of the fiduciary powers of the directors of Company B. The object is not to retain control as such but to prevent Company B from being reduced to impotence and beggary, and the only means available to the director for achieving this purpose is to retain control. That is quite different from directors seeking to retain control because they think that they are better directors than their rivals would be.'[227]

5.70   The justification for the action of the directors in this case is that they were doing what they believed was in the best interests of the company. The judgment might be said to be more limited in scope than *Teck* as the legitimacy of the issue depended on the directors foreseeing some detriment to the

---

[222] *Harlowe's Nominees Pty Ltd v Woodside (Lakes Entrance) Oil Co* [1968] HCA 37; (1968) 121 CLR 483 at [6].

[223] Referred to in *Criterion Properties plc v Stratford UK Properties LLC* [2002] EWHC 496 (Ch); [2002] 2 BCLC 151 at [15]. The judgment is noted in R P Austin, H A J Ford and I M Ramsay *Company Directors* (Sydney, LexisNexis Butterworths, 2005) at 298. The judgment was affirmed by the Court of Appeal at [1984] 2 All ER 225, but the appeal did not deal with the issue discussed in this chapter.

[224] (1938) 60 CLR 150.

[225] [1953] HCA 39 at [24]; at 438.

[226] [2002] EWHC 496 (Ch); [2002] 2 BCLC 151.

[227] The quotation is set out in the Court of Appeal's decision ([2002] EWCA Civ 1883; [2003] 1 WLR 2108; (2003) BCC 50; (2003) 2 BCLC 129 at [15]).

company. The obvious reason for the issue in *Cayne* is that the company would benefit from a rival's attempt to gain control being thwarted. Under *Teck* it would seem that provided that the directors believed that the company would benefit from their remaining in control as they could do a better job than a rival, they should be able to act to ensure they remain in control.[228] In contrast, in *Criterion Properties plc v Stratford UK Properties LLC*[229] Hart J at first instance, and later the Court of Appeal, took the view that it might be the proper use of powers to inhibit or prevent a takeover.

5.71 Although the Privy Council in *Ampol* referred to the judgment of Berger J in *Teck*, it distinguished the case on the basis that in the latter case the defeating of T's majority control had been incidental to the board's purpose of entering into a mineral exploitation agreement with its preferred partner. The Privy Council's approach to the problem was different. In its view the directors' motives in *Ampol* were not consistent with any purpose for which the power relating to the issue of share capital was conferred upon them. This has been criticised on the basis that the Judicial Committee ended up assuming that there was a limited list of purposes, not set out in the articles, for which the power was given. It then reasoned that the purposes of the directors were not on the list so they were in breach. In contrast Berger J simply took the view that where the statute and the articles are silent as to purpose, no purpose, save for the general one of the directors being required to look for the company's best interests, is imposed on the directors.[230] It has been argued that the problem with the Privy Council's reasoning is that it entails, as a matter of necessity, second-guessing what the board believes was the company's best interests, which is against the established, publicised practice of the courts.[231]

5.72 But, in the more recent Scottish case of *Dryburgh v Scotts Media Tax Ltd*,[232] Lord Glennie rejected the argument of a director being able to rely on the best interests of the company when he or she did not act for proper purposes. His Lordship said that:[233]

> 'On the other hand, where a power conferred on a director is used for a collateral purpose, it does not matter whether the director honestly believed that in exercising the power as he did he was acting in the interests of the company – if the power has been exercised for an improper purpose, its exercise will be set aside.'

His Lordship said this after referring to a significant number of English authorities.

---

[228] See D Bennett 'The Ascertainment of Purpose When Bona Fides are in Issue – Some Logical Problems' (1989) 5 Syd L R 5 at 13.

[229] [2002] EWHC 496 (Ch); [2002] 2 BCLC 151.

[230] B Welling *Corporate Law in Canada: The Governing Principles* (Toronto, Butterworths, 2nd edn, 1992) at 352–353.

[231] S Fridman 'An Analysis of the Proper Purpose Rule' (1998) 10 *Bond Law Review* 164.

[232] [2011] CSOH 147.

[233] Ibid at [91].

5.73 There has been occasional Australian support for the general approach in *Teck*. In *Whitehouse v Carlton Hotel Pty Ltd*,[234] in a dissenting judgment, Wilson J of the High Court of Australia, regarded the decision in *Teck* as:[235]

> '... a striking illustration of the propriety of directors taking action which they bona fide believed to be in the best interests of the company notwithstanding that it had the effect of destroying the voting power and intentions of the majority shareholder.'

5.74 His Honour had said that one must begin, in considering the issue of improper purpose, with the general proposition that the power to allot shares is a fiduciary power which must be exercised bona fide for the benefit of the company as a whole.[236] Shortly thereafter, Mahoney JA of the New South Wales Court of Appeal in *Darvall v North Sydney Brick & Tile Co Ltd*[237] said that there must be a distinction in principle between the case where a transaction is entered into for the purpose of defeating a takeover bid on the one hand, and a transaction which is prompted by the takeover offer but the ultimate purpose of which is to benefit the company as a whole, on the other.[238] This is a fine distinction in practice and it might well be difficult to determine whether a transaction was or was not improper on the basis laid down by the judge. It certainly does not auger well as far as certainty goes if such an approach is invoked.

G An assessment

5.75 It is arguable that the *Teck* case cannot apply to s 171(b) of the CA 2006 as the duty it provides for is not linked to the duty to act bona fide in the best interests of the company, as it once may have been.[239] It might be said that the legislature, in enacting s 171(b) and omitting any reference to acting bona fide in the best interests of the company, is coming down firmly on the side of the line of cases represented by *Ampol*, and eschewing the *Teck* approach. However, it might be argued by directors when confronted with the argument that they have breached the proper purposes duty that, while accepting the fact that all powers are conferred for particular purposes, they were exercising the relevant power in order to promote the success of the company, in accordance with s 172, for that is the overall purpose of the company, and that is consistent with acting in the best interests of the company. It might actually be said that the only proper purpose for which directors should be exercising powers is so as to promote the success of the company.[240] Certainly the foregoing argument,

---

[234] (1987) 162 CLR 285 at 292.
[235] [1987] HCA 11 at [16]; (1987) 162 CLR 285 at 297.
[236] [1987] HCA 11 at [11].
[237] (1989) 16 NSWLR 260.
[238] Ibid at 328.
[239] This point is supported by the fact that the duty to act in good faith in the best interests of the company and the duty to act for proper purposes are contained in the same provision in Australia (Corporations Act 2001, s 181), although in different paragraphs. As discussed earlier, many have argued that the duties have been and are certainly now separate.
[240] B Hannigan *Company Law* (London, LexisNexis Butterworths, 2003) at 219.

if mounted by the directors, might be stronger if directors can point to the fact that they had regard to the factors mentioned in s 172(1). The Australian legislature's approach has been somewhat different. It has included the duty to act for proper purposes in the same section with the duty to act in good faith for the interests of the company, s 181 of the Corporations Act 2001, and, therefore, there is, perhaps, more scope for arguing that it is related to the requirement to act in good faith. But, after saying that, two things need to be noted. First, while the proper purposes duty and the duty to act bona fide are in the same section, they are contained in separate paragraphs, and arguably in reading s 181 one is left in no doubt that they are distinct. Second, the judgment of the Court of Appeal of the Supreme Court of Western Australia in *Westpac Banking Corporation v Bell Group Ltd (in liq) [No3]*[241] does not support the notion that the proper purposes duty is related to the requirement of acting in good faith. In this case Drummond AJA emphasised the fact that the duties were separate and he did not approve of part of the judgment of Lewison J (as he then was) in *Ultraframe UK Ltd v Fielding*[242] on the basis that his Lordship, wrongly, in the view of Drummond AJA, conflated the duties.[243] With respect, I think that it is not clear from what Lewison J said in the relevant part of his judgment[244] that he was falling foul of what Drummond AJA alleged. His Lordship does mention the two duties in the same sentence, although separated by a semi-colon, but that alone is not enough, in my submission, to say that he was conflating the two duties. This is especially supported by the fact that soon after, Lewison J said:[245]

> 'The good faith of the directors is not, however, the be-all and end-all. If they act in good faith, but for a purpose which is outside the ambit of their powers, their good faith will not validate their action. Similarly if they act for a collateral purpose, their good faith will not validate their action.'

5.76 But somewhat later, in what is a very long judgment, Lewison J does make comments that suggest that he is ready to take into account the fact that the directors had the best interests of their company in mind in determining whether they had acted for an improper purpose.[246] Later, in *Madoff Securities International Ltd (in liq) v Raven*,[247] Popplewell J makes it clear that the two duties are distinct, although they do overlap.[248]

---

[241] [2012] WASCA 157; (2012) 89 ACSR 1.

[242] [2005] EWHC 1638 (Ch); [2005] All ER (D) 397 (Jul); [2006] FSR 17; [2004] RPC 24.

[243] *Westpac Banking Corp v Bell Group Ltd (No 3)* [2012] WASCA 157; (2012) 89 ACSR 1 at [2002].

[244] *Ultraframe UK Ltd v Fielding* [2005] EWHC 1638 (Ch) at [1292].

[245] Ibid at [1293].

[246] Ibid at 1643.

[247] [2013] EWHC 3147 (Comm).

[248] Ibid at [267].

5.77 The fact that the duties are separate led Drummond AJA to say in *Westpac Banking v Bell Group*, as with others, that whether directors acted bona fide or not is not relevant in determining whether directors have acted for an improper purpose.[249]

5.78 Some concern has been voiced as to whether the courts are, in their construction of the purposes of powers, limiting directorial power when the company has not done so, and this has enabled the courts to intervene in companies' decision-making.[250] The approach has been criticised on the basis that the courts are making value judgments, based on hindsight.[251] Professor Len Sealy argues that in this area of the law the courts work with hindsight, first ascertaining, from the evidence, the directors' purpose and then finding, without reasoned argument, whether or not it is a permissible purpose.[252] It might be possible to see the case-law as indicating an attempt by the courts to try to enforce the division of power between directors and the general meeting and to stop the former from going beyond their powers.[253] It might be thought that in fending off takeover attempts, the directors are usurping the role of the shareholders to determine who controls the company.[254]

5.79 In the first edition of her excellent company law text, Brenda Hannigan suggested that the cases indicate that another formulation of the proper purposes doctrine is that there is a responsibility imposed on the directors to act in a way that is in accordance with the company's constitution and particularly the constitutional division of power.[255] However, as mentioned earlier, that does not appear to sit so well with the new s 171 of the CA 2006, which includes a duty to act in accordance with the constitution and provides for a separate proper purposes duty.

5.80 Case-law demonstrates the fact that the courts have tended to defer to directors' judgments when it comes to commercial issues,[256] although there have been suggestions that the courts might use the proper purposes principle to review the business decisions of directors,[257] thus permitting the courts to do that which they had said expressly they would not do, namely intervene in matters of internal corporate management.[258] For while one has statements such as those of Malcolm CJ of the Western Australian Supreme Court (Full

---

[249] *Westpac Banking Corp v Bell Group Ltd (No 3)* [2012] WASCA 157; (2012) 89 ACSR 1 at [2014].

[250] B Hannigan *Company Law* (London, LexisNexis Butterworths, 2003) at 239.

[251] L S Sealy '"Bona Fides" and "Proper Purposes" in Corporate Decisions' (1989) 15 Mon U L R 265 at 276.

[252] Ibid.

[253] B Hannigan *Company Law* (London, LexisNexis Butterworths, 2003) at 240.

[254] L S Sealy '"Bona Fides" and "Proper Purposes" in Corporate Decisions' (1989) 15 Mon U L R 265 at 273.

[255] B Hannigan *Company Law* (London, LexisNexis Butterworths, 2003) at 241.

[256] For instance, see *Howard Smith Ltd v Ampol Ltd* [1974] AC 821 at 832, 835–836.

[257] B Hannigan *Company Law* (London, LexisNexis Butterworths, 2003) at 239.

[258] S Fridman 'An Analysis of the Proper Purpose Rule' (1998) 10 *Bond Law Review* 164.

Court) in the case of *Permanent Building Society v Wheeler*,[259] that courts are not to consider whether a decision was good or bad from a business perspective and that the courts do not attempt to ascertain whether what the directors have done is proper by objectively considering the interests of the company, but rather they examine the actions of the directors in terms of the proper purpose for the power,[260] it could be said that the courts are making value judgments about what the directors have done, and therefore intervening. The need to take this latter approach is consistent with the classic statement of Bowen LJ in *Hutton v West Cork Railways Co*:[261]

> 'Bona fides cannot be the sole test, otherwise you might have a lunatic conducting the affairs of the company, and paying away its money with both hands in a manner perfectly bona fide yet perfectly irrational.'

5.81 Thus it is possible to say that if no reasonable board would have made the decision that is being impugned because it is not in the best interests of the company, it would be a breach of duty. Hence, we can say that in relation to the duty to act for proper purposes that if no reasonable board would think that the decision was substantially for a purpose for which the power was conferred the court might infer that the decision was not made in good faith for a purpose within the power.[262] Whether that should make any difference or not is a matter for debate.

5.82 The upshot is that, leaving aside the 'but for' test embraced by the Australian High Court from time to time and embraced by at least two judges of the UK Supreme Court, there appears to be at least two distinct approaches invoked by the courts.[263] First, the power may only be used for the specific purpose for which it was conferred.[264] This approach is reliant on value judgments made by the courts as to the propriety of the director's action, viewed objectively. The second, and the one championed by *Teck*, is that directors are entitled to use their powers provided they do so honestly and in good faith with the best interests of the company in mind.

5.83 The first approach and the one taken by judges in English cases, such as *Hogg v Cramphorn*[265] and the Privy Council in *Ampol*, can be seen as a restrictive approach as it restricts the directors' exercise of power. This might, as suggested earlier, be an effort on the part of the courts to ensure that the directors are controlled in some way by the shareholders. That is, while they are

---

[259] (1994) 14 ACSR 109.
[260] Ibid at 137.
[261] (1883) 23 Ch D 654 at 671.
[262] See *Shuttleworth v Cox Bros and Co (Maidenhead) Ltd* [1927] 2 KB 9, 23 and 24; *Wayde v NSW Rugby League Ltd* (1985) 61 ALR 225 at 232.
[263] See R Nolan 'Maxwell's Improper Purposes' (1994) 15 Co Law 85 where the learned commentator identifies more approaches.
[264] One might see the 'but for test' as only building on this first test, and not as a distinctly different approach.
[265] [1967] Ch 254.

granted broad powers of management there has to be some limitation on them. Buckley J said[266] in his judgment in *Hogg v Cramphorn* that:

> 'Nor will this court permit directors to exercise powers, which have been delegated to them by the company in circumstances which put the directors in a fiduciary position when exercising those powers, in such a way as to interfere with the exercise by the majority of its constitutional rights.'

5.84

His Lordship then said[267] that the directors cannot say that they:

> 'genuinely believe that what we seek to prevent the majority from doing will harm the company and therefore our act in arming ourselves or our party with sufficient shares to outvote the majority is a conscientious exercise of our powers under the articles, which should not be interfered with.'

5.85 The approach in *Teck* involves more reliance being placed on the professionalism and integrity of the directors. It is consistent with a stewardship approach to directors. The general approach taken in the English courts might be seen as giving support to agency theory and to ensuring that agency problems, such as the directors using their position to benefit themselves (or protect themselves), are addressed.

5.86 Powers exercised by directors might be able to be classified in two ways; first, as internal powers, namely those relating to the workings of the company and its internal administration (and leading to the vast majority of case-law); second, as external powers, namely those used in dealing with outsiders.[268] Richard Nolan has asserted,[269] with some justification, that the courts appear to subject the powers of the directors to deal with internal matters, such as allotting shares, to greater scrutiny than powers that are used externally, such as dealing with company property.[270] Perhaps this is because the courts do not want to second-guess commercial decisions made by directors or delimit their management powers,[271] yet they are more ready, as a corporate governance concern, to ensure that directors treat the members properly. Although not expressing it this way, the courts might be endeavouring, from an economic analysis point of view, to deal, as mentioned above, with the agency problem and to control an agent's powers. This might be gleaned from what Buckley J had to say in *Hogg v Cramphorn*[272] in the first of the quotations set out above.

---

[266] Ibid at 268.

[267] Ibid.

[268] Richard Nolan draws the distinction: 'The Proper Purpose Doctrine and Company Directors' in B A K Rider (ed) *The Realm of Company Law* (London, Kluwer, 1998) at 23.

[269] Ibid at 24–25.

[270] Nolan argues that the remedies will differ when an external power as opposed to an internal power is abused: ibid at 26–29.

[271] For example, see *Carlen v Drury* (1812) 1 Ves & B 154 at 158.

[272] [1967] Ch 254.

According to his Lordship the majority should be allowed to pursue what course it chooses, however poor a judgment that might be, as long as it does not oppress the minority.

5.87 Nolan takes the view that when it comes to examining the exercise of powers affecting the internal workings of the company, in contrast to the powers used externally, it is meaningless to look at the interests of the company because the powers are mainly focused on shareholders' rights and their involvement in the company and not with the conduct of the endeavour for which the company exists.[273] And s 172(1) arguably appears to give support to that.

5.88 When it comes to the regulation of external powers, the effect is not as extensive as it once was. Since the enactment of s 40 of the CA 2006, and, to a great extent, its most recent forebears, the issue of using powers improperly is not going to affect third parties who deal with the company in good faith. If directors do abuse a power, that is not a concern of the third party. A member is entitled to attempt to stop any such exercise of power (under s 40(4)), but that is likely to be used infrequently, and is an internal matter.

5.89 The restrictive approach can be difficult to apply, especially where the directors have mixed purposes, as the courts have to identify the substantial one and, as indicated earlier, it might be hard, even impossible, to distinguish the weight or influence of the purposes on how the directors acted.

5.90 Nevertheless, the restrictive approach might not mean that directors are inevitably going to be liable for doing those things which are regarded as not normal exercises of a particular power. First, the articles are able to be formulated in such a way as to authorise the exercise of a power for what ordinarily will be an improper purpose.[274] It would seem that if directors are concerned that the scope of their powers is restricted in any way, they could seek to have the company's constitution altered in order to delete restrictions on the purposes for which they may exercise powers.[275]

5.91 Second, the fact that if the use of a power benefits directors incidentally will not of itself invalidate the use of the power, provided that self-interest was not the substantial or dominant reason for the exercise of the power.[276]

---

[273] R C Nolan 'The Proper Purpose Doctrine and Company Directors' in B A K Rider (ed) *The Realm of Company Law* (London, Kluwer, 1998) at 26. See the comments in the judgment of Latham CJ in *Mills v Mills* (1938) 60 CLR 150 at 164, where the learned judge made statements to a similar effect.

[274] *JD Hannes v MJH Pty Ltd* (1992) 7 ACSR 8 (NSWCA).

[275] *Peskin v Anderson* [2001] 1 BCLC 372.

[276] *Hirsche v Sims* [1894] AC 654; *Mills v Mills* (1938) 60 CLR 150 (Aust HC).

5.92   What is clear is that the ultimate conclusion as to whether the power has been exercised for a proper purpose is always for the court.[277] Interestingly, Drummond AJA in *Westpac Banking Corporation v Bell Group Ltd (in liq) [No3]*[278] characterised the test that applied as an objective one on the basis that it is a matter for the court as to whether, in the circumstances of the case, the power has been exercised for a proper or improper purpose.[279] This is because, in his Honour's view and the view of many others, as we have seen, whether directors acted bona fide is not relevant.[280] It was said that:[281]

> 'Because the powers of directors are generally very broadly framed and because they exercise those powers in what are often complex commercial contexts requiring contestable judgments on matters of business, the court in deciding whether the relevant power has been exercised for a proper purpose will pay greater or lesser respect, according to the circumstances of the case, to the course taken by the directors. But the directors' judgment will not be decisive when the issue is whether the relevant power has been exercised for a proper or an improper purpose.'

5.93   At first blush it might seem that the decision of the UK Supreme Court in *Eclairs Group Ltd v JKX Oil and Gas plc*[282] has clarified things. For the first time we have had a Supreme Court/House of Lords case that has tackled the issue of proper purposes and Lord Sumption provided a clear steer towards adopting a causative approach. But, a majority of judges did not feel that they could comment definitively in that case on the scope of s 171(1)(b), and the approach that Lord Sumption was advocating, so we still have to wait for a later case to provide more certainty. In subsequent cases that come to the Chancery Division or the Court of Appeal (or the Outer or Inner Houses of the Court of Session in Scotland) judges might feel that they could apply a causative approach in line with the reasoning of Lord Sumption, but others might be wary of doing so given the comments of the majority judges, feeling that they need to leave the matter to another case that makes its way to the Supreme Court. The problem with that is that we could be waiting for some time.

5.94   The upshot of directors not using their powers properly is that any transaction is voidable at the option of the company, except where the action could be ratified by the members.[283] An improper allotment, if invalidated by a court, will usually be declared to be void.[284]

---

[277] *Westpac Banking Corp v Bell Group Ltd (No 3) [2012] WASCA 157*; (2012) 89 ACSR 1 at [2010].

[278] Ibid.

[279] Ibid at [2012].

[280] Ibid at [2014].

[281] Ibid at [2017].

[282] [2015] UKSC 71; [2016] 1 BCLC 1; [2016] BCC 79 at [30].

[283] *Bamford v Bamford* [1970] Ch 212; [1969] 1 All ER 969 at 973 (CA); *Whitehouse v Carlton Hotel Pty Ltd* [1987] HCA 11; (1987) 162 CLR 285 (Aust HC); *Glover v Willert* (1996) 20 ACSR 182 (Qld S Ct (Full Court)).

[284] See *Piercy v S Mills & Co Ltd* [1920] 1 Ch 77 at 85; *Residues Treatment & Trading Co Ltd v Southern Resources Ltd (No 4)* (1989) 14 ACLR 569 at 572 (SA S Ct (Full Ct)).

5.95 Whether a party dealing with the company could rely on any transaction that the company entered into with the third party, and where the director who was involved in acting for the company was not using powers for proper purposes, will depend on agency law and s 40. Unless a third party could be said to be acting other than in good faith, he or she could rely on the transaction and enforce it against the company as the third party is not to be prejudiced by the fact that a director is not acting properly.[285]

5.96 More effects of a breach, including the remedies that are available are discussed in detail in **Chapter 15**.

IV SUMMARY

5.97 Section 171(a) of the CA 2006 appears to be uncontroversial, primarily because at common law the duty has been subject to little consideration. However, the same cannot be said of the duty set out in s 171(b) if its background is anything to go by, because at common law there have been different approaches to applying the duty. The predominant one has been what the Chapter has referred to as the restrictive approach. This states that it matters not if directors believe in good faith that their action is in the best interests of the company if the courts assess that the directors' substantial purpose in taking the action was improper, the action will be regarded as a breach of duty. The Chapter has indicated that there is case-law, particularly in Australia, that has advocated a causative approach and that has been favoured by two UK Supreme Court judges in a recent case, but that does not mean that English or Scottish courts will necessarily follow such an approach, especially given the traditional interpretation being in line with the restrictive approach.

---

[285] See *Criterion Properties plc v Stratford UK Properties LLC* [2002] EWHC 496 (Ch); [2002] 2 BCLC 151.

CHAPTER 6

DUTY TO PROMOTE THE SUCCESS OF THE COMPANY

I INTRODUCTION

6.1   Arguably, this chapter deals with the most controversial and challenging duty that was introduced in CA 2006, and the one that has given lawyers, academics, companies and their directors the most concern and been the most puzzling.[1] The fact that the provision can be described in this way is demonstrated by the fact that it precipitated more debate in the Parliament than any other provision contained in the whole of CA 2006. It has no obvious precursor, although it has strong links to the duty to act bona fide in the best interests of the company, which was the predominant duty and the core fiduciary duty owed by directors before the codification of the duties.[2] As with s 171, there has been some debate as to whether this duty is a fiduciary duty,[3] but recent English authority appears to come down firmly on the side of it being one.[4] Having said that, it is not common that the decision concerning a dispute that concerns breaches of directors' duties relies on whether a duty is classified as fiduciary or not.[5]

---

[1]   Institute of Chartered Secretaries and Administrators (ICSA), *Guidance on Directors' General Duties* – January 2008 at para 3.2.3.

[2]   *Item Software (UK) Ltd v Fassihi* [2004] EWCA Civ 1244; [2005] ICR 450; [2005] 2 BCLC 91 at [41]; *Madoff Securities International Ltd (in liq) v Raven* [2013] EWHC 3147 (Comm) at [188].

[3]   Some argue that to describe the duty of loyalty as a fiduciary obligation is a mistake: R Flannigan 'Fiduciary Duties of Shareholders and Directors' [2004] JBL 277 at 281; M Conaglen 'The Nature and Function of Fiduciary Loyalty' (2005) 121 LQR 452; E Waitzer and J Jaswal '*Peoples, BCE,* and the Good Corporate "Citizen"' (2009) 47 *Osgoode Hall Law Journal* 439 at 444; M Conaglen 'Interaction Between Statutory and General Law Duties Concerning Company Director Conflicts' (2013) 31 *Company and Securities Law Journal* 403.

[4]   For instance, see *Regentcrest plc v Cohen* [2002] 2 BCLC 80 at 105; *Extrasure Travel Insurances Ltd v Scattergood* [2003] 1 BCLC 59 at [87]; *Bell Group Ltd (in liq) v Westpac Banking Corporation [No 9]* [2008] WASC 239; (2008) ACSR 1 at [4527]–[4527]; *Roberts v Frohlich* [2011] 2 BCLC 571 at [83], [84], [97]; *Towers v Premier Waste Management Ltd* [2011] EWCA Civ 923; [2012] 1 BCLC 67; *Odyssey Entertainment Ltd v Kamp* [2012] EWHC 2316 (Ch) at [207]; *Maidment v Attwood* [2012] EWCA Civ 998 at [22]; *Madoff Securities International Ltd (in liq) v Raven* [2013] EWHC 3147 (Comm) at [188]; *Viviendi SA v Richards* [2013] EWHC 30006 (Ch) at [143]; *McTear v Engelhard* [2014] EWHC 1056 (Ch) at [91]; *Breitenfeld UK Ltd v Harrison* [2015] EWHC 399 (Ch); [2015] 2 BCLC 275 at [59].

[5]   A Stafford and S Ritchie *Fiduciary Duties: Directors and Employees* (Bristol, Jordan Publishing, 2nd edn, 2015) at 29.

6.2   It has been argued, although prior to the point when the duty in s 172 of the CA 2006 was put in force, that it is different from the duty to act bona fide in the best interests of the company.[6] Yet the cases that have mentioned the provision have generally stated that it sets out the pre-existing law on the subject.[7] Also, the duty which is the subject of the Chapter is probably the most wide-ranging duty of the general duties in the Act, and clearly the most difficult to interpret, even after it has now been on the statute books for nine years. Thus, and because it is not as closely aligned to any previous duty when compared with the position of other duties in Chapter 2 of Part 10 of the CA 2006, and we still have not had that much in the way of case-law, portions of this chapter still involve speculation, albeit based on existing case-law, legal and equitable principles, and comments by legislators, as to the meaning and application of the provision.

6.3   It is possible to say that this duty is the fundamental duty of directors, and that other duties mentioned elsewhere in Chapter 2 of the CA 2006 are applications of this duty.[8] For instance, the duty to avoid conflicts means that a director is proscribed from placing himself or herself in a position where his or her company either might be harmed or might not be able to benefit from a particular situation. An argument that there has been a breach of the s 172 duty might, in some circumstances, be coupled with a claim that the directors have breached their duty of care and skill under s 174 of the CA 2006.

6.4   The Chapter begins with an overview of s 172 of the CA 2006, and this is followed by a discussion of how the section emerged from the consideration of the relevant law review bodies, Government deliberations and Parliamentary examination. Next, the Chapter provides a lengthy consideration of how the section has been, and is likely to be in the future, interpreted by the courts, with special focus on the key elements of the section, such as 'good faith' and 'success.' After this discussion the Chapter explores the enforcement of the duty, followed by consideration of practical issues, such as consideration of what directors need to do to ensure that they comply with the provision. The final part of substance, before a conclusion, seeks to provide a few evaluative thoughts about the provision and its operation.

---

[6]   See, for example, Maclay Murray Spens *Guide to the Companies Act 2006*. Cf Cameron McKenna 'Companies Act 2006: Deferred Reform' Law-Now, 29 November 2006; Ashurst *The Companies Act 2006: Directors Duties* (November 2006).

[7]   For example, see *Re West Coast Capital (LIOS) Ltd* [2008] CSOH 72; 2008 Scot (D) 16/5 (Outer House, Court of Sessions, Lord Glennie) at [21]; *Odyssey Entertainment Limited (in liq) v Kamp, Timeless Films Limited, and Metropolis International Sales Limited* [2012] EWHC 2316 (Ch); *Madoff Securities International Ltd (in liq) v Raven* [2013] EWHC 3147 (Comm) at [260]. The last judgment did not go on to discuss the section at all.

[8]   See *Shepherds Investments Ltd v Walters* [2006] EWHC 836 at [106].

II THE SECTION

A Generally

6.5   The interpretation of s 172 of CA 2006 will be the subject of most of the Chapter. The section comprises three subsections. The Chapter focuses primarily on s 172(1) and will simply mention the operation of both s 172(2) and (3).

6.6   In this part the general content of the section will be considered as well as its general thrust. It provides, in the most important of the subsections, s 172(1), that directors are to act in the way that they consider, in good faith, would be most likely to promote the success of the company for the benefit of the members as a whole, and in doing so they are to have regard to various matters, such as the interests of employees etc which are set out in paras (a)–(f) in s 172(1).

6.7   It is interesting to note that aspects of the duty are reminiscent, in many ways, of what was said in a couple of cases. First, the classic case of *Aberdeen Railway Co v Blaikie Brothers*.[9] The court there said[10] that:

> 'The directors are a body to whom is delegated the duty of managing the general affairs of the company. A corporate body can only act by agents, and it is of course the duty of those agents so *to act as best to promote the interests of the corporation* whose affairs they are conducting.' (my emphasis)

6.8   Far more recently, in another notable case, *Scottish Co-operative Wholesale Society Ltd v Meyer*[11] Lord Denning said that the duty of directors 'was *to do their best to promote its business* and to act with complete good faith towards it'[12] (my emphasis).

6.9   The Government states that Chapter 2 can be viewed in one of two ways, either as simply codifying the existing equitable and common law obligations of company directors, or it marks a radical change in articulating the connection between what is good for a company and what is good for society at large, and s 172 of the CA 2006 falls, it has been submitted, into the latter category.[13] Certainly s 172 is the provision which potentially provides the most significant change in the law on duties. With respect, saying that the case-law over the past nine years, as well as the comments of academics, has demonstrated that to say that s 172 provided a radical change was hyperbolic.

---

[9]   (1854) 1 Macq 461.
[10]   Ibid at 471 HL (Sc) per Lord Cranworth LC.
[11]   [1959] AC 324.
[12]   Ibid at 367.
[13]   *Duties of Company Directors* (DTI, June 2007), Introduction and Statement of Rt Hon Margaret   Hodge,   and   available   at   http://webarchive.nationalarchives.gov.uk/ 20070603164510/http://www.dti.gov.uk/files/file40139.pdf.

6.10   The CLRSG accepted that the duty encapsulated in s 172 of the CA 2006 would not make a great deal of difference to the present situation but felt that it would 'have a major influence on changing behaviour and the climate of decision making'.[14]

6.11   Before dealing with the main part of s 172 of the CA 2006, the duty to promote the success of the company, which occupies most of the balance of the Chapter, we will deal with sub-ss (2) and (3).

B Companies not focused on member benefits

6.12   Section 172(2) of the CA 2006 provides something of an exception to the general duty found in sub-s (1). The second subsection provides that where there is a company that includes purposes other than the benefit of the members, it operates as if the reference to promoting the success of the company for the benefit of its members (in s 172(1)) were to achieving the purposes set by the company. According to the Explanatory Notes to the CA 2006 this deals with altruistic, or partly altruistic, companies. Examples that are given are charitable companies and community interest companies, but the notes accept that it is possible for any company to have objectives that are unselfish and are paramount over the members' own interests. As to what the purposes of the company are is a matter for the good faith judgment of the directors. It is also a matter for the good faith judgment of the directors, according to the Explanatory Notes 'where the company is partially for the benefit of its members and partly for other purposes, the extent to which those other purposes apply in place of the benefit of the members'.[15]

C Duties to creditors

6.13   Section 172(3) of the CA 2006 is discussed in detail in **Chapter 13** in the context of a responsibility for directors to consider creditor interests, but the provision will be introduced here. What the subsection does is to recognise the common law development of a duty of directors to consider the interests of the creditors of the company in certain circumstances. The provision does not state when creditors' interests intrude into the judgment and decision-making of directors. This is left to the common law. As we will see in **Chapter 13**, the circumstances which will lead to directors having to consider creditor interests involve situations where the company is insolvent or in some lesser form of financial difficulty.

6.14   Section 172(3) of the CA 2006 provides that the duty to promote the success of the company for the benefit of the members is subject to the obligation to creditors. What this actually means is unclear. Does it mean that the duty in s 172(1) still applies when a company is in financial difficulty? One

---

[14]   Company Law Review *Modern Company Law for a Competitive Economy: Developing the Framework* (London, DTI, 2000) at para 5.1.17.
[15]   Explanatory Notes to the CA 2006 at para 330.

would think that it should mean that when a company is in financial difficulty the directors must be concerned about ensuring that the loss to creditors is reduced rather than looking to boost shareholder returns. So, until the company has moved out of its financial mire the s 172(1) duty is suspended.[16]

III THE DEVELOPMENT OF THE DUTY[17]

6.15 The way that the duty has come to us is of primary interest. It provides a useful background to the duty and gives us an understanding why it is drafted in the way that it is.[18]

A The Company Law Review

6.16 In its deliberations the CLRSG identified two possible approaches to addressing the issue of how directors are to manage their companies, namely either a shareholder value approach or a pluralist approach, and it did this in connection with its recommendations to have the duties of directors codified. The CLRSG noted that shareholder value (discussed in **Chapter 3**) has generally been implemented in the UK, and pointed up, in its discussion of for whose benefit a company should be managed, many of the arguments that have been tossed to and fro by those in favour and those against the shareholder value principle. The CLRSG stated[19] that the present law reflects the fact that companies are managed for the benefit of the shareholders, and it confers on the shareholders ultimate control of the undertaking, such that '[t]he directors are required to manage the business on their behalf ....'[20] It went on to say that the ultimate objective of companies is to generate maximum wealth for shareholders.[21]

6.17 In its codification of directors' duties, the CLRSG advocated introducing an approach, which it referred to as 'enlightened shareholder value',[22] for guiding directors in how they are to manage companies. It felt the new approach would better achieve wealth generation and competitiveness for the benefit of all. This approach involves directors having to act in the collective

---

[16] I have sought to consider how this would work elsewhere: A Keay 'Formulating a Framework for Directors' Duties to Creditors: An Entity Maximisation Approach' (2005) 64 CLJ 614; A Keay 'Directors' Duties and Creditors' Interests' (2014) 130 LQR 443.

[17] This section of the chapter is based on parts of A Keay 'Enlightened Shareholder Value, the Reform of the Duties of Company Directors and the Corporate Objective' [2006] *Lloyds Maritime and Commercial Law Quarterly* 335.

[18] For an extended discussion of the development of the duty, see A Keay *Enlightened Shareholder Value Principle and Corporate Governance* (Abingdon, Routledge, 2013), Ch 3.

[19] Company Law Review *Modern Company Law for a Competitive Economy: Strategic Framework* (London, DTI, 1999) at para 5.1.4.

[20] Ibid at para 5.1.5.

[21] Ibid at para 5.1.12.

[22] Company Law Review *Modern Company Law for a Competitive Economy: Strategic Framework* (London, DTI, 1999).

best interests of shareholders,[23] but it eschews 'exclusive focus on the short-term financial bottom line' and seeks a more inclusive approach that values the building of long-term relationships.[24] It is said to involve 'striking a balance between the competing interests of different stakeholders in order to benefit the shareholders in the long run'.[25] The CLRSG emphasised in one of its consultation papers that this did not mean disregarding the short-term interests of shareholders, but it in fact envisaged directors taking a balanced approach and that the long-term view should not be paramount over the short term or vice versa.[26] The concept of the enlightened shareholder value approach found its way into the Government's White Papers of July 2002 and March 2005, the Companies Reform Bill 2005, and ultimately into the CA 2006.

6.18   In the process of embracing the enlightened shareholder value approach, the CLRSG rejected[27] the pluralist theory which would require the law being:

> 'modified to include other objectives [besides maximising shareholder value] so that a company is required to serve a wider range of interests, not subordinate to, or as a means of achieving shareholder value (as envisaged in the enlightened shareholder value view), but as valid in their own right.'

6.19   The CLRSG said that adopting the pluralist approach would necessitate substantial reform of the law on directors' duties,[28] and later, in another consultation paper, the CLRSG regarded the pluralist approach as neither workable nor desirable in the UK.[29] In a subsequent consultation paper, the CLRSG explained its approach further, stating that under the enlightened shareholder value principle directors were obliged to 'achieve the success of the company for the benefit of the shareholders by taking proper account of all the relevant considerations for that purpose' and this involved taking 'a proper balanced view of the short and long term; the need to sustain effective ongoing relationships with employees, customers, suppliers and others' as well as to 'consider the impact of its operations on the community and the environment'.[30] This was the beginning of what ultimately became s 172 of the CA 2006.

---

[23]   Company Law Review *Modern Company Law for a Competitive Economy: Developing the Framework* (London, DTI, 2000) at para 2.22.

[24]   Ibid.

[25]   J Armour, S Deakin and S Konzelmann 'Shareholder Primacy and the Trajectory of UK Corporate Governance' (2003) 41 *British Journal of Industrial Relations* 531 at 537.

[26]   Company Law Review *Modern Company Law for a Competitive Economy: Developing the Framework* (London, DTI, 2000) at para 3.54.

[27]   Company Law Review *Modern Company Law for a Competitive Economy: Strategic Framework* (London, DTI, 1999) at para 5.1.13.

[28]   Company Law Review *Modern Company Law for a Competitive Economy: Strategic Framework* (London, DTI, 1999) at para 5.1.30.

[29]   Company Law Review *Modern Company Law for a Competitive Economy: Completing the Structure* (London, DTI, 2000) at para 3.5.

[30]   Company Law Review *Modern Company Law for a Competitive Economy: Developing the Framework* (London, DTI, 2000) at para 2.19.

B Company Law Reform: the first Government White Paper

6.20 The Government published a White Paper in July 2002,[31] and it expressly endorsed many of the statements of the CLRSG.[32]

6.21 The draft Companies Bill that was part of the White Paper provided for the codification of the duties of directors. Clause 19 stated that Sch 2 to the draft Bill set out the general principles by which directors were to be bound. Paragraph 2 of the Schedule stated that:

'A director of a company must in a given case –

(a) act in the way he decides, in good faith, would be the most likely to promote the success of the company for the benefit of its members as a whole; and

(b) in deciding what would be most likely to promote that success, take account in good faith of all the *material factors* that it is practicable in the circumstances for him to identify.' (my emphasis)

6.22 The paragraph then went on to enumerate the 'material factors.' They were similar to those set out in paras (a)-(f) of s 172(1) of CA 2006.

C Company Law Reform: the second Government White Paper

6.23 In March 2005 a second White Paper, titled 'Company Law Reform',[33] appeared. This second White Paper encompassed many of the points raised in the earlier White Paper, but there were some interesting changes in how the approaches advocated in the CLRSG's Final Report and the first White Paper would be implemented.

6.24 The second White Paper, according to the explanatory notes relating to it, was said[34] to:

'embed in statute the concept of Enlightened Shareholder Value by making clear that shareholders must promote the success of the company for the benefit of its shareholders, and this can only be achieved by taking due account of both the long-term and short-term, and wider factors such as employees, effects on the environment, suppliers and customers.'

6.25 The White Paper provided, as with the earlier one, that there are two elements to the way in which directors are to run the company.[35] First, they are to do that which they consider, in good faith, is most likely to promote the success of the company for the benefit of the members as a whole. Second, in

---

[31] *Modernising Company Law* (Cm 5553, 2002, DTI). For a discussion of the White Paper, see R Goddard 'Modernising Company Law: The Government's White Paper' (2003) 66 MLR 402 at 407.

[32] For example, *Modernising Company Law* (Cm 5553-I, 2002, DTI) at para 3.6.

[33] Cm 6456, 2005, DTI.

[34] Cm 6456, 2005, DTI at p 5.

[35] *Company Law Reform* (DTI, 2005), Explanatory Notes at para B17.

carrying out the first element, the directors are to take into account, where relevant, and as far as is reasonably practicable, several factors (in order to reflect wider consideration of responsible business behaviour) that are listed, but not intended to be exhaustive. The factors enumerated in cl B3 of the draft Company Law Reform Bill that was part of the White Paper, and which was very similar to the notes relating to para 2 of Sch 2 of the first White Paper, were set out in cl B3(3) and were:

> '(a)   the likely consequences of any decision in both the long and the short term
> (b)   any need of the company –
>> (i)   to have regard to the interests of its employees
>> (ii)   to foster its business relationships with suppliers, customers and others
>> (iii) to consider the impact of its operations on the community and the environment, and
>> (iv)   to maintain a reputation for high standards of business conduct.'

6.26   The directors also had to consider the need to act fairly as between members of the company who had different interests. In addition, the draft Bill recognised that the directors had to take into account creditors' interests in certain circumstances.

6.27   Clause B3 encompassed two ideas. First, the long-term performance of the company has to be considered by directors. It has been a frequent criticism of directors that they overly focus on the short-term benefits for companies as this pleases shareholders. Short-termism has been defined as 'seeking short-term gain to the exclusion of long-term achievement'.[36] Second, the approach took into account an array of interests of those who might be categorised loosely as stakeholders. So, while the clause ensured the maintaining of the shareholder-centred paradigm, at the same time it is asserted that it permits, in appropriate circumstances, consideration being given to a wider range of interests.

D The Company Law Reform Bill

6.28   On 1 November 2005, the Company Law Reform Bill was introduced into the House of Lords. The Guidance to the Key Clauses, and published by the Government at the same time as the Bill was introduced, stated that the Bill enshrined the enlightened shareholder value principle.[37] Clause B3 in the draft Bill and included with the Second White Paper became cl 156. Clause 156(1) and (3) were very similar to the provisions in cl B3. These clauses stated:

> '(1) A director of a company must act in a way that he considers, in good faith, would be most likely to promote the success of the company for the benefit of the members as a whole.

---

[36]   D Mullins 'Foreword' in M Jacobs, *Short-term America* (Cambridge, Mass, Harvard Business School Press, 1991) and quoted in J Grinyer, A Russell and D Collison 'Evidence of Managerial Short-termism in the UK' (1998) 9 *British Journal of Management* 13 at 13.

[37]   This was contained in clause 62 of the Guidance. The Guidance is no longer available.

(3) In fulfilling the duty imposed by this section a director must (so far as is reasonably practicable) have regard to –

(a)   the likely consequences of any decision in the long term
(b)   the interests of the company's employees
(c)   the need to foster the company's business relationships with suppliers, customers and others
(d)   the impact of the company's operations on the community and the environment
(e)   the desirability of the company maintaining a reputation for high standards of business conduct, and
(f)   the need to act fairly between the members of the company.'

6.29   One interesting change from the draft Bill was the fact that there was no reference to the need to consider both short-term and long-term consequences; reference was made only to long-term consequences. This is possibly an admission that directors already focused on short-term results and that their responsibility to promote the success of the company for the benefit of the members implicitly demanded that they always consider the short-term results of any action.

6.30   Clause 156 became s 172 (eventually) when the CA 2006 was passed.

IV THE INTERPRETATION OF THE SECTION

A Introduction

6.31   In a way, the first part of the section codifies, although the terminology has changed, the established rule that directors must act in good faith for the benefit of what they believe are the interests of their company.[38] The task of the directors is to promote the success of the company, and this obviously means they are to advance and foster the company's aims and objectives.

6.32   In *Cobden Investments Ltd v RWM Langport Ltd (sub nom: Re Southern Counties Fresh Foods Ltd)*,[39] Warren J said that: 'The perhaps old-fashioned phrase acting *"bona fide* in the interests of the company" is reflected in the statutory words acting "in good faith in a way most likely to promote the success of the company for the benefit of its members as a whole". They come to the same thing with the modern formulation giving a more readily understood definition of the scope of the duty.'[40] In *Madoff Securities International Ltd (in liq) v Raven*[41] Popplewell J said that the section codified the common law that dealt with the duty to act in good faith, as did the judge in *Re HLC Environmental Projects Ltd.*[42]

---

[38]   *Re Smith and Fawcett Ltd* [1942] Ch 304.
[39]   [2008] EWHC 2810 (Ch).
[40]   Ibid at [52].
[41]   [2013] EWHC 3147 (Comm) at [260].
[42]   [2013] EWHC 2876 (Ch).

6.33 While the duty in s 172 is derived from the general duty to act bona fide in the best interests of the company, the wording of the duty indicates that the duty contained in s 172 of the CA 2006 is different and introduced a different concept. As a consequence a judge might take the approach that Millett J adopted in *Re M C Bacon Ltd*.[43] Millett J, in hearing a case on preferences under the then new insolvency legislation (s 239 of the Insolvency Act 1986), refused to consider cases on the previous preference provisions. Judges have not done that with s 172. On the contrary they have happily considered pre-codification cases dealing with the duty to act bona fide in the best interests of the company. This is probably because, as we saw in **Chapter 4,** the codified law is clearly based on the common law rules and equitable principles that the courts are going to have consideration for the existing case-law. While s 172 is somewhat different from the duty that it effectively succeeds the courts have had reference to the case-law that addressed the duty that might be said to be the lynchpin of the law developed by the courts, namely the duty to act bona fide in the interests of the company, and this is likely to continue. This duty provided that the directors had to exercise their discretion bona fide in what they considered was in the interests of the company.[44] This duty was regarded as subjective in that the courts would not impose their own views as to whether the decisions made by the director were in the best interests of the company.[45] This is in accordance with the classic statement in *Re Smith and Fawcett Ltd*[46] that directors were obliged to act 'bona fide in what they consider – not what a court may consider – is in the interests of the company...'[47] Whether a director had breached his or her duty came down to a consideration of the director's state of mind. It has been held that s 172 does, like its precursor duty, involve a subjective duty.[48]

6.34 While we have a few cases that involved a finding that a director is in breach of s 172(1), for instance in *Odyssey Entertainment Limited (in liquidation) v Kamp, Timeless Films Limited, and Metropolis International Sales Limited*,[49] thus far we still have not had a case where the provision has been analysed in any significant detail. There are several cases where s 172 has been referred to, but its substance not considered. The provision has been considered most often in applications brought by shareholders seeking permission to continue (or, in Scotland, leave to commence) a derivative action against a director(s). The issue of derivative actions is discussed in detail in **Chapter 14,** but it should be mentioned here that s 172 must be the subject of a judge's consideration where he or she has accepted that in an application to continue a derivative action the applicant/claimant has successfully convinced

---

[43]   [1990] BCLC 324.
[44]   *Re Smith and Fawcett Ltd* [1942] Ch 304.
[45]   *Regentcrest plc v Cohen* [2002] 2 BCLC 80. Also, see *Roberts v Frohlich* [2011] 2 BCLC 571 at [83], [84].
[46]   [1942] Ch 304.
[47]   *Re Smith and Fawcett Ltd* [1942] Ch 304 at 306 per Lord Greene MR.
[48]   *Re Pro4Sport Ltd; Hedger v Adams* [2015] EWHC 2540 (Ch); [2016] 1 BCLC 257 at [34].
[49]   [2012] EWHC 2316 (Ch).

the judge that the application discloses a prima facie case.[50] Section 263(2)(a) of the CA 2006 states an application for permission must be refused if the judge is satisfied that a person acting in accordance with s 172 would not seek to continue the claim. If a judge is not so satisfied he or she must still consider the importance that a person acting in accordance with s 172 would place on continuing the claim. So, in the Chapter we will consider what the courts have said in this context, although the caveat must be sounded that they are of limited help as they do not assist a great deal in getting either an overarching view of s 172 or an appreciation of the meaning of elements of the provision.

6.35 Although not overtly stated, it is likely that the duty to foster the success of the company for the benefit of the members and the duty to take into account other interests can be seen in a hierarchal way, with the former being regarded more highly than the latter. The CLRSG advocated a hierarchy of obligations when it proposed a similar approach,[51] and this involved the promotion of the benefit of the members' interests above those of the broader interests set out in paras (a)–(f) of s 172(1). There is no indication as to the extent to which directors are to have regard for wider interests, an issue that is discussed later. This, therefore, means that the shareholder value principle (and discussed in **Chapter 3**) will generally hold sway.

6.36 Lord Goldsmith summarised the Government's view on s 172 of the CA 2006 in the following manner:[52]

> 'it is for the directors, by reference to those things we are talking about – the objective of the company – to judge and form a good faith judgment about what is to be regarded as success for the members as a whole....they will need to look at the company's constitution, shareholder decisions and anything else that they consider relevant in helping them to reach that judgement...the duty is to promote the success for the benefit of the members as a whole – that is, for the members as a collective body – not only to benefit the majority shareholders, or any particular shareholder or section of shareholders, still less the interests of directors who might happen to be shareholders themselves.'

6.37 It is notable that the duty applies to the directors of all companies, without any focus on size or nature. Clearly what directors of a small family company must do compared with the directors of a large FTSE 100 public company is usually going to be completely different.

6.38 It would seem that courts will, if there is an allegation of breach on the part of directors, have to examine the good faith of the directors and this might, as we shall see, involve some consideration of the decision-making and reasoning of the directors and the matters which they took into account when coming to a decision. But it is not likely that courts will second-guess the decision which the directors came to, save where it was improper.

---

[50] Section 262(3).
[51] Company Law Review *Modern Company Law for a Competitive Economy: Completing the Structure* (London, DTI, 2000) at para 3.19.
[52] Lords Grand Committee, 6 February 2006, column 256.

6.39 Importantly, directors are granted a completely unfettered discretion in the actions which they take provided that they are acting in a way that they consider would most likely promote the success of the company for the benefit of the members. Yet the CLRSG, whose basic recommendations are implemented in the CA 2006, stated that the primary reason for rejecting the pluralist position was that it would grant an unpoliced discretion to directors,[53] and this appears to be what we have with the section.

6.40 It should be said that the duty is separate from that found in s 171(b) (duty to use powers for proper purposes) and discussed in the last chapter. Also of importance in this context is a point made in **Chapter 5** and that is highlighted by the case of *Eclairs Group Ltd v Glengary Overseas Ltd*.[54] In that case Mann J said that the duty in s 172 does not trump the provisions of s 171. His Lordship has said that a consideration of whether a director has used powers for proper purposes has to have been undertaken before examining whether s 172 has been complied with.[55] It is likely that if directors have not used powers for proper purposes then they will not be promoting the success of the company for the benefit of the members. Of course, directors in breach of s 171(b) might not be in breach of s 172 as they might have exercised the power in good faith believing that its exercise would promote the success of the company for the benefit of the members. Yet, if there is a breach of s 171(b) then the fact that there might not be a breach of s 172(1) is largely academic.

6.41 A word should be expressed about corporate groups, a widespread phenomenon in the United Kingdom (and elsewhere). How are directors of companies who are involved in a corporate group to act? Traditionally, directors have been required to act in the best interests of their own company, and not in the interests of the group,[56] and this seems to remain the same under s 172 of the CA 2006.

6.42 The final point to note before moving on to the main elements of s 172 is that for the purposes of s 414A, which requires companies (other than those eligible for the small companies regime for accounts (see s 414B)) to prepare a strategic report and its purpose is to inform members of the company and help them assess how the directors have performed their duty under s 172 (s 414C).[57] Section 414C sets out what must be contained in the report.

---

[53] Company Law Review *Modern Company Law for a Competitive Economy: Developing the Framework* (London, DTI, 2000) at para 3.24.

[54] [2013] EWHC 2631 (Ch).

[55] Ibid at [210].

[56] For example, see *Extrasure Travel Insurances Ltd v Scattergood* [2003] 1 BCLC 59.

[57] Formerly this was done in effect by s 417. The provision was repealed from 1 October 2013 by the Companies Act 2006 (Strategic Report and Directors' Report) Regulations 2013. For a discussion of the provision, see O Aiyegbayo and C Villiers 'The Enhanced Business Review: Has it Made Corporate Governance More Effective?' [2011] JBL 699; C Villiers 'Narrative Reporting and Enlightened Shareholder Value under the Companies Act 2006' in J Loughrey (ed) *Directors' Duties and Shareholder Litigation in the Wake of the Financial Crisis* (Cheltenham, Edward Elgar, 2012) at 97–129; A Keay *Enlightened Shareholder Value Principle and Corporate Governance* (Abingdon, Routledge, 2013), Ch 5.

B Good faith[58]

6.43 In line with its predecessor duty, s 172 requires directors to act in good faith. It is likely that in any particular case the issue of whether the directors acted in good faith will be the most singular issue. Directors are, as we have seen, to act in such a way that they consider, in good faith, that which will promote the success of the company. For many years, as we have seen, directors have been obliged to act 'bona fide in what they consider – not what a court may consider – is in the interests of the company …'.[59] So, how far the directors must go in considering the interests of constituencies (stakeholders) other than the members is a matter for the good faith of the directors and not what is reasonable in the circumstances. The Law Commission put it this way:[60]

> 'Directors therefore cannot use their powers to benefit third parties or themselves. The duty is a subjective one, which is not broken merely because the court would not have reached the same conclusion as the directors as to what was in the company's interests. Provided that the directors act in good faith in what they believe to be the company's interests, it does not matter that their decision also promotes their own interests.'

6.44 The duty is to promote the success of the company, and they must fulfil this while acting in good faith. Even if what they do is to promote the success of the company, they are in breach if they were to fail to act in good faith.

6.45 The difficulty of finding directors in breach under this provision is demonstrated by the fact that it is a matter for the directors, not the court, to determine what are the interests of the shareholders, and, again, it is a matter for the directors, not the court, to decide over what period the aim of promoting the success of the company for the shareholders can most appropriately be fulfilled – an issue of short term versus long term. The directors have to determine the extent to which the promotion of the shareholders' interests requires the company to be generous in relation to non-member interests.[61] Given all of this, save in cases of really bad behaviour, one can see that it is very difficult to demonstrate that the directors have breached their duty of good faith.[62] It is very difficult, in most cases, to impugn the actions of someone who is able to state clearly that he or she believed that what was done was for the company's best interests. Paul Davies has gone as far as saying that it is hard to prove that a director has not acted in good faith 'except in egregious cases or where the directors, obligingly, have left a clear

---

[58] Parts of this section of the chapter draws on A Keay *Enlightened Shareholder Value Principle and Corporate Governance* (Abingdon, Routledge, 2013) at 93–107.

[59] *Re Smith and Fawcett Ltd* [1942] Ch 304 at 306 per Lord Greene MR.

[60] Law Commission, *Company Directors: Regulating Conflicts of Interests and Formulating a Statement of Duties*, Law Com No 153, Scots Law Com No 105, 1998 at para 11.5, and referring to *Hirsche v Sims* [1894] AC 654.

[61] P Davies *Gower and Davies' Principles of Company Law* (London, Sweet and Maxwell, 7th edn, 2003) at 389.

[62] Ibid. This is also acknowledged by Richard Nolan in 'The Legal Control of Directors' Conflicts of Interest in the United Kingdom: Non-Executive Directors Following the Higgs Report' (2005) 6 *Theoretical Inquiries in Law* 413 at 424.

record of their thought processes leading up to the challenged decision'.[63] It is very difficult, in most cases, to challenge the actions of someone who is able to state clearly that he or she believed that what was done was for the company's best. Directors will normally assert that their motives were pure, and they are likely to be able to convince themselves after the event of these pure motives, for as one commentator said: 'Directors, like other people, are capable of deceiving themselves about the point and effect of their actions.'[64] Social psychological research has established the fact that a person can delude himself or herself and believe that he or she knows why a particular decision was reached.[65] Courts are going to be rather reluctant to decline to accept oral evidence given by directors concerning their motives, and especially because alleging improper motives is relatively serious.[66] Having said this, directors still have to give evidence and be cross-examined, and after all of that, and in light of the circumstances surrounding the alleged breach, it is permissible for a judge not to believe directors when they state that they believed they were acting in good faith for the benefit of the company.[67]

6.46 The consequence of the provision is said to prevent the courts from second-guessing the decision-making of the board as far as it relates to deciding where the interests of the company actually lie.[68] Along these lines, Paul Davies is of the opinion that it is appropriate that the courts are not permitted to substitute their view of the decision made for that of the directors, because the courts lack expertise.[69] Such a view is not new; it tends to be a constant refrain in much of the academic literature on company law.[70] Yet, it is submitted that courts are not as commercially inept as they are often portrayed. When reviewing what occurred to a company, often some years before the hearing of the action, they have, in recent years, demonstrated a good deal of understanding of the positions in which directors found themselves at the relevant time. It is submitted that the judges have carefully analysed the situation confronting directors, and have generally come down on the side of the directors, with the decision of Park J in *Re Continental Assurance Co of*

---

[63]   P Davies *Gower and Davies' Principles of Company Law* (London, Sweet and Maxwell, 2008) at 510.

[64]   'Puzzles and Parables: Defining Good Faith in the MBO Context' (1990) 25 *Wake Forest Law Review* 15 at 22.

[65]   A Tenbrunsel and D Messick 'Ethical Fading: The Role of Self-Deception in Unethical Behaviour' (2004) 17 *Social Justice Research* 223 at 225.

[66]   R Hollington *Shareholders' Rights* (London, Sweet and Maxwell, 5th edn, 2007) at 51.

[67]   See, for example, *Charterbridge Corp Ltd v Lloyds Bank Ltd* [1970] Ch 62; [1969] 3 All ER 1185; *Extrasure Travel Insurance Ltd v Scattergood* [2003] 1 BCLC 598.

[68]   P Davies *Gower and Davies' Principles of Company Law* (London, Sweet and Maxwell, 7th edn, 2003) at 389.

[69]   Ibid.

[70]   For example, see the views of Professor Dale Oesterle in 'Corporate Directors' Personal Liability for "Insolvent Trading" in Australia "Reckless Trading" in New Zealand and "Wrongful Trading" in England: A Recipe for Timid Directors, Hamstrung Controlling Shareholders and Skittish Lenders' in I M Ramsay (ed) *Company Directors' Liability for Insolvent Trading* (Melbourne, Centre for Corporate Law and Securities Regulation and CCH Australia, 2000).

London plc[71] in relation to a wrongful trading claim being a prime example. The judges generally appear to realise that directors have to make tough decisions in often difficult circumstances. Furthermore, judges make allowances for the risks of business as evidenced in *Re Brian D Pierson (Contractors) Ltd*[72] where the judge recognised that a reasonable businessperson would be 'less temperamentally cautious than lawyers and accountants'.[73] In any event prescribing judges not to second-guess the decision-making of directors does not prohibit courts, as suggested above, from declining to believe a director's stated good faith.[74]

6.47 While judges will, it is acknowledged, often have to wrestle with difficult questions flowing from differing views of what constitutes right action in the circumstances in which companies operated,[75] they are able to make a fair assessment of the actions of directors and are now able and better equipped to take practical and commercial decisions.[76] Judges have sought to achieve a balance between the protection of shareholders and the other parties mentioned in s 172 of the CA 2006, on the one hand, and ensuring that directors (acting on behalf of their companies) are not totally discouraged from taking appropriate business risks, on the other hand.

6.48 The one allegation that might be made against the process is that courts might not be apprised of all the necessary information for making a decision, due to time and cost. However, this is something that could be levelled at many areas of the law, such as actions brought by shareholders who argue that the affairs of their company are being conducted in an unfairly prejudicial manner (an action that is initiated pursuant to s 994 of the CA 2006).

6.49 Obviously 'good faith' is a critical issue. What does 'good faith' mean? The concept of good faith is rarely articulated although used frequently in the law and elsewhere. It is clearly an ambiguous expression.[77] Notwithstanding its wide use (or maybe because of it) there is no clear and common definition as to what it means, with the expression being regarded as 'loose and amorphous.'[78] It is such that it is probably easier to say what is not acting in good faith than to define what is actually meant by the words 'good faith'.[79] The expression is defined in the *New Oxford Dictionary of English* as meaning: 'honesty or

---

[71] [2001] BPIR 733.
[72] [2001] 1 BCLC 275.
[73] Ibid at 305.
[74] For instance, see the decision of HH Judge Norris QC in *Wrexham Association Football Club Ltd v Crucialmove Ltd* (referred to in the Court of Appeal judgment at [2006] EWCA Civ 237; [2008] 1 BCLC 508).
[75] W T Allen 'Ambiguity in Corporation Law' (1997) 22 Del J Corp L 894 at 899.
[76] A point accepted as far back as 1982 by the Report of the Insolvency Law Review Committee, *Insolvency Law and Practice* ('Cork Report') (Cmnd 858, HMSO) at para 1800.
[77] *Sharp v Blank* [2015] EWHC 3220 (Ch) at [23].
[78] F Juenger 'Listening to Law Professors Talk about Good Faith: Some Afterthoughts' (1995) 69 *Tulane Law Review* 1253 at 1254.
[79] M Eisenberg 'The Duty of Good Faith in Corporate Law' (2006) 31 *Delaware Journal of Corporate Law* 1 at 21.

sincerity of intention.'[80] In general, the expression tends to be used in law to connote honesty and propriety.[81] There are recurring themes in the cases and literature relating to good faith, such as: fairness;[82] sincere attempts at honouring obligations; providing full and fair disclosure; undivided loyalty; no intention to act improperly or defraud;[83] and non-violation of accepted corporate law norms.[84]

6.50 In some contexts good faith identifies an actual state of mind irrespective of the quality or character of the causes that induces it. In other contexts it might mean that a person has to exercise the caution and diligence that is to be expected of an ordinary person of ordinary prudence.[85] The expression is used frequently in the law and specifically in company law. Len Sealy identifies two meanings given to the phrase.[86] First, it provides the idea of acting honestly and with the best intentions. The second connotes the idea of an activity being genuine. Sealy points to the fact that the first tends to require a more subjective application while the latter a more objective application.[87] In the American case of *Siamo v Helvering*[88] Judge Clark also identified two meanings of good faith. His Honour said that they were divergent.[89] First, the expression describes a state of mind, irrespective of the results that are produced. Second, it is construed objectively in that the person must act with reasonable caution and diligence. In several English cases it has been held in different contexts that good faith may go beyond personal honesty and the absence of malice.[90]

6.51 Under the duty to act bona fide in the interests of the company, the focus was very much on what the directors themselves considered, and so there was an appraisal of the director's intentions. It was made clear by the courts that they would neither impose their own views as to whether the decisions made by

---

[80] J Pearsall (ed) *New Oxford Dictionary of English* (OUP, 2001) at 790.

[81] *Olifent v Australian Wine Industries Ltd* (1996) 14 ACLC 510 at 515. For a variety of works on the subject, see, J O'Connor *Good Faith in English Law* (Aldershot, Dartmouth Publishing, 1990); R Summers 'Good Faith in General Contract Law and the Sales Provisions of the Uniform Commercial Code' (1954) 54 *Virginia Law Review* 195; L Ponoroff 'The Limits of Good Faith Analyses: Unravelling and Redefining Bad Faith in Involuntary Bankruptcy Proceedings' (1992) 71 *Nebraska Law Review* 209; J Blanchard 'Honesty in Corporations' (1996) 14 *Company and Securities Law Journal* 4; S Litvinoff 'Good Faith' (1997) 71 *Tulane Law Review* 1645.

[82] O'Connor, ibid at 99–102.

[83] See E Nowicki 'Not in Good Faith' (2007) 60 *Southern Methodist University Law Review* 441 at 454; E Nowicki 'A Director's Good Faith' (2008) 55 *Buffalo Law Review* 457 at 483, 485.

[84] M Eisenberg 'The Duty of Good Faith in Corporate Law' (2006) 31 *Delaware Journal of Corporate Law* 1 at 5; J Kerr 'Developments in Corporate Governance: The Duty of Good Faith and its Impact on Director Conduct' (2006) 13 *George Mason Law Review* 1037 at 1042.

[85] *Mid Density Developments Pty Ltd v Rockdale Municipal Council* (1993) 116 ALR 460 at 468 (Aust Fed Ct (FC)).

[86] '"Bona Fides" and "Proper Purposes" in Corporate Decisions' (1989) 15 Monash ULR 263 at 269.

[87] Ibid.

[88] 13 F Supp 776.

[89] Ibid at 780.

[90] *Lucas v Dicker* (1880) 6 QBD 84 at 88; *Re Dalton* [1963] Ch 336 at 354–355.

the director were in the best interests of the company,[91] nor would they hold a director liable simply because his actions happen, in the event, to cause injury to the company.[92] Further, no reasonableness test was to be applied in relation to what directors had done and in judging their good faith. Whether a director had breached his or her duty came down to a consideration of the director's state of mind and provided that directors believed in good faith that they were acting in the best interests of the company they could not be said to be in breach. So, the former duty was regarded as subjective. In *Regentcrest plc v Cohen*[93] Jonathan Parker J emphasised the fact that the duty to act bona fide in the best interests of the company is subjective in that the crucial issue is the director's state of mind.[94] His Lordship went on to say that: 'The question is not whether, viewed objectively by the court, the particular act or omission which is challenged was in fact in the interests of the company.'[95] A director will not be held liable (because he or she did not believe that he or she was acting in the best interests of the company) *merely* because it seems to the trial judge that the court would have acted differently if in the position of the director.[96] Subsequently, in *Extrasure Travel Insurance Ltd v Scattergood*[97] Jonathan Crow (sitting as a deputy High Court judge) also stressed the fact that it is what the director honestly believed was in the best interests of the company that is critical, and not the court's view about what would be best for the company.[98] The deputy judge said:[99]

'if, having considered all the evidence, it appears that the director did honestly believe that he was acting in the best interests of the company, then he is not in breach of his fiduciary duty merely because that belief appears to the trial judge to be unreasonable, or because his actions happen, in the event, to cause injury to the company.'

6.52   What little we have in case-law seems to suggest that the approach just articulated will be employed in relation to s 172. Warren J, in dealing with a claim under s 172(1), in *Cobden Investments Ltd v RWM Langport Ltd*[100] said: 'it is accepted that a breach will have occurred if it is established that the relevant exercise of the power is one which could not be considered by any reasonable director to be in the interests of the company.'[101] This is apparently inconsistent with what he had said earlier, namely that the directors are to be judged subjectively. One explanation is that Warren J, in saying this, had in mind the statements of Jonathan Crow in *Extrasure Travel Insurance Ltd v*

---

[91]   *Re Smith and Fawcett Ltd* [1942] Ch 304 at 306; *Regentcrest plc v Cohen* [2001] 2 BCLC 80; *Extrasure Travel Insurance Ltd v Scattergood* [2003] 1 BCLC 598.

[92]   *Extrasure Travel Insurance Ltd v Scattergood* [2003] 1 BCLC 598 at [90].

[93]   [2002] 2 BCLC 80.

[94]   *Regentcrest plc v Cohen* [2002] 2 BCLC 80 at [120].

[95]   Ibid.

[96]   Ibid. Also, see *Cobden Investments Ltd v RWM Langport Ltd* [2008] EWHC 2810 (Ch) at [53].

[97]   [2003] 1 BCLC 598.

[98]   Ibid at [87], [90].

[99]   Ibid at [90].

[100]   [2008] EWHC 2810 (Ch).

[101]   Ibid at [53].

Scattergood[102] which indicated that where the assertion of good faith by directors is not plausible then courts may deign not to believe the directors and plausibility may be determined by the reasonableness of the actions of the directors. This is an issue that warrants further consideration and we will return to it later. Whether Warren J did have the comments of Jonathan Crow in mind or not, his Lordship was clearly of the view that the duty in s 172 is subjective just as its precursor was. Such a view is confirmed by the explanatory notes to the Act. They provide that the decision as to what will promote the success of the company, and what constitutes such success, is one for the director's good faith judgment, and this ensures that business decisions on, for example, strategy and tactics are for the directors, and not subject to decision by the courts, provided directors acted in good faith.[103] This suggests that directors will plead that they acted in good faith and believed that what they did would promote the success of the company, and it would be a matter for the claimant in the action against the directors to convince a court that they acted otherwise.

6.53 It is interesting that in the last few decades we have seen less emphasis placed on determining standards in subjective terms and greater emphasis on objective terms.[104] An example is the duty of care, and that is exemplified by s 174 of the CA 2006. Yet in s 172 we seem to have complete reliance on a subjective test. In *Fletcher v National Mutual Life Nominees Ltd*[105] Henry J of the New Zealand High Court expressed reservations concerning whether the use of subjective terms to assess directorial actions are appropriate factors to apply in the commercial world of today.[106] So, are there any objective considerations to be taken into account in determining whether a director has acted in good faith? Dr Rosemary Teele Langford asserts that objective considerations have become increasingly relevant.[107] The difficulty is in ascertaining when objective considerations are to be taken into account and to what extent. The problem of relying solely on a subjective test was made plain in the well-known comment of Bowen LJ in *Hutton v West Cork Rly Co*:[108]

> 'What would be the natural limit of their power...? Bona fides cannot be the sole test, otherwise you might have a lunatic conducting the affairs of the company, and paying away its money with both hands in a manner perfectly bona fide, yet perfectly irrational.'

---

[102] [2003] 1 BCLC 598.
[103] Explanatory Notes to the Companies Act 2006 at para 327. Also, see Clause 64 of the Guidance to Key Clauses in the Company Law Reform Bill 2005.
[104] L S Sealy 'Directors' Duties Revisited' (2001) 22 Co Law 79 at 82.
[105] [1990] 3 NZLR97.
[106] Ibid at 661.
[107] R Teele Langford *Directors' Duties: Principles and Application* (Sydney, Federation Press, 2014) at 59.
[108] (1883) 23 Ch D 654 (CA) at 671.

6.54   There have been some concerns emitted over the employment of a purely subjective test. Professor Ross Parsons propounded a similar view when he said[109] that one has to distinguish:

> 'What a director has done from what he feels he ought to have done. A principle which must be tuned to the wavelength of the directors' conscience may be welcome to a theologian but will be of little significance as a legal control.'

6.55   In Australia the objective consideration that might be used is that an action of a director is a breach if no reasonable director would have thought that the action would be of benefit to the company.[110] Sealy has said that there is an objective threshold of reasonableness below which the existence of good faith will not of itself suffice to safeguard a decision of a director.[111] Yet as the commentator notes, the test in *Hutton v West Cork Railway Co*[112] does not seem to have ever been applied.[113] But while the courts have not totally embraced objective considerations; they do have some relevance. The case of *Charterbridge Corp Ltd v Lloyds Bank Ltd*[114] may be seen as authority for permitting objective considerations to be introduced in making a decision as to whether the duty has or has not been breached,[115] but it only permits objective consideration of the actions of directors in limited circumstances. Here Pennycuick J said that the court had to ask whether an intelligent and honest man in the position of a director of the company involved, could, in the whole of the circumstances, have reasonably believed that the transaction was for the benefit of the company,[116] where the director had actually failed to consider whether an action would be in the interests of the company.[117] Where the

---

[109]   'The Director's Duty of Good Faith' (1967) 5 MULR 395 at 417.

[110]   *Darvall v North Sydney Brick & Tile Co Ltd* (1987) 12 ACLR 537 at 553; *Re HIH Insurance Ltd*; *ASIC v Adler* (2002) 41 ACSR 72 at [738]–[740].

[111]   L Sealy '"Bona Fides" and "Proper Purposes" in Corporate Decisions' (1989) 15 *Monash University Law Review* 265 at 277

[112]   (1883) 23 Ch D 654.

[113]   L Sealy '"Bona Fides" and "Proper Purposes" in Corporate Decisions' (1989) 15 *Monash University Law Review* 265 at 277.

[114]   [1970] Ch 62; [1969] 3 All ER 1185.

[115]   *Charterbridge* has been approved on many occasions. For example, see *Equiticorp Finance Ltd v Bank of New Zealand* (1993) 11 ACSR 642 (NSW CA) (although two of the judges (Clarke and Cripps JJA at 726) had some reservations about it); *Australian National Industries Ltd v Greater Pacific Investments Pty Ltd in Liq (No 3)* (1992) 7 ACSR 176; *Japan Abrasive Materials Pty Ltd v Australian Fused Materials Pty Ltd* (1998) 16 ACLC 1172 at 1180 (WA S Ct); *Linton v Telnet Pty Ltd* (1999) 30 ACSR 465 at 471–473; *Extrasure Travel Insurances Ltd v Scattergood* [2003] 1 BCLC 598 at [91]; *Simtel Communications Ltd v Rebak* [2006] EWHC 572 (QB); [2006] 2 BCLC 571 at [104]. However, note that Bryson J of the New South Wales Supreme Court in *Maronis Holdings Ltd v Nippon Credit Australia Ltd* [2001] NSWSC 448; (2001) 38 ACSR 404, held that the principle enunciated in *Charterbridge* had no application to the issue of whether a director had breached the duty to act in good faith (at [185]). His Honour was of the view that the test in *Charterbridge* should only be applicable in the course of considering whether, as a question of fact, the directors were abusing their powers (at [188]).

[116]   *Charterbridge Corp Ltd v Lloyds Bank Ltd* [1970] Ch 62 at 74; [1969] 3 All ER 1185 at 1194. Also, see *Shuttleworth v Cox Bros (Maidenhead) Ltd* [1927] 2 KB 9 at 23.

[117]   In this case the judge was dealing with a group of companies and held that the directors had to consider separately the interests of each company: ibid.

director had turned his or her mind to whether doing something was in the interests of the company, then the focus was solely on the director's subjective good faith. The *Charterbridge* reasoning has been approved of on many occasions by both English and Commonwealth courts,[118] even though on occasions it does not seem to have been applied in a uniform or correct manner.

6.56 While in cases like *Regentcrest plc v Cohen*[119] the duty is subjective in that the issue is the director's state of mind, courts have given clear indications that when a director states that he or she held the good faith belief that what he or she did was in the best interests of the company, they are not obliged to believe the director's statement. In other words, while a claim against a director under this duty has to establish that he or she did not act in good faith, this does not mean that a director's assertion that he or she acted in good faith is unassailable. The courts are not going to accept unquestioningly a bald statement by a director that he or she acted in good faith if the evidence does not support that fact. Harman J said in *Re A Company*[120] said that: 'It is, in my judgment, vital to remember that actions of boards of directors cannot simply be justified by invoking the incantation "a decision taken bona fide in the interests of the company."'[121] Courts may well dismiss a director's claim to have acted in good faith where he or she has benefited personally from the impugned action or for some purpose other than advancing the welfare of the company and its interests.[122] This was manifested in the recent judgment of Norris J in *Breitenfeld UK Ltd v Harrison*[123] where a director had said regularly in evidence that he had acted in good faith for the company's interests, but his Lordship said that he rejected this evidence of acting in good faith,[124] and it is also evident in the New Zealand case of *Morgenstern v Jeffreys*[125] where the transaction that had led to the director being sued had been for his benefit.[126] Earlier, according to Jonathan Parker J in *Regentcrest plc v Cohen*,[127] directors have a more difficult task in convincing the court that they honestly believed the action to be in the best interests of the company if a director's act led to significant detriment to the company.

6.57 Courts can come to the conclusion that a director was not acting in good faith when he or she took a particular action, not only from a consideration of the evidence of the director, but also from an examination of objective

---

[118] For example, see *Linton v Telnet Pty Ltd* (1999) 30 ACSR 465 at 471–473; *Colin Gwyer & Associates Ltd and another v London Wharf (Limehouse) Ltd* [2002] EWHC 2748 (Ch); [2003] 2 BCLC 153 at [73]; *Extrasure Travel Insurances Ltd v Scattergood* [2003] 1 BCLC 598 at [91]; *Simtel Communications Ltd v Rebak* [2006] EWHC 572 (QB); [2006] 2 BCLC 571 at [104].

[119] [2001] 2 BCLC 80 at 105.

[120] [1988] BCLC 570.

[121] *Re a Company* [1988] BCLC 570 at 577.

[122] L Strine et al 'Loyalty's Core Demand: The Defining Role of Good Faith in Corporation Law' accessible at http://ssrn.com/abstract=1349971 (accessed 5 May 2011).

[123] [2015] EWHC 399 (Ch).

[124] Ibid at [69].

[125] [2014] NZCA 449.

[126] Ibid at [85].

[127] [2001] 2 BCLC 80 at [120].

matters.[128] In *Bell Group Ltd (in liq) v Westpac Banking Corporation [No 9]*,[129] Owen J said that he would, in deciding upon the state of mind of the directors, take account of surrounding circumstances and this may involve objective considerations. Thus objective considerations might be employed as part of the evaluation of the credibility of the director's evidence and claim that he or she acted in good faith.[130] It would appear that the fact of the matter is that a judge, in certain circumstances, and given the evidence in general, would not believe that the director acted in good faith, despite what he or she said in evidence. Clearly, according to the approach of Jonathan Parker J, mentioned above, it would seem that courts are permitted to draw inferences concerning the director's state of mind from witness statements and circumstantial evidence. Therefore, it is not simply a matter of a director coming to court and saying that he or she acted in good faith and that will be accepted unreservedly. As indicated earlier, a judge is at liberty to disbelieve the director's evidence concerning his or her good faith. A good example is the New Zealand Court of Appeal took the view in *Morgenstern v Jeffreys*,[131] mentioned above, where the director who was the subject of a breach of duty action was held not to have acted in good faith. The court relied on a number of objective factors in coming to this decision.[132]

6.58 There are other indications in case-law that the courts would not accept a director's evidence of honest belief in his or her actions in situations where the facts seem to suggest the contrary. Some courts have included the reasonableness of what the director did or did not do in the assessment of the director's claim about good faith.[133] In *Extrasure Travel Insurance Ltd v Scattergood*[134] Jonathan Crow (sitting as a deputy judge of the High Court) said that 'the fact that his [the director's] alleged belief was unreasonable may provide evidence that it was not in fact honestly held at the time'.[135] In this case the court was of the opinion that there had been a breach of duty. The company had paid a sum, which amounted to most of its funds, to its holding company in a corporate group set-up. Subsequently, the subsidiary became insolvent and ultimately its business was sold off and the purchaser, together with the company, brought proceedings against two former directors who orchestrated the payment to the holding company. It was argued, inter alia, that the directors

---

[128] This approach has been invoked in the US: *Citron v Fairchild Camera and Instrument Corp* 1988 WL 53322 (Del Ch).

[129] [2008] WASC 239.

[130] D Kershaw *Company Law in Context: Text and Materials* (OUP, 2nd edn, 2012) at 344; R Teele Langford *Directors' Duties: Principles and Application* (Sydney, Federation Press, 2014) at 191.

[131] [2014] NZCA 449.

[132] Ibid at [85].

[133] *Shuttleworth v Cox Bros & Co (Maidenhead) Ltd* [1927] 2 KB 9 at 23–24; *Bell Group Ltd v Bell Group Ltd (in liq) v Westpac Banking Corporation [No 9]* [2008] WASC 239 at [4598] (although on appeal one of the appeal judges did question what the judge at first instance had said on this point (see *Westpac Banking Corporation v Bell Group Ltd (in liq) [No 3]* [2012] WASCA 157; (2012) 89 ACSR 1 at [2052]–[2078]).

[134] [2003] 1 BCLC 598.

[135] Ibid at [90] and accepted in *Westpac Banking Corporation v Bell Group Ltd (in liq) [No 3]* [2012] WASCA 157; (2012) 89 ACSR 1 at [2056].

had breached their duty to use their powers for the purpose for which they were conferred. The directors stated that they acted in the best interests of the company, and that the sum represented money owed to the holding company.[136] But Jonathan Crow had no hesitation in rejecting this assertion based on the proved circumstances existing at the time of the payment.[137] The deputy judge felt that the reason offered by the directors had been created *ex post*.[138] The deputy judge was of the view that the sum was paid because another subsidiary of the holding company needed the money to pay a third party who was pressing for payment, and this action was not in the best interests of the company which made the payment.[139] The deputy judge opined that the directors' evidence was not plausible, given the surrounding evidence, and he found against them.[140] He said: 'I am satisfied that the defendants did not think, on 17 August 1999, that the transfer of £200,000 was in the best interests of Extrasure.'[141]

6.59 In *Item Software (UK) Ltd v Fassihi*[142] Arden LJ took a similar view when she said that 'there is no basis on which Mr Fassihi [the director] could reasonably have come to the conclusion that it was not in the interests of Item [his company] to know of his breach of duty'. Arden LJ's comments in this case seem to support the fact that a judge may assess the facts objectively and is entitled to infer that a director did not hold the good faith view that what he or she did or did not do, by way of breach of duty, was in the best interests of the company.[143] In *Item Software* a director, knowing that his company wished to renew a contract with a third party, essentially sabotaged negotiations for that contract and sought to obtain it for himself. He was held liable for breach of his duty to act in good faith in the best interests of his company in not disclosing his improper attempts to secure the contract for himself and his family company.

6.60 Another instance of the use of objective considerations in this context can be seen in the well-publicised decision of the Supreme Court of Western Australia in *Bell Group v Westpac Banking Corp (No9)*[144] where the trial judge, Owen J, said that the indication in evidence by directors of their subjective intention was relevant, but a court could consider the surrounding circumstances, which are objective, in order to provide an indication of the directors' state of mind. The judge said that:

> 'Unless the party challenging the conduct in question can demonstrate a justifiable basis for asserting that the directors did not believe bona fide that the transactions were in the interest of the companies there is no breach of this duty. If the

---

[136] Ibid at [103].
[137] Ibid at [103]–[104].
[138] Ibid at [104].
[139] Ibid at [107].
[140] Ibid at [106].
[141] Ibid at [105].
[142] [2004] EWCA Civ 1244; [2005] 2 BCLC 91 at [52].
[143] Ibid at [41], [44].
[144] [2008] WASC 239 at [4598].

challenging party can show that there are no reasonable grounds on which the decision could have been made or the conduct undertaken [by the director], then an element of objectivity is introduced into the equation. But it seems to me that the objective considerations relate back to the question whether the directors honestly believed the transaction to be in the best interests of the company, not to whether (regardless of what the directors believed) it did not benefit the company.'[145]

In his judgment Owen J appeared to condone in this comment judicial assessment of the reasonableness of the director's actions as far as the benefit of the company is concerned, but later he makes it clear that reasonableness is only considered in the context of what the director actually believed.

6.61 The decision of Owen J was appealed. In the Court of Appeal of the Western Australian Supreme Court Drummond AJA essentially agreed with much of what Owen J said, but his Honour seemed to go further and support a broader objective approach when he said that:

'It is irrelevant that the directors may have honestly believed they were acting in the company's interests, if the court on an objective assessment of all the circumstances, considers that their conduct is manifestly unreasonable. In that event, the court will intervene e.g. by treating such a decision by the directors as voidable.'[146]

I think that it is fair to say that the approach of Drummond J was not supported fully by the other judges and it has been subject to some criticism.

6.62 Of course in many cases the evidence will not be there for a claimant to impugn successfully the assertion of a director that he or she acted in good faith in the interests of the company. It has been submitted that it would seem that except where the directors have acted very badly and clearly not in good faith it is probably difficult to demonstrate that the directors have breached their duty.[147] Courts are going to be rather reluctant to decline to accept oral evidence given by directors concerning their motives, and especially because alleging improper motives is relatively serious.[148] This may be true in many cases, but perhaps saying that the directors have to have acted very badly might be placing the bar too high. There are indications from several cases considered above that the director's actions have to be plausible. Directors have to give evidence and be cross-examined, and after all of that, and in light of the circumstances surrounding the alleged breach, it seems that it is permissible for

---

[145] Ibid at [4598].

[146] *Westpac Banking Corporation v Bell Group Ltd (in liq) [No3]* [2012] WASCA 157; (2012) 89 ACSR 1 at [1983].

[147] P Davies *Gower and Davies' Principles of Company Law* (London, Sweet and Maxwell, 7th edn, 2003) at 389. This is also acknowledged by Richard Nolan in 'The Legal Control of Directors' Conflicts of Interest in the United Kingdom: Non-Executive Directors Following the Higgs Report' (2005) 6 *Theoretical Inquiries in Law* 413 at 424.

[148] R Hollington *Shareholders' Rights*, (London, Sweet and Maxwell, 5th edn, 2007) at 51.

a judge not to believe directors when the latter state that they believed they were acting in good faith for the benefit of the company.

6.63   The approach taken above is similar to that taken in relation to an action against a director for breach of the duty to use powers for proper purposes. For it was indicated in *Howard Smith Ltd v Ampol Petroleum*[149] that a court can gather a director's intention by collecting from the surrounding circumstances all the materials which genuinely help in consideration of the question. Lord Wilberforce, in giving the advice of the Judicial Committee of the Privy Council, quoted and approved of what Viscount Finlay had to say in *Hindle v John Cotton Ltd*.[150] Viscount Findlay said:[151]

> 'Where the question is one of abuse of powers, the state of mind of those who acted, and the motive on which they acted, are all important, and you may go into the question of what their intention was, collecting from the surrounding circumstances all the materials which genuinely throw light upon that question of the state of mind of the directors so as to show whether they were honestly acting in discharge of their powers in the interests of the company or were acting from some bye-motive, possibly of personal advantage, or for any other reason.'

6.64   Sealy has said that the use of 'good faith' has led to the contention that a subjective honesty of purpose was all that needed to be shown so as to avoid any challenge to the exercise of a discretion, but in company law that has never been the case.[152] Furthermore, it is probable that to establish a breach of duty in this context does not mean that bad faith must be proved.[153]

6.65   One commentator has asserted that courts will be able to infer that a director did not consider, in good faith, a decision to promote the success of his or her company where they conclude that no reasonable director could have done so.[154] Nevertheless, while that might well be considered a justified and appropriate approach, and it has some Australian authority in support, it is submitted that it must be emphasised, as mentioned earlier, that this only applies where there is evidence that suggests no reasonable director would act in the way that the director had done and this is linked to the fact that the court cannot accept that the director did believe that he or she was acting in good faith. It must be underlined that the courts are not able to state simply that they would not have taken such action as it was not reasonable and so the director is liable.

---

[149]   [1974] AC 821.

[150]   (1919) 56 Sc LR 625.

[151]   Ibid at 630–631.

[152]   '"Bona Fides" and "Proper Purposes" in Corporate Decisions' (1989) 15 Monash ULR 263 at 269.

[153]   See *State Bank of South Australia v Marcus Clark* (1996) 14 ACLC 1019 at 1042.

[154]   D Drake 'Directors' Duties' in V Joffe et al *Minority Shareholders: Law, Practice and Procedure* (Oxford, OUP, 2008) at 368 and referring to *Gething v Kilner* [1972] 1 WLR 337 at 342; *Re a Company, ex p Burr* [1992] BCLC 724 at 731.

6.66 While objective consideration might be of relevance, clearly those impugning the actions of a director do have to overcome several difficulties. As noted earlier, the burden of establishing a lack of good faith lies squarely on those attacking the director's conduct.[155] The starting point is that a director will, if he or she can assert that they acted in good faith, not be liable for breach of duty. Added to this, and also mentioned earlier, is the fact that courts give so much deference to directors that this enables the latter to have wide discretion to act. It has been a long-standing approach in the courts not to interfere with the decisions of directors;[156] rather they defer to the actions of directors because they do not think that it is appropriate for them to substitute their views over those of the directors who have much greater knowledge, time and expertise at their disposal to assess what are the best interests of the company.[157] The courts take the view that they are not equipped to evaluate whether a particular decision would benefit the company. Courts will have little option but to defer to the directors if the latter acted in good faith.[158] In one of the first cases to consider s 172, *R (on the application of People and Planet) v HM Treasury*,[159] the judge took the traditional position concerning decisions about how the company was managed and said that they were matters for the directors and shareholders could only affect what directors did within the constraints that are imposed on directors according to their duties and in this situation they were governed by s 172.[160]

6.67 Thus, it is not likely that directors will be found liable on a regular basis. While it seems to be that objective considerations may be of importance, it is likely that provided a director does not seek to benefit personally, acts completely irrationally or admits to failing to really consider what was in the best interests of the company he or she is not going to be found liable for contravening the duty.

6.68 There are various views as to whether there will be successful challenges as to what the directors have done in any given situation. With respect, Professor John Birds is probably right when he states that the effect of the section is going to be largely educational and that decisions taken in good faith are not likely to be more easily challenged than under the existing law.[161]

---

[155] For example, see *Charterbridge Corp Ltd v Lloyds Bank Ltd* [1970] Ch 62 at 74.

[156] *Carlen v Drury* (1812) 1 Ves & B 154 at 158; *Darvall v North Sydney Brick & Tile Co Ltd* (1989) 16 NSWLR 260 at 281; (1989) 15 ACLR 230 at 247; *CW Shareholdings v WIC Western International Communications Ltd* (1998) 30 OR (3d) 755 at [57] (Ontario Superior Court of Justice).

[157] *Carlen v Drury* (1812) 1 Ves & B 154 at 158; *Darvall v North Sydney Brick & Tile Co Ltd* (1989) 16 NSWLR 260 at 281; (1989) 15 ACLR 230 at 247; *CW Shareholdings v WIC Western International Communications Ltd* (1998) 30 OR (3d) 755 at [57] (Ontario Superior Court of Justice). *BCE Inc v 1976 Debentureholders* [2008] SCC 69 at [38], [40].

[158] J Parkinson 'The Legal Context of Corporate Social Responsibility' (1994) 3 *Business Ethics: A European Review* 16 at 19.

[159] [2009] EWHC 3020 (Admin)

[160] See the discussion of the case in S Copp 'S.172 of the Companies Act 2006 Fails People and Planet" (2010) 31 *Company Lawyer* 406.

[161] A Alcock, J Birds and S Gale *Companies Act 2006: The New Law* (Bristol, Jordan Publishing, 2007) at 146.

6.69 Finally we should not that any allegations of want of good faith on the part of a director should be put to the director in cross-examination.[162]

C Success

6.70 The directors are to promote the success of the company. The critical question to ask is: what is success? Lord Goldsmith[163] asked this rhetorically in debates in Parliament and answered the question this way:

> 'The starting point is that it is essentially for the members of the company to define the objective they wish to achieve. Success means what the members collectively want the company to achieve. For a commercial company, success will usually mean long-term increase in value. For certain companies, such as charities and community interest companies, it will mean the attainment of the objectives for which the company has been established.'

6.71 Later his Lordship went on to say that in determining success the directors have to look at the objective of the company and decide what is to be regarded as success for the members as a whole, and this will involve consideration of 'the company's constitution, shareholder decisions and anything else that they consider relevant in helping them to reach that judgement'.[164] This is consistent with the fact a note in para 2 of the White Paper of July 2002,[165] which dealt with the promotion of the success of the company, stated the success of the company for the benefit of the members must be consistent with the company's constitution. What this means is that success must be determined on an individual basis – what is success for one company is not success for another. It suggests that members can dictate that the directors manage the company for short-term benefits if that is what they see as the objectives of the company even though the intention behind this provision was to permit companies to operate for the long term.

6.72 Lord Goldsmith went on, in his speech in February 2006, from what is quoted above, to say[166] that:

> '... for a commercial company, success will normally mean long-term increase in value, but the company's constitution and decisions made under it may also lay down the appropriate success model for the company. ... it is essentially for the members of a company to define the objectives they wish to achieve. The normal way for that to be done—the traditional way—is that the members do it at the time the company is established. In the old style, it would have been set down in the company's memorandum. That is changing ... but the principle does not change that those who establish the company will start off by setting out what they hope to achieve. For most people who invest in companies, there is never any

---

[162] *GHLM Trading Ltd v Maroo* [2012] EWHC 61 (Ch); [2012] 2 BCLC 369.
[163] Lord Goldsmith, Lords Grand Committee, 6 February 2006, col 255.
[164] Lords Grand Committee, 6 February 2006, col 256.
[165] *Modernising Company Law* (Cm 5553, 2002, DTI).
[166] Lords Grand Committee, 6 February 2006, col 258.

doubt about it—money. That is what they want. They want a long-term increase in the company. It is not a snap poll to be taken at any point in time.'

6.73 One would think that the purposes of the company will influence what a court would see as to what promotion of the success of the company would entail. The difficulty is that a company's purposes might not be that clear and/or there is no way to predict what a court will determine are a company's purposes in any given circumstances.

6.74 Nevertheless, the decision as to what will promote the success of the company, and what constitutes such success, is one for the director's good faith judgment. As a result decisions concerning the company's business strategy and tactics are for the directors, and not subject to decision by the courts, always provided the directors acted in good faith.[167] There might be evidence that suggests that the directors did not endeavour to promote the success of the company, but they were seeking to do something else. But the evidence would, one would think, have to be clear and convincing.

6.75 In the past, success could be said to mean an increase in the share value of the company's shares, or at least the maximisation of the company's profits. But is such a view restricted by the requirement to have regard for the factors set out in s 172(1) of the CA 2006? I do not think so. There appears to be no reason why the focus on share value and profit maximisation is wrong, but equally 'success' may now mean long-term increase in value.[168] What does 'the long term' mean? It might mean the long-term increase in the company's financial value. This is not always easy to assess. Does it mean that the company is more financially stable? Does it take into account whether the value of the company's shares is higher, or whether more dividends have been paid out? The meaning of long term is discussed later.[169] Could it also be argued that given the circumstances of the company in order to achieve success the directors need to do something that benefits one of the company's constituencies other than the shareholders, such as the employees? The answer might well be in the positive if the directors can demonstrate that they believe in good faith that the action will promote the success of the company and that will ultimately benefit the shareholders.

6.76 It might be said that success means the achievement of the business objectives that the company has laid down for itself, and these could include financial, strategic or others. As mentioned earlier, the Government's intention is that the decision as to what will promote the success of the company, and what constitutes such success, is one for the director's good faith judgment.[170] The directors' interpretation of any business objectives could be crucial but provided their interpretation is made in good faith they will be regarded as complying with their duty. It might be argued that what is done to fulfil that

---

[167] Explanatory Notes to the CA 2006 at para 327.
[168] See, for example, P Beale 'Directors Beware' (2007) 157 NLJ 1033.
[169] Below at **6.98–6.114**.
[170] Explanatory Notes to the CA 2006 at para 327.

interpretation cannot be impugned provided that it cannot be established that the directors did not have a good faith belief in their strategy promoting the company's success.

6.77 The Government is concerned that directors make business decisions on things like strategy and tactics and they are not a matter for court review, provided that the directors acted in good faith. Of course, if directors act negligently in making decisions they could well be liable under s 174 of the CA 2006 for breach of duty of care, although if what the directors have done can be regarded as the exercise of a business judgment the courts might well find the directors not to be liable on this score.[171] The Explanatory Notes to the CA 2006 state[172] that:

> 'It will not be sufficient to pay lip service to the factors [these set out in s 172(1)(a)-(f)], and, in many cases the directors will need to take action to comply with this aspect of the duty. At the same time, the duty does not require a director to do more than good faith and the duty to exercise reasonable care, skill and diligence would require, nor would it be possible for a director acting in good faith to be held liable for a process failure which would not have affected his decision as to which course of action would best promote the success of the company.'

6.78 Whether a company is able to be successful is likely to depend on its relations with its trading partners, customers and other stakeholders, so considering the interests of stakeholders could well contribute to success. Also, success is reliant on having a good reputation and this is related in many ways to how it deals with its stakeholders. Of course, 'reputation' is a factor that is included in those that are enumerated in s 172(1) and to which directors are to have regard.

6.79 Finally, in relation to this part of the Chapter, we must emphasise that success is always couched in terms of benefits for members. Indeed in a derivative action case,[173] HH Judge Keyser QC (sitting as a judge of the High Court) said that the notion of the success of the company in the present circumstances was in respect of the fair distribution of benefits to its members. The focus on members brings us to the next section of the Chapter.

D 'Benefit members as a whole'

6.80 Directors are to promote the success of the company so as to benefit the members as a whole. It is notable that the term, 'members', is used, rather than 'shareholders', the typical term used in the past. This is because the legislation will apply to companies limited by guarantee, as well as companies limited by shares, and the former type of companies do not have shareholders, only members.

---

[171] See the discussion in **Chapter 8**.
[172] Explanatory Notes to the CA 2006 at para 328.
[173] *Hughes v Weiss* [2012] EWHC 2363 (Ch) at [54].

6.81   The expression 'members as a whole' has been used on several occasions in company law and, consequently, one would assume that the judicial comments on the meaning of the expression would be pressed into service here. The courts have tended to hold that it means the present and future shareholders, certainly in relation to companies for profit.[174] As far as the meaning of the benefit involved, the courts have tended to hold that it means the financial well-being of the shareholders.[175]

6.82   The foregoing, if correct, makes the assessment of the decisions of directors difficult, for some actions can be more beneficial for the present shareholders than future ones because a long-term view is not taken.[176] But if a long-term approach is employed it might be thought to be beneficial for the interests of future shareholders.

E Factors to which regard is to be had

6.83   Directors must act in a way that is designed to promote the success of the company, and in doing so they must have regard to certain factors. Section 172(1) of the CA 2006 adumbrates a number of factors (in six paragraphs) which deal with groups, stakeholders or constituents that are linked to companies. Why are the constituents who are mentioned in s 172(1) important? Well, employees, suppliers, customers, and communities (as well as creditors) make firm-specific investments that tie their economic fortunes to the firm's fate.[177] R Edward Freeman and his co-authors expressed the rationale behind the need to consider constituencies, in this way:[178]

> 'Business is about putting together a deal so that suppliers, customers, employees, communities, managers and shareholders all win continuously over time. In short, at some level, stakeholder interests have to be joint – they must be traveling in the same direction – or else there will be exit, and a new collaboration formed.'

6.84   The inclusion of the factors set out indicates a significant change in approach, for under the Companies Act 1985 the only reference to 'constituencies' or 'stakeholders' was in s 309, and that was to employees. It provided that the matters which the directors had to have regard in performing

---

[174] For instance, see *Gaiman v National Association for Mental Health* [1971] Ch 317 at 330; *Brady v Brady* (1987) 3 BCC 535 at 552 (CA).

[175] For instance, see *Gaiman v National Association for Mental Health* [1971] Ch 317 at 330; *Brady v Brady* (1987) 3 BCC 535 at 552.

[176] In *Provident International Corp v International Leasing Corp Ltd* [1969] NSWR 424 at 440 it was said that directors should consider the interests of future members although in R Austin, H Ford and I M Ramsay *Company Directors: Principles of Law and Corporate Governance* (London, LexisNexis Butterworths, 2005) the learned commentators take the view that this is rather odd given the fact that the present members could have the company wound up and the assets distributed to themselves (at para 7.8).

[177] Professors Margaret Blair and Lynn Stout take issue with this: 'Director Accountability and the Mediating Role of the Corporate Board' (2001) 79 Wash U L Q 403 at 418.

[178] S Venkataraman 'Stakeholder Value Equilibration and the Entrepreneurial Process' in R E Freeman and S Venkataraman (eds) *The Ruffin Series No 3: Ethics and Entrepreneurship* (Charlottesville, Philosophy Documentation Center, 2002) at 45.

their functions include the interests of the employees in general, as well as the members. Everyone agreed that s 309 was pretty much of a lame duck, mainly because employees could not enforce it, and it is submitted that it is good that the new legislation has put the provision out of its misery. It is also to be noted that unlike previous versions of s 172(1) of the CA 2006, the requirement to have regard for the factors in this subsection is not restricted in any way. In one previous version of the section, cl B3 of the Company Law Reform Bill that was part of the White Paper of 2005 and titled 'Company Law Reform',[179] it was stated that the directors were to have regard for the matters now contained in s 172 'so far as reasonably practicable'. It has been pointed out that the deletion of these words means that directors are not permitted a defence based on ignorance, particularly when one considers the fact that the directors are obliged to exercise a duty of care, pursuant to s 174.[180]

6.85 Interestingly, one cannot find in any of the paragraphs that list the factors a reference to economic and financial factors, or certainly, at least, directly. But the factors stated are not to be seen as exhaustive and, in any event, it might be thought that the directors would take into account economic and financial factors when considering what benefits the members as a whole.

6.86 Arguably, there was nothing in the case-law that forbade directors from taking into account the interests of others besides shareholders, as long as the directors acted in good faith in the best interests of the company as a whole. In fact on several occasions businesspersons have said that it would be counter-productive for companies not to take into account the interests of their stakeholders in making decisions. But the new section does make it clear that directors are to consider stakeholder interests when it is in the interests of the members to do so. In the past much has turned on the meaning of 'interests of the company'. It has probably been one of the most problematical expressions in company law. Nourse LJ in *Brady v Brady*[181] opined that it was sometimes misunderstood. Many have said that it means the shareholders as a whole.[182] Yet there are cases in which judges have played down the pre-eminence of shareholders' interests. It has been argued that there is not a clear strain of authority running through UK or Commonwealth case-law that holds that only shareholder interests are to be the concern of the directors.[183] A number of cases do suggest that the focus should be on shareholders, while others either merely blandly state that the directors are to act in the interests of the company, or indicate that the interests of the company involves something more than the interests of shareholders.[184]

---

[179] Cm 6456, DTI, London.
[180] J Birds et al *Boyle and Birds' Company Law* (Bristol, Jordan Publishing, 6th edn, 2007) at 618.
[181] (1987) 3 BCC 535 at 552.
[182] Company Law Review *Modernising Company Law: Strategic Framework* (London, DTI, 1999) at para 5.1.5.
[183] A Keay 'Enlightened Shareholder Value, the Reform of the Duties of Company Directors and the Corporate Objective' [2006] *Lloyds Maritime and Commercial Law Quarterly* 335 at 345.
[184] Ibid.

6.87 The factors to which the directors have to have regard, and mentioned in s 172(1) of the CA 2006, are, as mentioned above, not exhaustive,[185] for the provision, after mentioning this requirement, states in parentheses the words 'amongst other matters'. The factors mentioned 'highlights areas of particular importance which reflect wider expectations of responsible business behaviour …'.[186] The words 'amongst other matters' lead one to ask what other matters might be envisaged here, and when should they be considered? The answer is that it will be left to the directors' good faith discretion and to the circumstances. One would think that other matters should be considered when it is relevant and appropriate to do so. But can we be more precise? It is perhaps strange that creditors were not expressly mentioned. It might be said that the reason that they are not mentioned is that they are protected by s 172(3) which, as I have noted already and discuss in detail in **Chapter 13,** provides that the duty imposed by s 172 is subject to any rule of law requiring directors in certain circumstances to take into account the interests of creditors. Also, creditors might be covered by the catchall 'others' in s 172(1)(c). But, if creditors are meant to be covered by s 172(1) then it is perhaps odd that creditors were not expressly mentioned.

6.88 A final issue in relation to lack of guidance, and one that is readily apparent to anyone that has followed the debate about what is the corporate objective, is how do directors have regard to the interests set out in s 172(1) where there is conflict between the various interests?[187] Even the CLRSG recognised the fact that where the long-term interests of the company are in view, there will be a clash between the interests of those mentioned in s 172(1), on the one hand, and those of the shareholders, on the other.[188] Examples given by the CLRSG include the closing down of a plant or the termination of a long-term supply contract when the continuation of either will impact adversely on shareholder returns.[189] If there is a conflict do the directors have to balance, in line with the stakeholder theory (discussed in **Chapter 3**), competing factors where they conflict? There are indications from one case, *Re Phoenix Contracts (Leicester) Ltd (sub nom: Shepherd v Phoenix Contracts (Leicester) Ltd)*[190] that directors are entitled to balance various factors set out in s 172(1). It must be noted that this case did not involve a claim pursuant to s 172, but involved a petition (under s 994 CA 2006) by a member of a company who was seeking relief because the affairs of the company had been undertaken in a way that

---

[185] See the comments of Lord Goldsmith, Lords Grand Committee, 9 May 2006, col 846.

[186] Explanatory Notes to the CA 2006, at para 326.

[187] The same concern that was expressed in regard to the US constituency statutes. These statutes, drafted in various ways in different states, provide generally that directors are permitted to take into account a range of interests when making their decisions. It has been said that these statutes place burdens on directors to consider a wide range of interests that might well conflict without 'establishing sufficient standards by which directors may evaluate them' (J D Springer 'Corporate Constituency Statutes: Hollow Hopes and False Fears' (1999) *Annual Survey of American Law* 85 at 107).

[188] Company Law Review *Modern Company Law for a Competitive Economy: Strategic Framework* (London, DTI, 1999) at para 5.1.15.

[189] Ibid.

[190] [2010] EWHC 2375 (Ch).

unfairly prejudiced him. There was some debate over whether the petitioner had acted in good faith because it was accepted that he had left an anonymous voicemail with a potential customer of the company's informing it that the company was being investigated by the Office for Fair Trading. In the course of her judgment Proudman J considered whether the petitioner had, in his role as a director of the company, acted in accordance with s 172. She said that the petitioner had acted properly. Her Ladyship said:

> 'Applying the criteria laid down in s. 172, Mr Shepherd [the petitioner and the director who informed] was balancing the deleterious consequences of his conduct as far as its relations with its [the petitioner's company] major customer was concerned, and the potential for damage to the Company's employees if the contract was not gained (s.172(1)(a)(b)(c)), against the Company's reputation as a whole (s.172(1)(d) and (e)) in light of the OFT investigation.'[191]

6.89 If directors are to engage in balancing, how are they to do it? For instance, should a company purchase new technology that might benefit the environment, but which might also affect employees as there might be job losses?[192] Also, what weight is to be given to each factor?[193] The glib answer might be that so long as the directors resolve any conflicts on the basis of their good faith judgment and exercise reasonable skill and care in reaching any decisions, their actions cannot be impugned. In addition, if the directors do act accordingly the courts may well be reluctant to interfere with such commercial decisions.[194] But surely we must not lose sight of the fact that the overarching requirement for directors is to promote the success of the company for the benefit of the members as a whole and that will be the final determining issue. It is submitted that any regard for the factors in s 172(1) must be such that it does not impinge on the members' benefits. This is acknowledged by the GC 100, a group of the general counsel and company secretaries of the FTSE 100 companies (Association of General Counsel and Company Secretaries of the FTSE 100 companies).[195] The Institute of Chartered Secretaries and Administrators (ICSA) Guidance on Directors' General Duties, provided in January 2008, accords with this as it states[196] that:

> 'At times these six factors, and any others that are being considered, may be in conflict but the key issue for decision making is that the directors should choose the action that will promote the overall success of the company for the benefit of members as a whole, even if that may sometimes have a negative impact on one or more of the six factors.'

---

[191] Ibid at [103].
[192] Example given in CMS Cameron McKenna 'Companies Act 2006: An Overview' September 2007.
[193] So long as directors can show that they considered the statutory factors, some lawyers believe that the courts are unlikely to scrutinise whether they have properly weighed them: Cameron McKenna 'Companies Act 2006: Deferred Reform' Law-Now, 29 November 2006, 6, http://www.law-now.com/law-now/default (last accessed on 22 March 2007) at 5; Bond Pearce LLP 'The Company Law Reform Bill' February 2006, at 2.
[194] P Beale 'Directors Beware' (2007) 157 NLJ 1033.
[195] 'Companies Act (2006) – Directors' duties,' 7 February 2007 at para 4.
[196] ICSA International *ICSA Guidance on Directors' General Duties* (January 2008) at para 3.2.2.

6.90 The fact that directors are required to have regard to other factors, besides shareholder interests, makes it potentially more difficult than before to challenge directors' decisions. A well-rehearsed objection to pluralist (stakeholder) models of governance is that in a true pluralist model directors can justify not acting in a complaining stakeholder's interests on the basis that they were pursuing the interests of another stakeholder – known as the 'too many masters problem'.[197] Directors might conceivably be able to defend what they did by saying that they did it because they felt that they were having appropriate regard for the interests of a particular constituency. However, it must always be noted that under s 172(1) the ultimate consequence is that the any action must benefit the members.

6.91 We might end up with what the position in the United States is said to be, under the business judgment rule, namely directors who wish to depart from the standard shareholder value approach have to find some objective reason to point to the fact that the decision assists the company.[198] One wonders what would happen with the facts of the American case of *Shlensky v Wrigley*[199] if decided under s 172. In that case the board that controlled the company which owned a baseball franchise refused to schedule night games because it would interfere with the lives of those who lived around the baseball stadium. Some shareholders took action against the board. The shareholders failed to get a ruling that the directors were in breach of their duties, as the directors could take into account the effect on the community. Could UK directors argue that they would not schedule night games as they were having regard to the community and that would be promoting the success of the company in the long-run?

6.92 The fact that directors have been entitled to consider the interests of others besides the shareholders is illustrated by the decision of Canada's highest court, the Supreme Court of Canada, in *Peoples' Department Stores v Wise*,[200] where it was said that directors had a duty to act in the best interests of the corporation and that 'the best interests of the corporation' meant acting to maximise the value of the corporation. Major and Deschamps JJ, in delivering the judgment of the Court, specifically stated that the expression acting in the 'best interests of the corporation' does not mean acting in the best interests of the shareholders or any one stakeholder's interests.[201] The judges went on to say[202] that:

> 'But if they [the directors] observe a decent respect for other interests lying beyond those of the company's shareholders in the strict sense, that will not…leave directors open to the charge that they have failed in their fiduciary duty to the

---

[197] S M Bainbridge 'Director Primacy: the Means and Ends of Corporate Governance' (2003) 97 *Northwestern University Law Review* 581.

[198] L Ribstein 'Accountability and Responsibility in Corporate Governance' (2006) 81 Notre Dame L Rev 1431 at 1470.

[199] 237 NE 2d 776 (Illinois, 1968).

[200] [2004] SCC 68; (2004) 244 DLR (4th) 564.

[201] Ibid at [42].

[202] Ibid at [42]–[43].

company…We accept as an accurate statement of law that in determining whether they are acting with a view to the best interests of the corporation it may be legitimate, given all the circumstances of a given case, for the board of directors to consider, inter alia, the interests of the shareholders, employees, suppliers, creditors, consumers, governments and the environment…At all time, directors and officers owe their fiduciary duties to the corporation. The interests of the corporation are not to be confused with the interests of the creditors or those of any other stakeholders.'

6.93   This wide approach is supported by professional associations. For while the demand to consider other factors has been criticised by some as placing an extra burden on directors, the Institute of Directors has said that most competent directors have been doing this already.[203] It might well be that directors will delegate consideration of some of the factors mentioned and will require reports for board meetings which will make decisions that might affect the factors mentioned.

6.94   Joan Loughrey, Andrew Keay and Luca Cerioni[204] found from a study of what lawyers believed concerning the duty in s 172(1) of the CA 2006, that the subsection cannot be viewed in isolation from the new derivative action in s 260. Taken together these have been described as subjecting directors to a 'double whammy'.[205] Lawyers have raised the prospect that that this could allow activist shareholders such as employee or environmental groups to bring tactical litigation alleging that directors have negligently failed to have regard to one of the factors in s 172, or placed undue weight on others.[206] It has been asserted that we live in a world where shareholder activism is becoming more widespread.[207] Hence, in **Chapter 14** the issue of derivative claims is considered in some detail.

6.95   Having regard for interests other than those of the members may produce some benefits for members. Some shareholders might take the view, adroitly it is suggested, that if there is not a concern for wider interests demonstrated by the company then when the time comes for them to exit, it is quite possible that new investors might not view the company as an attractive investment proposition. Also, taking into account factors other than shareholder interests might ultimately produce financial benefits for the company, and ultimately for

---

[203] 'Directors' Duties: Sleepless Nights or Business as Usual?' (no longer available online).

[204] 'Legal Practitioners, Enlightened Shareholder Value and the Shaping of Corporate Governance' (2008) 8 *Journal of Corporate Law Studies* 79 at 96.

[205] A phrase first used by Lord Hodgson of Astley Abbots in the Grand Committee Stage of the Bill, 27 Feb 2006, Hansard HL Vol 679, col GC2, and subsequently adopted by Herbert Smith: *In the Line of Fire-Directors Duties under the Companies Act 2006* and Mills and Reeve Briefing Oct 2006; Clifford Chance, *The Companies Act 2006* (November 2006) at 3-4; Not all lawyers take this approach – see Ashurst *The Companies Act 2006* (November 2006) at 3.

[206] G Milner-Moore and R Lewis (Herbert Smith) '"In the Line of Fire" – Directors' Duties under the Companies Act 2006' Practical Law; Norton Rose *Shareholder Rights*; Freshfields Bruckhaus Deringer *Companies Act 2006: Directors Duties* (November 2006) p 11; Clifford Chance *The Companies Act 2006* (November 2006) p 4. It should be stressed that not all lawyers took these views.

[207] G Milner-Moore and R Lewis, ibid.

the shareholders. There is a significant literature on the fact that having regard for stakeholder interests can benefit the company. Take, for instance, having regard for employee interests. Human resources are critical to all companies and consideration for employee interests can be key in attracting, retaining and motivating good employees.[208] All of this could lead to greater employee loyalty, morale, motivation, retention and identification with the company itself which can benefit the company,[209] in that it is likely to lead to higher productivity and less cost in addressing employee discontent and the need to replace employees leaving the company. This should foster the success of the company and benefit the members.

6.96 In assessing whether the directors have engaged in promoting the success of the company the courts might be seen as being rather hamstrung because they have no business experience, but they can listen to evidence and weigh that up. In civil cases in the UK there is no jury to confuse, and judges can make decisions on evidence and the credibility of witnesses.

6.97 The following sections of this Part of the Chapter focus on the factors that are identified in s 172(1). At the outset it should be noted that apparently the order of the factors is not intended by Parliament to indicate a hierarchy, with any factor having precedence over any others. But, obviously, in any given situation one or more might be considered of greater importance than others. For instance, companies engaged in certain types of industry might have to focus more on the issue of effects on the environment in making their decision when compared with other companies.

1 Long term

6.98 This provides that directors have a duty, when promoting the success of the company to have regard for 'the likely consequences of any decision in the long term'.

6.99 The objective of the shareholder value theory, hitherto predominant in the UK, is unclear as to whether it involves the increase of shareholder value in the short or the long term.[210] For the most part shareholder value has been linked to short-termism, which might be unfair and incorrect. Certainly some scholars adhering to this theory have not eschewed a long-term approach, particularly where it is appropriate. The theory does not really posit what shareholder value actually encompasses. It might mean 'immediate revenue or

---

[208] M Bernioff and K Southwick *Compassionate Capitalism: How the Corporations Make Doing Good an Integral Part of Doing Well* (Career Press, 2004) and referred to in D McBarnet at 19; Corporations and Markets Advisory Committee *Corporate Social Responsibility*, Discussion Paper, November 2005, Canberra at 17; E Klein and J du Plessis 'Corporate Donations, the Best Interest of the Company and the Proper Purpose Doctrine' (2005) 28 UNSWLJ 69 at 88.

[209] L Moir 'What Do We Mean By Corporate Social Responsibility?' (2001) 1 *Corporate Governance* 2 at 3.

[210] H Simon 'Theories of Decision-Making in Economics and Behavioral Science' (1959) 49 *American Economic Review* 253 at 262.

long range basic profitability of wealth-producing resources'.[211] Clearly short-term and long-term strategies differ, so there is the problem of whether short-term or long-term horizons should be set.[212]

6.100 Because of the threat of hostile takeovers, some directors have tended to act in the short-term interests of their shareholders – to keep the shareholders satisfied and so they would reject any takeover offer, and, therefore, keep them (it is hoped) in control of the management of the company. It is highly likely that if directors perceive that their positions might be under threat they will tend to manage for the short term as it is not going to be much use to them if the company is set to do well in the future, when they might not to be around when that occurs, or even around next month. Of course, managing for the long term does not mean, necessarily, that there will be lower profits in the short term, although it is likely that this will be the case.

6.101 Perhaps a good example of neglecting the long term is where a company engages in drastic cost-cutting that might achieve short-term results by improving the bottom line for a short while, but in the long-run this might deleteriously affect the company's business.[213] According to several finance academics, the shareholder value approach produces a short-term focus and short-term earnings performance overshadows all else,[214] and this fails to maximise social wealth.[215] While logically shareholder value should not necessarily lead to short-termism, with a concomitant fixation on the quarterly earnings of companies and their share value,[216] in practice this has often occurred. Henry Silverman, a chairman of a US public company, Realogy property services group, complained bitterly about shareholders being obsessed with the short term, so much that he advocated taking companies private.[217] Enron, the disgraced American energy company, is, because of the effects of its business approach, synonymous with short termism.

---

[211] P Drucker 'Business Objectives and Survival Needs: Notes on a Discipline of Business Enterprise' (1958) 31 *The Journal of Business* 81 at 82. For an instance of a court permitting a company to foster long-term benefits, see *Shlensky v Wrigley* 237 NE 2d 776 (Ill App Ct, 1968).

[212] See H Hu 'Risk 'Time and Fiduciary Principles in Corporate Investment' (1990) 38 UCLA L Rev 277. Also, see A Keay 'Getting to Grips With the Shareholder Value Theory in Corporate Law' (2010) 39 *Common Law World Review* 358.

[213] E Orts 'The Complexity and Legitimacy of Corporate Law' (1993) 50 *Washington and Lee Law Review* 1565 at 1592.

[214] S Wallman 'The Proper Interpretation of Corporate Constituency Statues and Formulation of Director Duties' (1991) 21 *Stetson Law Review* 163 at 176–177; M Lipton and S Rosenblum 'A New System of Corporate Governance: The Quinquennial Election of Directors' (1991) 58 U Chi L Rev 187, at 205–215; M E van der Weide 'Against Fiduciary Duties to Corporate Stakeholders' (1996) 21 Del J Corp L 27 at 61.

[215] Wallman, ibid at 176–177; Lipton and Rosenblum, ibid at 203; E Orts 'The Complexity and Legitimacy of Corporate Law' (1993) 50 *Washington and Lee Law Review* 1565 at 1591.

[216] See D Millon 'Why is Corporate Management Obsessed with Quarterly Earnings and What Should be Done About it?' (2002) 70 *George Washington Law Review* 890, especially, 902.

[217] T Bawden 'Surge in buyouts of quoted companies as hassled bosses line up to go private' *The Times*, 13 January 2007.

6.102   The CLRSG talked about the business relationships which companies have as important intangible assets of the company.[218] It then went on to say that 'the state of directors' duties at common law are often regarded as leading to directors having 'an undue focus on the short term and the narrow interests of members at the expense of what is in a broader and a longer term sense the best interests of the enterprise ...'[219] and so this is one reason that it favoured greater focus on the long term.

6.103   The introduction of the long term factor in s 172(1)(a) of the CA 2006 was introduced to ensure that directors did not feel compelled to think short term, something that some advocating shareholder value would say is the duty of the directors as that benefits the shareholders better. Yet, while many have said that directors have focused on short-termism, that is debatable and it is arguable whether it was ever the law of this country that directors had a duty to make short-term gains.[220] The CLRSG had said that directors were obliged to 'achieve the success of the company for the benefit of the shareholders by taking proper account of all the relevant considerations for that purpose' and this involved taking 'a proper balanced view of the short and long term'.[221] Directors were at liberty to use their commercial judgment in order to balance short- and long-term considerations.[222]

6.104   The common law, and now s 172 of the CA 2006, permits directors to consider short-term and long-term issues in making decisions. It enables directors not necessarily to aim for a high increase in the market value of the company's shares. In the Company Law Reform Bill that was part of the Government's 2005 White Paper,[223] cl B3 stated, inter alia, that directors have to have regard to: '(a) The likely consequences of any decision in both the long and the short term.' The omission of any reference to the short term in the CA 2006 led Mayson, French and Ryan to conclude that the long term is more important.[224] I am unsure whether one can necessarily draw that conclusion as undoubtedly the general thrust of the provision, with the benefit of members being the end result, would still permit consideration of the short term. Perhaps the omission of any reference to the short term is designed merely to emphasise the relevance of the long term when it has been eschewed in the past. It

---

[218] Company Law Review *Modern Company Law for a Competitive Economy: Strategic Framework* (London, DTI, 1999) at para 5.1.10.

[219] Ibid at para 5.1.17.

[220] See J Birds 'The Reform of Directors' Duties' in J de Lacy (ed) *The Reform of United Kingdom Company Law* (London, Cavendish, 2003) at 159.

[221] Company Law Review *Modern Company Law for a Competitive Economy: Developing the Framework* (London, DTI, 2000) at para 2.19.

[222] See Australian Parliamentary Joint Committee on Corporations and Financial Services 'Corporate Responsibility: Managing Risk and Creating Value,' 21 June 2006 at para 3.82 and accessible at www.aph.gov.au/Parliamentary_Business/Committees/Joint/Corporations_and_Financial_Services/Completed_inquiries/2004-07/corporate_responsibility/report/index (accessed 8 February 2016).

[223] Cm 6456, 2005, DTI.

[224] *Company Law* (OUP, 24th edn, 2007) at 457.

provides directors with a statutory base for withstanding pressure from shareholders and others to manage necessarily for the short term.

6.105 The law appears to be such that directors are not obliged, certainly now, to manage their companies so as to produce exclusively short-term benefits, such as maximising immediate profits. Courts in other jurisdictions have stated that directors may take account of the long-term well-being of a company.[225] The law has permitted directors to reduce the size of the wealth of the company by, for instance, granting bonuses to employees on the basis that to do so may benefit the company both immediately and in the future.[226] But, directors are not prevented from managing for short-term gains; it is a matter of a commercial judgment on their part. If they believe that it will promote the success of the company for the benefit of the members, provided that they have had regard for long-term considerations in their thinking and decision-making they can manage for the short-term.

6.106 Essentially, directors must now ask themselves: 'What is likely to result from the decisions we make today in the long term?'[227] Clearly, there appears to be a difference between what the case was before the advent of the CA 2006 and since its introduction, but, as suggested above, prior to the inclusion of s 172(1)(a) many directors did look at the long term in certain situations and did not generally only focus on the short-term effects of their decisions. For example, if a company were to expand and open a new factory, it would be clear that the short-term costs of facilitating this process[228] would be huge, but it might well produce handsome benefits in the long term.

6.107 It is sometimes thought that all shareholders necessarily want directors to focus on short-term benefits. But this is not necessarily correct. When the International Accounting Standards Board stated in a discussion paper that 'equity investors see companies as a source of cash in the form of dividends (or other cash distribution) and increase in the prices of shares or other ownership interests',[229] the Investment Management Association, the trade body representing the asset management industry in the UK, indicated that it disagreed and it asserted that members want financial reports from companies to enable them to carry out a stewardship role, as part of their role of assessing management and corporate strategy for the long-term benefit of the business. Along similar lines, the Australian Parliamentary Joint Committee on Corporations and Financial Services in its report, 'Corporate Responsibility: Managing Risk and Creating Value',[230] was of the view that most shareholders were happy to support corporate responsibility as that will lead to shareholder gains, either in the short or long term.

---

[225] *Provident International Corporation v International Leasing Corp Ltd* [1969] 1 NSWR 424 at 440; *Paramount Communications Inc v Time* Inc 571 A 2d 1140 (Del, 1989).

[226] *Hampson v Price's Patent Candle Co* (1876) 45 LJ Ch 437.

[227] S Sheikh *A Guide to the Companies Act 2006* (London, Routledge/Cavendish, 2008) at 403.

[228] Including building the factory, creating more jobs and so on.

[229] Referred to in the Investment Management Association's response. This used to be available at

6.108 Concern for long-term wealth is something that has been advocated even by those who have been the most fervent supporters of shareholder value. In their well-known article, 'The End of History for Corporate Law',[231] Professors Henry Hansmann and Reiner Kraakman said that there was 'no longer any serious competitor to the view that corporate law should principally strive to increase long-term shareholder value'. Professor Michael Jensen, a long-time advocate of shareholder value, agreed.[232] However the focus of these and other commentators is on long-term shareholder value, while s 172 talks rather vaguely about the fact that directors are to have regard for the likely consequences of any decision in the long term. In this regard it has been asserted that meeting the fair expectations of stakeholder groups is necessary for long-term profitability.[233] Yet that is not necessarily consistent with long-term shareholder value.

6.109 It has been suggested by Loughrey et al that:[234]

> 'It is at least possible though, that directors seeking to minimise *ex ante* the risks of derivative action, may take the view that section 172 requires them to consider the long-term consequences of their decisions and the other statutory factors when reaching decisions, where they had not done so previously.'

6.110 Challenging directors for allegedly failing to consider long-term issues is accompanied by evidential problems. Shareholders with a long-term perspective might take the view that despite the rhetoric from the directors that they have made a decision based on long-term considerations, 'the board in fact adopted a short-termist approach. However, as this would amount to a challenge to the board's good faith, such a claim would face evidential difficulties as well as other obstacles.'[235]

6.111 It might well be thought that it is only where shareholders embrace a long-term inclusive approach, but directors clearly do not, that there is the potential for shareholders to demonstrate that a decision does not comply with the general duty, using the same kinds of long-term performance benchmarks as directors adopting an inclusive long-term view might.[236]

---

www.investmentfunds.org.uk/news/research/2006/topic/corporate_governance/ imaresponsetoiasbdponconceptualframework.pdf, but is no longer.

[230] Australian Parliamentary Joint Committee on Corporations and Financial Services 'Corporate Responsibility: Managing Risk and Creating Value,' 21 June 2006 at para 4.22 and accessible at: www.aph.gov.au/Senate/committee/corporations_ctte/corporate_responsibility/report/ report.pdf.

[231] (2001) 89 *Georgetown Law Journal* 439.

[232] M Jensen 'Value Maximisation, Stakeholder Theory and the Corporate Objective Function' (2001) 7(3) *European Financial Management* 297 at 309.

[233] R S Karmel 'Implications of the Stakeholder Model' (1993) 61 *George Washington Law Review* 1156 at 1169.

[234] 'Legal Practitioners, Enlightened Shareholder Value and the Shaping of Corporate Governance' (2008) 8 *Journal of Corporate Law Studies* 79 at 100.

[235] Ibid at 107.

[236] Ibid.

6.112 There will be shareholders who internalise the requirements of s 172 of the CA 2006, and regard compliance with it as an indication of good practice in the conduct of their company's business. But other shareholders may have the opposite perception, and may take the view that the section simply institutes a more bureaucratic decision-making process, and ought not to affect the substantive outcome of directors' decisions. The former group will adopt a long-term view when assessing whether the company is being managed for their benefit. In contrast the latter group is more likely to include those who take a short-term approach, embracing the opinion that a company is run for their benefit when the outcomes of directors' decisions bring them immediately visible advantages, such as an increase in share price.[237]

6.113 One would think that no derivative action would be initiated by shareholders against directors for breach of the duty either when both shareholders and directors internalise the requirements of s 172 of the CA 2006 or where neither fails to do so. In the former circumstances shareholders will be content with the way that directors act where it involves a long-term, inclusive approach, especially if shareholders perceive that this approach is governed by objective yardsticks which will monitor the company's performance. Shareholders might seek to take proceedings against directors when they do not wish directors to consider long-term matters, and directors do so. In this situation, shareholders who wish to impugn the decision of a board because they, the shareholders, favour a short-term focus, may argue that the duty required the promotion of the short-term interests of members over other factors listed in s 172. Shareholders also might bring proceedings if they want directors to have regard to long-term considerations and the directors do not. In other cases directors will obviously fall back on the argument that what they did, they did in good faith and believed that it would promote the success of the company for the benefit of the members. Certainly the inclusion of the long-term factor in the section seems to mean that directors can consider long-term matters with potentially greater impunity from attack, when in the past they might have been concerned that shareholders might get restless and seek to initiate proceedings.[238]

6.114 Finally, what might constitute a failure to have regard to the long term? This depends on a lot of factors, such as the size of the company, the company's business and the nature of the relevant marketplace. The ICSA Guidance on Directors' General Duties gives the example of a failure to consider the long term where a pharmaceutical company cuts the research and development budget.[239]

---

[237] Ibid.

[238] Ibid at 106.

[239] February 2008 at para 3.2.1. Research and development is usually an investment made in order to generate future cash and profit flows: J Grinyer, A Russell and D Collison 'Evidence of Managerial Short-termism in the UK' (1998) 9 *British Journal of Management* 13 at 14.

2 Employees

6.115   The second factor mentioned in s 172(1) of the CA 2006 provides that directors, in making decisions, are to have in mind 'the interests of the company's employees'. Given the fact that s 309 of the CA 1985 made special provision for employees and that they do, in many businesses, form a critical element of the company, it is not surprising to see special mention of this group. Employees had, prima facie, some protection in s 309, as we have seen, but this provision gave no benefit to employees, and was described by one commentator as 'either one of the most incompetent or one of the most cynical pieces of drafting on record'.[240]

6.116   The inclusion of employees in the list of s 172 factors is especially pertinent when one considers the fact that employees invest firm-specific human capital in the company and they 'are not merely automata in charge of operating valuable assets but valuable assets themselves, operating with commodity-like physical assets'.[241] Nevertheless, employee interests have been given relatively little attention,[242] and this places them in a position where they are vulnerable to management caprice.[243] It has been suggested that because employees no longer 'enjoy' the position of being the sole stakeholder besides shareholders whose interests have to be considered by directors, because of the repeal of s 309, this potentially downgrades the importance of the interests of employees.[244] The case of *Parke v Daily News*[245] demonstrates the tendency to downgrade employees' interests. In this case the directors of a newspaper company decided to sell two of their company's newspapers, and the proceeds of the sale were to be divided up between the company's employees because they would be made redundant as a consequence of the sale. This was held to be contrary to the best interests of the company's shareholders, and while the directors' motives were generous, their action went beyond a legal entitlement.

6.117   Would the decision be any different if the facts of *Parke v Daily News* came before a court under the new law? The facts and the directors' rationale for their actions would be critical. This is because directors still have to consider what is best for the company's members as a whole, whilst only having regard to its employees' interests. The effect of this is that it is unlikely that directors will make a decision for the benefit of employees unless it will confer some further benefit on shareholders, possibly not in the short term, but certainly at some stage. However, s 172 is exempted from consideration when

---

[240]   L S Sealy 'Directors' "Wider" Responsibilities – Problems Conceptual, Practical and Procedural' (1987) 13 *Monash University Law Review* 164 at 177.

[241]   L Zingales 'In Search of New Foundations' (2000) 55 *Journal of Finance* 1623 at 1641.

[242]   K Wedderburn 'Companies and employees: common law or social dimension' (1993) 109 LQR 220.

[243]   See M O'Connor 'The Human Capital Era' (1993) 78 Cornell L Rev 899 at 905-917.

[244]   C Wynn-Evans 'The Companies Act 2006 and the Interests of Employees' (2007) 36 *Industrial Law Journal* 188 at 191.

[245]   [1962] Ch 927.

s 247 of the CA 2006 applies.[246] This latter provision provides that directors may make provision for employees on the cessation or transfer of a company's business even if this would otherwise constitute a breach of the general duty to promote the success of the company. So, if we were given the facts of *Parke v Daily News* under the new law, it is likely that the directors' action would be protected by s 247.

6.118 What might a court today do with the facts of *Hampson v Price's Patent Candle Co*?[247] In that case the directors made gratuitous payments to employees on account of their exertions in helping the company to be profitable. It was in effect an annual bonus. A disgruntled shareholder brought proceedings against the company arguing that the directors had acted beyond their powers. The court rejected the claim on the basis, inter alia, that giving payments to employees was likely to spur them on to work even harder in the future for the good of the company.[248] In his judgment Jessel MR said that the directors know how to conduct the company's business to the most advantage and they should be permitted to decide whether an action was advantageous for the company or not. The same result could well occur under the new law, particularly if employee payments can be tied to the development of the business and that is likely to benefit the members at some point. Would the payments in *Hampson v Price's Patent Candle Co* be permissible where the result was that the amount to be received by members is reduced? Arguably it is allowable under s 172(1) of the CA 2006 provided that there is some good reason for it and it is connected with promoting the success of the company, perhaps as it retains important employees or fosters morale (and that will lead to long-term member benefits). Of course, as with all of what we are considering the good faith of the directors is an essential element, and, as we have seen, save in a few situations, it is going to be hard to impugn the directors' actions on the basis that they did not act in good faith.

6.119 The kinds of matters that affect employees and might be taken into consideration by directors are: the payment of bonuses (with the rationale being the same as that discerned in *Hampson v Price's Patent*); taking into account employee views on relocation of company operations; redundancies; and health and safety issues related to the company's plants and offices. The ICSA Guidance on Directors' General Duties gives as an example of not having regard to the interests of the company's employees, the closing down of a plant to outsource abroad, thus leading to redundancies among the existing staff.[249]

6.120 Of course, having regard for the factors mentioned in s 172 of the CA 2006 is something that must occur along with promoting the success of the company. For instance, considering the interests of employees might enable it to

---

[246] The section became operative on 1 October 2007: Companies Act 2006 (Commencement No 3, Consequential Amendments, Transitional Provisions and Savings) Order 2007, SI 2007/2194.

[247] (1876) 45 LJ Ch 437.

[248] Ibid at 439.

[249] February 2008 at para 3.2.1.

recruit more qualified workers and to retain those who are invaluable to the operations of the company, thus producing future benefits for the company, and, as a result, for members.

3 Suppliers and customers

6.121 Directors must, according to s 172(1)(c) of the CA 2006, have regard to 'to the need to foster the company's business relationships with suppliers, customers and others'. No business is able to operate without links and dealings with other firms and people. In some shape or form all companies have suppliers and customers. The intention behind this is obviously to ensure relations which will produce long-term gains for the company. However, it has been suggested that this adds nothing to the case prior to the CA 2006 for, although directors owed no fiduciary duty to these groups, they still had a moral duty[250] to them. This is manifested by the regular dealings that many businesses have with such groups and the fact that a company is dependent upon them in order to function. Obviously all companies need goods and services to be supplied to them and to sell goods, services etc to customers, whether they be end of the line consumers or other companies in the production and marketing chain. An example of meeting this requirement in s 172 is ensuring that suppliers are paid on time. When the word 'customer' is referred to, most probably think of consumers and the marketing literature indicates that if one can retain a customer's loyalty to a product then that benefits the company as its marketing costs are reduced and production and sales volume are able to be firmed up.[251]

4 The community and the environment

6.122 Section 172(1)(d) of the CA 2006 requires directors to take into account 'the impact of the company's operations on the community and the environment'. It is particularly difficult to understand what this actually means and what actions are covered by it. For instance, the notion of the 'community' might be regarded as rather amorphous.[252] It is certainly a concept that is difficult to pin down. It could well be taken to include the people, businesses and institutions (including schools, hospitals, national and local governments) located in, and around, the places where the company operates.

6.123 With regard to the community, it is difficult to ascertain when it should be considered as many decisions taken by directors can have an adverse effect,

---

[250] S Sheikh *A Guide to the Companies Act 2006* (London, Routledge/Cavendish, 2008) at 408, fn 1772.

[251] F Webster 'The Changing Role of Marketing in the Corporation' (1992) 58 *Journal of Management* 1 and referred to in L Cerioni 'The Success of the Company in s.172(1) of the UK Companies Act 2006: Towards an Enlightened Directors' Primacy' (2008) 4 *Original Law Review* 1 at 6.

[252] W Carney 'Does Defining Constituencies Matter?' (1990) 59 *University of Cincinnati Law Review* 385 at 414.

or may have a potentially adverse effect, on the community.[253] Again, it turns upon the general requirement that the directors must be acting for the benefit of the company's members as a whole, which means that the community interests[254] might well be overlooked. Often the focus is on health issues for the local community, but a community will also be affected if the company decides to close its factory and relocate elsewhere. Clearly such action would affect employees first and foremost, but the effect can be far wider, especially if the company is large. Closure could mean that small businesses that supplied either the company or its workers (in their private capacities) would have to terminate their activities as well, leading to wider redundancies. Schools and community groups might be affected by the fact that workers might need to relocate with the company or, if made redundant, move elsewhere to obtain a new job. The effect of a termination of business is well illustrated by the insolvency of the car maker MGRover and the subsequent closure of its huge factory at Longbridge, near Birmingham in 2005. The company employed directly about 20,000 workers as well as having relationships with a host of suppliers that relied on orders from MGRover either in a major way or for their total business activities. Many business relied on the custom of Longbridge workers. The closure of the company's factory had a major impact, economically and socially, on the Longbridge area.

6.124 Having regard for the community might manifest itself in a number of ways, such as a donation to a local cause or refraining from certain actions which might deleteriously affect the community. However, directors must remember that they have to justify any such action as enhancing the success of the company. This does not, it is submitted, necessarily, mean that success has to be reduced directly to monetary terms. Having an input in the community might be seen as contributing to the success of the company as a respected local firm, and part of its role as a good citizen. This might enhance its reputation, which could arguably contribute to the company's success and ultimately benefit the members.

6.125 Of course, in a number of cases the interests of the community and those of the environment will overlap, but while the community tends to mean a focus on individuals and groups of individuals, the environment is likely to be limited to the natural world. Of course, a number of things that could affect the latter will also affect the former. For instance, if a company permits noxious liquids to escape from its factory, it will endanger the environment and also, as a result, it might be deleterious for the community.

6.126 Presumably, given the state of the world today, the Government included the requirement concerning the environment as part of its efforts to

---

[253] For example a company could open an unsightly factory which would be unfavourable in the community or may opt to close a factory which would have an adverse effect on the community through job cuts.

[254] A good example would be the closing of a factory – if it is seen that it is not in the interests of the members to keep the factory running (if it is losing money) the fact that it will have an adverse effect on the community will not prevent its closure.

encourage companies to protect the environment by reducing emissions and pollution. In having regard to the community and the environment may simply mean complying with proper procedures laid down by council by-laws, environmental regulations and health and safety measures. One effect of the provision might be that if called upon to adjudicate what the directors have done, courts may well not see expenditure for the benefit of the community as being contrary to the success of the company. Moreover, companies are increasingly having regard to communities and the environment. An example is the supermarket Tesco. In 2008 it had plans to open a large distribution centre outside Andover, but encountered considerable criticism from local people, primarily based on potential congestion caused by lorries arriving at the centre. The company indicated its intention to take into account the community and environment and introduced a 10-point community plan, with pledges to increase local sourcing and to consult local communities in an attempt to be viewed as a good neighbour.[255]

6.127 Of course, a company can be very cynical and seek to placate members of the local community with apparent positive actions, but where there is little substance. But failure to take action can damage a company's reputation, which can be seen as the most important intangible asset of a company.[256] Firms have economic incentives to have a good reputation in communities where they have offices and factories – they might be subject to higher taxes or find it harder to recruit workers if their reputation suffers.[257] A company might decline to take on a project that despite being potentially profitable could alienate the local or wider community and lead to the entity being derided, and see its reputation diminish.

6.128 Directors would be best advised, one would think, to instruct independent consultants who have expertise in environmental and health matters to assist them in determining what effect decisions might have on communities and the environment.

6.129 The ICSA in its Guidance on Directors' General Duties has said that:

> 'it is first necessary to identify the community or communities of which the company is a part (eg the board of a bank may need to consider the impact on the community in certain localities of a proposed programme of branch closures. On the environment, a manufacturing company would need to consider the effect of alternative proposed new industrial processes on its carbon footprint).'

---

[255] Julia Finch 'Arriving soon at Stonehenge: 480 trucks a day from Tesco's "megashed"' *The Guardian*, 23 February 2008.

[256] J Dean *Directing Public Companies: Company Law and the Stakeholder Society* (London, Cavendish, 2001) at 107. Also, see S Letza, X Sun and J Kirkbride 'Shareholding and Stakeholding: A Critical Review of Corporate Governance' (2004) 12 *Corporate Governance* 242 at, 255; R Woolley 'Shareholder Analysis' 31 *Company Secretary's Review* 62 (8 August 2007).

[257] L Ribstein, 'Accountability and Responsibility in Corporate Governance' (2006) 81 Notre Dame L Rev 1431 at 1457–1458.

5 High standards of business conduct

6.130 Section 172(1)(e) of the CA 2006 provides that directors must have regard for maintaining a reputation for high standards for business conduct. This is rather a vague requirement. It is unclear what it would mean for any company. It is something that one would expect a company's management to consider. It covers values and ethics, and perhaps adhering to a particular code of conduct – either one it formulates or one that has been drafted by a trade or business association to which the company belongs. Clearly it is highly desirable for a company to be regarded as credible and trustworthy, and holding high standards of conduct can have this effect.[258] One would think that it covers the company's dealing with customers and, where it sells to the public, consumers, and in some ways would overlap with s 172(1)(c).

6 Members

6.131 The final factor, found in s 172(1)(f) of the CA 2006 provides that directors are to have regard to the need to act fairly as between members of the company. It means that directors are not permitted to favour one group of members over and above another group. It is the case that at common law directors were not permitted to exercise their powers in a partial manner, improperly preferring one section of the shareholders over another.[259] So, in many ways it is a restatement of the previous law.[260]

6.132 An example of a case where it was argued that members had not been treated fairly as against other members is *Mutual Life Insurance v Rank Organisation Ltd*[261] In that case the directors of the company, Rank, had given shareholders, other than their North American shareholders, the right to subscribe for new shares of the same class. There was evidence that the North Americans had been excluded because the company did not wish to comply with the requirements for registration of the Securities and Exchange Commission (SEC) in the United States and equivalent authorities in Canada. The directors had had advice from merchant bankers, which they had accepted, and which was in turn based on an investigation by accountants, that to register with the SEC would not be in the interests of the company. The North American shareholders in Rank claimed the company had acted in breach of the articles. They claimed that their shares entitled them to equal treatment without discrimination. The argument was rejected by the court. In the light of the wide powers which the directors had under the articles the judge held that the directors' power of allotment was only to be restricted by two implied terms: first, directors' powers are to be exercised in good faith in the interests of the company; second, powers must be exercised fairly as between different

---

[258] See the Annotations to G20/OECD *Principles of Corporate Governance*, September 2015, at p 53 and accessible at www.oecd.org/corporate/principles-corporate-governance.htm.

[259] *Howard Smith Ltd v Ampol Petroleum* [1974] AC 821.

[260] See *Mills v Mills* (1938) 60 CLR 150 at 164; *Re BSB Holdings Ltd (No 2)* [1996] 1 BCLC 155 at 246–249.

[261] [1985] BCLC 11.

shareholders.[262] On the facts of the case, Goulding J held that the directors had acted in the best interests of Rank and that there had been no unfairness between the two groups of shareholders.

6.133 The ICSA Guidance on Directors' General Duties has stated that the directors need to ensure that private shareholders are not disadvantaged by the structure of corporate transactions or share issues, or by lack of information, and it suggests that the company's website is a useful way to address the last matter so as to avoid inequality.[263]

6.134 The benefit in a company treating its members fairly is, inter alia, that the existing members might be willing to take up new share issues, thereby reducing the cost of the company obtaining additional capital, and, of course, it is likely to reduce the likelihood of disaffected shareholders bringing legal actions against the company or using any other means of bringing pressure to bear on the directors.[264] Failure to have regard to this factor might form the basis for a s 994 application by a shareholder because the shareholder has been unfairly prejudiced.

7 Summary

6.135 There is a danger that s 172(1) of the CA 2006 can lead to unnecessary bureaucracy and record-keeping that might deflect boards from making wise and appropriate decisions. However, the Government's spokespersons, as well as many of those advising companies, have robustly said that this should not be the case. Obviously, what the courts say and how they interpret the provision in light of specific facts will be of critical importance and will be likely to determine the practice of boards in the future. Until cases provide more guidance concerning the section and its application, boards might continue to feel uneasy.

6.136 It would seem to be the case that directors cannot be expected, at all times, to make decisions which foster the interests of all those which have a stake in the company as in some cases the various interests are likely to conflict with each other. Does this mean that the directors must make a choice or effect a balance? This issue was broached earlier, when considering the judgment in *Re Phoenix Contracts (Leicester) Ltd (sub nom: Shepherd v Phoenix Contracts (Leicester) Ltd)*,[265] but it is taken up also in the next section of the chapter in the context of the meaning of 'have regard to'.

6.137 In any event it must be emphasised again that all of the factors mentioned above are subordinate to the requirement to promote the success of the company for *the benefit of the members* – their interests are primary.

---

[262] The decision was followed in *Re BSB Holdings Ltd (No 2)* [1996] 1 BCLC 155.
[263] February 2008, at para 3.2.1.
[264] Such as complaining to the media.
[265] [2010] EWHC 2375 (Ch).

F 'Have regard to'

6.138   As we have seen, s 172 of the CA 2006 requires directors to have regard to a menu of stakeholder interests. In what manner should regard be given by the directors to these interests? Neither s 172 nor any other provision in the CA 2006 explains what it means when it states that a director is 'to have regard to' the interests mentioned in the section, or how directors are to consider such interests other than those of the members, in the decisions that they are making. Furthermore, neither does the Guidance to Key Clauses issued with the draft Bill in the March 2005 White Paper, nor do the Explanatory Notes to the CA 2006 assist. An issue that is critical in this regard is whether enlightened shareholder value means that directors are merely to take other constituencies into account insofar as this promotes shareholder value – a purely instrumental concern with constituency interests – or whether it enables or even requires directors to be concerned with such interests as ends in themselves. The background to the provision, together with the way that it is drafted suggests that the former interpretation is probably correct. If so, then what relevance do other interests have? The phrase, 'have regard to' suggests, according to the *New Oxford Dictionary of English*, that one pays attention to or is concerned about something.[266] What does this mean in the context of s 172?

6.139   It has been suggested that these words mean that directors are required to be aware systematically of the listed factors just discussed, as well as any other factors which may pertain to the company's interests in respect of a particular matter, and to take them into account in the decision-making process.[267] It has been suggested further that the foregoing should not be done in isolation, but should occur in the broader context of determining whether a particular course of action would be likely to promote the success of the company.[268] It is likely that the situation which will lead to directors being at most risk of being in breach of their duty is if they did not give adequate attention to any of the factors addressed in s 172 of the CA 2006 and resultant decisions are clearly unsuccessful in business terms.[269] It has been said[270] that this might happen:

> 'where a company fails to put in place adequate environmental protection controls – a reference to point (d) above – which results in pollution, death or injury to employees or third parties and, consequently, loss of revenue and consumer confidence in the company. Directors might also be at risk of breaching their responsibilities under section 172 where they allow their company to engage in illicit business practices – a reference to point (e) above – and where the exposure

---

[266] J Pearsall (ed) (OUP, 2001) at 1561.
[267] J Davies 'A Guide to Directors Obligations Under the Companies Act 2006' Association of Chartered Certified Accountants, August 2007, at para 6.38, and accessible at www.accaglobal.com/content/dam/acca/global/PDF-technical/business-law/tech-tp-cdd.pdf.
[268] Ibid at para 6.38.
[269] Ibid.
[270] Ibid.

of those activities leads to bad publicity for the company, regulatory or criminal action against it and, in the long run, adverse consequences for the company's commercial and business interests.'

6.140 It will not be sufficient for directors merely to pay lip service to the factors, and, in many cases the directors will need to take action to comply with this aspect of the duty.[271] In a Ministerial Statement that purported to give guidance to directors the then Minister responsible for the legislation, Margaret Hodge MP, stated that 'have regard to' meant that directors were 'to give proper consideration to' the factors,[272] something that she said earlier in the Commons.[273]

6.141 During the passage of the Bill through Parliament, Margaret Hodge MP, said: 'We believe it is essential for the weight given to any factor to be a matter for the director's good faith judgement. Importantly, the decision is not subject to the reasonableness test.'[274] The Government promised to publish a plain English guidance explaining what directors must do to comply with the general duties. It did not do so, though it did in June 2007 publish the Ministerial Statement referred to above, but it was a document that included a very glib statement of what directors should do. This was contained in an introduction by the relevant minister and followed by some quotations made by ministers in the Parliamentary debates.[275] This is wholly inadequate. Many of the statements need legal interpretation, and while we cannot expect the Government to provide a detailed and authoritative interpretation, which is a matter for the courts, one would have thought that more could have been done by way of guidance for directors. Directors probably do not have much more guidance after nearly 10 years of the existence of the provision.

6.142 In having regard to the factors listed, the duty of care, skill and diligence found in s 174 of the CA 2006 will apply.

6.143 The lack of guidance for directors is particularly concerning where there is a conflict or a potential conflict between various interests, not, one would think, an infrequent occurrence. The CLRSG recognised the fact that where the long-term interests of the company are in view, there could well be a clash between the interests of some or all of those mentioned in s 172(1)(a)–(f), on the one hand, and those of the shareholders, on the other.[276] Examples given by the CLRSG included the closing down of a plant or the termination of a

[271] Explanatory Notes to the Companies Act 2006, at para 328.
[272] 'Duties of Company Directors' DTI, June 2007, Introduction and Statement of Rt Hon Margaret Hodge MP, at 9, and available at http://webarchive.nationalarchives.gov.uk/20070603164510/http://www.dti.gov.uk/files/file40139.pdf.
[273] HC Comm D 7 October 2006, col 789.
[274] HC Comm D 11 July 2006, cols 591–593.
[275] 'Duties of Company Directors' (DTI, June 2007), Introduction and Statement of Rt Hon Margaret Hodge, and available at http://webarchive.nationalarchives.gov.uk/20070603164510/http://www.dti.gov.uk/files/file40139.pdf.
[276] Company Law Review *Modern Company Law for a Competitive Economy*: 'The Strategic Framework' (London, DTI, 1999) at para 5.1.15.

long-term supply contract when the continuation of either will impact adversely on shareholder returns.[277] If there is a conflict, do the directors have to engage in a balancing exercise as demanded by stakeholder theory (discussed in **Chapter 2**)? This is considered below. Before doing so one might say that it is rather strange, as Stephen Copp notes, that one should 'promote some good cause A by having regard to some potentially conflicting causes B, C, D, and/or E'.[278]

6.144   What happens if the company could follow one of two avenues, let us refer to them as 'A' and 'B', with both benefiting the company equally, but where A will also benefit one or more constituency interests and B will not. Does A have to be followed? What if one option is marginally better for shareholders, but the other option fulfils one or more of the factors mentioned in s 172 of the CA 2006? Is having regard to the interests of others going to mean that directors will decide not to do something that is beneficial for the company's members? Surely this cannot be the case as that would not meet the overall obligation of directors, namely to promote the success of the company for the benefit of the members as a whole.

6.145   The term 'have regard to' does not give any idea as to what weight should be given to individual factors.[279] This is something that is left to the directors and their discretion which is to be exercised in good faith. It might mean that directors seek to balance the various interests in the company. What if a course of action is going to promote the success of the company and benefit the members, but the directors ascertain that this action can be implemented in one of two ways, with each way enhancing the interests of different constituencies? Are directors to engage in a balancing exercise in such circumstances? Clearly, the balancing of stakeholder interests is, of itself, a tricky issue, and it means that directors have to solve what some commentators see as impossible conflicts of interests.[280] Balancing involves an 'inherently subjective process',[281] and has been the subject of significant criticism over the years,[282] particularly in relation to the need to balance the interests of constituencies. For instance, in its response to the second White Paper and the

---

[277]   Ibid.

[278]   S Copp 'Corporate Social Responsibility and the Companies Act 2006' (2009) *Economic Affairs* 16 at 19 (December).

[279]   J Davies 'A Guide to Directors Obligations Under the Companies Act 2006' Association of Chartered Certified Accountants, August 2007, at para 6.38, and accessible at www.accaglobal.com/content/dam/acca/global/PDF-technical/business-law/tech-tp-cdd.pdf.

[280]   J Macey 'An Economic Analysis of the Various Rationales for Making Shareholders the Exclusive Beneficiaries of Corporate Fiduciary Duties' (1991) 21 *Stetson Law Review* 31 at 31; V Jelisavcic 'A Safe Harbour Proposal to Define the Limits of Directors' Fiduciary Duty to Creditors in the "Vicinity of Insolvency"' [1992] *Journal of Corporation Law* 145 at 148. This view gains some support from the Ontario High Court of Justice in *Royal Bank of Canada v First Pioneer Investments Ltd* (1980) 20 OR (2d) 352.

[281]   J Parkinson 'Models of the Company and the Employment Relationship' (2003) 41 *British Journal of Industrial Relations* 481 at 498.

[282]   For instance, see T Hurst and L McGuiness 'The Corporation, The Bondholder and Fiduciary Duties' (1991) 10 *Journal of Law and Commerce* 187 at 205; M Siems 'Shareholders, Stakeholders and the "Ordoliberalism"' (2002) 13 EBLR 139 at 141.

draft Bill, in 2005, the Law Society for England and Wales indicated significant concern in relation to directors having to weigh up the list of factors contained in the precursor of s 172 of the CA 2006, cl 156(3) of the Bill, when making decisions, fearing that it will lead to practical problems.[283] It might be argued that directors will not understand the interests of non-shareholder groups as directors are usually involved in exercising entrepreneurial skills.[284] Allied to this is the fact that directors' thinking is, generally, too centred on shareholder benefits, as, arguably, they have to be, especially in light of the fact that the directors are to promote the success of the company for the benefit of the members, to be able to focus on what are the interests of others.

6.146 Some might feel that directors could use a balancing exercise as an opportunity to foster their own self-interest.[285] With directors having greater discretion in deciding what interests to take into account, it might be thought that shareholders will have more difficulty in monitoring the performance of directors, and directors might resist claims of breach of duty on the basis that what they did was based on a consideration of the interests of one or more parties mentioned in s 172 of the CA 2006. Are a company's managers in a position to carry out a fair and efficient balancing of the interests on the basis that they might well be looking to take into account their own interests, often at odds with those of some constituencies?[286] This might be particularly pertinent when one considers s 172(1)(f) and the need to ensure that the directors act fairly between the members of the company. Directors might be minded to favour one group over another for personal reasons. Also, because executive directors have a compensation package that provides for share options some directors might be minded to take action that is likely to boost the share price.

6.147 Nevertheless, it might be argued that if directors were to engage in the balancing of interests, it has its attractions. First,[287] it has been argued that resolving conflicts is part and parcel of being a director. Some management specialists have even said that managing competing interests is a primary function of management.[288] The fact that the balancing of diverse interests is

---

[283] June 2005 at 35. The reply can be accessed at the Society's Website – www.lawsociety.org.uk.

[284] M van der Weide 'Against Fiduciary Duties to Corporate Stakeholders' (1996) 21 *Delaware Journal of Corporate Law* 27 at 60.

[285] M Roe 'The Shareholder Wealth Maximization Norm and Industrial Organization' (2001) U Pa L Rev 2063 at 2065.

[286] J Parkinson 'Models of the Company and the Employment Relationship' (2003) 41 *British Journal of Industrial Relations* 481 at 498.

[287] The ensuing points draw on material in A Keay 'Formulating a Framework for Directors' Duties to Creditors: An Entity Maximisation Approach' (2005) 64 CLJ 614 at 623–625.

[288] H Ansoff *Strategic Management* (Englewood Cliffs, Prentice-Hall, 1984) and referred to in J Harrison and R Freeman 'Stakeholders, Social Responsibility and Performance: Empirical Evidence and Theoretical Perspectives' (1999) 42 *Academy of Management Journal* 479 at 479. Management commentators have asserted that directors are in effect to act as referees between two stakeholder groups (M Aoki *The co-operative game theory of the firm* (Oxford, Clarendon Press, 1984) and referred to in T Donaldson and L Preston 'The Stakeholder Theory of the Corporation Concepts, Evidence, and Implications' (1995) 20 The *Academy of Management Review* 65 at 86).

within directors' abilities and skills is something that has been recognised as far back as 1973 by a UK Department of Trade and Industry Report,[289] and by some American courts.[290] Directors have been classified as fiduciaries and society regularly requires those who are fiduciaries to make balanced decisions that can be quite difficult.[291] Proponents of the need/ability of directors to balance might point to another kind of fiduciary, the trustee. Trustees have to make investment decisions sometimes with various categories of beneficiaries in mind. Second, while it is argued that it is easier to police how directors are acting when directors are only to act for shareholders and no one else,[292] it must not be forgotten that once all is said and done, that it is not always easy to perceive what is in the best interests of the shareholders, and directors have to balance various elements when deciding what is the best for shareholders. For example, directors might have to consider whether to take a particular action which, although it might boost the company's share price, it will also reduce the likelihood of dividends for a period.

6.148   Third, as adverted to above, there are different kinds of shares and it has been incumbent on directors to balance the interests of the various shareholders, so that they act fairly between them[293] for, on occasions, these different classes of shareholders have opposing interests.[294] Some shareholders intend only to retain shares for a short term, while others want to invest for a longer term. Other shareholders hold a diversified portfolio, with their investment spread amongst a number of different companies with divergent interests, and still others might have all their investment concentrated in the one company. In companies that are closely-held, one might have the problem of the conflicting interests of controlling and minority shareholders.

6.149   How have directors conducted themselves in the past? Have they engaged in balancing? There is evidence that directors are often seeking to balance interests in the decisions which they make.[295] The chairman of the US company, Standard Oil, stated, in 1946, that the business of companies should be carried on 'in such a way as to maintain an equitable and working balance among the claims of the various directly interested groups – stockholders,

---

[289]   *Company Law Reform* (Cmnd 5391) at paras 55–59.

[290]   For example, *Unocal Corp v Mesa Petroleum Corp* (1985) 493 A 2d 946.

[291]   R Campbell Jr 'Corporate Fiduciary Principles for the Post-Contractarian Era' (1996) 23 *Florida State University Law Review* 561 at 593.

[292]   For example, R Clark *Corporate Law* (1986) at 20 and referred to in Committee on Corporate Laws 'Other Constituency Statutes: Potential for Confusion' (1990) 45 Bus Law 2253 at 2270.

[293]   *Mills v Mills* (1938) 60 CLR 150 at 164; *Re BSB Holdings Ltd (No 2)* [1996] 1 BCLC 155 at 246–249.

[294]   M McDaniel 'Bondholders and Stockholders' (1988) 13 *Journal of Corporation Law* 205 at 273; R B Campbell Jr 'Corporate Fiduciary Principles for the Post-Contractarian Era' (1996) 23 Florida State University Law Review 561 at 593; R de R Barondes 'Fiduciary Duties of Officers and Directors of Distressed Corporations' (1998) 7 *George Mason Law Review* 45 at 78.

[295]   It has been noted that directors do already consider the interests of various constituents: *Report of the Committee on Corporate Governance* (chair, Sir Ronald Hampel) (1998) and referred to by J Dine 'Implementation of European Initiatives in the UK: The Role of Fiduciary Duties' (1999) 3 CfiLR 218 at 223.

employees, customers and the public at large'.[296] More recently, a corporate reputation survey of *Fortune 500* companies (the largest listed companies in the US) found that satisfying the interests of one stakeholder does not automatically mean that this is at the expense of other stakeholders.[297] This is supported by empirical evidence, obtained in a study by the *Financial Times* of Europe's most respected companies, which found that chief executive officers were of the view that one of the features of a good company director was the ability to ensure that there was a balancing of the interests of stakeholder groups.[298] Recent studies[299] suggest that many large public companies certainly have gone further than having regard to at least some of the factors enumerated in s 172(1). There are indications that company directors have exceeded the general expectations encapsulated in both s 172 and earlier comments made by academics, policymakers and practitioners. Ahmed A-Hawarndeh et al have suggested that 'many companies may have internal rankings of the importance of stakeholders depending on what is concerned'.[300]

6.150 So, while there is a case for balancing, it is undeniable that at times directors might have some difficulty if they have to balance the interests that are mentioned in paras (a)-(f) of s 172(1), especially now that the factors to be balanced are enumerated in statute, whereas before there was no statutory direction. But I think that directors are not in fact required to balance interests. There is no indication in the legislation that they are to do so, and the CLRSG was critical of the need to balance, and of pluralist approaches that require balancing.[301] However, of course, even if not required to do so, they may in fact undertake such action subconsciously, and there is evidence, as we have just seen, to the effect that directors have done this in the past. And effecting a balance might be the correct way for directors to proceed.

6.151 Consideration of whether directors should balance, and what weight they should place on particular interests might be all theoretical, for the fact is that it really does not matter what is a good result for any of the constituencies mentioned in the provision, after directors have had regard for these interests, as the ultimate concern of directors is that their action promotes the success of

---

[296] Quoted in M Blair *Ownership and Control* (Washington DC, The Brookings Institute, 1995) at 212. It is also quoted in N Craig Smith *Morality and the Market* (London, Routledge, 1990) at 65 and referred to in J Parkinson 'Models of the Company and the Employment Relationship' (2003) 41 *British Journal of Industrial Relations* 481 at 494, although the date given in the latter is 1950.

[297] L Preston and H Sapienza 'Stakeholder Management and Corporate Performance' (1990) 19 *Journal of Behavioral Economics* 361.

[298] Referred to in E Scholes and D Clutterbuck 'Communication with Stakeholders: An Integrated Approach' (1998) 31 *Long Range Planning* 227 at 230.

[299] A Keay and R Adamopoulou 'Shareholder Value and UK Companies: A Positivist Inquiry' (2012) 13 *European Business Organization Law Review* 1; A Al-Hawarndeh et al 'The Interpretation of the Director's Duty under Section 172 Companies Act 2006: Insights from Complexity Theory' [2013] JBL 417.

[300] A Al-Hawarndeh et al 'The Interpretation of the Director's Duty under Section 172 Companies Act 2006: Insights from Complexity Theory' [2013] JBL 417 at 430.

[301] Company Law Review *Modern Company Law for a Competitive Economy: Strategic Framework* (London, DTI, 1999), generally in section 5.1.

the company *for the benefit of the members as a whole*. This is supported by the ICSA when it states that directors are to have regard to 'traditional considerations' such as profitability and the financial effects on shareholders, as they are still of critical importance; they are central to the duty to promote the success of the company for the benefit of the members as a whole.[302]

6.152   It has been noted earlier in **Chapter 3** that many of those who argue for shareholder value, acknowledge that having regard for constituency interests is not necessarily going to disadvantage the shareholders. The consideration of factors other than shareholder interests might produce financial benefits for the company, and ultimately for the shareholders. In fact having regard for interests other than those of the members may produce some benefits for members hitherto not countenanced. If there is a concern for stakeholder interests and the long term, shareholders might find that when the time comes for them to exit, it is quite possible that new investors might view the company as more of an attractive investment proposition.

V WHAT WILL CONSTITUTE A BREACH?

6.153   As indicated earlier in the Chapter, there has been relative few cases that has considered s 172 and even less that has examined elements of it or given us indications of actions which will constitute a breach of the section. Section 172(3) appears to have received more attention, as indicated in Chapter 13.

6.154   It is contended that a broad range of facts could lead to a director being found liable for breach of s 172.

6.155   In *Odyssey Entertainment Ltd v Kamp*,[303] HH Judge Simon Barker QC (sitting as a High Court judge) indicated that it would be a breach if a director has decided or is seriously considering carrying on a business in the same field as that carried on by his or her company, and is recommending to the board of his or her company that the company closes its business in the field of interest, if he or she remains silent.[304] In this case his Lordship found that the defendant director had given overly pessimistic advice to his board, disengaged from the business of the company and failed to inform the board about matters which it had an interest in knowing.[305]

6.156   It is suggested that a breach of s 172 would be found where one has facts similar to those in the Australian case of *Ralph v Diakyne Pty Ltd*.[306] In this case the defendant director of X company authorised a payment by X to Y

---

[302]   Institute of Chartered Secretaries and Administrators *Guidance on Directors' General Duties* (January 2008) at para 3.2.3.

[303]   [2012] EWHC 2316 (Ch).

[304]   Ibid at [214].

[305]   Ibid at [231], [235].

[306]   [2012] FCAFC 18.

company, a company in which the director had a large majority shareholding. He believed in good faith that X owed the money to Y, but he knew that X disputed the fact that the sum was due. Such an action could not be said to be promoting the success of the company.[307]

6.157   There is a corpus of case-law that indicates that a director is in breach of s 172 if he or she fails to report his or her own misconduct to the company. That this is a breach of duty was first recognised by the Court of Appeal in *Item Software (UK) Ltd v Fassihi*[308] when the Court took the view that the obligation to report one's own misconduct was part of the general duty to act in good faith for the best interests of one's company.[309] Simply, the director could not have reasonably believed that it was not in the company's best interests that it was made aware of the director's breach. In this respect s 172 communicates a similar idea as the previous uncodified duty. The approach in *Item Software* has, notwithstanding some criticism, both judicial[310] and academic,[311] been applied in several cases both where breaches of pre-codified duties and s 172 have been alleged.[312] I considered this kind of breach in Chapter 4, where it was noted that the Full Court of the South Australian Supreme Court in *Southern Real Estate Pty Ltd v Dellow and Arnold*[313] held that a director owed, as part of her duty of good faith, a duty to advise her fellow directors of her intention to leave the company and set up a competing business, but that the Victorian Supreme Court in *P & V Industries Pty Ltd v Porto,*[314] said that directors are not obliged to disclose wrongdoing to their companies.[315] It could be argued, one would think, that the formulation of an intention to leave and establish a competing business as occurred in the South Australian case, was a wrong and needed to be disclosed.

6.158   One of the rationales behind the obligation to disclose is probably that the company needs to know what the director has done as that might colour what the company does in the future. In establishing a breach it would be

---

[307] It is likely that, as in the case itself the director would also be liable for a conflict of interest (under s 175). See **Chapters 9** and **10**.

[308] [2004] EWCA Civ 1244 (2004) BCC 994; (2005) 2 BCLC 91 (CA).

[309] Ibid at [41].

[310] See, *Commonwealth Oil & Gas Co Ltd v Baxter* [2009] CSIH; 2010 SC 156 at [14], [82].

[311] For instance, see B Hannigan 'Reconfiguring the No Conflict Rule – Judicial Structures, a Statutory Restatement and the Opportunistic Director' (2011) 23 *Singapore Academy Law Journal* 714; L Ho and P Lee 'A Director's Duty to Confer: A Matter Of Good Faith' (2007) 66 CLJ 348. Also, see R Nolan 'A Fiduciary Duty to Disclose?' (1997) 113 LQR 220.

[312] *Shepherds Investments Ltd v Walters* [2006] EWHC 836 (Ch), [2007] 2 BCLC 202 at [132]; *Brandeaux Advisers (UK) Ltd v Chadwick* [2010] EWHC 3241 at [47]; *GHLM Trading Ltd v Maroo* [2012] EWHC 61 (Ch); [2012] 2 BCLC 369 at [195]; *ODL Securities Ltd v McGrath* [2013] EWHC 1865 (Comm) at [17] (dealing with an employee whose position was said to be analogous to a director); *Electrosteel Castings (UK) Ltd v Metapol* [2014] EWHC 2017 (Ch) at [34]; *GHLM Trading Ltd v Maroo* [2012] EWHC 61 (Ch); [2012] 2 BCLC 369 at [192]–[194]; *First Subsea Ltd v Balltec Ltd* [2014] EWHC 866 (Ch) at [187]; *IT Human Resources plc v Land* [2014] EWHC 3812 (Ch) at [121], [125]; *Haysport Properties Ltd v Ackerman* [2016] EWHC 393 (Ch).

[313] [2003] SASC 318; (2003) 87 SASR 1 at [29].

[314] [2006] VSC 131; (2006) 24 ACLC 573 (Vic S Ct).

[315] The court relied on *Breen v Williams* (1996) 186 CLR 71 (Aust HC).

necessary to establish that the director subjectively concluded that disclosure was in the interests of the company or that he or she would have so concluded if acting in good faith.[316] In *Haysport Properties Ltd v Ackerman*[317] Peter Smith J said that a director owes a continuous duty to disclose any breaches of duty until he ceased to be a director. It has been suggested that the obligation will rarely, if ever, be adhered to because of the negative ramifications that will probably result.[318] But that does not limit its effectiveness as far as claimants are concerned. Indeed Arden LJ did say that the fact that a director is not likely to comply with the duty is not a reason for failing to impose the obligation if it is appropriate.[319]

6.159 In fact it has been said that it can be incumbent on a fiduciary to disclose matters other than wrongdoing if the director subjectively considered that it was in the company's interests for it to be disclosed for the 'single and overriding touchstone' is the duty of a director to act in what he considers in good faith to be in the best interests of the company, and so there is no reason to restrict disclosure only to the director's misconduct.[320]

6.160 In a very recent judgment, in *Wey Education plc v Atkins*,[321] HHJ Cooke (sitting as a judge of the High Court) has expressed caution in coming to a conclusion that a director is in breach for failing to disclose wrongdoing. His Lordship noted that the consequences of the application of the duty in this way raises difficult issues. He said that *Item Software* was not 'authority for the proposition that every breach of obligation by a director must be confessed to his company, or that there is an obligation to disclose in a particular case and the breach would justify dismissal'.[322] The judge said that it was easy to see how an obligation to confess ought to be implied where the director's conduct involves something that is done in secret and for the director's own benefit, such as involvement in a competing business. But Judge Cooke did not think that all breaches of duty might lead to the same conclusion.[323] Thus this judgment might be seen as limiting the ambit of the duty to disclose. It will be interesting to see whether other judges follow a similar approach.

6.161 Hart J was effectively saying that a director could not stand idle while some third party poached the company's staff. There is Australian authority to the effect that directors are obliged to take action to prevent other directors breaching their duties, and the decision in *British Midland Tool Ltd v Midland International Tooling Ltd*, as well as the decision in *Shepherds Investments Ltd v Walters* [2006] EWHC 836.

---

[316] *GHLM Trading Ltd v Maroo* [2012] EWHC 61 (Ch); [2012] 2 BCLC 369 at [194].
[317] [2016] EWHC 393 (Ch) at [117].
[318] I Moore 'Revisiting the Duty to Confess: A Director's Duty to Disclose His Own Misconduct' (2016) 384 *Company Law Newsletter* 1.
[319] [2004] EWCA Civ 1244; (2004) BCC 994; (2005) 2 BCLC 91 (CA) at [65].
[320] *GHLM Trading Ltd v Maroo* [2012] EWHC 61 (Ch); [2012] 2 BCLC 369 at [195].
[321] [2016] EWHC 1663 (Ch).
[322] Ibid at [146].
[323] Ibid.

If directors do not disclose to their companies attempts that are made by a potential competitor to poach them or their colleagues from the company, they could well be said to be in breach of s 172 as such action is potentially damaging for the company.[324] In *British Midland Tool Ltd v Midland International Tooling Ltd*[325] Hart J was effectively saying that a director could not stand idle while some third party poached the company's staff. There is Australian authority to the effect that directors are obliged to take action to prevent other directors breaching their duties, and the decision in *British Midland Tool Ltd v Midland International Tooling Ltd*, as well as the decision in *Shepherds Investments Ltd v Walters*,[326] seem to suggest that this is the case in the UK and s 172 would be the provision imposing the obligation.[327]

6.162 Finally, while not mentioning s 172, Peter Smith J in *Hemsley v Graham*[328] held that directors are under a duty to disclose to their company the misconduct of others, and one would think that this duty could come within s 172(1).

VI ENFORCEMENT OF THE DUTY

6.163 A critical issue seems to be that if directors fail to take into account the interests enumerated in s 172(1) of the CA 2006 in circumstances where the company needed to do so, there is no penalty imposed on directors. True, there could be a civil action brought against one or more directors for the breach of duty, but only the board itself, which is usually given the power to manage the company by the articles, has the right to initiate proceedings against the directors. For a number of reasons action might not be taken. For instance, if all the directors are in breach it would be highly unlikely that the board would be taking action against themselves.[329] Shareholders under a derivative action or, perhaps, pursuant to s 994 of the CA 2006,[330] might be able to bring proceedings, but it is submitted that this is not likely to be a frequent occurrence. Even if action against directors is taken later, perhaps following the company's entry into administration or liquidation, it is likely to be difficult to establish that the directors should not have done what they did, perhaps several years in the past. First, any administrator or liquidator would have to impugn successfully any claim on the part of the directors that they had acted in good

---

[324] *British Midland Tool Ltd v Midland International Tooling Ltd* [2003] EWHC 466 (Ch); [2003] 2 BCLC 523 at [89].

[325] Ibid at [92].

[326] [2006] EWHC 836.

[327] See the discussion in R Langford 'The Duty of Directors to Act Bona Fide in the Interests of the Company: A Positive Fiduciary Duty? Australian and the UK Compared' (2011) 11 JCLS 215 at 226.

[328] [2013] EWHC 2232 (Ch) at [411].

[329] More reasons were given earlier at **4.54**.

[330] This provision entitles shareholders to bring proceedings where the affairs of the company have been carried out in an unfairly prejudicial way. It is arguable that the provision cannot be employed in public companies save in very limited circumstances. See *Re Astec (BSR) plc* [1998] 2 BCLC 556.

faith in a way that was most likely to promote the success of the company for the benefit of members. Second, the courts have made it plain that they will not use hindsight in making their decision when assessing the actions of directors,[331] and it might be argued, certainly when one studies the cases involving claims of wrongful trading under s 214 of the Insolvency Act 1986, that courts have tended to place a benevolent interpretation on what directors have done, and they have not found them liable save where they have acted in a completely irresponsible manner.[332]

6.164 Traditionally courts have refrained from reviewing the business decisions of directors. However, whilst years ago the courts tended to defer to the decisions of the directors (taking the view that 'directors are businesspersons who are actually involved in the running of businesses and we should not interfere readily'), there is clear evidence that in more recent times courts have been more interventionist. Nevertheless, while there has been greater judicial intervention in the management of companies, it is likely to be the case that courts will not want to be seen as second-guessing decisions as a regular mode of approach, and particularly when it comes to gauging what is likely to promote the success of the company.

6.165 The problem with s 172 of the CA 2006 is that none of the constituencies mentioned in the list of factors set out in the provision have a right to take action against directors who breach the section. This was undoubtedly one of the primary problems with s 309 of the CA 1985. In relation to this section the employees had no right to bring an action against the directors if the latter contravened the section, a point acknowledged by the CLRSG.[333] The CLRSG said that the benefit of a provision like s 309 is that it will 'confer an immunity on the directors, who would be able to resist legal actions by the shareholders based on the ground that the directors had neglected their normal fiduciary duty to them ...'.[334] That might be true, but the problem is not usually that directors have considered the interests of non-shareholder interests too much and need protection; rather it is that the directors in fact failed to consider non-shareholder interests.

6.166 As noted above, one avenue available to disenchanted shareholders where a director's breach of duty is not the subject of company action, is to initiate derivative proceedings, but these proceedings are not available to non-shareholder stakeholders. It is highly unlikely that the UK would introduce

---

[331] For instance, see *Re Welfab Engineers Ltd* [1990] BCC 600; *Re Sherborne Associates Ltd* [1995] BCC 40; *Re Kudos Business Solutions Ltd*; [2011] EWHC 1436 (Ch); [2012] 2 BCLC 65; *Re Idessa (UK) Ltd*[2011] EWHC 804 (Ch); [2012] BCC 315 (sub nom *Burke v Morrison*). Lewison J in *Secretary of State for Trade and Industry v Goldberg* ([2004] 1 BCLC 597 at 613) made the same point in relation to an assessment of a director's conduct when hearing an application under the Company Directors' Disqualification Act 1986.

[332] For example, see *Re Continental Assurance Co Ltd* [2001] BPIR 733; *The Liquidator of Marini Ltd v Dickensen* [2003] EWHC 334 (Ch); [2004] BCC 172.

[333] Company Law Review *Modern Company Law for a Competitive Economy: Strategic Framework* (London, DTI, 1999) at para 5.1.21.

[334] Ibid.

derivative actions for non-shareholders.[335] The only possible action might be to allow proceedings for injunctive relief, stopping directors from doing something that manifests a lack of regard for the interests of particular stakeholders. Even here it is very questionable whether a court would accede to applications of non-shareholders, for the courts would have to consider evidence in order to make a decision as to whether directors did intend to act appropriately. Deciding this issue would be problematic even for a judge hearing the actual trial dealing with alleged breaches of duty, let alone on an application for an injunction. As it is there may be few occasions where a director is going to have to justify what he or she did. Of course, very often, and especially with what might be regarded as the day-to-day affairs of the company, constituencies will not know what the directors have done. In many situations they might not know what has been done for some appreciable time, and by then it might be too late to do anything that is effective.

6.167 While the CLRSG rejected the pluralist position, inter alia, on the basis that it would involve directors having to consider the interests of all constituencies, and it would give no formal remedy for abuse by the directors,[336] this is apparently what we have with s 172 of the CA 2006. Arguably, the section has the same failings that the CLRSG identified with the pluralist theory – how to choose between a number of competing and inconsistent constituent interests? We could end up with what has been said to be wrong with stakeholder theory, namely directors are left in a position of not being *accountable* for the stewardship of their company's resources.[337] Perhaps the real problem is that unlike in the past where the law has sought to require directors to meet acceptable standards of behaviour, such as not acting in self-interest, it is now seeking to compel directors to act in a particular manner,[338] and this is far harder to regulate.

6.168 It might be said that protection of the interests of stakeholders is left not to any specific rights, such as the right to be heard or represented, but wholly to the discretion of the directors.

6.169 As adverted to above, the only stakeholders in the company who are able to take action under the CA 2006 appear to be the shareholders. Shareholders are, under the Act, given the right to bring derivative proceedings (subject to court approval) against directors in respect of a cause of action vested in the company (s 260(1)(a) of the CA 2006). So, if directors fail to comply with s 172(1) in some way, does that lead to a claim that is vested in the company so that the members could initiate derivative proceedings? It would appear that the answer is in the affirmative given the fact that s 178 provides

---

[335] Unlike Canada, where creditors can initiate derivative proceedings if they can convince a court that they are a proper person to make an application (Business Corporations Act 1985, s 238).

[336] Company Law Review *Modern Company Law for a Competitive Economy: Strategic Framework* (London, DTI, 1999) at para 5.1.21 at 5.1.30.

[337] M Jensen 'Value Maximisation, Stakeholder Theory and the Corporate Objective Function' (2001) 7(3) *European Financial Management* 297 at 305.

[338] S Worthington 'Reforming Directors' Duties' (2001) 64 MLR 439 at 448.

that the consequences of breaches of ss 171–177 are the same as would apply with the corresponding common law rules or equitable principles. Under these latter rules and principles a right of action would redound to the company where directors breached one of their duties. Also, s 260(3) provides that a derivative claim may be brought only in respect of a cause of action arising from an actual or proposed act involving, inter alia, a breach of duty by a director of the company. Hence, it would seem that a cause of action would vest in the company, within the meaning of s 260, and members would be entitled to continue derivative proceedings. This whole area is discussed in depth in **Chapter 14.**

6.170   Shareholders might be prompted to take action if the directors either fail to act so as to promote the success of the company for the benefit of the members or fail to have regard to the need to act fairly as between members (s 172(1)(f)), but such action is not so likely to occur, if at all, in circumstances where the directors fail to have regard for the other interests adumbrated in s 172(1) of the CA 2006, especially when one takes into account the fact that there is likely to be a cost element in any derivative claim. As one commentator has said: 'Deep-pocketed hedge funds could be encouraged to take action to apply pressure on company boards to implement the sorts of strategy required to produce the high returns their investors demand',[339] but they are unlikely to do so where directors have not taken into account the interests of other stakeholders. There are only a few situations where one could envisage an action being brought by a member other than in the cases mentioned above. First, where a member makes an investment in the company for the long term, and it is felt that the action of the directors does not have regard for the long term. Second, a member is also an employee of the company and is concerned that the directors did not, in what they have done, have regard to the interests of the employees. Third, a member is concerned that the directors have not had regard for the need to promote business relationships with suppliers, customers or others and it is likely to damage the company in the future. Fourth, there are members of the company living in the community in which the company operates, and they believe that the community will be adversely affected by the actions of the directors, and that will, as a consequence, affect the lives of those members. An example might be where a company, which operates several factories, decides to close one that is in the community where a member resides or has other business interests. Fifth, so-called shareholder activists, who have concerns wider than their own interests take proceedings because of a heightened sense of community interest or concern for the environment, and they believe that directors failed to consider community interests and/or the environment in the decisions which they have made.

6.171   Of course, it is always an option for non-shareholder stakeholders to become very minor shareholders in companies with which they have dealings so that they have the option, as a last resort, of taking derivative action against the directors if the directors fail to have regard for the factors set out in

---

[339]   P Beale 'Directors Beware' (2007) 157 NLJ 1033.

s 172(1)(a)–(f) in making their decisions.[340] But this kind of strategy is unlikely to be invoked save in rare cases, and the chances of it succeeding could well be low.

6.172 Even if derivative proceedings are commenced, directors might well argue that they did have regard for all of the matters mentioned in s 172(1)(a)–(f) of the CA 2006 and simply believed in good faith that what they did promoted the success of the company for the benefit of the members. If so, as indicated earlier, it might well be difficult for a member to challenge such an assertion successfully, and to establish that the directors did not have regard for the relevant matters. Certainly, as we will see in **Chapter 14**, shareholders have not had a good success rate in securing permission (leave in Scotland) from the courts to continue derivative proceedings.

VII IN PRACTICE

6.173 What does this provision mean in terms of practice? How should directors proceed as far as demonstrating compliance with the section? A difficulty for directors is knowing what formal processes and/or records, if any, and what kind of paper trail, if any, is needed. The legislation does not provide any assistance for it does not prescribe any procedures and it might be argued that consequently none have to be implemented. The concern that directors might have in terms of guidance is likely to be exacerbated somewhat by the fact that the kinds of decision which directors have to make are very varied and all companies are different (such as in size, business and structure) so it is not possible to prescribe a single process. Due to a broad range of circumstances in which directors exercise their duties, and the very different kinds of companies that exist, it is not possible to suggest a particular process which will apply for all decisions made by boards. The GC 100 states that it would be completely unworkable to require all decisions, and the reasons for them, to be recorded in writing.[341]

6.174 Loughrey et al found, in their study, conducted before s 172 was put in force, of the views of practitioners concerning how directors should act, that there was a divergence of opinions amongst the large commercial law firms.[342] But there does appear to be two general approaches to addressing compliance with this duty. There are those who take the view that directors have to record in much greater detail than in the past the reasons for their decision-making with the factors in s 172(1) of the CA 2006 firmly in view. Loughrey et al found from their study that the great majority of lawyers believe that s 172 was likely to affect the procedural aspects of boards' decision-making. Their opinion was that the need to take account of the statutory factors will result in a more

---

[340] Unlike in some other jurisdictions a shareholder does not need to hold a required percentage of the company's shareholding before being entitled to bring derivative proceedings.

[341] GC100, Companies Act (2006) – Directors' duties, 7 February 2007 at para 6.1.

[342] J Loughrey, A Keay and L Cerioni 'Legal Practitioners, Enlightened Shareholder Value and the Shaping of Corporate Governance' (2008) 8 *Journal of Corporate Law Studies* 79.

bureaucratic decision-making process and that lengthier board minutes may be necessary as evidence that directors have taken the factors into account.[343] Loughrey et al state that if they take these steps the lawyers have advised, that the courts are unlikely to set aside or query the board's decisions.[344] Furthermore, it is also possible that detailed board minutes could reduce the risk of derivative litigation commencing, insofar as they demonstrate to the shareholders that the statutory factors have been properly considered.[345]

6.175 It is felt that it is likely that lawyers will advise their shareholder clients of the low possibility of success of litigation where directors have communicated, in the form of detailed board minutes, the Directors' Report, the Strategic Report or other communications with shareholders, that they have taken a long-term inclusive approach so as to foster the long-term success of the company. The more detailed, complete, and structured the board's explanation is, and the more the board's approach relies on professional advice and rational performance benchmarks, and adopts an integrated legal, economic-financial and social view, the more likely it is that shareholders will be advised that they will be unable to establish that directors have breached s 172 of the CA 2006.[346]

6.176 A second approach is that while directors may have to be precise, they do not have to do a lot more than they are, from a bureaucratic perspective, already doing. The ICSA has stated that the provision only re-enacts and consolidates existing statutory provisions, the common law and best practice.[347] This second view is characterised by the opinion that consideration of the factors should not mean that boards have to keep records of the thought processes which end up influencing their decisions. It will usually suffice for board minutes to provide that the directors, having taken into account their duty to promote the success of the company, considered the s 172 factors (as well as any other relevant factors) in arriving at their decisions.[348] Significant support for this view might be obtained from some of the comments of legislators. For example, the former Attorney General, Lord Goldsmith, said[349] in the House of Lords:

> 'There is nothing in this Bill that says there is a need for a paper trail .... I do not agree that the effect of passing this Bill will be that directors will be subject to a breach if they cannot demonstrate that they have considered every element. It will be for the person who is asserting breach of duty to make that case good ... [Derivative claims] will be struck out if there is no decent basis for them.'

---

[343] Ibid at 102.

[344] Ibid at 103 and referring to Clifford Chance *The Companies Act 2006* (November 2006) at 2; Bond Pearce LLP 'The Company Law Reform Bill' February 2006, at 3.

[345] J Loughrey, A Keay and L Cerioni 'Legal Practitioners, Enlightened Shareholder Value and the Shaping of Corporate Governance' (2008) 8 *Journal of Corporate Law Studies* 79 at 103.

[346] Ibid.

[347] Institute of Chartered Secretaries and Administrators *Guidance on Directors' General Duties* (January 2008) at para 3.2.3.

[348] See P Beale 'Directors Beware' (2007) 157 NLJ 1033.

[349] Lord Goldsmith, Lords Grand Committee, 9 May 2006, col 841.

6.177   While some have suggested that the directors would need to retain a paper trail, legislators have dismissed this, as indicated in the above quotation. Also, it has been said[350] that:

> 'The clause does not impose a requirement on directors to keep records, as some people have suggested, in any circumstances in which they would not have to do so now.'

6.178   Probably the most important practical issue that the provision raises is how do directors go about demonstrating that they have had regard to the factors listed in paragraphs (a)-(f) of s 172(1) of the CA 2006. Advice from professional bodies is such that there should not be an over-abundance of red tape. This is very much in line with the comments above and the statements of government spokespersons made in parliamentary debates. The GC 100 has said[351] that it is:

> 'of the view that directors are not currently, and should not be, as a result of this legislative codification, forced to evidence their thought processes whether that is with regard to the stated factors or any other matter influencing their thinking. Apart from the unnecessary process and paperwork this would introduce into the boardroom, it would inevitably expose directors to a greater and unacceptable risk of litigation, especially in light of the new derivative action also being brought in by the Companies Act 2006.'

and:

> 'where the nature of the decision being taken by directors is such that it is supported by a formal process, that process need only specifically record consideration of those duties where the particular circumstances make it particularly necessary or relevant. The default position should be *not* to include these references.'[352]

6.179   The GC 100 has said that it is not necessary to minute everything that is said in relation to each factor, except to the extent appropriate to reflect the points that were raised, and this approach will mean that there will not be a substantial increase in the length of minutes.[353] The ICSA concurs on this point, stating that the minutes should record decisions taken and do not necessarily need to give detail on how each factor was considered.[354] The emphasis has been on the fact that the directors must make a judgment in good faith for the success of the company having regard to all the information and having taken advice when appropriate.[355]

---

[350]   Margaret Hodge, Commons Committee, 11 July 2006, col 592.
[351]   GC100, Companies Act (2006) – Directors' duties, 7 February 2007 at para 4.
[352]   Ibid at para 6.1(ii).
[353]   GC100, Companies Act (2006) – Directors' duties, 7 February 2007 at para 6.3(h).
[354]   Institute of Chartered Secretaries and Administrators (ICSA) *Guidance on Directors' General Duties* – January 2008 at para 3.2.3.
[355]   Ibid.

6.180 So, it might be argued that board minutes will normally be limited to recording decisions, and every element that was considered in the course of making those decisions will not be included; minutes will be compiled in the same way that they have always been. It has been pointed out that, notwithstanding the existence of s 309 of the CA 1985, boards have not mentioned in minutes the provision when recording all decisions that affect company employees.[356] However, two points can be made in this respect. First, s 309, as already discussed, was widely regarded as a lame duck provision. Second, it might be argued that the CA 2006's intention is, inter alia, to introduce a greater measure of structure and formality into the decision-making process, and if a claim of breach is levelled against directors by shareholders, or either an administrator or a liquidator, their defence will be supported by records indicating the fact that they were endeavouring to comply with the statutory procedure.[357]

6.181 Those taking this view might assert that the new provision does not require the directors to do more than they have always done. For instance, Birds has said[358] that:

'There seems little doubt that the properly advised board of a large company has long considered the consequences of its decisions on the wide range of interests now contained in the statute [CA 2006, s 172(1)].'

6.182 The Australian Senate's Standing Committee on Legal and Constitutional Affairs put it well in its report, 'Company Directors' Duties' in 1989, when it said:[359]

'The courts have associated directors' duties with 'the interests of the company.' This does not mean that directors must not consider other interests. The 'interests of the company' include the continuing well-being of the company. Directors may not act for motives foreign to the company's interests, but the law permits many interests and purposes to be advantaged by company directors, as long as there is a purpose of gaining in that way a benefit to the company.'

6.183 Adherents to both of the views emanating from the advice of lawyers would probably agree that where a specific factor is of great significance or is of actual or potential importance it might be prudent for briefing papers to be prepared and discussed at the board meeting. The GC100 has suggested that the preparation of a background paper which discussed the factors that need to be considered is a key way of assisting directors in properly taking into account

---

[356] J Davies 'A Guide to Directors Obligations Under the Companies Act 2006' Association of Chartered Certified Accountants, August 2007, at para 6.41, and accessible at www.accaglobal.com/content/dam/acca/global/PDF-technical/business-law/tech-tp-cdd.pdf.

[357] Ibid.

[358] A Alcock, J Birds and S Gale *Companies Act 2006: The New Law* (Bristol, Jordan Publishing, 2007) at 145.

[359] Section 6.3 and referring to J D Heydon 'Directors' Duties and the Company's Interests' in P Finn (ed) *Equity and Commercial Relationships* (Sydney, Law Book Co, 1987) at 135.

all relevant factors relating to their decision,[360] and each director will have had the opportunity of considering it in advance and of raising any questions at or before the meeting. However, it is up to the directors concerned to use their business judgment in considering the proposal.[361] On controversial issues, or matters which may be open to challenge, lawyers have suggested that boards may need to commission advice from independent consultants and from lawyers themselves (of course the latter might be seen as self-serving).[362]

6.184 From a procedural perspective, it is particularly critical that accurate and thorough minutes are taken at board meetings and meetings of committees of the board, such as the audit committee. But the GC100 takes the view[363] that:

> 'board minutes should not be used as the main medium for recording the extent to which each of the factors of the Companies Act were discussed. Board minutes do not, after all, do so today insofar as either the common law or statutory duties require directors to consider particular factors. The minimum requirement for minutes should only be that they clearly state the decision reached.'

6.185 While it may well be sufficient for the minutes of board meetings to state that the directors have taken the factors into account, and points made in relation to any one or more of the factors that are particularly pertinent, it is probably prudent to record the background discussions entered into by directors and rationales for any decisions taken. When there has been consideration of issues that might affect the factors set out in s 172(1) of the CA 2006 the minutes should show that the board had regard to those factors. There is certainly, in all probability, a need to produce some records of what the directors have done in this regard, such as following up a matter that might need to be investigated or where further information is required. This is obviously to point out to anyone concerned that they have complied with the law, and also to absolve the director if there is a later investigation by a liquidator or administrator.

---

[360] GC100, Companies Act (2006) – Directors' duties, 7 February 2007 at para 6.3(b)). According to the ICSA a 'system of checking before any paper is finally included in the board pack should be introduced in order to ensure that all the factors regarding a decision that are relevant to directors' duties have been adequately covered in the paper. This checking process would normally be conducted by the Company Secretary or by the Chairman. Either would have authority to seek amendments to the paper to address the relevant points.' (Institute of Chartered Secretaries and Administrators (ICSA) *Guidance on Directors' General Duties* (January 2008) at para 3.2.3).

[361] Ibid at para 6.3(e).

[362] Clifford Chance, *The Companies Act 2006* (November 2006) at 2; Nabarro Nathanson *Companies Act 2006: A Modern and Effective Framework for Company Law* at 2; Mills and Reeve *Briefing* (February 2006). Not all law firms take this view, though it is a common one: Burges Salmon and Freshfields for example consider that most companies will be able to rely on existing systems: Freshfields Bruckhaus Deringer *Companies Act 2006: Directors Duties* (November 2006) at 5; Burges Salmon *Companies Act 2006: Provisions coming into effect in January 2007*, at 1.

[363] GC100, Companies Act (2006) – Directors' duties, 7 February 2007 at para 6.3(f)).

6.186   All in all it would seem prudent for directors to include in their minutes, as a minimum, a standard reference to the fact that the board adhered to the decision-making requirements in s 172 of the CA 2006 in relation to their considerations. If the nature of the matter under discussion demanded that directors had to consider several competing factors, and some decisions will clearly not, it is probably advisable that the directors record the reasons why the particular option embraced was considered to be the more likely to promote the success of the company.[364] But it must be noted that the more information that is given, such as providing a reason for following a particular option, and the more documentation a board brings into existence can be grist for a claimant's mill. It might be that directors have to aim for a happy medium where they provide clear evidence that they had regard to the s 172 factors, but they do not go into great detail.

6.187   It might be a temptation for a board to focus on the factors mentioned in s 172(1) of the CA 2006 and to tick them off as they address them, and feel that it is 'job done,' but it is necessary that directors do not ignore the fact that factors outside of those listed and that might need to be taken into account.

6.188   Furthermore, it has been said that where there is urgency in relation to any matter, then boards should not have to wait until all formal reports, which have been commissioned, have been received and studied.[365] To do so might well be against the promotion of the success of the company.

VIII ASSESSMENT[366]

6.189   Clearly s 172 of the CA 2006 is an interesting innovation. Its exact application and impact still cannot be completely divined some nine years after its coming into force. It introduces some concepts the effect and operation of which are not easily determined. While the law has built up judicial commentary on good faith, and this is likely to be considered by courts interpreting s 172, it is not so easy to say how the concept of success will be interpreted and how directors are to have regard to the factors enumerated in the section.

6.190   As far as the duty's effect on practice, it would seem that the views of practitioners before it came into force varied from the duty being a 'damp squib' which would not introduce any new liabilities or responsibilities for

---

[364] J Davies 'A Guide to Directors Obligations Under the Companies Act 2006' Association of Chartered Certified Accountants, August 2007, at para 6.41, and accessible at www.accaglobal.com/content/dam/acca/global/PDF-technical/business-law/tech-tp-cdd.pdf.

[365] CMS Cameron McKenna 'Companies Act 2006: An Overview' September 2007.

[366] For a broad assessment of the provision as a part of enlightened shareholder value, see A Keay *Enlightened Shareholder Value Principle and Corporate Governance* (Abingdon, Routledge, 2013) Ch 7.

directors,[367] to assertions that the duty to promote the success of the company would lead to 'radical change'[368] and a real prospect of increased litigation against directors.[369] Loughrey et al found that most lawyers were agnostic about whether the section would alter the outcome of directors' decisions in the ordinary course of business.[370] In a study conducted by Dr Peter Taylor in 2008–2009 it was revealed that only about one quarter of those who responded to the questionnaire that he sent out considered that the Act would cause the directors of their companies to have a higher regard for the duties required under s 172(1).[371] There has been some empirical work undertaken after the introduction of s 172 that does shine some light on the effect of the provision.[372] Perhaps the most wide-ranging study was an evaluation of the Act undertaken by Infogroup/ORC International for the Department of Business Innovation and Skills ('ORC study') in 2011,[373] and there was a reasonable focus on s 172 in the questions asked as part of the study. It found that there was a reasonably high awareness among directors concerning s 172 and its general effect,[374] but it also found that it had not changed behaviour at all amongst the vast majority of directors.[375] Several of the interviewees in another study in 2011 and conducted by the Association of Chartered Certified Accountants ('ACCA study') were of the view that enlightened shareholder value had made little or no difference.[376] Despite viewing s 172 as a gesture in the right direction, one respondent in the ACCA study who was not convinced that it would have the intended impact, said:

> 'My personal view on this is that it is a gesture in the right direction, but the way that the particular section is framed is unconvincing in its potential impact, because it uses this phrase "Directors must have regard to specified stakeholder related factors," nobody really understands exactly what the legal force of that is,

---

[367] Bruce Hanton of Ashursts, quoted in *Financial Director* 26 November 2006 www.financialdirector.co.uk/financial-director/analysis/2169965/companies-act (last accessed on 26 March 2007).

[368] J Gauntlett and R Dattani (Norton Rose) *Directors Duties Codified* (November 2006).

[369] G Milner Moore and R Lewis (Herbert Smith) *In the Line of Fire-Directors Duties under the Companies Act 2006* (hereafter '*In the Line of Fire*'), 4.

[370] J Loughrey, A Keay and L Cerioni 'Legal Practitioners, Enlightened Shareholder Value and the Shaping of Corporate Governance' (2008) 8 *Journal of Corporate Law Studies* 79 at 90 and referring to Cameron McKenna 'Companies Act 2006: Deferred Reform' *Law-Now* 29 November 2006, at 4-5; Freshfields Bruckhaus Deringer, *Companies Act 2006: Directors Duties* (November 2006), at 4.

[371] P Taylor 'Enlightened Shareholder Value and the Companies Act 2006' (unpublished PhD thesis, Birkbeck College, University of London, May 2010) at 161.

[372] There is more discussion of the studies in A Keay *Enlightened Shareholder Value Principle and Corporate Governance* (Abingdon, Routledge, 2013), and particularly at 50–56.

[373] S Fettiplace and R Addis 'Evaluation of the Companies Act 2006' 2 August 2010 at 62 and accessible at www.gov.uk/government/uploads/system/uploads/attachment_data/file/31655/10-1360-evaluation-companies-act-2006-volume-1.pdf.

[374] Ibid at 64–65.

[375] Ibid at 72–73.

[376] D Collison et al 'Shareholder Primacy in UK Corporate Law: An Exploration of the Rationale and Evidence', Research Report 125, Certified Accountants Educational Trust (London), 2011 at pp 34, 39, 44.

and also directors are faced with a situation whereby they are required to have regard to a number of stakeholder factors, some of which are almost by definition mutually exclusive.'[377]

6.191 It is questionable whether s 172(1) is really understood by company officers. One company secretary who answered questions for the ORC study said in relation to the provision that: 'Directors now must be aware of the need to wear a different hat and make decisions for the benefit of the entire community.'[378] The same company secretary said that: 'It [the section 172 duty] has sharpened up directors' attitudes and procedures rather than a cultural shift.'[379]

6.192 The CLRSG was confident that the statutory code would have 'a major influence in changing behaviours and the climate of decision-making' by deterring short termism.[380] This was not because the new formulation of directors' duties changed the law, for the CLRSG thought that it simply reflected existing law and best practice. However, it had noted considerable evidence that the law was widely misunderstood as a result of the manner in which it was expressed and interpreted.[381] As noted above, there is some doubt whether the provision has had much of an impact.

6.193 The approach adopted by the CLRSG, and then the Government, is criticised by Professor Sarah Worthington because a duty is being used to improve directorial standards, but duties have historically been used to set acceptable minimum standards and the learned commentator states that it is one thing, say, to prevent directors acting without due care, it is another thing to impose upon them an enforceable duty to act in such a way as to promote the success of the company. She notes that other methods are usually adopted to encourage good behaviour.[382]

6.194 Prima facie, s 172 of the CA 2006 might be regarded as virtually embedding a form of shareholder value in company law when this had not previously been the case. UK law has not unequivocally adopted shareholder value as the main concern for directors in managing the company. But s 172 makes it clear that the focus is to be on shareholder interests, because the duty of directors to promote the success of the company is always subject to the fact that it must be for the benefit of the members as a whole. For that reason alone it constitutes a critical development.

6.195 There does not appear to be any indication that the provision has led to greater benefits for non-shareholder stakeholders. Although it is arguable that

---

[377] Ibid at 63.

[378] Ibid at p 74 (Case Study 3).

[379] Ibid at p 74 (Case Study 3).

[380] Company Law Review *Modern Company Law for a Competitive Economy: Developing the Framework* (London, DTI, 2000) at para 3.58.

[381] See Company Law Review *Modern Company Law for a Competitive Economy: The Strategic Framework* (London, DTI, 1999) at para 5.1.20 (for instance).

[382] 'Reforming Directors' Duties' (2001) 64 MLR 439 at 448.

many large companies have been having regard for stakeholder interests for some time. A study of 50 of the companies making up the FTSE 100 showed in 2011 that stakeholders other than shareholders are indeed important to these companies and that companies desire to have good relations with them, and appear to take the interests of stakeholders into account in making decisions.[383]

6.196 Finally, anecdotal evidence seems to suggest that claimants are being advised by many practitioners to rely on breaches of other duties in **Chapter 10** rather than that contained in s 172, perhaps because the section remains a bit of an unknown quantity. This might well chime with the fact that we have seen relatively few cases that have got to court that have involved claims under s 172. This might change if we do see more cases being heard by the courts and the judges give us clearer indications as to how they interpret the provision.

IX CONCLUSION

6.197 In the House of Lords during the debate on the Company Law Reform Bill 2005, Lord Goldsmith, who led for the Government, said[384] that the enlightened shareholder value principle is proper as it:

> 'resolves any confusion in the mind of directors as to what the interests of the company are, and prevents any inclination to identify those interests with their own. It also prevents confusion between the interests of those who depend on the company and those of the members.'

6.198 However, I think that this chapter indicates that s 172 of the CA 2006 does not resolve confusion in the minds of directors. Rather it is likely that it in fact adds to the confusion.

6.199 Arguably, the benefit of the enlightened shareholder value model is that it enables directors to take into account non-shareholder interests when making decisions, without being in breach of their duties, always providing that their ultimate decisions do in fact promote the success of the company for the benefit of its members as a whole. Of course, if the actions of the directors do achieve this objective it is unlikely that shareholders would be complaining about the fact that directors have considered the interests of other stakeholders. Absent where activist shareholders are moved to object to the fact that directors have not considered certain factors set out in s 172 of the CA 2006, the only scenarios where shareholders might take umbrage at what the directors have done is where the company would have been more successful had the directors not taken into account non-shareholder interests, or shareholders with a vision for the long term would impugn the actions of the directors on the basis that the directors have not had regard to long-term considerations.

---

[383] See A Keay and R Adamopoulou 'Shareholder Value and UK Companies: A Positivist Inquiry' (2012) 13 *European Business Organizations Review* 1.

[384] Lords Grand Committee, 6 February 2006, col 255.

6.200   Certainly s 172(1) of the CA 2006 is an interesting innovation in that it provides, for the first time, a legislative mandate as to for whose interests directors are to act in their management of the affairs of companies. How the provision is applied might well depend on a number of factors. Perhaps the main point to note is that there does not seem to be any framework in place to ensure that directors are held accountable for their decision-making process.[385] As it is there are likely to be few occasions where a director is going to have to justify what he or she did. Of course, very often, and especially with what might be regarded as the daily affairs of the company, those constituencies who are mentioned in s 172(1) will not know what the directors have done, and when they do, it will too late to do anything that is effective. Members might be able to get permission to institute derivative proceedings against directors where there is thought to be a breach of s 172(1), but save where directors have failed to benefit the members from the action that they have taken, such proceedings are likely to be few and far between. Those who are numbered amongst other constituencies in the provision will not be entitled to initiate any legal proceedings against directors, so where directors fail to have regard for the interests set out in the subsection, it is unlikely that they will be brought to book.

6.201   The main concern with s 172 of the CA 2006 is that neither it nor any other document really provides significant guidance to directors as to what they should be doing and how they should be acting.

---

[385] Arguably this is provided for in the Strategic Report that is required under s 414A of CA 2006 (as it has been amended).

CHAPTER 7

DUTY TO EXERCISE INDEPENDENT JUDGMENT

I INTRODUCTION

7.1   Directors make many decisions in the life of a company, and this means that they exercise a number of discretionary powers. These include from whom, and when, to borrow, the issuing of shares and making calls in relation to those shares, and making decisions as to the contracts they will make on behalf of the company. In private companies directors often have a discretion as to whether they will register a transfer of shares from a shareholder to an outsider. In the carrying out of their functions, including exercising their discretions, directors are required to exercise independent judgment, so they must retain the power of making *their* decisions. Section 173 of the CA 2006, the provision that deals with this, states that directors must exercise independent judgment. It then goes on to provide virtual exceptions to that rule when it says that the duty is not breached if directors act in accordance with an agreement entered into by the company that restricts the future exercise of discretion by the directors or in a way authorised by the company's constitution.

7.2   While there is no exact equivalent duty at common law, this duty encapsulates what was essentially required at common law.[1] The duty at common law was seen as being that directors were prohibited from fettering their discretion in the exercise of their powers. Others regarded the requirement to exercise an independent judgment as part of a director's duty to act bona fide in the best interests of the company.[2] The Explanatory Notes to the CA 2006 were content to describe the obligation as a principle of the law. Professor Brenda Hannigan criticised the provision,[3] when it was included in the 2002 White Paper,[4] on the basis that it is meaningless to anyone who is not familiar with the case-law, so it is unlikely to assist in clarity and accessibility, which were aims of the codification exercise.

7.3   It has been clear at common law that directors are not able to delegate the exercise of their discretionary powers as that would interfere with their

---

[1]   See Explanatory Notes to the CA 2006, at para 333.
[2]   Professor Brenda Hannigan saw the obligation as a corollary of the wider duty to act bona fide: *Company Law* (London, LexisNexis Butterworths, 2003) at 231.
[3]   Ibid at 244.
[4]   Cmnd 5553-II.

independence.[5] The new provision says nothing on the topic directly, but the Explanatory Notes to the CA 2006[6] make it patent that a power is not conferred by s 173 on the directors to delegate. Nevertheless, the Notes state that the section does not stop a director from exercising a power to delegate where it is conferred by the company's constitution as long as the exercise of the power is in accordance with the company's constitution.

7.4 Companies, like individuals, might find, at times, that it is in their interests that the directors circumscribe the exercise of their discretionary powers in the future. But it has been asserted that directors are not permitted to agree either with each other or with third parties as to the manner in which they would act in the future, notwithstanding the fact that the directors are not receiving any benefit from the arrangement.[7] It must be noted that the question of directors fettering the future exercise of their powers is only an issue where the relevant persons contract or undertake to act in a particular way in their capacity as directors.[8] Also we must distinguish the case where the company fetters its options in the future, which is legitimate, and where the directors limit the exercise of their powers, which is not legitimate.

7.5 The cases and the literature that have considered the duty as it existed at common law have done so with the duty of directors to act bona fide in the best interests of the company in mind. As explained previously, this has traditionally been regarded as the premier duty of directors. It is not mirrored in the legislation that has codified the duties, although, as considered in **Chapter 6,** the duty to promote the success of the company probably encompasses many aspects of the original duty.

7.6 The rationale for the duty in s 173 of the CA 2006 is obviously that directors who do fetter their discretion could well be acting in a way that is opposed to the company's interests. In the language of s 172, they might be acting in a way that fails to promote the success of the company. Additionally, the directors could be placing themselves in a conflict situation, that is, future action that would benefit the company might be inconsistent with the undertaking or agreement that the directors have made earlier.

7.7 The Chapter begins with a substantial consideration of the common law at the time of the codification of the duty. A substantial discussion is warranted as, it is submitted, s 173 of the CA 2006 reflects the common law significantly. The Chapter then moves on to discuss the special case of nominee directors and ends with an examination of the terms of s 173.

---

[5] For instance, see *Re Leeds Banking Co* (1866) LR 1 Ch App 561; *Re County Palatine Loan & Discount Co* (1874) LR 9 Ch App 691.

[6] Paragraph 335.

[7] P Davies *Gower and Davies' Principles of Modern Company Law* (London, Sweet and Maxwell, 7th edn, 2003) at 390.

[8] T Courtney 'Fettering Directors' Discretion' (1995) 16 Co Law 227 at 227.

II THE EXISTING COMMON LAW

A The general rule

7.8 While most cases referred to in this area are reasonably modern, as far back as 1878 the duty can be seen in an incipient form. In *Re Englefield Colliery Co*[9] certain persons were induced by the promoter of a company, Sheridan, to become directors of the company on the basis that they would not be required to pay for qualifying shares that would be allotted to them. The directors resolved, without inquiry or seeking copies of vouchers or receipts from Sheridan as to expenditure, that Sheridan was to be paid £3,500 by way of preliminary expenses. The directors were held liable to repay this sum to the company. The Court of Appeal was concerned that the directors were beholden to Sheridan and could not exercise an independent judgment in the exercise of their functions and decisions.[10]

7.9 Somewhat later, in *Clark v Workman*[11] the chairman of a board of directors of a private company undertook to a transferee of some of the company's shares that he would do all that he could to obtain the approval of the board for the transfer. The company's shareholders successfully argued, inter alia, that the director had acted in breach of his fiduciary duty by fettering his discretion.

7.10 Moving into the modern era, in *John Crowther Group plc v Carpets International plc*[12] JC plc agreed to purchase the shares in CI Ltd from I plc. Under Stock Exchange rules, the agreement had to receive the approval of I plc's shareholders. The agreement included a provision that I plc would recommend the proposal to its shareholders and to propose resolutions of acceptance to its shareholders, and this would be done even if other offers were made. Initially, I plc's directors recommended to the shareholders that the bid should be accepted. But, subsequently a more attractive bid was made by another party, and I plc's directors decided to recommend the new bid to the shareholders, instead of JC plc's bid. JC plc took action against I plc on the basis that the I plc directors had breached the agreement to obtain the consent of I plc's shareholders.[13] Vinelott J found in favour of I plc on the basis that the directors agreed to use reasonable endeavours to secure the passing of the resolution, but the agreement had to be subject to anything that the directors were obliged to do in pursuance of their fiduciary duties. His Lordship said that it was for the directors to decide what they considered to be in the best interests of the company and to do whatever they considered to be in the best interests of the company at the relevant time.[14] A similar situation occurred in *Rackham v*

---

[9]   (1878) 8 Ch D 388 (CA).
[10]   Ibid at 401.
[11]   [1920] 1 IR 107.
[12]   [1990] BCLC 460.
[13]   Ibid at 464, 465.
[14]   Ibid at 465.

Peek Foods Ltd[15] with the same result, although the issue of the directors' independent judgment was not broached directly.

7.11 The decisions in *John Crowther Group plc v Carpets International plc*[16] and *Rackham v Peek Foods Ltd*[17] suggest that if directors were required to obtain the approval of shareholders for a contract then they are not bound by any undertaking previously given to a third party, for they must give full disclosure to the shareholders concerning the undertaking.

7.12 While in most cases the kind of issue which we are considering involves an undertaking given to a party which is outside of the company, in the Canadian decision of *Ringuet v Bergeron*,[18] the promises were given by directors to each other. The Canadian Supreme Court, whilst upholding the notion that directors are not to fetter their discretion, held that the undertakings were valid even when the undertakings were made in relation to how directors would act in the future. In his judgment Judson J (with whom the other judges concurred) said that the undertaking given by all directors was valid as the directors owned the shares in the company.[19] Thus the same result is not likely in a company whose shares are not closely-held.

7.13 It is possible that directors would be in breach of their duty where:[20]

- they agree in advance to convene a meeting of the company's board of directors so as to appoint specific persons as directors of the company;

- they agree in advance to convene a meeting at which shares will be allotted to specific persons;

- they agree, in advance of a board meeting, with X to vote to support the registration of X as a member of the company;

- they agree to register a transfer of shares at a subsequent meeting of the company's board of directors.

7.14 Other case-law also indicates that if directors placed themselves in a position where they exercise no discretion in carrying out company business, but do what they are told to do, they are acting improperly.[21]

7.15 In fettering his or her discretion a director might in effect be preventing himself or herself from ensuring that he or she acts bona fide in the best

---

[15]   [1990] BCLC 895.
[16]   [1990] BCLC 460.
[17]   [1990] BCLC 895.
[18]   (1960) 24 DLR (2d) 449 (S Ct (Can)).
[19]   Ibid at 459.
[20]   The following are based on T Courtney 'Fettering Directors' Discretion' (1995) 16 Co Law 227 at 228.
[21]   For instance, see *Selangor United Rubber Estates Ltd v Craddock (No 3)* [1968] 1 WLR 1555; [1968] 2 All ER 1073; *Belmont Finance Corp Ltd v Williams Furniture Ltd (No 2)* [1980] 1 All ER 393 at 406.

interests of the company. It matters not, at common law, that the director in entering into an agreement fettering discretion was not seeking to gain personally from the agreement.

B The exceptions

7.16 In the case of *Boulting v ACTT*[22] Upjohn LJ considered the issue at hand and said that it is the company which is owed a fiduciary duty, and hence it is able to release the director owing that duty from its strict application. This is not quite provided for in s 173 of the CA 2006, but the section does state, in sub-s (2)(b) that directors do not infringe the duty encompassed by the section if the company's constitution authorises the action of the directors. This means that, as long as the constitution provides, the directors could, for instance, undertake to a majority shareholder that they will refrain from exercising certain of their powers, something that they cannot ordinarily do.[23]

7.17 The leading English case on this subject is the Court of Appeal decision in *Fulham Football Club Ltd v Cabra Estates plc*[24] In this case the defendant, a subsidiary of V, which owned the ground at which Fulham FC played their football matches, applied for planning permission to develop the ground for residential purposes. The council also submitted a planning application and issued a compulsory purchase order in relation to the ground. Before a public inquiry into the purchase order and planning applications began, Fulham FC and its shareholders and directors made an agreement with V and the defendant that related to the future development of the ground and at the same time the shareholders and directors entered into a letter of undertaking under seal covenanting to obtain the support of Fulham FC concerning V's planning applications, not to object to them, not to support the purchase order, and not to support the council's case at any inquiry which considered a purchase order or planning application. The shareholders and directors complied with this undertaking at the first inquiry, with the result that the purchase order was not confirmed and planning permission sought by the council and V was refused. Following this V submitted new applications which were refused by the council and a further public inquiry was ordered. The directors of Fulham FC advised V that because of a change in the situation, they intended to give such evidence at the inquiry as they considered to be in the best interests of the football club. It was argued by V that the directors were bound to support V's application. One of the directors' arguments in their defence was that they were not able to be bound by the undertakings to the extent that they conflicted with their fiduciary duties to the club as directors. While the other arguments of the directors were accepted at first instance, this argument was not. The Court of Appeal agreed with the judge on this point. Neill LJ (with whom the other judges agreed) said:[25]

---

[22] [1963] 2 QB 606.
[23] See *Automatic Self-Cleansing Filter Syndicate Co Ltd v Cunninghame* [1906] 2 Ch 34.
[24] [1994] 1 BCLC 363; [1992] BCC 863.
[25] Ibid at 392; 875.

'It is trite law that directors are under a duty to act bona fide in the interests of their company. However, it does not follow from that proposition that directors can never make a contract by which they bind themselves to the future exercise of their powers in a particular manner, even though the contract taken as a whole is manifestly for the benefit of the company. Such a rule could well prevent companies from entering into contracts which were commercially beneficial to them.'

7.18 The Court of Appeal relied substantially on the Australian High Court decision in *Thorby v Goldberg*[26] which involved a similar point. In that case the directors of a company had argued that an agreement was illegal or was otherwise void because it tied the hands of the directors with regard to the exercise of their powers and duties in the future. The court, agreeing with all of the members of the court below, the New South Wales Court of Appeal, said that if the directors bona fide think that a contract which they negotiate is, at the time, in the interests of the company as a whole, they may bind themselves by the contract to do whatever is necessary to implement it. One of the judges in the High Court, Owen J, stated that:[27]

'For all that appears from the plea, the directors of the Company may, before the execution of the agreement, have given proper consideration to the desirability of entering into it and decided that it was in the best interests of the Company that it should be made. If so, it would be impossible to argue that they had, by executing the document, improperly fettered the future exercise of their discretion. In fact they would already have exercised it and, in the absence of an allegation that they had done so improperly, the suggested defence could not be sustained.'

7.19 Importantly in both cases the courts provided that a distinction must be made between directors fettering their discretion in the future and directors exercising their discretion so that their future conduct is circumscribed. In only the former situation is a director liable for breach.

7.20 At the end of its judgment in *Fulham Football Club Ltd v Cabra Estates plc*[28] the Court of Appeal referred to *Rackham v Peek Foods Ltd*[29] and *John Crowther Group plc v Carpets International plc*,[30] which were considered earlier in this chapter. Neill LJ, who delivered the judgment of the Court of Appeal, noted that *Thorby v Goldberg* was not cited in either case. His Lordship said that the *Rackham* and *Crowther* decisions might be able to be justified on their own facts,[31] but in any event they should not be seen as establishing a general proposition that directors can never bind themselves as to the future exercise of their fiduciary powers. He added that if they could be seen to do so then they would be wrong.[32] Professor Andrew Griffiths has

---

[26] (1964) 112 CLR 597.
[27] Ibid at 617-618. Kitto J also said something similar (at 605–606).
[28] [1994] 1 BCLC 363; [1992] BCC 863.
[29] [1990] BCLC 895.
[30] [1990] BCLC 460.
[31] At first instance, Chadwick J distinguished the cases.
[32] [1994] 1 BCLC 363 at 393; [1992] BCC 863 at 876.

distinguished the cases from *Fulham Football Club Ltd v Cabra Estates plc* on the basis that in the former cases the directors were limited in their contracting power (they had to obtain shareholder approval for the agreement) whereas in the latter case they were not.[33]

7.21   So, at common law directors would not be in breach of the duty to fetter their discretion if they exercised their discretion to agree that they would act in a certain way in the future. This action might well assist the company in that the directors could commit the company to certain conduct in the future, and, obviously, if directors could not commit the company to a long-term contract then third parties might see the company as an unreliable business contact. The concern is that directors are not to prevent themselves from exercising an independent judgment on all matters on which they must make decisions for the company. The duty to exercise an independent judgment is an essential element to the proper and effective discharge of a director's functions.

III THE SPECIAL CASE OF NOMINEE DIRECTORS

7.22   One of the main issues that have been encountered in relation to this duty is with nominee directors,[34] namely those directors who have been nominated to the board by particular parties with the idea that the nominee would represent their interests. The situation often occurs with subsidiary companies,[35] where the holding company has nominees on the board of the subsidiary (sometimes executive directors of the holding company) or it can occur where a major shareholder, a class of shareholders, bondholders or employees have the right to appoint a director. Another prevalent instance is where joint venturers incorporate a joint venture company and are permitted to nominate directors to the board of the company.[36] The right to appoint a nominee might be provided for under the company's constitution or pursuant to contract. In some cases there is no constitutional or contractual right to appoint, but the appointor has so much influence that the persons who have the legal power to appoint will agree to the appointor's desire for representation on the board of directors.[37]

7.23   The following does not purport to be a detailed consideration of nominee directors, but merely a discussion of them in the context of the duty under consideration. The discussion makes a distinction between those directors who are merely nominated by a shareholder and whose responsibility to the

---

[33]   'The Best Interests of Fulham FC: Directors' Fiduciary Duties in Giving Contractual Undertakings' [1993] JBL 576 at 583.

[34]   Known as 'constituency directors' in the United States.

[35]   For instance, see *Kuwait Asia Bank EC v National Mutual Life Nominees Ltd* [1991] 1 AC 187 (PC).

[36]   For example, see *Gwembe Valley Development Co Ltd (in receivership) and another v Koshy and others (No 3)* [2003] EWCA Civ 1048; [2004] 1 BCLC 131.

[37]   R Austin, H Ford and I M Ramsay *Company Directors: Principles of Corporate Governance* (Sydney, LexisNexis Butterworths, 2005) at 557.

nominator terminates on appointment and those directors who owe some responsibilities to their nominating shareholder after their appointment.[38] The book focuses on the latter.

7.24 While it might be said that the term 'nominee director' has no clear meaning,[39] nominee directors have been defined as:[40]

> ' ... persons who, independently of the method of their appointment, but in relation to their office, are expected to act in accordance with some understanding or arrangement which creates an obligation or mutual expectation of loyalty to some person or persons other than the company as a whole.'

7.25 The use of nominee directors is quite wide in practice.[41] Such directors encounter certain problems and these were well articulated by Barron J, of the Irish High Court in the case of *Irish Press plc v Ingersoll Irish Publications Ltd*,[42] when he said:

> 'The position of nominee directors can be a difficult one if they disagree with the views of the person or body appointing them. Their duty is to act in the interests of the company. They have also got a duty to act on the instructions of their nominating party. But acting in the interests of the company is no more than acting in the interests of all its shareholders. If what they are asked to do involves seeking to damage the interests of one section of the shareholders in favour of another then as a Director they have a duty not to do that. However, if what they are required to do is merely something that they themselves personally think is not the way to approach the matter then they must give way. There is nothing wrong with the appointing body or party from having a view as to where the interests of the company lie and ensuring that its nominees follow that direction provided that in so doing they are not seeking to damage anybody else's interest in the company.'

7.26 As Dr Deidre Ahern has said: 'Nominee directors have provided a conundrum for company law and this is an area where commercial reality and

---

[38] A distinction made by the Australian Companies and Securities Law Review Committee in its discussion paper *Nominee Directors and Alternate Directors* Discussion Paper No 7 (1987) at [101]. The distinction is acknowledged by Stanley Burnton J in *R (on the application of Inland Revenue Commissioners) v Kingston Crown Court* [2001] EWHC 581 (Admin) at [20].

[39] P Redmond 'Nominee Directors' (1987) 10 UNSWLJ 194 at 194; E Thomas 'The Role of Nominee Directors and the Liability of their Appointors' in F MacMillan Padfield (ed) *Perspectives on Company Law* (London, Kluwer, 1997) vol 2, at 236.

[40] Companies and Securities Law Review Committee (NSW, Australia) *Nominee Directors and Alternate Directors* Report No 8, 2 March 1989 at 7. See also the earlier discussion paper of the same title, Discussion Paper No 7 (December 1987) at pp 1–2 and quoted in E Boros 'The Duties of Nominee and Multiple Directors: Part 1' (1989) 10 Co Law 211 at 211.

[41] P Redmond 'Nominee Directors' (1987) 10 UNSWLJ 194 at 194; E Boros 'The Duties of Nominee and Multiple Directors: Part 1' (1989) 10 Co Law 211 at 211; E Thomas 'The Role of Nominee Directors and the Liability of their Appointors' in F MacMillan Padfield (ed) *Perspectives on Company Law* (London, Kluwer, 1997) vol 2, at 235.

[42] High Court, 13 May 1994, at p 77 of the transcript and noted in T Courtney 'Fettering Directors' Discretion' (1995) 16 Co Law 227 at 229.

legal niceties frequently collide.'[43] In the words of another commentator, a nominee director is: 'between the devil and the deep blue sea.'[44] It is clear that a nominee could rather easily be placed in a conflict situation,[45] where the interests of the company as a whole diverge from the interests of his or her appointor. In such a scenario if the director fails to act in accordance with the interests of the company, he or she is failing in that duty, but if he or she does not act for the interests of the appointor, then he or she is likely to incur the wrath of the appointor and be dismissed.

7.27 Where there is a nominee situation, it is not unusual for the nominated director to agree informally or formally to act according to the instructions of his or her nominator.[46] Nominee directors are in breach of the duty to fetter discretion if they were to contract with an outsider to act in a particular way at board meetings, or to favour the nominator's interests over those of the company in the event of conflict.[47] Often though there will be an informal arrangement that is not binding. But, the nominator expects loyalty. Whether the director is in breach where there is such a situation will depend on the extent to which the director is entitled to consider the interests of the nominator in acting in the best interests of the company.[48] The traditional position in English law has been that the nominee is not to act in the interests of the nominator except where the interests of the nominator coincide with that of the company, or else he or she would not be exercising discretion independently,[49] and the director could face a conflict of interest. In *Dairy Containers Ltd v NZI Bank Ltd*[50] Thomas J of the New Zealand High Court noted that the: 'very nature or understanding of the arrangement by which directors are appointed as "nominee directors" means that they have fettered their discretion to act independently'.[51] In *Boulting v ACTT*[52] Lord Denning MR said by way of obiter[53] that:

> 'It seems to me that no one, who has duties of a fiduciary nature to discharge, can be allowed to enter into an engagement by which he binds himself to disregard those duties or to act inconsistently with them. No stipulation is lawful by which he agrees to carry out his duties in accordance with the instructions of another

---

[43]   'Nominee Directors' Duty to Promote the Success of the Company: Commercial Pragmatism and Legal Orthodoxy' (2011) 128 LQR 118 at 119.

[44]   R Parsons 'The Director's Duty of Good Faith' (1967) 5 MULR 395 at 418.

[45]   And essentially in breach of the no conflict rule. See *Aberdeen Rly Co v Blaikie* (1854) 1 Macq 461 at 471–472.

[46]   For an American view, see, for example, E Veasy and C Guglielmo 'How Many Masters Can a Director Serve? A Look at the Tensions Facing Constituency Directors' (2008) 63 Bus Law 761.

[47]   See *Kregor v Hollins* (1913) 109 LT 225 (CA); *Clark v Workman* [1920] IR 107 (Ir HC).

[48]   E Boros 'The Duties of Nominee and Multiple Directors: Part 1' (1989) 10 Co Law 211 at 211.

[49]   *Boulting v ACTT* [1963] 2 QB 606 at 626 (CA); *Kuwait Asia Bank EC v National Mutual Life Nominees Ltd* [1991] 1 AC 187 (PC).

[50]   [1995] 2 NZLR 30.

[51]   Ibid at 95.

[52]   [1963] 2 QB 606.

[53]   Ibid at 626. Lord Denning dissented as to the overall decision in the case.

rather than on his own conscientious judgment; or by which he agrees to subordinate the interests of those whom he must protect to the interests of someone else.'

7.28 His Lordship then went on[54] to consider the issue of a nominee director and said that:

'Or take a nominee director, that is, a director of a company who is nominated by a large shareholder to represent his interests. There is nothing wrong in it. It is done every day. Nothing wrong, that is, so long as the director is left free to exercise his best judgment in the interests of the company which he serves. But if he is put upon terms that he is bound to act in the affairs of the company in accordance with the directions of his patron, it is beyond doubt unlawful ....'

7.29 His Lordship had taken a similar line earlier in *Scottish Co-Operative Wholesale Society Ltd v Meyer*,[55] when sitting in the House of Lords. Some years after the decision in *Boulting,* Harman LJ in *Lindgren v L & P Estates Ltd*[56] thought, in relation to the liability of a director, that it was quite irrelevant that the director had been appointed to represent the interests of the parent company,[57] thus suggesting that courts should not give any due consideration to the position in which a nominee finds himself or herself.

7.30 The English case-law makes it clear that nominee directors must not put the interests of their nominators higher than those of the company. Such directors, notwithstanding their position, are required to do that which is in the interests of the company and not what might correspond with the interests of his or her appointors.[58] Likewise, the Privy Council in *Kuwait Asia Bank EC v National Mutual Life Nominees Ltd*[59] said: 'In the performance of their duties as directors ... [the nominee directors] were bound to ignore the interests and wishes of their employer, the bank'.'[60] HH Judge Havelock-Allan QC (sitting as a High Court judge) in *Re Neath Rugby Ltd*[61] applied what has been the traditional English approach and said[62] that:

'the appointee's primary loyalty is to the company of which he is a director. He is obliged to act in the best interests of that company. He is quite entitled to have regard to the interests or requirements of his appointor to the extent that those interests or requirements are not incompatible with his duty to act in the best interests of the company.'

---

[54] Ibid at 626–627.
[55] [1959] AC 324.
[56] [1968] Ch 572.
[57] Ibid at 594.
[58] *Selangor United Rubber Estates Ltd v Craddock (No 3)* [1968] 1 WLR 1555; [1968] 2 All ER 1073. Also, see the Australian decision of *SGH Ltd v FCT* [2002] HCA 18; (2002) 188 ALR 241 at [30].
[59] [1991] 1 AC 187.
[60] Ibid at 221–222.
[61] [2007] EWHC 1789 (Ch); [2008] 1 BCLC 527.
[62] Ibid at [27].

7.31 In a judgment handed down after a later hearing in the Neath Rugby litigation[63] Lewison J (as he then was) concluded that the duties of a nominee director, are owed to the company alone.[64] His view was that the company was entitled to the best independent judgment of a nominee director in deciding where its interests lay.[65] His Lordship went on to say that a nominee director was not required to prefer the interests of his nominator, and certainly not required to do so where in his judgment the interests of his nominator conflicted with those of the company.[66] The judgment of Lewison J was appealed,[67] but it was dismissed by the Court of Appeal which agreed with his Lordship's approach to nominee directors.

7.32 It would appear to be clear that under English law nominee directors do owe the same duties as all directors.[68] Recently the Privy Council has propounded the same view.[69]

7.33 While the English position is quite strict, Professor Paul Davies has wondered whether this is actually the situation in practice.[70] It was stated by Professor Jim Gower[71] that:

> 'to deny a director, openly appointed under the articles to represent a particular class, the right to think primarily of the interests of that class, instead of exclusively of the members and creditors as a whole, may be to defeat the whole object of his appointment.'

7.34 In *Cobden Investments Ltd v RWM Langport Ltd,*[72] Warren J did provide for a more liberal view, than the one traditionally voiced, when he said that the shareholders could, by unanimous consent, approve of a nominee director being able to negotiate with the company on behalf of his nominator and without regard for the best interests of the company. In taking this view his Lordship was accepting what the Australian court in *Japan Abrasive Materials Pty Ltd v Australian Fused Materials Pty Ltd*[73] had said.[74] The judge did take the view that it was doubtful whether it is possible to release a director from his or her general duty to act in the best interests of the company.[75] But, if it were possible then Warren J opined that before he would allow it he would want

---

[63]   *Hawkes v Cuddy; Re Neath Rugby Ltd* [2007] EWHC (Ch) 2999 [2008] BCC 390.
[64]   Ibid at [189].
[65]   Ibid at [194].
[66]   Ibid.
[67]   *Re Neath Rugby Ltd* [2009] EWCA Civ 291; [2010] BCC 597.
[68]   *Cobden Investments Ltd v RWM Langport Ltd* [2008] EWHC 2810 (Ch) at [67].
[69]   *Central Bank of Ecuador and others v Conticorp SA* [2015] UKPC 11; [2016] 1 BCLC 26 at [45].
[70]   P Davies *Gower and Davies' Principles of Modern Company Law* (London, Sweet and Maxwell, 7th edn, 2003) at 391.
[71]   L C B Gower *Principles of Modern Company Law* (London, Sweet and Maxwell, 4th edn, 1979) at 580.
[72]   [2008] EWHC 2810 (Ch).
[73]   (1998) 16 ACLC 1172.
[74]   [2008] EWHC 2810 (Ch) at [63]-[64], [67].
[75]   Ibid at [67].

ideally an express written agreement signed by all of the shareholders.[76] His Lordship did say that he was not saying that a director may act in the interests of his or her appointor regardless of the impact on the company of which he or she is a director.[77] But he said that he saw 'no reason in principle why in relation to specific areas of interest, a director should not be released from his fiduciary duty to give his best independent judgment to the company.'[78] So, the decision does suggest that the shareholders can by way of contract attenuate the duties that are owed by directors. What the decision does not do is to set the parameters for that approach.

7.35 Lewision J referred to shareholder agreements in *Hawkes v Cuddy; Re Neath Rugby Ltd*[79] and he did not appear to rule out the possibility of the approach subsequently taken by Warren J in *Cobden Investments Ltd v RWM Langport Ltd*. The Court of Appeal in the appeal in *Re Neath Rugby Ltd*[80] did not dismiss the idea of a director's duties being attenuated by contractual agreement. Certainly in recent times the courts appear to be more ready to accept the opting out of aspects of company law by way of contractual arrangement.[81]

7.36 Certainly Jacobs J of the New South Wales Supreme Court in *Re Broadcasting Station 2GB Pty Ltd*[82] recognised the realities of the situation, and said that nominees would not be in breach if they acted in favour of the interests of their nominators unless it was possible to infer that they would have acted in that way even if their actions were not in the interests of the company.[83] In such a situation the director must have a reasonable belief that what he or she is doing is in the interests of the company as well as the nominator. Jacobs J acknowledged that it was not realistic to expect a nominee director to approach each company issue with an open mind.[84] Subsequently, in the Federal Court of Australia, Bowen CJ in *Re News Corp Ltd*[85] said[86] that:

> 'It is both realistic and not improper to expect that such directors will follow the interests of the company which appointed them subject to the qualification that they will not so act if of the view that their acts would not be in the interests of the company as a whole.'

---

[76] Ibid.
[77] Ibid at [64].
[78] Ibid at [67].
[79] [2007] EWHC (Ch) 2999 [2008] BCC 390.
[80] [2009] EWCA Civ 291; [2010] BCC 597 at [44].
[81] See, for instance, *Fulham Football Club (1987) Ltd v Richards* [2011] EWCA Civ 855; [2012] Ch 333 where the Court of Appeal said that there was nothing to prevent a dispute which formed the basis of an unfair prejudice petition under s 994 of the Companies Act 2006 being referred to arbitration where such a dispute was covered by an arbitration agreement.
[82] [1964–65] NSWR 1648.
[83] Ibid at 1663.
[84] Ibid at 1663.
[85] (1987) 70 ALR 419.
[86] Ibid at 437.

7.37 Subsequently, and again in the Federal Court, a similar view has been propounded. In *Canwest Global Communications Corporation v Australian Broadcasting Corp*,[87] Hill J observed that:

> 'Directors usually act in accordance with the wishes and interests of a party that has brought about their appointment and on whose goodwill their continuation in office depends unless that places them in breach of their duties.'

7.38 It has been stated, again by Jacobs J, in *Levin v Clark*[88] that it might well be in the interests of the company that someone represents, and acts for, the interests of an outsider, and that the fact that the articles allows for this representation to take place indicates that this state of affairs is in the best interests of the company. Templeman J of the Supreme Court of Western Australia in *Japan Abrasive Materials Pty Ltd v Australian Fused Materials Pty Ltd*[89] took the same sort of approach. In this case a joint venture company was involved, and it is submitted that a court is more likely to accept that directors will favour their appointors when appointed to these kinds of companies.[90] With such companies the wishes of shareholders, and hence the company's interests, could be determined from the articles and any shareholders' agreement. The articles or agreement could state that the directors have been appointed to act in such a way as to represent the interests of their appointors. As a consequence the obligations of one class of director could be made different from those of other directors.[91]

7.39 The upshot of the Australian jurisprudence is that nominees need not enter into their duties with an open mind and they *may* pursue the interests of their appointor provided that when there is a conflict they favour the company's broader interests. While it seems that the Australian position remains as discussed above, it might be notable that the Australian High Court, in *SGH Ltd v Federal Commission of Taxation*,[92] refrained from agreeing with the approach taken in the earlier Australian cases. But it must be stated that the Court did not have to make any ruling on the issue and did not intimate any disagreement with the earlier approach adopted in cases like *Re Broadcasting Station 2GB*.[93]

7.40 The general Australian approach has been adopted in New Zealand. Mahon J of the New Zealand High Court in *Berlei Hestia (NZ) Ltd v*

---

87 [1997] FCA 731; (1997) 24 ACSR 405.
88 [1962] NSWR 686 at 700–701.
89 (1998) 16 ACLC 1172.
90 Such companies are virtually partnerships utilising the corporate form and a board meeting is a meeting of partners (E Thomas 'The Role of Nominee Directors and the Liability of their Appointors' in F MacMillan Padfield (ed) *Perspectives on Company Law* (London, Kluwer, 1997) vol 2, at 237). In such companies it is common to see articles permitting shareholders to appoint and remove directors who represent them.
91 E Thomas 'The Role of Nominee Directors and the Liability of their Appointors' in F MacMillan Padfield (ed) *Perspectives on Company Law* (London, Kluwer, 1997) vol 2, at 248.
92 [2002] HCA 18; (2002) 188 ALR 241 at [30].
93 [1964–65] NSWR 1648.

Ferryhough,[94] a case involving a joint venture company, took the same position as Jacobs J in *Re Broadcasting Station 2GB*.[95] His Lordship felt that it did not seem unreasonable for the corporators of the company to be able to agree on an adjusted form of fiduciary liability for directors so that outsiders would not be prejudiced.[96] Subsequently, in *Trounce and Wakefield v NCF Kaiapoi*[97] the same view was taken by Heron J of the New Zealand High Court and endorsed by Thomas J in *Dairy Containers Ltd v NZI Bank Ltd*.[98]

7.41   The position in Singapore appears to cause more uncertainty. It has been held by the Court of Appeal in that jurisdiction, in *George v Jenton Overseas Investment Pte Ltd*,[99] that a nominee who is a director of a corporate nominator owes undivided loyalty to both companies and must act in good faith for the best interests of both. Accordingly a nominee must ensure that he or she does not place himself or herself in a position where there was actual conflict and the director was in a situation where he or she could not fulfil obligations to one company without failing in his or her obligations to the other. If a nominee prefers the interests of one company over the other then the director is liable. This approach is likely to cause severe problems for nominees in many situations. It might well be unrealistic to ignore the fact that on occasions a director in the kind of situation envisaged in the Singaporean case might be faced with two ways to approach something, one that favours the nominator and one that favours the company.

7.42   It is probably fair to say that overall, and certainly from an historical viewpoint, the Australian and later New Zealand position has been a pragmatic one and more relaxed, compared with the stricter view espoused by Lord Denning, the Privy Council and other English judges. Although one must note that the approach of Upjohn LJ in *Boulting v ACTT*[100] was more liberal than the approach of Lord Denning and those evident in other cases, for he said that persons such as directors can properly and honestly give their services so that they serve two masters to the great advantage of both. In the corporate context if the company is content with that position and understands its rights there is no reason why the general rule that this conflict would not be permitted, should not be relaxed.[101] But this latter approach does not seem to have attracted a lot of English support until recently and as explained above.

7.43   It seems that the approach of the Australian courts and of Upjohn LJ has much going for it. First, it does not require nominees to tie themselves in knots

---

94   [1980] 2 NZLR 150.
95   [1964–65] NSWR 1648.
96   Ibid at 166. The Australian High Court in *Whitehouse v Carlton Hotel Pty Ltd* [1987] HCA 11; (1987) 162 CLR 285, effectively accepted that the company may, in its articles, relieve directors of part of their fiduciary duties.
97   [1985] 2 NZCLC 99, 422.
98   [1995] 2 NZLR 30 at 96.
99   [2007] SGCA 13; [2008] 1 LRC 231.
100 [1963] 2 QB 606.
101 Ibid at 637.

trying to serve two masters – an impossible task.[102] Second, it is realistic. Third, in some cases the interests of the company might involve keeping the nominator content.

7.44 It may be particularly difficult for nominees not to subordinate themselves to the will of their nominators. It might well be that under the new legislation a nominee director may be in a more difficult position unless the constitution acknowledges the nominee's situation and that he or she is to act for the nominator.[103] Certainly, the most optimum situation for a nominee is to ensure that the company's constitution permits him or her to consider the interests of his or her nominator.[104] This would seem, under s 173 of the CA 2006, to be permitted,[105] and make life easier for a nominee.[106] But, the director must remember that a statutory duty is owed to promote the success of the company, consequently there might be occasions where he or she is in the position of having to take a view that is against his or her nominator if there is to be an escape from the clutches of s 172.

IV THE PROVISION – SECTION 173

7.45 The general rule provided by s 173 of the CA 2006 is very similar to that laid down at common law, hence, prima facie, it would seem likely that the case-law will be applied by the courts when construing s 173. It is in relation to the exceptions where things are different and this might have an effect on how the common law is regarded.

7.46 It will be remembered that directors would not be in breach of the duty to fetter their discretion if they exercised their discretion to agree that they would act in a certain way in the future. But this is subject to the proviso that the action of the directors was taken at that time bona fide in the best interests of the company. The new legislation has not used this formula at all. Section 173 of the CA 2006 does not include any such or like qualification. But it must be borne in mind, as indicated earlier, that directors must comply with the duty in s 172, so we might substitute 'promote the success of the company' for 'acting bona fide in the best interests of the company', with the result that

---

[102] Something acknowledged by Lord Denning, a proponent of the strict approach (*Scottish Co-Operative Wholesale Society Ltd v Meyer* [1959] AC 324 at 366).

[103] See Pey-Woan Lee 'Serving Two Masters – The Dual Loyalties of the Nominee Director in Corporate Groups' [2003] JBL 449 at 463 (it is to be noted that this article was written before the present legislation was drafted).

[104] The Australian High Court seemed to endorse such a view in *SGH Ltd v Federal Commissioner of Taxation* [2002] HCA 18; (2002) 210 CLR 51; (2002) 188 ALR 241 at [30] (Aust HC) and referring to *Bennetts v Board of Fire Commissioners of NSW* (1967) 87 WN (Pt 1) (NSW) 307, which tended to side with the stricter approach evident in England.

[105] Compare the view of Professor Paul Redmond who has argued that while nominees might be allowed to consider the interests of their appointor, they should not be permitted to fetter their discretionary powers: 'Nominee Directors' (1987) 10 UNSWLJ 194 at 207.

[106] It is arguable whether this would have been permitted at common law, although there is authority that appears to be in support of the approach, certainly in relation to conflict issues: *New Zealand Netherlands Society 'Oranje' Inc v Kuys* [1973] WLR 1126.

directors are entitled to fetter their discretion if they do so in order to promote the success of the company. However, that is not the end of the matter. In s 173(2)(a) the general principle to exercise independent judgment does not apply where there is an agreement entered into *by the company* that restricts the future exercise of discretion by its directors. It is submitted that this might mean that the scope of the exception to the general principle under the section is not as wide as it was at common law. In the cases that have been decided the agreement circumscribing the actions of directors has not always been made by the company, yet the courts have been willing to say that the duty is not breached, provided that the director(s) acted bona fide in the best interests of the company. Obviously, under the new regime, if the board makes an agreement with another party, and this agreement fetters powers then this would fall within the exception in s 173 as the board will usually have the power to act on behalf of the company.[107] But a fettering of powers by one or more directors will not be covered unless the director(s) has the power to make contracts for the company, and is in fact acting for the company.

7.47 Importantly, when considering directorial liability, the effect of the provisions in the CA 2006 is cumulative so more than one duty may apply to a particular state of affairs.[108] As we noted in **Chapter 4**, where this occurs a director must comply with each applicable duty. The result is that a director cannot claim immunity if he or she was fulfilling one duty but fails to comply with another.[109] So, a director who does not retain independent judgment, but can rely on the exceptions in s 173(2), still might conceivably breach another duty. The Explanatory Notes to the Act provides the following example:

> 'Taking a bribe from a third party would, for example, clearly fall within the duty not to accept benefits from third parties (section 176) but could also, depending on the facts, be characterised as a failure to promote the success of the company for the benefit of its members (section 172) or as an aspect of failing to exercise independent judgment (section 173).'

7.48 All of this is consistent with the position that has been often put, namely that the fiduciary duties owed by directors overlap.

7.49 Finally, we can say that the point at which it will be determined whether there was a breach of another duty is likely to be at the time of the entering into of the agreement that is alleged to fetter powers.[110]

V CONCLUSION

7.50 The duty provided for in s 173 of the CA 2006 that directors are to exercise independent judgment is clearly based on the duty at common law that

---

[107] Such as under the Companies (Tables A–F) Regulations 1985, Table A, reg 70.

[108] CA 2006, s 179. See Explanatory Notes at paras 311, 312.

[109] Explanatory notes at para 313.

[110] See *Thorby v Goldberg* [1964] HCA 41; (1964) 112 CLR 597 at 601; *Fulham Football Club Ltd v Cabra Estates plc.* [1994] 1 BCLC 363 at 392; [1992] BCC 863 at 875.

directors are not to fetter their discretion. Again, as under the common law, there are exceptions to the general rule, and the duty is not breached if directors act in accordance with an agreement entered into by the company that restricts the future exercise of discretion by the directors or in a way authorised by the company's constitution. But while the section is based on a common law duty the provision, it is submitted, has a different ambit. While the exceptions in s 173(2) are similar to those exceptions developed at common law, they are not identical. At common law directors would not be in breach of the duty to fetter their discretion if they exercised their discretion to agree that they would act in a certain way in the future. It is possible to construe the exceptions under the section as not being as broad as that at common law. The critical aspect is that any agreement which affects a director's exercise of independent judgment must be one that has been entered into by the company, so unless directors have the power to make a contract for the company, they are likely to be in breach of s 173.

7.51 Also, it is critical that directors realise that while fulfilling the strict letter of the law in relation to the s 173 duty, they could actually be in breach of another duty. This requires directors to have regard to the general duties in Chapter 2 of Part 10 of the CA 2006 as a whole.

CHAPTER 8

DUTY OF CARE, SKILL AND DILIGENCE[1]

I INTRODUCTION

8.1   Thus far we have been focusing on fiduciary duties. Before continuing to consider fiduciary duties, we now turn our attention in this chapter to the second type of duty owed by directors, namely the duty of care, skill and diligence.[2] At common law while a director could not be held to be in breach of the duty to act bona fide in the best interests of the company (arguably the primary fiduciary duty prior to the enactment of s 172 of the CA 2006) by simply acting negligently, provided he or she believed that what he or she were seeking to do was in the best interests of the company, the director, however, could be liable for a breach of the duty of care.[3] It is interesting to note at the outset that fiduciary duties and duties of care produced separate bodies of case-law and that the latter introduced concepts of tort law, which play no part in a consideration of fiduciary duties. Historically, any actions that might be regarded as serious tended to be considered under the heading of breach of fiduciary duty rather than thoughts turning to whether the action might in fact have been a breach of a duty of care. However, times have changed. As we will see later in the chapter, the approach of the judiciary in the past 25 years has meant that there is more focus on the duty of care. This is perhaps indicated by the fact that in Chapter 2 of Part 10 of the CA 2006 Parliament has inserted the breach of duty provision ahead of those dealing with the duties of directors to avoid conflicts of interest and not to accept benefits from third parties. It would seem that the recent case-law and the approach of Parliament mean that there has been a fundamental change in the climate. The message that is being given both by the courts and the legislature is that breach of duties of care is something to be taken very seriously. However, we must add that there are still relatively few cases where directors have been held to be in breach of this duty. Possible reasons for this are offered later in the Chapter.

---

[1]   For an excellent discussion of some theoretical issues pertaining to this kind of duty, see C A Riley 'The Company Director's Duty of Care and Skill: The Case for an Onerous but Subjective Standard' (1999) 62 MLR 697.

[2]   American law provides that the duty of care is not a common law rule, but a fiduciary duty. American law divides fiduciary duties into two, namely duties of loyalty and duties of care. See T Frankel 'Fiduciary Duties as Default Rules' (1995) 74 Oregon LR 1209 at 1210. Some jurists and commentators in other common law jurisdictions take the view that the duty of care is fiduciary. For instance, see the judgment of Lee AJA in *Westpac Banking Corp v Bell Group Ltd (No 3)* [2012] WASCA 157; (2012) 89 ACSR 1 at [841]. [845], [895]–[896].

[3]   *Colin Gwyer & Associates Ltd v London Whark (Limehouse) Ltd* [2003] 2 BCLC 153.

8.2   The duty of care (unless it is necessary to do otherwise, I will in the chapter refer to the duty of care as a catch-all expression for the duty of care, skill and diligence) is designed to combat the shirking of directors. It is not, according to s 178 of the CA 2006, a fiduciary duty; as suggested above, this was the existing position when codification occurred.[4] Prior to the CA 2006 directors owed both an equitable and common law duty of care.[5] The common law duty was based on tort, and breach of it could be described as negligence. The equitable duty is linked to the director's fiduciary duties in that they were required to exercise reasonable care in discharging their fiduciary powers, just as trustees were and are.[6] Section 170 indicates that the common law rules and equitable principles that applied in relation to the duty before codification will apply, but any distinction between the equitable duty and the common law duty should be of little consequence in light of codification. The duty of care is now covered by s 174.

8.3   The difficulty for a director is that a director's remit can cover a variety of business activities, all involving different care and attention and a different skill level.

8.4   A breach of the duty can consist of a failure to act when a director should have done so, or, conversely, making a decision which is one that could be impugned in some way. There are, clearly, circumstances where the duty could overlap with other duties.[7] For example, the directors of a company make a contract that is not one made in good faith in order to promote the success of the company, and constitutes, therefore, a breach of s 172 of the CA 2006. If the contract was one that no reasonable directors would have made then it is likely that there is also a breach of s 174.

8.5   Generally speaking there is not a significant amount of case-law in the UK to guide us in our consideration of this duty. There is a significant dearth of

---

[4]   *Extrasure Travel Insurances Ltd v Scattergood* [2003] 1 BCLC 598; *Permanent Building Society (in liq) v Wheeler* (1994) 11 WAR 187 at 238; *O'Halloran v R T Thomas & Family Pty Ltd* (1998) 45 NSWLR 262 at 274. See W Heath 'The Director's Fiduciary Duty of Care and Skill: A Misnomer' (2007) 25 CSLJ 370.

[5]   *Lagunas Nitrate Co v Lagunas Syndicate* [1899] 2 Ch 392 at 435 (CA); *Base Metal Trading Ltd v Shamurin* [2004] EWCA Civ 1316; [2005] 2 BCLC 171 at [19]. This is also the case in *Australia: Permanent Building Society (in liq) v Wheeler* (1994) 14 ACSR 109 at 155. For an interesting discussion of the difference between the two types of duty, see S Worthington 'The Duty to Monitor: A Modern View of the Director's Duty of Care' in F Patfield (ed) *Perspectives on Company Law* (London, Kluwer, 1997) vol 2 at 186–188. In the United States the duty of care is regarded as a fiduciary duty. There has been some questioning in the Australian journal literature concerning the denial of the duty of care as fiduciary. See, A Goldfinch 'Trustee's Duty to Exercise Reasonable Care: Fiduciary Duty?' (2004) 78 *Australian Law Journal* 678; W Heath 'The Director's "Fiduciary" Duty of Care and Skill: A Misnomer' (2007) 25 *Company & Securities Law Journal* 370. More importantly, in obiter comments in the Western Australian Court of Appeal, *Westpac Banking Corporation v Bell Group Ltd (in liq) (No 3)* [2012] WASCA 157; (2012) 89 ACSR 1 at [840], [874]–[884], Lee AJA indicated that the view of Owen J at first instance that the duty of care was not a fiduciary duty was open to question.

[6]   *Re Chapman* [1896] 2 Ch 763.

[7]   Acknowledged by the Explanatory Notes to the CA 2006 at para 311.

case-law on s 174 itself. However, there are two fields in which we can find some additional guidance. First, some of the many disqualification cases that have been brought in the past 25 years or so have produced some useful guidance as to how courts view the director's duty of care,[8] for, on numerous occasions, it has been alleged that directors should be disqualified because of their failure to devote sufficient care to their functions and that they are unfit for office.[9] Second, further assistance can be found in the quite considerable number of Australian cases that have been decided under the statutory duty of care applicable in that jurisdiction (presently s 180 of the Corporations Act 2001). Several of the cases have emanated from the collapse of large, substantial companies. Australia has embraced a business judgment rule, a rule that is applied regularly in the United States, but unlike the United States there does not appear to be judicial reluctance, notwithstanding the rule, in holding directors liable in appropriate cases. I should add that under Australian law a director owes both a duty of care at common law as well as a duty of care under the relevant companies legislation.[10] The Australian legislatures saw fit to retain the common law duties when introducing statutory duties, something that the United Kingdom did not do. The Australian statutory provisions impose essentially the same standards as those applying at common law.[11]

8.6 So, while each case involving a claim for a breach of the duty of care must be taken on its own merits, the various previous decisions dealing with the common law and equitable duties, both here and elsewhere in common law jurisdictions, together with the disqualification cases, are of assistance in determining general principles and the principles that are to operate to enable us to ascertain what are the actual duties of directors in a particular case.[12] As much will turn on the facts of individual cases, it is intended not to labour the facts of all authorities considered. The focus will be on principles and practice. The case-law developed prior to codification will be of importance as s 174 effectively follows s 214 of the Insolvency Act 1986 which was the provision by which the judges, immediately before the advent of s 174, have said the duty of care was governed.

8.7 Often executive directors who have contracts of employment (non-executives do not usually have contracts) will have in those contracts

---

[8] As in Australia. For example, see *ASC v Donovan* (1998) 28 ACSR 583.

[9] For example, see *Baker v Secretary of State for Trade and Industry* [2001] BCC 273, where former senior executive directors of Barings Bank were disqualified from acting as directors for not having ensured that the company had adequate systems in place to control and monitor the activities of a trader whose unauthorised dealings had led to the bank's total collapse. Also, see *Re Barings plc (No 5)* [1999] 1 BCLC 433.

[10] The first enactment of legislation to cover a breach of duties by directors occurred in the early 1960s for most States (eg Companies Act 1961 (NSW)), although Victoria enacted the first statutory duty in the British Commonwealth in its Companies Act 1958 (Vic), s 107. This section dealt with directors acting honestly and using reasonable diligence.

[11] For example, see *Re HIH Insurance Ltd (in prov liq); ASIC v Adler* [2002] NSWSC 171; (2002) 41 ACSR 72; (2002) 20 ACLC 576 at [372] (NSW S Ct); *Sheahan v Verco* [2001] SASC 91; (2001) 37 ACSR 117 at [97] (SA S Ct); *Daniels v Anderson* (1995) 13 ACLC 614 at 657 (NSWCA).

[12] *ASC v Gallagher* (1993) 10 ACSR 43 at 52 (WA S Ct (Full Ct)).

express terms to the effect that they are to exercise the care and skill that would be expected of a person in their position.[13] If there is no express term then there will be an implied term.[14] A director will be taken to have promised the company that he or she has the skills of a reasonably competent person in his or her category of appointment and that he or she will act with reasonable care, diligence and skill.[15] Consequently, executive directors will often be sued for breach of contract, but breach of duty of care might be pleaded as an alternative ground in a claim.

8.8   A factor in favour of directors is that boards have been reluctant in the past to bring actions against directors.[16] There are probably a number of reasons for this. First, if boards did instigate proceedings against one or more directors, other board members might be implicated or be embarrassed by evidence given at any subsequent trial. Second, directors might have a feeling of solidarity with the miscreant(s) and realise that they might be the subject of possible litigation at some time in the future,[17] and they would need all the friends on the board that they can muster. Third, proceedings could affect confidence in the company itself and generate negative publicity. Finally, directors might reason that the potential recovery might not be worth the cost and time in taking action. This last reason is exemplified to a degree by the case of *Equitable Life Assurance Society v Bowley*.[18] Proceedings were issued against a number of former directors of the company, but were eventually discontinued at great cost. But, of course, even if the board decides not to take action, a director is not totally safe. As with most breaches of duty, actions will be most often initiated by liquidators and administrators who assume control of companies when they fall into insolvency.[19] Liquidators will usually commence proceedings under the so-called misfeasance procedure in s 212 of the Insolvency Act 1986, which permits actions, inter alia, against directors for negligent conduct.[20] Administrators have a similar action, under para 75 of Schedule B1 of the Insolvency Act. Other actions might be commenced by the

---

[13]   For example, see *Simtel Communications Ltd v Rebak* [2006] EWHC 572 (QB); [2006] 2 BCLC 571 at [104].

[14]   *Lister v Romford Ice & Cold Storage Co Ltd* [1957] AC 555. See *Circle Petroleum (Qld) Pty Ltd v Greenslade* (1998) 16 ACLC 1577; *Bairstow v Queen's Moat Houses plc* (2000) 1 BCLC 549.

[15]   *Re HIH Insurance Ltd (in prov liq); ASIC v Adler* [2002] NSWSC 171; (2002) 41 ACSR 72; (2002) 20 ACLC 576 at [372].

[16]   H Hirt 'The Company's Decision to Litigate Against its Directors: Legal Strategies to Deal with the Board of Directors' Conflict of Interest' [2005] JBL 159 at 159. But the learned author notes that this state of affairs seems to be changing.

[17]   Ibid at 165.

[18]   [2003] EWHC 2263 (Comm); [2004] 1 BCLC 180.

[19]   Liquidators might assign actions in some cases. For example, see *Condcliffe v Sheingold* [2007] EWCA Civ 1043, although this case involved a breach of fiduciary duty.

[20]   See, for example, *Re D'Jan of London Ltd* [1993] BCC 646; *Re Westlowe Storage and Distribution Ltd (in liq)* [2000] 2 BCLC 590; *Re Idessa (UK) Ltd* [2011] EWHC 804 (Ch); *Roberts v Frohlich* [2011] EWHC 257 (Ch) [2011] 2 BCLC 635; *Re Kudos Business Solutions* [2011] EWHC 1436 (Ch); *GHLM Trading Ltd v Maroo & others* [2012] EWHC 61. Others, such as creditors are also entitled to employ s 212. See, for example, *Mullarkey v Broad* [2007] EWHC 3400 (Ch); [2008] 1 BCLC 638.

company after a takeover or by disgruntled shareholders (pursuing derivative proceedings[21]). Another situation where the conduct of directors may be examined is where the company sues its auditors, and the auditors argue contributory negligence, namely that the directors have breached their duty (this is on the basis that the acts of the directors are those of the company).[22]

8.9   Undoubtedly, the law is seeking to ensure that directors can continue their activities, including entrepreneurial ones, and one must have regard for the fact that:[23]

> 'commercial decisions, in the dynamic context of an ongoing commercial relationship and a complex development project, even important decisions, are not unusually taken on imperfect or partial information and reasonably in reliance upon the advice of colleagues and other officers in the common enterprise.'

8.10   But at the same time the directors must be accountable for what they do and their actions assessed on a reasonable scale. The tendency is to make directors more accountable, but it always must be remembered that there is an element of risk taking in what the directors have to do, and if decisions are overly scrutinised directors will refrain from risk taking and that will not, in many cases, maximise corporate wealth. Ipp JA, a former Australian judge, writing extra-judicially some 20 years ago,[24] felt that there was a tendency to see directors as ready targets because of the failures of some companies, and this was not always fair.

8.11   While there has been some uncertainty as to whether fiduciary duties apply to shadow directors,[25] the duty of care will apply to such directors. Furthermore, there is an indication that directors who are members of a parent company board, as well as the boards of subsidiaries, might be liable to the parent company for the way that they have acted in relation to the affairs of the subsidiaries.[26]

8.12   This chapter begins with a consideration of the way that the duty has developed over the past 150 years or so and the approaches taken by the courts. This is followed by a discussion of an apparent change in judicial approach towards the end of the last century. Next the Chapter considers s 174 and then this leads on to an examination of the issues that relate directly to the various components of the duty, namely care, skill and diligence. It is to be noted that in

---

[21]   See **Chapter 14** for a discussion of such proceedings.

[22]   As occurred in *AWA v Daniels* (1992) 10 ACLC 933 (and on appeal (1995) 13 ACLC 614). An English court has stated that auditors would not be prevented from alleging contributory negligence: *Barings v Coopers and Lybrand* [2003] EWHC 1319 (Ch).

[23]   *Martech International Pty Ltd v Energy World Corp Ltd* [2006] FCA 1004; [2007] 234 ALR 265 at [351].

[24]   'The Diligent Director' (1997) 18 Co Law 162 at 162.

[25]   See **2.29** above.

[26]   *Gardner v Parker* [2003] EWHC 1463 (Ch) at [13]–[24]; (on appeal at [2004] EWCA Civ 781 at [19]) and referred to by R Reed 'Company Directors – Collective or Functional Responsibility' (2006) 27 Co Law 170 at 175.

many ways some issues overlap both care and diligence, such as attentiveness, but it is probably helpful for exposition purposes to discuss the contemporary law separately under these respective duties.

II BACKGROUND

8.13   The duty of care has had rather a chequered history. For many years the courts had low expectations of the standard of care to be provided by directors and as a consequence, historically, the courts refrained from imposing liability for breach except in the most obvious cases.[27] This is in contrast with the courts' approach to fiduciary duties, which has been stringent, and breaches treated severely.[28] The courts have been generally reluctant to pass judgment on the merits of management decisions when taken in good faith. However, while accepting the fact that directors are appointed to take certain risks, they have been expected to act with a reasonable degree of care and demonstrate reasonable skill.

8.14   The low expectations of the courts, and the fact that the courts were tolerant of director inactivity, is demonstrated by the rather infamous *Marquis of Bute's Case*.[29] In this case the defendant had been appointed as a director of a bank at the age of six months. Henceforth, he only attended one meeting in 39 years.[30] He was sued, on the basis of a breach of duty of care, for losses sustained by the bank as a result of the irregular activities of the managers and trustees of the bank. The court noted that directors' duties were intermittent in nature, and while a director must exercise care and skill at the meetings which he or she attended, there was no obligation for a director actually to attend meetings. The director was held not liable. Earlier, in *Re Montrotier Asphalte Co*[31] it was said that if a director was called away (by business or even pleasure) and could not attend a meeting then it would be wrong to say that he could be held liable for what was done in his absence.[32] This led the New South Wales Court of Appeal in *Daniels v Anderson*[33] to say that the law seemed to suggest that if there was trouble likely to occur as a result of decisions taken at a board meeting the best action was to absent oneself from the meeting.

8.15   Another aspect of the fact that there were low expectations is found in *Re Brazilian Rubber Plantations and Estates Ltd*[34] where Neville J said that a director is not obliged to take any precise role in the company's affairs. It is only when a director does take on a role that he or she must use reasonable

---

[27]   Professor Brenda Hannigan notes that in practice directors have rarely been sued for breach of the duty of care: *Company Law* (London, Lexis Nexis Butterworths, 2003) at 298.

[28]   For example, see *Regal (Hastings) Ltd v Gulliver* [1967] 2 AC 134 (HL).

[29]   [1892] 2 Ch 100.

[30]   Contrast the early case of *Charitable Corp v Sutton* (1742) 2 Atk 400; 26 ER 642, where a director was found liable for not attending a meeting.

[31]   (1876) 34 LT 716.

[32]   Ibid at 717.

[33]   (1995) 13 ACLC 614 at 657 (NSWCA).

[34]   [1911] 1 Ch 425.

care. But, in any event, according to Neville J, directors were not to be held liable for errors of judgment, just as trustees would not be liable.[35] His Lordship said that a director must take reasonable care and that is to be measured by what is expected of an ordinary person in the relevant circumstances if acting for himself of herself.[36] The test of the ordinary prudent person of business using the care that he or she would apply to his or her own affairs is the one that was, of course, applied to trustees.[37] It was emphasised by the judge that the actions of directors were not to be tested by considering what a court itself would think was reasonable.[38]

8.16 The courts in the nineteenth century and early twentieth centuries, in particular, tended to treat issues of care, skill and diligence from a perspective of good faith, that is: was the director acting in good faith when he or she did what is complained of? If good faith were displayed then liability would, ordinarily, not be imposed. The approach in *Overend Gurney & Co v Gurney*[39] of Lord Hatherley LC, who said that the directors in the case before him had been imprudent and unwise, that is negligent, but were not to be held liable, for to be liable they had to be guilty of gross or culpable negligence in a business sense, which was typical of the general trend of opinion in the early cases.[40] Even what might be regarded as extreme conduct did not lead the court to find the defendants in *Re Brazilian Rubber Plantations and Estates Ltd*[41] liable for breach. In that case the directors sanctioned the purchase of a rubber plantation for £150,000 even though they knew that the seller had purchased it for £15,000 and that the number of trees fit for tapping had been grossly exaggerated. In the course of his judgment Neville J confessed that he found it difficult to distinguish between negligence and gross negligence.[42] His Lordship expressed the view[43] that as far as the issue of care was concerned there was a lack of precision in saying that a director's liability existed when there was gross negligence.[44]

---

[35] Ibid at 436. The case of *Re Chapman* [1896] 2 Ch 763 is authority for the proposition that trustees are not liable for errors of judgment provided that they meet certain requirements such as acting with reasonable care and prudence. The recent case of *Roberts v Frohlich* [2011] EWHC 257 (Ch) [2011] 2 BCLC 635 at [106] is authority for the view that errors of judgment on their own does not constitute a breach of care.

[36] *Re City Equitable Fire Insurance* Co. [1925] Ch 407 at 437.

[37] *Speight v Gaunt* (1883) 22 Ch D 727 at 739.

[38] [1911] 1 Ch 425 at 437–438.

[39] (1869) LR 4 Ch App 701.

[40] For example, see *Turquand v Marshall* (1869) 4 Ch App 376; *Lagunas Nitrate Co v Lagunas Syndicate* [1899] 2 Ch 392 (CA); *Re National Bank of Wales Ltd* [1899] 2 Ch 629 (CA); *Re Brazilian Rubber Plantations and Estates Ltd* [1911] 1 Ch 425. The first reported case to involve a claim of a breach of duty of care in English law, *Charitable Corp v Sutton* (1742) 2 Atk 400; 26 ER 642, required directors to have acted with gross negligence for liability to be imposed.

[41] [1911] 1 Ch 425.

[42] Ibid at 437.

[43] Ibid.

[44] Ibid at 436–437.

8.17   There are instances of courts holding directors liable, but they do involve situations where the directors' actions are clearly in breach. For example, in *Gould v Mt Oxide Mines Ltd (in liq)*[45] the directors of a company permitted X who was not a director or even a shareholder of their company to draw cheques on the company's bank account, and the directors were held liable for the loss sustained by the company following X drawing a cheque for an unauthorised purpose.

8.18   For many years, the courts regarded directors as amateurs,[46] who were only involved in a part-time activity, and whose duties were regarded as intermittent. In *Re Denham & Co*[47] the director who was sued was referred to as a 'country gentleman' and it was said that because of his background and lack of experience he could not be expected to understand the financial statements of the company and the circumstances surrounding the fraud perpetrated by the chairman. The courts took the view that shareholders had a vote when it came to appointment of directors, so they deserved the directors they got. In *Overend & Gurney & Co v Gurney*[48] Lord Hatherley LC said that: 'The company must take the consequences of having intrusted their moneys to persons of sanguine temperament who have made a purchase which turns out to be a bad one.'[49] In *Turquand v Marshall*[50] the court emphasised the fact that it was the shareholders who chose such unwise directors.[51] At this time in the development of company law the company was clearly associated with the shareholders, and this led, for instance, to the courts, when referring to company property, talking about 'their property' and not 'its property'.[52] Hence, if the shareholders voted for negligent directors it was seen as only affecting their interests/benefits. The idea of separate legal entity had not been fleshed out at this point.

8.19   Perhaps the most important of the earlier cases, certainly in terms of influence and longevity, was *Re City Equitable Fire Insurance Co*.[53] In this case an action was brought against directors by the Official Receiver as liquidator of their former company. He claimed that the directors, while acting honestly, had been negligent in not ascertaining the fact that the chairman had made on behalf of the company certain investments and loans, and paid dividends out of capital, and these actions were tantamount to fraud. Romer J said that directors had not only to act honestly, but must exercise some degree of care and skill.[54]

---

[45]   (1916) 22 CLR 490.
[46]   It is interesting to note that in as far back as 1742 Lord Hardwicke stated that it was no excuse for directors to say that their role was merely honorary: *Charitable Corporation v Sutton* (1742) 2 Atk 400 at 405–406.
[47]   (1884) 25 Ch D 752.
[48]   (1869) LR 4 Ch App 701 (CA).
[49]   Ibid at 720.
[50]   (1869) 4 Ch App 376.
[51]   Ibid at 386.
[52]   See P Ireland, I Grigg-Spall and D Kelly 'The Conceptual Foundations of Modern Company Law' (1987) 14 *Journal of Law and Society* 149 at 150.
[53]   [1925] Ch 407.
[54]   Ibid at 427.

However, his Lordship observed that the case-law did not give any clear answer to the question: what particular degree of care and skill had to be exercised by a director?[55] Romer J devoted a fair amount of time to establishing what is meant by wilful negligence, for if the conduct of the directors could be so classified, they would be liable. He expressed the view, keeping company with Neville J in *Re Brazilian Rubber Plantations and Estates Ltd,* that he found it difficult in understanding the difference between negligence and gross negligence.[56] His Lordship said that directors must take reasonable care and that is measured, using the same approach as propounded by Lord Hatherley LC in *Overend & Gurney & Co v Gurney,*[57] against the care an ordinary person might be expected to take in the circumstances on his or her own behalf.[58] Romer J said[59] that the practical duties of a director in one company will be different from those owed by a director in another company (comparing a director of a small retail business and a director of a railway company). This case is famous for the fact that it established three propositions that encapsulated the law and that were to act as guiding principles in this area for 60 years, and still have some impact. The three propositions, together with some additional explanatory comments, are:

- A director need not exhibit in the performance of his or her duties greater skill than may be reasonably expected from a person of his or her knowledge and experience. This meant that directors were not liable for mere errors of judgment,[60] and they only needed to exhibit as much skill as someone as competent or as inexperienced as they were.

- A director is not bound to give continuous attention to the affairs of his or her company, as the duties of a director are intermittent. His Lordship regarded the director's responsibilities as being limited to attending board meetings and the meetings of board committees of which he or she was a member.[61] All of this is obviously directed at non-executive directors for executive directors are obliged to give continuous attention to their companies.

- If it is prudent from a business sense that some duty be left to some other official, then in the absence of grounds for suspicion, a director is justified in trusting that official to perform those duties honestly.[62]

8.20 Although the case went on appeal these points were not directly relevant, as only limited aspects of the case were argued before the Court of Appeal. Consequently, as mentioned above, the three propositions were relied on in most subsequent cases.

---

[55] Ibid at 426.
[56] Ibid at 427–428.
[57] (1871–72) LR 5 HL 480 (HL).
[58] *Re City Equitable Fire Insurance Co.* [1925] Ch 407 at 427–428.
[59] Ibid at 426.
[60] Ibid at 428–429. This is the same for all professionals. See *Saif Ali v Sydney Mitchell & Co* [1980] AC 198 at 220; [1978] 3 All ER 1033 at 1043 (HL).
[61] *Re City Equitable Fire Insurance Co.* [1925] Ch 407 at 429.
[62] Ibid at 429. This effectively follows what was said in *Dovy v Cory* [1901] AC 44 at 492.

8.21 Notwithstanding the fact that the duty outlined in the case appeared to provide for some degree of objectivity, something not always acknowledged, the law often regarded the duty as purely subjective. Importantly the courts refrained from imposing objective standards of competence or skill in the field in which the company operated. It has been argued[63] that the case has been misrepresented by writers who have over-emphasised the subjective test referred to above in the first proposition, for, it is argued, substantial objective elements are clearly apparent in what Romer J had to say. Notably he said that the necessary standard is that of 'reasonable care' to be measured by the care an ordinary person ought to be expected to take in the circumstances when acting for himself or herself.[64] It is pointed out that the three propositions were expressed to be 'in addition' to this basic objective standard.[65] This interpretation seems to be consistent with the much earlier comments of Lord Hatherley in *Overend & Gurney & Co v Gurney*,[66] when he said that the test was basically objective as courts have to ask what an ordinary prudent person would be expected to have done in the situation if that person were acting for himself or herself.[67]

8.22 The propositions in *Re City Equitable* focused, as did much of the preceding law, on the non-executive director and arguably did not apply to the modern executive, or even the modern non-executive. Case-law now suggests that no distinction is made between executives and non-executives in the sense that both can be held liable.[68] But there must surely be significant distinctions made at a practical level,[69] as we shall see later in the Chapter. Nevertheless, *Re City Equitable* indicated that directors were under a duty to at least become familiar with the affairs of their company and its business.[70] But directors did not need to have special abilities and, for instance, a director of an insurance company would not be expected to have the skill and ability of an actuary.[71]

8.23 The duty of directors remained ill-defined for many years.[72] We can sum up the duty of the director according to the older cases as undemanding.[73] The reasons for this are undoubtedly legion, but the primary ones appear to be that: directors were clearly appointed with little or no experience; the difficulties in

---

[63] A Hicks 'Directors' Liabilities for Management Errors' (1994) 110 LQR 390.

[64] It is certainly questionable whether a person should be permitted to risk other people's money to the same degree as his or her own. See M Trebilcock 'The Liability of Company Directors for Negligence' (1969) 32 MLR 499 at 501.

[65] A Hicks 'Directors' Liabilities for Management Errors' (1994) 110 LQR 390 at 392.

[66] (1871–72) LR 5 HL 480 (HL).

[67] Ibid at 487.

[68] *Dorchester Finance Co Ltd v Stebbing* [1989] BCLC 498; *Equitable Life Assurance Society v Bowley* [2003] EWHC 2263 (Comm); [2004] 1 BCLC 180 at [35]. This is the case also in New Zealand (*Deloitte Haskins and Sells v National Mutual Life Nominees Ltd* (1991) 5 NZCLC 67, 442-3) and Australia (*Daniels v AWA Ltd* (1995) 13 ACLC 614 at 662 (NSWCA)).

[69] This appears to have been the case at first instance in *Daniels v AWA Ltd* (1992) 10 ACLC 933, but not in the New South Wales Court of Appeal ((1995) 13 ACLC 614 (NSWCA)).

[70] See *Re Australasian Venezolana* (1962) 4 FLR 60 at 66.

[71] *Re City Equitable Fire Insurance Co.* [1925] Ch 407 at 428.

[72] *Daniels v Anderson* (1995) 13 ACLC 614 at 656 (NSWCA).

[73] *Bishopsgate Investment Management Ltd v Maxwell* [1993] BCC 120 at 139.

bringing actions led to a paucity of case-law; the courts were decidedly reluctant to make adverse judgments about the decisions of directors.[74] Also, as we have seen, post- *Re City Equitable* it was often suggested that the standard of care was wholly subjective,[75] even though this seems to be an incorrect interpretation of the case, and this might well have discouraged the bringing of proceedings. Furthermore, the lenient way that the duty was applied was another probable reason for the initiation of relatively few actions.

III THE PERCEIVED CHANGE IN JUDICIAL APPROACH

8.24 For the best part of 65 years the law did not move on in any major way. The exposition of Romer J in *Re City Equitable* was regarded as explaining and laying down the law. This is somewhat surprising when one notes the development of the neighbour principle in relation to negligence in the early 1930s and subsequent developments relating to that tort.[76] According to a leading text, by the late 1980s the common law on the duty of care in this area was lamentably out of date.[77] Nevertheless, in more recent times the courts have become more pro-active and acknowledged that they 'ought not to remain "wholly aloof"'.[78] The first decision that arguably marked this approach (of the modern era), even if did not take things too far, was the 1989 case of *Dorchester Finance Co Ltd v Stebbing*[79]. In this case the defendant directors signed blank cheques and left the making of loans to another director, the chairman, who was not supervised,[80] and this permitted the subsequent misapplication of company funds. All three defendant directors were held to be in breach of their duty. Foster J only found one director, the chairman, to be guilty of gross negligence, while the other two defendants were guilty of negligence. The judge rejected the argument of counsel for the defendants that only directors guilty of gross negligence were in breach. Also, the judge did not accede to the notion that non-executive directors were able to do nothing about the company's finances and had to rely on the company's auditors.[81]

8.25 The next major development came in the case of *Norman v Theodore Goddard*.[82] Hoffmann J, with 'minimal analysis',[83] stated that s 214 of the

---

[74] S Worthington 'The Duty to Monitor: A Modern View of the Director's Duty of Care' in F Patfield (ed) *Perspectives on Company Law* (London, Kluwer, 1997) vol 2 at 189.

[75] J H Farrar 'The Duty of Care of Company Directors in Australia and New Zealand' in R Rider (ed) *The Realm of Company Law* (London, Kluwer, 1998) at 42. The last point is well illustrated by *Shuttleworth v Cox Bros and Co (Maidenhead)* [1927] 2 KB 9 at 23.

[76] S Worthington 'The Duty to Monitor: A Modern View of the Director's Duty of Care' in F Patfield (ed) *Perspectives on Company Law* (London, Kluwer, 1997)vol 2 at 181.

[77] J Farrar et al *Farrar's Company Law* (London, Butterworths, 3rd edn, 1991) at 396.

[78] L S Sealy 'The Director as Trustee' [1967] CLJ 83 at 101.

[79] [1989] BCLC 498.

[80] While such action was regarded as a breach of duty, in *Re Hitco 2000 Ltd* [1995] BCLC 63; [1995] BCC 161, the action was not regarded as sufficient to warrant a disqualification order being made against the director.

[81] This resonates with the more recent judgment in *ASIC v Healey* [2011] FCA 717.

[82] [1992] BCC 14.

[83] B Hannigan *Company Law* (London, Lexis Nexis Butterworths, 2003) at 297.

Insolvency Act 1986 correctly stated the common law duty of care of a director.[84] No authority was cited to his Lordship and he mentioned no case in support of his view. Clearly no case had, previously, taken this approach, although the section had only commenced operation in 1986. The judge did not find the director in the case before him to be liable as he held that the director had acted reasonably. His Lordship followed the approach that he had accepted as representing the common law in the subsequent case of *Re D'Jan of London*,[85] although in this latter case the defendant director was found liable. The director signed an insurance form, which had been completed by his insurance broker without first checking whether the contents of it were in fact accurate, and subsequently the insurance company repudiated liability in relation to an event covered by the insurance on the basis of the wrong answers provided on the insurance form by the defendant. Again, his Lordship said, with no discussion, that s 214 of the Insolvency Act stated the common law.

8.26 While the aforementioned case-law has undoubtedly led to a more strict approach from the courts, it is arguable that the test propounded by Hoffmann J did not depart significantly from that put forward by Romer J in *Re City Equitable Fire Insurance Co*.[86] Andrew Hicks has asserted[87] that:

> 'Romer J was setting out a dual standard, first the minimum and irreducible objective standard of the reasonable care of the ordinary man acting on his own behalf; and secondly, the subjective test that relieves him if he does not have highly specialised expertise. Romer J's subjective test is not intended to reduce the standard of care below that of the reasonable ordinary businessman.'

8.27 At about the same time as the UK courts were implementing a stricter approach, the New South Wales Supreme Court heard and ruled in a very important duty of care case, *AWA Ltd v Daniels*,[88] that has had implications not only for the Australian courts, but also for the UK's courts.[89] Rogers CJ (Comm Div) in *AWA Ltd v Daniels* made several comments that indicated that the common law in relation to the duty of care had changed by 1992. His Honour said:[90]

> 'Of necessity, as the complexities of commercial life have intensified the community has come to expect more than formerly from directors whose task is to govern the affairs of companies to which large amounts of money are committed by way of equity capital or loan. The affairs of a company with a large annual

---

[84] [1992] BCC 14 at 15. Interestingly, while the Australian courts did not apply the Australian provisions governing the equivalent to wrongful trading, insolvent trading (see Corporations Act 2001, ss 588G and following), these provisions appear to have influenced the development of the duty in Australia (eg see *Daniels v Anderson* (1995) 13 ACLC 614 at 656 (NSWCA)) and convinced the courts of the need for a higher standard of care.

[85] [1993] BCC 646.

[86] [1925] Ch 407.

[87] A Hicks 'Directors' Liabilities for Management Errors' (1994) 110 LQR 390 at 392.

[88] (1992) 10 ACLC 933.

[89] For instance, see Jonathan Parker J in *Re Barings (No 5)* [1999] 1 BCLC 433 who adopted what was said in *AWA v Daniels* (1992) 10 ACLC 933.

[90] Ibid at 1013.

turnover, large stake in assets and liabilities, the use of very substantial resources and hundreds, if not thousands of employees demand an appreciable degree of diligent application by its directors if they are to attempt to do their duty.'

8.28 On appeal in the AWA case (*Daniels v Anderson*) the New South Wales Court of Appeal recognised the fact that much had changed since the decision in *Re City Equitable*.[91] As the Australian jurisprudence is dealt with here, we should note that notwithstanding the importance of *Daniels* in the development of the law in Australia, in the 1990s there was not the same opening up of the duty[92] as there was in the United Kingdom. But, there appears to have been a change in the new millennium with cases like *Re HIH Insurance Ltd (in prov liq)*,[93] *Re OneTel Ltd (in liq)*,[94] *ASIC v Vines*,[95] and *ASIC v Healey*[96] and so on suggesting a more stringent application of the law. Reference is made to these and other cases later.

8.29 Returning to s 214 of the Insolvency Act 1986, it provides that a director will be liable to contribute to the assets of a company that is in liquidation if he or she knew or ought to have concluded that there was no reasonable prospect of the company avoiding insolvent liquidation.[97] Of critical importance for our examination is s 214(4) that provides, for the purposes of the section, that the facts a director ought to know or ascertain, the conclusions that he or she ought to reach and the steps that ought to be taken, are those which would be known, ascertained, reached or taken by a reasonably diligent person having:

- the general knowledge, skill and experience that may be reasonably expected of a person carrying out the same function, and

- the general knowledge, skill and experience that the director has.

8.30 Interestingly both factors have objective and subjective aspects. While the first factor is essentially objective (how would the reasonable person act in discharging the director's function?), there must be reference to the director's function, so the test is employed in light of the subjective circumstances of the director.[98] The second factor is subjective in that reference is made to the general knowledge, skill and experience of the director, namely something that is specific to the director, but the standard is objective in the sense that the law looks at how the reasonable person would operate with the knowledge, skill and experience that the director possesses.

---

[91] *Daniels v Anderson* (1995) 13 ACLC 614 at 659.
[92] For example, see the decisions of *Vrisakis v ASC* (1993) 11 ACSR 162; *ASC v Gallagher* (1993) 10 ACSR 43; *Biala Pty Ltd v Mallina Holdings Ltd* (1994) 15 ACSR 1.
[93] [2002] NSWSC 171; (2002) 41 ACSR 72; (2002) 20 ACLC 576 (NSW S Ct).
[94] (2003) 44 ACSR 682 (NSW S Ct).
[95] (2003) 48 ACSR 322 (NSW S Ct).
[96] [2011] FCA 717.
[97] See A Keay *Company Directors' Responsibilities to Creditors* (Abingdon, Routledge/Cavendish, 2007) ch 8.
[98] Ipp 'The Diligent Director' (1997) 18 Co Law 162 at 166.

8.31 It might be argued that UK case-law in the late 1980s and early 1990s saw a change in the approach of the courts rather than an essential change in the law. The courts merely applied the law in cases, such as *Re City Equitable Fire Insurance*,[99] in a modern context.[100]

IV THE NEW PROVISION

8.32 Section 174 of the CA 2006 encapsulates the developments that took place in the case-law in the 15 to 20 years preceding it, and provides that the duty is that which is contained in s 214(4) of the Insolvency Act 1986.[101] The wording is aligned with the provisions of s 214. After stating that directors have to exercise reasonable care, skill and diligence in carrying out their functions, s 174(2) explains what this means. The subsection, in explaining this, combines both objective and subjective standards. The subsection provides:

> 'This means the care, skill and diligence that would be exercised by a reasonably diligent person with –
>
> (a)   the general knowledge, skill and experience that may reasonably be expected of a person carrying out the functions carried out by the director in relation to the company, and
> (b)   the general knowledge, skill and experience that the director has.'

8.33 While knowledge, skill and experience are mentioned in para 2(b), care is not mentioned. It is only mentioned in s 174(1) and then again in the preamble to sub-s (2). This suggests that while knowledge, skill and experience will differ between directors, there is only one standard of care; the element of care cannot be taken as personal.

8.34 Undoubtedly the provision is going to be interpreted and applied in conformity with the law developed in the past 25 years and which focused on s 214 of the Insolvency Act 1986.

8.35 A director will be judged by two tests and the director has to attain the higher of the standards set by the tests.[102] So, if a director were to meet the standard of a reasonable person carrying out the director's functions in relation to the company, but a court took the view that the director did not act in such a way as one would reasonably expect of someone with his or her knowledge, skill and experience, the director could be held liable for breach of duty. In the reverse situation, where a director does act as a reasonably diligent person with

---

[99]   [1925] Ch 407.
[100] S Worthington 'The Duty to Monitor: A Modern View of the Director's Duty of Care' in F Patfield (ed) *Perspectives on Company Law* (London, Kluwer, 1997) vol 2 at 189.
[101] CA 2006, s 174 is based on recommendations from the Law Commission ('Company Directors: Regulating Conflicts of Interest and Formulating a Statement of Duties,' No 261, 1999, Pt 5) and the CLRSG (Draft Clauses, Sch 2, para 4).
[102] The first part of this paragraph is based on A Keay *Company Directors' Responsibilities to Creditors* (Abingdon, Routledge/Cavendish, 2007), Chapter 8.

his or her own knowledge, skill and experience would have acted, but the director cannot be said to have acted in line with how the reasonable person would have acted in carrying out the director's functions (perhaps a poorly qualified director with little experience), the director again will be liable, not being able to hide behind his or her lack of expertise. The director must fulfil both tests to avoid liability. This prevents a highly experienced director being immune from liability where he or she might act as a reasonable person carrying out his or her function would have, but fails to live up to the standard that one would reasonably expect of a person of his or her experience. Likewise, the tests mean that very inexperienced directors are not able to duck liability merely because they did what reasonable persons of their experience would have done, if their conduct falls below that expected of a reasonable person acting in his or her position. A director cannot rely on his or her inexperience or deficiencies,[103] and ignorance is not an excuse.[104] In a wrongful trading case, *Re DKG Contractors Ltd*,[105] one of the directors said that he did not know about companies and had no idea what was involved in being a director.[106] But this did not save him from liability under the same kinds of tests as set out in s 174 of the CA 2006. In *Gamble v Hoffman*,[107] whilst not deciding the matter, Carr J of the Australian Federal Court doubted whether he could take into account, in assessing liability, the director's very humble background and experience, namely the fact that the director had left school at the age of 14, had no tertiary qualifications and had worked as a fruit and vegetable market gardener (an occupation that was not related to the business of the company) for all of his life. Such a background would not, it appears, affect the final decision of a court. Obviously, the concern of the legislature would be that neither inexperienced nor incompetent directors are to be protected because of the mere fact that they are inexperienced or incompetent, and those who are experienced are not able to say that while they did not live up to their standards, they did what a reasonably diligent person would have done.

8.36 Section 174(2)(a) of the CA 2006 requires a court to consider the 'functions carried out by the director in relation to the company'. This does not embrace the Law Commission's recommendation that the duty should encompass the circumstances of the company as well as the function of the director.[108] Consequently the section appears to limit the ambit of a court's considerations, namely only to the director's functions. In contrast s 180(4) of the Australian legislation (Corporations Act 2001) provides:

---

[103] This is consistent with the general law on negligence: *Wilsher v Essex Area Health Authority* [1987] QB 730 and affirmed at [1988] AC 174.
[104] *Re Brian D Pierson (Contractors) Ltd* [1999] BCC 26 at 55; [2001] BCLC 275 at 309 (a wrongful trading case).
[105] [1990] BCC 903.
[106] Ibid at 912.
[107] (1997) 24 ASCR 369 at 373.
[108] 'Company Directors: Regulating Conflicts of Interest and Formulating a Statement of Duties,' No 261, 1999 at para 5.15.

'In the exercise of his or her powers and the discharge of his or her duties, an officer of a corporation must exercise the degree of care and diligence that a reasonable person in a like position in a corporation would exercise in the corporation's circumstances'

and it appears to be somewhat broader as it permits courts to refer to the circumstances of the company as well as the position of the director.[109] But, it is submitted, that given the jurisprudence that has developed, particularly in relation to s 214(4), the UK courts will be able to consider more than just the actual functions of the directors, including things like the size and nature of the company as well as the make-up of the board and the way that functions are distributed.[110] If this were not the case then the ambit of the provision would be too narrow.

8.37 One commentator has suggested that the greater strictness in relation to this duty has resulted from the more demanding statutory standards imposed on directors where their companies are faced with, or the prospect of, insolvency.[111] This might be true to a point, although the courts have tended to be relatively relaxed in their requirements when it comes to claims for wrongful trading brought when companies have entered insolvent liquidation.[112]

8.38 Whilst what is expected of directors today is more than what was expected in previous times, in assessing directors, we must be careful to scrutinise only the behaviour of directors and not the results of what they do, for they cannot control certain exogenous events,[113] nor can they foresee their occurrence as they are not omniscient.[114] The courts have indicated some understanding of the difficulties facing directors in the discharge of their duty of care. For instance, in the Australian case of *Vrisakis v ASC*[115] Ipp J of the Full Court of the Western Australian Supreme Court said that directors are involved in activities that have foreseeable risk of harm to the company's interests, and just because something goes wrong does not mean that they are liable for a breach of their duty of care. He went on to say that the section in the legislation (Corporations Law, s 234, the forerunner to s 180(4) of the Corporations Act 2001) that provides for the duty (and not unlike s 174 of the CA 2006) is not intended to dampen business enterprise and activity.

---

[109] See the comments on this in *ASIC v Healy* [2011] FCA 707.

[110] The distribution of functions was a factor Romer J in *Re City Equitable Fire Insurance* [1925] Ch 407 at 428 said should be taken into account.

[111] P Davies *Gower and Davies' Principles of Company Law* (London, Sweet and Maxwell 7th edn, 2003) at 433.

[112] See A Keay *Company Directors' Responsibilities to Creditors* (Abingdon, Routledge/ Cavendish, 2007) at 137-147 where it is argued that the courts have not been overly strict on directors subject to wrongful trading proceedings. A prime example is *Re Continental Assurance Ltd* [2001] BPIR 733.

[113] See C A Riley 'The Company Director's Duty of Care and Skill: The Case for an Onerous but Subjective Standard' (1999) 62 MLR 697 at 705, 710.

[114] *Morley v Statewide Tobacco Services Ltd* [1993] 1 VR 423.

[115] (1993) 11 ACSR 162 at 212.

8.39 It is interesting to note, lest it be thought that the provision places onerous requirements on directors, that the courts have not been overly harsh in applying the tests in s 214 cases or breach of duty cases. In fact, it might be said that they have been quite lenient. What must be taken into account today is that the complexity of commercial life has developed significantly, certainly since the days of the gentlemen directors of the mid-late nineteenth century (and beyond). More and more is probably expected of those to whom large amounts of money and the futures of a lot of people (in terms of equity investments and pensions) are committed. This is, to a degree, reflected in the case-law.

8.40 The duty has been under development for some time and it is true to say that at the time when the duty was codified development was still occurring. There have been relatively few cases where s 174 has been considered, but it seems that at the moment we can say that the section is following the case-law that was decided immediately before codification. The courts have not taken the advent of the section as an opportunity to develop the ambit of the duty further.

8.41 It is provided now by statute, and it was the case at common law, that all directors must display a degree of care, skill and diligence. The critical issue is how much must they display? This cannot be legislated for. It has been said that in deciding whether there has been a breach or not, especially if the breach concerns the way that the company ran its business, 'evidence of what is normal in the field of commerce in which the company operates is of considerable relevance.'[116] One of the problems in this area is the fact that there is no prescribed, or even recognised, body of detailed expert knowledge involved in acting as a director.[117] Each case will undoubtedly be decided on its own merits, because whether or not a breach of s 174 has occurred is an intensely fact-specific issue.[118]However, there are some principles that have been laid down which will guide the consideration and we will examine them in the following parts of the Chapter. It is likely that commercial practice will set the standards and courts will adopt many of those as the law on the issue. For a case where the requirements of s 174 are considered in relation to the evidence adduced, see *Weavering Capital (UK) Ltd (in liquidation) v Petersen.*[119]

8.42 In considering the provision a judge is only required in deciding that the duty has been breached, to recognise the requirements of s 174 and to review

---

[116] *Abbey Forwarding Ltd (in liq) v Hone* [2010] EWHC 2029 (Ch) at [198 per Lewison J.

[117] Although in some cases Australian judges have referred to evidence given by experienced directors or published reports. See, for example, in relation to the evidence of directors, *Re HIH Insurance Ltd; ASIC v Adler* [2002] NSWSC 171; (2002) 41 ACSR 72 at [385]; *ASIC v Vines* [2003] FLR 405, [2003] NSWSC 1116, SC, NSW; (2005) 23 ACLC 1387. In *ASIC v Rich* [2003] NSWSC 85; (2003) 21 ACLC 450 at [68]–[70] the judge referred, inter alia, to the Higgs Report. In *ASIC v Healey* [2011] FCA 717 the judge, in his judgment, referred to the Australian institute of Company Directors' publication titled, 'How to Review a Company's Financial Reports: A Guide for Boards'.

[118] *Brumder v Motornet Service and Repairs Ltd* [2013] EWCA Civ 195 at [54].

[119] [2012] EWHC 1480 (Ch).

the facts; it is not necessary for the judge to expand and set out what he or she regards as the standard of care to be exercised by the relevant director.[120]

8.43 We will now examine the various duties that are contained in s 174 of the CA 2006. As indicated earlier, there are overlaps between care, skill and diligence.

V CARE

8.44 What courts find difficult on many occasions is distinguishing the responsibility and conduct of individual directors from that of the board as a whole.[121] Presumably if the responsibility is that of the whole board then all are liable, for directors owe their duties individually and collectively.[122] Directors have a duty to join in with the other directors in supervising and controlling the managers.[123] Lord Woolf CJ in *Re Westmid Packing Services Ltd (No 3)*[124] emphasised the fact that directors as a board have a collective responsibility and it is fundamental to corporate governance, but this is based on individual responsibility.[125] One of the problems that was identified as far back as 1997 is that the actual role of the board of directors 'in modern companies has not been realistically defined with a degree of particularity'.[126] Anyway, leaving aside collective liability, we now focus on the issues that pertain directly to individual directors, although, of course, more than one director might be the subject of an action in any given situation.

8.45 We have to begin with the acknowledgment that it is not possible for a law to state exhaustively what roles a director is to play. It is necessary to rely on generally composed standards. In some Australian cases evidence from experienced company directors and officers has been drawn upon by courts as part of their determination of the appropriate standards to be applied.[127] In other cases material published by professional associations and government bodies dealing with directors and their roles have been relied upon.[128]

---

[120] [2013] EWCA Civ 71 at [29].

[121] *Re Landhurst Leasing plc* [1999] 1 BCLC 286 at 346; *Re Queens Moat Houses plc (No 2)* [2004] EWHC 1730 (Ch); [2005] 1 BCLC 136 at [26].

[122] *Re Barings (No 5)* [1999] 1 BCLC 433 at 489; *Secretary of State v Thornbury* [2007] EWHC 3202 (Ch); [2008] 1 BCLC 139 at [36]. Also see *Gold Ribbon (Accountants) Pty Ltd v Sheers & Ors* [2006] QCA 335 at [234] (Qld S Ct (CA)).

[123] *Re Vintage Hallmark plc* [2006] EWHC 2761 (Ch); [2007] 1 BCLC 788.

[124] [1998] 2 All ER 124; [1998] BCC 836; [1998] 2 BCLC 646.

[125] [1998] 2 All ER 124 at 130; [1998] 2 BCLC 646 at 653. Approved of in *Re Kaytech International plc* [1999] 2 BCLC 351 at 425 (CA).

[126] L Griggs and J Lowry 'Finding the Optimum Balance for the Duty of Care Owed by the Non-Executive Director' in F Patfield (ed) *Perspectives on Company Law* (London, Kluwer, 1997) vol 2 at 206.

[127] For example, *Re HIH Insurance Ltd; ASIC v Adler* [2002] NSWSC 171; (2002) 41 ACSR 72 at [385]; *ASIC v Vines* [2003] FLR 405, [2003] NSWSC 1116, SC, NSW; (2005) 23 ACLC 1387.

[128] For example, *ASIC v Rich* [2003] NSWSC 85; (2003) 21 ACLC 450 at [68]–[70] where the judge referred, inter alia, to the Higgs Report. In *ASIC v Healey* [2011] FCA 717 the judge

8.46 There are certain functions that executives should be able to discharge, and they will be in breach if: they fail to put the board in the position where it can assess certain occurrences in the affairs of the company; and they fail to establish proper systems that enable the preparation of financial information that is accurate and can be relied upon.[129] This is an issue that is discussed later under the heading 'Records and Accounts'.

8.47 For non-executives we know that they are to engage in monitoring, making themselves aware of the business in which their company is involved, and keeping themselves informed concerning the affairs of the company, including, most importantly, the company's finances.[130] The problems for the non-executives are at least three-fold. First, the executives and senior managers control the flow of information to the board and so the amount and quality of information that the non-executives have is often limited. Secondly, being part-time the non-executives will not devote large amounts of time to their role, thus they do not, certainly in large companies, often have the chance to keep apprised of company affairs. They are likely then to rely on the information that is fed to them by management. Thirdly, the non-executives will usually lack expertise concerning the business of the company, again meaning that they will rely heavily on management for advice.

8.48 Clearly, it would be unfair and improper to expect every director, even in the same company, to have equal knowledge and experience of all elements of a company's business. A person's performance is dependent on the role in the management of the company which he or she is required to undertake, and the responsibilities which he or she has assumed.[131]

8.49 Some directors might be retained as specialists and they have particular functions to fulfil. They will have special responsibilities in this regard, something discussed later under the heading of 'Skill,' but they are not entitled to ignore areas outside of their immediate remit and expertise.[132] In New Zealand, a case indicated that higher standards would be expected of professional directors.[133] There have been suggestions in the Australian jurisprudence that the directors of professional trustee companies have to meet a higher duty than directors of other companies.[134]

---

referred to the Australian institute of Company Directors' publication titled, 'How to Review a Company's Financial Reports: A Guide for Boards'.

[129] *Cashflow Finance Pty Ltd v Westpac Banking Corp* [1999] NSWSC 671 (NSW S Ct); *Re OneTel Ltd (in liq); ASIC v Rich* [2003] NSWSC 85; (2003) 44 ACSR 682 (NSW S Ct).

[130] See, for instance, *Secretary of State for Trade and Industry v Thornbury* [2007] EWHC 3202 (Ch); [2008] BCC 768.

[131] *Re Barings (No 5)* [1999] 1 BCLC 433 at 484.

[132] *Re Property Force Consultants Pty Ltd* (1995) 13 ACLC 1051 at 1061; *Re HIH Insurance Ltd (in prov liq); ASIC v Adler* [2002] NSWSC 171; (2002) 41 ACSR 72; (2002) 20 ACLC 576 at [372] (NSW S Ct).

[133] *Re Global Print Strategies Ltd* (24 November 2004, unreported), High Court (Salmon J).

[134] *Wilkinson v Feldworth Financial Services Pty Ltd* (1998) 29 ACSR 642 at 693; *ASC v AS Nominees Ltd* (1995) 133 ALR 1; (1995) 18 ACSR 859.

8.50 Whilst it may be regarded as a basic point, it perhaps needs to be said that directors are not inevitably liable for all management decisions that turn out to be bad. Furthermore, directors are not to be held liable for mere errors of judgment.[135] It is when directors themselves are negligent and that negligence causes the company to lose out that they are liable.

8.51 One last thing to say at this point is that the old distinction between gross negligence and negligence, a distinction which a number of judges have said that they have found difficult to make, is clearly no longer of any relevance.[136]

A Monitoring

8.52 Perhaps the most critical aspect of the job of a director is to monitor and, in some cases, to supervise the work of subordinates and colleagues. For the non-executive director this is part of the watchdog function that they have, and perhaps this is the most demanding one. The *Report on the Financial Aspects of Corporate Governance* (known commonly as 'the Cadbury Report' after its chairman) specifically stated that all directors have a responsibility to monitor and to ensure that appropriate controls over the activities of their companies exist.[137] In the case of *ASIC v Healey*[138] Middleton J stated that monitoring was: 'a core, irreducible requirement of directors to be involved in the management of the company and to take all reasonable steps to be in a position to guide and monitor.'[139]

8.53 The kind of monitoring that will be required of executives compared with non-executives will usually differ. It is more likely that executives will monitor the work of non-board managers in the company, while the non-executives will monitor the work of the executive directors and some very senior managers. A significant part of the case-law has focused on this obligation. The law recognises though that directors cannot monitor everyone's work and every activity that goes on in a company, especially when the company is not small. Courts have always said that it is permissible for directors to rely on others. However, there are limits to when one can rely on others. Primarily the limits to reliance are where the directors' suspicions are, or should have been, aroused. The issue of reliance is discussed later in detail.[140]

8.54 It is obviously absolutely critical that to comply with these responsibilities directors should take reasonable steps to place themselves in a situation where they can guide and monitor the management of the

---

[135] *Re Brazilian Rubber Plantations and Estates Ltd* [1911] 1 Ch 425 at 436; *Roberts v Frohlich* [2011] EWHC 257 (Ch) [2011] 2 BCLC 635 at [106]; *Australian Securities and Investments Commission v Lindberg* (2012) 91 ACSR 640; [2012] VSC 332 at [72].

[136] See, for example, *State of South Australia v Clarke* (1996) 19 ACSR 606 (SA S Ct).

[137] London, Gee, 1992 at para 1.8.

[138] [2011] FCA 717.

[139] Ibid at [16].

[140] Below at **8.88–8.99**.

company.[141] To enable them to be able to do this independently and competently, directors must ensure that they do not allow one or more directors to dominate them, for to allow that situation is for directors to fail in discharging their duties;[142] directors need to come to an independent judgment.[143] Leaving responsibility for certain matters to domineering colleagues opens passive directors up to possible liability. But there have been studies indicating that the chief executive officers (CEOs) of large companies, in particular, will often dominate boards.[144] Other executive directors might use their expertise and experience to do the same. Of course, in such circumstances domineering directors often simply refuse to comply with requests for information etc, and so the directors who seek such information are in a difficult position as to what they can or ought to do. Clearly though the 'burying the head in the sand' approach does not work and is fraught with danger. Naturally if a domineering director has support at board level, as is often the case, a concerned director's position is made even more precarious. While it is impossible to catalogue a defined list of actions that can be taken by directors to save themselves from possible liability, the following might be worth considering by directors (depending on the relevant circumstances):

- making inquiries of other directors;
- ensuring questions (and possibly concerns) are raised at board meetings and carefully minuted;
- resigning[145] (this has a greater chance of protecting a director from a duty of care breach than in a wrongful trading action), although the judgment of Briggs J (as he then was) in *Lexi Holdings Ltd (in administration) v Luqman*[146] provides that if a director does resign he or she:

> 'may nonetheless be required to take steps to deal before departure with a pressing matter calling for attention, or to put her continuing colleagues on the board in possession of information known to her relevant to the matter in question, so as to enable them to deal with it. Exceptionally, a director may upon departure be obliged to put relevant information in the hands of the company's shareholders or other stakeholders, if not satisfied that continuing colleagues on the board have the inclination or the ability to deal with a matter of concern';

---

[141] *Dairy Containers Ltd v NZI Bank Ltd* [1995] 2 NZLR 30 at 79; *Sheahan v Verco* [2001] SASC 91 at [101]; *Re HIH Insurance Ltd (in prov liq)*; *ASIC v Adler* [2002] NSWSC 171; (2002) 41 ACSR 72; (2002) 20 ACLC 576 at [372]; *DCT v Clark* (2003) 45 ACSR 332 at 335.

[142] *Re Westmid Packing Services Ltd* [1998] 2 BCLC 646 at 653; [1998] BCC 836 at 842; *Re Landhurst Leasing plc* [1999] 1 BCLC 286 at 346; *Re Queens Moat Houses plc (No 2)* [2004] EWHC 1730 (Ch); [2005] 1 BCLC 136 at [26].

[143] *Equitable Life Assurance Society v Bowley* [2003] EWHC 2263 (Comm); [2004] 1 BCLC 180 at [41].

[144] For example, see S Hill 'The Social Organization of Boards of Directors' (1995) 46 *The British Journal of Sociology* 245.

[145] See *Re Park House Properties Ltd* [1998] BCC 847 at 865. Also, see, *Sheahan v Verco* [2001] SASC 91 at [101] where the South Australian Supreme Court referred to the US decisions of *Dodd v Wilkinson* 42 NJ Eq 647, at 651; 9 A 685 (E & A 1887); *Williams v Riley* 34 NJ Eq 398 at 401 (Ch 1881).

[146] [2008] EWHC 1639 (Ch) at [39].

- obtaining professional advice; seeking information from the company's accountants where financial issues are at stake.

8.55 It is equally critical that directors do not allow themselves to be manipulated and deceived by other directors, and particularly the senior executives.[147] There is empirical evidence from the United States that non-executive directors tend to defer, as suggested earlier, to the CEO or chairman rather than monitoring as they should.[148] There are cases that suggest that this occurs in the United Kingdom. An example is *Dorchester Finance Co Ltd v Stebbing*.[149] In that case two non-executives signed blank cheques at the behest of the chairman who did what he pleased with them.

8.56 There is another aspect to non-executives failing to monitor adequately, or following through on issues that they have discovered from some preliminary monitoring. This is failing to challenge the executives on management issues[150] because of a desire on the part of non-executives not to 'rock the boat'. Directors might not want to be seen as endangering the cohesion of the board,[151] or causing unnecessary work to be done.[152] However, this can lead to liability as the defendant in *Gold Ribbon (Accountants) Pty Ltd v Sheers*[153] found. In this case, the director of X, Mr Dunn, objected to the appointment of a company to run X's business, which was providing unsecured loans to practising accountants. He attempted to alter the arrangements concerning the appointment, but he was told that there would be no changes made, and he took the position that it would not be in the interests of the company 'to continue to rock the boat'. He felt that his decision was reasonable having regard to 'the dynamics of the board' and the fact that 'apparently competent professional people had the day to day running of the operation of the business'.

8.57 Another factor that might precipitate less than adequate monitoring is where directors, and particularly non-executives, become overly familiar with

---

[147] See *Re Westmid Services Ltd* [1998] 2 BCLC 646 at 653; [1998] BCC 836 at 842 where the defendants were manipulated and deceived by a director who treated the company as his own (at 652; 841).

[148] Jay W Lorsch *Pawns or Potentates: The Reality of America's Corporate Boards* (Cambridge, Mass, Harvard Business School Press, 1989) at 41–49.

[149] [1989] BCLC 498.

[150] Andrew Hill Lombard ('Deferential Directors Need to Stir up the Boardroom' *The Financial Times*, 27 September 2007) suggests that there is not enough challenging of executive directors' plans.

[151] See Felix Robatyn 'An Agenda for Corporate Reform' *Wall Street Journal*, 24 June 2002.

[152] For a discussion of this issue in the context of the approval of directors' conflicts, see A Keay 'The Authorising of Directors' Conflicts of Interests: Getting a Balance?' (2012) 12 *Journal of Corporate Law Studies* 129.

[153] [2005] QSC 198 at [105] (Qld S Ct). The decision was reversed on appeal (*Gold Ribbon (Accountants) Pty Ltd v Sheers* [2006] QCA 335 (Qld CA)) but the appeal court did not contradict what the trial judge had to say about the duty of care. The reason for the reversal was that the appellate court was of the view that the trial judge was wrong in his conclusions on causation.

other directors, and especially the CEO. In such situations there is likely to be the tendency for directors to be restrained in their monitoring and questioning.[154]

8.58 It was indicated by Sir Richard Scott V-C in *Re Barings plc*[155] that in general terms the higher the office of a director within a company, the greater the responsibilities that fall upon him or her. Those who gain high office are required to exercise diligent supervision. They must realise that they need to consider the whole system over which they have supervision and control, whether it is working properly, ensuring that those to whom tasks have been given are discharging their roles efficiently, and that they should see the warning signs when they occur.[156]

8.59 A classic instance in the United Kingdom of a failure to monitor adequately is to be found with the Barings Bank collapse. The bank collapsed after one of their traders, Nick Leeson, had been involved in unauthorised trading activities. Disqualification proceedings were brought against three directors on the basis that they were unfit to act as directors (with no allegations of dishonesty being made) because they were guilty of serious failures of management and this demonstrated incompetence of a high degree. Generally speaking the executive directors did not monitor the work of Leeson. Specifically the case of the Secretary of State was that: Leeson was left in control of both the dealing and settlement functions (a very powerful position to be in) at the bank's Singapore branch and notwithstanding the fact that an internal audit specifically recommended that his roles be divided, the directors took no action; there was no imposition and enforcement of risk limits; Leeson's requests for large amounts of funding were met and funds paid over without any proper investigation; and there was a failure in the bank's internal controls. It would appear from *Barings that if, as in this case, directors make mistakes, in the process of monitoring, that are 'elementary and fundamental'*[157] *or they fail to take steps that are obvious, they would be held liable.*

8.60 The celebrated Australian case of *AWA Ltd v Daniels*,[158] whilst not a disqualification case, but a case involving, inter alia, alleged directorial breach of the duty of care, was similar to *Barings* in that the executive directors had failed to put in place adequate controls in relation to a relatively inexperienced manager. The failure was exacerbated by the fact that the foreign exchange dealing over which the manager had oversight was a new venture for the company and it might have been assumed that the CEO would have ensured that tighter controls were put in place. As he had not done so, he was liable. In

---

[154] See A Keay 'The Authorising of Directors' Conflicts of Interests: Getting a Balance?' (2012) 12 *Journal of Corporate Law Studies* 129.

[155] [1998] BCC 583.

[156] Ibid at 586.

[157] *Re Barings plc (No 5)* [1999] 1 BCLC 433 at 451.

[158] (1992) 10 ACLC 933 at 1014 and approved of on appeal (*Daniels v Anderson*) by the New South Wales Court of Appeal (1995) 13 ACLC 614.

another English case, *Re Continental Assurance Ltd*[159] a director who had been a corporate financier failed to read the accounts of the company to which he had been appointed and the court said that he was seriously incompetent and that he should be disqualified as a consequence. Given the way that the law has developed the director would probably be held responsible even if he was not a trained financier.

8.61 To ensure that supervision functions, like record keeping, are adequate and not glossed over, they should be kept separate from the day-to-day operations of the company.[160] Likewise, board meetings should not be strictly scheduled pursuant to a uniform pattern, such as occurring monthly, if circumstances dictate that it is necessary for them to be held more frequently so as to enable directors, inter alia, to carry out their supervising functions properly.[161] In *AWA Ltd v Daniels*[162] there was judicial criticism that the board met rigidly on a monthly basis, whereas there was a real need to meet more often at times.

8.62 Clearly, directors need to ensure that any operation conducted by their company needs to have proper records, internal controls and the provision of full reports when called for by management,[163] as well as systems that exist in relation to delegation, decision-making, information flow and financial controls.[164] Directors need to makes sure that there is a reasonable strategy in place. As Professor Sarah Worthington notes, negligence is usually found where there are inadequate strategies in existence, rather than in cases where a particular decision has been made that is seen to be wrong ultimately.[165]

8.63 If the company is to be party to a transaction involving the potential for conflict between interest and duty for a director(s), the duty of care and diligence falls to be exercised in a context requiring special vigilance, calling for scrupulous concern on the part of those officers who become aware of that transaction to ensure that any necessary corporate approvals are obtained and safeguards put in place. While the primary responsibility will fall on the director proposing to enter into the transaction, this does not excuse other directors who become aware of the transaction.[166]

8.64 The Australian case of *Re HIH Insurance Ltd (in prov liq); ASIC v Adler*[167] provides an interesting case as far as monitoring goes. The case resulted from the fall-out from the collapse of HIH Insurance, one of Australia's

---

[159] [1997] BCLC 48.
[160] *Daniels v Anderson* (1995) 13 ACLC 614 (NSWCA).
[161] Ibid.
[162] (1992) 10 ACLC 933.
[163] *Daniels v Anderson* (1995) 13 ACLC 614 at 652 (NSWCA).
[164] *Dairy Containers Ltd v NZI Bank Ltd* [1995] 2 NZLR 30 at 79–80.
[165] S Worthington 'The Duty to Monitor: A Modern View of the Director's Duty of Care' in F Patfield (ed) *Perspectives on Company Law* (London, Kluwer, 1997) vol 2 at 197.
[166] *Re HIH Insurance Ltd (in prov liq); ASIC v Adler* [2002] NSWSC 171; (2002) 41 ACSR 72; (2002) 20 ACLC 576 at [372].
[167] Ibid.

largest insurance companies. A number of actions were commenced by the Australian corporate regulator, the Australian Securities and Investments Commission ('ASIC'),[168] against directors of HIH. The main claim might be regarded as being against Rodney Adler, a non-executive director of HIH, who had a high-profile in the Australian insurance market and in general commercial life. The actions commenced involved allegations of breaches of duties covered by several sections of the Australian legislation. Importantly for our purposes here ASIC claimed that there had been breaches of the Australian equivalent of s 174 of the CA 2006. One of the transactions that was subject to scrutiny was the investment by HIH in a body in which one of Adler's companies was heavily involved, and it was Adler who had asked for the investment to be put in place. An executive director, Williams, was the subject of a number of claims and one of them was that he was in breach of his duty of care (under s 180 of the Corporations Act). Unusually, Williams as an executive director responded to the request of a non-executive, Adler, without performing sufficient checks, whereas with many duty of care breaches, it is non-executives who respond to requests, or accept the advice, of executive directors without the necessary checks. Williams was found to be in breach because he wrongly relied on the advice of Adler and delegated authority to him. The court held him liable for failing to ensure there were put in place proper safeguards including independent appraisal of the investments made. According to Santow J, the director should have put in place a proper due diligence process before the investment arrangements were effected.[169] The learned judge made the point that Williams should have been more vigilant because he was dealing with a fellow director. In something of a like situation directors were found liable in *Weathering Capital (UK) Ltd v Peterson*[170] because they had failed to prevent the actions of a fraudulent director.

8.65   In the wake of the collapse of HIH the Australian Government convened a Royal Commission and it found that in large public companies many significant decisions are made by the managers of the company without any reference to the board, thereby making the task of non-executive directors even harder.[171]

8.66   So, it would seem that the courts will not permit directors to get away with a total abrogation of their responsibility in relation to their monitoring duties.[172] Besides being in breach of their duty of care they would probably also be breaching their duty of diligence. It is likely to be situations such as where

---

[168]   Under the Australian Corporations Act 2001, ASIC has the power to initiate civil and criminal proceedings against directors for breach of statutory duties.

[169]   *Re HIH Insurance Ltd (in prov liq); ASIC v Adler* [2002] NSWSC 171 (2002) 41 ACSR 72; (2002) 20 ACLC 576 at [453].

[170]   [2012] EWHC 1480 (Ch) and affirmed by the Court of Appeal ([2013] EWCA Civ 71).

[171]   The Commonwealth of Australia, The HIH Royal Commission *The Failure of HIH Insurance* (2003) vol 1 at 121–122.

[172]   *Re Westmid Services Ltd* [1998] 2 BCLC 646 at 653; [1998] BCC 836 at 842. Also see *Re Barings (No 5)* [1999] 1 BCLC 433.

directors have taken some steps to monitor, or risks are not obvious, where it will be more difficult to establish liability.[173]

B Keeping themselves informed

8.67 This can also be seen as part of the monitoring task. It is not realistic for all of the directors to manage the modern day medium-large company. The critical thing is to put in place the framework for supervision and to ensure that they monitor the workings of the company. Nevertheless, directors need to inform themselves concerning two kinds of matters. First, they need to inform themselves of the actual nature of the company's business. Directors must become familiar with the kind of business in which the company engages as well as the way that the business is conducted.[174] Second, they must keep up-to-date with what is generally happening in the development and management of the business.[175] It is likely today that a director of a rubber company could not, in defending proceedings against him or her for breach of duty of care, rely on what Neville J said in *Re Brazilian Rubber Plantation & Estates Ltd*,[176] namely that he could undertake management of such a company in complete ignorance of everything relating to rubber and not be liable. Both public and judicial expectations have greatly increased. But one must take into account the fact that a non-executive director is not able to have a detailed knowledge of the workings of a large company that is part of a large corporate group[177] when the situation is that they only meet on occasions and do not see all information about the company's affairs.

8.68 In *Re Westmid Packing Services Ltd (No 3)*[178] the Court of Appeal emphasised the fact that each director had a duty to keep himself or herself informed of the company's affairs, particularly its financial position, in order to enable them to be able to have sufficient understanding of the company's business and to discharge their duties.[179] Doing this would allow directors to make independent judgments.[180] What happens though if a director is denied access to documents? For example, what if a new director seeks access to particulars relating to an earlier corporate transaction and is denied access as the transaction was highly confidential? How would a court assess the

---

[173] J Loughrey 'The Directors' Duty of Care and Skill and the Financial Crisis' in J Loughrey (ed) *Directors' Duties and Shareholder Litigation in the Wake of the Financial Crisis* (Cheltenham, Edward Elgar, 2012) at 25–26.

[174] *Sheahan v Verco* [2001] SASC 91 at [121].

[175] *Mason v Lewis* [2006] 3 NZLR 225 at 235 (NZCA).

[176] [1911] 1 Ch 425.

[177] This was acknowledged by Rogers CJ in *AWA v Daniels* (1992) 10 ACLC 933 at 1014 and approved of on appeal by the New South Wales Court of Appeal (1995) 13 ACLC 614.

[178] [1998] 2 All ER 124; [1998] BCC 836 at 842; [1998] 2 BCLC 646 at 653. A similar view was taken in the disqualification case of *Galeforce Pleating Co Ltd, Re [1999] 2 BCLC 704* [1999] 2 BCLC 704 which applied *Re Westmid Packing Services Ltd* [1998] 2 BCLC 646; [1998] BCC 836.

[179] Also, see *Re Vintage Hallmark plc* [2006] EWHC 2761 (Ch); [2007] 1 BCLC 788; *Secretary of State v Thornbury* [2007] EWHC 3202 (Ch); [2008] 1 BCLC 139 at [36]; *Sheahan v Verco* [2001] SASC 91 at [101] (SA S Ct).

[180] *ASC v Gallagher* (1993) 10 ACSR 43 at 54.

director's conduct if he or she accepts the denial of access, but later it turns out that the information that was sought was critical? Surely it is necessary for the director to ask: what would the reasonably diligent person in the director's position have done, and for a court to judge him or her on the response made to the question posed. On a practical level perhaps the director in the above position has to consider whether or not to resign on the basis that he or she cannot fulfil the oversight role that he or she is called upon to fulfil.[181]

8.69 When it comes to the finances, it is difficult, if not impossible, to lay down any specific rules; clearly it will depend on the company's circumstances. For instance, if a company was struggling financially, it would be prudent for directors to seek regular updates at every meeting, and, perhaps, for the number of meetings to increase.

8.70 In the last 25 years we have seen helpful comments on the duty of care and skill in many of the large number of disqualification cases that have considered the conduct of directors. One such case was *Re Barings plc (No 5)*,[182] a case already outlined. In his judgment, Jonathan Parker J (as he then was) provided some useful propositions summarising his view of the law concerning directors' obligations. One of these was that directors have a continuing duty to acquire and maintain a sufficient knowledge and understanding of the company's business to enable them to discharge their duties to the company.[183] This statement did not exempt non-executives, so, unlike, in the early cases, these directors are not able to remain aloof, for although different things will be required of them compared to executive directors they will be expected to be up to date with company affairs.

8.71 In *Morley v Statewide Tobacco Services Ltd*,[184] the court was concerned with a claim against a director who had played no part in the affairs of a small family company from the time of its incorporation until the time of its liquidation, a period of nearly 30 years, for debts incurred when the company was commercially insolvent. She had been a director when the affairs of the company had been administered by her late husband, and after his death by her son, both of whom were directors. Ormiston J of the Victorian Supreme Court said that directors should not be entitled to hide behind ignorance of the company's affairs the state of which they have contributed to by their own failure to make further necessary inquiries about what is going on. Passivity is no excuse for directors in today's world of commerce.

8.72 Directors' responsibility to be informed includes, it would seem, the need to monitor company debt and related matters to ensure that the company is not

---

[181] See G Santow 'Codification of Directors' Duties' (1999) 73 *Australian Law Journal* 336 at 341.
[182] [1999] 1 BCLC 433. The Court of Appeal endorsed the judgment on appeal ([2000] 1 BCLC 523; sub nom *Baker v Secretary of State for Trade and Industry* [2001] BCC 273).
[183] [1999] 1 BCLC 433 at 489.
[184] [1993] 1 VR 423.

falling into insolvency and so that they are not engaging in wrongful trading.[185] Obviously executive directors must keep themselves informed about any risks in taking any particular action. In *Mistmorn Pty Ltd (in liq) v Yasseen*[186] a de facto director, whose company operated a duty free shop, built up to undue and unnecessarily large levels of stock at a time when he knew that there had been three previous thefts from the shop. He also knew that the stock was uninsured (renewal of insurance was refused in light of the earlier thefts). The company went into liquidation and the liquidator brought misfeasance proceedings against the director because, after the build up of stock, there was a fourth theft from the shop. Subsequently, he was held liable for breach of duty of care, the judge describing his actions as irresponsible in the circumstances. This decision seems to place a heavy burden on directors, although the decision might be regarded as being limited to its facts as the judgment indicates that the de facto director had acted in very questionable ways preceding the liquidation of his company. As mentioned earlier in this chapter,[187] executives and senior managers control information and might not pass on to the board important matters, so it is necessary for non-executives in particular to be pro-active when they can to secure information that will permit them to keep apprised of what is going on in the company.

8.73 It is perhaps good to finish this part of the Chapter by quoting what Middleton J said in the Australian case of *ASIC v Healey*,[188] which is discussed in several places throughout the Chapter. His Honour said that:[189]

> 'a director should acquire at least a rudimentary understanding of the business of the corporation and become familiar with the fundamentals of the business in which the corporation is engaged; a director should keep informed about the activities of the corporation; whilst not required to have a detailed awareness of day-to-day activities, a director should monitor the corporate affairs and policies; a director should maintain familiarity with the financial status of the corporation by a regular review and understanding of financial statements; a director, whilst not an auditor, should still have a questioning mind.'

C Delegation

8.74 Many cases have unequivocally recognised the fact that directors are permitted to delegate, as a matter of necessity, particularly when a business reaches a particular size.[190] For as Romer J stated in *Re City Equitable*: 'The larger the business carried on by the company the more numerous, the more important, the matters that must of necessity be left to the managers, the

---

[185] For a study of wrongful trading, see A Keay *Company Directors' Responsibilities to Creditors* (Abingdon, Routledge/Cavendish, 2007) Chs 7–10 and 20.

[186] (1996) 21 ACSR 173; (1996) 14 ACLC 1387.

[187] Above at **8.47**.

[188] [2011] FCA 717.

[189] Ibid at [17].

[190] For example, see *Re Barings plc (No 5)*. Also, see Companies and Securities Law Review Committee 'Company Directors and Officers: Indemnification, Relief and Insurance' Report No 10 (Canberra, Australian Government Printer, 1990) at para 29.

accountants and the rest of the staff.'[191] The approach of Romer J was applied in many cases, including in *Norman v Theodore Goddard*[192] by Hoffmann J, and in *Re Westmid Packing* Lord Woolf MR said that a proper degree of delegation and division of responsibility was certainly permissible.[193] This has been necessary given the complexity of business life and the expectations of the community that involve expecting more from directors in the government of the affairs of companies.

8.75 Delegation in the context of a company involves 'the delegation of authority to exercise of particular powers by one person or group of people, to another person or group of people'.[194] Before relying on anyone or delegating tasks to a director or other managers of the company, the directors should ensure that it is appropriate to delegate in the circumstances[195] and that the persons to whom directors are intending to delegate are suitable persons. Delegation does not mean that the authority of the one delegating ends. On the contrary, in delegation both the one delegating and one to whom power is delegated hold authority to exercise the power delegated.[196] Hence, where a board of directors appoints a person, such as a specialist director, it is critical that it ensures that the person to whom tasks will be delegated is assessed not only for competence to perform those functions, but for trustworthiness.[197] The relationship between the director and the delegate, must be such that the director honestly holds the belief that the delegate is trustworthy, competent and someone on whom reliance can be placed. Knowledge that the delegate is dishonest or incompetent will make reliance unreasonable,[198] and even more so if the person has (and this is known to the director) been found guilty of dishonesty and imprisoned.[199] But once the decision to delegate to an apparently trustworthy person has been made, that is not the end of it. A director can forget about the function delegated and how it is discharged, even if the delegate could be properly regarded as trustworthy and deemed capable, on reasonable grounds, of discharging the delegated function.[200] Directors should continue to monitor and be aware of what the delegate is doing. It is not enough for directors to wait for issues concerning the delegate's role or work to

---

[191] [1925] Ch 407 at 426–427.

[192] [1992] BCC 14.

[193] [1998] 2 BCLC 646 at 653; [1998] BCC 836 at 842. Also see *Re Barings (No 5)* [1999] 1 BCLC 433.

[194] A Gibbs and J Webster 'Delegation and Reliance by Australian Company Directors' (2015) 33 *Company and Securities Law Journal* 297 at 301.

[195] For cases where it was held that it was not appropriate to delegate, see *ASIC v MacDonald (No 11)* (2009) 256 ALR 199 at [260]; *ASIC v Healey* [2011] FCA 717 at [125].

[196] A Gibbs and J Webster 'Delegation and Reliance by Australian Company Directors' (2015) 33 *Company and Securities Law Journal* 297 at 301.

[197] J Davies 'A Guide to Directors Obligations under the Companies Act 2006' Association of Chartered Certified Accountants, August 2007, para 6.55, and accessible at www.accaglobal. com/content/dam/acca/global/PDF-technical/business-law/tech-tp-cdd.pdf.

[198] *Biala Pty Ltd v Mallina Holdings Ltd* (1994) 15 ACSR 1 at 62 (WA S Ct); *Re HIH Insurance Ltd (in prov liq); ASIC v Adler* [2002] NSWSC 171; (2002) 41 ACSR 72; (2002) 20 ACLC 576 at [372].

[199] *Lexi Holdings Ltd (in administration) v Luqman* [2008] EWHC 1639 (Ch) at [51]–[55].

[200] *Re Barings (No 5)* [1999] 1 BCLC 433 at 487.

be brought to their attention; they must be pro-active in their monitoring.[201] In *Re R D Industries Ltd*[202] a disqualification order was made against a managing director who failed to supervise the finance manager's activities carefully as well as failing to deal with accounting problems of which he was aware. In particular the director was aware of breaches of an invoice discounting agreement with the company's bank and he was held to be responsible for the breaches. This contributed to the financial downfall of the company and it ending up in administration.

8.76 While directors are entitled to delegate certain tasks and responsibilities, they cannot delegate the management function itself.[203] In *Re Barings plc (No 5)*[204] Jonathan Parker J said that although directors are entitled (subject to the articles of association of the company) to delegate particular functions to others who are subordinate to them in the management chain, and also to trust their competence and integrity to a reasonable extent, exercising the power of delegation does not absolve a director from the duty to supervise the delegate's discharge of the delegated functions.[205] So, while delegation is allowed, and is often necessary, it does not permit total abrogation of the responsibility of directors.[206]

8.77 Although the director delegating retains a residual duty of supervision and control, there are, of course, limits to the extent of supervision that can be undertaken. It is impossible to lay down detailed ground rules that stipulate the amount and nature of oversight that directors must provide for when it comes to delegation. What is acceptable delegation is a matter that depends on the actual circumstances,[207] and these encompass a host of factors, such as the kind of business, the size of the company and the nature and extent of the delegation.[208] In *ASIC v Adler*[209] Santow J said that the following factors should be taken into account in determining the reasonableness of the extent of delegation:

- whether the function could be properly left to the ones to whom it had been delegated;

---

[201] For instance, see the case of one of Baring Bank's directors, Tuckey who seemed to only get involved if some extraordinary issue came to his notice: [1999] 1 BCLC 433 at 503–504, 519 and referred to in J Loughrey 'The Directors' Duty of Care and Skill and the Financial Crisis' in J Loughrey (ed) *Directors' Duties and Shareholder Litigation in the Wake of the Financial Crisis* (Cheltenham, Edward Elgar, 2012) at 30–31.

[202] [2014] EWHC 2844 (Ch).

[203] *Dairy Containers Ltd v NZI Bank Ltd* [1995] 2 NZLR 30 at 80.

[204] [1999] 1 BCLC 433.

[205] [1999] 1 BCLC 433 at 489. See *Lexi Holdings plc (In Administration) v Luqman* [2007] EWHC 2652 (Ch) at [219].

[206] *Re Westmid Services Ltd* [1998] 2 BCLC 646 at 653; [1998] BCC 836 at 842. Also see *Re Barings (No 5)* [1999] 1 BCLC 433.

[207] *Dairy Containers Ltd v NZI Bank Ltd* [1995] 2 NZLR 30 at 80.

[208] *Australian Securities and Investments Commission v Maxwell* (2006) 59 ACSR 373 at [100]; *Australian Securities and Investments Commission v Warrenmang Limited* [2007] FCA 973 at [23].

[209] [2002] NSWSC 171; (2002) 41 ACSR 72; (2002) 20 ACLC 576; (2002) 168 FLR 253.

- the extent to which the directors was or should have been made to make inquiries;

- the relationship between the one delegating and the one to whom power is delegated;

- whether the directors believed that the delegate was trustworthy, competent and someone who could be relied on;

- the steps that were taken by the director.[210]

Clearly directors are not required to consider everything that a delegate does, and the precise nature of that will depend on the particular circumstances,[211] but they are required to oversee to a reasonable extent any delegation and to ensure that appropriate internal controls are put in place. This requirement was not fulfilled in *Barings* as the directors had little idea as to what Leeson was doing; they certainly were not supervising his activities. In *Re Landhurst Leasing plc*,[212] the court distinguished between the sort of functions that could be delegated and those that remained the duty of the board. It was said that a director should be at liberty to rely on the actions of his or her colleagues in relation to the matters that fall within these colleagues' areas of responsibility, provided that the director has no grounds for suspicion that he or she should not so rely. The court indicated that directors might be liable if they abdicated responsibility for matters for which the whole board should be responsible, even if there was no reason why the person on whom the functions had been delegated was not to be trusted.[213]

8.78   The Federal Court of Australia in *ASIC v Healey*,[214] a decision discussed in more detail in the next part of the Chapter, addressed the issue of delegation. It provided that, as other cases have held, directors can delegate functions to others and they can rely on other officers unless it should be recognised that reliance is misplaced.[215] For instance, directors cannot substitute reliance upon the advice of management for their own attention and examination of an important matter that falls specifically within the board's responsibilities as is the case with the reporting obligations considered in this decision.[216] Middleton J stated that the companies legislation imposes ultimate responsibility for the financial reports upon the directors and that responsibility cannot be delegated.[217] This does not mean that the directors are not entitled to seek assistance in carrying out their responsibilities, and may rely on others.[218] His Honour accepted that directors could delegate their responsibilities such as preparing the company's accounts, but directors cannot merely 'go through the

---

[210] Ibid at [372].
[211] *Re Barings (No 5)* [1999] 1 BCLC 433 at 487.
[212] [1999] 1 BCLC 286 at 346.
[213] Ibid.
[214] [2011] FCA 717.
[215] Ibid at [167].
[216] Ibid at [175].
[217] Ibid at [125].
[218] Ibid at [129].

motions' with,[219] or 'wave through,' financial statements that are based on the accounts,[220] and for which the directors are responsible. As these documents are important and significant, the directors must understand and focus upon the content of financial statements, and if necessary, make further inquiries if matters revealed in these financial statements call for such action.[221]

D Records and accounts

8.79 While directors are not expected to be accountants or to have any particular financial or administrative expertise, courts will assume that certain minimum standards are attained. It is expected that as a minimum the directors will ensure that proper records are created and maintained, and that they will cause accounting records to be prepared and maintained accurately.[222] In addition, it is expected that directors will have a basic understanding of the financial position of the company,[223] and some financial awareness.[224] Failure to do so could always leave them open to a liquidator's action under s 214 of the Insolvency Act 1986 if the company were to end up in insolvent liquidation. Directors should maintain familiarity with the financial status of the company by a regular review of financial statements,[225] for a failure to examine the company's books could be a breach of the duty.[226] In *Sheahan v Verco*[227] directors were held liable because, inter alia, when they became directors, they did not ask to see even the basic financial statements of the company such as the annual statements for previous years.[228] But while directors might be expected to view statements, they are not expected to query financial statements except to the extent that their business experience would dictate that they should do so.[229] If there is concern when reviewing financial statements, it may give rise to a duty to inquire further into matters revealed by those statements,[230] but they will not be compelled to make their own investigations or undertake an audit of the accounts personally, although they should ensure that there are appropriate systems established so accurate and reliable information gets to the board.[231] In *Cashflow Finance Pty Ltd v Westpac*

---

[219] Ibid 717 at [174].
[220] Ibid at [20]
[221] Ibid at [20].
[222] See *Re Produce Marketing Consortium Ltd* (1989) 5 BCC 569 at 595 (a wrongful trading case).
[223] *Re Westmid Packing Services Ltd* [1998] 2 BCLC 646; [1998] BCC 836.
[224] *Secretary of State for Trade and Industry v Thornbury* [2007] EWHC 3302 (Ch); [2008] BCC 768.
[225] *ASIC v Plymin* (2003) 46 ACSR 126 at 224.
[226] *Sheahan v Verco* [2001] SASC 91.
[227] Ibid.
[228] Ibid at [112].
[229] *Re Queens Moat Houses plc (No 2)* [2004] EWHC 1730 (Ch); [2005] 1 BCLC 136 at [35].
[230] *Sheahan v Verco* [2001] SASC 91 at [101].
[231] *Re One.Tel Ltd (in liq); ASIC v Rich* [2003] NSWSC 85; (2003) 44 ACSR 682.

Banking Corp[232] liability was visited on a director because he failed to put adequate systems of control or audit in place so as to prevent fraud being perpetrated by employees.[233]

8.80 Companies are required by s 386 of the CA 2006 to keep adequate accounting records, and they must, according to s 388(1)(b), be open to inspection by the company's officers at all times. 'Officer' is not defined for general purposes in the Act, but it does include directors of the company for the purposes of Part 36 which deals with offences under the CA 2006.[234] In any event the common law confers on directors the right to apply to the courts for an order permitting inspection of the accounting records so as to enable them to carry out their duties,[235] and the courts have a discretion as to whether or not they will make the necessary order. It has been held that save where a director is likely to be removed, the courts will rarely withhold an order from a director.[236]

8.81 While it is expected that directors will engage professional advisers, the former are not entitled to hide behind professionals in certain respects. For instance, the retaining of an accountant to prepare financial records is not an action that would excuse the directors from their duty to understand the financial position of the company.[237] Also, directors are not able to defer totally to auditors because the directors have a statutory duty to prepare financial statements giving a true and fair view of the company's affairs[238] for consideration of the auditors and the duty should not be affected by the auditor's view of the accounts prepared for them.[239]

8.82 The decision of Middleton J of the Federal Court of Australia in *ASIC v Healey*[240] is of particular note here, although arguably the principles that it lays down are not limited to accounts, which was its focus. In summary this case (it is long and consists of 589 paragraphs) dealt with the accounting requirements and the statutory demands that are placed on Australian directors in terms of accounts by the companies legislation (Corporations Act 2001). The case revolves around the approval by the directors of the consolidated financial statements of Centro, Centro Property Trust (the then second largest retail property owner/manager in Australia) and Centro Retail Trust (which then had an interest in 29 quality shopping centres across Australia) for the financial year ending on 30 June 2007[241] at a board meeting attended by the defendant directors on 6 September 2007. There were several public companies and a managed investment scheme registered under the Act that made up the Centro

---

[232] [1999] NSWSC 671.

[233] *Cashflow Finance Pty Ltd v Westpac Banking Corp* [1999] NSWSC 671 at [298].

[234] CA 2006, s 1121(2).

[235] *Oxford Legal Group Ltd v Sibbasbridge Services plc* [2007] EWHC 2265 (Ch) at [34].

[236] *Conway v Petronius Clothing Co Ltd* [1978] 1 WLR 72 at 89–90.

[237] *Re OneTel Ltd (in liq); ASIC v Rich* [2003] NSWSC 85; (2003) 44 ACSR 682.

[238] See CA 2006, s 393.

[239] *Re Queens Moat Houses plc (No 2)* [2004] EWHC 1730 (Ch); [2005] 1 BCLC 136 at [32].

[240] [2011] FCA 717.

[241] Most Australian companies have a financial year that is the same as the tax year in Australia (1 July to 30 June).

Property Group and Centro Retail Group. The structure of the group is not critical for our purposes. As under UK law,[242] each Centro company had to prepare a financial report and a directors' report for the financial year, and the accounts that were the subject of the decision were those relating to the year ending on 30 June 2007.[243] By s 295 of the Corporations Act, the financial report of each Centro company had to include a declaration by the directors: whether, in the directors' opinion, there are reasonable grounds to believe that the company will be able to pay its debts as and when they become due and payable; and whether, in the directors' opinion, the financial statement and notes are in accordance with the Corporations Act (including a declaration of compliance with accounting standards and that they provide a true and fair view[244]). Also by s 296(1) of the Corporations Act, the financial report of each of the Centro companies for the financial year ending on 30 June 2007 was required to comply with the accounting standards made by the Australian Accounting Standards Board ('AASB').[245] The claim was brought by the Australian corporate regulator, Australian Securities and Investments Commission ('ASIC') and it alleged was that the directors had breached their duty of care under s 180 (akin to s 174 of the UK legislation)(and the duty under s 344 of the Corporations Act to take all reasonable steps to ensure compliance with the parts of the Act dealing with the company's financial records and reporting) in that the accounts produced and published did not comply with the Corporations Act and accounting standards. Specifically it was alleged that: the accounts failed to classify correctly a number of borrowings as non-current liabilities when they were current liabilities; shortly after the close of the 2007 financial year Centro had granted guarantees as a part of a major transaction that it entered into, and the directors should have disclosed this fact in the annual report as it was a material post balance date event; the non-executive directors gave the declarations required by s 295 of the Corporations Act, but, in breach of s 295A of that Act, they did so before receiving declarations from the CEO and CFO, that, inter alia, the annual accounts complied with the AASB standards. The directors were held liable.

8.83 The decision provides that, as other cases have held, directors can delegate functions to others and they can rely on other officers unless it should be recognised that reliance is misplaced.[246] For instance, directors cannot substitute reliance upon the advice of management for their own attention and examination of an important matter that falls specifically within the board's responsibilities as with the reporting obligations considered in this case.[247] His Honour accepted that directors could delegate their responsibilities such as preparing the company's accounts, but, as mentioned earlier, directors cannot just merely 'go through the motions' with,[248] or 'wave through,' financial

---

[242] See s 394 of the Companies Act 2006.
[243] See s 292 of the Act.
[244] See s 393 of the Companies Act 2006.
[245] See Chapter 2-4 of Part 15 of the Companies Act 2006 for similar UK requirements.
[246] [2011] FCA 717 at [167].
[247] Ibid at [175].
[248] Ibid at [174].

statements that are based on the accounts,[249] and for which the directors are responsible. As these documents are important and significant, the directors must understand and focus upon the content of financial statements, and if necessary, make further inquiries if matters revealed in these financial statements call for such action.[250]

8.84 Some have taken the view that the decision in *Healey* might diminish the pool of directors from which directors can be appointed, because many lack significant financial literacy,[251] but Middleton J said that identification of the errors in the statements did not require a high standard of financial literacy.[252] While he said that, it may well be that directors should have a degree of accounting literacy that requires a knowledge of accounting practice and accounting standards, it was not a matter for resolution in the case before him and so he did not make a definitive statement concerning the amount of knowledge required.[253]

8.85 A very short time after the decision in *ASIC v Healey*, the New Zealand High Court adopted a similar approach in *R v Moses*,[254] a case in which directors were convicted, inter alia, of distributing investment statements that were untrue. The judge, Heath J, specifically held that independent consideration of the accuracy of financial statements is a non-delegable duty of directors of finance companies. Heath J stated, in terms reminiscent of the judgment of Middleton J, that:

> 'It is axiomatic that a director of a finance company will be assumed to have the ability to read and understand financial statements and the way in which assets and liabilities are classified. For example, a director of a finance company should be expected to know that a current asset is one expected to be realised within one year. Without those basic skills, it would not be possible for directors to monitor and guide the finance company's business.'[255]

8.86 It is likely that the issue of failing to check or make inquiries in relation to the accounts of a company might be more of a live issue at a time a company was in distress or on the brink of becoming insolvent,[256] and the company subsequently enters liquidation, although we must not forget that the Centro companies which were the subject of the *Healey* case were solvent. Where a company is in distress or insolvent directors will need to consider the interests of creditors[257] and this will undoubtedly include an examination of the accounts and perhaps in a different way than where the company is clearly solvent.

---

[249] Ibid at [20].

[250] Ibid at [20].

[251] H Low 'Directors Face More Pressure' *The Australian Financial Review*, June 28, 2011 at 63.

[252] [2011] FCA 717 at [23].

[253] Ibid at [206].

[254] [2011] NZHC 646.

[255] Ibid at [83]–[84].

[256] See **Chapter 13** for a discussion of this issue.

[257] See s 172(3) of the Companies Act 2006 and common law developments. For example, see;

8.87 Clearly directors are not required to have in-depth knowledge of accounting standards but they are expected to be financially literate to a point and have a rudimentary understanding of accounting concepts. In *Healey* Middleton J indicated that the directors are not to read the financial statements merely in order to correct typographical or grammatical errors or even immaterial errors of arithmetic. He went on to state that the reading of financial statements is:

> 'to ensure, as far as possible and reasonable, that the information included therein is accurate. The scrutiny by the directors of the financial statements involves understanding their content. The director should then bring the information known or available to him or her in the normal discharge of the director's responsibilities to the task of focussing upon the financial statements. These are the minimal steps a person in the position of any director would and should take before participating in the approval or adoption of the financial statements and their own directors' reports.'[258]

E Reliance

8.88 We have already considered the issues surrounding the delegation of tasks and the fact that the directors who delegate cannot rely totally on the delegate; the director has to supervise. In *Re City Equitable*[259] it was said that if it is prudent from a business sense that some duty be left to some other official, then in the absence of grounds for suspicion, a director is justified in trusting that official to perform those duties honestly and relying on them in the sphere of their responsibility.[260] This remains correct. Far more recently, in *Re OneTel Ltd (in liq); ASIC v Rich*,[261] Austin J said that even where a director is entitled to trust subordinates, he or she is not necessarily exonerated from ensuring that he or she is adequately informed.[262] The same view was essentially expressed in Court of Appeal dicta in *Bishopsgate Investment Management Ltd (in liq) v Maxwell*.[263]

8.89 Directors are able to rely in their decision-making on information and advice supplied by those to whom functions have been delegated within a company. Often, a major issue is going to be: how much can non-executive directors rely on executives and other managers? In *Lexi Holdings plc (In Administration) v Luqman*[264] it was argued by M, a non-professional non-executive, that it was reasonable for her to rely on the fact that the activities of a manager of the company was being monitored by three other

---

Liquidator of West Mercia Safetywear v Dodd (1988) 4 BCC 30; Re Pantone 485 Ltd [2002] 1 BCLC 266; Gwyer v London Wharf (Limehouse) Ltd [2003] 2 BCLC 153; [2002] EWHC 2748 (Ch); Re MDA Investment Management Ltd [2004] BPIR 75 at 102; [2003] EWHC 227 (Ch). This issue is discussed in detail in **Chapter 13**.

[258] [2011] FCA 717 at [22].
[259] [1925] Ch 407.
[260] Ibid at 429.
[261] [2003] NSWSC 85.
[262] Ibid at [77].
[263] [1993] BCC 120 at 140.
[264] [2007] EWHC 2265 (Ch) at [224].

directors who were professionals in the area in which the company operated. But Briggs J (as he then was) said that while a person in M's position might be able to say that such reliance may reasonably reduce the obligations on a non-professional non-executive director to appraise the company's affairs and to supervise colleagues, it cannot totally absolve that person from supervising to the point of justifying complete inactivity. The facts of each case are, naturally, going to be critical to this issue.

8.90 This section of the Chapter is more concerned about the reliance of non-executives on the information that is given to them by management. The fact of the matter is that non-executives will often rely on, and in most of the cases they probably have to rely on much of, what they get told by management and what documentation they are given. In the somewhat distant past courts have found that directors have not been liable for breach in depending on information or advice of executive committees,[265] chairmen of directors[266] and CEOs.[267] This reliance was not merely limited to the daily operations of the company, but went as far as policy-making issues, such as to what dividends were to be declared.[268] But while directors are entitled to rely on management to a point, they cannot always merely rely without question on the information that is provided to them.[269] In *Daniels v Anderson*[270] the New South Wales Court of Appeal said that no directors have an untrammelled right to rely on others. Furthermore, the court opined that where directors know, or by the exercise of ordinary care should have known, any facts that should put them on their guard and would suggest that there should be no reliance on others, then reliance may not prevent liability being imposed.[271] This approach was adopted subsequently by Santow J in *ASIC v Adler*.[272] His Honour went on to say that the reasonableness of delegation forms part of an overall assessment of whether directors have complied with the duties that they owe to their company.

8.91 What is difficult to determine is how far directors need to go out and obtain information. Are they actively to go and get it or can they rely justifiably on what they are given by directors and/or managers? The problem is one of information asymmetry, that is, not all members of the board are going to be apprised of the same amount and quality of information at any one time. The CEO and other executives will know more and may not share with others the full details. The task of non-executive directors is to try and ensure that at

---

[265] *Land Credit Company of Ireland v Lord Fermoy* (1870) LR 5 Ch App 763.

[266] *Re Denham & Co* (1884) 25 Ch D 752.

[267] *Lucas v Fitzgerald* (1903) 20 TLR 16.

[268] M Trebilcock 'The Liability of Company Directors for Negligence' (1969) 32 MLR 499 at 508.

[269] *Weavering Capital (UK) Ltd (In Liquidation) v Peterson* [2013] EWCA Civ 71; *Deloitte Haskins and Sells v National Mutual Life Nominees Ltd* (1991) 5 NZCLC 67,442-3; *Daniels v AWA Ltd* (1995) 13 ACLC 614 at 662 (NSWCA); *Re Landhurst Leasing plc* [1999] 1 BCLC 286 at 346; *Equitable Life Assurance Society v Bowley* [2003] EWHC 2263 (Comm); [2004] 1 BCLC 180 at [41].

[270] (1995) 13 ACLC 614.

[271] The Court relied on US authority in the form of *Federal Deposit Insurance Corp v Bierman* 2 F 3d 1424 (1993).

[272] [2002] NSWSC 171, (2002) 41 ACSR 72, (2002) 20 ACLC 576 (NSW S Ct).

appropriate times they are given all of the relevant information that the executive members of the board have. Of course, at times, in some company situations, it is going to be advantageous for a CEO not to disclose certain information. But this could, of course, mean that a non-executive is unaware of key data. The difficulty of getting the correct information has been a major contributing factor to many corporate collapses, such as Enron in the US and Maxwell Communications in the UK.

8.92 It is quite possible that an executive director is, in the distribution of work, given an unreasonable load. If this occurs, is it unreasonable for other directors to rely on this overloaded director? Might it be argued that if directors are aware of this overload, they should not be able to rely on what they are told by the director as he or she might not be on top of the work? The difficulty for any claimant might be establishing the fact that non-executives, in particular, were aware of the full extent of the director's workload and could not be said to have known that he or she was overloaded. What about the liability of overloaded directors? If a director is overloaded perhaps it is more understandable that he or she relies on someone else. For instance, in *Martech International Pty Ltd v Energy World Corp Ltd*[273] French J said that a managing director was not in breach of his duty of care when he relied on the head of business development of the company because the managing director had a complex role to play. The fact that the head of business development was a senior, long-serving, experienced and trusted officer of the company[274] was critical, for the suggestion was that the managing director could only rely on the other officer because he was so well-regarded.

8.93 Directors have an obligation to discern situations where, if they do rely on others they might be placing themselves in jeopardy, and they should not rely on what they are told. In *Equitable Life Assurance Society v Bowley*,[275] Langley J stated that the law as set out in *Re City Equitable* did not accurately depict the law as we now have it. His view was that non-executives could not be expected to rely on executives to perform their duties without a greater degree of scrutiny. Non-executives had to engage in more inquiring than traditionally expected. However, after saying that, the judgment in *Re City Equitable* has not been totally overtaken by either subsequent cases or s 174 of the CA 2006. The statement concerning dependence on others is generally correct. There is not some kind of overwhelming trend for directors in modern cases to be held liable despite relying on the actions of others. This is perhaps demonstrated in *AWA v Daniels*[276] where the non-executives were said to be able to assume that the CEO had given them a full account of the problems that had beset the company. In *Biala Pty Ltd v Mallina Holdings Ltd (No 4)*[277] Ipp J dismissed a claim in negligence at common law against directors, who relied on false information provided to them by the person alleged to be a de facto

---

[273] [2006] FCA 1004; (2007) 234 ALR 265.
[274] Ibid at [350].
[275] [2003] EWHC 2263 (Comm); [2004] 1 BCLC 180.
[276] (1995) 13 ACLC 614.
[277] (1994) 13 WAR 11.

director of a company. Even a director with executive responsibilities in the company was excused when he acted on the basis of false information supplied to him. He did so having regard to a long relationship that had existed between himself and the alleged de facto director and the fact that he had relied on and trusted the other person in numerous other dealings. Such reliance in these circumstances was found not to be negligent. This holding was upheld on appeal.[278] In the wrongful trading case of *Re Sherborne Associates Ltd*[279] the judge indicated that two of the directors against whom proceedings had been brought, being non-executives, were entitled to rely on the third director sued, a highly experienced chairman, because he had had greater involvement with the company and the accounts.[280] More recently *DCT v Clark*[281] said that directors are permitted to rely on assurances from those whom they have come to trust.

8.94 Yet, one wonders if the standard is now stricter than adopted in the cases just mentioned. For instance, the clear indication from *Sheahan v Verco*[282] is that whatever the reputation of executives of the company, directors are to be cautious in relying on others. In this case two non-executive directors were held liable. They had relied on the CEO, Linke, and had failed to inform themselves about the affairs of the company. The court found that one of the directors held liable, Verco, regarded Linke as a fair, honest and successful businessman who had acquired substantial assets and was successful in the fuel retailing business, the business in which the company was involved.[283] The non-executive directors did not, at any time, look at the company's books, or seek either to investigate the businesses run by the company or to verify information about the company which had been provided to them by Linke.[284] According to the court, if the directors had informed themselves appropriately about the company and found it to be financially healthy and well managed with appropriate procedures for reporting through the CEO to the board, it may be expected that they could have relied on the CEO's statements without being in breach of their duty as directors.[285] All of this points to the fact that the issue of reliance is always a matter of degree. Importantly, directors must ensure that they do not allow dominant directors to demand that reliance be placed upon them, so that they are not accountable.[286] In *Re AG (Manchester) Ltd*[287] directors were held liable in a situation where, as Patten J (as he then was) explained, an inner group of directors had 'reduced the role of the other directors to departmental managers with no serious input at board meetings on

---

[278] See *Dempster v Mallina Holdings Limited* (1994) 13 WAR 124, especially at 186.
[279] [1995] BCC 40.
[280] Ibid at 55.
[281] [2003] NSWCA 91 at [107].
[282] [2001] SASC 91.
[283] Ibid at [15].
[284] Ibid at [113] and [121].
[285] Ibid at [121].
[286] *Re Westmid Packing* [1998] 2 BCLC 646 at 653; [1998] BCC 836 at 842; *Re Landhurst Leasing plc* [1999] 1 BCLC 286 at 346; *Re Queens Moat Houses plc (No 2)* [2004] EWHC 1730 (Ch); [2005] 1 BCLC 136 at [26]. Also, see *Re AG (Manchester) Ltd* [2008] EWHC 64 (Ch); [2008] 1 BCLC 321.
[287] [2008] EWHC 64 (Ch); [2008] 1 BCLC 321.

issues affecting the running of the company'.[288] In the case of *ASIC v Healey*[289] Middleton J said that a director is not entitled to rely blindly on others in areas whether he or she lacks expertise.

8.95 The fact that a director has had a long relationship with another director and the latter had proven to be trustworthy, might save the former from liability in some situations where he or she has relied on the other director and that other director has acted appropriately.[290] But it is hard to know where to draw the line. The extent to which a director may reasonably rely on the executives and other professionals to perform their duties continues to develop and is 'fact sensitive'.[291] In determining whether reliance was reasonable a court might consider the extent of steps taken by the director, for example inquiries made or other circumstances that engender 'trust'.[292] In *Daniels v Anderson*[293] the New South Wales Court of Appeal said that no principles could be laid down as far as the extent to which a non-executive could rely on others. Like many principles in this area there is a lack of precision, unfortunately as a matter of necessity.

8.96 The issue of trust can obviously be a sensitive issue in many companies. A director might feel that in questioning, or even merely inquiring about certain things, particularly from very senior managers, he or she might be seen as undermining the authority and position of the senior manager or meddling in someone else's area of control. If that is the reaction then there is always the possibility that the director will receive less assistance in the future. Of course, if offence is taken by the senior manager it might mean that there is something to hide. It is difficult for a director to know how to take a rebuff from a senior manager, but obviously the general circumstances are critical.

8.97 Directors may, even where their reliance on another is not misplaced, constitute a breach if he or she leaves to other people responsibility for issues for which the board as a whole ought to take responsibility.[294]

8.98 So, while things might have got tougher for directors, they can still rely on others, but perhaps in fewer situations. Again, as it is with other issues considered in this chapter, the Australian decision of *ASIC v Healey*[295] is of interest in relation to reliance. It provides that, as other cases have held, directors can delegate functions to others and they can rely on other officers unless it should be recognised that reliance is misplaced.[296] For instance,

---

[288] Ibid at [178].
[289] [2011] FCA 717.
[290] *Biala v Mallina Holdings Pty Ltd* (1993) 11 ACLC 1082 at 1199-1110 (WA S Ct).
[291] *Equitable Life Assurance Society v Bowley* [2003] EWHC 2263 (Comm); [2004] 1 BCLC 180 at [41].
[292] *Re HIH Insurance; ASIC v Adler* [2002] NSWSC 171; (2002) 41 ACSR 72; (2002) 20 ACLC 576 at [372].
[293] (1995) 13 ACLC 614.
[294] *Re Landhurst Leasing plc* [1999] 1 BCLC 286 at 346.
[295] [2011] FCA 717.
[296] Ibid at [167].

directors cannot substitute reliance upon the advice of management for their own attention and examination of an important matter that falls specifically within the board's responsibilities as with the reporting obligations considered in this case.[297]

8.99 In this case Middleton J stated that the companies legislation imposes ultimate responsibility for the financial reports upon the directors and that responsibility cannot be delegated.[298] This does not mean that the directors are not entitled to seek assistance in carrying out their responsibilities, and may rely on others.[299] According to Middleton J, the reason that the directors failed to see the 'obvious errors' in the financial statements was that they all adopted the same approach in relying exclusively upon the processes that had been put in place, as well as their advisers. The problem was none of the directors stood back, armed with their own knowledge, and examined and considered for themselves the financial statements.[300] The Court indicated that while directors can rely on others to prepare the accounts, they need to review them carefully and thoroughly. Specifically, they must at least understand the terminology used in the financial statements.[301] The case manifests the danger that looms for directors of overly relying on officers of the company. It is a temptation for any director to defer to what is said or done by an officer who is experienced and working full-time in the affairs of the company. But clearly directors are still permitted to rely on officers. How they do so and to what extent remains a primary issue.

F The objective standard

8.100 We have seen that s 174 imposes both a subjective standard and an objective standard. This section of the Chapter considers what the objective standard involves. The answer is far from easy. It involves determining what care a reasonable person would exercise in discharging the functions of the relevant director, and given the director's background. But clearly no precise and detailed statements can be formulated. Obviously it is going to depend on the type of functions that the director carries out and also his or her experience and knowledge. In relation to both of these issues one has to consider the specific situation of each director.

8.101 The court in *Daniels v Anderson* held that non-executive directors must as a minimum 'take reasonable steps to place themselves in a position to guide and monitor the management of the company'.[302] But such an injunction does not, of itself, provide a great deal of practical assistance. The assertion of Professor Paul Davies that, while not binding on the courts, it is likely that the

---

[297] Ibid at [175].
[298] Ibid at [125].
[299] Ibid at [129].
[300] Ibid at [569].
[301] Ibid at [567].
[302] (1995) 13 ACLC 614 at 664. See *Dairy Containers Ltd v NZI Bank Ltd* [1995] 2 NZLR 30 at 79.

courts will take into account, where apposite and appropriate, what the Combined Code (now the UK Corporate Governance Code) provides concerning directors' responsibilities, and determine what is reasonable as a result,[303] seems to be adroit and helpful as far as it can go, but it might well have little or no application to closely-held companies.

8.102 While the same duty is imposed on all directors, the extent of that duty and the standard of care are varying factors and will depend on the facts and the director's position.[304] There can be an immense number of different situations to which the law needs to apply the same test,[305] and the performance of the director must be assessed in light of the function that was allocated to the director and the responsibilities that he or she assumed in fulfilling that function. A director's competence is to be assessed in relation to the role in the management that he or she has taken on, and the duties and responsibilities that are required by that role.[306] For instance, in *Daniels v Anderson*, while the chief executive officer of the company was held liable for failing to find out that an employee had committed foreign exchange frauds, the non-executives were not. It has been stated that there is a universal requisite standard of competence, no matter what the company's business and the director's role, but this had to be applied to each set of facts.[307] So, if a person is appointed as the finance director of the company, or some other specialist position, his or her performance will be judged as against the reasonable person acting in that capacity.[308] While the section only refers to functions of the director, it is submitted that besides considering that the nature of the company, as well as its size, will be taken into consideration. In addition, the way that the company's business is organised and the role that the director is required to play will determine whether a director has breached his or her duty.[309] This point reflects the fact that in each case the court is called upon to exercise a value judgment, and while earlier decisions are important in laying down general principles, it clearly remains a question of fact requiring an investigation into the specific role and duties pertaining to the director in the particular case in question.[310]

8.103 Courts may well infer an objective standard of financial competence from other parts of the CA 2006 such as the accounts provisions,[311] and particularly provisions such as s 393 which requires directors not to approve

---

[303] P Davies *Gower and Davies' Principles of Company Law* (London, Sweet and Maxwell, 7th edn, 2003) at 436.

[304] *Daniels v Anderson* (1995) 13 ACLC 614 at 662.

[305] *Re Landhurst Leasing plc* [1999] 1 BCLC 286 at 346.

[306] *Re Vintage Hallmark plc* [2006] EWHC 2761 (Ch); [2007] 1 BCLC 788.

[307] *Re Barings plc (No 5)* [1999] 1 BCLC 433 at 484.

[308] *Re Brian D Pierson (Contractors) Ltd* [1999] BCC 26; [2001] BCLC 275.

[309] *Bishopsgate Investment Management Ltd v Maxwell* [1993] BCC 120 at 139; *DCT v Clark* [2003] NSWCA 91; (2003) 45 ACSR 332 at [108].

[310] *ASC v Gallagher* (1993) 10 ACSR 43 at 52 (WA S Ct (Full Ct)). See *Dovey v Cory* [1901] AC 477 at 488.

[311] This has occurred in Australia: R P Austin, H A J Ford and I M Ramsay *Company Directors: Principles of Law and Corporate Governance* (Sydney, LexisNexis Butterworths, 2005) at 63.

accounts unless satisfied that the accounts give a true and fair view of the assets, liabilities and financial position of the company. Failing to ensure that the company had and maintained appropriate financial statements and records is a breach.[312]

8.104 In determining liability, it is necessary for a court to consider not only the functions of the director, and the nature of the business of the company, but also the composition of the board[313] and the way work is distributed between directors and others.[314]

8.105 Is it such that the rewards that a director receives in discharging his or her functions are to be taken into account in determining the relevant standard? The answer is uncertain. According to Jonathan Parker J in *Re Barings plc (No 5)*,[315] when it comes to the extent of a director's duties the level of a director's reward may be a relevant element. However, his Lordship hastened to add that the expected competence of a director does not depend on how much he or she is paid, although the judge did say that the greater the reward, the greater the responsibilities.[316]

8.106 A couple of examples of the application of the test which is being considered in this section follow. In *Circle Petroleum (Qld) Pty Ltd v Greenslade*[317] the managing director of a company was held liable for permitting a trading partner of his company to have $A2.2m credit when previously the limit had been $A700,000 as this was not in accordance with usual business practice in the industry concerned and it was against the wishes of the board. Importantly it was found that what the director did involve the taking of abnormally high risks as he was aware that the trading partner of his company was experiencing financial difficulties at the time of the extension of the credit. Clearly, this was not something that the reasonable person acting as a managing director would do. In *Re QLS Superannuation Ltd*[318] a director was held liable for both his failure to ensure that the loan conditions fixed by the board were satisfied before he permitted funds to be loaned, and his failure to make proper inquiry into the history of repayment by the borrower and any inquiry into his repayment history in respect of borrowings from other lenders.

---

[312] *Sheahan v Verco* [2001] SASC 91 at [101].

[313] *DCT v Clark* [2003] NSWCA 91; 45 ACSR 332 at [108]; *Australian Securities and Investments Commission v Maxwell* (2006) 59 ACSR 373 at [100]; *Australian Securities and Investments Commission v Warrenmang Ltd* [2007] FCA 973 at [23].

[314] *ASC v Gallagher* (1993) 10 ACSR 43 at 53; *Australian Securities and Investments Commission v Maxwell* (2006) 59 ACSR 373 at [100]; *Australian Securities and Investments Commission v Warrenmang Ltd* [2007] FCA 973 at [23]. This effectively follows on from what was said in *Re City Equitable* [1925] Ch 407 at 427.

[315] [1999] 1 BCLC 433.

[316] Ibid at 488.

[317] (1998) 16 ACLC 1577.

[318] [2003] FCA 262; (2003) 21 ACLC 888 at [115].

8.107 On the basis of the decision of the Supreme Court of New South Wales in *ASIC v Vines*,[319] where a court permitted a person to give expert evidence of what one would expect of a reasonably competent chief financial officer (this was a non-director post, but officers of the company, along with directors, can be held liable for breach of statutory duties under the Australian Corporations Act 2001), it might be that a court in the United Kingdom would allow expert evidence in relation to a director carrying out a specialised role.

8.108 In a later hearing in the *Vines* litigation, Austin J said that the general law of torts may now be called in aid as a source of guiding principles for the content of the statutory standard of care of company directors.[320] Austin J said that the statutory standard in the Australian Act should not be treated as 'an idiosyncratic and isolated phenomenon',[321] and this could be applied to the UK provision particularly given the fact that s 170(4) of the CA 2006 states that the provisions are to be interpreted and applied in the same way as prevailing common law rules and equitable principles.

8.109 It could be argued that an objective test assists companies in the process of selecting directors, as they cannot know all about the competence of a potential director and any prospective director has to meet the standard of the reasonable person. Perhaps the test might dissuade a person who knows that they are not up to standard from applying for, or accepting an offer of, appointment.[322]

8.110 In sum, it is not possible to formulate a rule of universal application as to how the duty is to be fulfilled.[323] The extent of the duty and the question whether it has been discharged must depend critically on the facts of each particular case, including the role that the director has in the management of the company.[324]

G Decisions and hindsight

8.111 It has been asserted by Muir J of the Queensland Supreme Court in *Circle Petroleum (Qld) Pty Ltd v Greenslade*[325] that while changes have occurred since *Re City Equitable* there does not seem to be a major change in the fact that courts are reluctant to find directors liable for breach of duty as a result of business judgments, particularly where they are exercising their functions for entrepreneurial reasons. With respect, this seems to ring true. It is

---

[319] [2003] NSWSC 1116.

[320] *ASIC v Vines [2003] FLR 405, [2003] NSWSC 1116, SC, NSW* at [1070].

[321] Ibid at [1070].

[322] C A Riley 'The Company Director's Duty of Care and Skill: The Case for an Onerous but Subjective Standard' (1999) 62 MLR 697 at 713. The learned writer argues that this argument fails.

[323] A view expressed in Australia some years before this: *Gould and Birbeck and Bacon v Mount Oxide Mines Ltd (in liq)* (1916) 22 CLR 490 at 531 (Aust HC).

[324] *Re Barings (No 5)* [1999] 1 BCLC 433 at 489. CA 2006, s 386 imposes a duty on companies to keep such accounting records.

[325] (1998) 16 ACLC 1577 at 1592.

perhaps based on the fact that the business decisions of an entrepreneurial nature that directors make are not easy for judges to evaluate. If a decision is successful the director is regarded as having adopted a reasonably obvious course of action, but if the decision leads to a bad result then there is a tendency to assume that the director got it wrong. Psychologists have demonstrated from experiments that individuals tend to exaggerate how easy the outcomes of a decision could be foreseen when they have hindsight.[326] It is certainly easy to be wise after the event, and UK courts have been mindful of this,[327] and generally they have not second-guessed the decisions that directors have made. The judges have generally been careful not to employ hindsight to find directors liable and have extended to directors reasonably wide latitude in interpreting how they have acted.[328] See, for example, the decision of Hoffman J in *Re Welfab Engineers Ltd*.[329] The action involved a claim that directors had breached their duty to the company, in that they failed to take into account the interests of creditors, because they accepted one bid for the company's property, while rejecting what appeared to be more substantial bids at a time when the company was in desperate financial straits. The court, in coming to a decision that the directors were not liable for breach of their duties, took into account the commercial environment at the time of the making of the transaction alleged to constitute the breach, even though it occurred some seven years before the hearing. At the time of the alleged breach the geographical region in which the company's business operated was suffering a harsh recession and this impacted markedly on the decision made. The approach of the courts highlighted here is, perhaps, implicit acceptance of the fact that directors cannot be seen as insurers of the success of any action and the decisions which they make. In addition the courts have tended to be reluctant to engage in assessing the merits of commercial judgments.[330] As mentioned before in the Chapter, courts do not hold directors liable for mere errors of judgment.[331]

8.112 It is not easy to establish that a director is liable because of a judgment that he or she made, especially if it is clear that they did their best. But one would think that they could be liable in such circumstances based on, perhaps, the failure to fulfil the objective element of s 174. Courts have, in a limited way, held directors liable for the decisions that they have made. Take for instance the case of *Simtel Communications Ltd v Rebak*[332] where a director made a decision to purchase a large quantity of goods for his company without having in place any arrangements for them to be sold on. He was held liable by the

---

[326] See the research cited by M Eisenberg 'The Duty of Care and the Business Judgement Rule in American Corporate Law' (1997) 2 *Company Financial and Insolvency Law Review* 185 at n.21.

[327] For example, see *Re Sherborne Associates Ltd* [1995] BCC 40 (a wrongful trading case); *Re Welfab Engineers Ltd* [1990] BCC 600.

[328] This is also the case in wrongful trading actions. For example, see *Re Continental Assurance Ltd* [2001] BPIR 733.

[329] [1990] BCC 600.

[330] For example, see *Howard Smith Ltd v Ampol Petroleum Ltd* [1974] AC 821.

[331] *Re Brazilian Rubber Plantations and Estates Ltd* [1911] 1 Ch 425 at 436; *Roberts v Frohlich* [2011] EWHC 257 (Ch) [2011] 2 BCLC 635 at [106].

[332] [2006] EWHC 572; [2006] 2 BCLC 571.

judge who said that what the director had done had gone beyond a mere error of judgment and involved an unacceptable level of risk-taking.[333] The directors in *Re Brian D Pierson (Contractors) Ltd*[334] were held liable for transferring a part of the company's business without requiring any payment for goodwill, and this was even though in the circumstances the only potential purchaser of the goodwill was the ultimate purchaser and the goodwill was not capable of significant realisation in the market.

8.113   A final case worth mentioning is *Roberts v Frohlich*,[335] where the judge held the directors liable for various decisions that they made on the basis that they breached their duty of care, only after clearly stating that an assessment of what a director has done was to be made without the benefit of hindsight.[336] Courts will not hold directors liable if they have considered all of the information that is reasonably available to them.[337] In some cases courts will find that when examining a director's decision-making, the director has not used powers for proper purposes (see **Chapter 5**) as well as or instead of acting in breach of the duty of care.[338]

8.114   It is outside of the scope of the book to investigate in any detail the normative issue of whether directors should be held liable or not for a breach of their duty of care when they make bad judgments. Of course, one concern that might be voiced is that when it comes to assessment of the decisions of the directors, the latter are at the mercy of the judgment of the courts. This is an understandable concern. But while judges are not businesspersons, they are experienced in legal affairs and they can hear, and make judgments based on, evidence. It is up to directors to lead evidence to support their case that they have acted quite competently, provided that they have a case to answer on the claimant's submissions and evidence. Also, when looking at the recent case-law, it is submitted that where courts have held directors to be liable, the cases have been clear-cut, with *Dorchester Finance Ltd v Stubbing*[339] and *Re D'Jan of London*,[340] cases discussed earlier, being prime examples. A far more recent example is *Secretary of State for Trade and Industry v Swan*.[341] In this case a director, who was the chairman and CEO of a company, was held in breach in that he failed to inquire as to the purpose of cheques which he signed and which involved large amounts of money. The cheques were in fact part of a cheque kiting policy, which everyone involved in the case accepted was wholly unacceptable and an improper practice, if not dishonest.[342] The essence of

---

[333]   Ibid at [39].

[334]   [1999] BCC 26.

[335]   [2011] EWHC 257 (Ch) at [102].

[336]   Ibid at [106].

[337]   *Re Welfab Engineers Ltd* [1990] BCC 600.

[338]   For instance, *Simtel Communications Ltd v Rebak* [2006] EWHC 572; [2006] 2 BCLC 571; *Bishopsgate Investment Management Ltd (in liquidation) v Maxwell* (No 2) [1994] 1 All ER 261, [1993] BCLC 1282, [1993] BCC 120.

[339]   [1989] BCLC 498.

[340]   [1993] BCC 646.

[341]   [2005] EWHC 603 (Ch).

[342]   *Secretary of State for Trade and Industry v Swan* [2005] EWHC 603 (Ch) at [212].

cheque kiting is the utilisation by the kiter of the period taken by the bank to clear a cheque so as to obtain a fictional increase in the balance of the payee's account before the cheque is cleared and its amount is deducted from the payer's account.[343]

8.115 It is often said that courts should not be able to review the wisdom of particular business decisions made by directors.[344] But why not? Is this because they can only view the decision retrospectively and they cannot view it objectively enough? But someone has to be able to assess, based on evidence, what others have done. Judges regularly make decisions about the actions of all kinds of professionals and non-professionals.

8.116 Some jurisdictions apply what is known as the business judgment rule when it comes to determining whether directors are liable for a breach of their duty of care. The prime example is the United States. However, Australia provides a better example for us as the Australian legislation was originally based on the UK Companies Act and it is still generally much closer to the UK's in content, and, of course, the common law has developed along very similar lines. A few words about the business judgment rule are appropriate given the impact that it has had generally in some common law jurisdictions.

H The business judgment rule

8.117 It must be emphasised that the following is only an overview of what can be seen as a complicated rule. This is especially so as far as the United States is concerned where there is some uncertainty in the case-law as to aspects of the rule.

8.118 In the United States the business judgments of directors are only reviewed in extraordinary circumstances.[345] This is because of what might be regarded as US corporate law's central doctrine,[346] the business judgment rule. The rule tends to insulate directors from liability for negligent acts.[347] The rule takes the focus of the court away from whether the director made the correct decision to whether the director adhered to adequate and appropriate processes that led to the decision. Consequently, it is said to provide a 'safe harbour' for directors. So, US directors are entitled to rely on the business judgment rule if they can establish in relation to the particular judgment in question that: they exercised a business judgment (this includes a decision to refrain from taking any action – where no decision to act or not to act was made then directors are subject to review under the duty); the judgment was made in good faith for a proper purpose; they do not have a material personal interest in the subject

---

[343] Ibid at [13].
[344] R Reed 'Company Directors – Collective or Functional Responsibility' (2006) 27 Co Law 170 at 171.
[345] D Rosenberg 'Galactic Stupidity and the Business Judgment Rule' (2006–07) 32 *Journal of Corporation Law* 301 at 301–302.
[346] S Bainbridge *Corporation Law and Economics* (New York, Foundation Press, 2002) at 241.
[347] Ibid at 243.

matter of the judgment, so that there is no conflict of interest; they informed themselves about the subject matter of the judgment to the extent that they reasonably believed to be appropriate;[348] and they rationally believe that the judgment is in the best interests of the company.[349] The presumption[350] is that the director has acted properly and it is the job of the plaintiff (claimant) to rebut this presumption. If the plaintiff can do so, and rebutting is not easy, then the burden shifts to the director who has to establish the fairness of the transaction that is impugned.[351]

8.119 The rule pervades every aspect of corporate law in the United States.[352] It is designed to preserve directors' discretion and to protect the directors from courts using hindsight to find them liable. The rule provides, in a nutshell, that courts will not substitute their business judgment for that of the informed, reasonable director who acts bona fide in the best interests of the company,[353] and an action will fail even if the claimant can demonstrate that the action of the directors has caused loss to the company unless the director's actions do not meet the aforementioned qualities.[354] So, a US director cannot be held liable for breach of the duty of care if he or she makes a bad judgment or a decision which he or she makes is unsuccessful,[355] provided the above factors can be established on his or her behalf.

8.120 The review of a director's action by a court, applying the business judgment rule, will involve a review of the objective financial interests of the directors, a review of the director's motivation and an objective review of the process by which a decision was reached by the director.[356] Importantly, directors' actions cannot be second-guessed by a court, provided that the directors made informed, reasonable decisions in good faith, and which were based on the details that were available to them when making the decisions.

---

[348] See *Cede and Co v Technicolor Inc* (1993) 634 A 2d 345 (Delaware) for a case where the directors were held not to have informed themselves appropriately.

[349] American Law Institute *Principles of Corporate Governance and Structure: Restatement and Recommendations* (1982) at s 4.01. See, for example, *Aronson v Lewis* (1984) 473 A 2d 805; *Parnes v Bally Entertainment Corp* (1999) 722 A 2d 1243 (Delaware). Also, see S Bainbridge *Corporation Law and Economics* (New York, Foundation Press, 2002) at 270–283.

[350] Professor Stephen Bainbridge argues that it is really an assumption and not a presumption in the evidentiary sense of 'presumption' (*Corporation Law and Economics* (New York, Foundation Press, 2002) at 269–270).

[351] L Johnson 'The Modest Business Judgment Rule' (2000) 55 *Business Lawyer* 625 at 628.

[352] S Bainbridge 'Director Primacy: The Means and Ends of Corporate Governance' (2003) 97 *Northwestern University Law Review* 547 at 601.

[353] For instance, see *Moran v Household International Inc* (1983) 500 A 2d 1346, 1356 (Delaware); *Aronson v Lewis* (1984) 473 A 2d 805 at 812 (Delaware); *Spiegel v Buntrock* 571 A 2d 767, 774 (1990) (Delaware); R Cieri, P Sullivan, and H Lennox 'The Fiduciary Duties of Directors of Financially Troubled Companies' (1994) 3 *Journal of Bankruptcy Law and Practice* 405 at 408.

[354] See D Millon 'Why is Corporate Management Obsessed with Quarterly Earnings and What Should be Done About it?' (2002) 70 *George Washington Law Review* 890 at 917.

[355] *Joy v North* (1983) 692 F 2d 880 at 885.

[356] *Re RJR Nabisco Inc. Shareholders' Litigation* (31 January 1989, unreported), Delaware Chancery Court, referred to by A Tompkins 'Directors' Duties to Creditors: Delaware and the Insolvency Exception' (1993) 47 *Southern Methodist University Law Review* 165 at 188.

Incorporating elements that are derived from the business judgment rule serves to provide some significant protection for directors in an area where concern has been voiced that directors have to endure uncertainty.[357] Some have said that the rule has all but eviscerated the duty of care,[358] for it seriously undermines the accountability of directors for what they do.[359] Another commentator has suggested that it is easy for directors to satisfy the standard of business judgment.[360] It is generally thought that the only time when courts will review what directors have decided to do or not to do, is when their decision has reached the borderline of good faith.[361]

8.121 The primary problem facing the implementation of the rule seems to be that there are two conceptions of the rule in US case-law (and it must be remembered that there are courts from many jurisdictions in the United States making decisions on this rule), and these compete with one another. These are: first, the rule is used as a standard of review, with the result that directors have to be found to have acted with gross negligence;[362] and, second, the rule is regarded as an abstention principle,[363] which involves the existence of a presumption against a review of the director's actions by a court that are alleged to constitute a breach of the duty of care except where the presumption can be rebutted by demonstrating that one (or more) of the preconditions for the rule to apply has not been fulfilled.[364]

8.122 Australia, with a company law system that, while not as close as it once was, is more similar to the UK's than the US, is an interesting case. It decided to embrace the rule in the late 1990s, in legislation[365] (arguably courts had taken aspects of it into account for many years), but if the number of reported cases are anything to go by, the rule is not preventing successful proceedings being brought against directors as much as in the United States.[366] There have only been two cases, *ASIC v Rich*[367] and *ASIC v Mariner Corporation Ltd*,[368] where a defendant director had successfully employed the rule to save himself or

---

[357] R Cieri, P Sullivan, and H Lennox 'The Fiduciary Duties of Directors of Financially Troubled Companies' (1994) 3 *Journal of Bankruptcy Law and Practice* 405.

[358] It is suggested that the duty of care has no relevance in the most important US jurisdiction for company law, namely Delaware: S Lubben and A Darnell 'Delaware's Duty of Care' (2006) 31 *Delaware Journal of Corporate Law* 589. Also, see A Palmiter 'Reshaping the Corporate Fiduciary Model: A Director's Duty of Independence' (1989) 67 *Texas Law Review* 1351 at 1353.

[359] M Blair and L Stout 'A Team Production Theory of Corporate Law' (1999) 85 Va L R 247 at 299–300.

[360] M Eisenberg 'The Duty of Care and the Business Judgement Rule in American Corporate Law' (1997) 2 *Company Financial and Insolvency Law Review* 185 at 186.

[361] D Rosenberg 'Galactic Stupidity and the Business Judgment Rule' (2006-07) 32 *Journal of Corporation Law* 301 at 301–302.

[362] See *Cede and Co v Technicolor Inc* (1993) 634 A 2d 345 (Delaware).

[363] See *Shlensky v Wrigley* (1968) 237 NE 2d 776 (Illinois).

[364] S Bainbridge, *Corporation Law and Economics*, (New York, Foundation Press, 2002) at 243.

[365] Corporate Law Economic Reform Program 1999 (Cth).

[366] The rule has rarely been discussed by Australian courts. An example is *Re HIH Insurance Ltd; ASC v Adler* [2002] NSWSC 171; (2002) 41 ACSR 72; (2002) 20 ACLC 576.

[367] [2009] NSWSC 1229; (2009) 236 FLR 1; (2009) 75 ACSR 1.

[368] [2015] FCA 589.

herself from liability. Both decisions are at first instance only. Section 180(2) of the Corporations Act 2001 provides (s 180(1) provides the duty of care) the rule in the following terms:

> 'A director or other officer of a corporation who makes a business judgment is taken to meet the requirements of subsection (1), and their equivalent duties at common law and in equity, in respect of the judgment if they:
>
> (a)   make the judgment in good faith for a proper purpose; and
> (b)   do not have a material personal interest in the subject matter of the judgment; and
> (c)   inform themselves about the subject matter of the judgment to the extent they reasonably believe to be appropriate; and
> (d)   rationally believe that the judgment is in the best interests of the corporation.
>
> The director's or officer's belief that the judgment is in the best interests of the corporation is a rational one unless the belief is one that no reasonable person in their position would hold.'

8.123   It has been held that the director has the onus of proving all of elements of the rule, namely those found in paras (a)–(d) above,[369] and the requirements are demanding.

8.124   The most detailed discussion of the Australian statutory business judgment rule has been given by Austin J in *Australian Securities and Investments Commission v Rich*.[370]

8.125   In one of the leading cases, *Re HIH Insurance Ltd; ASC v Adler*,[371] the judge, Santow J, denied a director the right to invoke the rule because he either failed to make a business judgment at all or to the extent that he did, he failed to establish that it was made in good faith for a proper purpose. Also, the director had a material personal interest in the subject matter of the judgment and had failed to inform himself to the extent he could reasonably believe to be appropriate.[372] The rule can protect directors in relation to a range of managerial conduct and this includes planning, budgeting and forecasting.[373] The Australian jurisprudence is such that the rule has not been frequently employed by the courts in relation to breaches of the duty of care,[374] although it is an important element of the law.

---

[369]   *Australian Securities and Investments Commission v Fortescue Metals Group Ltd* (2011) 190 FCR 364 at [197]. This case, a decision of the Full Court of the Federal Court, was overruled by the High Court in *Forrest v Australian Securities and Investments Commission* [2012] HCA 39; (2012) 91 ACSR 128; 30 ACLC 12-034, but on another issue, and the High Court did not disapprove of what was said by the Full Court of the Federal Court.

[370]   [2009] NSWSC 1229; (2009) 75 ACSR 1 at [7248]–[7295].

[371]   [2002] NSWSC 171; (2002) 41 ACSR 72; (2002) 20 ACLC 576.

[372]   Ibid at [453].

[373]   *ASIC v Rich* (2009) 75 ACSR 1 at [125]; [7273]–[7276].

[374]   For example, see *ASIC v Vines [2003] FLR 405, [2003] NSWSC 1116, SC, NSW*; (2005) 55

8.126 While the business judgment rule[375] does not apply in the United Kingdom,[376] a derivation of it arguably applies, just as it did in Australia before it embraced the legislative rule that it has now. Should the United Kingdom embrace the business judgment rule? Well the question might be rather academic especially given the fact that the CA 2006 is still in relative infancy; government might think that things need to settle down now for a while before it takes any further action. The danger with the American model is that the courts become deferential to decisions of boards, almost feeling that they cannot question decisions that are made by businesspersons,[377] and it means that the level of accountability is effectively low. The result is that unless a claimant can establish that the directors engaged in fraud, bad faith, gross overreaching or abuse of discretion, the courts will not interfere.[378] Also, some might argue that the United Kingdom has a quasi-business judgment rule in any event, as indicated earlier, in that the courts do not second guess what directors have done. Certainly one would think that if a business judgment rule did exist the legislature would have, like Australia, incorporated it in the CA 2006. It is perhaps interesting to note that the Company Law Review Steering Group made few mentions of the business judgment rule in its many papers and its Final Report. In fact UK judges have consistently refrained from reviewing business judgments made by directors,[379] but as mentioned earlier in the Chapter there have been occasions where courts have held directors liable for their decisions and judgments. It might be argued that it is difficult to see any clear differences in principle between some of the cases that fall on one side of the line, and where directors' decisions have not been reviewed, and those that fall on the other said of the line and where decisions of directors have been reviewed by the courts.

8.127 Some in Australia argued against the introduction of a business judgment rule on the basis that the long-established general law doctrines, applying in the United Kingdom as well as Australia, protected directors from

---

ACSR 617; *Gold Ribbon (Accountants) Pty Ltd v Sheers & Ors* [2006] QCA 335. Also, see R Baxt 'How Forgiving Can a Court be of a Directors' Breaches of Duty? (2007) 35 ABLR 370 at 372–373.

[375] For example, see *In re Healthco International Inc* (1997) 208 BR 288 at 306 (Massachusetts). Also, see American Law Institute, *Principles of Corporate Governance and Structure: Restatement and Recommendations*, 1982; M Eisenberg 'The Duty of Care and the Business Judgement Rule in American Corporate Law' (1997) 2 *Company Financial and Insolvency Law Review* 185.

[376] The Law Commission in its 1999 Report on 'Company Directors: Regulating Conflicts of Interest and Formulating a Statement of Duties' (No 261) thought that such a rule was not necessary (Pt 5). The CLRSG agreed: Company Law Review, *Modern Company Law for a Competitive Economy: Developing the Framework* (London, DTI, 2000) at para 3.69–3.70. The CLRSG felt that such a rule would add complexity and would be unfair as it would be overly harsh in some cases and give too much leeway in others.

[377] See D Millon 'Why is Corporate Management Obsessed with Quarterly Earnings and What Should be Done About it?' (2002) 70 *George Washington Law Review* 890 at 917.

[378] For example, see *Treadway Co v Care Corp* 638 F 2d 357 at 382 (1980); *Crouse-Hinds Co v Inter-North Inc* 634 F 2d 690 at 702 (1980).

[379] R Reed 'Company Directors – Collective or Functional Responsibility' (2006) 27 Co Law 170 at 170.

the use of judicial hindsight.[380] Perhaps one of the differences between the US and UK positions is that under the former's system, provided that the conditions that constitute the rule are fulfilled, a director will not be liable if he or she makes a decision that is unreasonable and causes loss to the company provided that the decision is rational,[381] whilst in the United Kingdom the director could possibly be liable. In sum, the position in the United Kingdom is arguably more flexible than that which applies in the US, and many might find that to be more attractive. Nevertheless, it is questionable whether there is a great deal of flexibility in that the UK courts seem to shy away from finding directors liable if there is any suggestion that what is being argued for by the claimant is that the director did not exercise care in making a business judgment.

I Professional advice

8.128   The issue of the taking of professional advice is a multifaceted one. Initially we can say that in some circumstances directors might be in breach of their duty if they make a decision without first obtaining expert advice. Second, what if directors do take advice? On one side of the coin, directors are likely to be placing themselves in jeopardy if they take action which flies in the face of advice provided by experienced professionals who have expertise relating to the kind of action contemplated.[382] For example, in *AWA Ltd v Daniels*[383] it was said that one of the failings of the CEO was not acting on the warnings of an auditor. In the Irish case of *Coyle v Callanan*[384] O'Leary J found that a director had acted reasonably in acting on express and specific legal advice. In *Re Stephenson Cobbold Ltd*,[385] a disqualification case, the court found that a director was entitled to take the advice of the company's auditors, when he questioned payments made by the company in relation to the personal matters of another director, and when he got the answer that the financial affairs of the company were being conducted properly. In *Green v Walkling*[386] the court found the director not liable because he had acted reasonably in seeking legal advice and acting pursuant to it. The judge indicated that the fact that a director has taken advice is a relevant factor in determining whether a director should be held liable.[387] In the same case the court made it plain that provided that a director had acted properly it did not matter that the advice given was incorrect or that a different adviser would have proffered different and, perhaps, correct advice. The adviser needs to be qualified and independent if a director is going to be able to rely on what he or she was advised when resisting

---

[380]   For example, see P Redmond 'Safe Harbours or Sleepy Hollows: Does Australia Need a Statutory Business Judgment Rule?' in I M Ramsay (ed) *Corporate Governance and the Duties of Company Directors* (Melbourne, Centre for Corporate Law and Securities Regulation, University of Melbourne, 1997).

[381]   See *Selheimer v Manganese Corporation of America* (1966) 224 A rd 634 (Penn).

[382]   *ASC v Donovan* (1998) 28 ACSR 583.

[383]   (1995) 13 ACLC 614.

[384]   [2006] 1 IR 447.

[385]   [2000] 2 BCLC 614.

[386]   [2007] EWHC 2046 (Ch);[2008] BCC 256.

[387]   Ibid at [38].

a liability claim.[388] Also, the director must have provided the adviser with correct information.[389] In another situation, namely consideration of whether a person fulfilled the fit and proper test for investment advisers, the Financial Market and Services Tribunal adopted the view that the fact that the person followed legal advice was an important issue to take into account.[390]

8.129 In *Re D'Jan of London Ltd*[391] Hoffmann LJ said that if a director were to sign a long agreement 'of turgid legal prose'[392] after the solicitor for the company assured the director that it accurately reflected the board's instructions, he may well be excused from reading it all. Yet on the other side of the coin, while directors are entitled to rely on professional advisers they must not do so blindly accepting all that they are told and failing to ask reasonable questions, where appropriate.

8.130 As Professor Brenda Hannigan points out, the risk involved in permitting directors to rely on professional advice without question is that directors will instruct advisers in all matters and shift the risk of liability.[393] So, a distinction has to be made between reliance that is merited and blind dependence. The bottom line is: was it reasonable, given all of the facts, for the directors to depend totally on the advice of the professional? In answering that question, the director and his or her experience and qualifications, as well as the kind of company in which the director holds office, are relevant issues to be taken into account.[394] Of course a director is not usually expected to possess the necessary skills to evaluate the advice given in relation to a specialist area. A recent example of a case where the judge held that a director had acted reasonably in relying on advice is *Re Pro4Sport Ltd; Hedger v Adams*.[395] HHJ Behrens (sitting as a judge of the High Court) in that case made it clear that relying on advice could be an important factor in determining if a director was in breach of his or her duty to exercise reasonable care.[396] Interestingly, the New Zealand Companies Act 1993 provides that a director may rely on advice given by a professional where the latter is a professional adviser or expert in relation to matters which the director believes on reasonable grounds to be within the person's professional or expert competence.[397] In the much earlier

---

[388] *Iesini v Westrip Holdings Ltd* [2009] EWHC 2526 (Ch); [2011] 1 BCLC 498 and referred to in W Wan 'Directors' Defence of Reliance on Professional Advisers under Anglo-Australian Law' (2015) 44 *Common Law World Review* 71 at 76.

[389] *ASIC v Adler* [2002] NSWSC 171; (2002) 41 ACSR 72; *ASIC v Hobb* [2012] NSWSC 1276.

[390] J Gray 'Financial Services and Market Tribunal Adjudication on "Fit and Proper" Test for FSA Approved Persons' (2004) 12 *Journal of Financial Regulation and Compliance* 75. But note that the Singaporean High Court in *Ong Chow Hong v Public Prosecutor* [2011] SGHC 93 said that the fact that the defendant directors relied on legal advice did not exonerate them as they needed to make their own independent assessment of the facts.

[391] [1993] BCC 646.

[392] Ibid at 648.

[393] B Hannigan *Company Law* (London, Lexis Nexis Butterworths, 2003) at 309.

[394] *Australian Securities and Investments Commission v Maxwell* (2006) 59 ACSR 373 at [100].

[395] [2015] EWHC 2540 (Ch); [2016] 1 BCLC 257.

[396] Ibid at [46].

[397] Section 138.

case of *Re McNulty's Interchange Ltd*[398] Browne-Wilkinson V-C said that if a person relies on advice it is not correct to hold him or her liable because he or she failed to appreciate that the advice was wrong.[399] In a recent decision of the New Zealand Court of Appeal, *Morgenstern v Jeffreys*,[400] it was said that if a director wishes to put the argument that he or she relied on the advice of a professional adviser he or she:[401]

> 'will therefore need to adduce evidence establishing the nature and scope of the advice and the circumstances justifying the director's reliance on the advice. At the very least the director would be expected to adduce direct evidence from the professional advisers and make them available for cross-examination.'

These requirements seem to be reasonable and might well be followed by a UK court.

8.131 Directors cannot simply instruct a professional and think that they can wash their hands of the matter totally.[402] For instance, the retaining of an accountant to prepare financial records is not something that would excuse the directors from their duty to understand the financial position of the company.[403] In other instances, it is submitted that it would be incumbent on directors once they have sought advice, to contact their advisers from time to time, if they hear nothing from their advisers, to ascertain what is happening. As foreshadowed already, it would also seem necessary for directors to ask appropriate and timely questions of their advisers rather than just accepting everything they are told without question. There are instances of directors being found not liable when they have asked questions.[404] Of course it might become an issue in any given case about the kind and depth of the questions asked by directors.

8.132 Over-reliance on advisers is something about which directors must be concerned. It is the directors whose job it is to make decisions on the basis that they are commercially sound and without unnecessary and inappropriate risk.

---

[398] (1988) 4 BCC 533.

[399] Ibid at 535.

[400] [2014] NZCA 449.

[401] Ibid at [76].

[402] For an example of a case where a director was held to be unfit for office and disqualified on the basis that he relied totally on professional advice and without asking appropriate questions, see *Re Bradcrown Ltd* [2000] 2 BCLC 614. Also, see the Singaporean High Court decision in *Ong Chow Hong v Public Prosecutor* [2011] SGHC 93 where it said that the fact that the defendant directors relied on legal advice did not exonerate them as they needed to make their own independent assessment of the facts.

[403] *Re One.Tel Ltd (in liq); ASIC v Rich* [2003] NSWSC 85; (2003) 44 ACSR 682.

[404] For example, see *Norman v Theodore Goddard* [1991] BCLC 1028; [1992] BCC 14.

Directors also have to evaluate whether they have taken an adequate amount of advice, and from the right kind of people[405] to enable them to make a decision.[406]

8.133 In sum, directors are entitled to rely on the advice of professionals who are appropriately qualified and independent, where the advice is within the expertise of the adviser and where the directors has provided the adviser with the correct information and context, and assessed the advice as far as his or her expertise and knowledge permits.

VI SKILL

8.134 'Skill' does not have any specialised meaning. In their joint judgment in *Daniels v Anderson*[407] Clarke and Sheller JJA defined it as:[408]

> 'That special competence which is not part of the ordinary equipment of the reasonable man but the result of aptitude developed by special training and experience which requires those who undertake work calling for special skill not only to exercise reasonable care but measure up to the standard of proficiency that can be expected from persons undertaking such work.'

8.135 Initially we must note that it was stated in *Re Brazilian Rubber Plantations and Estates Ltd*[409] that a director is not bound to bring any special skills or qualifications to his or her office, and it is submitted that this still holds true unless the director is being appointed to a specialist role.

8.136 If a person is designated as the 'sales director', 'marketing director' or 'finance director' then special skills must be expected of that person.[410] In *ASC v Vines*[411] the court recognised the fact that the position of finance director or chief financial officer is an accepted post in large companies such that there is clear specialised skill relevant to the office. A good example of a finance director's position and responsibility is to be found in *Re AG (Manchester) Ltd*.[412] In this case the finance director was a qualified accountant who had spent time as the financial controller of a sizeable company, namely Matalan plc.[413] At proceedings brought for his disqualification, the director

---

[405] In *Coleman Taymar Ltd v Oakes* [2001] 2 BCLC 749 the judge said that the director was not able to rely on the advice of the lawyer from whom he had sought advice as the lawyer was not a company lawyer and company law advice was what was needed.

[406] J Loughrey 'The directors' duty of care and skill and the financial crisis' in J Loughrey (ed) *Directors' Duties and Shareholder Litigation in the Wake of the Financial Crisis* (Cheltenham, Edward Elgar, 2012) at 32.

[407] *Daniels v Anderson* (1995) 13 ACLC 614 (NSWCA).

[408] Ibid at 665.

[409] [1911] 1 Ch 425 at 437.

[410] *Brian D Pierson* at [1999] BCC 26 at 55; [2001] BCLC 275 at 309; *ASIC v Vines* (2003) 48 ACSR 322.

[411] *ASIC v Vines* (2003) 48 ACSR 322.

[412] [2008] EWHC 64 (Ch); [2008] 1 BCLC 321.

[413] Ibid at [38].

was held to be unfit to be a director because he had failed to put into place aspects of corporate governance that pertained to finance matters, including failing to ensure that the company was able to pay dividends and other expenses, and informing the board about his concerns over the affordability of proposals in respect of dividends and expenses.[414] The director had left final decisions to a small group of directors who had always 'called the tune' when it came to finance matters[415] and he was someone who did not consult the full board.[416]

8.137 No specific skill is prescribed for non-executives, but each one will be judged on the basis of the experience that he or she has and what a reasonable person would have done in his or her position. In *Re City Equitable*,[417] for example, it was said that a director of an insurance company would not be expected to have the skill and ability of an actuary.[418] This position can be contrasted with other jurisdictions, where some training or set of abilities are required. For instance, in Singapore, directors have to show a reasonable level of knowledge of company law before being able to be appointed.[419]

8.138 Skill might be regarded as the most difficult of the trio of factors included in s 174 of the CA 2006 to get a handle on. Compared with care and diligence, skill suggests that it is something that has more substantive content. Whilst an element of ability comes within care, it is largely a matter of being committed, perceptive and aware. As far as skill goes, it is a problem in prescribing the skills that the reasonable person acting in the position of the director should have. Would one include basic accountancy skills, ability to understand accounts and other financial statements, capacity to manage and an understanding of how companies operate? The difficulty with this is that many persons might not be able to meet such a level, and the pool of available persons might diminish significantly. Loose et al say that '*all* directors must show some skills, but professionally qualified or experienced directors must show more'.[420] However, the learned authors do not identify the skills that must be held by all directors. Obviously all directors have some skills, but they might not be those which a reasonably diligent person operating as a director would have. It might be argued that in a more complicated commercial world the standards of directors' skills should be heightened. On the other side of the

---

[414] Ibid at [82], [181].

[415] Ibid at [85].

[416] Ibid at [86].

[417] [1925] Ch 407.

[418] Ibid at 428.

[419] L Roach 'The Director's Duty of Skill and Care: Has the Law Commission Got it Right?' (1999) 20 BLR 51 at 52.

[420] P Loose, M Griffiths and D Impey *The Company Director* (Bristol, Jordan Publishing, 9th edn, 2007) at 278.

argument are the points that commerce does not want either to deter appropriate people from willing to accept appointments[421] or stultify enterprise and a certain amount of risk-taking.[422]

8.139 It has been said that if a non-executive director were a professionally qualified person, such as a solicitor, he or she is expected to show the same care as any non-executive director and not as a solicitor.[423] But this seems to fly in the face of a number of judicial statements as well as s 174 of the CA 2006. In *Re Brazilian Rubber Plantations and Estates Ltd*[424] it was said that if directors have special skills or qualifications they are expected to apply them in the course of their functions. Section 174 provides that the skills of a director are to be taken into account in determining whether the duty has been fulfilled. As John Davies of the Association of Chartered Certified Accountants states:[425]

> 'Under this test [s 174], where a director has particular professional or business skills, for example as a qualified accountant, that will have a bearing on whether the standard of skill and diligence he or she displays in practice, both generally and in respect of specific matters, is 'reasonable' and thereby meets the statutory test. A director who has such special skills will be expected by virtue of section 174(2)(b) to pay particular attention to, demonstrate an appropriate level of competence in and be prepared to assume a higher degree of responsibility in relation to issues which relate to the area in which he or she specialises: in the case of a director who is an accountant, this will clearly mean issues relating to accounting and finance.'

8.140 The problem with this interpretation is that specialists might decline to serve as they may feel that it places too great an onus on them. Yet can or should the law ignore the skills a director possesses?

8.141 It is a totally different situation where directors are appointed because of their skills, for it is only reasonable that they be judged against the standards of their profession.[426] There would need to be some indication, probably in a

---

[421] This is acknowledged in the case-law. For example, see *Australian Innovation Ltd v Paul Andre Petrovsky* (1994) 13 ACLC 1357. Also, see the extra-judicial comments of Lord Hoffmann in (1997) 18 Co Law 194 at 196.

[422] V Finch 'Company Directors: Who Cares About Skill and Care?' (1992) 55 MLR 179 at 202. Also, see R J Daniels 'Must Boards Go Overboard? An Economic Analysis of the Effects of Burgeoning Statutory Liability on the Role of Directors in Corporate Governance' in J S Ziegel (ed) *Current Developments in International and Comparative Corporate Insolvency Law* (Oxford, Clarendon Press, 1994) at 569; L S Sealy 'Director's Wider Responsibilities – Problems Conceptual Practical and Procedural' (1987) 13 Mon ULR 164 at 186; S R McDonnell 'Geyer v Ingersoll Publications Co: Insolvency Shifts Directors' Burden From Shareholders to Creditors' (1994) 19 Del J Corp L 177 at 209; C C Nicholls 'Liability of Corporate Officers and Directors to Third Parties' (2001) 35 Can Bus L J 1 at 5.

[423] J H Farrar 'The Duty of Care of Company Directors in Australia and New Zealand' in R Rider (ed) *The Realm of Company Law* (London, Kluwer, 1998) at 45.

[424] [1911] 1 Ch 425.

[425] J Davies 'A Guide to Directors Obligations Under the Companies Act 2006' Association of Chartered Certified Accountants, August 2007, para 6.22, and accessible at www.accaglobal.com/content/dam/acca/global/PDF-technical/business-law/tech-tp-cdd.pdf.

[426] R Reed 'Company Directors – Collective or Functional Responsibility' (2006) 27 Co Law 170 at 192.

letter of appointment or some other document, which establishes the fact that the director has been appointed because of his or her skills. Subsequent conduct and actions post-appointment might, however, suffice to indicate that a director has been appointed to a specialist position.

VII DILIGENCE

8.142   Diligence involves conscientiousness, energy and attentiveness, and the duty of diligence covers the work of directors that involves ensuring that the company's affairs are being managed carefully.

8.143   A director is not able to argue that he or she left all management functions to others without question;[427] there are minimum responsibilities that must be met and there is no such thing as a 'sleeping director', for the function of 'directing' demands that the director has some consideration of the company's affairs.[428] In *Metal Manufacturers Pty Ltd v Lewis*[429] Kirby P said that:

> 'The time has passed when directors and other officers can simply surrender their duties to the public and those with whom the corporation deals by washing their hands, with impunity, leaving it to one director or a *cadre* of directors or to a general manager to discharge their responsibilities for them.'[430]

8.144   A director is also not able to say that he or she had a confined area of responsibility and the matter which relates to the alleged breach was outside of that.[431] Likewise, if directors are appointed because of their particular skills they are not relieved from paying attention to the company's affairs in general even if they involve matters that are outside their expertise.[432]

8.145   Directors in the case of *Re Park House Properties Ltd*[433] were disqualified on the ground of unfitness because of their inactivity in the conduct of the company's affairs.[434] Neuberger J was scathing in his appraisal of the director's performance, and particularly the director's failure to keep himself

---

[427]   See *Cohen v Selby* [2000] BCC 275 at 286; *Re AG (Manchester) Ltd* [2008] EWHC 64 (Ch); [2008] 1 BCLC 321 at [187].

[428]   *Re Brian D Pierson (Contractors) Ltd* [1999] BCC 26 at 55; [2001] BCLC 275 at 309. Also, see; *Mason v Lewis* [2006] 3 NZLR 225 at 237 (NZCA); *Lexi Holdings plc (In Administration) v Luqman* [2007] EWHC 2265 (Ch).

[429]   (1988) 13 NSWLR 315.

[430]   Ibid at 318-319. This was actually even the case in the nineteenth century. See *Ashurst v Mason* (1875) LR 20 Eq 225 at 234; *Land Credit Company of Ireland v Lord Fermoy* (1870) LR 5 Ch App 763 at 770.

[431]   *Weavering Capital Ltd (in liq) v Dabhia* [2012] EWHC 1480 (Ch) at [173].

[432]   *Re Property Force Consultants Pty Ltd* (1995) 13 ACLC 1051 at 1061.

[433]   [1997] 2 BCLC 530.

[434]   The Court of Appeal in *Re Kaytech International plc* [1999] BCC 390 at 403 said that a policy of inactivity in relation to a company's affairs is tantamount to misconduct and warrants a director's disqualification.

informed of the affairs of the company and leaving all matters to another director who had made the sort of errors that should not imbue confidence in others.[435]

8.146 Directors cannot continue in office and receive remuneration on the one hand, and yet abdicate responsibility for the affairs of the company, on the other.[436] The alternative is for the director to resign.[437] This particularly affects spouses (although far from exclusively[438]), where in small family companies one of the spouses leaves the responsibility for the business almost totally to the other spouse. An example where this occurred in the family context is *Cohen v Selby*.[439] In this case the director of a company had to resign as he entered an individual voluntary arrangement (under the Insolvency Act 1986), and his son, a 19-year-old student, was appointed as a director. He was in fact only 17 when appointed. The original director continued to run the business as a de facto or shadow director and the son left management of the affairs of the company to his father and never addressed the responsibilities of being a director. The son just did everything that his father asked him to do. The son was held liable.[440]

8.147 It should be noted that if directors resolutely shut their eyes to the obvious or refrain from asking pertinent and appropriate questions in case they discover the truth, they will be liable for they cannot shut their eyes to what is happening around about them.[441] One aspect that comes to mind in considering the issue of diligence is what happens when the distribution of work is such that a particular director is given an unreasonable load. Is he or she breaching the duty in either not recognising this or if he or she does, not pointing it out to the board, and suggesting a re-jigging of responsibilities? How do the courts view such a director if he or she has, for instance, not done something that a reasonable director would have done? Does the court take into account his or her workload? It would seem to be harsh not to do so, but perhaps it might said that the professional thing for the director to do is to point out the heavy workload and the possible consequences that might flow from such a situation.

8.148 One of the important elements of any director's role is to attend board meetings. It is only if a director attends meetings that he or she is able to contribute to debate and persuade others on particular actions. What is the position now with respect to attendance at meetings? In *Re City Equitable*[442] it

---

[435] [1999] 2 BCLC 530 at 556–557.

[436] *Galeforce Pleating Co Ltd, Re [1999] 2 BCLC 704* [1999] 2 BCLC 704 at 716. Also, see *Re Stephenson Cobbold Ltd* [2000] 2 BCLC 614 at 625; *Lexi Holdings plc (In Administration) v Luqman* [2007] EWHC 2265 (Ch) at [224].

[437] *Galeforce Pleating Co Ltd, Re [1999] 2 BCLC 704* [1999] 2 BCLC 704 at 716. Also, see *Re Park House Properties Ltd* [1998] BCC 847 at 865.

[438] See *Secretary of State v Thornbury* [2007] EWHC 3202 (Ch); [2008] 1 BCLC 139 at [36].

[439] [2000] BCC 275.

[440] *Cohen v Selby* [2000] BCC 275. The son succeeded on appeal because of the way that the case against him had been pleaded: see [2002] BCC 82.

[441] *Daniels v Anderson* (1995) 13 ACLC 614; *Sheahan v Verco* [2001] SASC 91 at [101].

[442] [1925] Ch 407.

was said that a director's duties are intermittent. In some old cases there is incredible evidence of lack of attendance. The classic one often cited is the case of *Marquis of Bute's Case*,[443] which was mentioned early in the Chapter,[444] and involved the defendant only attending one meeting in 39 years. In *Re Montrotier Asphalt Co*[445] Bacon V-C said that a director is not bound to attend every meeting of the directors, and it is not part of the duty of a director to take part in every transaction which is considered at a board meeting. The latter point is probably still true to an extent. Clearly, there is now far more of an onus on directors to attend meetings. In *Vrisakis v ASC*[446] Malcolm CJ of the Supreme Court of Western Australia said: 'a director is expected to attend all meetings unless exceptional circumstances, such as illness or absence from the State prevent him or her from doing so'.[447] Since his Honour's statement, in 1993, things might be said to be even stricter, for in *Gold Ribbon (Accountants) Pty Ltd v Sheers*[448] Muir J of the Queensland Supreme Court said that unless a director regularly attends board meetings he or she will be unable to participate in the governance of the company and thus fulfil one of a director's primary responsibilities.[449] If a director cannot attend meetings on a regular basis then he or she should carefully consider resigning or else appointing an alternate.[450] But directors will not be saved from liability merely because they attend meetings. They should ensure that they are concentrating at the meetings as inattention may lead to liability.[451] Besides being attentive, directors should ensure that any concerns that they have are voiced and minuted at board meetings.[452]

8.149 Meeting on a regular basis is one thing that directors need to do to ensure that they are discharging their duty. This requirement was highlighted by the Combined Code on Corporate Governance.[453] In *Sheahan v Verco*[454] non-executive directors were held to be liable for failing to make sure that there were sufficient meetings of the board. In this case there was no meeting from June 1990 until December 1991.

---

[443] [1872] 2 Ch 100.

[444] Above at **8.14**.

[445] [1876] WN 170.

[446] (1993) 9 WAR 395; (1993) 11 ACSR 162.

[447] Ibid at 170 (ACSR).

[448] [2005] QSC 198.

[449] Ibid at [74].

[450] R P Austin, H A J Ford and I M Ramsay *Company Directors: Principles of Law and Corporate Governance* (Sydney, LexisNexis Butterworths, 2005) at 236. One of the respondents in *Re Park House Properties Ltd* [1998] BCC 847 at 865 saved themselves from some liability by resigning.

[451] *Ashurst v Mason* (1875) LR 20 Eq 225 at 234. In *Land Credit Company of Ireland v Lord Fermoy* (1870) LR 5 Ch App 763 the court acknowledged that a director could not be excused from liability because he was asleep at a board meeting.

[452] This is recognised indirectly by the UK Corporate Governance Code, Financial Reporting Council, 2012 at para A.1.2 and accessible at: http://www.frc.org.uk/Our-Work/Codes-Standards/Corporate-governance/UK-Corporate-Governance-Code.aspx (accessed 21 November 2013).

[453] Ibid at para A1.1 (p 5).

[454] (2001) 37 ACSR 117.

8.150 It is not just attendance and concentration at meetings that are important. It is also important that directors are well-prepared for meetings. Obviously, directors will often be sent a lot of material to read and consider for meetings. In fact the directors in *ASIC v Healey*[455] complained that they had too much information to digest for the meeting at which the annual accounts were signed off. Middleton J had little sympathy with this attitude. To avoid this problem the judge indicated that directors must seek to manage information overload. This is not an easy task to achieve. Directors might be concerned that if they instruct management not to include particular items in briefing papers etc, then they might be missing something that is important or potentially so. It would seem that there is a balance to be struck, but striking it is a potentially difficult matter.

8.151 Finally, on the question of diligence, executive directors must ensure that in performing their duty they adhere both to any express wishes that the board has laid down in relation to a particular matter,[456] and to any particular instructions.[457]

VIII NON-EXECUTIVES

8.152 While the whole of this chapter covers issues that affect non-executives, it is appropriate to devote a section to consideration of non-executives and their particular position, for given the fact that many executives will be liable under their contract of employment if they act without care, it is non-executives who are likely to be more often the defendants in breach of duty actions.

8.153 Gone is the idea that the non-executive directors are mere figureheads, recruited because of their name, title or previous positions. Clearly at no point are non-executives to see themselves as 'window dressing',[458] even if others do.

8.154 Such directors have important corporate governance roles to play, namely to act as independent directors. Now such directors do not merely get paid a modest honorarium. They are generally paid a sum that reflects a more substantial amount of involvement with the company than previously was the case.[459] The court in *Daniels v Anderson*[460] stated that non-executive directors must, as a minimum, 'take reasonable steps to place themselves in a position to guide and monitor the management of the company'.[461]

8.155 Although it is said that there is no distinction between executive and non-executive directors in the sense that the same duties are applied to both, it

---

[455] [2011] FCA 717.
[456] *Circle Petroleum (Qld) Pty Ltd v Greenslade* (1998) 16 ACLC 1577.
[457] *Vines v ASIC* [2007] NSWCA 75 at [452].
[458] *Re City Equitable Fire Insurance Co Ltd* [1925] Ch 407 at 444.
[459] *AWA Ltd v Daniels* (1992) 10 ACLC 933 at 1013.
[460] (1995) 13 ACLC 614.
[461] Ibid at 664. See *Dairy Containers Ltd v NZI Bank Ltd* [1995] 2 NZLR 30 at 79.

is submitted that s 174 of the CA 2006 allows for a distinction to be drawn between them in that it refers to 'carrying out the functions carried out by a director'. This clearly suggests that there will be different applications of the standard and this would be consistent with the case-law. The thing that differentiates the non-executive from the executive is the fact that the former has not got the same responsibility for the execution of company strategies and policies formulated by the board.[462] It is necessary for the functions of non-executives to be clarified in law, for while there are many statements in the academic literature and in corporate governance codes, there is no hard law on the subject, and this hinders the assessment of whether directors are in breach of s 174.

8.156 It is submitted that to exercise care, directors have to be aware of what the company is about, and, hence, when taking up a new post a director should read into the board's minute book and speak to the key office holders in the company in order to ascertain what are the critical issues that are affecting the company and its affairs.

8.157 For non-executives it is a matter of knowing how far they need to go in asking questions and requiring documents. How far can they rely on management, an issue that we have just considered? Non-executives might take the view that if they make an inquiry that action could, possibly, require them to go further and ask other questions or peruse other documents. But if they do not make that inquiry they might well be regarded as being in breach. Arguably, it is not an option for non-executives to refrain from making inquiries on the basis that to do so might 'open up a can of worms'.

8.158 There is evidence from Australia that non-executives are not highly involved in the governance of their companies. A survey conducted in 2007 by the Australian Institute of Management found that only 39 per cent of directors who responded to the survey said that they were highly or very highly involved in the corporate governance agenda.[463] It has been found in a study of non-executive directors undertaken by the Chartered Institute of Internal Auditors (CIIA) in 2011 and involving the surveying of Heads of Internal Audit, that they have little knowledge of the risks in their companies.[464] The CIIA asserts that this is due to the fact that non-executives have a limited range of information on key issues and they are wholly dependent on the management for the information that they receive.[465] Failing to be involved could open up the possibility of the initiation of legal actions.

8.159 The biggest concern for non-executives, according to the Institute of Directors in its response to the Department of Trade and Industry's

---

[462] L Griggs and J Lowry 'Finding the Optimum Balance for the Duty of Care Owed by the Non-Executive Director' in F Patfield (ed) *Perspectives on Company Law* (London, Kluwer, 1997) vol 2 at 208.

[463] 20 September 2007 and formerly available at www.aim.com.au/research/aimags.html.

[464] N Clark 'Non Execs Have "Little Idea" on Risk' *The Independent*, 19 September 2011.

[465] Ibid.

Consultation Paper on 'Director and Auditor Liability' in 2004, was liability for errors of omission.[466] Another matter of potential concern is that non-executives, because they are to be regarded as independent, will have little, or no, experience in relation to the business conducted by the company and this will inevitably mean that they will have to rely on the managers for assistance and information.[467] We have already considered the potential problems with this and what directors should do in this regard.

8.160 As discussed earlier, information asymmetry is often a problem for non-executives, and the Institute of Directors has said that it is difficult for such directors to identify areas where more information should be brought to the board and then to identify what might be regarded as a culpable failure to take action.[468] Often the problem for non-executive directors is that they do not know what they don't know and, therefore, are unable to seek out specific materials, advice and papers. They simply may not know what will assist them.

8.161 The difficulty for a non-executive who has recently been appointed to an established board is that he or she can find it hard to get to grips with what needs to be done and the priorities that face the company.[469] According to the Institute of Directors, such directors often encounter a dilemma. If they act without all of the necessary information they risk alienating their directorial colleagues, but if they wait while they gather sufficient information and make inquiries, they could be held liable for not taking the most appropriate steps.[470]

8.162 There are suggestions from the Australian case of *Re OneTel Ltd (in liq); ASIC v Rich*[471] that it is certainly arguable that if a non-executive acts as the chairman of a listed company or the chairman of an audit committee or some other sub-committee of the board he or she has special responsibilities. According to Austin J of the New South Wales Supreme Court the responsibilities are to reflect contemporary community expectations.[472] This is despite the fact that case-law[473] and soft corporate governance law[474] has indicated that the chairman of a board has no legal status or any position that is superior to other directors. But the UK's Corporate Governance Code 2012[475] provides some principles that relate to chairmen, obviously emphasising the role of the chairman and his or her leadership position and

---

[466] March 2004 at p 7.

[467] H Birds 'The Rise and Fall of the Independent Director' (1995) 5 *Australian Journal of Corporate Law* 235 at 253.

[468] Institute of Directors '*Directors and Auditors Liability*' Institute of Directors, March 2004 at p 7.

[469] Ibid.

[470] Ibid.

[471] [2003] NSWSC 85; 44 ACSR 341 at [61].

[472] Ibid at [71].

[473] *Wishart v Henneberry* (1962) 3 FLR 171 at 173.

[474] *Report on the Financial Aspects of Corporate Governance* (Gee, London, 1992) at p 34.

[475] Financial Reporting Council *The UK Corporate Governance Code* (September 2012) at para A.3 and accessible at: www.frc.org.uk/getattachment/a7f0aa3a-57dd-4341-b3e8-ffa99899e154/UK-Corporate-Governance-Code-September-2012.aspx.

responsibility for the board's performance. This might, of course, assume that the chairman is an executive. In *ASIC v Rich* the chairman was held liable for failing both to ensure that the board was fully advised concerning all material financial information and to detect any adverse developments that affected the financial position of the company.

IX ENFORCEMENT OF A BREACH

8.163 It will be necessary for anyone wishing to enforce a claim against directors for a breach of the duty of care to prove causality,[476] namely that the breach lead to the company's loss (that is, no loss would have occurred had there been no breach[477]), and that the loss sustained by the company was foreseeable.[478]

8.164 Of concern is actually fixing on the action that can be regarded as a breach that can be enforced. Sometimes several actions or transactions might arguably constitute the breach. In *ASIC v Vines*[479] the New South Wales Supreme Court accepted the submission of counsel that, when assessing an alleged breach that involves several transactions, it is necessary to consider the transactions as a whole with an eye to reality, but the court did caution that care must be taken in applying this approach. Where there are numerous particular allegations against the directors, it was said in *Vines* that it would be unacceptable if the law were to require or even permit a claimant to separate a series of events and transactions that involve moving towards a common purpose, by taking each step along the way and alleging a separate breach in relation to that step, and have them considered in isolation. However, the court made it plain that in a situation where events and transactions are connected, the claimant need not necessarily identify a single breach as if there were only a single transaction.

8.165 Most of the discussion concerning breach of this duty has been in the context of directors being sued either by company liquidators following the commencement of liquidation or by shareholders bringing a derivative action on behalf of the company. In either of these scenarios, the argument is that the directors breached their duty *to the company*. Yet, in the past there has been some suggestion that directors could be held liable to people other than the company for the breach they committed because of damage suffered by those others.[480] Under the law prior to codification this suggestion had undoubted strength. Has it now? The first thing to note is that s 170(1) of the CA 2006 states that the duties in Chapter 2 of Part 10 are owed *to the company*. Second,

---

[476] *Lexi Holdings plc (In Administration) v Luqman* [2007] EWHC 2652 (Ch) at [225].
[477] See *Re Dawson (deceased)* [1966] 2 NSWR 211.
[478] *Dairy Containers Ltd v NZI Bank Ltd* [1995] 2 NZLR 30 at 81.
[479] *ASIC v Vines* [2003] FLR 405, [2003] NSWSC 1116, SC, NSW; (2005) 55 ACSR 617 at [1068].
[480] S Worthington 'The Duty to Monitor: A Modern View of the Director's Duty of Care' in F Patfield (ed) *Perspectives on Company Law* (London, Kluwer, 1997) vol 2 at 198–199.

the duties at common law and in equity are, according to s 170(3), replaced by the duties set out in statute. So, it would appear, absent any special relationship between the director and a third party that might create a duty of care,[481] a third party would find it difficult to take action against the director personally. However, of course, the actions of the director might be imputed to the company, which might owe a duty of care to the third party. The action brought by the third party would, of course, then have to be brought against the company. On the basis of the concept of separate legal entity, the directors could not be held liable, in the normal course of things.

8.166 If a director has committed a breach of duty, relief from liability might still be available for the director. First, his or her company might decide not to take action. If this occurs a shareholder might, conceivably, file a derivative action against the director, that is, taking action on behalf of the company. If this is done then the shareholder must apply for permission (leave in Scotland) from the courts to continue the derivative action. This is discussed in detail in **Chapter 14**, although it is relevant in this context to say that while at common law shareholders were not able, save where directors had benefited from their negligence, to initiate derivative actions against directors for negligence,[482] under the new statutory derivative scheme in Part 11 of the CA 2006, shareholders are now able to bring proceedings where directors have been negligent. Lawyers have raised the prospect that that this could allow activist shareholders to bring a derivative action alleging that directors have negligently failed to have regard to one of the factors in s 172(1) of the CA 2006, or placed undue weight on others.[483] This does not appear to have occurred thus far.

8.167 An alternative to taking derivative proceedings is for a shareholder to consider taking action under the unfair prejudice provision, s 994 of the CA 2006. It has been a matter of debate whether the negligence of directors constitutes unfair prejudice. While mismanagement was not regarded as constituting 'oppression' pursuant to s 210 of the Companies Act 1948,[484] one of the legislative precursors to s 994, it appears to be open to a court to hold that in any given case negligence constitutes unfairly prejudicial conduct. However, in *Re Elgindata Ltd*[485] Warner J said that a court would normally be hesitant in doing so and that the argument that the petitioner had a right to expect from the defendant a reasonable standard of management was to be

---

[481] For a case where directors were not held liable, see *Red Sea Tanker Fund v Papachristidis* (unreported, but noted in D Kavanagh 'UK court keeps duty of care high' (1997) 19 *International Financial Law Review* 31). Directors might, of course, in exceptional circumstances, be liable for other torts, such as negligent misstatement: *Williams v Natural Life Health Foods* [1997] 1 BCLC 131 (CA).

[482] *Daniels v Daniels* [1978] Ch 406.

[483] G Milner Moore and R Lewis (Herbert Smith) *In the Line of Fire-Directors Duties under the Companies Act 2006*, at 3; Norton Rose *Shareholder Rights*; Freshfields Bruckhaus Deringer *Companies Act 2006: Directors Duties* (November 2006) at 11; Clifford Chance, *The Companies Act 2006* (November 2006) at 4.

[484] *Re Five Minute Car Wash Service Ltd* [1966] 1 WLR 745.

[485] [1991] BCLC 959.

rejected.[486] His Lordship thought that when investing in a company shareholders take the risk that management may prove not to be of the highest quality. But his Lordship did indicate that a court was not prevented from finding that mismanagement constituted unfair prejudice. Having said this, the learned judge felt that the mismanagement would have to be serious before the provision could be applied. Whilst *Re Macro (Ipswich) Ltd*[487] was not a case that was solely about mismanagement (the petitioner was also arguing that he had not been consulted on policy decisions, something to which he was entitled), Arden J acceded to the relief sought under an unfair prejudice petition where there had been persistent and serious mismanagement.

8.168 It is submitted that the view of Warner J should not be accepted by a court today in light of the common law developments in the early 1990s and the enactment of s 174 of the CA 2006. Surely it is clear that the ideas that the shareholders have to put up with sub-standard performance from directors, and they get the directors that they deserve, are ones that have been put to bed.

X DEFENCES

8.169 Apart from taking issue with the claim of the company that what he or she did was not in breach of his or her duty, the defendant director might, of course, dispute the facts on which the claim is made. There are other possible defences. First, the defendant might argue, in respect of any claim based on the common law principles, that the loss suffered was not foreseeable and/or there was a lack of causation. It is usually necessary for a claimant to establish that the breach of duty that is argued for caused the loss alleged,[488] that is, for the causation element to be satisfied it must be possible to say that the company's loss would not have been suffered but for the director's breach.[489] Courts are cautious in applying hindsight to their analysis of causation[490] as it is possible that some time down the track the actions or omissions of any directors might look wrong. Second, the defence of contributory negligence may be put forward. A third is that the company failed to mitigate its loss.[491]

8.170 Reed has suggested that a pleading of contributory negligence would be best suited where there is a financially substantial or insured defendant with impecunious co-defendants.[492] One possible consequence of the director's actions could still be that the company might have a negligence claim against a third party, such as auditors, reduced in size, if the director is found to be

---

[486] [1991] BCLC 959 at 994.
[487] [1994] 2 BCLC 354; [1994] BCC 781. See G Stapledon 'Mismanagement and the Unfair Prejudice Provision' (1993) 14 Co Law 94.
[488] *Weavering Capital (UK) Ltd v Dabhia* [2013] EWCA Civ 71 at [49].
[489] See *Gold Ribbon (Accountants) Pty Ltd v Sheers* [2006] QCA 335 at [272].
[490] *Lexi Holdings Plc (in administration) v Luqman* [2008] EWHC 1639 (Ch); [2008] 2 BCLC 725.
[491] R Reed 'Company Directors – Collective or Functional Responsibility' (2006) 27 Co Law 170 at 178.
[492] Ibid at 178.

negligent and in breach of his or her duty to the company. This would be on the basis of contributory negligence. Such a scenario occurred in *AWA Ltd v Daniels*[493] where the court took the view that the CEO's actions constituted a breach of duty and it meant that the company was guilty of contributory negligence.[494]

8.171 The duty of care is owed collectively by a board and individually by each director.[495] A director might be sued for a breach, and he or she might argue that other directors or other persons, even, were also responsible for the loss and should contribute to any award of damages. The director would claim contribution under s 1(1) of the Civil Liability (Contribution) Act 1978. In *Equitable Life Assurance Society v Bowley*[496] one of the non-executives did plead the fact that the society had contributed to the negligence, because its actuarial directors and managers failed to do certain things, such as bring certain points to the attention of the board.

8.172 Worthington has asserted that directors cannot excuse themselves by demonstrating the fact that even if they took the action that their duty required of them it would not have changed what the board decided to do; the end result would be the same.[497] For instance, a director made decision X without asking questions of managers, and he or she asserts that even if any pertinent questions were asked by the director, the managers would have lied to him or her, so, rather than doing Y, the director would have still taken decision X.

XI CONCLUDING REMARKS

A What will the courts consider?

8.173 The following are the kinds of factors that the courts are likely to consider in determining whether or not there has been a breach of duty:

- the type and size of the company's business;
- how responsibilities in the company are allocated;
- any specific role given to the director;
- has the director made a business judgment;
- any exceptional circumstances that existed;

---

[493] (1992) 10 ACLC 933.

[494] In *AWA v Daniels* (ibid), because of the chief executive officer's actions, responsibility for 20 per cent of the liability was laid at the door of AWA.

[495] *Re Barings (No 5)* [1999] 1 BCLC 433 at 486. Also, see *Gold Ribbon (Accountants) Pty Ltd v Sheers* [2006] QCA 335 at [234].

[496] [2003] EWHC 2263 (Comm); [2004] 1 BCLC 180.

[497] S Worthington 'The Duty to Monitor: A Modern View of the Director's Duty of Care' in F Patfield (ed) *Perspectives on Company Law* (London, Kluwer, 1997) vol 2 at 192 and referring to *Ramskill v Edwards* (1885) 31 Ch D 100; *Bishopsgate Investment Management Ltd v Maxwell* [1994] 1 All ER 261, [1993] BCC 120, [1993] BCLC 1282, *Times*, February 16, 1993 at 140. This is invoking an argument that is similar to the rule in *Brickenden v London Loan & Savings Co* [1934] 3 DLR 465 at 469 which applies in relation to disclosure.

- the extent to which the director has informed himself or herself concerning the company's business, affairs and finances;

- the director's entitlement to rely on others;

- the extent to which the director has monitored the activities of those to whom he or she has delegated authority;

- the way that the director has monitored the company's affairs and his or her colleagues.[498]

B Assessment

8.174   Chris Riley stated 24 years ago[499] that the precise scope and effect of the various recent developments at common law was an argument in favour of codification. It is perhaps arguable as to whether codification has produced the needed precision. Yet it might be said that it is not possible to have greater precision, certainly in relation to the duties considered in this chapter, when one takes into account the fact that directors serve diverse functions in diverse companies.

8.175   It has been said that the severity of the rule on director's duty must be tempered if we are not going to put off the type of people we want as directors taking up the post. This argument has been mounted by some who oppose the inclusion of a provision preventing wrongful trading type of conduct,[500] as well as in relation to the potential liability of directors for breach of duty. Professor Ron Daniels, for instance, states that the 'liability chill will deter talented individuals from accepting a nomination for board service'.[501] There has been some anecdotal evidence to the effect that people are now more wary about becoming directors,[502] but other evidence has been to the contrary, such as the following view: '[T]he truth is that there is no shortage of candidates for the board ... It seems that people still want to belong to the club [FTSE 100

---

[498] Based on the following: S Worthington 'The Duty to Monitor: A Modern View of the Director's Duty of Care' in F Patfield (ed) *Perspectives on Company Law* (London, Kluwer, 1997) vol 2 at 173; R Reed 'Company Directors – Collective or Functional Responsibility' (2006) 27 Co Law 170 at 190; *Daniels v Anderson* (1995) 13 ACLC 614; *Vrisakis v ASC* (1993) 11 ACSR 162; *Australian Securities and Investments Commission v Maxwell* (2006) 59 ACSR 373 at [100].

[499] 'The Company Director's Duty of Care and Skill: The Case for an Onerous but Subjective Standard' (1999) 62 MLR 697 at 698.

[500] For example, D Oesterle 'Corporate Directors' Personal Liability for 'Insolvent Trading in Australia 'Reckless Trading' in New Zealand and 'Wrongful Trading' in England: A Recipe for Timid Directors, Hamstrung Controlling Shareholders and Skittish Lenders' in I M Ramsay (ed) *Company Directors' Liability for Insolvent Trading* (Melbourne, Centre for Corporate Law and Securities Regulation and CCH Australia, 2000) at 29.

[501] R J Daniels 'Must Boards Go Overboard? An Economic Analysis of the Effects of Burgeoning Statutory Liability on the Role of Directors in Corporate Governance' in J S Ziegel (ed) *Current Developments in International and Comparative Corporate Insolvency Law* (Oxford, Clarendon Press, 1994) at 569. Also, see S R McDonnell 'Geyer v Ingersoll Publications Co: Insolvency Shifts Directors' Burden From Shareholders to Creditors' (1994) 19 Del J Corp L 177 at 209; C C Nicholls 'Liability of Corporate Officers and Directors to Third Parties' (2001) 35 Can Bus L J 1 at 5.

[502] F Gibb 'Directors chilled by the fear of financial liability' *The Times*, 23 September 2003.

companies] that continues to exist at the top of British business.'[503] These comments are a little dated now, but there is nothing to suggest that anything has changed. Allied to the view that there is still a goodly number of people seeking directorships is the fact that there is no suggestion in any study that there has been a shortage of persons willing to be appointed as directors. Whether those appointed are as capable as one would expect is another issue, and very difficult to assess. In fact the strictness of the duty could deter those who are incompetent, and that is a favourable consequence of the development of the duty.

8.176 There is a clear tension between discretion given to directors and their accountability, and the law has to address that. There has to be a balance.[504] Perhaps the law has addressed this with the courts ensuring that hindsight alone does not convict a director. Errors of directors are going to continue to occur and that needs to be accepted, and while we should not return to the notion that only gross negligence can be regarded as a breach, it is only in cases of clear carelessness where directors will be found liable.

C Summary

8.177 This chapter has discussed the fact that in fulfilling their duties of care, skill and diligence, directors must: be attentive, be informed concerning the business and affairs of their company, inquire about and understand the financial position of the company, use their skills appropriately and, while being entitled to rely on others, refrain from overly relying on them, and failing to ensure that they supervise to a reasonable extent.

8.178 Clearly, assuming that the new provision that covers the duty of care is interpreted along the lines of the common law extant at the time of its advent, the application of the law will be fairly strict. It now reflects the change in the role and position of the company director in the twenty-first century, when compared with the nineteenth, and even much of the twentieth, century.

8.179 It is assumed in this chapter that the new s 174 of the CA 2006 will be interpreted in such a way that the case-law developed over the past 25 years has been applied. Many think that this is the correct position. While the law is reasonably settled, it is not the law but its application that is the real concern. This chapter has sought to suggest the manner in which the courts will apply the case-law decided both here and elsewhere in dealing with claims under s 174. This provides some guidance for directors to ensure that they act in such a way as to allow them to remain free from the threat of any litigation. It is generally recognised that the application of the principles discussed here is difficult. Nevertheless, there must be an attempt to apply them carefully and fairly, having in mind the fact that there should be a balance between being overly benign in relation to director's actions on the one hand, and being overly

---

[503] P Wheatcroft 'Let Some Others Join the Club' *The Times*, 15 October 2003.
[504] A Keay *Board Accountability in Corporate Governance* (Abingdon, Routledge, 2015).

harsh, on the other; there must be a balance between prudence (and accountability) and entrepreneurialism (and power).[505] Adopting either extreme position will have adverse effects on commercial life. Everyone would probably agree that the commercial world (and companies individually) does not want to see directors who are not taking their jobs seriously, are shirking in some way, or are 'completely lost' in what they are doing retaining their posts. There has to be a duty of care, skill and diligence, but the questions are: what is the duty to be and what standards are to be applied? What the law does not want to do is to make the duty overly onerous and deter appropriate people from taking up office.

---

[505] Ibid.

CHAPTER 9

AVOIDING CONFLICTS OF INTEREST: THE DUTY

I INTRODUCTION

9.1 This Chapter is the first of four that focus on the issues relating to directors' interests and duties being in conflict with the duties that they owe to their companies. This chapter and the immediately succeeding one deal squarely with conflicts of interests, and **Chapters 11** and **12** address benefits to directors and the need for disclosure of interests respectively. As will be clear in the following discussion, the four chapters are related. Section 175 of the CA 2006 deals with conflicts of interest and it has links with ss 176 and 177 for the latter two sections deal with the prohibition of actions that could lead to a conflict. In fact it has been said that the duty to avoid a conflict embraces the duty not to make a secret profit,[1] the duty covered by s 176. While the duties covered by s 175 and the following two sections might be seen as distinct duties, they are connected, probably by the concept of loyalty and the duty to promote the success of the company. I mention the latter duty in this context as the duties in ss 175-177 are, in a sense, applications of the duty to promote the success of the company.[2] The duties to avoid conflicts and profit which are contained in these sections are regarded as fiduciary by all commentators, even by those equity scholars who dissent from the view that the duty to promote the success of the company (duty to act in the best interests of the company) and the duty to use powers for proper purposes are fiduciary duties.[3] A critical aspect of equity in the form of the law of fiduciaries is that the one owing fiduciary duties should not allow his or her personal interests to conflict with the interests of the one to whom the duties are owed.[4] Avoiding a conflict is at the heart of the fiduciary relationship.[5] If directors do not avoid conflicts then they might be

---

[1] *Towers v Premier Waste Management Ltd* [2011] EWCA Civ 923; [2012] 1 BCLC 67; [2012] BCC 72.

[2] See the comments in *Shepherds Investments Ltd v Walters* [2006] EWHC 836 at [106], [132].

[3] For example, R Flannigan 'Fiduciary Duties of Shareholders and Directors' [2004] JBL 277; M Conaglen 'The Nature and Function of Fiduciary Loyalty' (2005) 121 LQR 452; E Waitzer and J Jaswal '*Peoples, BCE,* and the Good Corporate "Citizen"' (2009) 47 *Osgoode Hall Law Journal* 439; M Conaglen 'Interaction Between Statutory and General Law Duties Concerning Company Director Conflicts' (2013) 31 *Company and Securities Law Journal* 403. Also, some practitioners take the same view. For instance, see A Stafford and S Ritchie *Fiduciary Duties: Directors and Employees* (Bristol, Jordan, 2nd edn, 2015) at [1.10].

[4] *Aberdeen Rly Co v Blaikie Bros [1854] 2 Eq Rep 1281, [1854] 1 Macq 461, [1843–1860] All ER Rep 249 (HL)* at 471–472.

[5] See T Frankel 'Fiduciary Law' (1983) 71 *California Law Review* 795 at 811.

said to be acting in a disloyal fashion, so underlying the duty to avoid conflicts is the idea that the director is to be loyal to his or her beneficiary.[6] Clearly the law on conflicts of interest is one of the more difficult areas of company law, primarily because of the complexity of some of the case-law in which careful distinctions are made and the fact that the courts appear to be most concerned that they ensure that directors act loyally and remain accountable for what they do when there is any prospect of a conflict.

9.2   The conflict situations that are charted in the reported case-law are first, where directors have a conflict between their obligations to their company and their interest in benefiting themselves, and, second, where they have responsibilities to two competing companies.

9.3   The Chapter begins by providing some substantial background to s 175 of the CA 2006 by a general consideration of the conflict rules that applied in equity before codification, for without an appreciation of these it is likely to be difficult to appreciate the operation of s 175. This is followed by: a consideration of the section; what is involved with a conflict of interest; and the fact that the section encompasses possible conflicts as well as real conflicts. Next, the Chapter discusses exceptions to the principle that directors are not to place themselves in conflict situations. The final parts of the chapter examine the position of directors who hold directorships in competing companies and the position of former directors. The Chapter ends with a brief consideration of the effect of a breach and whether companies can opt out of s 175. The next chapter then moves on to consider the section in light of a number of practical situations, such as directors retiring in order to pursue a business in opposition to their former companies and the taking up by directors of business opportunities that might have been available to the company.

9.4   It is to be noted that the duty provided for in s 175 of the CA 2006 came into force on 1 October 2008. This was formalised in art 5(1)(d) of the Companies Act 2006 (Commencement No 5, Transitional Provisions and Savings) Order 2007.[7] As pointed out earlier in the book, 'the old law' on duties generally is likely to be of some importance. In a case dealing with a pre-codification time period Mummery LJ said in *Towers v Premier Waste Management Ltd*[8] that: 'it is unrealistic to ignore the terms in which the general statutory duties have been framed for post-2006 Act cases. They extract and express the essence of the rules and principles which they have replaced.' Moreover it must not be forgotten that s 170(3) provides that the codified duties are based on certain common law rules and equitable principles. Also, s 170(4) provides that the duties are to be interpreted and applied in the same way as common law rules and equitable principles and regard should be had to the corresponding common law rules and equitable principles in interpreting and applying the duties in the Act.

---

6   *Bristol & West Building Society v Mothew* [1998] Ch 1 at 18.
7   SI 2007/3495.
8   [2011] EWCA Civ 923; [2012] 1 BCLC 67; [2012] BCC 72 at [3].

II BACKGROUND

9.5   Before tracing some of the developments in this area it is worthwhile beginning by including reference to *Aberdeen Rly Co v Blaikie* Bros,[9] a classic case involving conflict involving a director. X was a director, and chairman, of A company. X, on behalf of A, entered into a contract to purchase chairs from a partnership, B, in which X was a partner. A, when the true state of affairs was discovered, sought to set aside the contract. It was held that X was in a position where he was to get the best deal that he could for A. He did not. In such a case unless there is disclosure by the director, the contract is voidable. The court said that directors should not be allowed to enter into engagements in which they have, or can have, personal conflicting interests, or which may possibly conflict, with the interests of those whom they are bound to protect.

9.6   In equity directors were subject to two rules that supplemented the general duties. These are the no-conflict and no-profit rules. The two undoubtedly overlap to some degree and this resulted in the courts mixing the two,[10] something that can be seen in Lord Herschell's speech in *Bray v Ford,*[11] where his Lordship talked of the principle which outlawed conflicts encompassing two themes, namely directors are not to be in conflict and they are not to profit from their position. His Lordship said that:

> 'It is an inflexible rule of a court of equity that a person in a fiduciary position ... is not, unless otherwise expressly provided, entitled to make a profit; he is not allowed to put himself in a position where his interest and duty conflict.'

In *O'Donnell v Shanahan,*[12] Richard Sheldon QC (sitting as a deputy judge of the High Court) observed[13] that:

> 'The distinction between the "no-conflict rule" and the "no-profit rule" is not always easy to identify and there are a number of reported decisions where the distinction has not been rigidly observed.'

9.7   There has been debate[14] over whether the no conflict and no profit rules are indeed separate or whether the latter is a specific application of the former. It is submitted that the two rules have tended to be treated by the courts as separate.[15] Having said that, in many cases they were considered and applied

---

[9]   (1854) 1 Macq HL 461.

[10]   S M Beck 'The Saga of Peso Silver Mines: Corporate Opportunity Reconsidered' (1971) 51 Can Bar Rev 80 at 89–90.

[11]   *Bray v Ford* [1896] AC 44.

[12]   [2008] EWHC 1973 (Ch).

[13]   Ibid at [176].

[14]   For instance, see P Koh 'Once a Director, Always a Fiduciary? (2003) 62 CLJ 403; D Kershaw 'Does it Matter How the Law Thinks About Corporate Opportunities' (2005) 25 *Legal Studies* 533.

[15]   For example, see *Kak Loui Chan v Zacharia* (1984) 154 CLR 178 at 198 (Aust HC) per Deane J; *O'Donnell v Shanahan* [2008] EWHC 1973 (Ch) at [176] and on appeal at [2009]

together, to the point where one without the other would be incomplete.[16] The no-conflict rule arguably underlies the no-profit rule and s 175 of the CA 2006 reflects that fact. Take the case of *Industrial Development Corp v Cooley*[17] as an example. In that case, the defendant director, who was an architect, was for a period the managing director of his company, the plaintiff in the case. The plaintiff company offered construction services to large public and private industrial enterprises. The defendant's duties included procuring new business for the company. In particular the director worked at obtaining contracts from the various gas boards in England. The company was interested in securing a contract relating to a project with one gas board, E, to construct four depots. The director, on behalf of the company, entered into unsuccessful negotiations with E. Subsequently, the deputy chairman of E approached the director for advice in his private capacity about E's affairs. The director realised that if he could resign from the plaintiff company he would have a good chance of obtaining for himself a valuable contract from E. During the course of his meeting with E's deputy chairman, the director acquired information, not possessed by the company, but which the company would have found to be helpful. Within a few days of his meeting with E the director secured a release from the company to be effective within a couple of weeks. The director was able to do this by dishonestly telling the company that he was ill. The company would not have agreed to the release if it had been aware of the true state of affairs. Following his release the director was given the contract, which the plaintiff had been pursuing, by E because of the work which, unknown to the plaintiff, he had performed at a time when he was still the company's managing director. The director made profits from the contract with E. The company sued the director and he was held liable as the contract was offered to him because he was the director of a company which operated in the relevant field. Roskill J said: 'if the defendant is not required to account he will have made a large profit as a result of having deliberately put himself into a position in which his duty to the claimant and his personal interests conflicted'.[18]

9.8   All of the foregoing perhaps explains the fact that the rules are not clearly divided in the CA 2006. The two sections that cover the no-conflict and no-profit rules, ss 175 and 176 do not clearly delineate the two rules. The former provision contains aspects of both rules, notwithstanding the fact that the title only suggests conflicts, while the latter section tends to represent a specialist aspect of the no-profit rule and is limited to the receipt of benefits from third parties. According to the Explanatory Notes to the CA 2006, s 175 deals with the no-conflict rule, but states that situations that involved the director profiting from his or her position are also covered by the section.[19] Critically the profit must involve a conflict of interest. This is not usually a

---

EWCA Civ 751; [2009] BCC 822. Simon Whitney accepts that is the case: 'Corporate Opportunities Law and the Non-Executive Director' (2016) 16 *Journal of Corporate Law Studies* 145 at 153.

[16]   *Kak Loui Chan v Zacharia* (1984) 154 CLR 178 at 199.

[17]   [1972] 1 WLR 443.

[18]   [1972] 1 WLR 443 at 453.

[19]   Explanatory Notes to the CA 2006, at para 338.

matter of concern as any profiting by directors will normally constitute a conflict of interest. This is exemplified in s 175(2) where the provision covers exploitation by directors of corporate property, information or opportunities. As Simon Whitney notes, it is likely that Parliament did not intend there to be any major change in the law following codification to the point of a single duty to avoid conflicts of interest.[20] The case-law seems to bear out that view.[21] Some jurisdictions retain a distinction between the two duties. Australia does not actually refer to either of them in its provisions, but that is not a major issue as the duties that have developed at common law and in equity remain in operation in Australia and one of those is the duty to avoid conflicts. The Canadian position is somewhat similar. Many Australian courts have actually regarded directors acting in a conflict situation to be in breach of s 181 of the Corporations Act 2001 which encompasses the duties to act in the best interests of the company and for proper purposes.[22] In particular the focus is on directors who are in conflict and who are not acting in good faith in the best interests of their company. Thus, having a conflict is said to be a prime example of not acting in good faith in the interest of the company.[23]

9.9   The advent of the no-profit rule as a separate rule occurred in the middle of the nineteenth century.[24] The rule was well explained in the Australian decision of *Furs Ltd v Tomkies*[25] as:

> '... the inflexible rule that, except under the authority of a provision in the articles of association, no director shall obtain for himself a profit by means of a transaction in which he is concerned on behalf of the company unless all the material facts are disclosed to the shareholders and by resolution a general meeting approves of his doing so or all the shareholders acquiesce. An undisclosed profit which a director so derives from the execution of his fiduciary duties belongs in equity to the company.'

This explanation was approved of in England in *Gwembe Valley Development v Koshy (No 3)*.[26]

---

[20]   'Corporate Opportunities Law and the Non-Executive Director' (2016) 16 *Journal of Corporate Law Studies* 145 at 155.

[21]   For instance, see *Thermascan v Norman* [2009] EWHC 3694 (Ch); *Sharma v Sharma* [2013] EWCA Civ 1287 at [52].

[22]   For instance, see *Darvall v North Sydney Brick & Tile Co Ltd* (1989) 7 ACLC 659; *Mid Density Developments Pty Ltd v Rockdale Municipal Council* (1993) 44 FCR 290; *Southern Real Estate Pty Ltd v Dellow and Arnold* [2003] SASC 318; (2003) 87 SASR 1; *Crusader Marine Holdings Pty Ltd v Ballantyne* [2011] QSC 152.

[23]   *Parker v Tucker* (2010) 77 ACSR 525 at [72] and referred to in R Teele Langford, 'Directors' Fiduciary Duties: The Relationship Between Conflicts, Profits and Bona Fides' (2013) 31 *Company and Securities Law Journal* 423 at 431.

[24]   J Glover *Commercial Equity: Fiduciary Relationships* (Butterworths, Sydney, 1995) at 147.

[25]   (1936) 54 CLR 583 at 592.

[26]   [2004] 1 BCLC 131 at [44].

9.10 The no-profit rule only barred the making of unauthorised profits and did not apply to all profits,[27] but the problem was knowing which profits did not fall foul of the rule. A good part of this and the next chapter will explore that issue.

9.11 In equity the no-conflict and no-profit rules are said to have two purposes, namely, first, 'to ensure that the fiduciary accounts for what has been acquired at the expense of the trust'[28] and, second, 'to ensure that fiduciaries generally conduct themselves at a level higher than that trodden by the crowd'.[29]

9.12 The idea behind the no-conflict rule is to ensure that the fiduciary is not swayed by concerns for his or her personal interests in any given situation.[30] If the director was swayed then he or she would be contravening his or her obligation of loyalty to the company.[31] The rule covers not only conflicts between the director's interests and the duty to the company, but also conflicts which the director might have in relation to his or her duty to the company and the director's duties to others.[32]

9.13 At the outset, in order to set the scene, it is worth again quoting what Lord Herschell had to say in *Bray v Ford*.[33] His Lordship said that:

'It is an inflexible rule of a court of equity that a person in a fiduciary position...is not, unless otherwise expressly provided, entitled to make a profit; he is not allowed to put himself in a position where his interest and duty conflict.'

9.14 In more modern times Millett LJ in *Bristol & West Building Society v Mothew*[34] put it this way:

'The distinguishing obligation of a fiduciary is the obligation of loyalty. The principal is entitled to the single-minded loyalty of his beneficiary. This core liability has several facets. A fiduciary must act in good faith; he must not make a profit out of his trust; he must not place himself in a position where his duty and his interest may conflict.'

9.15 This approach followed a long line of trust cases that finds its starting point in the case of *Keech v Sandford*,[35] where Lord King took the view that the rules of liability 'should be strictly pursued, and not in the least relaxed'.[36] It has led some commentators to say that the prohibitions are extreme in their

---

[27]   *Murad v Al-Saraj* [2005] EWCA Civ 959 at [62].
[28]   *Warman International Ltd v Dwyer* (1995) 182 CLR 544 at 557.
[29]   Ibid.
[30]   *Wilkinson v West Coast Capital* [2005] EWHC 3009 (Ch); [2005] BCC 717 at [251].
[31]   Ibid at [252].
[32]   *Transvaal Lands Company v New Belgium (Transvaal) Land and Development Company* [1914] 2 Ch 488; *In Plus Group Ltd v Pyke* [2002] EWCA Civ 370; [2002] 2 BCLC 201 (CA).
[33]   [1896] AC 44 (HL).
[34]   [1998] Ch 1 at 18.
[35]   (1726) Sel Cas Ch 61; (1726) 25 ER 223; [1726] All ER Rep 230.
[36]   (1726) Sel Cas Ch 61 at 62.

absolutism.[37] The principle carries out a prophylactic purpose.[38] Certainly the House of Lords has been most rigorous in ensuring that there is no suggestion that directors are able to continue in conflict positions or are going to profit from their positions. The cases make it clear that issues of fairness do not intrude, when it comes to deciding whether there has been a breach of the rules, for the courts are not able to engage in such considerations.[39] However, issues of fairness might be considered when the courts assess the extent of a director's liability.

9.16 The no-conflict rule in its essence is strict. For a start, *Aberdeen Rly Co v Blaikie Bros*[40] and other cases provide that it is not possible, in order to excuse the conflict, for the director to establish that the same contract with the same terms would not have been made by the company absent any conflict. It might have been noticed that in both of the earlier quotes from *Bray v Ford* and *Furs Ltd v Tomkies* that the respective judges referred to the rule as 'inflexible'.

9.17 A more recent case, to which we will return on many occasions in this chapter and the next, is *Regal (Hastings) Ltd v Gulliver*[41] and it demonstrates clearly the strictness of the general approach of the law. In this case R Ltd was a company that owned and managed a very successful cinema. Its directors, with a view to the future development or sale of the company, wanted to extend its business operations by the acquiring of other cinemas. They wished to acquire the leases of two particular cinemas. To do so the idea was to create a subsidiary of R Ltd, H Ltd. The directors of the subsidiary were essentially the directors of R Ltd. H Ltd was to be incorporated with a capital of £5,000 in £1 shares. It was thought that only £2,000 of the capital was to be issued and that it would be subscribed by R Ltd, which would control it. At this time R Ltd was contemplating the sale of its own cinema as well as the leases of the cinemas it was seeking to acquire through H Ltd. An offer was made to R Ltd for the cinemas. But difficulties began with the securing of the leases to the cinemas. The directors of R Ltd and H Ltd met. It was resolved that R Ltd should apply for 2,000 shares in H Ltd. It was agreed that £2,000 was the total sum which R Ltd could find to contribute, but more was needed. To overcome the problem, all but one of the directors of R Ltd agreed to apply for 500 shares. Thus, the capital of H Ltd was fully subscribed. The shares were duly paid for and allotted. The leases of the new cinemas were executed in favour of H Ltd. The purchase of the cinemas from R Ltd by the third party collapsed, but instead it was suggested that the shares of R Ltd and H Ltd be purchased by the third party. This occurred (with the directors making a substantial profit on

---

[37] J Lowry and R Edmunds 'The No Conflict-No Profit Rules and the Corporate Fiduciary: Challenging the Orthodoxy of Absolutism' [2000] JBL 122 at 122. See R Teele 'The Necessary Reformulation of the Classic Fiduciary Duty to Avoid a Conflict of Interest or Duties' (1994) 22 ABLR 99 at 100.

[38] J Lowry and R Edmunds 'The Corporate Opportunity Doctrine: the Shifting Boundaries of the Duty and its Remedies' (1998) 61 MLR 515 at 517.

[39] For example, see *Regal (Hastings) Ltd v Gulliver* [1967] 2 AC 134 (HL) at 154; *Furs Ltd v Tomkies* (1936) 54 CLR 583 at 592.

[40] (1854) 1 Macq HL 461.

[41] [1967] 2 AC 134.

their shares in H Ltd) and a new board of R Ltd was appointed. This new board brought proceedings on behalf of R Ltd against its former directors, in order to recover from them profits made by them upon the sale of their shares in H Ltd. The action was based on the allegations that: the directors had used their position as such to acquire the shares in H Ltd for themselves, with a view to enabling them at once to sell them at a very substantial profit; they had obtained that profit by using their positions as directors and were, therefore, accountable for it to R Ltd; in so acting they had placed themselves in a position in which their private interests were likely to be in conflict with their duty to R Ltd.

9.18 The judge at first instance, and the Court of Appeal, found for the defendants on the basis that they were only able to obtain the leases for the subsidiary company by contributing their own funds and purchasing some of the shares, and they acted in good faith. However, on appeal to the House of Lords R Ltd succeeded and it was held that the directors should account for the benefits that they had received. A critical thing for the House of Lords was that the shares, when acquired by the directors, were acquired by reason, and only by reason, of the fact that they were directors of R Ltd, and in the course of their execution of that office.[42] Their Lordships dismissed the good faith of the directors as irrelevant and also said that the fact that R Ltd could not have taken the leases of the cinemas without the assistance of the directors was not a reason for absolving the directors. And it has been held recently in *Breitenfeld UK Ltd v Harrison*[43] by Norris J that the law is still, under s 175, to the effect that good faith is not able to excuse a director from breach of the duty to avoid conflicts. Whether a breach of s 175 has occurred or not is determined objectively and it is not necessary to prove bad faith on the part of the director or an awareness that his or her conduct put him or her in breach for a director to be liable.[44] The directors in *Regal (Hastings)* were acting in good faith, but were arguably in a conflict situation.

9.19 The decision of the Court of Appeal in *Towers v Premier Waste Management Ltd*[45] also manifests the strictness of the rule as the Court made it plain that a defendant cannot plead in defence to a conflict claim that he or she did not make a significant profit or that it had not been established that he or she had obtained a valuable benefit. Also, it was said that it was not necessary for the claimant to prove fault on the part of the defendant or that the company had suffered a loss.

9.20 Despite the strictness of the rule, Upjohn LJ said in the Court of Appeal in *Boulting v Association of Cinematograph, Television and Allied Technicians*[46] that:

---

[42]   [1967] 2 AC 134 at 145, 147.
[43]   [2015] EWHC 399 (Ch); [2015] 2 BCLC 275 at [70].
[44]   *Richmond Pharmacology Ltd v Chester Overseas Ltd* [2014] EWHC 2692 (Ch) at [72].
[45]   [2011] EWCA Civ 923; [2012] 1 BCLC 67; [2012] BCC 72.
[46]   [1963] 2 QB 606 at 637–638.

'However, a broad rule like this must be applied with common sense and with an appreciation of the sort of circumstances in which, over the last two hundred years and more it has been applied and thrived. It must be applied realistically to a state of affairs which discloses a real conflict of duty and interest, and not to some theoretical or rhetorical conflict.'

9.21 As Professor Brenda Hannigan has stated, the no-conflict rule's strictness led to certainty, but it also led to commercial inconvenience.[47] To overcome this, clauses in companies' articles typically permitted directors to have interests in a contract with the company as long as the nature and extent of the interest was disclosed to the board.[48] This did not mean that improprieties would necessarily occur, for directors were still under the duty to act bona fide in the best interests of the company. Directors could only be excused from being in a conflict situation or retain a profit that they had made, if they made disclosure to a general meeting and it approved of the conflict or profit.[49] The fact that there are, under the CA 2006, new procedures for dealing with conflicts of interest might be regarded as diminishing, to some small extent, the strictness of the rule. These procedures are discussed later.[50]

9.22 It has been asserted, adroitly it is respectfully submitted, that the law in this area is an attempt to obtain a balance between safeguarding companies and permitting directors to engage in entrepreneurial activity.[51] Arguably, historically UK law has favoured the former side of the equation, by applying an inflexible approach, whilst in recent times there has been, perhaps, a move in some cases to effect more of a balance, with a tendency to be a little more flexible, as evidenced to some degree by the case-law and the provisions permitting authorisation of conflicts.

9.23 Under the pre-codified law some have said that directors had a duty to avoid conflicts, or it is an aspect of the fiduciary duty to act in good faith for the best interests of the company.[52] Others, with whom I respectfully concur, have said that there was no duty,[53] although directors should have ensured that their interests and those of the company would not come into conflict, hence the tag, 'the no-conflict rule'. Vinelott J explained in *Movitex Ltd v Bulfield*[54] that the obligation under which directors found themselves was not a duty,[55] but it was a disability to which all fiduciaries were subject. The fact is that a court simply will accede to a request to set aside a contract where a director is in a conflict situation; there is no consideration of whether the director is in

---

47   *Company Law* (London, LexisNexis Butterworths, 2003) at 247.
48   The Companies (Tables A–F) Regulations 1985, Table A, reg 85.
49   *Regal (Hastings) Ltd v Gulliver* [1967] 2 AC 134 (HL).
50   See below at **9.38–9.48**.
51   J Lowry and R Edmunds 'The Corporate Opportunity Doctrine: the Shifting Boundaries of the Duty and its Remedies' (1998) 61 MLR 515 at 515.
52   *Coleman Taymar Ltd v Oakes* [2001] 2 BCLC 749 at 768.
53   For example, B Hannigan *Company Law* (London, LexisNexis Butterworths, 2003) at 247–250.
54   [1988] 1 BCLC 104.
55   See F Jordan *Select Legal Papers* (Sydney, 1983) at 112 and referred to in P Koh 'Once a Director, Always a Fiduciary?' (2003) 62 CLJ 403 at 405.

breach of a duty.[56] There is Australian authority that agrees with this approach.[57] To avoid the setting aside of a contract where there is a conflict the director should disclose the conflict. Naturally, in any action for a setting aside of the contract, a director could be in breach of his or her duties, and subject to additional orders.[58]

9.24 Principles relating to the no-conflict and no-profit rules are not difficult to identify, but it is the circumstances of the alleged breach that are critical.[59] The cases[60] demonstrate that the facts of each case are critical and that the authorities can only go so far in assisting the courts and those giving advice. This merely reflects the fact, as Lord Upjohn stated in *Boardman v Phipps*:[61] 'Rules of equity have to be applied to such a great diversity of circumstances that they can be stated only in the most general terms and applied with particular attention to the exact circumstances of each case.' Also in that case Lord Cohen stated that simply because an agent acquires information and opportunity while acting as a fiduciary does not mean that he or she is accountable to principals for any profit obtained from the use of the information or opportunity, as the facts are the crucial issue.[62]

9.25 The way to prevent a breach of the no-conflict rule was, as indicated earlier, for the director to disclose the conflict. What form that was to take was usually provided under the articles. Also, the Companies Act 1985 in s 317 laid down some requirements. These are considered in **Chapter 12**. Directors were obliged to declare the nature of his or her interest in a contract or a transaction to a meeting of the board. This is now covered by s 177 of the CA 2006 in the case of proposed transactions, or under s 182 in the case of existing transactions, unless an exception applies under those sections.

9.26 We know from s 170(4) of the CA 2006 that the codified duties should be interpreted and applied in the same way as the common law rules and equitable principles, and regard is to be had to the corresponding rules and principles in the process of interpreting and applying the general duties. The issue of conflict is one area where there is likely to be a significant drawing on developments that have occurred in equity over many years. In one case where

---

[56]   *Movitex Ltd v Bulfield* [1988] 1 BCLC 104 at 120.

[57]   For example, see *Hospital Products Ltd v United States Surgical Corporation* (1984) 55 ALR 417 (Aust HC); *Kak Loui Chan v Zacharia* (1984) 154 CLR 178 (Aust HC); *Gemstone Corp of Australia Ltd v Grasso* (1993) 12 ACSR 47 (SA S Ct).

[58]   For example, see *JJ Harrison (Properties) Ltd v Harrison* [2002] 1 BCLC 162 (CA).

[59]   *In Plus Group Ltd v Pyke* [2002] EWCA Civ 370; [2002] 2 BCLC 201 at [90]; *Foster Bryant Surveying Ltd v Bryant* [2007] EWCA Civ 200; [2007] 2 BCLC 239 at [65].

[60]   In particular, see *Bhullar v Bhullar* [2003] 2 BCLC 241; [2003] BCC 711 at [36]. Also, for example, see *Wilkinson v West Coast Capital* [2005] EWHC 3009 (Ch); [2005] BCC 717 at [245].

[61]   [1967] 2 AC 46 at 123.

[62]   Ibid at 102.

s 175 was involved, *Thermascan Ltd v Norman*,[63] the parties agreed that the section did not alter the pre-existing law, and the judge did not disagree with this view.[64]

III THE RATIONALE FOR THE AVOIDANCE OF CONFLICTS

9.27 The justification for a rule that forbids directors being in conflict situations appears to be based on two grounds: first, to deter directors from even contemplating allowing themselves to be placed, or putting themselves, in a conflict situation;[65] second, to prevent directors from exploiting opportunities to make profits.[66] Jonathan Parker LJ in *Murad v Al-Saraj*,[67] referring to *ex p James*,[68] said that one of the policy reasons behind equity's no-conflict rule is the perceived difficulty in determining what might have happened but for the fact that the fiduciary had placed himself in a position of conflict. This appears to be what Professor Paul Davies was saying when he suggested its existence is due to the fact that a court is unlikely to be able to assess the fairness of a transaction if the director argues that the same transaction would have been made in circumstances where there was not a conflict.[69]

IV THE SECTION

9.28 It is helpful to set out broadly the structure of s 175 of the CA 2006. The section begins in sub-s (1) with a general rule that directors must avoid circumstances where they have, or can have, a direct or indirect interest that conflicts or may conflict with the company's interests.[70] The next subsection provides a particular illustration of the rule in that it states that the exploitation of any company property, information or opportunities is not permitted.[71] Subsections (3)–(6) then provide for exceptions to the general rule, together with the processes that must be followed to ensure that a director is not in breach. We consider the exceptions later.[72] Finally, sub-s (7) indicates that any reference in s 175 to a conflict of interest includes a conflict of an interest and a duty on the one hand, and a conflict of duties on the other.

---

[63] [2009] EWHC 3694 (Ch); [2011] BCC 535.
[64] Ibid at [14].
[65] *Bray v Ford* [1896] AC 44 at 51; *Murad v Al-Saraj* [2005] EWCA Civ 959 at [107]; *Kingsley IT Consulting Ltd v McIntosh* [2006] EWHC 1288 (Ch); [2006] BCC 875 at [55].
[66] *Kingsley IT Consulting Ltd v McIntosh* [2006] EWHC 1288 (Ch); [2006] BCC 875 at [55].
[67] [2005] EWCA Civ 959 at [107].
[68] (1803) 8 Ves 337 at 345.
[69] P Davies *Gower and Davies' Principles of Modern Company Law* (London, Sweet and Maxwell, 7th edn, 2003) at 392–394.
[70] CA 2006, s 175(1).
[71] CA 2006, s 175(2).
[72] Below at **9.36–9.50**.

9.29 So s 175 in fact includes elements of the strictness of the conflict rule, as discussed above, in s 175(1) and (2) which require respectively that a director is to avoid conflicts and that this avoidance does not depend on whether the company could have taken advantage of the property, information or opportunity that is available to the director. But the strictness is somewhat softened by s 175(4)(a) and (b) in that the former provides that the duty is not breached if the situation cannot be regarded as likely to give rise to a conflict, and the latter provides that the duty is not breached if the conflict has been authorised by the board.

V CONFLICT OF INTEREST

9.30 The critical aspect of s 175 is that directors must avoid a conflict of interest. As indicated at the end of the last part of the Chapter, s 175(7) provides that any reference to a conflict of interest in the section includes a conflict of interest and duty and a conflict of duties. This provision, therefore, is not exhaustive. In other words, there can be conflicts of interest that do not involve a conflict of interest and duty on the one hand and a conflict of duties on the other. However, it has been said that this duty covers all conflicts, actual and potential, between the interests of the director and the interests of the company.[73] The reference to conflicts of duties makes it clear that the judicial view that the no-conflict rule covered conflicts of interest and duty and conflicts of duties, is to prevail.

9.31 The test under the old law as to whether something constitutes a conflict has been whether a reasonable person looking at the facts would think that there was a real sensible possibility of conflict.[74]

9.32 'Interest' is not defined in s 175 of the CA 2006, but for the purposes of the no-conflict rule in the past it has been said to signify 'the presence of some personal concern of possible significant pecuniary value in a decision taken, or a transaction effected, by the [the] fiduciary'.[75] What is involved does not necessarily have to result in advantage for the director, provided that there is a possibility of advantage.[76] In determining whether or not there is a conflict courts will examine the extent of the director's interest to ascertain whether a conflict does in fact exist.[77] Section 175(1) codifies the old law in that an indirect interest is sufficient for a conflict to exist.[78] There is nothing in s 175 to indicate that conflicts are limited to those which involve pecuniary interests, although most conflicts will inevitably deal with pecuniary issues.

---

[73] Explanatory Notes to the CA 2006 at para 339.
[74] *Boardman v Phipps* [1967] 2 AC 46 at 124 (HL); *Queensland Mines Ltd v Hudson* (1978) 52 ALJR 399, (1975–76) ACLC 40-266, PC at 401 (PC); *Bhullar v Bhullar* [2003] 2 BCLC 241; [2003] BCC 711.
[75] P Finn *Fiduciary Obligations* (Sydney, Law Book Company, 1977) at 203.
[76] Ibid at 204.
[77] *Farrar v Farrars Ltd* (1888) 40 Ch D 395.
[78] *Baker v Palm Bay Island Resort Pty Ltd (No 2)* [1970] Qd R 210.

9.33 The interest can be direct or indirect. The former is relatively straightforward. The latter might be a little more problematic. An example would be in a situation where a director represents a major shareholder in a company whose interests conflict with those of the company.[79]

9.34 While it is possible to point to certain situations as examples of conflicts of interest within s 175, we must be careful, according to Norris J in *Breitenfeld UK Ltd v Harrison*,[80] not to see particular categories as ones into which a given set of facts must be shoe-horned for a director to be held liable.[81] His Lordship made the point in this case that the principles identified in *Boardman v Phipps*[82] by Lord Upjohn concerning conflicts needed to be applied to the facts of a case to determine whether there was in fact a breach.

VI POSSIBLE CONFLICT

9.35 For a breach of s 175 it is not necessary to prove an actual conflict existed, for under s 175(1) the possibility of a conflict suffices. This is the same as the old law.[83] The conflict must be a real possibility. The point was made in *Boulting v Association of Cinematograph Television and Allied Technicians*[84] by Upjohn LJ that for there to be a breach there must be circumstances that disclose a real conflict of duty and interest and not some theoretical or rhetorical conflict. The same judge, when sitting in the House of Lords in *Boardman v Phipps*,[85] stated that for a breach there had to be a 'real possibility of conflict' between the duty and the interest of the director. This seems to be captured in part, at least, in s 175(4) where it states that 'The duty is not infringed if the acceptance of the benefit cannot reasonably be regarded as likely to give rise to a conflict of interest.' Lord Upjohn stated[86] that these words meant that:

> 'the reasonable man looking at the relevant facts and circumstances of the particular case would think that there was a real sensible possibility of conflict, not that you could imagine some situation arising which might, in some conceivable possibility in events not contemplated as real sensible possibilities by any reasonable person, result in a conflict.'

9.36 Rix LJ (with whom Moses and Buxton LJJ agreed) in *Foster Bryant Surveying Ltd v Bryant*.[87] referred to the above statement with apparent approval and made the point that while Lord Upjohn dissented in *Boardman v*

---

[79] GC100, *Companies Act 2006 - Directors' conflicts of interest*, Association of General Counsel and Company Secretaries of the FTSE 100, 18 January 2008 at para 2.2(b).
[80] [2015] EWHC 399 (Ch).
[81] Ibid at [67].
[82] [1967] AC 46 at 124.
[83] For example, see *Boardman v Phipps* [1967] 2 AC 46.
[84] [1963] 2 QB 606 at 637–638.
[85] [1967] 2 AC 46.
[86] Ibid at 123 and quoting from *Aberdeen Rly Co v Blaikie Bros [1854] 2 Eq Rep 1281, [1854] 1 Macq 461, [1843–1860] All ER Rep 249 (HL)*.
[87] [2007] EWCA Civ 200; [2007] 2 BCLC 239.

Phipps the above statement has never been doubted.[88] In fact Roskill J in *IDC v Cooley*[89] said that the judgments of the other Law Lords in *Boardman v Phipps* did not differ as far as principle was concerned.

9.37 In the Australian High Court Deane J in *Kak Loui Chan v Zacharia*[90] talked about a 'significant possibility' of conflict[91] and in the same court in *Hospital Products Ltd v United States Surgical Corp.*[92] Mason J referred to the 'real or sensible possibility of a conflict'.[93] All of this means that a director of Company A that is engaged in selling women's clothing would not be in conflict if she became a director of Company B that has as its business the distribution of farm machinery,[94] because there is no real possibility of a conflict. According to Warren J in *Wilkinson v West Coast Capital*[95] the situation would be different if, in my example, Company A was thinking of diversifying into distributing farm machinery or something similar. But, on the old law, the director could take up the post with Company B, even if A was considering diversifying as suggested, as holding competing directorships was not disallowed, something we will consider shortly. The situation is likely to be different under the new law.

VII EXCEPTIONS

9.38 Section 175 of the CA 2006 is very broad. However, as already mentioned, conflicts relating to transactions or arrangements with the company are not covered;[96] they are an exception. This is clearly stated in *Burns v FCA*[97] which said that where a director has a conflicting interest in relation to a transaction with the company, the director cannot comply with s 175, because of s 175(3). One then moves to s 177 which provides that interests in transactions or arrangements with the company must be declared in the case of proposed transactions. If existing transactions are involved then s 182 applies. This is all subject to the possibility of the application of an exception applying under those sections. The matter of disclosure is discussed in **Chapter 12**. The reason for not outlawing conflicts a director might have in a transaction which he or she has with his or her company is probably a recognition that invariably companies have allowed in their articles for directors to have interests in such transactions as long as they were declared.

9.39 A second exception is found in s 175(4)(a) of the CA 2006, which provides that the duty is not infringed where the situation cannot reasonably be

---

88   Ibid at [62].
89   [1972] 1 WLR 443 at 450–451.
90   (1984) 154 CLR 178.
91   Ibid at 199.
92   (1984) 55 ALR 417 (Aust HC).
93   Ibid at [103].
94   See *Wilkinson v West Coast Capital* [2005] EWHC 3009 (Ch); [2005] BCC 717 at [253].
95   Ibid.
96   CA 2006, s 175(3).
97   [2014] UKUT 509 (TCC) at [75].

regarded as likely to give rise to a conflict of interest. This might mean that in the situation where a company decides, after being adequately informed and having investigated the circumstances, not to proceed with a project and permits a director to pursue it for himself or herself, the director will not be in breach.[98] Adequately informed in this context would mean full and frank disclosure of all material facts in line with that requirement referred to in *New Zealand Netherlands Society 'Oranje' Inc v Kuys*,[99] by Lord Wilberforce in delivering the advice of the Privy Council. The level of disclosure that is required if a fiduciary duty is to be restricted or abrogated goes well beyond anything that is required in an ordinary contractual relationship.[100] Where there is disclosure that involves properly informing the company this would encompass the company being advised of all the relevant facts but would not entail an understanding of the legal effect and it need not be appreciated by the company that the proposed action if taken by a director would be characterised as a breach of duty.[101] There is clearly no precise formula as to what constitutes adequately informing the company, and it will depend on all of the circumstances.[102]

9.40 A third, and the main, exception is covered by s 175(4)(b). This provides that the section is not infringed if the matter has been authorised by the directors.[103] Prior to codification, if directors were in a conflict position or they wished to retain a profit, they were obliged to make disclosure at a general meeting of members which had to give its approval,[104] unless some alternative procedure was properly provided for in the articles. This also applied where the director did not receive the benefit himself or herself personally, but it was received by a company that he or she incorporated to take the profit.[105] The CLRSG was of the opinion that the common law requirement of convening a meeting of the members was impractical and onerous, and was not consistent with the idea that the board makes business decisions for the company.[106] Added to this is the fact that the process of calling a meeting is costly and the time involved in the convening of a meeting could mean that the director loses the chance to take up the opportunity that is the subject of the conflict

---

[98] For example, see *Queensland Mines Ltd v Hudson* (1978) 52 ALJR 399, (1975–76) ACLC 40-266, PC at 401 (PC).

[99] [1973] 1 WLR 1126 at 1131H–1132A.

[100] *Park's of Hamilton (Holdings) Ltd v Campbell* [2014] CSIH 36; 2014 S.C. 726 at [38].

[101] *Sharma v Sharma* [2013] EWCA Civ 1287.

[102] This seems to be self-evident, but the case of *Cornerstone Property & Development Pty Ltd v Suellen Properties Pty Ltd* [2014] QSC 265 is authority for the proposition.

[103] Davies makes the point that this is consistent with the law as it applies to promoters who only have to disclose to an independent board: *Gower and Davies' Principles of Modern Company Law* (London, Sweet and Maxwell, 7th edn, 2003) at 394.

[104] *Regal (Hastings) Ltd v Gulliver* [1967] 2 AC 134 (HL). If they profit and do not receive approval then they are obliged to account for the profit received: *Keech v Sandford* (1726) Sel Cas Ch 61; (1726) 25 ER 223; [1726] All ER Rep 230; *Boardman v Phipps* [1967] 2 AC 46 at 123.

[105] *Cook v Deeks* [1916] AC 554; *CMS Dolphin Ltd v Simonet* [2001] 2 BCLC 704; [2002] BCC 200.

[106] Company Law Review *Modern Company Law for a Competitive Economy: Final Report* (London, HMSO, 2001) at para 3.23.

situation.[107] The CLRSG felt that the old law process fettered entrepreneurial and business start-up activity by existing company directors. These views were taken into account by the Government and s 175 addresses the concerns. It replaces, in s 175(4)(b), the rule that conflicts of interest must be authorised by the members of the company,[108] unless some alternative procedure is properly provided for, and permits, in certain cases, authorisation by the directors.[109] Naturally, any authorisation by the directors must be on a properly informed basis. In making a decision to authorise or not authorise, the directors are subject to the duty to promote the success of the company as found in s 172(1). A properly informed basis would involve being advised of all the relevant facts but this would not entail an understanding of the legal effect and the directors need not appreciate the proposed action would be characterised as a breach of duty.[110]

9.41 The legislation makes a distinction between private and public companies. In the case of a private company, a conflict can be authorised by the directors of the board unless the company's constitution prevents this.[111] The position with respect to public companies is that the constitution must expressly permit authorisation by the board.[112] Perhaps this difference can be justified on the basis that in many private companies the shareholders are also the directors, therefore they have a say in whether a conflict is permitted, and in other private companies it can at least be said that the members do have real power in electing the directors, while in many public companies a lot of shareholders have small holdings and little input as far as the election of directors is concerned.[113]

9.42 It is important to note that where the authorisation of the directors is sought, s 175(6) of the CA 2006 provides that any authorisation is effective only if:

'(a) any requirement as to the quorum at the meeting at which the matter is considered is met without counting the director in question or any other interested director, and

(b) the matter was agreed to without their voting or would have been agreed to if their votes had not been counted.'

---

[107] B Clark and A Benstock 'UK Company Law Reform and Directors' Exploitation of "Corporate Opportunities"' (2006) 17 ICCLR 231 at 238. For a discussion of the arguments favouring board sanction of conflicts, see A Keay 'The Authorising of Directors' Conflicts of Interests: Getting a Balance?' (2012) 12 *Journal of Corporate Law Studies* 129 at 136–138.

[108] If authority is needed, see *Crown Dilmun v Sutton* [2004] EWHC 52 (Ch); [2004] 1 BCLC 468.

[109] For a detailed discussion about the provision and the approval process, see A Keay 'The Authorising of Directors' Conflicts of Interests: Getting a Balance?' (2012) 12 *Journal of Corporate Law Studies* 129.

[110] *Sharma v Sharma* [2013] EWCA Civ 1287.

[111] CA 2006, s 175(5)(a).

[112] CA 2006, s 175(5)(b).

[113] For the predicament that shareholders of public companies can find themselves in, see A Keay 'Company Directors Behaving Poorly: Disciplinary Options for Shareholders' [2007] JBL 656.

9.43 This provision seeks, obviously, to ensure that any authorisation is granted by independent directors as the interested director himself or herself or any other interested director is unable to be counted in the quorum or in any subsequent vote. 'Interested director' is not defined in the section. It is an issue that is discussed in more detail shortly. For the purposes of the no-conflict rule, in the past interest has been said to signify 'the presence of some personal concern of possible significant pecuniary value in a decision taken, or a transaction effected, by [the] fiduciary'.[114] To have an interest does not mean that the conflict situation necessarily results in an advantage for the relevant director; it suffices if there is a possibility of advantage,[115] and this is line with s 175(4)(a). Importantly, the section does not stop allies, and those under the influence, of the director from attending the meeting, taking part in discussions and then voting, provided that they do not have an interest in the conflict, so in some companies one might question whether the board is truly independent. But, even with the previous position, where general meeting approval was required, there might not be a completely independent vote for the allies of the director would be entitled to vote their shares. If authorisation is to be sought at a board meeting it might be appropriate for any allies of the directors to excuse themselves when it comes to a vote. If this were done then a vote of authorisation is not likely to be challenged and the conflicted director can proceed with a degree of certainty. It is not unlikely that in some small companies it is not going to be possible to have a vote by a totally independent board, and so it would be more appropriate for the decision to go to the members, as the general meeting can always authorise the situation, pursuant to s 180(4), as it preserves any current ability of the members of a company to authorise conflicts that would otherwise be a breach of this duty.[116] This is discussed in **Chapter 16**.

9.44 In the construction or amending of the articles on the subject of authorisation, the company might seek to indicate how any matter is to be proposed to the board and how it is to be authorised by them and what the quorum requirements to approve any conflict must be.[117]

9.45 It is interesting to note that s 175 only prohibits a conflicted director from being counted in the quorum and from voting on the motion of authorisation. The director is still entitled to participate in discussion relating to consideration of any authorisation decision. It would have been more fitting to have required the director not to have any involvement in the decision-making process. It is in fact recommended by the Institute of Chartered Secretaries and Administrators, as being more appropriate, that a director who is subject to the conflict that is to be discussed by the board leaves the meeting when discussions take place on the matters pertaining to it.[118] The Institute also has

---

[114] P Finn *Fiduciary Obligations* (Sydney, Law Book Company, 1977) at 203.
[115] Ibid at 204.
[116] Explanatory Notes to the CA 2006 at para 340.
[117] GC100 *Companies Act 2006 – Directors' conflicts of interest* (Association of General Counsel and Company Secretaries of the FTSE 100, 18 January 2008) at para 3.1.
[118] ICSA International *ICSA Guidance on Directors' General Duties* (January 2008) at para 3.5.3.

recommended that the board retains a register of conflicts that records all conflicts for each director, and it states that it is advisable to present periodically the list of conflicts to the board, so that authorisation regarding any resultant conflict can be given.[119] In determining whether to authorise the conflict it is important for the directors to remember that they must consider whether their action is most likely to promote the success of the company,[120] as required by s 172.[121]

9.46 Section 180(1) of the CA 2006 confirms all of the foregoing by providing that if s 175 is complied with then any transaction or arrangement is not liable to be set aside as a result of any common law rule or equitable principle requiring the consent or approval of the members. But, the articles of a company can always specify more arduous demands for approval, such as requiring the matter to be taken to the general meeting. Section 175 does not prevent the requirement that other conditions, in addition to authorisation by the board, must be fulfilled for the conflict situation to be sanctioned. For instance, the constitution of the company may lay down extra, more demanding requirement(s).[122] Rather than obtaining board approval, authorisation can always be sought from the shareholders.

9.47 Now, subject to the limits contained in s 175(5), a director is clearly not liable if he or she obtains the authorisation of non-conflicted directors under s 175(4)(b) and this authorisation would include permission for the exploitation of a corporate opportunity. What if all the directors are going to avail themselves of the opportunity? No authorisation in such a situation can be given (see s 175(6)), so one assumes we are thrown back to the old law and there is a need for general meeting approval. It would seem that general meeting approval would still be required in the *Regal (Hastings) Ltd v Gulliver* type situation.

9.48 Although the fact that the directors may authorise a conflict under s 175 might appear to be totally new, there was some authority for the view that the directors all along have been able to authorise the taking up of an opportunity.[123] It was critical in the case of *Queensland Mines Ltd v Hudson*,[124] where it was held that a director had not breached the no-profit rule, that the board was apprised of all of the facts relating to an opportunity which the defendant director had taken up, and renounced the opportunity, as well as saying that the director could do whatever he liked with the opportunity for his benefit, but at his risk.[125] What is objectionable, possibly, about the

---

[119] Ibid.
[120] Ibid; GC100 *Companies Act 2006 - Directors' conflicts of interest* (Association of General Counsel and Company Secretaries of the FTSE 100, 18 January 2008) at para 1.3.
[121] See **Chapter 6** above.
[122] Lord Goldsmith in Lords Grand Committee, 9 February 2006, Hansard vol 678, col 326.
[123] *Queensland Mines Ltd v Hudson* [1978] 52 ALJR 379.
[124] Ibid.
[125] Ibid at 403.

decision-making process, is that in that case, discussed in detail later,[126] the board was not truly independent because the director appeared to have had input into its deliberations.[127]

9.49 As far as authorisation is concerned it will, as one would expect, only cover the conflict issue and not any other possible breach of duty. So, for example, authorisation can save a director from liability under s 175 of the CA 2006, but it cannot absolve him or her from liability under s 172. Nevertheless, a director may be able to grasp protection from s 180(4)(b) which provides that in a situation where a company's articles contain provisions for dealing with conflicts, general duties are not infringed by anything done (or omitted to be done) by the directors, or any of them, when adhering to those provisions. In addition, s 232(4) of the CA 2006 permits the articles to protect directors from liability by continuing to include provisions dealing with conflicts of interest where they were lawful under the old law. This would allow companies to continue to rely on an article dealing with conflicts, such as art 85 of Table A.[128] The GC100 (the Association of General Counsel and Company Secretaries of the FTSE 100 companies) has stated that there are two views taken in relation to addressing the s 180(4)(b) issue. The first is that the articles need to indicate that a director will not be in breach of duty if, for instance, he or she withholds information from the company. The second view is that the articles should allow the board, when it authorises a conflict, to state that the director is not required to disclose information received from a conflict situation.[129]

9.50 Whether or not directors should be able to authorise a conflict is debatable. Elsewhere I have been rather critical of the process and I have considered other options, before accepting that the present system with some modifications is probably the best option.[130] There are a number of possible problems with the process in the legislation. For example, in considering a conflict the directors might see themselves in a similar position in the future and they would expect some understanding and support from their fellow directors. The danger is that this is likely to engender generosity in their evaluation of a director's position,[131] and implicit reciprocity if the situation arises with other directors. But the major concern might well be that, as discussed briefly above, the legislation does not define who an interested director is and it could well be that persons connected with the conflicted director will attend and vote on whether approval should be given. So it is a matter for the courts as to whether

---

[126] Below at para **10.64**.

[127] But it would seem that under s 175 a director can have input to discussions about authorisation, although he or she cannot vote.

[128] The Companies (Tables A–F) Regulations 1985.

[129] GC100 *Companies Act 2006 - Directors' conflicts of interest* (Association of General Counsel and Company Secretaries of the FTSE 100, 18 January 2008) at para 3.2.

[130] See A Keay 'The Authorising of Directors' Conflicts of Interests: Getting a Balance?' (2012) 12 *Journal of Corporate Law Studies* 129.

[131] See R Nolan 'The Legal Control of Directors' Conflicts of Interest in the United Kingdom: Non-Executive Directors Following the Higgs Report' (2005) 6 *Theoretical Inquiries in Law* 413 at 424.

someone is interested or not. One would expect any director who has a direct or indirect pecuniary interest in the conflict situation would be regarded as 'interested.' What about directors who have family connections to the conflicted director? Section 190 of the Act extends the operation of some provisions in the Act to directors and connected persons. 'Connected person' is defined in s 252 so as to cover a director's family (further defined in s 253), but s 175 does not embrace the notion of connected person. Would spouses and children of conflicted directors be regarded as interested as a matter of course even if they have no specific interest in the conflict situation? It could be argued that they should be because it is possible that they could benefit from the circumstances constituting the conflict and that could influence them to vote for approval. In *Newgate Stud Co v Penfold*[132] David Richards J dealt with the issue of family interest in a different context. His Lordship said that spouses and domestic partners are not nominees for each other, but in any such relationship there exists the potential for the exercise of fiduciary duties to be influenced by personal considerations and the related director will be compromised by a desire to favour the relative.[133] Perhaps the related director should be excluded from voting in any event because he or she has a conflict of interest in relation to the action of approval,[134] that is, the director is conflicted in having to make a decision that involves the interests of his or her company on the one hand and the interests of his or her family member on the other. Those directors who might be regarded as allies of the director who is conflicted are not, prima facie, excluded. Hannigan refers to the case where there are directors on the board who are business associates of the conflicted director, and she asserts that 'there is a risk of mutually supportive collusion' between the parties who might then share opportunities that come the way of the company.[135] While this is a potential problem, it is acknowledged that it would be exceedingly difficult to draft legislation that would bar such persons from being able to vote. The concept of an ally is difficult to define and express in legislation, and, of course, there are different levels of allies. A director might be seen as an ally of a conflicted director in relation to a particular matter relating to the company's affairs, but he or she would not be when it comes to personal matters. It is to be noted that even with the pre-codified position, where general meeting approval was required, there might not be a completely independent vote as shareholders who are the allies of the director would be entitled to vote their shares.

9.51 It has been argued by Bryan Clark that the category of 'interested director' should extend to including those who are under the influence of the conflicted director. But while this is meritorious, the learned commentator accepts that determining when directors, not involved personally in the conflict,

---

[132] [2004] EWHC 2993 (Ch); [2008] 1 BCLC 46.
[133] Ibid at [237]–[240].
[134] B Hannigan *Company Law* (OUP, 2nd edn, 2009) at 266.
[135] Ibid at 266–267.

may have been under the influence of the conflicted director is likely to be problematic from an evidential perspective.[136]

9.52   The GC100 has suggested that when a public company is amending its articles to address s 175(4) of the CA 2006 and including a power for the board to authorise conflicts, it may want to consider how s 180(4)(b) might be employed as far as conflict situations authorised by the board are concerned. It might be regarded as desirable for the articles to provide unequivocally that a director will not be in breach of duty in respect of an authorised conflict situation where it involves receiving from a third party confidential information as a result of the conflict situation, and the director fails to disclose this to the company or uses it for the company's benefit, or where the director seeks to mitigate the consequences of his or her actions, when the actual conflict occurs as a result, for instance, from his or her non-attendance at board meetings or failure to read board papers.[137]

VIII EXAMPLES OF CONFLICT

9.53   The GC100 has, helpfully, suggested the following instances where a conflict situation will arise and the section will apply:[138]

'if a director of Company A is a competitor in some respects of Company A;

if a director of Company A is a major shareholder in Company A;

if a director of Company A is a potential customer of, or supplier to, Company A;

if a director of Company A owns property adjacent to Company A's property, the value of which could be affected by the activities of Company A;

if a director of Company A has an advisory relationship (for example, financial or legal) with Company A or a competitor;

if a director of Company A is a director of Company A's pension trustee company;

if a director wants to take up an opportunity that had been offered to, but declined by, Company A;

if a director is in a situation where he can make a profit as a result of his directorship whether or not he discloses this to Company A; and

---

[136] 'UK Company Law and Directors' Exploitation of "Corporate Opportunities"' (2006) 17 ICCLR 231 at 239.

[137] GC100 *Companies Act 2006 – Directors' conflicts of interest* (Association of General Counsel and Company Secretaries of the FTSE 100, 18 January 2008) at para 2.12.

[138] GC100 *Companies Act 2006 – Directors' conflicts of interest* (Association of General Counsel and Company Secretaries of the FTSE 100, 18 January 2008) at para 2.3.

if in each of the above situations, the director is a director of another company and that other company has the relevant relationship with Company A or is in the situation described above.'

IX COMPETING DIRECTORSHIPS

9.54 Should directors be able to act as directors of other companies? This has been a vexed issue, and the judges in England have expressed some unease with the concept of multiple directorships.[139] As far as executive directors are concerned the answer to the question posed above might be a qualified 'no', as typically they have to devote the whole of their energies to the company that employs them on a full-time basis.[140] However, an executive director might seek the approval of his or her company to act as a non-executive director of another company, and his or her employer might give its consent if it feels that this could be beneficial for the company. It might, for instance, enable the director to make helpful contacts that will benefit his employer company. For non-executive directors there does not seem to be any reason preventing them from acting on the boards of several companies as the very nature of the role of a non-executive is part-time. There is also the issue that is not discussed here as to whether a director can acquire and/or maintain a satisfactory understanding of the businesses of each of the companies, especially where the number is more than a couple. All of the foregoing is very straightforward. What is of particular concern and has been a vexed issue for many years and somewhat controversial, and is highly relevant to the duty at hand, is the matter of competing directorships. Can a director occupy positions on the boards of competing companies? If a director were to do so is he or she in a conflict situation that is prohibited by the law? This will mainly involve non-executives as executive directors will normally, as indicated above, be obliged, by contrast, to devote all of their time to working for their company.

9.55 It has been argued by Len Sealy and Sarah Worthington[141] that the effect of s 175 is to place a director who holds multiple directorships into a conflict situation. Parker Hood is of the view that this is stating the position too widely,[142] and Worthington, at least, might have had a change of mind for in her jointly authored edition of *Gower and Davies' Principles of Modern*

---

[139] P Hood 'Directors' Duties Under the Companies Act 2006: Clarity or Confusion?' (2013) 13 JCLS 1 at 41. The learned writer refers to *In Plus Group Ltd v Pyke* [2002] EWCA Civ 370; [2003] BCC 332 at [75], [78], [80].

[140] The UK Corporate Governance Code, Financial Reporting Council, September 2012, actually provides that directors of listed companies 'should be able to allocate sufficient time to the company to discharge their responsibilities effectively' at para B.5 (accessible at: www.frc.org.uk/Our-Work/Codes-Standards/Corporate-governance/UK-Corporate-Governance-Code.aspx (accessed 21 November 2013)).

[141] L S Sealy and S Worthington *Cases and Materials in Company Law* (OUP, 9th edn, 2010) at 341–342.

[142] P Hood 'Directors' Duties Under the Companies Act 2006: Clarity or Confusion?' (2013) 13 JCLS 1 at 43.

Company Law,[143] published since emitting the view mentioned above, she does not put forward the same opinion. One would think that provided the companies in which the directorships are held are not in competition then no conflict exists. The problem is likely to exist where either it is difficult to assess whether the companies are actually in competition. Another problem is that while companies are not in competition today, they could be tomorrow. For instance, X is a director of both A and B. If either A or B decides to commence business in the area occupied by the other there is a conflict. There also could be concern that X might use his influence to dissuade A or B from entering the domain of the other because he is concerned about the fact that if they did, he would then be in a conflict situation. And in such circumstances it is unlikely that either company would be willing to approve of it under s 175(5).

9.56 The classic case in favour of permitting directorships of competing companies is *London & Mashonaland Co Ltd v New Marshonaland Exploration Co Ltd*[144] where it was said that a director may serve in the same capacity in a competing company provided that the articles do not prohibit this or the director is not in breach of his or her duties. The case involved an application for an injunction by a company to prevent one of its directors from acting as a director of a rival company. Chitty J, who gave judgment, said that holding directorships in rival companies was permitted, although clearly it is not easy for directors who are in such a situation. There were three limits on the permissibility of acting in this way, according to Chitty J. First, a company is able to restrict the activities of its directors by terms in its articles which forbid them to act on the board of any other company or companies that are engaged in a substantial amount of business in competition with the company. Second, Chitty J indicated that there might be an express or implied contract with the director whereby the director's activities are restricted. As indicated above, the norm is for the service contracts of executive directors to limit them from being involved in other companies and as such directors are usually employees and they would be unable to hold competing positions.[145] Third, Chitty J stated that a director is not to disclose to a company any confidential information that was obtained in his or her role with another company, and in the case before him there was no evidence that the director had made any such disclosures. On this point one would think that it would be appropriate for a director holding competing positions to withdraw from any discussions of the board of one company that might touch on his or her knowledge of confidential information about the other company. If the director were to remain in the decision-making process of one company he or she might find that points he or she made might make in one company's board could compromise the other company's position. But, if he or she did not make such points it might be said that the director was not contributing appropriately to the discussion in the board meeting. The director simply could be in a no-win situation.

---

[143] P Davies and S Worthington *Gower and Davies' Principles of Modern Company Law* (London, Sweet and Maxwell, 9th edn, 2012) at 609.

[144] [1892] 3 Ch 577.

[145] *Hivac Ltd v Park Royal Scientific Instruments Ltd* [1946] Ch 169 (CA).

9.57 The following comment of Lord Cranworth in the case of *Aberdeen Railway Co* v *Blaikie Bros*[146] is somewhat difficult to square with the approach adopted in *London & Mashonaland Co Ltd* v *New Marshonaland Exploration Co Ltd*:[147]

> 'A corporate body can only act by agents and it is, of course, the duty of those agents so to act as best to promote the interests of the corporation whose affairs they are conducting. Such agents have duties to discharge of a fiduciary nature towards their principal. And it is a rule of universal application that no one having such duties to discharge shall be allowed to enter engagements in which he has, or can have, a personal interest conflicting, or which possibly may conflict, with the interests of those whom he is bound to protect ... So strictly is this principle adhered to that no question is allowed to be raised as to the fairness or unfairness of a contract to be entered into ...'

9.58 In *Bell* v *Lever Bros Ltd*,[148] Lord Blanesburgh, in obiter comments, assumed the correctness of the principle propounded in *Mashonaland,* and the *Mashonaland* principle has become regarded as the traditional approach.

9.59 While Gibbs J in *Consul Developments* v *DPC Estates Pty Ltd*[149] did not implicitly follow the approach in *Marshonaland,* and one can point to the odd occasion in Australia where judges have been less inclined to accept the *Marshonaland* view,[150] the traditional line has been generally sanctioned in Australia and the most recent cases have followed that approach, although pointing out that a director might well have to disclose conflicts to each company. The Australian High Court in *R* v *Byrnes*[151] said:

> 'A director of a company who is also a director of another company may owe conflicting fiduciary duties. Being a fiduciary, the director of the first company must not exercise his or her powers for the benefit or gain of the second company without clearly disclosing the second company's interests to the first company and obtaining the first company's consent.'

9.60 Why should directors be entitled to hold positions in competing companies given the fact that it is likely to place the director in almost impossible positions? Louis Brandeis, before his elevation to the bench of the Supreme Court of the United States, said that permitting directors to act in such a way was the root of many evils and suppressed competition and encouraged disloyalty. He went on to say that it led to a conflict situation with a person not being able to serve two masters.[152] While in *Bell* v *Lever Bros Ltd,*[153]

---

[146] (1854) 1 Macq 461 at 471–472.
[147] This was approved of by the House of Lords in *Phipps v Boardman* [1967] AC 46. It was cited as authority by the Privy Council in *Queensland Mines Ltd v Hudson* (1978) 52 ALJR 399, (1975–76) ACLC 40-266, PC at 400.
[148] [1932] AC 161 at 195.
[149] (1975) 132 CLR 373.
[150] For example, see *Mordecai v Mordecai* (1988) 6 ACLC 370 (NSWCA).
[151] [1995] HCA 1; (1995) 183 CLR 501 at [29].
[152] 'Breaking the Money Trusts' *Harper's Weekly,* 6 December 1913 at 13 and referred to in J

Lord Blanesburgh, in obiter comments, assumed the correctness of the principle propounded in *Mashonaland*, his Lordship did accept that serving two masters is not possible.[154]

9.61 In *On the Street Pty Ltd v Cott*,[155] the Australian court accepted the fact that there was nothing prohibiting a director from being involved in competing firms, but the director was obliged not to divulge information for the benefit of the rival. The same view was expressed by Young J in the New South Wales Supreme Court in *Rosetex Company Pty Ltd v Licata*.[156] In *Fitzsimmons v R*[157] a director was held liable for breach of duty when holding directorships in competing companies, but the reason for that was that he divulged the financial position of company A to company B's board when a member of both companies.

9.62 The general approach in New Zealand has, as in Australia, also been to follow *Mashonaland*.[158]

9.63 Back in England, in more recent times the Court of Appeal has acknowledged that directors can hold directorships in companies that are in competition. In *Plus Group Ltd v Pyke*,[159] it was said by Brooke LJ that: 'There is no completely rigid rule that a director may not be involved in the business of a company which is in competition with another company of which he is a director.'[160] Sedley LJ said that the court was bound by the decision of *Bell v Lever Bros*[161] and it had approved of *Mashonaland*.[162] But the learned judge went on to say, in a similar vein to Brooke LJ, that the facts of each case must be carefully examined, so there is no blanket rule that holding positions with competitors is permissible.[163] His Lordship did think that the *Mashonaland* principle warranted reconsideration in light of modern standards.[164]

9.64 The principle provided in *Mashonaland* has been the subject of criticism and it has been said that the principle is becoming more and more difficult to affirm.[165] Besides the rather critical comments in the Court of Appeal in *Plus*

Lawrence 'Multiple Directorships and Conflicts of Interest: Recent Developments' (1996) 14 *Company and Securities Law Journal* 513 at 513.

[153] [1932] AC 161 at 195.

[154] Ibid at 172.

[155] (1990) 3 ACSR 54.

[156] (1994) 12 ACSR 779. Also, see *SEA Food International Pty Ltd v Lam* [1998] FCA 130; (1998) 16 ACLC 552 (Aust Fed Ct).

[157] (1997) 23 ACSR 355 (WA CCA).

[158] *Berlei Hestia (NZ) Ltd v Fernyhough* [1980] 2 NZLR 150.

[159] [2002] EWCA Civ 370; [2002] 2 BCLC 201.

[160] Ibid at [72].

[161] [1932] AC 161.

[162] [2002] EWCA Civ 370; [2002] 2 BCLC 201 at [79].

[163] Ibid at [80].

[164] Ibid at [88].

[165] P Davies *Gower and Davies' Principles of Modern Company Law* (London, Sweet and Maxwell, 7th edn, 2003) at 415.

Group Ltd v Pyke the decision has been criticised in other English cases,[166] as well as in Scotland,[167] Australia[168] and most recently in Hong Kong.[169] *Mashonaland* was only a decision at first instance, although approved of by Lord Blanesburgh in *Bell v Lever Bros Ltd*,[170] and it does seem rather anomalous that directors can hold posts in competing companies, but employees and partners cannot.[171] Surely, as indicated by Millet LJ in *Bristol and West Building Society v Mothew*,[172] a fiduciary who acts for two principals with potentially conflicting interests has divided loyalty. Moreover, while a director might obtain consent to act in relation to two competing companies, he or she is going to have to constantly consider whether he or she is in a conflict position. One might ask whether a person can adequately serve one company, let alone both companies, in such a situation. Christie argues that if it is not legally possible for trustees to act in positions that involve competition,[173] it is as necessary that such a rule applies to the directors of public companies, with their diversified membership, and where shareholders have little say in those who become directors and how they operate.[174]

9.65 The problems that can arise when competing directorships are held are illustrated in two decisions. First, in the Delaware Supreme Court decision of *Broz v Cellular Information Systems Inc.*[175] In that case Broz was the sole shareholder and president of RFB Cellular Inc (RFBC), a company which held telecommunications licences for a number of districts of Michigan. Broz was also an outside director (non-executive) on the board of CIS, which was engaged in the same business, and operating licences in different parts of the same general region of the United States. Early in 1994, Broz, in his role as the sole shareholder of RFBC, was approached by a broker, Mackinac, acting on behalf of a company that was interested in selling the telecommunications licence it held for a part of Michigan (Michigan-2), an area which was located between the areas in which RFBC and CIS already operated their businesses. On behalf of RFBC, Broz began negotiations with Mackinac, but did not formally disclose the opportunity to the CIS board. It seems that neither Mackinac nor Broz believed that there was any real likelihood that CIS was interested in, or able to acquire, the Michigan-2 licence. This belief emanated principally from the fact that they were aware that CIS had been disposing of

---

166   *British Midland Tool Ltd v Midland International Tooling Ltd* [2003] EWHC 466 Ch; [2003] 2 BCLC 523 at [81]–[85]; *Foster Bryant Surveying Ltd v Bryant* [2007] EWCA Civ 200; [2007] 2 BCLC 239 at [70].

167   *Commonwealth Oil and Gas Company Ltd v Baxter* [2007] CSOH 198 at [175]–[176] and on appeal in the Inner House in *Commonwealth Oil and Gas Company v Baxter* [2009] CSIH 75; [2010] SC 156 at [4]–[5], [75]–[78].

168   *Eastland Technology Australia Pty Ltd v Whisson* [2005] WASCA 144; (2005) 223 ALR 123 at [69]; *Links Golf Tasmania Pty Ltd v Sattler* [2012] FCA 634; (2012) 292 ALR 382 at [545]–[547], [555]–[556], [559]–[563].

169   *Chen Wai Too v Poon Ka Man Jason* [2016] HKCFA 23 at [92]–[104].

170   [1932] AC 161 at 195.

171   P Watts 'The Transition from Director to Competitor' (2007) 123 LQR 21 at 24.

172   [1998] 1 Ch 1 at 18 (CA).

173   See *Re Thomson* [1930] 1 Ch 203.

174   M Christie 'The Director's Fiduciary Duty Not to Compete' (1992) 55 MLR 506 at 513–514.

175   637 A 2d 148 (1996) (Del).

similar licences and other assets as part of its strategy to survive financial collapse. Broz also had informal discussions with all of his fellow directors on the CIS board about his plans for RFBC to acquire the licence for Michigan-2. However, later in the same year, CIS's financial fortunes changed dramatically when a majority of its shares were acquired by Pri-Cellular Communications Inc. Pri-Cellular had become involved in a bidding war with Broz to acquire the licence for Michigan-2. Broz won the battle, and completed the purchase of the Michigan-2 licence on behalf of RFBC shortly before Pri-Cellular completed its takeover of CIS. Following the takeover, Broz and the other directors were removed from the CIS board, and their successors brought an action against Broz, claiming that he was liable for breach of his fiduciary duty of loyalty by diverting to his own company an opportunity to which CIS was entitled in equity, and that he was holding the Michigan-2 licence on constructive trust for Pri-Cellular.

9.66 A second instance is *State Bank of South Australia v Marcus Clark*.[176] Here, C was the CEO of the plaintiff (the Bank) and also a director of E in which he held a great many shares. E had lent money to A. A began experiencing financial problems. C was contacted at the Bank by a representative of A, who advised that A was considering selling one of its subsidiaries, O. C then was the prime mover in the proposal of the Bank to purchase O from A. C did not disclose his interests and participated in board meetings of the Bank when the purchase was considered. The Bank decided, without an independent valuation of O, to buy the company. The Bank paid A\$59m when the company was worth somewhere between A\$17m and A\$21m. A directed that part of the purchase price be paid to E in discharge of A's debt to E. In this case C had competing duties to the Bank and to E.

9.67 Notwithstanding the difficulties that might exist for directors, essentially the UK position has certainly been that competing directorships do not per se breach the no-conflict rule, while accepting that a director in such a situation might be laying himself or herself open to a prohibited conflict. There appear to be all sorts of possible scenarios that might lead to a director being in breach when acting for competing companies. For example, what about where a person is director of both X and Y, which are competitors, and an opportunity comes to her knowledge? Is she in breach to Y if she informs X and not Y? Or, is the director to advise both simultaneously to ensure fairness? What determines which company the director favours with the opportunity? It cannot surely be based on the caprice of the director. Of course, the facts might dictate that X is preferred to Y, because the opportunity arose because of the way that X is set up and it is more appropriate that X gets the opportunity, but this is too marginal a consideration and could place the director in a very difficult position involving difficult judgment calls.

9.68 Does s 175 of the CA 2006 change the position at common law? Section 175(7) provides that any reference to a conflict of interest includes a

---

[176] (1996) 14 ACLC 1019.

conflict of duties, so prima facie it would appear that holding competing directorships is a conflict of interest within s 175. If not a conflict, it would definitely appear to be a possible conflict within s 175(1). This provision follows equity which states that whether something constitutes a conflict is whether a reasonable person looking at the facts would think that there was a real sensible possibility of conflict.[177] It appears reasonable to assert that a director must avoid serving on the board of two competing companies' boards because in doing so he or she is in a situation where there is at least a possible conflict.[178] Certainly the GC100 has taken the view that holding competing directorships is a conflict situation and it would be necessary for the director to have his or her position authorised according to the terms of s 175.[179] The GC100 says that the provision applies even if the director does not have any influence over a particular situation for a conflict to arise. It has said:[180]

> 'For example, if a director of Company A is also a director of Company B, which is a competitor of Company A, it appears that the duty would be breached even if the director is not involved in any decision-making in the area in which the companies compete unless the boards of Company A and Company B have authorised the matter.'

9.69 In light of the requirement in s 170(4) of the CA 2006 that general duties should be interpreted and applied in the same way as common law rules or equitable principles, there may be sufficient grounds for a judge legitimately to follow the *Mashonaland* approach, particularly given the fact that the law on possible conflicts has existed for many years and that did not affect the decision in *Mashonaland* or the acceptance of the case in *Bell v Lever Bros*. But surely the safest position for directors to take is to follow the view propounded by the GC100 and have the situation authorised by the relevant boards of directors. In addition, it seems that that is the fairest action to adopt. Also, as discussed above, a director with competing directorships must surely be in a position where there is a possibility of conflict and that is not permitted because of s 175(1).

X FORMER DIRECTORS

9.70 While in equity a fiduciary obligation does not generally continue after the determination of the relationship that gave rise to it,[181] probably because the reason for imposing the obligation on the director (to ensure loyalty) no longer exists (it was stated in *Ultraframe (UK) Ltd v Fielding*[182] that once a director has resigned, the no-conflict rule ceased to apply in relation to the

---

[177] See *Boardman v Phipps* [1967] 2 AC 46 at 124; *Bhullar v Bhullar* [2003] 2 BCLC 241; [2003] BCC 711.

[178] See M Christie 'The Director's Fiduciary Duty not to Compete' (1992) 55 MLR 506 at 508.

[179] GC100 *Companies Act 2006 – Directors' conflicts of interest* (Association of General Counsel and Company Secretaries of the FTSE 100, 18 January 2008) at para 2.2(e).

[180] Ibid at para 2.2(e).

[181] *A-G v Blake* [1998] Ch 439 at 453; *CMS Dolphin Ltd v Simonet* [2001] 2 BCLC 704 at [95].

[182] [2005] EWHC 1638 (Ch); [2006] FSR 17.

former director's future activities),[183] former directors might still be in breach after the termination of their appointment.[184] This is particularly the case where they profit from their former post and they make use of information which belongs to their former company, such as confidential customer lists,[185] or they leave the company with the intention of exploiting an opportunity that came to the company, but they do not do so until they had retired from the company.[186] But, in an interesting decision, *Baker v Gibbons*,[187] the court did not find a former director liable for recruiting some of his former company's selling agents to his competing business. Pennycuick V-C rejected the company's argument that the names and addresses of the agents was confidential information that the former director obtained while a director and his Lordship rejected the idea that he could not use it following the termination of his post. This is consistent with the fact that courts are reluctant, it would seem, as will be discussed later (in **Chapter 10**), to prevent a person from furthering his or her right to conduct a business, save where it is a clear breach of duty. In *Island Export Finance Ltd v Umunna*[188] Hutchison J rejected the submission of the company's counsel that, because a director is in a fiduciary position, a director after cessation of his or her appointment is precluded from exploiting either any market of which he or she has become aware, or any knowledge he has gained, while employed by the company. That was regarded as far too broad a proposition.[189] The decision in *Thermascan Ltd v Norman*[190] is along similar lines, and what is more it was a case decided pursuant to s 175. In this case the defendant was a director of the claimant company, a commercial surveying company. He had entered into certain covenants, one of which was that for a period of six months following his termination of employment by the claimant he would not canvass customers of the claimant. The defendant resigned his directorship and he took up a post as an employee at another commercial surveying company. The claimant became aware that the defendant was canvassing the claimant's customers. The claimant applied for injunctive relief to enforce the covenants that the defendant had agreed to while an employee of the claimant. The defendant had given undertakings to the claimant, one of which was that he would honour the covenant concerning the non-canvassing of the claimant's customers for six months starting from the time that he left the claimant. After the close of the six month period the defendant established his

---

[183] Ibid at [1309]. Also, see *CMS Dolphin Ltd v Simonet* [2001] 2 BCLC 704; [2002] BCC 200; *Quarter Master UK Ltd v Pyke* [2004] EWHC 1815 (Ch); [2005] 1 BCLC 245.

[184] *IDC v Cooley* [1972] 1 WLR 443; *Island Export Finance Ltd v Umunna* [1986] BCLC 460 at 480; *SEA Food International Pty Ltd v Lam* [1998] FCA 130; (1998) 16 ACLC 552 (Aust Fed Ct); *Quarter Master UK Ltd v Pyke* [2004] EWHC 1815 (Ch) at [57]; [2005] 1 BCLC 245 at 264.

[185] For example, see *Roger Bullivant Ltd v Ellis* [1987] FSR 172; *Faccenda Chicken Ltd v Fowler* [1986] Ch 117 (this involved employee-employer relationship but the same principles can apply to companies and directors); [1986] 3 WLR 288; [1986] FSR 291; *Mordecai v Mordecai* (1988) 6 ACLC 370 (NSWCA); *Ferrari v Ferrari Management Services Pty Ltd (in liq)* [1999] QCA 230 (Qld S Ct).

[186] *Island Export Finance Ltd v Umunna* [1986] BCLC 460 at 481.

[187] [1972] 2 All ER 759.

[188] [1986] BCLC 460.

[189] Ibid at 483.

[190] [2009] EWHC 3694 (Ch); [2011] BCC 535.

own commercial surveying company and began to canvass some of the claimant's customers. The claimant sought, under s 175, from the court an injunction preventing the defendant from canvassing its customers. The court refused, saying that while the defendant remained subject to fiduciary duties, they did not extend to a blanket prohibition on canvassing business from the claimant's customers. The case of *Safetynet Security Ltd Coppage*[191] also involved a six month non-canvassing period, but the former director was held liable as he sought to canvass during the six months following the termination of his directorship. In *Killen v Horseworld Ltd*[192] a former director was held liable, but no time period had been set concerning competition and the actions of the former director alleged to be in conflict went to the very heart of the company's business.

9.71 Section 170(2) of the CA 2006 makes it clear that former directors remain responsible to their former company and must avoid a conflict[193] by the use of company property, information or opportunities that came to his or her knowledge whilst a director. To the extent mentioned, the duties apply to former directors as they do to directors, but subject to any necessary adaptations. The inclusion of former directors effectively accords with the old law position for a former director is, as the court in *CMS Dolphin Ltd v Simonet*[194] said, 'just as accountable as a trustee who retires without properly accounting for trust property'.[195] In equity the rule not only applied to opportunities exploited while a director is serving a term, it also applies to opportunities taken up when he or she has left the company if the opportunity arose during the course of his or her term of office.[196] Section 170(2) affirms this principle. This subsection does not appear to affect the general view that directors are permitted to use knowledge and expertise gained while acting as directors, but the decision of *Baker v Gibbons* might be decided differently now on the basis that the addresses of agents might be regarded as information within s 170(2).

9.72 The fact that the no-conflict rule ceases to apply to a director in relation to future activities is likely to be applied to the case where an administrator is appointed to a company, for such an appointment means directors' powers effectively cease.[197] That is, once administration commences a director is freed from his or her no-conflict duties. However, there may be situations where

---

[191] [2012] All ER (D) 57 (Dec).

[192] [2012] EWHC 363 (QB); [2012] All ER (D) 03 (Mar).

[193] In English law equity provided that a fiduciary obligation did not continue after the determination of the relationship which gave rise to it, so the duty to avoid conflicts ended on termination of the post of director: *Kingsley IT Consulting Ltd v McIntosh* [2006] EWHC 1288 (Ch); [2006] BCC 875 at [51]. For a discussion of the application of s 170(2) in this context, see *Killen v Horseworld Ltd* [2012] EWHC 363 (QB); [2012] All ER (D) 03 (Mar). Also, see *Safetynet Security Ltd Coppage* [2012] All ER (D) 57 (Dec).

[194] [2001] 2 BCLC 704.

[195] Ibid at 733.

[196] *CMS Dolphin Ltd v Simonet* [2002] BCC 600; *Wilkinson v West Coast Capital* [2005] EWHC 3009 (Ch); [2005] BCC 717 at [251].

[197] Insolvency Act 1986, Sch B1, paras 59–64.

directors are required to co-operate with the administrator and, in that situation, the no-conflict rule is likely to remain.[198] But all of the foregoing does not apply to the no-profit rule and in the situation where a director, after resigning, uses company property or information for his or her own benefit if it was obtained whilst a director, as the director is liable.[199]

XI THE EFFECTS OF A CONFLICT

9.73 In equity the effect of entering into a contract where one or more of the directors have a conflict is that the contract is voidable, at the option of the company,[200] and can be avoided without any consideration of the nature or fairness of the contract.[201] The company will lose the right to avoid under the usual equitable principles that apply to voidable contracts, namely: delay; affirmation; restitutio in integrum is not possible; or third parties acting in good faith have intervened. The miscreant director can be held to account for any profit which he or she has earned,[202] whether or not the company has suffered any loss,[203] or he or she might be held liable to pay damages if the company has sustained a loss. Interestingly, in *Murad v Al-Saraj*[204] Jonathan Parker LJ said that the no-conflict rule is neither compensatory nor restitutionary, but rather, it is designed to strip the fiduciary of the unauthorised profits he has made whilst he is in a position of conflict. The issue is discussed in more detail in **Chapter 15.**

XII OPTING OUT

9.74 Essentially in company law it is possible to see rules as either mandatory or enabling.[205] Where rules are enabling, companies can agree to opt out of their application. Some commentators advocate no mandatory rules for companies, or as few as possible so that companies are able to have complete freedom in entering into transactions, because those involved in and with companies are in a better position than government to decide what should

---

[198] D Prentice and J Payne 'Director's Fiduciary Duties' (2006) 122 LQR 558 at 559. This appears to be the case according to *Wilkinson v West Coast Capital* [2005] EWHC 3009 (Ch); [2005] BCC 717 at [251].

[199] *Ultraframe (UK) Ltd v Fielding* [2005] EWHC 1638 (Ch); [2006] FSR 17 at [1309] (there was an appeal only on the issue of costs – [2006] EWCA Civ 1660; [2007] 2 All ER 983). Also, see *Wilkinson v West Coast Capital* [2005] EWHC 3009 (Ch); [2005] BCC 717 at [251].

[200] *Guinness plc v Saunders* [1990] 2 AC 663.

[201] *Aberdeen Rly Co v Blaikie Bros* [1854] 2 Eq Rep 1281, [1854] 1 Macq 461, [1843–1860] All ER Rep 249 (HL) at 471–472.

[202] Ibid.

[203] *Consul Development Pty Ltd v DPC Estates Pty Ltd* (1974) 132 CLR 373 at 397 per Gibbs J.

[204] [2005] EWCA Civ 959 at [108].

[205] I M Ramsay 'Models of Corporate Regulation: the Mandatory/Enabling Debate' in C Rickett and R Grantham *Corporate Personality in the 20th Century* (Oxford, Hart Publishing, 1998) at 221; J Coffee 'The Mandatory/Enabling Balance in Corporate Law: An Essay on the Judicial Role' (1989) 89 Colum L Rev 1618; J Macey 'Corporate Law and Corporate Governance: A Contractual Perspective' (1993) 18 *Journal of Corporation Law* 185 at 186.

govern the relationships between a company and others. With that in mind we should ask whether companies can opt out of s 175 of the CA 2006 by including a clause in the articles preventing a conflict from actually arising in any shape or form. Koh thought that the director could do this as far as the old law was concerned.[206] There has been no little debate as to whether rules should be mandatory, but clearly there are many mandatory provisions in the CA 2006, and it would appear that s 175 is to be regarded as one of those. But, of course, the rule can effectively be side-stepped by board authorisation or authorisation under s 180(4) by the company.

XIII CONCLUSION

9.75   Section 175 seems to adopt in general terms the strict approach that was laid down by the mainstream of UK cases when operating under the no-conflict and no-profit rules. However, it does provide for directors to obtain authorisation for a conflict more easily, by gaining board approval rather than having to go to the general meeting.

9.76   The chapter has sought to provide a background to s 175 and to discuss how it is likely to be interpreted and applied. It has been submitted in this chapter that the new provision will prevent directors from holding more than one directorship in competing companies, without disclosing the conflicting roles and having them authorised by the boards of all companies involved. The next chapter continues to deal with s 175, but seeks to examine how it might apply practically in various situations.

---

[206] P Koh 'Once a Director, Always a Fiduciary?' (2003) 62 CLJ 403 at 415.

CHAPTER 10

AVOIDING A CONFLICT OF DUTY: APPLICATION

I INTRODUCTION

10.1 The last Chapter introduced s 175 of the CA 2006, the provision that makes it a duty for directors to avoid conflicts of interest. The makeup and general application of the provision was discussed, including consideration of whether directors holding directorships in competing companies are in breach of s 175 if they do not obtain the authorisation of the relevant boards, and the position of former directors. This chapter now takes s 175 and considers it in light of some kinds of situation that have regularly occurred in the past, and are likely to occur in the future. In particular the Chapter examines the position of directors who retire in order to establish a business in opposition to their former companies and/or take up business opportunities that might be available to the company. The kinds of situations discussed are not to be seen as exhaustive of the kinds of conflicts that might emerge. They are merely representative. One major aim of the Chapter is to ascertain when directors might be in breach of s 175. The largest part of the Chapter examines the exploitation of opportunities by directors in general, where those opportunities arose whilst they were acting as directors.

II RESIGNATION OF DIRECTORS

A Introduction

10.2 First we turn to focus on the situation where a director resigns from his or her company, with perhaps the intention of either establishing a competing business or exploiting a business opportunity of which he or she became aware while acting as a director. Undoubtedly, this has become a very important issue.

10.3 The first point that must be made in this area is that a director may resign if he or she chooses to do so even if it is likely to damage the company, as the power to resign is not a fiduciary power.[1] So resignation per se cannot constitute a breach of duty.

---

[1]   *CMS Dolphin Ltd v Simonet* [2001] 2 BCLC 704; [2002] BCC 200 at [87], [95].

10.4   In some circumstances there is likely to be some difficulty in establishing whether a director resigned in order to benefit himself or herself at the expense of the company. The problem primarily occurs where there are several reasons for resigning, and taking advantage of a benefit or establishing a competing business, is one of them. In this regard we are thrown back to the considerations we examined in **Chapter 5** in relation to the proper purpose test. We noted there the difficulty in establishing the purpose behind a director's particular course of action, particularly where directors might have a number of purposes in taking the action which is impugned. Would it be necessary, in the context of avoiding conflicts, for the company to prove, as it must with the proper purpose test, that in resigning it was the director's primary purpose to escape his or her obligations to the company? In *Island Export Finance Ltd v Umunna*[2] the judge accepted that it might have been in the mind of the director to take advantage of his position once he resigned, but it was not 'a primary or indeed an important motive.'[3] This suggests the need for consideration of the primary purpose of the director in resigning.

10.5   The obligations of a director may remain post-resignation, but when do the obligations end, as they must do at some point? In *Southern Real Estate Pty Ltd v Dellow and Arnold*[4] the South Australian Supreme Court said that: 'There is an obvious tension between a reasonable period [after leaving the company] during which the former director remains subject to his or her fiduciary duties, and freedom of competition.'[5] Obviously the longer the period after resignation before the former director begins in competition, the less likely there is a breach. Pearlie Koh has suggested a year,[6] but surely it is impossible to lay down any definite time. The period must depend on a number of elements, such as the type of company, the kind of business in which it is involved, the director's position in the company, and the ambit of operations of the competitor business that has been established.

10.6   Obviously there are a myriad of different situations that can exist as far as the resignation of directors is concerned. Koh notes that a director could be a controlling director with great power over what the company does, or he or she could be a director who has influence over certain customers or areas of the company's business. In these cases Koh submits that resignation should not put an end to a director's duties. But she contrasts these aforementioned situations with directors who have little control or influence in companies. In the latter case she argues that a director's obligations should end on resignation unless the company is able to prove that it has an interest in the opportunity exploited by the director subsequent to his or her resignation.[7] This is consistent with the general approach in *Foster Bryant Surveying Ltd v Bryant*.[8] In that case F set

---

2   [1986] BCLC 460.
3   Ibid at 476.
4   [2003] SASC 318; (2003) 87 SASR 1 at [29].
5   Ibid at [36].
6   P Koh 'Once a Director, Always a Fiduciary?' (2003) 62 CLJ 403 at 427.
7   Ibid at 425.
8   [2007] EWCA Civ 200; [2007] 2 BCLC 239.

up a company, F Ltd, with the assistance of a former client, A Ltd. A Ltd provided F Ltd with a lot of work and, as a result, it was F Ltd's largest client. A Ltd agreed to deal exclusively with F Ltd in relation to its surveying projects. F approached B to join him in the business. B agreed, subject to an agreement that provided he would work for five months unpaid and then receive 40 per cent of the company's shares. F and B were the only directors. Eventually, B's fiancée, soon to become wife, joined F Ltd as an employed surveyor. As time went on B and his wife increasingly performed the work given to F Ltd by A Ltd. The relationship between F and B deteriorated and F blocked B from using the company's bank account. F indicated he was dissatisfied with B's performance and B became very unhappy, leading him to apply for a job with another surveyor. F then made B's wife redundant and B decided to leave and advised F accordingly. B informed A Ltd by telephone that he had resigned and his wife had been made redundant. A few days later, W, A Ltd's managing director, asked B if he would work for A Ltd as he did not think that F could cope with all of A Ltd's work. During the period when B was working his resignation notice, A Ltd agreed with B that when A Ltd's exclusivity arrangement with F Ltd ended B would do all of A Ltd's work on a retainer basis plus salary. Until the end of his notice period B worked conscientiously but took no part in the management of F Ltd as a director. A few days before the end of B's notice period ended he incorporated a company that would do the work that he had agreed to do for A Ltd. The exclusivity arrangement terminated and A Ltd proposed that its work was to be divided between F Ltd and B's company. F refused and brought, on behalf of F Ltd, legal proceedings against B, B's company and A Ltd claiming that B had breached his duty to F Ltd by diverting a business opportunity. F Ltd failed at first instance, and on appeal failed again.

10.7 In the Court of Appeal Rix LJ (with whom Moses and Buxton LJJ agreed) considered the various situations that might arise where a director is resigning. At one extreme there is the director who has planned his or her resignation carefully having in mind the destruction of the company and with competition in view, or exploitation of its property in the form of business opportunities in which he or she was involved. At the other extreme is the situation where the defendant was a director in name only and had little or no involvement in the management of the company.[9] In the latter case the director will ordinarily not be liable, as was the situation with B in the case before the court.

10.8 The case of *Industrial Development Corp v Cooley*[10] undoubtedly falls into the former of the scenarios painted above, for he acted as the company's representative in negotiations entered into with those with whom the company might make contracts. What the defendant did in relation to negotiations was critical and his discretion was very wide; with aforethought the defendant

---

[9]   Ibid at [77].
[10]   [1972] 1 WLR 443.

planned his resignation, feigning illness, and was expecting to end up in competition with his former company. The case is discussed in detail in Chapter 9.[11]

B Exploiting opportunities

10.9 We deal with diverting and exploiting business opportunities in detail later in the Chapter so in this part we are more concerned with the situation where the resignation is precipitated by a desire to take up a business opportunity.

10.10 A person who has resigned as a director is able to take up any opportunity that arises after his or her resignation even if it is in the same area of business as that of his or her former company provided that it is not related in any way to information he or she obtained while a director, for the former director would, in the latter situation, be procuring an opportunity that may well come to the company.[12] The case of *Crown Dilmun v Sutton*[13] is a good example of the latter situation. In that case S was managing director of the two companies that had taken action against him. S had been instrumental in enhancing the reputation of the companies in the property market, and securing some lucrative developments. In 2002 he was approached in his capacity as managing director of the companies by H with the opportunity to buy, for £50m, the football stadium of Fulham Football Club. S diverted this opportunity to a company of which he was part, and away from the claimant companies. In 2003, after S had left the claimant companies, they became aware of S's involvement in the transaction and took proceedings against S. S was held liable.

10.11 In this case the opportunity was exploited while the director was in post, but if an opportunity arises whilst the director was in office and he or she exploits it after resignation, the issue is complex for it depends heavily on the facts. Generally speaking the director will not be able to exploit the opportunity.[14] The view of Laskin J of the Supreme Court of Canada in *Canadian Aero Service Ltd v O'Malley*[15] is apposite when he said[16] that a director is precluded from acting to divert a maturing business opportunity to himself:

> 'even after his resignation where the resignation may fairly be said to have been prompted or influenced by a wish to acquire for himself the opportunity sought by the company, or where it was his position with the company rather than a fresh initiative that led him to the opportunity which he later acquired.'

---

[11] Particularly at 9.7.
[12] *CMS Dolphin Ltd v Simonet* [2001] 2 BCLC 704; [2002] BCC 200.
[13] [2004] EWHC 52 (Ch); [2004] 1 BCLC 468.
[14] For example, see *CMS Dolphin Ltd v Simonet* [2001] 2 BCLC 704; [2002] BCC 200.
[15] (1973) 40 DLR (3d) 371.
[16] Ibid at 382.

10.12 This approach has been adopted in England.[17] In *Island Export Finance Ltd v Umunna*[18] the judge rejected the notion that a director, provided he or she does nothing contrary to the interests of the company while a director, may with impunity conceive the idea of resigning so that he or she may exploit some opportunity of the company and, having resigned, proceed to exploit it for himself or herself.[19] In *News International plc v Clinger*,[20] Lindsay J said: 'It would surely be an unacceptable incursion into a director's accountability if ... a director could avoid accountability by the simple expedient of ... resigning.'[21]

10.13 The company does not end its interest in an opportunity merely because the director has resigned. The nub of the issue is not when the director exploits the opportunity, but how and when the opportunity came to the director. If it came while he or she was acting as a director then he or she is obliged as a fiduciary not to exploit the opportunity as it belonged to the company to which the director owed fiduciary obligations. Whether the opportunity was one that related to the time when the former director was a director is a matter of evidence, and the longer the time between resignation and the making of the profit, post-resignation, the greater the chance, one would think, that the former director will not be held liable on the basis that it suggests that the opportunity was something that the director was not aware of whilst a director, or it did not arise as a result of his or her former role.[22] Perhaps the classic case is *IDC v Cooley*[23] (discussed in **Chapter 9**[24] and mentioned above) where the director was held liable. Here the director did not profit at all during his tenure as a director, but only exploited the opportunity following his resignation. The facts were set out earlier.[25] The director's wrongdoing had commenced while he was a director, but it only came to full fruition after he had left the company. This decision did not state that a director had to be in breach before he or she resigned. As Koh has stated:

> 'there must nevertheless be some concrete link between the acts or omissions of the director during the course of his directorship, and his resignation and the subsequent accrual of the benefit'.[26]

---

[17]   *Hunter Kane Ltd v Watkins* [2002] EWHC 186 (Ch) and referred to with apparent approbation *In Plus Group Ltd v Pyke* [2002] EWCA Civ 370; [2002] 2 BCLC 201 at [71]; *Foster Bryant Surveying Ltd v Bryant* [2007] EWCA Civ 200; [2007] 2 BCLC 239 at [8]. This was based on the statements of Laskin J in *Canadian Aero Service Ltd v O'Malley* (1973) 40 DLR (3d) 371 at 391.

[18]   [1986] BCLC 460.

[19]   Ibid at 480.

[20]   [1998] All ER (D) 592, unreported, 17 November 1998, ChD and referred to in B Hannigan *Company Law* (London, LexisNexis Butterworths, 2003) at 280.

[21]   Also, see *SEA Food International Pty Ltd v Lam* [1998] FCA 130; (1998) 16 ACLC 552 (Aust Fed Ct).

[22]   B Hannigan *Company Law* (London, LexisNexis Butterworths, 2003) at 280.

[23]   [1972] 1 WLR 443.

[24]   Particularly at **9.7**.

[25]   See ibid.

[26]   P Koh 'Once a Director, Always a Fiduciary?' (2003) 62 CLJ 403 at 418.

10.14 In *Kingsley IT Consulting Ltd v McIntosh*[27] Terence Mowschenson QC (sitting as a deputy judge of the High Court) said that a director could not set the groundwork for diverting a corporate opportunity whilst a director. Where a director had given notice of resignation, but was still in post, it is difficult to articulate the circumstances that would constitute a breach.[28] The matter would very much depend on the facts.[29] There are multifarious scenarios involving directors' resignations, so it is not possible to lay down firm statements. In such situations where there was not a clear line between where the defendant was a director, and where he or she was not a director, it was often hard to police and the courts have adopted a pragmatic approach, based on commonsense and the merits of the situation.[30] It was opined in *Foster Bryant Surveying Ltd v Bryant*[31] that this approach reflected the equitable principles on which the duty was based.

10.15 Whether Y, a director of company X, who resigns and takes up a an opportunity that she was led to because of her position as a director with X, rather than being a new initiative, is liable for a breach will depend on several factors, including: the post held; the nature of the opportunity; how developed the opportunity was; how specific was the opportunity and how the director related to it; the volume of knowledge possessed by the director; the circumstances in which the knowledge was obtained; whether the knowledge was special and private; how much time had elapsed after resignation when the alleged breach occurred; and the way in which the director left the company.[32] A director will not be in breach if either the company's hope of obtaining a benefit was not a maturing business opportunity and it was not seeking further business, or if the director's resignation was not prompted by a desire to acquire opportunities for himself or herself.[33] It is possible that the latter factor might have to be qualified to the extent that the defendant director had not acted in breach before the resignation.[34]

---

[27] [2006] EWHC 1288 (Ch); [2006] BCC 875 at [53].

[28] *Foster Bryant Surveying Ltd v Bryant* [2007] EWCA Civ 200; [2007] 2 BCLC 239 at [76].

[29] Ibid.

[30] Ibid.

[31] [2007] EWCA Civ 200; [2007] 2 BCLC 239.

[32] *Hunter Kane Ltd v Watkins* [2002] EWHC 186 (Ch) at [25] and referred to with apparent approbation *In Plus Group Ltd v Pyke* [2002] EWCA Civ 370; [2002] 2 BCLC 201 at [71]; *Foster Bryant Surveying Ltd v Bryant* [2007] EWCA Civ 200; [2007] 2 BCLC 239 at [8]. A number of the factors listed in the text were considered by the courts in *Island Export Finance Ltd v Umunna* [1986] BCLC 460; *CMS Dolphin Ltd v Simonet* [2001] 2 BCLC 704; [2002] BCC 200. The judge in *Hunter Kane* was relying heavily on statements in the judgment of Laskin J in *Canadian Aero Service Ltd v O'Malley* (1973) 40 DLR (3d) 371 at 391.

[33] *Hunter Kane Ltd v Watkins* [2002] EWHC 186 (Ch) at [25]. Note that in *Quarter Master UK Ltd v Pyke* [2004] EWHC 1815 (Ch); [2005] 1 BCLC 245 Paul Morgan QC (sitting as a deputy High Court judge) said that it was not clear whether liability attaches where the resignation was not prompted by a desire to take advantage of an opportunity, but advantage is taken later (at [73]).

[34] See *Quarter Master UK Ltd v Pyke* [2004] EWHC 1815 (Ch); [2005] 1 BCLC 245 at [73].

10.16 Perhaps one of the clearest instances of a resignation being prompted by an intention to exploit a corporate opportunity came in *IDC v Cooley*,[35] where, it will be recalled, the defendant diverted to himself a contract that it was his job to obtain for his company. This can be contrasted with the decision in *Island Export v Umunna*[36] where the defendant director was held not liable because his resignation was not in any way linked to exploiting a corporate opportunity.

C Establishing a competing business

10.17 Once he or she has resigned, a director is not prevented from utilising his or her skill and knowledge in relation to a competing business,[37] including the use of personal connections which have been made as a result of acting previously as a director,[38] but what we are really concerned with in this part of the Chapter is where the director takes steps towards competition while he or she is still a director. If the director does so, is he or she in breach of s 175 of the CA 2006?

1 Preliminary/preparatory steps

10.18 Until recently the unequivocal view taken in England was that the taking of preliminary steps towards establishing a competing business, and even the forming of an intention to compete, were permissible provided that there was no competition with the company before termination of the directorship.[39] Two cases will suffice as examples where directors were held not to be in breach when they set up businesses that could be said to be competing with their former companies. In *Island Export Finance Ltd v Umunna*[40] U was the managing director of IEF Ltd, the claimant company, which did business in West Africa. In 1976 U obtained a contract for IEF Ltd with the Cameroon's postal authorities for postal caller boxes. IEF Ltd did hope for subsequent contracts, but it had not received any indication from the postal authorities that they would be forthcoming. In 1977 U resigned as managing director due to his dissatisfaction with IEF Ltd and at the way he was being treated, including the lack of rewards coming his way from all of his work. At this time IEF Ltd was not actively pursuing further contracts with the Cameroon postal authority. U subsequently obtained for his own company, from the Cameroon's postal authorities, an order for postal caller boxes and for a travelling post box. IEF Ltd brought proceedings against U and his company on the basis that U, in entering into the contracts for his own company, had breached his fiduciary

---

[35] [1972] 1 WLR 443.
[36] [1986] BCLC 460.
[37] *British Midland Tool Ltd v Midland International Tooling Ltd* [2003] EWHC 466 (Ch); [2003] 2 BCLC 523 at [90], [93].
[38] *Hunter Kane Ltd v Watkins* [2002] EWHC 186 (Ch) and referred to with apparent approbation *In Plus Group Ltd v Pyke* [2002] EWCA Civ 370; [2002] 2 BCLC 201 at [71]; *Foster Bryant Surveying Ltd v Bryant* [2007] EWCA Civ 200; [2007] 2 BCLC 239 at [8].
[39] For example, see *Balston Ltd v Headline Filters Ltd* [1990] FSR 385 at 412.
[40] [1986] BCLC 460.

duty to IEF Ltd. It was argued, inter alia, by IEF Ltd that U remained under such a duty following his resignation as a director. However, the court found U not to be liable.

10.19 The second case involves a director that did more than the one in the previous case when still acting as a director. In *Balston Ltd v Headline Filters Ltd*,[41] B Ltd manufactured and sold glass microfibre filter tubes graded according to their air-flow resistance. Each grade of glass tube was manufactured using a particular recipe of glass fibres of different measurements. On 17 March H, a director of B Ltd, gave notice of termination of his employment. His employment was to expire on 11 July so that H would be able to exercise a share option on 9 July. On 14 March H had entered an agreement to take a lease over business premises. H said that he had not decided at that time whether to establish a business as a dealer in filtration products or as a manufacturer of filter tubes. On 16 April it was agreed that H would resign his post as a director of B Ltd and that he needed not to perform any duties after 18 April. H formally resigned his directorship on 18 April. On 25 April H purchased a shelf company, H Ltd. On 2 May H was contacted by someone who represented one of B Ltd's customers, C Ltd, concerning a meeting the previous day involving representatives of B Ltd and C Ltd at which B Ltd had informed C Ltd of a price increase for its filter tubes and had said that B Ltd was only prepared to continue to accept orders for those tubes for a limited period. Whilst in discussion with C Ltd's representative, H informed him that he was leaving B Ltd and that after 12 July he would be in a position to supply filter tubes to C Ltd. On 8 May H went to C Ltd's premises and C Ltd agreed to take filter tubes from H Ltd, to be delivered from 14 July for a period of about 18 months. After the discussions on 2 May with C Ltd's representative, H embarked on preparations for H Ltd to commence the manufacture of filter tubes on 14 July or as soon as possible thereafter. This involved purchasing equipment and the hiring of employees for H Ltd. Some of those employed had been employees and ex-employees of B Ltd. H commenced manufacture of sample tubes for C Ltd on 13 July. B Ltd instituted proceedings against H and H Ltd. It alleged, inter alia, breaches of H's fiduciary duty as a director. B Ltd's principal argument in relation to the claim, was that H had formed the intention to set up in competition with B Ltd while still a director of B Ltd, that the intention had caused a conflict between his personal interest and that of B Ltd, and that by failing to disclose that intention and the resulting conflict of interest H had acted in breach of his fiduciary duty. Falconer J indicated that H was not in breach when he decided to set up a competing business in the future and was not in breach in failing to disclose this to his company.[42] His Lordship said that directors would only be liable if their activities involved actual competition that were in conflict with particular interests of the company.[43] An interest in a business opportunity that was pertinent to the company's business would constitute a particular interest.[44]

---

[41]   [1990] FSR 385.
[42]   Ibid at 412.
[43]   Ibid.
[44]   Ibid.

10.20   The decision in *Balston Ltd v Headline Filters Ltd* was, arguably, more liberal than that in *Island Export Finance Ltd v Umunna*[45] given the fact that the director embarked on a number of substantial preparatory steps, such as the leasing of premises, to enable him to compete with his former company when his directorship terminated formally. The *Balston Ltd* approach was followed in *Coleman Taymar Ltd v Oakes*[46] where it was said that a director may form the intention or take preliminary steps to set up a competitive business when he or she leaves as a director, provided the competitive activity does not commence until his or her post is terminated.[47] The problem will often be whether the director has gone past the point of taking preliminary steps and actually commenced competition or is deemed to be in competition.[48] Where a director takes improper steps, that is, going past the taking of acceptable preliminary steps, before resigning to obtain a benefit in the future, the breach survives the resignation.[49] Clearly, the taking of preliminary steps that are permissible does not include taking advantage of corporate opportunities.[50]

10.21   Hart J in *British Midland Tool Ltd v Midland International Tooling Ltd*[51] took a more restrictive approach than the one adopted in *Balston Ltd*, a decision that his Lordship distinguished, when he said that in his view once a director forms the irrevocable intention to compete with his or her company, and has begun to take preparatory steps to effect that intention, the director should resign unless he or she is willing to disclose that intention to the company. In *British Midland Tool Ltd v Midland International Tooling Ltd* his Lordship held that the steps taken by the directors went beyond preliminary steps that were permissible when they not only failed to advise the company of the fact that they were aware of attempts by a competitor to poach members of the company's workforce, but actually promoted the success of the poaching process.[52] It is clear that seeking to poach staff of the company for a new venture, whilst still a director, is a breach.[53] In this case a director, X, had left the company and established a competing business, which he was entitled to do. But three other directors, who had agreed with X that they would join him in due course, were aware, while still acting as directors, that X was enticing employees away to come and join X's business, but they did not disclose this fact to their company. In addition, in *British Midland* a wider approach than that expressed in the past was posited, namely, holding that directors are not immune from liability simply by refraining from being involved in activities that are not in conflict with the particular interests of their company. Directors can

---

[45]   [1986] BCLC 460.

[46]   [2001] 2 BCLC 749.

[47]   *Coleman Taymar Ltd v Oakes* [2001] 2 BCLC 749 at 769. Also, see *LC Services Ltd v Brown* [2003] EWHC 3024 (QB).

[48]   *Coleman Taymar Ltd v Oakes* [2001] 2 BCLC 749 at 769.

[49]   *Canadian Aero Service Ltd v O'Malley* (1973) 40 DLR (3d) 371 at 382; *CMS Dolphin Ltd v Simonet* [2001] 2 BCLC 704; [2002] BCC 200 at [91].

[50]   *Kingsley IT Consulting Ltd v McIntosh* [2006] EWHC 1288 (Ch); [2006] BCC 875 at [53].

[51]   [2003] EWHC 466 (Ch); [2003] 2 BCLC 523 at [89].

[52]   Ibid at [90], [108].

[53]   *Balston Ltd v Headline Filters Ltd* [1990] FSR 385; *British Midland Tool Ltd v Midland International Tooling Ltd* [2003] EWHC 466 (Ch); [2003] 2 BCLC 523.

be regarded as culpable for omissions, such as not advising their company of something that was happening where it was contrary to the company's interests. In this case it was the poaching of staff.

10.22   Other cases have not gone as far as Hart J in *British Midland*, but the reasoning of Hart J was approved of by Etherton J (as he then was) in *Shepherds Investments Ltd v Walters*[54] to the point where the latter said that to the extent that the approach of Hart J and the approach in *Balston Ltd* differed, he favoured the former.[55] However, Etherton J opined that Hart J in *British Midland* might have been wrong when he said that a director must resign when he or she has formulated the intention to set up a competing business and, without disclosing his intentions to the company, begins to take preliminary steps.[56] The learned judge in *Balston Ltd* was only concerned with positive actions, while in *Shepherds Investments v Ltd v Walters* Etherton J was also concerned with omissions, namely non-disclosure.[57] This, as mentioned above, seemed to be a concern of Hart J in *British Midland* where it was said that omissions by a director mean that the director is as culpable as when he or she is undertaking positive actions. Etherton J in fact said that besides advising of their intention to leave, directors should disclose what preparatory steps they are taking and obtain permission before taking them,[58] but no other case has gone that far and it has been submitted that directors should not have to go to such an extent.[59] Simply directors will not seek permission because they know that permission will be refused.

10.23   An argument for adopting the rather strict approach of Hart and Etherton JJ is that given by Professor Peter Watts when he says, in relation to the director who has decided to leave and compete, that: 'His pending move is likely to colour every decision he takes, or omits to take, for the company, and by suppressing his intentions he inhibits the steps that the company might take to protect its goodwill, to his potential advantage.'[60] Other cases, while dealing with different facts and directorial goals, have also adopted a rather strict approach. For instance, in *Bhullar v Bhullar*[61] directors discovered that a property situated next to their company's property was for sale and they purchased it for themselves, at a time when the company had suspended its usual business of property development, which had been a decision made by the board. The court said that the directors should have made the purchase of the property for the company as it would make the company's land more valuable. Thus, the directors were held liable.

---

[54]   [2006] EWHC 836 (Ch).
[55]   Ibid at [105].
[56]   Ibid at [108].
[57]   P W Lee and L Ho 'A Director's Liberty to Compete' [2007] JBL 98 at 100.
[58]   [2006] EWHC 836 (Ch) at [132].
[59]   P Watts 'The Transition from Director to Competitor' (2007) 123 LQR 21 at 26.
[60]   Ibid at 24.
[61]   [2003] 2 BCLC 241; [2003] BCC 711.

10.24 Ascertaining whether a director has engaged in what might be regarded as a preparatory step towards competition is critical. For, under *British Midland,* engaging in preparatory steps would constitute a breach. Under the *Balston Ltd* approach, there must be a two-fold examination. First, the court must determine whether a director has undertaken preparatory steps to enable himself or herself to compete with the company and, second, if he or she has, do the steps go too far and consequently has the director in fact engaged in actual competition? Perhaps one of the reasons for supporting the *British Midland* approach is that there is a fine line between allowing directors to take preparatory action for competing with the company once the director has resigned on the one hand, and finding that the director has gone too far and breached his or her duty, on the other. So if one permits any preparatory action for competition a court is left with having to undertake some difficult analysis and knowing where to draw the line. The *British Midland* approach is more 'black and white', and produces greater certainty, much in the same way as the strict application of the no-conflict and no-profit rules did.

10.25 The point made by Etherton J in *Shepherds Investments,* and adverted to by other judges in earlier cases, is that 'the precise point at which preparations for the establishment of a competing business by a director becomes unlawful will turn on the actual facts of any particular case'.[62] So, for instance, in *Balston Ltd* the fact that the director only leased premises, and had not decided in which trade to engage once his directorship came to an end, was important. He had not gone as far as the directors in *Shepherds Investments*[63] who had decided to establish a business to compete with their company (S), and their business plan stated that the business would be established by core members of the management team of S who had identified significant improvements that could be made to S's business model. But, as we noted above, in *British Midland* the directors, who had taken preliminary steps to join a former director of the company in a competing business, were held liable notwithstanding the fact that they had refrained from actually being engaged in the poaching of staff from the company. The problem was that they remained silent concerning the fact that they knew that some of their colleagues were being approached by the former director. In *Coleman Taymar v Oakes*[64] the defendant did nothing which could properly be regarded as competing with his company before his contract terminated, but his actions in indirectly purchasing unwanted equipment belonging to the company went beyond the taking of preliminary steps towards the commencement of his competing business.[65]

10.26 The following have been regarded as permissible preparatory steps to competing with the company:

- having an intention to establish a competing business at some stage;

---

[62] [2006] EWHC 836 (Ch) at [108].
[63] Etherton J distinguished *Balston Ltd v Headline Filters Ltd* [1990] FSR 385.
[64] [2001] 2 BCLC 749.
[65] Ibid at [98].

- identifying suitable premises for the business and negotiating and signing a lease for the premises;

- purchasing a shelf company through which the future business will be conducted;

- negotiating and agreeing terms of employment with a competing business; and

- entering into heads of agreement for the formation of a company to carry on a competing business.[66]

10.27 Consulting professionals for advice might also be regarded as an action that does not constitute a breach.[67] Etherton J in *Shepherds Investments*[68] said that merely making a decision to establish a business at some future time and discussing that matter with friends and family did not constitute a breach.[69] Competition, which leads to a breach, has been said to be constituted by:

- actual competitive trading by way of the sale of goods or services of the type sold by the company;

- competitive tendering for customers or supplies; using a rival patent;

- competing for staff and equipment;

- compiling a list of the company's clients;

- preparing letters to the company's clients advising them of the fact that the director was leaving the company; and

- soliciting the custom of the company's clients.[70]

10.28 More recently H H Judge Hodge QC (sitting as a High Court judge) in *Berryland Books Ltd v BK Books Ltd*[71] said that:

'I am satisfied from the authorities cited to me that, when drawing the line between legitimate preparation for future competition and undertaking illegitimate competitive activity before an employee has left his employment, the law regards it as unlawful to undertake the following: (1) working for a competitor while still employed; (2) personally competing while still employed; (3) concealing or diverting matured or maturing business opportunities; (4) misusing the employer's property, including confidential information and assets; and (5) taking the steps

---

[66]   See *Balston Ltd v Headline Filters Ltd* [1990] FSR 385; *Framlington Group plc v Anderson* [1995] BCC 611; *Saatchi and Saatchi Company plc v Saatchi* (unrep, 13 February 1995, Ch D, Jonathan Parker J); *Coleman Taymar v Oakes* [2001] 2 BCLC 749; *Shepherds Investments Ltd v Walters* [2006] EWHC 836 at [108].

[67]   *Shepherds Investments Ltd v Walters* [2006] EWHC 836 (Ch) at [108].

[68]   Ibid.

[69]   Ibid.

[70]   See *Balston Ltd v Headline Filters Ltd* [1990] FSR 385 at 412; *Coleman Taymar Ltd v Oakes* [2001] 2 BCLC 749; *Framlington Group plc v Anderson* [1995] BCC 611; *Cranleigh Precision Engineering Ltd v Bryant* [1965] 1 WLR 1293; *Southern Real Estate Pty Ltd v Dellow and Arnold* [2003] SASC 318; (2003) 87 SASR 1; *Shepherds Investments Ltd v Walters* [2006] EWHC 836 (Ch) at [108].

[71]   [2009] EWHC 1877 (Ch); [2009] 2 BCLC 709.

necessary to establish a competing business so that it is 'up and running' or 'ready to go' as soon as the employee leaves his employment.'[72]

The judge's decision was reversed on appeal,[73] but on other grounds.

10.29 The reason for permitting directors to take preliminary steps is based in the public interest concept of not restraining trade.[74] In *Item Software (UK) Ltd v Fassihi*,[75] Arden LJ also indicated that the law should not be overly intrusive or else entrepreneurial activity would be deterred and this would not be beneficial. This issue is discussed later in relation to corporate opportunities.[76]

10.30 There might appear to be some inconsistency with allowing directors to take preparatory steps to set up a competing business and their duty to promote the success of the company, as found in s 172 of the CA 2006, so it might be that in a given case a court could find a director not liable under s 175, but liable under s 172. It is to be remembered that s 179 provides that more than one of the general duties owed by directors might apply to any given situation.

2 Other factors

10.31 Besides the nature of preparatory steps that have been taken, other factors have some apparent importance in determining whether a director is liable or not. For instance, *In Plus Group Ltd v Pyke*,[77] discussed later in the Chapter,[78] the Court of Appeal was heavily influenced by the fact that the defendant director had effectively been excluded from management of the company.[79] In *Foster Bryant Surveying Ltd v Bryant*,[80] discussed earlier,[81] the judges were influenced by the fact that the actions of the director (B) were virtually forced on him by the attitude of the other director (F), who had dismissed the defendant's wife from employment with the firm, and by the fact that when he resigned the defendant intended to find employment with a firm of chartered surveyors, and not set up in business for himself.[82] While serving out his notice period the defendant did not act as a director, for he was excluded from management, and he acted merely as an employed chartered surveyor.[83] Rix LJ appeared to approve of the comment of Lawrence Collins J in *CMS Dolphin v Simonet*[84] that there had to be a relevant connection between resignation and the obtaining of business in order for a director to be

---

[72] Ibid at [23].
[73] *Berryland Books v Baldwin* [2010] EWCA Civ 1440.
[74] *Balston Ltd v Headline Filters Ltd* [1990] FSR 385 at 412.
[75] [2004] EWCA Civ 1244 (2004) BCC 994; (2005) 2 BCLC 91 at [63] (CA).
[76] Below at **10.73–10.77**.
[77] [2002] EWCA Civ 370; [2002] 2 BCLC 201 (CA).
[78] Below at **10.66**.
[79] [2002] EWCA Civ 370; [2002] 2 BCLC 201 at [89].
[80] [2007] EWCA Civ 200; [2007] 2 BCLC 239.
[81] Above at **10.6**.
[82] *Foster Bryant Surveying Ltd v Bryant* [2007] EWCA Civ 200; [2007] 2 BCLC 239 at [79].
[83] Ibid at [80]–[83].
[84] [2001] 2 BCLC 704; [2002] BCC 200.

in breach.[85] Whilst it might appear that the court was also influenced by the fact that the director was approached by a third party to do some work for that third party, Buxton LJ said that a director is unable to use such a situation as a defence to a claim for breach of duty.[86] This is perhaps consistent with the fact that Sedley LJ in *In Plus Group* had said that if a director finds that he or she is accidentally in a conflict position the director must act appropriately and regularise[87] or abandon the conflict situation.[88]

10.32 An element that might be taken into consideration, when a competing business is established, is the length of time that has elapsed between the termination of a director's involvement with a company and the setting up of the competing business. One would think that the longer the time between resignation and the establishment of the business, post-resignation, the greater the chance that the former director will not be held liable on the basis that it suggests that the resignation and the setting up of the business were not linked. In *Southern Real Estate Pty Ltd v Dellow and Arnold*[89] a director took preliminary steps to establish a competing business by, inter alia, compiling a list of half of her company's clients, preparing letters to those clients advising them of the fact that she was departing the company and establishing another business, and soliciting their custom. The director resigned subsequently and the company sued her for breach of duty when she established the new business and received the custom of many of the company's clients. The court referred to *Robb v Green*[90] which indicated that a director may not solicit the custom of his or her company's clients whilst a director and for a reasonable period following resignation. The court did not need to consider what constituted a reasonable period, for the director commenced trading immediately on her termination of office. The court did not rely on the no-conflict rule, but found the director liable for breaching her duty of good faith.[91]

III EXPLOITATION

A Introduction

10.33 Section 175(2) of the CA 2006 is clearly designed to stop directors from exploiting three things: corporate property, corporate opportunities and corporate information. There has never been any real debate about the liability of company directors misappropriating and/or using company property, and most directors would be aware of their obligations in relation to property.[92] In

---

[85] *Foster Bryant Surveying Ltd v Bryant* [2007] EWCA Civ 200; [2007] 2 BCLC 239 at [88]. Also, see *Canadian Aero Service Ltd v O'Malley* (1973) 40 DLR (3d) 371 at 382.

[86] *Foster Bryant Surveying Ltd v Bryant* [2007] EWCA Civ 200; [2007] 2 BCLC 239 at [100].

[87] One assumes by advising his or her company.

[88] This point is made in T Singla 'The Fiduciary Duties of Resigning Directors' (2007) 28 Co Law 275 at 275.

[89] [2003] SASC 318; (2003) 87 SASR 1.

[90] [1895] 2 QB 1.

[91] [2003] SASC 318; (2003) 87 SASR 1 at [29], [32].

[92] Although, as Davies adroitly points out, any duty not to use company property is often

fact, directors assume the duties of a trustee in relation to company property.[93] There has been some uncertainty concerning the meaning of property of the company in this sort of context. Some items are clearly able to fall within the term. Examples are land, equipment and cars. But other items do cause some concern. Of particular concern are business opportunities and confidential information. There is authority for the proposition that both are to be regarded as property of the company.[94] However, it might be questionable to see an opportunity, such as a possible contractual arrangement, as property, although the Privy Council appeared to do so in *Cook v Deeks*.[95] In *Boardman v Phipps*[96] Lord Upjohn, although in dissent, disagreed that information should be seen as property for the purposes of fiduciary liability.[97] The case-law suggests that there is clearly overlap between property, information and opportunities and courts should not be concerned how they categorise what directors have obtained through their actions. Therefore, it is appropriate that the legislation, to be all-encompassing, covers property, information and opportunity. This drafting pre-empts any likely debates over whether opportunities and information constitute property of the company.

10.34 Little needs to be said specifically about property, as it has not tended to be a controversial issue. Most of what will be said relates to opportunities. As indicated above, in some cases opportunities have been classified as property,[98] and in *In Plus Group Ltd v Pyke*[99] Brooke LJ said that any profits obtained by a director from exploiting an opportunity are treated by equity as company property.

B Corporate information

10.35 Naturally, during his or her tenure a director will be aware of information that belongs to the company, such as client lists, or information about the company, such as a report by the company's solicitors on the legal implications of a particular business venture. A director cannot exploit this information. For instance, in *McNamara v Flavel*[100] a director of Duna World Pty Ltd, the name of which was a specialist trade name that had compiled significant goodwill, became aware of the fact that the company was in financial straits. The director was involved in a board decision that led to the change of the name of the company as part of a plan to reinvigorate the company's business. A little while later the director obtained the registration of

---

overlooked by directors in one person companies: P Davies *Gower and Davies' Principles of Modern Company Law* (London, Sweet and Maxwell, 7th edn, 2003) at 416.

[93] *J J Harrison (Properties) Ltd v Harrison* [2002] 1 BCLC 162 (CA).

[94] *CMS Dolphin Ltd v Simonet* [2001] 2 BCLC 704; [2002] BCC 200 at [96]; *Bhullar v Bhullar* [2003] 2 BCLC 241 (CA).at 256; *Quarter Master UK Ltd v Pyke* [2004] EWHC 1815 (Ch); [2005] 1 BCLC 245 at [72].

[95] [1916] AC 554.

[96] [1967] 2 AC 46.

[97] Ibid at 127–128.

[98] *CMS Dolphin Ltd v Simonet* [2001] 2 BCLC 704.

[99] [2002] EWCA Civ 370; [2002] 2 BCLC 201 at [71].

[100] (1988) 13 ACLR 619.

Duna World as a business name. A company, of which he was a director and shareholder, then commenced business under the business name, Duna World. Subsequently, the original company, entered liquidation and action was taken by the liquidator against the director for breach of duty. The South Australian Supreme Court found against the director on the basis that he used information about the company to get an advantage for himself. In like manner a director would be liable if he or she were to ascertain information that had come to the company and to use it. For instance, a director ascertains that in a call for tenders his company has made a tender of £100,000. The director then has his own family company submit a price slightly lower in order to secure the contract.

10.36 It has been suggested that the information that cannot be exploited is limited to that which equity would protect by way of injunction if a director sought to avail himself or herself of it.[101] This might well be an unreasonable limitation as to when companies can take action, but certainly the use of the information, one would think, would have to be regarded as improper.

10.37 A director is entitled to use information and methods gleaned from his or her time as a director, provided that this does not include trade secrets, which constitutes things like customer and supplier information.[102]

C Corporate opportunities

1 Introduction

10.38 Section 175(2) of the CA 2006 specifically states that the duty to avoid conflicts applies to the exploitation of corporate opportunities. Historically, this has been a very difficult area and has attracted a reasonable amount of academic comment. The Chapter has already broached some issues that pertain to this subject, such as the situation where directors retire in order to take advantage of an opportunity.

10.39 At the outset it must be noted that the courts have not defined what is actually meant by an opportunity in the context of this area of the law, but it is submitted that it is regarded broadly. Later the Chapter considers the kind of opportunities directors are not permitted to exploit.

10.40 What has to be taken into account in relation to the issue of exploitation of corporate opportunities is the fact that directors must ensure that they do their very best for their companies, and should only be able to avail themselves of opportunities that come to them as representatives of their company, in very limited circumstances, if at all. But, on the other side of the coin, the law must not hinder the entrepreneurial efforts of directors.

---

[101] *Rosetex Company Pty Ltd v Licata* (1994) 12 ACSR 779 at 784.
[102] *Item Software (UK) Ltd v Fassihi* [2004] EWCA Civ 1244 (2004) BCC 994; (2005) 2 BCLC 91; *Quarter Master UK Ltd v Pyke* [2004] EWHC 1815 (Ch); [2005] 1 BCLC 245.

10.41   In equity if a director diverted an opportunity to himself or herself while in post he or she could be liable under either the no-conflict rule or the no-profit rule (and perhaps sometimes under both), whereas if he or she is no longer a director it would only be the no-profit rule,[103] for there could no longer be any conflict. Now, with codification, the actions would generally be caught by s 175 of the CA 2006. The corporate opportunity doctrine has developed as a specific application of the no-profit rule, as it really simply involves a director exploiting an opportunity to make a profit.

10.42   Section 175(2) of the CA 2006 obviously encapsulates what was one aspect of the no-profit rule, namely that directors are not permitted to usurp an opportunity that effectively belongs to the company. A classic instance of a case where directors did this, and the kind of thing that s 175(2) is seeking to stop, is *Cook v Deeks*,[104] a decision of the Privy Council, on appeal from Canada. This case is a leading example of the application of the no-profit rule. It will be remembered that in this case three directors of a four director company, X, which was involved in the construction of railways, negotiated on behalf of X to secure some construction contracts. During the course of their negotiations, the directors arranged for the contracts to be performed by them rather than X. The directors formed a new company especially to carry out the contracts. The fourth director of X learned of this, but the other three controlled X and passed a resolution at a general meeting ratifying what had been done. They then resigned from the board of X. The fourth director brought proceedings as a minority shareholder to enforce the rights of X. The upshot was that the Privy Council held that the three directors were liable as they had profited from their roles as directors, and they held the contracts in trust for X.

10.43   What has been of major debate is what kinds of opportunities, if any, are immune from the application of the no-profit rule. It has been a vexed question. The fundamental issue is whether a gain made by a person has resulted from opportunities or knowledge flowing from his or her role as a fiduciary. Professor Brenda Hannigan puts it well, as far as the no-profit rule was concerned, when she states:[105]

> 'In essence, what the courts are attempting to do is to identify an ambit of opportunity emanating from the company which comprises its circle of activities which the directors must not exploit for their personal benefit. As directors, they are trustees of the company's property and opportunities and the protection of that property and opportunities is expressed in terms of a fiduciary duty on directors not to profit from their position or from opportunities or knowledge resulting from it.'

10.44   Where a director in post has exploited a clear opportunity that was his or her company's, then s 175(2) will apply. The difficult situations, and the ones

---

[103]   *Ultraframe (UK) Ltd v Fielding* [2005] EWHC 1638 (Ch); [2006] FSR 17 at [269].
[104]   [1916] AC 554. A more recent example of a clear breach is found in *Cranleigh Precision Engineering Ltd v Bryant* [1965] 1 WLR 1293.
[105]   B Hannigan *Company Law* (LexisNexis Butterworths, 2003) at 281.

that are most likely to lead to argument, are where a company has decided not
to pursue a particular opportunity, it cannot pursue it, or it has no interest in
the opportunity. These kinds of cases seem to be addressed in *Warman
International Ltd v Dwyer*,[106] where it was said that '… it is no defence that the
plaintiff [the company] was unwilling, unlikely or unable to make the profits
for which an account is taken …'.

10.45 As will become patently clear, the difficulty is to know where to draw
the line. On occasions the courts have drawn the line at a point where some
would see it as being harsh, while in other cases courts have been more liberal.

10.46 Another difficulty, for the court, may well be ascertaining what really
occurred. In many cases the only ones who can give evidence on particular
issues are the defendants and/or their associates.[107] Can the court rely on the
evidence as there is a chance that it will be couched in a way that will benefit
the case of the defendants? Of course, judges have to evaluate the testimony of
witnesses carefully and decide who is and who is not to be believed on
particular issues.

10.47 There have been two approaches invoked by the courts in dealing with
the issues at hand. Before dealing with those, another aspect of corporate
opportunities needs to be mentioned in passing. If a director becomes aware of
an opportunity, which he or she is not minded to exploit for his or her benefit,
but the director does not inform the company of the opportunity, he or she
might well be liable for breach of either or both the duty of care in s 174 of the
CA 2006 or the duty to promote the success of the company in s 172(1).

2 A strict approach

10.48 The actions of the directors in *Cook v Deeks*,[108] and discussed above,
involved a blatant attempt to exploit a company opportunity. But, historically,
the law is so strict that the courts have tended to be suspicious of any
directorial benefits and the no-profit rule caught situations where the directors
acted quite properly and certainly not fraudulently. This is probably best
illustrated in the case of *Regal (Hastings) Ltd v Gulliver*[109] to which we will
come to shortly, and which was considered in the previous Chapter in some
depth.[110]

---

[106] [1995] HCA 18; (1994-1995) 182 CLR 544 at 558.
[107] For example, see *Peso Silver Mines Ltd v Cropper* [1965] 56 DLR (2d) 117.
[108] [1916] AC 554.
[109] [1967] 2 AC 134.
[110] Above at paras **9.17–9.18**.

10.49 The law is so strict in this area that it has been described as 'draconian'.[111] Sir W M James LJ in *Parker v McKenna*[112] emphasised the strictness of the rule when he said[113] that:

> 'I do not think it is necessary, but it appears to me very important, that we should concur in laying down again and again the general principle that in this Court no agent in the course of his agency, in the matter of his agency, can be allowed to make any profit without the knowledge and consent of his principal; that that rule is an inflexible rule, and must be applied inexorably by this Court, which is not entitled, in my judgment, to receive evidence, or suggestion, or argument as to whether the principal did or did not suffer any injury in fact by reason of the dealing of the agent; for the safety of mankind requires that no agent shall be able to put his principal to the danger of such an inquiry as that.'

10.50 As Deane J of the Australian High Court noted in *Kak Loui Chan v Zacharia*[114](*Chan*), in giving the leading judgment:[115]

> 'Many of the statements of the general principle requiring a fiduciary to account for a personal benefit or gain are framed in absolute terms – "inflexible," "inexorably", "however honest and well-intentioned", "universal application" – which sound somewhat strangely in the ears of the student of equity and which are to be explained by judicial acceptance of the inability of the courts, "in much the greater number of cases", to ascertain the precise effect which the existence of a conflict with personal interest has had upon the performance of fiduciary duty.'

10.51 The rule is so inflexible that the courts do not investigate the facts of the conflict, for the breach occurs as soon as conflict arises.[116] The reason for this inflexibility is the concern that the beneficiary in a fiduciary relationship should not have to prove loss.[117] A classic instance of this is the case of *Regal (Hastings) Ltd v Gulliver*[118] where the company had not suffered any loss, but was entitled to recover from the directors in any event. The facts and decision were discussed earlier.[119] The House of Lords, significantly, made the point that it did not matter that the company was in no position to take advantage of the business opportunity which the directors took up. Importantly, Lord Russell said that the opportunity and special knowledge needed to obtain the shares had come to the directors in their role as directors, and, therefore, as fiduciaries. All of this was notwithstanding that the directors had acted at all

---

[111] G Sullivan 'Going It Alone – Queensland Mines v Hudson' (1979) 42 LQR 711 at 711.

[112] (1874) LR 10 Ch App 96.

[113] Ibid at 124–125.

[114] (1984) 154 CLR 178.

[115] [1984] HCA 36; (1984) 154 CLR 178 at [30].

[116] *IDC v Cooley* [1972] 1 WLR 443.

[117] J Lowry and J Sloszar 'Judicial Pragmatism: Directors' Duties and Post-resignation Conflicts of Duty' [2008] JBL 83 at 84. See *Furs Ltd v Tomkies* (1936) 54 CLR 583; *Fexuto Pty Ltd v Bosnjak Holdings Pty Ltd* [2001] NSWCA 97; (2001) 37 ACSR 672.

[118] [1967] 2 AC 134 (HL). The case has been the subject of many critiques. For a recent one, see C Sing 'Avoidance of Loss: Regal Hastings and the No Conflict Rule' (2013) 34 *Company Lawyer* 73.

[119] Above at **9.17–9.18**.

times in good faith[120] and that without the directors using their own money to purchase shares the company could not take on the project. This case, while being the leading case in the area, is also probably the best instance of the strictness of the rule.

10.52   In this case Lord Russell succinctly summarised the position at law:[121]

> 'The rule of equity which insists on those, who by use of fiduciary position make a profit, being liable to account for that profit, in no way depends on fraud, or absence of bona fides, or upon such questions or considerations as whether profit would or should otherwise have gone to the plaintiff, or whether the profiteer was under a duty to obtain the source of the profit to the plaintiff, or whether he took a risk or acted as he did for the benefit of the plaintiff, or whether the plaintiff has in fact been damaged or benefited by his action. The liability arises from the mere fact of a profit having, in the stated circumstances, been made.'

10.53   At its strictest the *Regal Hastings* approach is that if an opportunity occurs that is within the ambit of protected activities, any claim on the part of the directors that they acted in good faith or that the company could not take up the opportunity, will fail. This approach has the attraction of certainty[122] and simplicity of application, but, of course, it lacks flexibility. The idea behind prohibiting exploitation is to ensure that directors are not unjustly enriched. But in some cases the company will be unjustly enriched. This is the objectionable aspect of the judgment in *Regal Hastings*, according to Davies, for the company's claim 'was wholly unmeritorious'.[123] The purchasers of the company received an undeserved windfall, yet the directors did all the work and took on the extra risk. What is perhaps ironic in *Regal Hastings* is that the company made profits only because of the willingness of the directors to purchase shares in the subsidiary company. Yet, as Davies observes, only Lord Porter seemed to be disturbed by this fact.[124] Also, and not taken into account, the directors held a majority of the shares in the company and could have easily passed a ratification resolution in the general meeting. The fact that resolving the circumstances which the case addressed is not easy is demonstrated by the fact that the court at first instance and the Court of Appeal (unanimously) found for the directors, although it is fair to say that the House of Lords was unanimous in reversing the earlier opinions. It is probably surprising that the directors did not seek, and were not granted, relief under the then equivalent of s 1157 of the CA 2006 (discussed in **Chapter 17**), given the fact that they appeared to have acted honestly and reasonably. One matter that is often overlooked is that the subsidiary could have secured the leases without an issue of shares to the directors if the directors had given guarantees concerning the payment of rent until the issued capital of the subsidiary reached £5,000. So there was a way of securing the leases other than the directors

---

[120]   [1967] 2 AC 134 (HL) at 144.

[121]   Ibid at 144–145.

[122]   B Hannigan *Company Law* (London, LexisNexis Butterworths, 2003) at 289.

[123]   P Davies *Gower and Davies' Principles of Modern Company Law* (London, Sweet and Maxwell, 7th edn, 2003) at 417.

[124]   Ibid.

taking shares in the subsidiary. Taking the share purchase option meant that the company had been deprived of the power to acquire the shares. This would result in the company's shareholders only receiving a reduced proportion of the eventual sale price of the two cinemas.[125] It might be said, of course, that the directors should not have been obliged to place themselves under the risks inherent in the giving of guarantees.

10.54 Several cases that followed *Regal Hastings* in time adopted a similar approach. For instance, *IDC v Cooley*[126] can also be viewed as an example of the strict approach, despite the fact that the director did not act in good faith, unlike the directors in *Regal Hastings*, and the opportunity was never presented to the company. Cooley had not done his case any good by lying to his company when he resigned. It is argued by some that anything less than implementation of the strict approach in absolute terms might tempt directors to fail to do all that they can to obtain an opportunity for their company.[127]

10.55 The fact that the strict approach appears to hold sway is manifested by the comments of the Court of Appeal in *Towers v Premier Waste Management Ltd*.[128] The Court made it plain that a defendant cannot plead in defence to a conflict claim that he or she did not make a significant profit or that it had not been established that he or she had obtained a valuable benefit. Also, it was not necessary for the claimant to prove fault on the part of the defendant or that the company had suffered a loss.

3 A more liberal/flexible approach

10.56 Notwithstanding the general strictness of the law there are indications of a more liberal, or, at least, a more flexible, approach from some courts. The most prominent cases are usually seen as the Canadian cases of *Peso Silver Mines Ltd v Cropper*[129] and *Canadian Aero Service Ltd v O'Malley*,[130] and the Australian case of *Queensland Mines Ltd v Hudson*,[131] but as we will see there are indications of a more liberal approach in some English decisions.

10.57 In *Peso Silver Mines Ltd v Cropper*,[132] P Ltd owned land next to some mineral claims. The claims were owned by X who offered to sell them to P Ltd. P Ltd's board of directors, after due investigation and because of several factors such as it was felt that the company had enough land, the state of the development of the claims and the amount asked for the claims, rejected the offer by X. Then X approached C, a director of P Ltd, and offered the claims to him. A company incorporated by C and other directors of P Ltd purchased the

---

[125] At 146.
[126] [1972] 1 WLR 443.
[127] B Hannigan *Company Law* (London, LexisNexis Butterworths, 2003) at 288.
[128] [2011] EWCA Civ 923; [2012] 1 BCLC 67; [2012] BCC 72.
[129] [1966] 56 DLR (2d) 117 and on further appeal at [1966] 58 DLR 1.
[130] (1973) 40 DLR (3d) 371.
[131] (1978) 52 ALJR 399 at 401 (PC).
[132] [1966] 56 DLR (2d) 117 and on further appeal at [1966] 58 DLR 1.

claims. Subsequently, a sale of control of P Ltd was effected, with the directors who set up the company to take the claims leaving the board. The new management that had been installed in P Ltd initiated legal proceedings against the former directors. P Ltd claimed that C was in breach of his duty to it by making profits from an opportunity, namely taking up the mineral claims first offered to P Ltd. At first instance the director succeeded and P Ltd appealed to the British Columbia Court of Appeal.[133] In a majority decision the appeal was dismissed. P Ltd appealed again, this time to the Supreme Court of Canada. The Supreme Court unanimously dismissed the company's appeal.[134]

10.58 In finding that the former director was not in breach of his duty to the company, the Supreme Court of Canada essentially agreed with the court below. In his leading judgment in the British Columbia Court of Appeal Bull JA pointed to the findings of fact that C and the other directors of P Ltd acted in good faith, solely in the interests of the company and with sound business reasons in rejecting the offer made to P Ltd by X. There was no suggestion in the evidence that the offer to the company was accompanied by any confidential information unavailable to any prospective purchaser or that C had access to any information by reason of his office. The evidence was that the company received on average two to three offers to purchase claims per week. Bull JA found, applying what was said in *Regal Hastings*, that when the offer was presented to C it did not come to him in his capacity as director, and he could be liable if the opportunity came to him only by reason of the fact that he was a director of P Ltd.[135]

10.59 Bull JA was of the view that the principles developed in trust law and applied in the corporate setting, and acceded to by *Regal Hastings*, must be interpreted in light of modern practices.[136] C, in *Peso Silver*, was held to have acted in good faith,[137] but so had the directors in *Regal Hastings*. Importantly, in *Peso Silver* the board, at a properly constituted board meeting, made a decision in good faith and after obtaining professional advice that the offer to buy the claims should not be accepted. It was only after this point that C participated in the transaction that was challenged. Bull JA acknowledged that if the transaction had occurred at a point when no offer had been made to P Ltd or the offer was still being considered by the company, then C may well have been liable. The problem that this case throws up is the difficulty for courts of ascertaining whether the company's rejection of an opportunity was bona fide or not.

10.60 A little later the Supreme Court of Canada was again laying down a somewhat more liberal approach than that found in England. In *Canadian Aero Service Ltd v O'Malley*[138] C Ltd was involved in topographical mapping and

---

[133] Reported at [1966] 56 DLR (2d) 117.
[134] Reported at [1966] 58 DLR 1.
[135] [1966] 56 DLR (2d) 117 at 157.
[136] Ibid at 155.
[137] Ibid.
[138] (1973) 40 DLR (3d) 371.

geophysical exploration. O had been a part of C Ltd in one capacity or another for many years and became president and CEO of it in due course. Z was another director of C Ltd. O and Z formed a company, T, shortly before they resigned from C Ltd. For a number of years C Ltd had, through the efforts of O and Z, among others, been pursuing a contract in Guyana (to be sponsored by the Canadian government as part of its overseas aid) and doing a lot of preparatory work. It was thought that C Ltd had a very good chance of securing the contract. However, very soon after the incorporation of T, and after the resignation of O and Z from C Ltd, T obtained the contract. C Ltd brought proceedings against O and Z for breach of duty.

10.61   The court seemed to endorse the 'pervasiveness of a strict ethic in this area of the law,'[139] and Laskin J, in delivering the judgment of the Court, said[140] that:

> 'In my opinion, this ethic disqualifies a director or senior officer from usurping for himself or diverting to another person or company with whom or with which he is associated a maturing business opportunity which his company is actively pursuing; he is also precluded from so acting even after his resignation where the resignation may fairly be said to have been prompted or influenced by a wish to acquire for himself the opportunity sought by the company, or where it was his position with the company rather than a fresh initiative that led him to the opportunity which he later acquired.'

10.62   However, what was said by the learned judge later in his judgment appeared to provide more latitude to directors. Laskin J said that he did not regard the principles stated in *Regal Hastings,* and which grew out of the early cases dealing with fiduciaries (and not directors), as providing 'a rigid measure'.[141] He went on to say that in his view neither the conflict test nor the test of accountability for profits deriving solely from holding the post of director should be seen as 'the exclusive touchstones of liability'.[142] The judge felt that new fact situations might well demand a 'reformulation of existing principle to maintain its vigour in the new setting'.[143]

10.63   Nevertheless, the Supreme Court found against O and Z as they diverted a maturing business opportunity from C Ltd to T.

10.64   In *Queensland Mines Ltd v Hudson*[144] H, a director of Q and acting in that capacity, entered into negotiations for mining concessions from the State of Tasmania. He applied for the licences in his name, but he was supported, and funded by, Q, and when the licences were awarded he acknowledged that he held them on behalf of Q. When it was indicated to him by Q that the company could not and would not proceed, because of financial constraints, and it gave

---

[139] Ibid at 382.
[140] Ibid.
[141] Ibid at 383.
[142] Ibid.
[143] Ibid.
[144] (1978) 52 ALJR 399 (PC).

its approval to H taking the licences, H set up a company that took the licences forward. H took on considerable risk and eventually his company entered into arrangements with an American company whereby H's company would be paid substantial royalties. Q subsequently took proceedings against H for breach of duty, claiming all profits obtained from the licences. The action went to the Privy Council from the New South Wales Supreme Court. The Judicial Committee accepted the fact that the opportunity to earn the royalties initially arose from H's position as a director of Q.[145] But the Judicial Committee held that because the board of Q, when fully informed as to all the facts, decided to renounce all interest in the concessions and approved of H going on alone and taking over the venture for his own account, H was not liable.[146] It is noteworthy that the board did not formally resolve that H could take the licences, and H actually participated in the decision-making and had significant influence at board level.[147] The general meeting did not provide approval for H to take the licences on his own account.

10.65 The English case of *Island Export Finance Ltd v Umunna*,[148] the facts of which were set out earlier,[149] might be regarded as an instance of a case where a more liberal approach was implemented. In this case the court did not find the director liable in doing business with a third party, who had previously had dealings with his company because he was not, either when he resigned from his company or when he was approached by the third party (a few months following his resignation from his company), seeking to foster business relations with the third party. The judge was influenced by the fact that the company was not actively seeking further contracts of the kind which it claimed the former director had improperly diverted to himself. Also, the judge rejected the submission of counsel for the company that, because a director is in a fiduciary position, after cessation of his or her appointment, he or she is precluded from exploiting any market of which he or she has become aware while employed.[150]

10.66 There is even evidence of a less harsh trend in some recent English cases and, perhaps, notably in the Court of Appeal decision in *In Plus Group Ltd v Pyke*.[151] In this case M and P established three companies in which they were equal shareholders and directors. One of the companies in the group took over P's existing business of refurbishing commercial premises. P transferred, as a loan, £200,000 to one of the other companies, IP. IP was involved in working on office interiors, and its main work came from doing business with C Ltd, with whom contact had been made earlier by P. Due to a number of events, the working relationship between P and M gradually broke down. P did not receive any remuneration and was not able to obtain information concerning accounts

---

[145] Ibid at 403.
[146] Ibid.
[147] G R Sullivan 'Going It Alone – Queensland Mines v Hudson' (1979) 42 MLR 711 at 713.
[148] [1986] BCLC 460.
[149] Above at **10.18**.
[150] [1986] BCLC 460 at 483.
[151] [2002] EWCA Civ 370; [2002] 2 BCLC 201.

and the companies' financial positions. C Ltd stopped giving work to IP and disputed amounts alleged to be owed to IP. P established his own interiors company and after some months began doing work for C Ltd. The group of companies initiated legal proceedings against P claiming the profits made by P and his new company. P succeeded at first instance, and on the appeal by the companies. The Court of Appeal referred to the circumstances of the case as 'unusual'[152] and placed emphasis on the fact that P had been excluded from the companies for more than six months prior to taking on work from C Ltd.[153]

10.67 Subsequently, the Court of Appeal in *Foster Bryant Surveying Ltd v Bryant*[154] said that the application of the principles in some circumstances required care and sensitivity as to the facts and other principles such as the freedom of people to compete in business where there is no misuse of company property whether in the form of business opportunities or trade secrets.[155] The court felt that some flexibility had to be shown in the circumstances before it, namely where a director is retiring and seeking to set up a competing business.[156]

10.68 While some, such as Norris JA in his dissenting judgment in *Peso Silver Mines Ltd v Cropper*,[157] call for the maintenance of the strict standard,[158] others believe that it is time to consider a more liberal approach. In *Murad v Al-Saraj*[159] Arden LJ mused that it may be time for the courts to revisit the operation of the inflexible rule of equity where it appears to be harsh, such as where the trustee has acted in perfect good faith and without any deception or concealment, and in the belief that he or she was acting in the best interests of the beneficiary.[160] Her Ladyship stated that: 'it would not be impossible for a modern court to conclude as a matter of policy that, without losing the deterrent effect of the rule, the harshness of it should be tempered in some circumstances'.[161] In the same case, Jonathan Parker LJ agreed with her Ladyship,[162] although he felt that the day had not arrived when there should be a change of direction.[163] The decision in *Peso Silver* adverted to the fact that the world has changed and a more liberal approach might be needed,[164] and this

---

[152] For example, ibid at [94].

[153] Dignam and Lowry mused that it was curious that the court did not find the director liable but excused him from liability under s 727 of the CA 1985 (now s 1157 of the CA 2006): *Company Law* (OUP, 5th edn, 2008) at 331.

[154] [2007] EWCA Civ 200; [2007] 2 BCLC 239.

[155] Ibid at [76].

[156] Ibid.

[157] [1966] 56 DLR (2d) 117 at 139.

[158] Norris JA thought that the complexities of modern commercial life was a good reason for retaining the strict approach (ibid).

[159] [2005] EWCA Civ 959.

[160] However, in *Wrexham AFC Ltd v Crucialmove Ltd* [2006] EWCA Civ 237; [2007] BCC 139 at [51] Sir Peter Gibson, with whom Dyson LJ agreed, did not think that there could be any tempering of the harshness of the principle by any court below the House of Lords.

[161] [2005] EWCA Civ 959 at [82].

[162] Ibid at [121].

[163] Ibid at [122].

[164] [1966] 56 DLR (2d) 117 at 155.

was some 40 years ago! There is academic opinion that supports such an approach.[165] The fact is that the inflexible rule is based on rules developed in the eighteenth century whereas the courts today are confronted with the commercial world of the twenty-first century. The downside in adopting a more liberal approach, for some commentators, is that monitoring costs will increase.[166] It might also mean that it might not be as clear where the line of acceptability is actually located.

10.69 The decisions in *In Plus Group* and *Foster Bryant,* as well as others, might be evidence of the judiciary relinquishing strict formulations in favour of a more practical approach. However, this is not to suggest that the rules are going to be bent substantially, if at all, for in the latter case Rix LJ, after he recognised the principles relating to the no-conflict and no-profit rules were 'exacting' and 'exactingly enforced,' said that he doubted whether it remains true to say that the principles are inflexible and to be applied 'inexorably,'[167] and said that he favoured a 'commonsense and merits-based approach'.[168]

10.70 Despite the fact that some courts have adopted an apparently more liberal or flexible approach, the strict approach of the courts remains evident in some recent cases. Take, for instance, the cases of *Gencor ACP Ltd v Dalby*[169] and *Bhullar v Bhullar.*[170] Also, the British Columbia Court of Appeal in *Canadian Metals Exploration Ltd v Wiese*[171] indicated, without qualification, approval of *Regal Hastings*, even though it has been suggested that the Canadian approach is more liberal.

10.71 In *Wiese, Peso Silver* was distinguished.[172] The former involved Canadian Metals Exploration Ltd (the company), a mining exploration company, which had mineral claims, known as the Turnagain project, over a large mineral deposit in British Columbia. The company had been conducting a drilling programme on the deposit for many years. W was the directing mind of the company until early 2004, when he was replaced by J. Prior to J becoming involved in the company, W had another person, S, stake, on his behalf and that of Q Ltd, a company he controlled, claims adjacent to and a few miles away from the company's claims. The company sought an order that the title of the claims staked by W be transferred to it on the basis that he had breached his fiduciary obligation to the company. W's defence was that the company agreed he could stake the disputed claims at a meeting in May 2003 that was not formally convened and for which there were no minutes. The participants at the meeting gave divergent views as to what occurred at the meeting. The company maintained that it was decided that W would have S

---

[165] For example, see P Chew 'Competing Interests in the Corporate Opportunity Doctrine' (1989) 67 *North Carolina Law Review* 435 at 448.
[166] P Koh 'Once a Director, Always a Fiduciary?' (2003) 62 CLJ 403 at 410.
[167] [2007] EWCA Civ 200; [2007] 2 BCLC 239 at [76].
[168] Ibid.
[169] [2000] 2 BCLC 734.
[170] [2003] 2 BCLC 241; [2003] BCC 711 (CA).
[171] [2007] BCCA 318 (CanLII) at [28].
[172] Ibid at [32].

stake claims for the company while W said that it was agreed that W could instruct S to stake the claims for W and Q Ltd. Gerow J upheld the claims to be a corporate opportunity for the company. Her Honour added that adjacent unstaked mineral claims are somewhat of a unique corporate opportunity in that they do not yet belong to the company, they could be lost at the instance of staking by a third party, and they are analogous to a contract being pursued by a company. Her Honour referred to them as 'an emerging corporate opportunity'.[173] She held that there was no rejection of the corporate opportunity by the company.[174]

10.72 One of the problems with diluting the strict approach is that this might tempt directors to shift from impartial positions and to favour their own interests. Specifically, they might be moved to decide that the company should not or could not embrace a particular opportunity, and pursue the opportunity for themselves. This might well have occurred in *Wiese*.

4 Restraint of trade and hindering entrepreneurialism

10.73 The courts will not stop directors from exploiting general knowledge and expertise that they have gained whilst acting as directors on the basis that this would be tantamount to restraint of trade.[175] While the company has the right to expect a director to discharge his or her duties, the courts have indicated that the director has the right to earn a living.[176] How he or she goes about doing that could be critical.

10.74 In *Island Export Finance Ltd v Umunna*[177] Hutchison J said[178] that:

> 'It would, it seems to me, be surprising to find that directors alone, because of the fiduciary nature of their relationship with the company, were restrained from exploiting after they [sic] had ceased to be such any opportunity of which they had acquired knowledge while directors. Directors, no less than employees, acquire a general fund of knowledge and expertise in the course of their work, and it is plainly in the public interest that they should be free to exploit it in a new position... it is an altogether different thing to hold former directors accountable whenever they exploit for their own or a new employer's benefit information which, while they may have come by it solely because of their position as directors of the plaintiff company, in truth forms part of their general fund of knowledge and their stock-in-trade.'

---

[173] Ibid at [23].
[174] Ibid at [32].
[175] *Island Export Finance Ltd v Umunna* [1986] BCLC 460 at 482; *Balston Ltd v Headline Filters Ltd* [1990] FSR 385 at 412. See *Dranez Amstalt v Hayek* [2002] EWCA Civ 1729 [2003] 1 BCLC 278 (CA) for a case involving specialist ability, where it was felt that it was in the public interest that this ability was exploited.
[176] For example, see *Foster Bryant Surveying Ltd v Bryant* [2007] EWCA Civ 200; [2007] 2 BCLC 239 at [48].
[177] [1986] BCLC 460.
[178] Ibid at 482.

10.75   As mentioned earlier, in *Item Software (UK) Ltd v Fassihi*,[179] Arden LJ also indicated that the law should not be overly intrusive or else entrepreneurial activity would be deterred and this would not be beneficial to society. In *Shepherds Investments v Ltd v Walters*[180] Etherton J (as he then was) did not think that the restraint of trade point trumped the need to enforce a director's duties strictly.[181] But in that case the judge was considering action being taken pre-termination of post.

10.76   Courts do not prohibit directors from using expertise and information gleaned from his or her work with the company.[182] A useful illustration is to be found in the case of *Framlington Group plc v Anderson*.[183] In that case three of the defendants were employed as private client fund managers by the claimants, which were companies in a corporate group. The defendants were also directors of one or more companies in the group. I shall refer to the claimants collectively as F. Under the terms of the directors' employment they were permitted, if they ceased to be employed by, or directors of, F, to establish or join a competing business and to take with them or to solicit Fs' clients. The directors were offered contracts of employment with R plc, which they decided to accept. R plc then negotiated with F for F to sell that part of F's business which was represented by the clients who would transfer their managed funds to R plc when the three directors moved to R plc. The transfer price consisted mainly of F receiving shares in R plc and it was calculated by reference to the value of the managed funds transferred. The directors were instructed not to, and did not, participate in the negotiations conducted between F and R plc concerning the transfer of managed funds. R plc offered to the directors, as part of their new employment, shares in R plc, the number of which was to be based on the value of the managed funds transferred. When F discovered the term concerning the issuing of shares in favour of the directors, F issued proceedings claiming that the shares, together with any income and other profits which those shares had earned since they were beneficially acquired by the three managers, were secret profits for which the three managers were accountable to F and that they held them on constructive trust for F. It was argued that the effect of the share consideration to be awarded to the directors was to deprive F of part of the purchase price which they could otherwise have obtained from R plc on the transfer of the managed funds.

10.77   The judge, Blackburne J, said[184] that the shares were issued to the directors as consideration for bringing to the new employer an asset, being one which belonged to them and which, on leaving their former company's employment:

---

[179]   [2004] EWCA Civ 1244 (2004) BCC 994; (2005) 2 BCLC 91 at [63] (CA).
[180]   [2006] EWHC 836.
[181]   Ibid at [107].
[182]   *Crown Dilmun v Sutton* [2004] EWHC 52 (Ch); [2004] 1 BCLC 468 at [184].
[183]   [1995] BCC 611.
[184]   Ibid at 628.

'they were free to exploit for themselves, namely, the client goodwill which attached to them as the persons who had, over many years, managed their clients' investments. The consideration shares were the price which the three were willing to accept in return for binding themselves under five-year service contracts to make that goodwill available to Rathbone [R plc – the new employer] and for restricting their freedom, after the termination of their service contracts, to exploit that client goodwill for themselves or for others.'[185]

5 Company not being able to exploit the opportunity

10.78 It was asserted by the House of Lords in *Regal Hastings* that it was not material that the company was not in a position to exploit the opportunity, because it could not obtain the necessary funds to increase the capitalisation of the subsidiary company. More recently it has been said that the fact that the company could not take advantage of the opportunity is no defence.[186] Spigelman CJ of the New South Wales Court of Appeal in *Fexuto Pty Ltd v Bosnjak Holdings Pty Ltd*[187] said that:

'The issue is not whether the beneficiary – relevantly the company entitled to the opportunity – would, or even could, otherwise have availed itself of that opportunity. Equity is concerned with the protection of the fiduciary relationship and frequently does so with a strictness which has a consequence that an errant fiduciary must account for profits which the beneficiary would never have obtained (see *Furs v Tomkies* (supra) at 592) eg by reason of a legal disability or an insufficiency of funds (eg *Regal (Hastings) v Gulliver*).'[188]

10.79 The view encapsulated in the decisions referred to above has found its way expressly into s 175(2) of the CA 2006, for the provision states that it is immaterial whether the company could take advantage of the opportunity.

10.80 It is asserted that even if an opportunity cannot be taken up by the company, and, it would seem, according to *Wilkinson v West Coast Capital*[189] the company had the power to take up the opportunity, if a director takes it up then he or she would need to account for any profits made on the basis of a conflict of interest.[190] It is argued that if directors could plead by way of defence that the company could not or chose not to avail itself of an opportunity, then it would mean that courts would · have to indulge in determining what the company's attitude was in fact and what was said and done, which could well involve some significant factual disputes.[191] Hannigan points out that in *Regal Hastings* there was nothing to suggest that the directors

---

[185] R Austin, H Ford and I M Ramsay (*Company Directors* (Sydney, LexisNexis, 2005) at 375) have queried the decision on the basis that it is unusual to say that a director is the owner of client goodwill built up while he or she was a director.

[186] *Murad v Al-Saraj* [2005] EWCA Civ 959 at [59]; *Wrexham AFC Ltd v Crucialmove Ltd* [2006] EWCA Civ 237; [2007] BCC 139 at [40].

[187] [2001] NSWCA 97; (2001) 37 ACSR 672.

[188] Ibid at [120].

[189] [2005] EWHC 3009 (Ch); [2005] BCC 717 at [261].

[190] *Company Law* (London, LexisNexis Butterworths, 2003) at 288.

[191] Ibid.

could not have obtained finance elsewhere to capture the project for the company, thus suggesting that the directors' submission that the company could not avail itself of the opportunity to be questionable.[192] But it must not be forgotten that the proof of a negative, namely, the company could not obtain finance, is impossible.

10.81 It has been suggested that if a company is unable to take up an opportunity, the opportunity cannot be the company's.[193] Although a fair point, it is probably only academic now that s 175(2) upholds the position articulated in *Regal Hastings* that a director is liable even if the company was unable to exploit the opportunity. Straun Scott argues that if directors were not liable in exploiting an opportunity that the company found it impossible to exploit, there would be an inconsistency with the duty in s 172, to promote the success of the company, because it would raise real prospects of conflicts of interest, for directors who can raise the issue of impossibility may encounter the 'temptation to refrain from exerting [their] strongest efforts on behalf of the company since, if [the company] does not meet the obligations, an opportunity of profit will be open to [the fiduciary] personally'.[194] The advantage of s 175(2), like the strict approach to this area, is probably certainty, and it also makes the judge's job somewhat easier.[195] The drawback with certainty can well be inequity as deserving parties may be unable to obtain a remedy.[196]

6 *The company would not have succeeded in obtaining the opportunity*

10.82 A director cannot plead by way of a defence to usurping an opportunity that his or her company would not have been able to succeed in obtaining or exploiting it.[197] It is sufficient that the director or some other party obtained a commercial benefit as a result of a breach of duty.[198] Scott puts it well when he states that: '[t]o the extent that fairness to the company is seen as not harming the company, there is a logic in allowing a corporate fiduciary to raise arguments that the company was not harmed by the action in issue'.[199] If this were applied to *Regal Hastings* (where the cinemas could not have been leased without directorial assistance) and *IDC v Cooley*[200] (where the director argued,

---

[192] Ibid.

[193] S Scott 'The Corporate Opportunity Doctrine and Impossibility Arguments' (2003) 66 MLR 852 at 867.

[194] *Irving Trust* 73 F2d 121 (Cal, 2nd Cir 1934) and quoted by Scott, ibid.

[195] See the comments of Moses LJ in *Foster Bryant Surveying Ltd v Bryant* [2007] EWCA Civ 200; [2007] 2 BCLC 239 where his Lordship rather bemoans the movement away from inflexible rules (at [97]).

[196] B Clark and A Benstock 'UK Company Law Reform and Directors' Exploitation of "Corporate Opportunities"' (2006) 17 ICCLR 231 at 236.

[197] *CMS Dolphin Ltd v Simonet* [2001] 2 BCLC 704; [2002] BCC 200.

[198] *Regal (Hastings) Ltd v Gulliver* [1967] 2 AC 134 at 144; *Warman International Ltd v Dwyer* (1995) 182 CLR 544 at 558; *Humphris v Jenshol* (1997) 25 ACSR 212 at 224 (Aust Fed Ct).

[199] 'The Corporate Opportunity Doctrine and Impossibility Arguments' (2003) 66 MLR 852 at 854.

[200] [1972] 1 WLR 443.

adroitly, that the company would not have been acceptable to the party with whom he finally contracted) there might have been a different result.

10.83 If the situation was not as discussed above, courts might have to engage in second-guessing whether a company might have succeeded in obtaining the benefits of the opportunity, and this would not probably be palatable to the courts.

7 The company chooses not to pursue an opportunity

10.84 While s 175(2) addresses the situation where the company cannot take up the opportunity, it does not say anything about the case where the company chooses not to pursue it, for one reason or another. Bull JA in *Peso Silver*, speaking on behalf of the majority, said that it would seem that 'an out-and-out *bona fide* rejection by the company would be the best evidence that any later dealings with the property by anyone would not be against its interests'.[201] *Regal Hastings* was distinguished, because in that case the company wanted to take up the shares, but could not. As indicated earlier, in *Queensland Mines* the director was not liable because the company had decided not to take up the licences and gave informal consent to the director doing what he wished or could do with the licences.[202] The issue in this case, as it could be in other cases, was whether there was a bona fide rejection of the opportunity. An aspect of the *Queensland Mines* decision that is potentially critical was that the director participated in the decision-making and had significant influence.[203] The danger with permitting directors to take up an opportunity in the circumstances envisaged here is that it might be difficult to ascertain what influence he or she has had on the decision of the company to refrain from pursuing an opportunity, unless the director were excluded from discussions.

10.85 There is a related issue. What is critical is the fact that the company's information about commercial matters will often be relayed by directors as a result of what they have ascertained. The directors are 'in a position to manipulate and distort information, both about a disputed project as well as about the company's financial capacity, just so as to prevent the company from securing the project'.[204] What is more, the directors could embark on such a strategy to set up a protective screen for their future behaviour. The directors could always place a negative 'spin' on any situation, such that the company decides that it is not an attractive proposition. This might lead to allegations against the director involved that he or she acted improperly, but it might be difficult to prove.

---

[201] [1966] 56 DLR (2d) 117 at 156.
[202] (1978) 52 ALJR 399 at 403–404.
[203] G R Sullivan 'Going It Alone – Queensland Mines v Hudson' (1979) 42 MLR 711 at 713.
[204] P Koh 'Once a Director, Always a Fiduciary?' (2003) 62 CLJ 403 at 424.

8 *Third party preference*

10.86   There are instances in the case-law, and it is not unlikely to happen, that a third party is desirous of a director taking up an opportunity that the third party can provide, because the third party has a high regard for the director's ability, but would not want the director's company taking it on. Can it be said that this is taking up a company's opportunity? The no-profit rule applied even where a third party actually approached a director personally, wanting him or her to be involved in the exploitation of an opportunity.[205] The law would be concerned that offers could be engineered in such a way as to protect the director if directors were allowed to take up third party offers. Also, it might encourage directors to act in such a way that they advertise their abilities at the expense of the company.[206] The situation envisaged here is what occurred in *IDC v Cooley*.[207]

10.87   Whilst it might appear that the Court in *In Plus Group*[208] was influenced by the fact that the director was approached by a third party to do some work for that third party, Buxton LJ said that a director is unable to use such a situation as a defence to a claim for breach of duty.[209] This is perhaps consistent with the fact that, as mentioned earlier, Sedley LJ had said that if a director finds that he or she is accidentally in a conflict position, the director must act appropriately and regularise[210] or abandon the conflict situation.[211] In being approached by a third party the director in *IDC v Cooley* found himself in a conflict situation and he should have disclosed this to the company.

9 *The role in which the director is acting*

10.88   In *Regal Hastings* Lord Russell was of the view that a director is liable if he or she makes a profit by reason of, and in the course of carrying out, his or her role.[212] However, whilst this seems to mean that directors are not liable if the opportunity came to them not as a result of their position as a director, or once they have left office, later case-law does not seem to support that limitation. While in *Regal Hastings* the decision was predicated on the directors becoming aware of, and going through with, the transaction while they were directors, in *Canadian Aero Service Ltd v O'Malley*[213] Laskin J rejected any idea that *Regal Hastings* was to be limited to the situation where the director completes the opportunity while still a director. His Honour felt that it was

---

[205] *IDC v Cooley* [1972] 1 WLR 443; *Pacifica Shipping Co Ltd v Andersen* [1986] 2 NZLR 328.
[206] Of course, it might be said that many career directors who are ambitious are seeking to put themselves and their abilities forward at most times.
[207] [1972] 1 WLR 443.
[208] [2002] EWCA Civ 370; [2002] 2 BCLC 201.
[209] Ibid at [100].
[210] One assumes by advising his or her company.
[211] Above at **10.31**.
[212] [1967] 2 AC 134 at 149.
[213] (1973) 40 DLR (3d) 371.

necessary not to put the principle emanating from that case 'in the strait jacket of special knowledge acquired while acting as directors ...'.[214]

10.89 Clearly, where the opportunity is actually presented to the directors themselves, or they receive information while acting as directors, they are obliged to relay that to the company, and this might be the case even if the director obtains this in some other capacity.[215] This follows from *IDC v Cooley*, where the director was approached by the third party for his personal view. The problem with saying that the director is responsible for passing on any information to the company is that some might not come to him or her in the capacity of a director. Directors do not receive information 'marked for them in their different capacities.'[216]

10.90 The main contention by the company in *Peso Silver*, and relying on what Lord Russell said in *Regal Hastings*, namely that a director is liable if he or she makes a profit by reason of, and in the course of carrying out, his or her role,[217] was that the director was in breach because he acquired knowledge about the claims when acting as a director of P Ltd[218] Bull JA disagreed with the contention and said[219] that:

'the authorities require that to come within the rule [as stated in *Regal Hastings*] the impugned transactions must, as stated by Lord Russell, be by reason of the fact, and *only by reason* of the fact, that they were directors and in the *course of the execution* of that office.'

10.91 His Honour recognised that in *Regal Hastings* the directors were indeed carrying out their duties as required by their company in a company transaction, but that was not the case before him, because the negotiations and acquisition of the claims, while based on knowledge obtained while directors, was not done 'only' in their capacity as directors and not 'in the execution of that office'.[220] Certainly if the *Peso Silver* decision is not correct, then a person who knows of a particular opportunity when acting as a director at one point (and his or her company does not take up the opportunity), then resigns for reasons not connected with the opportunity and enters into a transaction involving the opportunity at a later date, he or she is liable. That does not seem either to be fair or an implementation of the rationale behind the no-conflict and no-profit rules.

10.92 In *Peso Silver* the court accepted the fact that if an opportunity comes to a director in a non-directorial role, then it may be exploited with no liability

[214] Ibid at 383.
[215] *Bhullar v Bhullar* [2003] 2 BCLC 241; [2003] BCC 711; *Item Software (UK) Ltd v Fassihi* [2004] EWCA Civ 1244 (2004) BCC 994; (2005) 2 BCLC 91 at [12].
[216] S M Beck 'The Saga of Peso Silver Mines: Corporate Opportunity Reconsidered' (1971) 51 Can Bar Rev 80 at 82.
[217] [1967] 2 AC 134 at 149.
[218] Ibid at 156.
[219] Ibid.
[220] Ibid at 156–157.

attaching. The difficulty for the courts is probably establishing, in some cases, what is a non-directorial role. Is a person who holds the office of a director to be regarded as acting in that role all day every day, or – to use the modern vernacular – 24/7? As companies are usually interested in exploiting all or any opportunities that might come their way, it might be argued that the rule should cover every situation of profit-making in which the director is involved.[221] But in some cases can it really be said that the opportunity has 'come the company's way?'

10.93   In *Crown Dilmun v Sutton*[222] Peter Smith J[223] identified two instances where there would be a breach when a director receives an opportunity.

> '[first] where a fiduciary obtains knowledge or information which is not available to the general public and is obtained by him as confidential information in the course of his fiduciary relationship and had a special value, in that it enables him to assess the commercial feasibility of a purchase by him and the appropriate terms of a purchase offer and thereby substantially contributes to the successful purchase by him ... The second situation is where a fiduciary obtains confidential information in the course of his fiduciary relationship and then enters into a purchase for his own benefit in circumstances where his personal interest conflicts or may conflict with his fiduciary duties, for example his duty to consider a purchase on behalf of the trust or even an application to the court for authority to purchase.'

10.94   This exposition seems to assume that a director will not always be in breach, that is, there might well be cases where information and/or opportunities do come to a director in some other capacity, and he or she is not liable if the opportunities are exploited.

10.95   What is perhaps more problematic is the case where a director ascertains that an opportunity to exploit exists and whether it is really something that is the company's or something which the director can exploit in a personal capacity. *Bhullar v Bhullar*[224] is a case in point. The Court of Appeal denied the assertion that for the director to be accountable there should have been some improper dealing with property belonging to the company.[225] The question to ask in the kind of case I have posited is not, according to the Court of Appeal, whether the company had some type of beneficial interest in the opportunity, as that would be a too restrictive approach, but rather whether the director's exploitation of the opportunity is the kind that would attract the application of the rule.[226] The Court said that the rule is simple, but not easy to apply in all cases.[227]

---

[221]   R Austin, H Ford and I M Ramsay *Company Directors* (Sydney, LexisNexis, 2005) at 365.
[222]   [2004] EWHC 52 (Ch); [2004] 1 BCLC 468.
[223]   Ibid at [185].
[224]   [2003] 2 BCLC 241; [2003] BCC 711.
[225]   Ibid at [27].
[226]   Ibid at [28].
[227]   Ibid at [30].

10.96 If a director remains in post then it matters not that he or she make a profit from an opportunity in some other capacity. In *Bhullar* the directors, who purchased for themselves a property next to their company's, obtained knowledge that it was for sale not in their capacity as directors, but as passers-by. The Court of Appeal said, and this was approved of in *Item Software (UK) Ltd v Fassihi*,[228] that at the critical point of time the directors had one capacity only in which they were carrying on business, that is as directors of the company.[229] Again this sounds like expecting directors to be acting in that capacity 24/7. Crucially Roskill J said[230] in *IDC v Cooley* that:

> 'Information which came to [the director] while he was managing director and which was of concern to [the company] and was relevant for [the company] to know, was information which it was his duty to pass on to [the company] because between himself and [the company] a fiduciary relationship existed ....'

10.97 This illustrates the fact that the fiduciary relationship is all encompassing. Is the role of director, therefore, so all-consuming that a director has no commercial life outside of the company? Nevertheless there are aspects of the case-law that seem to suggest that if an opportunity is remote from the director's role it might be permissible for him or her to exploit it. It is likely that this will be relatively rare in most situations in which directors find themselves. It is probable that it will only apply where the opportunity is not related to the company's existing or future area of business, and one must remember that companies are generally always looking for opportunities to expand and develop. It is likely that executive directors will be more constrained than non-executives, because of the part-time nature of the latter's role. While many authorities focus on the all-encompassing obligations of the director, the Federal Court of Australia in *SEA Food International Pty Ltd v Lam*[231] attempted to place some restriction on the scope of directorial responsibility. Cooper J said that it is necessary to look at the connection between the opportunity and the fiduciary position. His Honour said that there had to be 'a sufficient temporal and causal connection between the obligations and the opportunity'.[232] Ascertaining whether there is a sufficient connection will depend on a number of factors, 'including the circumstances in which the opportunity arises and the nature of it and the nature and extent of the company's operations and anticipated future operations.' In this case Cooper J said that it is necessary initially to ascertain the scope of the director's fiduciary obligations to the company in the circumstances of the case at hand and to identify the conduct that is said to constitute the breach. In *O'Donnell v Shanahan*,[233] a case considered shortly in relation to a different aspect of conflict and profit, Richard Sheldon QC (sitting as a deputy judge of the High Court) held that the defendant director was not liable in acquiring real estate,

---

[228] Ibid at [12].
[229] Ibid at [41].
[230] [1972] 1 WLR 443 at 451.
[231] [1998] FCA 130.
[232] At this stage of reporting, the Federal Court judgments did not contain paragraph numbers, so, unfortunately no specific reference within the judgment can be given.
[233] [2008] EWHC 1973 (Ch); sub nom *Re Allied Business and Financial Consultants Ltd*.

even though the opportunity to acquire came to him while acting as a director. The reason for that decision was that the company's business did not involve any activity that related to acquiring property.

10.98 The general thrust of the authorities, *Peso Silver* aside,[234] might be seen as suggesting that a director is in the role of a director at all times, at least wherever there is a commercial benefit to be secured. If so, does that mean that if a director does something, such as buying shares that leads to a profit, he or she is in breach? The answer might well be: it depends on the company's operations and the shares purchased.

10 The North American experience

10.99 While in the United Kingdom the law on the subject of corporate opportunities is a 'supplemental adjunct'[235] to the duty of loyalty as manifested by the no-conflict and no-profit rules, this is to be contrasted with the developed jurisprudence on the subject in the United States and now in Canada, where there tends to be a dedicated corporate opportunities doctrine. The American approach has not been to restrict the doctrine to playing a part in the no-conflict and no-profit rules, but it has been specially formulated.[236] Obviously the UK Parliament had a chance to take the same, or a similar, approach when considering the codification question, but decided not to embrace it.

10.100 It will be interesting to see if the courts use the opportunity of new legislation to embrace different approaches, particularly that which is extant in the United States. In the United States a far more flexible approach is taken. For instance, in *Broz v Cellular Information Systems Inc*,[237] the facts of which were discussed in **Chapter 9**,[238] the Delaware Supreme Court explained the corporate opportunity doctrine in somewhat contrasting terms to that found in the orthodox UK case-law. It said[239] that:

> '[a] corporate officer or director may not take a business opportunity for his own if: (1) the corporation is financially able to exploit the opportunity; (2) the opportunity is within the corporation's line of business; (3) the corporation has an interest or expectancy in the opportunity; and (4) by taking the opportunity for his own, the corporate fiduciary will thereby be placed in a position inimicable to his duties to the corporation.'

10.101 The approach in s 175(2) of the CA 2006 is to be contrasted with that which applies in the United States, where the fact that a company is not able to

---

[234] And, possibly *O'Donnell v Shanahan* [2008] EWHC 1973 (Ch), *but the decision was overturned on appeal. See O'Donnell v Shanahan* [2009] EWCA Civ 751; [2009] BCC 822.

[235] J Lowry and R Edmunds 'The No Conflict-No Profit Rules and the Corporate Fiduciary: Challenging the Orthodoxy of Absolutism' [2000] JBL 122.

[236] Ibid at 123.

[237] 673 A 2d 148 (1996).

[238] Above at **9.65**.

[239] 673 A 2d 148 at 155 (1996).

take up an opportunity is a factor which a court will take into account in deciding whether or not a director acted properly.[240]

11 What is an opportunity?

10.102   What is a corporate opportunity? Few courts have tried to address this issue. Laskin J in *Canadian Aero* has been one of the few judges to consider it. The learned judge was of the view that an opportunity had to be more than maturing (to constitute a corporate opportunity), but one that is actively pursued by the company. This cannot be right when a director has kept an opportunity from the company. Is not there room for saying that opportunity can cover potential benefits – is not that what opportunities are? Clearly there are going to be matters of degree. For instance, in *Canadian Aero Service Ltd v O'Malley*[241] the company was more likely to gain the contract in that case than the company in *IDC v Cooley*. However, as discussed earlier, the fact that a company is not likely to succeed in bringing an opportunity to fruition is not the critical issue.

10.103   The approach in the United States under its corporate opportunities doctrine is to provide that a director is not entitled to exploit a corporate opportunity for his or her benefit whilst still in a fiduciary position (unless there is consent), but the director is able to exploit anything that is not within the concept of a corporate opportunity. The difficulty lies as already foreshadowed in defining: what is a corporate opportunity? This is something that has occupied significant court time in the United States, and led to the formulation of several different tests.[242]

10.104   Koh has concluded in an examination of the subject[243] that:

> 'The concept of the corporate opportunity which may be subject to this continuing obligation, should be confined only to those business opportunities in which the company already has an interest, or in the fruition of which the company has a real and almost certain expectancy.'

10.105   The former qualification for an opportunity (where the company already has an interest) is clear. But the second, dealing in expectancy, is far more difficult to define. Perhaps it might be said that a corporate opportunity exists where an opportunity relates to an entity with whom continuing relations is anticipated. But is this the case where the completion of the opportunity is doubtful, such as where there is significant competition? In *Island Export Finance Ltd v Umunna*[244] the judge found that the fact that the company was far from assured of gaining a contract, even though the company had been involved with the third party who could grant the opportunity, was an

---

[240] For example, see *Guth v Loft Inc* 5 A 2d 503 (Del, 1939).
[241] (1973) 40 DLR (3d) 371.
[242] P Koh 'Once a Director, Always a Fiduciary?' (2003) 62 CLJ 403 at 411.
[243] Ibid at 443.
[244] [1986] 1 BCLC 460.

important factor in ruling against the company, for there was no 'maturing business opportunity'.[245] According to Roskill J the fact that the company was not actively pursuing the matter was also of importance.[246]

10.106 Professors Alan Dignam and John Lowry conclude that 'any opportunity within the company's line of business is off-limits to the director unless the company's permission to proceed is first obtained'.[247] 'The line of business'[248] is a factor taken into account by American courts in analysing whether directors are liable in exploiting an opportunity, and the American Law Institute (ALI) has defined 'corporate opportunity' as:

> 'one that comes to a director or senior executive in connection with the performance of their functions or in such away as reasonably to lead them to conclude that the person offering the opportunity expects it to be disclosed to the company (a modified capacity approach)30 or where a senior executive knows an opportunity is closely connected to a business in which the company is engaged or expects to engage.'[249] (footnotes in the original are excluded)'

10.107 There have been two references to the line of business concept in reasonably modern English decisions. In *Wilkinson v West Coast Capital*[250] Warren J said that the directors in *Regal Hastings* were liable as the opportunity of which they availed themselves was within the scope of the company's business.[251] His Lordship pointed out that Lord Macmillan said, in *Regal Hastings*:

> 'The plaintiff company has to establish ... that what the directors did was *so related to the affairs of the company* that it can properly be said to have been done in the course of their management and in the utilisation of their opportunities and special knowledge as directors.' (Warren J's emphasis)[252]

10.108 Subsequently, in *O'Donnell v Shanahan*[253] Richard Sheldon QC (sitting as a deputy judge of the High Court) said[254] that:

---

[245] Ibid at 482.

[246] Ibid.

[247] *Company Law* (OUP, Oxford, 5th edn, 2008) at 333 and referring to *Quarter Master UK Ltd v Pyke* [2004] EWHC 1815 (Ch); [2005] 1 BCLC 245; and *Wrexham AFC Ltd v Crucialmove Ltd* [2006] EWCA Civ 237; [2007] BCC 139.

[248] Sometimes referred to as 'the scope of business'.

[249] D Ahern, "Guiding Principles for Directorial Conflicts of Interest: *Re Allied Business and Financial Consultants Ltd*; *O'Donnell v Shanahan*' (2011) 74 MLR 596 at 602, and referring to American Law Institute, Principles of Corporate Governance: Analysis and Recommendations (St Paul, Minnesota: American Law Institute Publishers, 1994) sections 5.05(b)(1)(2).

[250] [2005] EWHC 3009 (Ch); (2007) BCC 717.

[251] Ibid at [287].

[252] *Regal (Hastings) Ltd v Gulliver* [1967] 2 AC 134(HL) at 153 and quoted in *Wilkinson v West Coast Capital* [2005] EWHC 3009 (Ch); (2007) BCC 717 at [290].

[253] [2008] EWHC 1973 (Ch).

[254] Ibid at [193]. The deputy judge relied on P Finn *Fiduciary Obligations* (1977) at para 547 (see, for example, [199]).

'I find it necessary to have regard to the scope of the company's business in applying the "no profit rule", although in so doing I recognise that I have to take into account at least the "expanded line of business" test.'

10.109 In *Aas v Benham*[255] the Court of Appeal applied a scope of business test in the context of a partnership and this decision was relied on substantially by Richard Sheldon QC. In *Aas v Benham* Lindley LJ said that:[256]

'Suppose a partner to become, in the course of carrying on his business, well acquainted with a particular branch of science or trade, and suppose him to write and publish a book on the subject, could the firm claim the profits thereby obtained? Obviously not, unless, by publishing the book, he in fact competed with the firm in their own line of business.'

10.110 The learned deputy judge in *O'Donnell v Shanahan* adopted a line of business approach,[257] in a similar way to Lindley LJ, rejecting the argument that the approach only applied to partnerships.[258] But the development of any established line of business approach in England was truncated when the Court of Appeal reversed the decision of Richard Sheldon QC on appeal.[259] Rimer LJ (with whom the other judges agreed) distinguished *Aas v Benham* and said that the authorities relating to directors' accountability did not support the so called 'scope of business' exception as far as the no profit rule was concerned.[260] His Lordship added that the authorities were in fact contrary to the concept of the scope of business.[261]

10.111 The approach of the Court of Appeal is to require directors to disclose all opportunities that directors encounter in their capacity as directors to the company. It then is a matter for the company whether it wishes to pursue them, even if they are in an area that they had not at that point sought to do business. Rimer LJ said that:

'It may have been improbable that the company could or would want to be able to take up the opportunity itself. But the opportunity was there for the company to consider and, if so advised, to reject and it was no answer to the claimed breach of the "no profit" rule that property investment was something that the company did not do.'[262]

---

[255] [1891] 2 Ch 244.
[256] Ibid at 256.
[257] [2008] EWHC 1973 (Ch) at [193], [21].
[258] Ibid at [193].
[259] *O'Donnell v Shanahan* [2009] EWCA Civ 751; [2009] BCC 822; sub nom *Re Allied Business and Financial Consultants Ltd*. For an analytical discussion of the case, see D Ahern, 'Guiding Principles for Directorial Conflicts of Interest: *Re Allied Business and Financial Consultants Ltd; O'Donnell v Shanahan*' (2011) 74 MLR 596.
[260] [2008] EWHC 1973 (Ch) at [56].
[261] Ibid. For a critique of the decision not to accept the scope of business approach, see E Lim, 'Directors' fiduciary duties : a new analytical framework' (2013) 139 LQR 242 at 248–249.
[262] *O'Donnell v Shanahan* [2009] EWCA Civ 751; [2009] BCC 822 at [71].

10.112   Rightly, it is submitted with respect, this approach, as Deirdre Ahern says, leads one to the conclusion that in effect this gives the company 'a right of first refusal in respect of all opportunities which come a director's way'.[263]

10.113   Rimer LJ emphasised the fact that a company should be able to expect the undivided loyalty of directors and one manifestation of how that is to be discharged is disclosing all opportunities to the company. His Lordship said that it is not for the director to decide whether his or her company would be interested in a particular opportunity.[264] The learned judge went even further and said that there was no room in this area of the law for a scope of business inquiry.[265] While the majority of the Hong Kong Court of Final Appeal in *Chen Wai Too v Poon Ka Man Jason*[266] felt that Rimer LJ was going too far in what he said in this respect, the Hong Kong Court did find that a director of a company, S, was in breach when he opened up restaurants which were similar to that ran by S even though there was evidence to indicate that S was only established for a single purpose, namely the running of a particular restaurant with no indications that it would open up other such restaurants. In fact if other restaurants were to be opened, they were to be controlled by a separate company, although the shareholders of these companies were to be the shareholders of S. A majority of the Hong Kong Court felt that it was not right to distinguish *Aas v Benham* and that a scope of business inquiry might not be improper; it all depended on the facts.[267]

10.114   As with the general thrust of the strict approach to conflicts evident over time in English law, the approach advocated by the Court of Appeal in *O'Donnell v Shanahan* does provide for certainty.[268] That means that it provides that everyone should know where they are, but, of course, directors, save in larger companies, rarely get legal advice before embarking on a particular course of action that they believe is profitable. The approach does take into account the fact that companies might wish to expand into hitherto unexploited areas of commerce at any point and it should be permitted to do so, and it should not be pre-empted from taking up relevant business opportunities. However, perhaps one of the principal concerns with the approach favoured by the Court of Appeal is that if one does not lay down some parameters every opportunity encountered by a director might be seen as a potential corporate opportunity requiring disclosure to the company before it can be exploited.[269] One might say that the courts should balance the interests

---

[263] D Ahern "Guiding Principles for Directorial Conflicts of Interest: *Re Allied Business and Financial Consultants Ltd*; *O'Donnell v Shanahan*' (2011) 74 MLR 596 at 604.

[264] *O'Donnell v Shanahan* [2009] EWCA Civ 751; [2009] BCC 822 at [70].

[265] Ibid.

[266] [2016] HKCFA 23 at [85].

[267] Ibid at [86]–[87].

[268] Regarded by commerce as the 'the great object': *Vallejo v Wheeler* (1774) 1 Cowp 143.

[269] See S Scott 'The Corporate Opportunity Doctrine and Impossibility Arguments' (2003) 66 MLR 852 at 859; D Ahern 'Guiding Principles for Directorial Conflicts of Interest: *Re Allied Business and Financial Consultants Ltd*; *O'Donnell v Shanahan*' (2011) 74 MLR 596 at 601.

of the directors and the company and that with the conservative approach generally applied in England the courts are coming down too heavily in favour of the company.

10.115 The undoubted problem with the concept of the line of business is actually ascertaining the line of business of a company. At first instance in *O'Donnell v Shanahan* the deputy judge was able to do so. He said that the defendant director had not been in breach when he acquired some property, because the company's business had, in essence, been the provision of financial and business advice and assistance, including, in particular, arranging bank loans, mortgages and insurance, and the acquisition of property for investment had not been within the scope of the business of the company. In the view of the deputy judge this meant that there had been no real sensible possibility of a conflict in the defendant director acquiring an interest in the property as an investment. The view could be put, one would think, on the basis of what the deputy judge said, that if there is an opportunity that becomes available, but it is not one that it is clearly within the scope of the company's business, a director is not in breach if he or she exploits it. *O'Donnell v Shanahan* is to be contrasted with *Bhullar v Bhullar*[270] where the defendant directors, it will be remembered, acquired real estate that was adjacent to their company's property and were found liable; but in that case the company was involved in developing real estate.[271] The opportunity was far closer to the company's line of business.

10.116 It is not appropriate to say that line of business is anything that is covered in the company's objects, because for years the tendency has been to draft very wide objects (to enable a company to do virtually anything) in order to circumvent the ultra vires doctrine.[272] This is arguably exacerbated by s 31(1) of the CA 2006 because it provides that unless the articles place restrictions on the company, it has unrestricted objects.[273] *Island Export Finance Ltd v Umunna*[274] is a case where the court was of the view that the opportunity was remote from the business interests of the company and consequently the director was not liable. There is great difficulty in knowing where to draw the line. Can a company argue that it was considering moving into a new area, the area in which the director exploited the opportunity, and so it was denied a corporate opportunity? If so, one would think that it would need to provide evidence of this strategy.

10.117 The difficulty is that there is a temptation for directors not to pursue a possible contract as vigorously as possible for a company, so that he or she can keep open the possibility of he or she being able to take up the contract. The

---

[270] [2003] 2 BCLC 241; [2003] BCC 711.

[271] In his judgment in *O'Donnell* Richard Sheldon QC actually contrasted the case before him with *Cook v Deeks* [1916] AC 554, where the directors took advantage of a contract which clearly related to the business of the company: at [200].

[272] The strength of this doctrine has been arguably weak for many years, but lawyers have continued to draft wide objects clauses.

[273] B Clark and A Benstock 'UK Company Law Reform and Directors' Exploitation of "Corporate Opportunities"' (2006) 17 ICCLR 231 at 237.

[274] [1986] 1 BCLC 460.

more interest shown by a company, or the more a director is seen to be inquiring about it, the greater the chance it might be seen as a maturing corporate opportunity.

10.118 In *Hunter Kane Ltd v Watkins*[275] the deputy judge deciding the case rejected the notion that a maturing business opportunity was limited to a unitary contract. It is broader than that and could extend to an opportunity, as in the subject case, where there was a formal arrangement between the company and other parties that gave the company the reasonable expectation of doing business with the other parties.[276]

10.119 According to Hannigan: 'Once the profit-making opportunity is within the protected ambit of the company's activities and opportunities, there can be no personal exploitation of that opportunity ....'[277] The role of directors is to exploit all opportunities of which they become aware for their companies' benefit, unless they have made full and frank disclosure and the company gives full and informed consent.[278] The courts will stamp down on any attempt by directors to exploit a maturing business opportunity that has come to their company. But they will permit any exploitation of an opportunity where the director has not pursued it or it has not come about as a result of his or her fiduciary position, or does not involve the use of confidential information.[279]

12 Directorial conduct

10.120 The rule behind s 175 of the CA 2006 is so strict that it applies even if the director has acted in good faith, as the directors did (as everyone agreed) in *Regal Hastings*.[280] Lord Russell in that case said that: '[t]he profiteer, however honest and well-intentioned, cannot escape the risk of being called upon to account.'[281] Nevertheless, some of the cases also suggest a resonance with some of the US case-law where it is important to investigate and consider the director's conduct which is being challenged. Earlier cases, most notably *IDC v Cooley*, indicate some judicial consideration of directorial conduct. In that case Roskill J was influenced by the fact that the director lied to the company when seeking release.

10.121 From the decision in *Foster Bryant Surveying Ltd v Bryant*[282] it would seem that a court will be influenced by the fact that a director acted in bad faith

---

[275] [2002] EWHC 186 (Ch).
[276] *Hunter Kane Ltd v Watkins* [2002] EWHC 186 (Ch) at [57].
[277] *Company Law* (London, LexisNexis Butterworths, 2003) at 287.
[278] *Crown Dilmun v Sutton* [2004] EWHC 52 (Ch); [2004] 1 BCLC 468; *Quarter Master UK Ltd v Pyke* [2004] EWHC 1815 (Ch); [2005] 1 BCLC 245 at [70].
[279] An example is *Framlington Group plc v Anderson* [1995] BCC 611.
[280] [1967] 2 AC 134 at 144.
[281] Ibid at 145.
[282] [2007] EWCA Civ 200; [2007] 2 BCLC 239.

and/or secretively.[283] In that case the director clearly had not acted in such a way. In fact the director had acted transparently at all times and this appeared to influence the court.[284]

10.122   In *In Plus Group*[285] the Court of Appeal did not think that the director was liable even though he had established his own company and entered into contracts with a major customer. The reasons were that he had not used company property or exploited confidential information belonging to the company, and he had been excluded totally from management of the company. This last reason sounds a little dangerous and might be seen by some as the basis for making profits on the excuse that he or she could not exercise directorial powers. But, as Professors Dan Prentice and Jenny Payne, point out:[286]

> 'it should always be remembered that a director cannot abdicate his or her status without formally resigning. Accordingly, it must be only in the most exceptional circumstances that a director can avoid the no conflict rule by pleading impotence when it is his or her duty to act in the interests of the company and avoid conflict.'

IV CONCLUSION

10.123   This Chapter has sought to examine the position of directors who retire in order to establish a business in opposition to their former companies and/or take up business opportunities that might be available to the company. It has also focused on the exploitation of opportunities by directors where those opportunities arose whilst they were acting as directors.

10.124   The legislation importantly proscribes any exploitation of any property, information or opportunities, and makes the point expressly (and thus affirms the case of *Regal Hastings*) that it does not matter that the company could not take up an opportunity. But, the section does not address some situations, such as where a company gives up a corporate opportunity, or the director arguably comes by the opportunity in his or her private capacity and exploits it. But, given the fact that s 170(3) and (4) of the CA 2006 provide that the duties shall be interpreted and applied in the same way as common law rules and equitable principles and regard should be had to the corresponding rules and principles, it is likely that the law as it developed before codification will be applied.

10.125   It has been argued that the old law 'needlessly inhibits the development of opportunities by the entrepreneurial-minded director',[287] and not only affects

---

[283]   Ibid at [48]. Also, see *CMS Dolphin Ltd v Simonet* [2001] 2 BCLC 704; [2002] BCC 200.
[284]   [2007] EWCA Civ 200; [2007] 2 BCLC 239 at [48].
[285]   [2002] EWCA Civ 370; [2002] 2 BCLC 201.
[286]   'Director's Fiduciary Duties' (2006) 122 LQR 558 at 559.
[287]   J Lowry and R Edmunds 'The No Conflict-No Profit Rules and the Corporate Fiduciary: Challenging the Orthodoxy of Absolutism' [2000] JBL 122 at 124.

individual directors, but the economy as a whole.[288] It will be interesting to see if the courts use the opportunity of new legislation to embrace different approaches, particularly those extant in the United States. In the United States a far more flexible approach is taken. In comparison with the UK's generally strict line, which does not allow for any examination of the facts of a case and consideration of the equity of the situation, for any transaction that involves a director in potential conflict is regarded absolutely as improper, the US courts will consider the facts that led to the alleged breach, what are the equities involved and how did the director act. If he or she acted in good faith then the courts might not hold that the director is liable, whereas under the line of authority following *Regal Hastings*, the directors are liable even though they had acted in good faith. My feeling is that it is unlikely that the courts will adopt any American style approaches, although there is a clear indication that English courts have applied a form of 'line of business' test. The historical UK approach might not be regarded as fair, but the courts have resolutely stuck to it and given the new legislation it does not appear that there will be little, or any, change. Such an approach does, it is argued by some, have the advantage of providing certainty. Also, the strictness of the rule might be seen as efficient as it means that, under the agency rule, the principals do not have to expend costs in monitoring the fact that the agents, namely the directors, are acting appropriately.

10.126 In this area the facts are going to be of critical importance. It would seem that there is a big difference between, for example, the defendant director in *Foster Bryant* whose relationship with the other director had broken down, who had no ulterior motive in resigning, and who was approached by a third party about doing some work that involved his former company getting fewer instructions, and the director in *Southern Real Estate Pty Ltd v Dellow and Arnold*[289] who acted in a calculating and clandestine fashion, and who had set out, well before her resignation, to compete with her company, as well as taking information such as client records. In the former case the director was passive whereas in the latter the director was very active.

10.127 In this area of law the task it seems is to arrive at a fair balance where the company is not 'ripped off' on the one hand, and on the other hand directors are not prohibited from engaging in commerce and using some of the expertise and knowledge gleaned from their former posts. Fiduciary law does indeed tread a fine line,[290] and knowing where to draw the line is difficult. Some might feel that the present law does not provide an adequate balance.

---

[288] Ibid.
[289] [2003] SASC 318; (2003) 87 SASR 1 at [29].
[290] P Koh 'Once a Director, Always a Fiduciary?' (2003) 62 CLJ 403 at 443.

CHAPTER 11

DUTY NOT TO ACCEPT BENEFITS

I INTRODUCTION

11.1 In equity directors were under an obligation not to profit from their positions as directors and it was known as the 'no-profit' rule, something which was considered in detail in the previous two chapters. The general rule is that directors are not to profit from their positions unless they are expressly permitted to do so. The idea has always been that directors should receive nothing, save their remuneration, unless the articles of association or the general meeting permit them to do so. As we saw in the two previous chapters, the law is so strict that the courts are suspicious of any directorial benefits outside of remuneration. The rule against benefits flows from trust law, and is applied generally to fiduciaries. The law's concern is that directors are in a position where they can exploit circumstances to their own benefit and at the expense of the company. But directors are in place to act for and protect the company, not to obtain benefits for themselves. The articles may allow a director to profit, but any benefit must be sanctioned by the general meeting.

11.2 This chapter deals with the duty set out in CA 2006, s 176. The duty came into force on 1 October 2008. This was formalised in art 5(1)(d) of The Companies Act 2006 (Commencement No 5, Transitional Provisions and Savings) Order 2007.[1]

11.3 While s 175 of the CA 2006 dealt with issues formerly encompassed by the no-profit rule (as well as the no-conflict rule), s 176 provides a specialist aspect of the no-profit rule and is limited to the receipt of benefits from third parties.[2] The rule provided under the duty is connected with the one discussed in the two previous chapters, essentially the no-conflict rule. The idea behind the no-conflict rule was to prevent fiduciaries misusing their position so as to benefit themselves. The two rules overlap to the extent that they both address improper directorial conduct. Where directors accept benefits from third parties, certainly if some service is expected or required, then it is likely that the directors are not acting loyally to their companies, and this goes to the very heart of a director's role and obligations.

---

[1] SI 2007/3495.
[2] In fact it has been said that the duty to avoid a conflict embraces the duty not to make a secret profit: *Premier Waste Management Ltd v Towers* [2011] EWCA Civ 923; [2012] 1 BCLC 67.

11.4   The Chapter first provides a brief exposition of s 176 of the CA 2006. This is followed by consideration of benefits that are excepted from the application of s 176, and an examination of the types of benefits that might fall under the provision. Thereafter the Chapter considers secret profits and bribes as the prime examples of the benefits at which the section is aimed, and finally the effects of a breach of the provision are considered. The Chapter draws in a limited way on the law that has developed in relation to agents and third party benefits. As with the position relating to directors, an agent must not put himself or herself in a position where there is a conflict between the agent's interest in getting a commission and his or her duties to the principal.[3]

II THE PROVISION

11.5   CA 2006, s 176 begins with a bald, broad proscription that directors are not to accept a benefit from a third party which is given because they are directors or for doing something as directors.[4] To establish a case against a director it will be necessary to prove a nexus between the granting of the benefit and either the fact that the recipient is a director or he or she has done, or will do, something as a director. The fact that a benefit that is not related to his or her directorial position is not disallowed is consistent with the law that has developed in relation to agency, where it has been held that an agent may receive a benefit if it is outside his or her agency relationship.[5] The proscription here is against making secret profits because that will usually require him or her to do something for a third party's benefit rather than the benefit of his or her company. This has always been proscribed as far as agents are concerned. A director is liable for a breach of s 176 even if his or her company is not damaged in any way. The law is concerned that there is the potential for the company to suffer loss. Also, as we saw in the two previous chapters the law applies inflexibly in these kinds of situations.

11.6   It is likely that the fact that a director is in a situation where he or she is given a benefit by a third party might well constitute a conflict. As Lord Upjohn said in *Boardman v Phipps*,[6] and approved in *FHR European Ventures LLP v Cedar Capital Partners LLC*[7] by the Supreme Court:[8]

> 'A fiduciary who acts for two principals with potentially conflicting interests without the informed consent of both is in breach of the obligation of undivided loyalty; he puts himself in a position where his duty to one principal *may* conflict with his duty to the other.'

---

[3]   *Barry v The Stoney Point Canning Co* (1917) 55 SCR 51 at 73; *Meadow Schama and Co v C Mitchell and Co Ltd* (1973) 228 EG 1511 at 1512; *Anangel Atlas Compania Naviera SA v Ishikawajimaa-Harima Heavy Industries Co Ltd* [1990] 1 Lloyd's Rep 167 at 171.

[4]   CA 2006, s 176(1).

[5]   *Aas v Benham* [1891] 2 Ch 244 at 256.

[6]   [1967] 2 AC 46.

[7]   [2014] UKSC 45; [2015] AC 250; [2014] 3 WLR 535 at [5].

[8]   Ibid at 123.

Any mention of a conflict of interest (in fact the only mention is in s 176(4)) includes a conflict of interest and of duty as well as a conflict of duties.[9]

11.7 Besides a director running foul of s 176 of the CA 2006, the acceptance of a benefit giving rise to an actual or potential conflict of interest will fall, as indicated above, within the duty to avoid conflicts of interest in s 175.[10] However, unlike s 175, this duty is not subject to any provision for board authorisation of the receipt of a benefit. Nevertheless, any current ability of the members of a company to authorise the acceptance of benefits which would otherwise be a breach of this duty is preserved by s 180(4).[11] It might be possible for the articles to contain a provision permitting a director to receive and retain a benefit.

11.8 It is likely that the section will be interpreted strictly even if the director has had to undertake significant risk in what he or she has done for the company, for equity has provided such an approach in the past.[12] But the director should be entitled to claim any expenditure in gaining the benefit that he or she received.[13]

III EXCEPTIONS

11.9 Essentially there are two exceptions. First, as with s 175 of the CA 2006, there is no breach if the acceptance of the benefit cannot reasonably be regarded as likely to cause a conflict of interest.[14] This seems to mean that any benefit received must be secret in order to contravene s 176, or else the giving of the benefit might not be regarded as constituting a conflict as the company knows about it. In the agency case of *Shipway v Broadwood*[15] Chitty LJ said that: '[t]he real evil is not the payment of money, but the secrecy attending it'.[16]

11.10 The second exception is where the benefit given is by a party through whom the director's services are provided to the company.[17] An example of the application of the exception was given in Grand Committee by Lord Goldsmith, the then Attorney-General. This involved a director providing services to the company through his or her own company.[18]

---

[9] CA 2006, s 176(5).
[10] Explanatory Notes to the CA 2006 at para 344.
[11] Ibid at para 345.
[12] For example, see *Burrell v Mossop* (1888) 4 TLR 270; *Williams v Stevens* (1866) LR 1 PC 352.
[13] *Boardman v Phipps* (1967) 2 AC 46 (HL).
[14] CA 2006, s 176(4).
[15] [1899] 1 QB 369.
[16] Ibid at 373.
[17] CA 2006, s 176(3).
[18] *Hansard*, GC Day 4, vol 678, column 330, 9 February 2006.

IV 'THIRD PARTY'

11.11   CA 2006, s 176 outlaws benefits given by third parties to directors. The expression 'third party' is defined in s 176(2) in exclusionary terms. The following are *not* third parties: the company, an associated corporate body or a person acting on behalf of the company or an associated corporate body. Consequently, anyone else is a third party, leaving a wide range of possibilities. 'Associated bodies corporate' is defined in s 256. The effect of this provision is that if we are seeking to ascertain whether a body is associated with X Ltd, the following would be covered: a holding company of X Ltd; a subsidiary company of X Ltd; or a company that is a subsidiary of the same holding company as X Ltd.

V FORMER DIRECTORS

11.12   Former directors (see CA 2006, s 170(2)) are subject to the duty not to accept benefits from third parties as regards things done or omitted to be done by them before ceasing to be directors. To the extent mentioned, the duty applies to former directors as it does to directors, but subject to any necessary adaptations. The inclusion of former directors effectively accords with the common law for a former director is, as the court in *CMS Dolphin Ltd v Simonet* said: 'just as accountable as a trustee who retires without properly accounting for trust property.'[19]

VI 'BENEFIT'

11.13   'Benefit' is not defined in s 176. During debates in Parliament the Solicitor-General stated that the ordinary meaning of the word should be applied.[20] It has been defined as 'an advantage or profit gained from something.'[21] The provision probably has commissions and bribes and any sort of secret benefit in mind.

11.14   Clearly there are some benefits which can be identified easily. These are financial rewards or money's worth such as tickets to prestigious sporting, entertainment or cultural events.[22] Will it be applied to the receipt of corporate hospitality? The GC100 has suggested that company boards will need to review their policies on, for example, corporate hospitality taken up by directors.[23] Whether the giving or receipt of corporate hospitality may be considered as creating a conflict of interest should be decided according to the context in which it is given or received. It is likely that in the following situation the benefits might offend: a director, who at the time that he or she is involved in

---

[19]   [2001] 2 BCLC 304 at 733.
[20]   HC Comm D 11 July 2006, columns 621–622.
[21]   J Pearsall (ed) *The New Oxford Dictionary of English* (OUP, 2002) at 162.
[22]   *ICSA Guidance on Directors' General Duties*, January 2008, at para 3.6.5.
[23]   GC100, *Companies Act 2006 - Directors' conflicts of interest*, Association of General Counsel and Company Secretaries of the FTSE 100, 18 January 2008 at para 2.6.

negotiating a contract with another company, is offered corporate hospitality by that other company. Having said that the Institute of Chartered Secretaries and Administrators ('ICSA') feel that liability might depend on what was the 'norm' and whether the benefit was excessive within the particular environment.[24]

11.15 The ICSA has said that proportionate and defensible policies need to be formulated as far as benefits are concerned and it has stated[25] that these policies should provide:

> 'how to deal with benefits offered by or received from third parties and which state what levels of corporate entertainment are significant for this policy or which need prior authorisation. The policies (including any updates) should be approved by the board, perhaps on a recommendation from the audit committee. All relevant employees and contractors should be informed of the policy and any updates and, for the company's protection, required to sign a receipt and acknowledgement to study and comply with the terms of the policy and any updates to it.'

11.16 Professor John Birds has suggested that if a director, who has knowledge of confidential information because of his or her position as a director, such as an impending takeover, makes a profit from the buying and selling of his or her company's shares, the director will be liable under s 176.[26]

11.17 It is possible that if a small gift is given to a director after the completion of a transaction and related to services performed by the director, then the position in equity as far as an agent is concerned may apply. With agents such a gift would not constitute a secret commission,[27] provided that the gift was not expected when the transaction was entered into or was not intended to affect subsequent transactions.[28] Likewise an inexpensive gift at Christmas is not likely to lead to a breach of the provision.[29]

VII SECRET PROFITS AND BRIBES[30]

11.18 Although not specifically mentioned, s 176 is directed at directors receiving secret profits and bribes. The provision effectively applies the rule in equity that fiduciaries are not to accept secret commission or bribes.[31]

---

[24] *ICSA Guidance on Directors' General Duties*, January 2008 at para 3.6.5.
[25] Ibid.
[26] J Birds et al *Boyle and Birds' Company Law* (Bristol, Jordan Publishing, 6th edn, 2007) at 631. Of course, it is likely that the director would also be guilty of insider dealing.
[27] *The Parkdale* [1897] P 53.
[28] F Reynolds *Bowstead and Reynolds on Agency* (London, Sweet and Maxwell, 16th edn, 1996) at 247.
[29] B Griffiths 'Dealing with Directors' Conflicts of Interest under the Companies Act 2006' (2008) 6 JIBFL 292.
[30] Clarke J provides an excellent, and succinct discussion of bribes in *Novoship (UK) Ltd v Mikhaylyuk* [2012] EWHC 3586 (Comm) at [104]–[112].
[31] *Attorney-General for Hong Kong v Reid* [1994] 1 AC 324 (PC).

Lord Reid said in *Attorney-General for Hong Kong v Reid*[32] that 'bribery is an evil practice which threatens the foundations of any civilised society'[33] and the Supreme Court in *FHR European Ventures LLP v Cedar Capital Partners LLC*[34] repeated the statement and gave it its approbation. It might be thought that bribery is not something that one would see a lot of in the UK, but in *Novoship (UK) Ltd v Mikhaylyuk*[35] the Court of Appeal emphasised the fact that bribery remains widespread.

11.19   The law has a significant dislike for secret profits.[36] The courts do not consider, in determining the issue of liability, whether the one to whom a duty is owed has in fact lost out. In *Regal (Hastings) Ltd v Gulliver*,[37] a case discussed in detail in **Chapter 9**, Lord Wright said that: 'both in law and equity, it has been held that, if a person in a fiduciary relationship makes a secret profit out of the relationship, the court will not inquire whether the other person is damnified or has lost a profit which otherwise he would have got.'[38]

11.20   An example of a case where a fiduciary (not a director) was compelled to account, inter alia, for secret profits was *Murad v Al-Saraj*[39] and the case provides some useful commentary on the effects of a fiduciary receiving secret profits. In that case A approached two sisters, whom we will call collectively, M, with a proposition related to the purchase of a hotel. The proposition involved the purchase of the hotel for £4.1m with M contributing £1m and A £500,000 in cash. The balance was to be raised by way of loans to a company, D, that was going to be set up by A and M in order to buy the property. D would be owned equally by M and one of A's companies. Profits from the running of the hotel would be divided two-thirds to M and one-third to A. A further element of the proposition was that if the hotel was sold the profit, if any, would be divided equally between A and M. M agreed, and the hotel was purchased by D. Subsequently M discovered that the situation was not quite as it was portrayed by A to M. A did not contribute £500,000 in cash, but his 'contribution' involved discharging debts he was owed by the vendor of the hotel, namely a secret commission of £369,000 for finding a buyer and £131,000 in unenforceable business and moral debts. M sued A for breach of fiduciary duty on the basis that A did not disclose how his contribution was made up and that he was receiving a secret profit. M was successful as A, as a fiduciary, was liable to account for profits that he had made within the scope and ambit of the duty that conflicted with his personal interest.[40]

---

[32]   Ibid.
[33]   Ibid at 330.
[34]   [2014] UKSC 45; [2015] AC 250; [2014] 3 WLR 535 at [42].
[35]   [2014] EWCA Civ 908.
[36]   For example, see *Boston Deep Sea Fishing & Ice Co v Ansell* (1888) 39 Ch D 339 (CA).
[37]   [1967] 2 AC 134 (HL).
[38]   Ibid at 154.
[39]   [2005] EWCA Civ 959.
[40]   The case is discussed on several occasions in **Chapter 15**.

11.21 Much has been said about secret profits and bribes in the context of agency. In *Boston Deep Sea Fishing and Ice Co Ltd v Ansell*[41] the defendant was held liable to account to the plaintiff company of which he was director for secret bribes or bonuses which he had received from persons making contracts with the company. The defendant's liability flowed from the fiduciary relationship which applied to his dealings with the company, for he acted as the company's agent.

11.22 The Explanatory Notes to the CA 2006 mentions bribes specifically.[42] They are a form of secret profit. According to Leggatt J in *Anangel Atlas Compania Naviera SA v Ishikawajimaa-Harima Heavy Industries Co Ltd*,[43] a bribe 'consists in a commission or other inducement, which is given by a third party to an agent as such, and which is secret from his principal'.[44] A bribe was described by Romer LJ in *Hovenden & Sons v Millhoff*[45] in the following way:

'a gift made…with the view of inducing the agent to act in favour of the donor in relation to transactions between the donor and the agent's principal and that gift is secret as between the donor and the agent – that is to say, without the knowledge and consent of the principal – then the gift is a bribe in the view of the law.'

In *Ross River Ltd v Cambridge City FC*[46] Briggs J (as he then was) described bribery as something:[47]

'committed where one person makes or agrees to make a payment to the agent of another person with whom he is dealing without the knowledge and consent of the agent's principal.'

11.23 At first instance in *Novoship (UK) Ltd v Mikhaylyuk*[48] Clarke J said that 'the essential character of a bribe is, thus, that it is a secret payment or inducement that gives rise to a realistic prospect of a conflict between the agent's personal interest and that of his principal'. This indicates the fact that conflict of interest is an essential element of a bribe.

11.24 There appear to be five components to a bribe:

1. there is a gift or other benefit given to the agent (or other fiduciary) or a promise to give something;
2. the gift is related to the agent's position (the bribe giver knowing that the agent is the agent of a person with whom the bribe giver is dealing) but need not relate to any specific arrangement;

---

[41] (1888) 39 Ch D 339.
[42] Explanatory Notes to the CA 2006 at para 344.
[43] [1990] 1 Lloyd's Rep 167.
[44] Ibid at 171. Also, see *Industries and General Mortgage Co Ltd v Lewis* [1949] 2 All ER 573.
[45] (1900) 83 LT 41 at 43.
[46] [2007] EWHC 2115; [2008] 1 All ER 1004.
[47] Ibid at [203].
[48] [2012] EWHC 3586 (Comm) at [106].

3.   the gift induces the agent to do something in favour of the one giving the gift;

4.   the giving of the gift puts the agent into a situation where his or her interest is in conflict, actually or potentially, with that of his or her principal;

5.   the gift is kept secret from the agent's principal.

All of the foregoing accords with the definition of a bribe in the Bribery Act 2010. Under this legislation a bribe is 'an inducement intended to gain an improper advantage whether or not the inducement or intended inducement has that effect'.[49]

11.25   A classic bribe would be for a director to be paid a sum of money by X, a supplier, to argue for, and favour, a company contract being given to X to supply goods which are needed by the director's company.[50]

11.26   A bribe involves corruption and where a payment is not for corrupt purposes, it is more appropriate to talk about the arrangement as a secret commission.[51]

11.27   Much is likely to turn on how the courts view a particular transaction or arrangement. An example is *Framlington Group plc v Anderson*.[52] The case was discussed in the last Chapter, but in relation to a different issue and so it is helpful to set out the facts again. In the case three of the defendants were employed by the plaintiffs, companies in a corporate group, as private client fund managers. They were also directors of one or both of companies in the group. I shall refer to the plaintiffs collectively as F. Under the terms of the directors' employment they were permitted, if they ceased to be employed by, or directors of, F, to establish or join a competing business and to take with them or to solicit Fs' clients. The directors were offered contracts of employment with R plc, which they decided to accept. R plc then negotiated with F for F to sell that part of F's business which was represented by the clients who would transfer their managed funds to R plc when the three directors moved to R plc. The transfer price consisted mainly of shares in R plc and was calculated by reference to the value of the managed funds transferred. The directors were instructed not to, and did not, participate in the negotiations conducted between F and R plc concerning the transfer of managed funds. R plc offered to the directors, as part of their new employment, shares in R plc, the number of which was to be based on the value of the managed funds transferred. When F discovered the term concerning the issuing of shares in favour of the directors, F issued proceedings claiming that the shares, together with any income and other profits which those shares had earned since they were beneficially

---

[49]   W Christopher, 'Trillion dollar bribery' (2011) 161 NLJ 25.
[50]   For example, see *Boston Deep Sea Fishing and Ice Co Ltd v Ansell* (1888) 39 Ch D 339.
[51]   F Reynolds *Bowstead and Reynolds on Agency* (London, Sweet and Maxwell, 16th edn, 1996) at 246–247.
[52]   [1995] 1 BCLC 475.

acquired by the three managers, were secret profits for which the three managers were accountable to F and that they held them on constructive trust for F. It was argued that the effect of the share consideration to be awarded to the directors was to deprive F of part of the purchase price which it could otherwise have obtained from R plc on the transfer of the managed funds.

11.28 Blackburne J indicated that the shares issued to the directors for coming to the new employer could not be regarded as a secret commission, and hence the benefits, it would seem, would not fall foul of s 176. The consideration for which the shares were payment was securing the long-term service of the three managers and with it their client goodwill. The learned judge distinguished the decision of the Australian High Court in *Furs Ltd v Tomkies*.[53] In that case the plaintiff company was carrying on the business of manufacturing furs for coats and ladies' stoles, and of tanning, dyeing, and dressing skins. The defendant, T, was the managing director of the company; he was also the manager of the tanning, dyeing and dressing branch of the business. He had special knowledge of this branch of the business which had been developed under his management. T had recommended that the company sell off this branch of the business. A New Zealand company, X, was interested in buying it. L, one of X's officers, was sent to Australia to negotiate for it. He indicated that if X bought the business then it would want to avail itself of T's services. T advised the chairman of his company about what L had said and the chairman said that as the company would not be able to retain T's services when the business was sold he should make the best deal that he could for himself. T and L agreed that T would be employed by X for three years and that he would receive £5,000[54] worth of shares in X and some promissory notes.

11.29 L and T negotiated a price to be paid to the plaintiff, and T advised the chairman who agreed to the price. Neither the directors nor the shareholders were told that the defendant was receiving a sum of £5,000, and the defendant made every effort to prevent this becoming known. The chairman knew that T was receiving some benefit but was not able to ascertain the exact provision, and T would not disclose it. Subsequently, the plaintiff brought proceedings against T claiming the benefits which he received from X. The Australian High Court held T liable for receiving a secret profit, and ordered him to pay the benefit he received to his former company.

11.30 With the granting of secret commissions, there is a presumption that the agent is influenced by it in doing his or her job,[55] and that is essentially the objectionable aspect of the benefit. However, it is not necessary for the company to establish the fact that the giving of the benefit has affected the way that the agent/director has conducted himself or herself in the role as an agent or director.

---

[53] (1936) 54 CLR 583.
[54] This was pre-decimalisation of currency which saw Australia change to dollars.
[55] *Hovenden & Sons v Millhoff* (1900) 83 LT 41 at 43.

11.31 If a benefit given to a director satisfies the criteria of a bribe then: it is irrelevant what was the intention of the one paying the bribe;[56] there is no need to establish that the one making the gift intended to induce the action of the agent;[57] it is presumed that the director was influenced to act by the bribe;[58] it is presumed that the company has experienced loss as far as the amount of the bribe is concerned.[59]

11.32 For an instance of a director receiving a secret profit, see *DEG-Deutsche Investitions- und Entwicklungsgesellschaft mbH v Koshy (No 2); Gwembe Valley Development Co Ltd (in receivership) v Koshy (No 3)*.[60]

VIII AUTHORISATION AND DEFENCE

11.33 Unlike with a conflict that is covered squarely by s 175, there is nothing in s 176 that provides that a director is able to seek the board's approval for the reception and retention of benefits from third parties. Obviously the whole idea of a benefit that constitutes a secret profit is that it is secret as far as the company is concerned. The articles could permit directors to receive certain benefits, but the drafting of the relevant article could be problematic. The case-law does suggest that the only certain way for a director as the recipient of an alleged bribe to defend himself or herself is to do what a director must do under s 175, that is, disclose the benefit to the company and secure its consent.[61] The director would need to ensure that the company is totally informed and so it is aware of the nature of the benefit and the circumstances of its giving.[62] There is nothing to suggest that disclosure to the board would be ineffective.

IX EFFECTS

11.34 It is not intended to embark on a prolix discussion of either the effects of a director receiving a bribe or secret commission or the remedies that are available to a wronged company as a result of a bribe or secret commission as Chapter 15 focuses on relief for breach of duty, but it is appropriate to say something given that bribes and secret commissions can be seen as somewhat different to other kinds of breaches.

---

[56] *Hovenden & Sons v Millhoff* (1900) 83 LT 41 at 43; *Industries & General Mortgage Co v Lewis* [1949] 2 All ER 573; *Ross River Ltd v Cambridge City FC* [2007] EWHC 2115; [2008] 1 All ER 1004.

[57] *Industries & General Mortgage Co v Lewis* [1949] 2 All ER 573.

[58] *Shipway v Broadwood* [1899] 1 QB 369; *Tesco Stores Ltd v Pook* [2003] EWHC 823 (Ch) at [38]–[45].

[59] *Mahesan v Malaysia Housing Corporation* [1979] AC 374.

[60] [2002] 1 BCLC 478. An appeal was allowed in part ([2003] EWCA Civ 1048; [2004] 1 BCLC 131).

[61] *Imageview Management Ltd v Jack* [2009] EWCA Civ 63; [2009] 1 BCLC 724 at [7].

[62] Ibid.

11.35   The first thing to say is that the director's action could be ratified by the shareholders. Unlike with s 175 there can be no process for board approval established, but as indicated above, full disclosure to the company will be a defence. If disclosure is made to the board or the general meeting of the shareholders then that should suffice. If a shareholder believes that there has been a breach and the disclosure is not full disclosure then he or she would need to consider initiating the derivative action process in order to claim against the errant director.

11.36   While Chapter 15 deals broadly with the effects of a breach and specifically relief, it is appropriate to say a few words about relief where secret commissions and bribes are involved. The following does not purport to be anything close to exhaustive.

11.37   A principal like a company could make a claim against the agent/director for money had and received.[63] A principal is entitled to seek equitable compensation or an account of profits against a fiduciary who receives a bribe.[64] In *Boston Deep Sea Fishing and Ice Co Ltd v Ansell*[65] Bowen LJ said:[66]

> '... the law implies a use, that is to say, there is an implied contract, if you put it as a legal proposition – there is an equitable right, if you treat it as a matter of equity – as between the principal and agent that the agent should pay it over, which renders the agent liable to be sued for money had and received, and there is an equitable right in the master to receive it, and to take it out of the hands of the agent, which gives the principal a right to relief in equity.'

11.38   While it is clear that a fiduciary is not entitled to profit from receiving a bribe or some undisclosed benefit as it constituted a breach of his or her fiduciary duty,[67] there has been a long-running debate as to whether a principal/beneficiary is able to rely on a proprietary right to recover from his or her agent/fiduciary the benefits of a bribe that the latter has received. If a principal was entitled to have a proprietary interest in the benefit of an agent then that would give the principal a priority over the agent's unsecured creditors and the principal could trace and follow the benefit in equity.[68] According to the Privy Council in *Attorney-General for Hong Kong v Reid*[69] and the courts in other Commonwealth jurisdictions,[70] the principal/beneficiary has a proprietary right to the benefits that constitute a bribe given to his or her

---

[63]   *Mahesan v Malaysia Housing Corporation* [1979] AC 374 at 383.
[64]   See *Fyffes Group Ltd v Templeman* [2000] 2 Lloyd's Rep 643; *Novoship (UK) Ltd v Mikhaylyuk* [2012] EWHC 3586 (Comm) at [86] and affirmed on appeal (*Novoship (UK) Ltd v Mikhaylyuk* [2014] EWCA Civ 908 at [93]).
[65]   (1888) 39 Ch D 339 (CA).
[66]   Ibid at 367–368.
[67]   See, *FHR European Ventures LLP v Mankarious* [2013] EWCA Civ 17; [2013] 3 All ER 29 at [13].
[68]   *FHR European Ventures LLP v Cedar Capital Partners LLC* [2014] UKSC 45; [2015] AC 250; [2014] 3 WLR 535 at [1].
[69]   [1994] 1 AC 324.
[70]   Notably, Australia, New Zealand, Singapore and Canada (as well as jurisdictions where the

agent/fiduciary. This is because an undisclosed profit, such as a bribe, which a director secures as a result of his or her acting as a director, belongs in equity to the company[71] (the director can be said to hold the benefit as a constructive trustee). This was inconsistent with an old Court of Appeal decision in *Lister v Stubbs*,[72] which was much more limited in scope. Relatively recently the Court of Appeal in *Sinclair Investments Ltd v Versailles Trade Finance Ltd*[73] refused to follow the Privy Council decision and held that it was bound by the reasoning in the decisions of *Lister v Stubbs*,[74] and another case, *Metropolitan Bank v Heiron*.[75] The Court in *Sinclair Investments* said that while a beneficiary is entitled to equitable compensation from the fiduciary, he or she is not able to claim a proprietary interest in the benefits acquired in breach of duty by the fiduciary except in two situations, namely where either the asset or money was or had been beneficially the property of the beneficiary or the fiduciary acquired the asset or money by taking advantage of an opportunity or right that was properly that of the beneficiary.[76] The Court said that if either of the two exceptions to the general rule applied then the beneficiary had the benefit of a constructive trust. The *Sinclair Investments* decision was a highly controversial decision, and it divided legal scholars in the common law world, with some[77] applauding the decision, while others, such as Lord Millett,[78] criticising it severely.

11.39   In a subsequent Court of Appeal judgment in *FHR European Ventures LLP v Mankarious*,[79] the Court found that the principal had a proprietary interest in the benefits as the case fell within the second of the exceptions identified in *Sinclair Investments*, and the Court distinguished *Lister*. In *FHR European Ventures* the secret commission that was given was paid out of funds of the principal, but if the commission had been out of non-principal funds then the principal would not have had a proprietary remedy available to it. The decision of the Court of Appeal was appealed to the Supreme Court and in *FHR European Ventures LLP v Cedar Capital Partners LLC*[80] which sought to resolve the divergence of opinion in the UK. In the unanimous opinion of all justices the appeal was dismissed. While the judgment of the Court recognised that if a principal was granted a proprietary right the agent's unsecured creditors could lose out, as the principal would have a priority right to the

---

decisions of the Privy Council remain binding). For an example of a case, see *Grimaldi v Chameleon Mining NL (No 2)* [2012] FCAFC 6 (Full Court of the Federal Court of Australia).
[71]   *Eden v Ridsdales Railway Lamp and Lighting Co* (1889) 23 QBD 368; *Attorney-General for Hong Kong v Reid* [1994] 1 AC 324 (PC); *Furs Ltd v Tomkies* (1936) 54 CLR 583 at 592 and approved of by the Court of Appeal in *Gwembe Valley Development v Koshy (No 3)* [2004] 1 BCLC 131 at [44]; *Mainland Holdings Ltd v Szady* [2002] NSWSC 699.
[72]   (1890) 45 Ch D 1.
[73]   [2011] EWCA Civ 347; [2011] 2 BCLC 501.
[74]   (1890) 45 Ch D 1.
[75]   (1880) 5 Ex D 319.
[76]   [2011] EWCA Civ 347; [2011] 3 WLR 1153; [2011] 2 BCLC 501 at [88]–[89].
[77]   For example, G Virgo 'Profits obtained in breach of fiduciary duty: personal or proprietary claim?' (2011) 70 CLJ 502 at 503.
[78]   P Millett 'Bribes and secret commissions again' (2012) 71 CLJ 583.
[79]   [2013] EWCA Civ 17; [2013] 3 All ER 29 at [79].
[80]   [2014] UKSC 45; [2015] AC 250; [2014] 3 WLR 535.

benefit given to the agent by way of a bribe or secret commission, and be able to trace the benefit into the hands of knowing receipts,[81] the Court was of the view that the preferable result was to grant to principals a proprietary right, especially where the agent's benefit consisted of secret commissions or bribes.[82] The Court noted that other common law jurisdictions had adopted the rule that a principal had a proprietary interest in the benefit obtained by the agent and felt that it was highly desirable that it should lean in favour of harmonisation across the common law world which would mean following the approach in *Attorney-General for Hong Kong v Reid*.[83] The Court concluded that the courts took a wrong turn in *Lister* and it and the cases that followed its approach were overruled. Thus, any secret commission or bribe received by an agent/fiduciary is held on trust for the principal. This effectively ends the spirited debate that we have seen for some years.

11.40 When undertaking the account against a director, the court adopts a broad approach and is not limited to profits which directly result from the transaction so as to exclude profits which can be said to be the result of another event, because the court does not enter into an investigation as to what would have happened if the fiduciary had complied with his obligations.[84] But a director cannot be made to account for profits that had not been made as a consequence of the breach of duty. Besides the director who received the benefit being required to account for what he or she had received, anyone who assisted the director is also liable to account.[85] The benefit to which the company would be entitled is extended to any properties in which the benefit had been invested.[86]

11.41 If a director receives a secret profit in breach of his or her duty then the director has the onus of establishing that certain profits are not to be accounted.[87]

11.42 The same applies in relation to the receipt of a bribe on the basis that it is being held on trust for the company.[88] The company can, in addition to claiming the benefit received by the fiduciary, sue the agent for any loss that the company has sustained because of the bribe.

11.43 The director could also be summarily dismissed for what he or she has done.[89]

11.44 It is possible that the third party who bribes or grants a secret commission to the director, could also be subject to a claim for damages from

---

[81] Ibid at [43], [44].
[82] Ibid.
[83] Ibid at [45].
[84] *Murad v Al-Saraj* [2005] EWCA Civ 958 at [76].
[85] Ibid at [69]; *Novoship (UK) Ltd v Mikhaylyuk* [2014] EWCA Civ 908 at [93].
[86] *Attorney-General for Hong Kong v Reid* [1994] 1 AC 324 (PC).
[87] *Murad v Al-Saraj* [2005] EWCA Civ 959 at [77].
[88] *De Busche v Alt* (1878) 8 Ch D 286.
[89] *Boston Deep Sea Fishing and Ice Co Ltd v Ansell* (1888) 39 Ch D 339 (CA).

the company, as occurred in an agency setting in *Fyffes Group Ltd v Templeman*.[90] Damages could be awarded if the company could demonstrate that the giving of the benefit caused some loss for the company. In this kind of situation the company would rely on tort on the basis that the company has been subjected to fraud.[91] It has been submitted that such a claim against the person who gives the bribe or commission depends on the existence of a transaction entered into between the company and the one giving the bribe.[92]

---

[90]   [2000] 2 Lloyd's Rep 643.
[91]   Ibid; *Mahesan v Malaysia Housing Corporation* [1979] AC 374 at 383; *Otkritie International Investment Management Ltd v Uromov* [2014] EWHC 191 (Comm) at [71].
[92]   A Stafford and S Ritchie, *Fiduciary Duties* (Bristol, Jordan Publishing, 2nd edn, 2015) at 325.

CHAPTER 12

DUTY TO DECLARE AN INTEREST

I INTRODUCTION

12.1   This is the fourth and final chapter that is linked to the idea of ensuring that directors are not in conflict situations. The duty covered in this chapter, and found in s 177 of the CA 2006, is concerned with requiring directors to disclose interests which they have in relation to a proposed transaction or arrangement with the company, so that their company is able to take that state of affairs into account in considering the director's position on issues relating to the transaction or arrangement. Naturally, a director's view on a matter might well be swayed if he or she has an interest in a transaction or arrangement, and, thus, it prevents the company from having the unbiased advice of a director on any particular issue.[1] Disclosure prevents the director from being in a true conflict situation as his or her interest is out in the open.

12.2   As part of the law that regulated directors, and flowing from the no-conflict rule, was the requirement in equity for directors to disclose to the company in general meeting any interest which they might have in transactions or arrangements in which the company is a party.[2] The reason for this was expressed[3] in the following way:

> 'The requirement for disclosure seems therefore to be intended not to protect the company against bad bargains or the consequences of arrangements into which they enter as a result of the partisan interest of a director, but simply to ensure that the honesty and integrity which should inform corporate dealings and, in particular, the internal management of corporations is scrupulously observed.'

12.3   In practice the articles of companies have often permitted disclosure by directors to the board, rather than the general meeting.[4] This process is now expressly permitted by s 177 of the CA 2006, and resolves any argument that there was a conflict between articles like reg 85 of Table A (Companies (Tables

---

[1]   *Benson v Heathorn* (1842) 1 Y & C Ch Cas 326 at 351; *Imperial Mercantile Credit Association v Coleman* (1871) LR 6 Ch App 558 at 567–568.

[2]   *DEG-Deutsche Investitions und Entwicklungsgesellschaft mbH v Koshy; Gwembe Valley Development Co Ltd v Koshy* [2003] EWCA Civ 1048; [2004] 1 BCLC 131 at [65].

[3]   *Woolworths Ltd v Kelly* (1991) 22 NSWLR 189 at 211; (1991) 4 ASCR 431 at 442 per Samuels JA.

[4]   For example, reg 85, Table A. See Explanatory Notes to the Companies Act 2006 at para 303. For a case example, see *Centoanti v Eekimitor Pty Ltd* (1994) 15 ACSR 629.

A–F) Regulations 1985) and s 310 of the Companies Act 1985.[5] Section 177, together with s 182, largely assumes the role once played by former s 317 of the CA 1985.

12.4 Like the duties discussed in the three previous chapters, the duty considered in this chapter deals with an issue of loyalty. A director who fails to disclose an interest is failing in his or her responsibility to be loyal to the company.

12.5 The duty provided for in s 177 came into force on 1 October 2008. This was formalised in art 5(1)(d) of the Companies Act 2006 (Commencement No 5, Transitional Provisions and Savings) Order 2007.[6]

12.6 The Chapter begins with a consideration of the terms of s 177 of the CA 2006 and then it considers the exceptions to the application of the provision and the meaning of 'interest'. This is followed by an examination of issues surrounding the disclosure, including how directors may legitimately make disclosure and what is the situation with the special case of single director companies. The consideration of s 177 ends with a brief discussion of the effects of a breach of the provision. The Chapter is completed by a short discussion of s 182, which although not a section that is part of the Act that deals with directors' general duties warrants some consideration in the context of a director's duties.

II THE PROVISION

12.7 CA 2006, s 177(1) provides the essential disclosure requirement of directors, and is that if they are in any way, directly or indirectly, interested in a proposed transaction or arrangement with the company, they must declare the nature and extent of that interest to the other directors. The next subsection then explains the various ways that this can be done. The subsection is not intended to be exhaustive as it begins by saying that 'the declaration *may* (but need not) be made ...' (my emphasis). The ways that a declaration can be made are:

> '(a) at a meeting of the directors, or
> (b) by notice to the directors in accordance with-
>   (i)   section 184 (notice in writing), or
>   (ii) section 185 (general notice).'

12.8 If at any time the declaration of interest proves to be, or becomes, inaccurate or incomplete, then the director must make a further declaration.[7] But this is only necessary 'if the company has not yet entered into the

---

[5] Vinelott J in *Movitex Ltd v Bulfield* [1988] BCLC 104 sought to reconcile the two.
[6] SI 2007/3495.
[7] CA 2006, s 177(3).

transaction or arrangement at the time the director becomes aware of the inaccuracy or incompleteness of the earlier declaration (or ought reasonably to have become so aware)'.[8]

12.9 A declaration is not permitted to be made *ex post facto*. It must be made before the company enters into the transaction or arrangement.[9]

12.10 Section 177(1) makes it clear that the director who has an interest is required not merely to indicate that he or she has an interest, for the director must specify the nature and extent of his or her interest.[10] Under the old law (s 317(1) of the CA 1985) a director also had to declare the nature of an interest, but not the extent of the interest. Consequently, s 177(1) might be regarded as wider than s 317(1) although under the latter it was said that the director was required to make a full and frank disclosure.[11] Also, in *Movitex Ltd v Bullfield*,[12] Vinelott J did say, and this was approved of in *DEG-Deutsche Investitions- und Entwicklungsgesellschaft mbH v Koshy (No 2); Gwembe Valley Development Co Ltd (in receivership) v Koshy (No 3)*,[13] that the disclosure under s 317 must be such that the other director or directors can see what his interest is and how far it goes.[14] But how far one has to go, under s 177, in identifying the interest is unclear. It might well depend on the circumstances, including the nature of the arrangement and the context in which it is made. It is worth noting that reg 85 of Table A does include a requirement to disclose the extent of the interest as well as the nature.

12.11 While s 177 of the CA 2006 is broader than s 317 of the CA 1985 in some respects, in one instance s 177 might be narrower. While s 317 expressly applied to shadow directors (s 317(8)), s 177 makes no such statement. Whether it applies to shadows directors hinges on s 170(5) which provides that general duties apply to shadows where and to the extent that the corresponding common law rules or equitable principles so apply. It was discussed in **Chapter 2** that there is some divergence of opinion as to whether shadow directors can be regulated by fiduciary duties.

12.12 As noted earlier, s 177 requires a director to disclose any interest, direct or indirect. So, the director does not need to be a party to the transaction for the duty to apply. An interest of another person in a contract with the company may require the director to make a disclosure under this duty, if that other person's interest amounts to a direct or indirect interest on the part of the director. An obvious example of an indirect interest is if the director's spouse was a shareholder in the company with whom the director's company was considering entering an arrangement.

---

[8]   Explanatory Notes to the CA 2006, at para 351.
[9]   CA 2006, s 177(4).
[10] See the Explanatory Notes to the CA 2006, at para 350.
[11] *Fine Industrial Commodities Ltd v Powling* (1954) 71 RPC 253 at 262.
[12] [1988] BCLC 104.
[13] [2002] 1 BCLC 478 at [255].
[14] [1988] BCLC 104 at 121.

12.13 Professor Paul Davies has indicated that one might be somewhat sceptical about the shareholders being protected by the disclosure where it is only made to the directors, for the directors might tend towards leniency, compared with shareholders, when it comes to any conflict of interests, especially if they feel that leniency might be extended to them in the future when disclosing interests.[15]

12.14 The classic case involving conflict, *Aberdeen Rly Co v Blaikie Bros*,[16] to which reference was made in **Chapter 9**, provides a good example of a situation where disclosure should be made. In that case X was a director in, and chairman of, A company. X, on behalf of the company, entered into a contract to purchase shares from a partnership, B, in which X was a partner. A company then sought to set aside the contract on the basis of X's conflict. It was held that X was in a position where he was to get the best deal that he could for A company. He did not. X should have disclosed his interest in B. In such a case it was said that unless there is disclosure by the director, the contract is voidable. A case today with the facts of *Aberdeen Rly Co* would not be dealt with under s 175 of the CA 2006 as conflicts that arise in relation to transactions with the company are excluded.[17] This type of situation would now be covered by s 177.

12.15 A more modern example of where disclosure should have occurred, and did not, was *State Bank of South Australia v Marcus Clark*.[18] Although this case also was discussed earlier,[19] it is helpful to set out the facts again. C was the chief executive officer of the plaintiff (the Bank) and also a director of E in which he held a great many shares. E had lent money to A. A began experiencing financial problems. C was contacted at the Bank by a representative of A, who advised that A was considering selling one of its subsidiaries, O. C then was the prime mover in the proposal of the Bank to purchase O. C did not disclose his interests and participated in board meetings of the Bank when the purchase was considered. The Bank decided, without an independent valuation of O, to buy the company. The Bank paid A\$59m when the company was worth somewhere between A\$17m and A\$21m. After the purchase, A directed that part of the purchase price be paid to E in discharge of its debt to E. On learning of this and C's interests the Bank took proceedings against C to recover the difference between the purchase price paid for O and its true value. The South Australian Supreme Court held that C had a duty to disclose his interests to the Bank's board, and because he did not do so he was in breach and liable to compensate the Bank.

12.16 To emphasise, s 177 is only concerned with the need to disclose in relation to a proposed transaction or arrangement with the company. The Attorney-General stated in Grand Committee, when the Bill was passing

[15] P Davies *Gower and Davies' Principles of Modern Company Law* (London, Sweet and Maxwell, 7th edn, 2003) at 400.
[16] (1854) 1 Macq HL 461.
[17] Section 175(3).
[18] (1996) 14 ACLC 1019.
[19] Above at **9.66**.

through Parliament, that different consequences emanated from a failure to disclose an interest in a proposed transaction compared with an existing arrangement.[20] Section 177 is supported by s 182 in that the latter covers existing transactions in which the company is involved. Section 182 repeats much of s 317 of the CA 1985. A declaration under s 182 is not required if the director had earlier made a declaration under s 177. The process that has to be followed for disclosure where there is a need to disclose in relation to an existing transaction or arrangement is set out in s 182 and is discussed briefly below.

12.17 Of course, a failure to disclose might well suggest that there is a conflict. If there is then a director could be in breach of both s 175 and s 177 of the CA 2006.

12.18 Unlike with a breach of its precursor, s 317 of the CA 1985, the failure to disclose if required by s 177 of the CA 2006 is not a criminal act.[21]

12.19 Section 180(1) of the CA 2006 provides that if s 177 is complied with then any transaction or arrangement is not liable to be set aside as a result of any common law rule or equitable principle requiring the consent or approval of the members. But, the articles of a company can always specify more arduous demands for approval, such as requiring the matter to be taken to the general meeting. The effect of s 180 is that if a director complies with s 177 he or she does not need to get approval from the shareholders. What s 177 does not do is to state what is the effect of compliance with the section. One might assume that it is that the director is exempt from any liability in relation to the benefit he or she receives as a result of the proposed transaction or arrangement with the company. But does it have a wider effect? What about a third party who might be involved in the transaction? Compliance with s 177 should, one would think, mean that the company is not able to avoid the transaction after it is entered into, and so the third party is safeguarded.[22]

12.20 The fact that directors comply with s 177 does not make them immune from being liable for a breach of any other of the duties set out in Chapter 2 of Part 10.[23]

III EXCEPTIONS

12.21 Section 177 provides for several exceptions to the requirement to make a declaration. First, under s 177(5) a director does not need to make a

---

[20] *Hansard*, HL GC Day 4, vol 678, cols 33-334 (6 February 2006).

[21] See CA 1985, s 317(9).

[22] P Hood 'Directors' Duties Under the Companies Act 2006: Clarity or Confusion?' (2013) 13 JCLS 1 at 35.

[23] This was the case under the old law. It was held in *Neptune (Vehicle Washing Equipment Ltd) v Fitzgerald* [1995] 1 BCLC 352 that the director was liable for breach of duty, absent any consideration of his failure to disclose.

declaration of an interest of which he or she is not aware, or where the director is not aware of the transaction or arrangement in question.[24] The exception does not lay down an exclusively subjective approach for determining directorial awareness, as objective considerations are to be taken into account. Thus, for the purposes of the section a director is treated as being aware of matters of which he or she ought reasonably to be aware. This provides two disadvantages for directors. First, it means that a director has greater difficulty in pleading ignorance of the transaction or arrangement. Second, a director could conceivably be in breach of the provision when he or she is genuinely ignorant of a need to make a disclosure.

12.22   The second exception is found in s 177(6). It provides that a director is not required to declare an interest in any of the following situations: it cannot reasonably be regarded as likely to give rise to a conflict of interest;[25] if, or to the extent that, the other directors are already aware of it (and for this purpose the other directors are treated as aware of anything of which they ought reasonably to be aware); if, or to the extent that, it concerns terms of his or her service contract that have been or are to be considered by a meeting of the directors, or by a committee of the directors appointed for the purpose under the company's constitution. One assumes that this last exclusion exists because the directors can be treated as being aware of the director's position. This addresses the problem that was before the court in *Runciman v Walter Runciman plc*.[26] In that case the plaintiff (R) had been chairman of WR. WR had been acquired through the process of a hostile takeover bid and R had been dismissed. Subsequently, WR accepted the fact that the dismissal had been unfair. There was disagreement as to the amount of damages that could be awarded to R. WR argued that a purported extension of R's contract of service, entered into before the takeover, was invalid because, inter alia, if the extension had been properly authorised the contract was voidable as R had not made disclosure of his interest in it. Simon Brown J refused to say that there was a breach of s 317 of the CA 1985 because while there was not, technically, a disclosure, it was self-evident that R had an interest in the extension of the contract.[27] His Lordship felt that any declaration by the director would be absurd because of the knowledge of WR's directors,[28] and he eschewed any focus on form rather than substance.[29] Simon Brown J seemed to go further and said that disclosure can be implied where the circumstances were such that all directors were aware of the interest of the director that was at issue.

---

[24]   This effectively duplicates reg 86(b) of Table A articles (Companies (Tables A–F) Regulations 1985).

[25]   This reflects reg 86(a) of Table A articles (Companies (Tables A-F) Regulations 1985) and the Companies (Model Articles) Regulations 2008, SI 2008/3229, reg 2, Sch 1, art 14(3)(b) (private companies); reg 4, Sch 3, art 14(3)(b) (public companies).

[26]   [1992] BCLC 1084.

[27]   Ibid at 1094.

[28]   Perhaps no less absurd than the disclosure required in *Lee Panavision Ltd v Lee Lighting Ltd* [1991] BCLC 575.

[29]   [1992] BCLC 1084 at 1094.

IV AN INTEREST

12.23 Section 177(1) provides that a director is to declare an interest in a transaction or arrangement, but nowhere in the provision is there any explanation of what is to be seen as an interest. It is probable that a director of X Ltd would have an interest within the section if he or she was a shareholder of a company with which X Ltd was proposing to enter a transaction or arrangement, or the director was a member of a partnership with which X Ltd was proposing to enter a transaction or arrangement.[30]

V THE DISCLOSURE

A Generally

12.24 Under s 317 of the CA 1985 disclosure had to be made to a meeting of the directors. Admittedly, this was interpreted liberally, but s 177 of the CA 2006 provides, potentially, more leeway. As indicated above under the heading 'The Provision,' in s 177(2) Parliament has set out some ways in which a director may disclose any interest that he or she has in a proposed transaction. The critical thing is that the provision is not exhaustive. It merely states some actions that the director can take and that will see him or her fulfil the duty of disclosure. The fact that the provision is not exhaustive is a double-edged sword. It is perhaps helpful that there are obviously other ways in which a director can disclose legitimately, but in not being exhaustive the provision leaves open the issue of what will actually constitute adherence to the section as a whole. Clearly, there will be instances where directors make disclosure in a way that is not covered by the ways mentioned in s 177(2) and there will be arguments about whether in fact they have acted properly or not. It is advisable, one would think, for directors to ensure that they disclose pursuant to one of the ways that is set out in the legislation, where at all possible, and to make sure that there is a proper record of the disclosure.

12.25 Notwithstanding s 177, the articles might require *additional* demands on directors, and how they can disclose to the directors.

B The manner of disclosure

12.26 Under s 177(2) a director discloses properly if he or she were to make a declaration:

- at a meeting of directors;
- by notice to the directors in accordance with s 184;
- by notice to the directors in accordance with s 185.

---

[30] *Imperial Mercantile Credit Association v Coleman* (1873) LR 6 HL 189.

12.27 Section 184 of the CA 2006 provides that notices that are sent to the other directors are to be in writing.[31] A notice must be sent in hard copy form unless the recipient has agreed to accept it in an electronic form.[32] The notice may be sent by hand or post, or, if it has been agreed that it can be sent electronically, by agreed electronic means.[33] Under the old s 317 a declaration had to be made at the next meeting of directors after a director became interested in a proposed transaction[34] and, in a similar vein, s 184(5)(a) provides that where a declaration has been made in the manner permitted by s 184, the making of the declaration is deemed to form part of the proceedings at the next meeting of directors after the notice is given.

12.28 Section 185 of the CA 2006 permits, again in a similar vein to that provided for in s 317 of the CA 1985, that if a director gives a general notice it is to be regarded as a sufficient declaration of interest in relation to the matters to which it relates.[35] The notice, which must be given to the directors of the company, should provide to the effect either that the director disclosing has an interest (as a member, officer, employee or otherwise) in a particular body corporate or firm and is to be regarded as being interested in any transaction or arrangement that may, following the date of the notice, be made with that body corporate or firm, or the director is connected with a particular person, other than a body corporate or firm, and is to be regarded as being interested in any transaction or arrangement that may, following the date of the notice, be made with that person.[36] The director is obliged to state the nature and extent of the director's interest in the body corporate or firm, or the nature and extent of the director's connection with the person.[37] Section 185 ends with an indication that a notice under the provision is not effective unless it is given at a meeting of the directors or the disclosing director takes reasonable steps to ensure that it is raised and read at the next meeting of the directors after it has been given.[38]

C To whom is disclosure to be made?

12.29 When s 177(1) of the CA 2006 states that the disclosure is to be made to 'the other directors' one assumes that this means to a full complement of directors and not just a committee of directors. Under the previous provision, s 317 of the CA 1985, it was not possible only to disclose to a committee,[39] and one would think that the same would apply under s 177.

---

[31]   CA 2006, s 184(1)(2).
[32]   CA 2006, s 184(3).
[33]   CA 2006, s 184(4).
[34]   CA 1985, s 317(2).
[35]   CA 2006, s 185(1).
[36]   CA 2006, s 185(2).
[37]   CA 2006, s 185(3).
[38]   CA 2006, s 185(4).
[39]   *Guinness plc v Saunders* [1990] 2 AC 663.

D Implied disclosure?

12.30 What is interesting is to consider whether there would be a breach of s 177 if a director did not actually do something to disclose his or her interest, but all of the directors were aware of the interest. Certainly the rationale behind the law would have been satisfied. But is that enough? Under s 317 of the CA 1985, Dillon LJ, giving the leading judgment of the Court of Appeal in *Lee Panavision Ltd v Lee Lighting Ltd*,[40] indicated that he would hesitate to find that the failure formally to declare at a board meeting an interest common to all members and, as a consequence already known to all of the board, was a breach.[41] Theoretically, it would seem that a director in the position of the directors in this latter case could argue that there had been effective compliance. One difficulty might be that under s 177, as opposed to s 317, directors have to declare the extent of their interest, as well as the nature of it, and it is likely that that is not going to happen where there is an informal disclosure.

E Participation of the disclosing director

12.31 While directors are not permitted by s 175 of the CA 2006 to be counted towards a board's quorum when the board is considering authorisation of a conflict, directors who have made a declaration under s 177, may, subject to the company's articles of association, be counted towards the quorum at the meeting that is convened to consider the transaction or arrangement involved, participate in any decision relating to such transaction with the company, and actually vote.[42] Regulation 94 of Table A forbids from voting directors who have disclosed, but often companies exclude that article. Nevertheless, ICSA has suggested that it is good practice for the board to take decisions on related matters without the director being present.[43] The reason for this is self-evident.

F Disclosure and single directors

12.32 Under s 317 of the CA 1985, where there was a company with a sole director then, according to the decision in *Neptune (Vehicle Washing Equipment Ltd) v Fitzgerald*,[44] the director was required to declare his or her interest at a board meeting even though he or she was the only director present. This seemed to be rather bizarre. In this case F was a sole director of N Ltd. At a board meeting attended by F and the company secretary, F resolved to pay himself £100,000 as compensation for the termination of his service contract. Subsequently, the company sought to avoid the contract and have the money returned. In a preliminary hearing Lightman J held that a sole director must disclose to the board meeting the interest he had in a transaction, and even pause for thought. The critical thing was that the minutes must record this fact. This rather farcical process is now unnecessary, because the situation is

---

[40] [1992] BCLC 22 (the decision at first instance can be found at [1991] BCLC 575).
[41] Ibid at 33.
[42] Explanatory Notes to the CA 2006 at para 354.
[43] *Guidance on Directors' General Duties* (January 2008) at para 3.7.5.
[44] [1995] 1 BCLC 352.

different under s 177 of the CA 2006 in that the disclosure only has to be made to the other directors,[45] and, of course, there are none to whom disclosure can be made if there is a sole director situation. The Explanatory Notes to the CA 2006 have confirmed that no disclosure is required in the *Neptune (Vehicle Washing Equipment Ltd)* type of case.[46] If the director is the only member of the company then he or she has to comply with s 231 which governs the case where a sole member of the company is also a director. Section 231(2) requires the terms of the service contract of the director, if not in writing, to be set out in a written memorandum or recorded in the minutes of the first board meeting following the making of the contract.

12.33   While a single director will not be required to disclose, this will not free the director from his or her other duties, so a director might be liable for a breach of s 175 of the CA 2006 if he or she were to act on behalf of the company in making a contract with a partnership in which he or she is a partner. Also, one would think that a director could be held liable for a breach of s 172 if he or she were to do something that was not intended to promote the success of the company, something that was probably the case in *Neptune (Vehicle Washing Equipment Ltd) v Fitzgerald*. Certainly in this case Lightman J was concerned about the director's lack of good faith.

VI EFFECTS

12.34   As mentioned earlier, a breach of s 177 does not lead to criminal liability: the section does not set out the consequences of a director's failure to make proper disclosure. However, it is probable that the courts will follow what was done when there was a contravention of s 317 of the CA 1985. Like s 177, s 317 did not state the civil consequences of a breach. When s 317 was breached the relevant contract was voidable.[47] It is submitted that the company would be able to claim an account of profits or equitable compensation on the basis of s 178. This is discussed in detail in **Chapter 15**. Where a company does seek compensation then it must demonstrate a causal link between the failure to disclose and loss.[48] If a company was only seeking rescission then the onus is on the director to prove disclosure, but if the company is seeking compensation it has the onus of establishing non-disclosure.

12.35   A director is not able to excuse himself or herself by establishing that the non-disclosure of the director had no real effect because the company would have entered into a transaction in any event, even if disclosure had been made.

---

[45]   Explanatory Notes to the CA 2006 at para 352.
[46]   Ibid.
[47]   *Craven Textile Engineers Ltd v Batley Football Club Ltd* [2001] BCC 679 (CA).
[48]   See *Target Holdings Ltd v Redferns* [1996] AC 421 at 432, 434 (HL); *Swindle v Harrison* [1997] 4 All ER 705 at 718, 733 (CA).

In *Brickenden v London Loan and Savings Co*,[49] in giving the judgment of the Privy Council, Lord Thankerton said:[50]

> 'When a party, holding a fiduciary relationship, commits a breach of his duty by non–disclosure of material facts, which his constituent is entitled to know in connection with the transaction, he cannot be heard to maintain that disclosure would not have altered his decision to proceed with the transaction, because the constituent's action would be solely determined by some other factor, such as the valuation by another party of the property proposed to be mortgaged. Once the Court has determined that the non–disclosed facts were material, speculation as to what course the constituent, on disclosure, would have taken is not relevant.'

12.36 More recently, Jonathan Parker LJ in *Murad v Al-Saraj*[51] approved of the comments. They are essentially consistent with what the Court of Appeal had to say in *Gwembe Valley Development Co Ltd (in receivership)v Koshy (No 3)*.[52] In that case Mummery LJ said that what would have happened if the required disclosure had been made was irrelevant.[53] This was all in the context of a claim for an account of profits which does not depend on the company experiencing loss. Mummery LJ said that when determining whether any compensation should be paid for loss claimed as a result of non–disclosure, the court is not precluded from considering what would have happened if there had been disclosure. If the commission of the wrong has not caused loss to the company then the company should not be entitled to elect to recover compensation.[54]

VII DISCLOSURE UNDER SECTION 182

12.37 This book deals with the general duties of directors in Chapter 2 of Part 10, but it is appropriate to discuss in brief the obligation on directors under s 182 of the CA 2006 as it is a close relative of s 177. It, together with s 177, replaces s 317 of the CA 1985. There are distinct similarities between sections 177 and 182 and in fact some parts of s 182 duplicate s 177 with necessary changes to take into account the thrust of s 182. It is submitted that where s 182 is the same, or nearly the same, as s 177, what has been discussed thus far will be applied by the courts.

12.38 Section 182(1) provides that if directors are in any way, directly or indirectly, interested in a transaction or arrangement that the company has entered into, they must declare the nature and extent of that interest to the other directors. The provision has no application where directors have already declared, under s 177, the nature and extent of the interest.

---

[49]   [1934] 3 DLR 465.
[50]   Ibid at 469.
[51]   [2005] EWCA Civ 959 at [105].
[52]   [2003] EWCA Civ 1048, [2004] 1 BCLC 131 at [135] per Mummery LJ.
[53]   Ibid at [145]–[146].
[54]   Ibid at [147].

12.39 While s 177 does not prescribe the only ways in which disclosure can take place, s 182(2) does. A declaration must be made at a meeting of the directors, by notice in writing in accordance with s 185 or by general notice according to s 185.

12.40 As with the position under s 177, if at any time the declaration of interest proves to be, or becomes, inaccurate or incomplete, then the director must make a further declaration.[55]

12.41 It is incumbent on a director to make the required declaration as soon as reasonably practicable.[56] But if the director does not make the declaration as soon as reasonably practicable, he or she is not freed from the obligation to make a declaration.

12.42 A director is excused from the obligation to make a declaration of an interest of which he or she is not aware or where the director is not aware of the transaction or arrangement in question.[57] As with s 177, the exception does not lay down an exclusively subjective approach for determining directorial awareness, as objective considerations are to be taken into account. Thus, for the purposes of the section a director is treated as being aware of matters of which he or she ought reasonably to be aware.

12.43 A further exception to the application of s 182 is provide for in s 182(6). The subsection duplicates s 177(6), and that which was discussed above[58] can equally apply to the provision.

12.44 Where there is a director who would ordinarily be required to disclose under s 182, but he or she is a sole director, there are requirements laid down by s 186 if the company is required to have more than one director. Section 186 provides that in such a case the declaration must be in writing and the making of the declaration is deemed to form part of the proceedings at the next meeting of directors after the notice is given.[59]

12.45 Section 182 is said to apply to shadow directors but with some adaptations.[60] These are as follows:

- the requirement in s 182(2)(a) that a declaration is to be made at a directors' meeting is not applicable;[61]
- in relation to general notice under s 185, s 185(4) does not apply;[62]

---

[55] CA 2006, s 182(3).
[56] CA 2006, s 182(4).
[57] CA 2006, s 182(5). This effectively duplicates reg 86(b) of Table A.
[58] See above at **12.22**.
[59] CA 2006, s 186(1).
[60] CA 2006, s 187(1).
[61] CA 2006, s 182(2).
[62] CA 2006, s 187(3).

- general notice is not effective unless given by written notice under s 184.[63]

12.46 Finally, unlike with s 177, it is an offence not to comply with s 182, namely failing to declare an interest that a director has in an existing transaction or arrangement.[64]

---

[63] CA 2006, s 187(4).
[64] CA 2006, s 183(1). The actual consequences are set out in s 182(2).

CHAPTER 13

DUTY TO CONSIDER THE INTERESTS OF CREDITORS[1]

I INTRODUCTION

13.1 Earlier, in **Chapter 6**, we considered the duty provided for under s 172. The focus of the chapter was completely on s 172(1). It was indicated in the chapter that s 172(3) provided a different approach, compared with s 172(1), and its consideration would be left until this chapter.

13.2 Section 172(3) of the CA 2006 provides that the duty imposed by s 172(1), the duty to promote the success of the company for the benefit of the members of the company, is subject to any enactment or rule of law requiring directors, in certain circumstances, to take into account the interests of creditors, so that in certain cases s 172(3) trumps the duty set out in s 172(1) because it makes the latter subject to the former. Section 172(3) makes a clear reference to the case-law that has developed over the past 35–40 years in the United Kingdom,[2] Australia,[3] New Zealand[4] and elsewhere in the Commonwealth and in Ireland[5] and which provides that if a company is in some form of financial difficulty the directors must consider the interests of creditors in the decisions which they make in running the company's affairs. This is clearly affirmed by the Court of Appeal in *Bilta (UK) Ltd (In Liquidation) v Nazir.*[6] In giving the leading judgment, with which

---

[1]   For a fuller discussion of this topic, see A Keay *Company Directors' Responsibilities to Creditors* (Abingdon, Routledge-Cavendish, 2007) at 151–286. Parts of the Chapter are based on the discussion in the aforementioned book.

[2]   For example, see *Winkworth v Edward Baron Development Co Ltd* [1986] 1 WLR 1512; [1987] 1 All ER 114; *Liquidator of West Mercia Safetywear v Dodd* (1988) 4 BCC 30; *Facia Footwear Ltd (in administration) v Hinchliffe* [1998] 1 BCLC 218; *Re Pantone 485 Ltd* [2002] 1 BCLC 266; *Gwyer v London Wharf (Limehouse) Ltd* [2002] EWHC 2748 (Ch); [2003] 2 BCLC 153; *Re MDA Investment Management Ltd* [2004] BPIR 75; [2003] EWHC 227 (Ch); *Re Cityspan Ltd* [2007] EWHC 751 (Ch); [2007] 2 BCLC 522.

[3]   For instance, see *Walker v Wimborne* (1976) 137 CLR 1; 3 ACLR 529; *Grove v Flavel* (1986) 4 ACLC 654; (1986) 11 ACLR 161; *Kinsela v Russell Kinsela Pty Ltd* (1986) 4 ACLC 215; (1986) 10 ACLR 395; *Jeffree v NCSC* (1989) 7 ACLC 556; (1989) 15 ACLR 217; *Galladin Pty Ltd v Aimnorth Pty Ltd (in liq)* (1993) 11 ACSR 23; *Linton v Telnet Pty Ltd* (1999) 30 ACSR 465; *Spies v The Queen* [2000] HCA 43; (2000) 201 CLR 603; (2000) 173 ALR 529.

[4]   For instance, see *Nicholson v Permakraft (NZ) Ltd* (1985) 3 ACLC 453; *Hilton International Ltd (in liq) v Hilton* [1989] NZLR 442.

[5]   See *Re Frederick Inns Ltd* [1991] ILRM 582 (Irish HC) and affirmed at [1994] ILRM 387 (Irish SC); *Jones v Gunn* [1997] 3 IR 1; [1997] 2 ILRM 245.

[6]   [2013] EWCA Civ 968.

Lord Dyson MR and Rimer LJ agreed, Patten LJ said that the 'obligation to act in the interests of creditors arises in circumstances where the company is or is likely to become insolvent and is no more than a statutory recognition of the decision of this court in *West Mercia Safetywear Ltd v Dodd* [1988] BCLC 250.'[7]

13.3   This chapter, after explaining the policy and legislative background to the position that exists with respect to the subject of the Chapter, goes on to consider the rationale for the duty and then the case-law as it has developed. These sections of the Chapter are then followed by consideration of: the circumstances that trigger the obligation; the way that directors should act when subject to the obligation to creditors; whether the obligation is in fact a direct or indirect duty to creditors; and to which creditors is the obligation owed? The duty provided for in s 172(3) is almost exclusively of interest to liquidators and administrators, as we will see. A breach of the duty is often pleaded by a liquidator, as part of a misfeasance claim under s 212 of the Insolvency Act 1986, along with a claim that a director has engaged in wrongful trading, and, therefore, in breach of s 214 of the Insolvency Act 1986.

II POLICY AND LEGISLATIVE BACKGROUND

13.4   The issue of directors considering creditors' interests posed a problem for the Company Law Review Steering Group ('CLRSG') commissioned to review UK company law in the latter years of the 1990s. Originally the CLRSG rejected (provisionally) at one stage, the idea of including any specific obligation to creditors in its proposals to the Government, taking the view that such an action might cut across the operation of s 214 of the Insolvency Act 1986, a provision which empowers liquidators to seek court orders requiring contributions to be made by directors who engaged in wrongful trading in failing to protect creditor interests.[8] Later, in its Final Report on 26 July 2001, a majority of the CLRSG had a change of mind,[9] certainly in relation to the situation where insolvency threatens a company. In a relatively long discussion on the topic, the CLRSG said,[10] inter alia, that:

> 'In providing a high level statement of directors' duties, it is important to draw to directors' attention that different factors may need to be taken into consideration where the company is insolvent or threatened by insolvency. To fail to do so would risk misleading directors by omitting an important part of the overall picture.'

13.5   The CLRSG proposed that directors should be required to take a balanced view of the risks to creditors at an earlier stage in the onset of

---

[7]   Ibid at [22]. See the discussion in the case of *Re HLC Environmental Projects Ltd* [2013] EWHC 2876 (Ch) and especially at [87]–[100].

[8]   *Modern Company Law for a Competitive Economy: Developing the Framework* (London, DTI, 2000) at para 3.73.

[9]   *Modern Company Law for a Competitive Economy: Final Report* (London, DTI, 2001) vol 1 at para 3.13.

[10]   Ibid at para 3.12.

insolvency,[11] so that where directors know or should know that the company is more likely than not at some point going to be unable to pay its debts as they fall due, they must, inter alia, take action that will achieve a reasonable balance between reducing the risk that creditors will not get paid and promoting the success of the company.[12]

13.6 In July 2002 the Government, in response to the Final Report of the CLRSG, published a White Paper, 'Modernising Company Law',[13] and in volume 1 it addressed the issue of directors having some responsibility to consider the interests of their companies' creditors when financial distress strikes their companies. The White Paper stated that the Government had concluded that the weight of the argument favoured the exclusion of any duties to creditors in the statutory statement envisaged by the CLRSG.[14] The Government maintained that if there was a statement of duties to creditors in the statute then it would be incumbent on directors to make finely balanced judgments and they might err on the side of caution because of fear of personal liability, and this would be inconsistent with the rescue culture which the Government was trying to foster.[15] In March 2005 the Government published a second White Paper, titled 'Company Law Reform',[16] that was said to build on the work of the CLRSG and the 2002 White Paper. As far as the changes to be effected in relation to directors, the new White Paper saw the duties of directors being included in the proposed sections of a new Act, rather than being placed in a Schedule, which had been the strategy employed by both the Final Report[17] of the CLRSG and the White Paper of 2002. Importantly, while the Government did not propose to codify a duty to creditors, it did state in the draft Company Law Reform Bill that it put forward that the duty imposed on directors to promote the success of the company for the benefit of its members 'has effect subject to any enactment or rule of law requiring directors, in certain circumstances, to consider or act in the interests of creditors of the company'.[18] In its explanatory notes the Government stated that this provision 'preserves the current legal position that, when the company is insolvent or is nearing insolvency, the interests of the members should be supplemented, or even replaced, by those of the creditors'.[19]

13.7 When the Company Law Reform Bill was introduced into the House of Lords, cl B3 in the draft Bill, included with the Second White Paper, had essentially become cl 156. Again, the Government confirmed in the Guidance to Key Clauses, released with the Bill, that the law dealing with directors' duties to

---

[11]   Ibid at para 3.17.
[12]   Ibid at Annex C, para 8.
[13]   Cm 5553-1, TSO, July 2002.
[14]   *Modern Company Law for a Competitive Economy: Final Report* (London, DTI, 2001) vol 1 at para 3.10.
[15]   Ibid at para 3.11.
[16]   Cm 6456.
[17]   *Modern Company Law for a Competitive Economy: Final Report* (London, DTI, 2001) vol 1 Annex C, cl 17 and Sch 2 of a draft Bill.
[18]   Clause B3(4).
[19]   Clause B19.

take into account creditors' interests should not be subject to legislation, but allowed to develop at common law.[20] This approach has carried over into the CA 2006. Interestingly in the Explanatory Notes to the Act, para 331 provides that s 172(3) of the CA 2006 recognises that the duty to promote the success of the company is displaced when the company is insolvent. It then goes on to note that s 214 of the Insolvency Act 1986 provides a mechanism under which the liquidator can require the directors to contribute towards the funds available to creditors in an insolvent winding up, where they ought to have recognised that the company had no reasonable prospect of avoiding insolvent liquidation and then failed to take all reasonable steps to minimise the loss to creditors. It is not clear why the Notes refer to insolvency here. As we will see, the law does not limit the existence of the obligation to consider creditor interests to the point where the company is insolvent. The Notes seem to acknowledge this, because in para 332 they provide that the requirement 'to promote the success of the company will be modified by the obligation to have regard to the interests of creditors as the company *nears* insolvency' (my emphasis). This is inconsistent with the statement in the former paragraph, but is closer to the state of the law. The upshot of the provision is that the duty to promote the success of the company will be modified by the obligation to have regard to the interests of creditors when the law requires it.[21]

13.8 As mentioned in **Chapter 6**, those creditors who are suppliers of companies might find some solace from the fact that directors are required, by s 172(1)(c) of the CA 2006, in fulfilling their duty to act in such a way as to promote the success of the company for the benefit of its members as a whole, to take account, inter alia, of any need of the company to foster its business relationships with suppliers and others. Also, any creditor of the company might argue that 'creditors' are covered by the catch-all 'others' in the provision and directors should have regard to its, and other creditors, interests. However, this does not stop a company from running up debts with a supplier and then ditching the supplier and moving on to some other supplier to establish a new relationship. If this occurs then the original supplier has no alternative but to sue the company for the amount owed or petition for either administration or liquidation of the company, as it has no standing to bring a derivative claim. These actions are fraught with disadvantages, not least being that the company is wound up with few assets and the supplier gets little or nothing back.

13.9 Leaving aside the legislation at this point we now turn to the rationale for the obligation and then the case-law as it has developed over the past 40 years. The Chapter discusses the obligation considered here as a duty, although this is not technically correct, for it is only an aspect of a duty.[22] Nevertheless, the literature often talks of a duty to creditors as a short-hand way of describing the obligation involved.

---

[20] Clause 170.
[21] Explanatory Notes to the CA 2006 at para 332.
[22] This appeared to be the view of the Court of Appeal in *Bilta (UK) Ltd (In Liquidation) v Nazir* [2013] EWCA Civ 968.

13.10   This chapter majors on the case-law developments in relation to when directors must take into account the interests of their companies' creditors. But it is to be remembered that s 172(3) provides that the duty in s 172(1) is subject to any rule of law or any enactment that requires directors to consider the interests of creditors. So, besides the circumstances set out in the case-law that has developed the requirement that directors consider creditors' interests, in certain situations, the s 172(1) duty may also be subject to other enactments. One obvious one is s 214 of the Insolvency Act 1986. This provision requires directors to take every step with a view to minimising the potential loss to the company's creditors. But this is only when the directors knew or ought to have concluded that there was no reasonable prospect that the company would avoid going into insolvent liquidation. The requirement in s 214 must surely be seen as an enactment which makes it incumbent on directors to see s 172(1) as subject to their consideration of the creditors' interests. This interpretation ensures that there is no conflict between s 172 and s 214. So, if the circumstances envisaged by s 214 exist, a director must put aside the requirement of s 172(1) and focus on ensuring that he or she takes into account the needs of creditors.

III THE BASIS OF THE DUTY

13.11   Before moving on to consider the jurisprudence in this area, this section of the Chapter examines briefly the reason for the existence of the obligation under study. The obligation acts as a form of creditor protection, inhibiting companies externalising the cost of their debts at the time of financial distress. The reason given for this obligation is that if the company is insolvent, near it or embarking on a venture which it cannot sustain without relying totally on creditor funds, 'the interests of the company are in reality the interests of existing creditors alone.'[23] At this time, the shareholders are no longer the owners of the residual value of the firm (the residual owners being those whose wealth directly rises or falls with changes in the value of the company[24]), having been, in effect, transplanted by the creditors,[25] whose rights are transformed

---

[23]   *Brady v Brady* [1989] AC 755, [1988] 2 All ER 617, [1988] 2 WLR 1308, (1988) 4 BCC 390, [1988] BCLC 579, [1988] 2 FTLR 181, (1988) PCC 316, 132 SJ 820, HL, reversing (1987) 3 BCC 535, [1988] BCLC 20, [1987] 2 FTLR 414, (1987) 137 NLJ 898, (1977) PCC 434, C at 552; *Dairy Containers Ltd v NZI Bank Ltd* [1995] 2 NZLR 30 at 97.

[24]   D Baird 'The Initiation Problem in Bankruptcy' (1991) 11 *International Review of Law and Economics* 223 at 228–229; S Gilson and M Vetsuypens 'Credit Control in Financially Distressed Firms: Empirical Evidence' (1994) 72 *Washington University Law Quarterly* 1005 at 1006. This seems to be what was being said in *Brady v Brady* [1989] AC 755, [1988] 2 All ER 617, [1988] 2 WLR 1308, (1988) 4 BCC 390, [1988] BCLC 579, [1988] 2 FTLR 181, (1988) PCC 316, 132 SJ 820, HL, reversing (1987) 3 BCC 535, [1988] BCLC 20, [1987] 2 FTLR 414, (1987) 137 NLJ 898, (1977) PCC 434, C. Professor Lynn LoPucki criticises the use of residual ownership: 'The Myth of Residual Owner: An Empirical Study' (2004) 82 Wash U L Q 1341. Mr Leslie Kosmin QC (sitting as a deputy judge of the Chancery Division in *Gwyer v London Wharf (Limehouse) Ltd* [2002] EWHC 2748 (Ch); [2003] 2 BCLC 153 specifically stated that creditors' interests should be paramount at the time of insolvency (at [74]). Overall the cases provide little guidance.

[25]   *Dairy Containers Ltd v NZI Bank Ltd* [1995] 2 NZLR 30 at 96.

into equity-like rights.[26] Thus, the directors are effectively playing with the creditors' money,[27] and so the creditors may be seen as the major stakeholders in the company,[28] and, as a consequence, the directors are obliged not to sacrifice creditor interests.[29]

13.12 It is the view of financial economists that directors might well, when their companies are in difficulty, undertake actions which involve more risk;[30] a position accepted by the CLRSG.[31] Shareholders are happy for this to occur, when the company is in financial distress, as they have little to lose for it will be the creditors who will lose out if the risk fails. There is empirical evidence to support the fact that this tends to occur,[32] and it has become axiomatic that this

---

[26] S Schwarcz 'Rethinking a Corporation's Obligations to Creditors' (1996) 17 *Cardozo Law Review* 647 at 668; R Millner 'What Does it Mean for Directors of Financially Troubled Corporations to Have Fiduciary Duties to Creditors?' (2000) 9 *Journal of Bankruptcy Law and Practice* 201 at 206–207. Whether this gives creditors a proprietary interest in the assets of the company is a matter for debate. It is suggested in *Kinsela v Russell Kinsela Pty Ltd* (1986) 4 ACLC 215 at 221 that they do, but compare the discussion in S Worthington 'Directors' Duties, Creditors' Rights and Shareholder Intervention' (1991) 18 MULR 121 at 141. For the view that several groups could be regarded as exposed to residual risk, see, G Kelly and J Parkinson 'The Conceptual Foundations of the Company: A Pluralist Approach' (1998) 2 CfiLR 174.

[27] Millner ibid at 207; R Hartman 'Situation Specific Fiduciary Duties for Corporate Directors: Enforceable Obligations or Toothless Ideals' (1993) 50 *Washington and Lee Law Review* 1761 at 1771; R Lipson 'Directors' Duties to Creditors: Volition, Cognition, Exit and the Financially Distressed Corporation' (2003) 50 *University of California at Los Angeles Law Review* 1189 at 1212. See *Brady v Brady* [1989] AC 755, [1988] 2 All ER 617, [1988] 2 WLR 1308, (1988) 4 BCC 390, [1988] BCLC 579, [1988] 2 FTLR 181, (1988) PCC 316, 132 SJ 820, HL, reversing (1987) 3 BCC 535, [1988] BCLC 20, [1987] 2 FTLR 414, (1987) 137 NLJ 898, (1977) PCC 434, C at 552.

[28] *Kinsela v Russell Kinsela Pty Ltd* (1986) 4 ACLC 215 at 221.

[29] Ibid. See J Sarra 'Taking the Corporation Past the 'Plimsoll Line' – Director and Officer Liability When the Corporation Founders' (2001) 10 *International Insolvency Review* 229 at 235; M Moffat 'Directors' Dilemma – An Economic Evaluation of Directors' Liability for Environmental Damages and Unpaid Wages' (1996) 54 *University of Toronto Faculty of Law Review* 293 at 302.

[30] See *Credit Lyonnais Bank Nederland NV v Pathe Communications Corp* 1991 Del Ch WL 277613; LEXIS 215; reproduced in (1992) 17 *Delaware Journal of Corporate Law* 1099 (Delaware Chancery Court). Also, see CC Nicolls 'Liability of Corporate Officers and Directors to Third Parties' (2001) 35 Can Bus L J 1 at 35; R Hartman 'Situation Specific Fiduciary Duties for Corporate Directors: Enforceable Obligations or Toothless Ideals' (1993) 50 *Washington and Lee Law Review* 1761 at 1771; R de R Baronds, 'Fiduciary Duties of Officers and Directors of Distressed Corporations' (1998) 7 *George Mason Law Review* 45 at 46; J Armour 'The Law and Economics of Corporate Insolvency: A Review' (2001) ESRC Centre for Business Research, University of Cambridge, Working Paper No 197, at 1.

[31] *Modern Company Law for a Competitive Economy: Final Report* (London, DTI, 2001) vol 1 at para 3.15.

[32] R Daniels 'Must Boards Go Overboard? An Economic Analysis of the Effects of Burgeoning Statutory Liability on the Role of Directors in Corporate Governance' in J Ziegel (ed) *Current Developments in International and Comparative Corporate Insolvency Law* (Oxford, Clarendon Press, 1994) at 549. However, R Barondes 'Fiduciary Duties of Officers and Directors of Distressed Corporations' (1998) 7 *George Mason Law Review* 45 at 62 challenges this view.

risk-taking will take place,[33] particularly where the directors are also the controlling shareholders.[34] It might be argued that as the unsecured creditors are protected only by contractual rights, when companies are financially stressed their position warrants some form of added protection,[35] whereby the directors become accountable, principally, to the creditors,[36] something that s 172(3) seems to require.

13.13 Another reason for protecting the creditors is that company directors might, in order to sustain the company's business, when it is failing, offer higher priority to new creditors, thereby weakening the position of existing creditors.[37]

13.14 A third reason for the obligation is that the level of risk upon which credit was calculated and extended by creditors has changed, and the duty compensates the creditors accordingly. The duty provides 'the greatest protection at the time of the greatest risk, and, by changing what the board can reasonably justify as being in the corporate interest'[38] stops improper use of the corporate power to incur liabilities.

13.15 If a company is subject to circumstances that mean that creditor interests have to be taken into account, the case-law indicates that the shareholders cannot ratify any breach by directors where the company is insolvent or even in financial difficulty.[39]

IV THE CASE-LAW DEVELOPMENT

13.16 Section 172(3) has indirectly indicated that it is the case-law that is highly critical as to how s 172(3) operates. The problem is that in dealing with some highly significant issues the case-law is not as clear as one would like to see.

13.17 The obligation that we are examining is very much of a Commonwealth development, but which has also been embraced in Ireland. The advent of the duty to consider the interests of creditors can be traced to several decisions delivered in Australasia, with the first decision being that of the High Court of

---

[33] R Adler 'A Re-Examination of Near-Bankruptcy Investment Incentives' (1995) 62 *University of Chicago Law Review* 575 at 590-598; Barondes, ibid at 46, 49.

[34] R Mokal 'An Agency Cost Analysis of the Wrongful Trading Provisions: Redistribution, Perverse Incentives and the Creditors' Bargain' (2000) 59 CLJ 335 at 353–354.

[35] M van der Weide 'Against Fiduciary Duties to Corporate Stakeholders' (1996) 21 *Delaware Journal of Corporate Law* 27 at 43; R Rao, D Sokolow and D White, 'Fiduciary Duty a la Lyonnais: An Economic Perspective on Corporate Governance in a Financially-Distressed Firm' (1996) 22 *The Journal of Corporation Law* 53 at 64.

[36] See the comments in *Re Pantone 485 Ltd* [2002] 1 BCLC 266 at 285–286.

[37] A Keay 'Directors' Duties to Creditors: Contractarian Concerns Relating to Efficiency and Over-Protection of Creditors' (2003) 66 MLR 665 at 669.

[38] R Grantham 'The Judicial Extension of Directors' Duties to Creditors' [1991] JBL 1 at 15.

[39] For instance, see *Re Horsley & Weight Ltd* [1982] 3 All ER 1045; *Kinsela v Russell Kinsela Pty Ltd* (1986) 4 ACLC 215; (1986) 10 ACLR 395; *Re DKG Contractors Ltd* [1990] BCC 903.

Australia in *Walker v Wimborne*.[40] In that case a liquidator had brought misfeasance proceedings (under the equivalent of s 212 of the Insolvency Act 1986 ('the misfeasance provision')), against several directors of the company being liquidated, Asiatic. The claim was based on the fact that the directors had moved funds from Asiatic to other companies in which they held directorships. The relevant companies, including Asiatic, were treated by the directors as a group. The directors were accustomed to moving funds between companies and when this was done no security was usually taken, and no interest charged or paid. At the time of the movement of funds that was the subject of the action, Asiatic was insolvent, and it later entered liquidation. In his leading judgment, Mason J (whose judgment was approved of by Barwick CJ) said:[41]

> 'In this respect it should be emphasised that the directors of a company in discharging their duty to the company must take into account the interests of its shareholders and its creditors. Any failure by the directors to take into account the interests of creditors will have adverse consequences for the company as well as for them.'

13.18

His Honour said that for there to be a misfeasance there had to be a breach of duty, and in his view the actions of the directors constituted a breach of duty. While the comments of Mason J were obiter, it might be argued that his comments have become authoritative.[42]

13.19 The approach provided in *Walker v Wimborne* was not apparently followed in the UK for some time. Occasionally, a judge said something that indicated that the *Wimborne* approach might be favoured, but there was no direct application of the principle. In *Lonrho Ltd v Shell Petroleum Co Ltd*,[43] Lord Diplock said that the best interests of the company are not exclusively those of the shareholders, but they may include those of its creditors.[44] A little later in *Re Horsley & Weight Ltd*,[45] in a case involving a claim by the liquidator of a company that the granting of a pension to a former director constituted a breach of duty, Templeman LJ said[46] that:

---

[40] (1976) 137 CLR 1; (1976) 3 ACLR 529.
[41] Ibid at 6–7; 531.
[42] J McConvill 'Directors' Duties to Creditors in Australia after Spies v The Queen' (2002) 20 *Company and Securities Law Journal* 4 at 12 and referring to R Tomasic, J Jackson, and R Woellner *Corporations Law: Principles, Policy and Process* (Sydney, Butterworths, 1996) at 413-418.
[43] [1980] 1 WLR 627 (HL).
[44] Ibid at 634.
[45] [1982] 1 Ch 442.
[46] Ibid at 455.

'If the company had been doubtfully insolvent at the date of the grant [of the pension] to the knowledge of the directors, the grant would have been both a misfeasance and a fraud on the creditors for which the directors would remain liable.'

13.20   In 1985 what became the leading case in New Zealand, *Nicholson v Permakraft (NZ) Ltd,*[47] a decision of the Court of Appeal, was decided. In this case P Ltd held shares in two companies. The shares in P Ltd were nearly all held by three persons. P Ltd experienced liquidity problems and in mid-1975 a reconstruction plan that was proposed involved the incorporation of a new company that would acquire nearly all of the shares of P Ltd and the companies in which it held shares (X and Y). The new company, Z Ltd, was to purchase the land and buildings owned by P Ltd at valuation, as well as the shares P Ltd held in X and Y. The shareholders of P Ltd would be paid a dividend from the funds paid to P Ltd. Z Ltd would charge P Ltd rent for the use of its former buildings. This plan was put into effect. In mid-1976 P Ltd encountered difficulties, consistent with those experienced by the industry generally, and the bank put in receivers and eventually the company went into liquidation. The liquidator commenced an action against the shareholders of P Ltd in order to recover the dividend that was paid to them. At first instance, the directors were found to be in breach of duty, and an appeal was instituted. While the appeal was successful, all three members of the Court held that when a company is insolvent the directors owe a duty to take into account creditor interests. In the case before it the court said that no duty existed.

13.21   Soon after the New Zealand decision the New South Wales Court of Appeal dealt with the duty in the case of *Kinsela v Russell Kinsela Pty Ltd.*[48] This case involved the commencement of an action by the liquidator of a company, RK, which carried on business as a funeral director. The action sought the setting aside of a lease over premises granted by RK to directors of the company. The lease had been granted three months before the commencement of winding up, and at a time when the company's financial position was precarious. The company had sustained a significant loss during the previous year, had suffered less severe losses for several years and the accounts some six months before the lease was entered into showed that the company's liabilities exceeded its assets by nearly A$200,000. Also of importance, was the fact that the company had committed itself to performing services in relation to pre-paid funerals. The lease involved the directors being given a term of three years at a below market rental, there was no escalator clause to cover inflation and the directors were entitled, during the life of the lease, to purchase part of the premises for a sum which was well below true value. The court found that the intention of the directors was to put the assets of RK beyond the reach of its creditors, and to preserve what had been a family business for many years.[49] The leading judgment (with which the other members of the court concurred) was handed down by Street CJ and it has

---

[47]   (1985) 3 ACLC 453.
[48]   (1986) 4 ACLC 215; (1986) 10 ACLR 395.
[49]   Ibid at 219; 399.

become one regularly cited by judges in subsequent decisions in the UK, throughout the Commonwealth and in Ireland. Street CJ said that when a company is insolvent, the creditors' interests intrude.[50] In this case the directors were liable.

13.22 The first comments in a UK decision that apparently embraced the duty expressly were in the House of Lords case of *Winkworth v Edward Baron Development Co Ltd*.[51] Here X and his wife, Y, were the directors and shareholders of a company, Z, having used company money to purchase their shares. Z bought a property that X and Y occupied as their home. As a consequence of this and other payments, the company was overdrawn on its bank account. The company's bank was given an undertaking by X that the deeds of the property purchased by Z would be held to the order of the bank. Y was unaware of this as she did not take an active part in the company. X and Y sold their former marital home and paid part of the proceeds into Z's bank account. Then X, without the knowledge of Y, initiated the mortgage of Z's property to W in order to raise funds to discharge the indebtedness on the overdraft. Z subsequently became insolvent and went into liquidation. W commenced an action for possession against Z as it has defaulted on its mortgage payments. Y opposed these proceedings on the basis that the payment of the funds from the former marital home gave her an equitable interest in the property. Ultimately the House of Lords held that Y did not have an equitable interest. Lord Templeman, in delivering a judgment unanimously supported by the other Law Lords, said that the equitable doctrine that a legal owner held in trust for those who contributed to the purchase of the property did not apply here because the payment made by X and Y to the bank account of Z was not referable to the acquisition of the property mortgaged to W as the property had been paid for before X and Y deposited their payment in Z's account. Also his Lordship said that X and Y had breached their duties to Z and Z's creditors when the company's funds were used for the purchase of their shares and when the company's overdraft was incurred and increased, partly to benefit X and Y.

13.23 What is crucial in this case is a dictum of Lord Templeman, which caused a significant amount of academic response, some of it highly critical. His Lordship said[52] that:

> '[A] company owes a duty to its creditors, present and future. The company is not bound to pay off every debt as soon as it is incurred and the company is not obliged to avoid all ventures which involve an element of risk, but the company owes a duty to its creditors to keep its property inviolate and available for the repayment of its debts.... A duty is owed by the directors to the company and to the creditors of the company to ensure that the affairs of the company are properly administered and that its property is not dissipated or exploited for the benefit of the directors themselves to the prejudice of the creditors.'

---

[50]   Ibid at 221; 401.
[51]   [1986] 1 WLR 1512.
[52]   Ibid at 1516.

13.24 The Full Court of the Western Australian Supreme Court in *Jeffree v NCSC*[53] subsequently followed the approach of Lord Templeman. In that case, at a time when arbitration proceedings were extant against a company, W, the controlling director, J, established a new company and sold the assets of W to the new company for value but not including anything for goodwill. When the person who initiated the arbitration proceedings succeeded against W there were no assets held by W. Subsequently, the then Australian corporate regulator, the National Companies and Securities Commission, brought criminal proceedings against J on the basis that he had breached his directorial duties.[54] The court held the director liable.

13.25 Meanwhile in England the Court of Appeal, in *Liquidator of West Mercia Safetywear Ltd v Dodd*,[55] in delivering what has probably become the leading case in the UK on the issue,[56] and cited and applied on many occasions, considered the matter. In this case, D was the director of two companies, X and Y. X was the parent company of Y. At the relevant time both companies were in financial difficulty. X had a large overdraft that D had guaranteed and it also had a charge over its book debts. One debt owed to X was £30,000, and this was owed by Y. A few days before there was a meeting of the members of Y, which was going to consider a motion that Y wind up, D transferred the sum of £4,000 that had been paid to Y by one of its debtor to X's overdrawn bank account. On liquidation of Y, the liquidator sought from the bank repayment to Y of the £4,000. The bank refused and so the liquidator sought both a declaration that D was guilty of misfeasance and breach of duty in relation to the transfer of the money to X, and repayment of the £4,000. At first instance, in the county court, the liquidator failed. He then appealed to the Court of Appeal. Dillon LJ, who gave the leading judgment with which the other members of the Court (Croom-Johnson LJ and Caulfield J) concurred, found that the payment constituted a fraudulent preference (under the Bankruptcy Act 1914, the precursor of s 239 of the Insolvency Act 1986). As far as the claim that there had been a breach of duty, his Lordship approved of what Street CJ said in *Kinsela,* particularly in relation to the directors having a duty to consider creditor interests when a company is in financial difficulty, and came to the view that there was a breach of duty on the part of D.

13.26 Since this decision there have been several English cases that have held directors liable for failing to take into account the interests of creditors when making decisions and when their company has been in financial straits. These decisions either expressly or in effect[57] have sought to apply what was said in

---

[53] (1989) 7 ACLC 556.
[54] While there have been changes, a breach of some duties by directors who act recklessly or in an intentionally dishonest manner can lead to criminal liability. Directors have never been liable under criminal law in the UK for breach of duties.
[55] (1988) 4 BCC 30.
[56] Professor Paul Davies has said that the case provides the clearest recognition of the duty in English law: *Gower's Principles of Company Law* (London, Sweet and Maxwell, 6th edn, 1997) at 603.
[57] For instance, see *Yukong Lines Ltd of Korea v Rendsburg Investments Corporation* [1998] BCC 870; *Facia Footwear Ltd (in administration) v Hinchliffe* [1998] 1 BCLC 218; *Re Pantone*

Liquidator of West Mercia Safetywear Ltd v Dodd, and, arguably, have not taken the law much further, although the decision in *Gwyer v London Wharf (Limehouse) Ltd*[58] and the fairly recent decision in *Re HLC Environmental Projects Ltd* might be seen as exceptions.[59] Also, since the 1980s, decisions in both Australia[60] and Ireland[61] have propounded the same view. In addition, for the first time, the Canadian courts[62] have also accepted the existence of the duty.[63]

V THE TRIGGERING OF THE DUTY

13.27 While most commentators and all courts take the view that the obligation that we are considering here is not applicable at all times, and while there is general agreement that it applies when a company is in some form of financial difficulty, courts have been rather reticent about stating the precise point when the obligation arises. Section 172(3) does not indicate when the duty in s 172(1) is trumped by s 172(3). This is left to the case-law.

13.28 At one extreme, namely the clear insolvency of the company, there seems to be general agreement that the obligation undoubtedly operates. In *Kinsela v Russell Kinsela Pty Ltd*[64] Street CJ found against the directors of the company because of the fact that the company was clearly insolvent when the lease was executed. While his Honour left open the possibility of the duty being extended in order to encompass other states of financial distress short of insolvency, he plainly accepted the fact that when a company is insolvent the directors have responsibilities to the creditors.[65] The Supreme Court of Ireland

---

485 Ltd [2002] 1 BCLC 266; *Gwyer v London Wharf (Limehouse) Ltd* [2002] EWHC 2748 (Ch); [2003] 2 BCLC 153; *Re MDA Investment Management Ltd* [2003] EWHC 227 (Ch); [2004] 1 BCLC 217; [2004] BPIR 75; [2003] EWHC 227 (Ch); *Ultraframe (UK) Ltd v Fielding* [2005] EWHC 1638 (Ch); *Re Bakewell Management Ltd* (unreported, 22 February 2008, High Court, Robin Knowles QC); *Williams v Farrow* [2008] EWHC 3663 (Ch); *Re Kudos Business Solutions Ltd* sub nom *Earp v Stevenson* [2011] EWHC 1436 (Ch); [2012] 2 BCLC 65; *Roberts v Frohlich* [2011] EWHC 257 (Ch); [2012] BCC 407; [2011] 2 BCLC 625. Also, see the Scottish case of *Dryburgh v Scotts Media Tax Ltd* [2011] CSOH 147.

[58]   [2002] EWHC 2748 (Ch); [2003] 2 BCLC 153 at [74].
[59]   [2013] EWHC 2876 (Ch) at [94]–[95].
[60]   For instance, see *Grove v Flavel* (1986) 11 ACLR 161 (SA S Ct); *Re New World Alliance Pty Ltd* (1994) 51 FCR 425 at 444-445; (1994) 122 ALR 531 (Aust Fed Ct); *Linton v Telnet Pty Ltd* (1999) 30 ACSR 465 (NSW CA); *Spies v The Queen* [2000] HCA 43; (2000) 201 CLR 603; (2000) 173 ALR 529; (2000) 74 ALJR 1263 (Aust HC).
[61]   For instance, see *Re Frederick Inns Ltd* [1991] ILRM 582 (Irish HC) and affirmed at [1994] ILRM 387 (Irish SC); *Jones v Gunn* ([1997] 3 IR 1; [1997] 2 ILRM 245.
[62]   *Sidaplex-Plastic Supplies Inc v Elta Group Inc* (1998) 40 OR (3d) 563; *Canbook Distribution Corporation v Borins* (1999) 45 OR (3d) 565; *Millgate Financial Corporation Ltd v BCED Holdings Ltd* (2003) CanLII 39497 (Ontario SC); *Peoples' Department Stores v Wise* [2004] SCC 68; (2004) 244 DLR (4th) 564.
[63]   There have been many cases in the UK and elsewhere where directors have been found to be in breach of the duty under consideration, and a number of them have made important points. They are discussed later in various parts of the Chapter.
[64]   (1986) 4 ACLC 215; (1986) 10 ACLR 395.
[65]   Ibid at 223; 404.

in *Re Frederick Inns Ltd*[66] appeared to agree for it took the view that if companies are insolvent then creditors have the right to petition for their winding up, and if that is the case, the directors should not be dealing with company property in any way other than for the betterment of the creditors.[67] In New Zealand in *Nicholson v Permakraft (NZ) Ltd*[68] Cooke J included near insolvency, along with insolvency or doubtful solvency, as the trigger for the imposition on directors of a duty to creditors.

13.29 There is clear authority in England that insolvency triggers the obligation to creditors. This can be seen in the decision of *Liquidator of West Mercia Safetywear Ltd v Dodd*[69] where the court said that where a company is insolvent the interests of the creditors overrode those of the shareholders. More recently, English courts in a large corpus of cases, such as *Re Pantone 485 Ltd*,[70] *Gwyer v London Wharf (Limehouse) Ltd*,[71] *Re Cityspan Ltd*,[72] *Roberts v Frohlich*[73] and *Re HLC Environmental Projects Ltd*,[74] have indicated that where a company is insolvent the interests of its creditors are paramount.[75] We will return to this point later in the Chapter.

13.30 Perhaps one of the major problems here is determining whether a company is or is not insolvent. The two ways that are used to ascertain whether a company is insolvent in the United Kingdom are the cash flow and balance sheet tests.[76] This is not the appropriate place to discuss the tests, but it suffices to say that determining whether a company was insolvent, on either test, is not easy[77] and both tests have their problems.[78]

---

[66] [1994] ILRM 387; [1993] IESC 1.
[67] Ibid at [38] (IESC).
[68] (1985) 3 ACLC 453 at 459.
[69] (1988) 4 BCC 30 at 33.
[70] [2002] 1 BCLC 266.
[71] [2002] EWHC 2748 (Ch); [2003] 2 BCLC 153.
[72] [2007] EWHC 751 (Ch); [2007] 2 BCLC 522; [2008] BCC 60.
[73] [2011] EWHC 257 (Ch); [2012] BCC 407; [2011] 2 BCLC 625 at [85].
[74] [2013] EWHC 2876 (Ch) at [92].
[75] Professors LoPucki and Whitford ('Corporate Governance in the Bankruptcy Reorganization of Large Publicly Held Companies' (1993) 141 U Pa L Rev 669 at 709) disagree, taking the view that management owes duties to both creditors and shareholders of an insolvent company until a bankruptcy reorganization occurs. But from their empirical research LoPucki and Whitford found that the managers of large public companies that are insolvent aligned with creditors more frequently than shareholders (at 745).
[76] See Insolvency Act 1986, s 123(1)(e), (2).
[77] The leading UK cases are: *Re Cheyne Finance Plc* [2007] EWHC 2402 (Ch); [2008] 1 BCLC 741; [2008] BCC 182; *BNY Corporate Trustee Services Ltd v Eurosail – UK 2007-3BL plc* [2013] UKSC 28; *Re Casa Estates Ltd* [2013] EWHC 2371 (Ch).
[78] For a discussion, see R Goode *Principles of Corporate Insolvency Law* (London, Sweet and Maxwell, 4th edn, 2011) Chapter 4; A Keay 'The Insolvency Factor in the Avoidance of Antecedent Transactions in Corporate Liquidations' (1995) 21 *Monash University Law Review* 305; P Walton, 'Inability to Pay Debts: Beyond the Point of No Return' [2013] JBL 160; A Keay *McPherson's Law of Company Liquidation* (London, Sweet and Maxwell, 3rd edn 2013) at 103–119.

13.31 Some cases have given indications that a duty to take into account creditors' interests is actually triggered before the company enters an insolvent state. There are various points identified by the courts, and these get further away from the state of insolvency as we go. First, it is said that directors can be subject to the obligation when their company is nearing insolvency.[79] In the Supreme Court of Western Australia in the case of *Geneva Finance Ltd v Resource & Industry Ltd*[80] it was held that the duty applied where the company was insolvent or approaching insolvency. Probably the most publicised decision has been the American case of *Credit Lyonnaise Bank Nederlander, NV v Pathe Communications Corp*,[81] where Chancellor Allen of the Delaware Court of Chancery stated that:

> 'At least where a corporation is operating in *the vicinity of insolvency*, a board of directors is not merely the agent of the residual risk bearers[the shareholders], but owes its duty to the corporate enterprise.'(my emphasis)

13.32 Chancellor Allen failed to explain exactly what he meant by 'in the vicinity of insolvency', but he seemed to be suggesting that the duty to creditors arises when the company is nearing insolvency.[82] Similarly, in *Gwyer v London Wharf (Limehouse) Ltd*,[83] Leslie Kosmin QC (sitting as a deputy judge of the High Court) said that the duty arose where the company was on the verge of insolvency, and that is probably close or near to insolvency.

13.33 Another mooted trigger for the obligation is where the company is of doubtful solvency.[84] Directors could probably ascertain when the solvency of their company is doubtful more easily than when insolvency has occurred. Insolvency occurs at one point. Doubtful solvency appears to be much broader.

---

[79]   *Nicholson v Permakraft (NZ) Ltd* (1985) 3 ACLC 453 at 459; *Re New World Alliance* (1994) 51 FCR 425 at 444-445; (1994) 122 ALR 531.

[80]   (2002) 20 ACLC 1427.

[81]   (1991) Del Ch WL 277613; LEXIS 215; reproduced in (1992) 17 *Delaware Journal of Corporate Law* 1099.

[82]   *Geyer v Ingersoll Publications Co* 621 A 2d 784 (1992). The duty was said to be owed, in the US, to creditors, and not, as in Commonwealth jurisdictions, to the company to take into account creditor interests. Interestingly, a Minnesota court in *Snyder Elec Co v Fleming* (305 NW 2d 863 at 869 (1981)) referred to directors owing duties to creditors when a company was on the verge of insolvency. The decision in *Credit Lyonnaise Bank Nederlander, NV v Pathe Communications Corp* has now been overturned. Directors now only have to take into account creditors' interests when the company is insolvent, not when the company is in the vicinity of insolvency. See, *Quadrant Structured Products Co v Vertin* 2015 WL 2062115 (Del Ch, 4 May 2015).

[83]   [2002] EWHC 2748 (Ch) at [74]; [2003] 2 BCLC 153 at 178.

[84]   *Nicholson v Permakraft (NZ) Ltd* (1985) 3 ACLC 453 at 459; *Brady v Brady* [1989] AC 755; [1988] 2 All ER 617; [1988] 2 WLR 1308; (1988) 4 BCC 390; [1988] BCLC 579; [1988] 2 FTLR 181; (1988) PCC 316; 132 SJ 820, HL, reversing (1987) 3 BCC 535; [1988] BCLC 20; [1987] 2 FTLR 414; (1987) 137 NLJ 898; (1977) PCC 434, C at 552; *Gwyer v London Wharf (Limehouse) Ltd* [2002] EWHC 2748 (Ch) at [4]; [2003] 2 BCLC 153 at 178. Also, see the comments of Templeman LJ in *Re Horsley & Weight Ltd* [1982] 1 Ch 442 at 455.

13.34 A third point that triggers the duty, according to some cases, is where there is a risk of insolvency.[85] In *West Mercia Safetywear v Dodd*[86] Dillon LJ referred to his earlier judgment in *Multinational Gas and Petrochemical Co v Multinational Gas and Petrochemical Services Co,* a case in which the Court of Appeal rejected the argument that the directors owed a duty to take into account creditors' interests following the fact that directors made a bad decision and this led to the company becoming insolvent.[87] His Lordship said that the reason for his decision in *Multinational Gas* was the fact that the subject company was amply solvent at the time that the directors made their decision, and the decision was made in good faith.[88] His Lordship implied in *West Mercia Safetywear* that if the company in *Multinational Gas* had not been amply solvent and there was a risk of insolvency as a result of the directors' decision, then he would have held there to have been a duty. But in the case of *Re HLC Environmental Projects Ltd,*[89] it was made clear that before the duty is triggered there must be a real rather than a remote risk of insolvency. John Randall QC (sitting as a deputy High Court judge) in *Re HLC Environmental Projects Ltd,*[90] said that in ascertaining what triggers the duty:

'The underlying principle is that directors are not free to take action which puts at real (as opposed to remote) risk the creditors' prospects of being paid, without first having considered their interests rather than those of the company and its shareholders.'

13.35 The focus on real risk of insolvency is reminiscent of what the New South Wales Court of Appeal said in *Kalls Enterprises Pty Ltd v Baloglow:*[91]

'It is sufficient for present purposes that, in accord with the reason for regard to the interests of creditors, the company need not be insolvent at the time and the directors must consider their interests if there is a real and not remote risk that they will be prejudiced by the dealing in question.'

13.36 In a very recent case that addressed the issue, *Bti 2014 Llc v Sequana SA,*[92] Rose J said:[93]

'a test set at the level of "a real (as opposed) to remote risk of insolvency" would appear to set a much lower threshold than a test set at the level of being "on the verge of insolvency" or of "doubtful" or "marginal" solvency.'

---

85 For example, see *Wright v Frisina* (1983) 1 ACLC 716; *Grove v Flavel* (1986) 11 ACLR 161 at 170; *Kinsela v Russell Kinsela Pty Ltd* (1986) 4 ACLC 215 at 223 (agreeing with Cooke J in *Nicholson v Permakraft (NZ) Ltd* (1985) 3 ACLC 453); *Winkworth v Edward Baron Development Ltd* [1986] 1 WLR 1512; *Hilton International Ltd (in liq) v Hilton* [1989] NZLR 442.

86 (1988) 4 BCC 30.

87 Ibid at 33.

88 Ibid.

89 [2013] EWHC 2876 (Ch) at [94]–[95].

90 [2013] EWHC 2876 (Ch) at [94]–[95].

91 [2007] NSWCA 191; (2007) 25 ACLC 1094.

92 [2016] EWHC 1686.

93 Ibid at [477].

13.37 Her Ladyship rejected the fact that whenever a company is 'at risk' of becoming insolvent at some indefinite point in the future, then the creditors' interests duty arises unless that risk can be described as 'remote'.[94] She went on to say that the essence of the real risk test was that 'the directors ought in their conduct of the company's business to be anticipating the insolvency of the company because when that occurs, the creditors have a greater claim to the assets of the company than the shareholders'.[95]

13.38 In *Nicholson v Permakraft* Cooke J also indicated that directors might be under a responsibility to creditors where the company was risking insolvency. His Lordship said that directors owed a duty where a 'contemplated payment or other course of action would jeopardise solvency,'[96] and similar language was used by Giles JA of the New South Wales Court of Appeal in *Linton v Telnet Pty Ltd*.[97]

13.39 It has been argued[98] that it would be difficult for this trigger to work if it must be established that the directors were aware, when considering a course of action, that there was a risk of insolvency, for requiring knowledge is leaving the creditors too exposed. Such a requirement could too easily favour the indigent director who has not sought to apprise himself or herself of the state of the company's affairs and, consequently, did not know that there was a risk of the company becoming insolvent. Consequently, in addition to prescribing knowledge of the risk of insolvency, an objective test should be employed. Therefore, the trigger for the duty would be either where the directors knew of the risk of insolvency resulting from their decision, or where they ought to have known of the risk of insolvency or that one of the reasonably expected consequences of their action could be insolvency. This is the approach that appeared to be favoured by Cooke J in *Nicholson v Permakraft*.[99] In giving his judgment in *Re HLC Environmental Projects Ltd*,[100] John Randall QC (sitting as a deputy High Court judge) rejected the submission that the duty is only triggered if the director was aware that the company fulfilled the conditions for the application of the sub-section. Thus the test is not dependent on subjective considerations.

13.40 There are other cases which have not sought to be precise when determining when the duty arises, for they have been content merely to say that the company must be in a dangerous financial position,[101] financially unstable,[102] or in financial difficulties.[103] It is difficult to be specific concerning the meaning of these phrases, but it is fair to say that for the most part, from a

---

[94] Ibid.

[95] Ibid at [478].

[96] (1985) 3 ACLC 453 at 459.

[97] (1999) 30 ACSR 465 at 478.

[98] A Keay *Company Directors' Responsibilities to Creditors* (Abingdon, Routledge-Cavendish, 2007) at 215–217.

[99] (1985) 3 ACLC 453 at 460.

[100] [2013] EWHC 2876 (Ch) at [94]–[95].

[101] *Facia Footwear Ltd (in administration) v Hinchliffe* [1998] 1 BCLC 218.

[102] *Linton v Telnet Pty Ltd* (1999) 30 ACSR 465.

financial economist's viewpoint, they mean that the company is facing insolvency,[104] and this appears to have been the meaning given in the cases. Therefore, the trigger point is probably close to 'doubtful solvency' or a 'risk of insolvency'.

13.41 In the Australian case of *Grove v Flavel*,[105] the Full Court of the Supreme Court of South Australia said that it was not persuaded that any duty could be owed save where there is 'insolvency *or* financial instability',[106] thereby clearly indicating that insolvency is not the only factor that will cause the duty to arise, but making it equally clear that there had to be some feature of financial instability in existence. What that actually means, however, was not considered by the court. In the US case of *Re Healthco International Inc*[107] the court said that directors had a duty in relation to creditors when the company is suffering from a 'condition of financial debility short of insolvency but which makes the insolvency reasonably foreseeable'.[108]

13.42 Clearly nominating a precise point when the obligation should arise is far from easy. In *Kinsela* Street CJ refrained from attempting to provide a general test of the degree of financial instability which must exist before directors are subject to an obligation to consider the interests of creditors.[109] Nevertheless, for the sake of certainty for both directors and others (particularly liquidators who are most often going to bring proceedings for breach) it is necessary to seek to formulate some test. Of course, in many cases, such as *Kinsela* and *West Mercia Safetywear* things are pretty straightforward. Most would agree that the directors in those respective cases should be held liable. At the other end of the spectrum to these cases there are going to be other cases like *Multinational Gas and Petrochemical Co v Multinational Gas and Petrochemical Services Ltd* that are as straightforward, and the director will not be liable for breach, for in such cases the companies concerned will be amply solvent at the time of the impugned transactions and the director made business decisions in good faith.

13.43 John Randall QC (sitting as a deputy High Court judge) in *Re HLC Environmental Projects Ltd*,[110] said, after referring to the various ways, short of insolvency, that courts have said the duty was triggered, said that they were essentially the same. He then stated:

---

[103] *Re MDA Investment Management Ltd* [2003] EWHC 227 (Ch) at [70]; [2004] BPIR 75 at 102.

[104] R Rao, D Sokolow and D White 'Fiduciary Duty a la Lyonnais: An Economic Perspective on Corporate Governance in a Financially-Distressed Firm' (1996) 22 *The Journal of Corporation Law* 53 at 62.

[105] (1986) 11 ACLR 161.

[106] Ibid at 169.

[107] 208 BR 288 (1999) (Massachusetts).

[108] Ibid at 302.

[109] (1986) 4 ACLC 215 at 223.

[110] [2013] EWHC 2876 (Ch) at [94]–[95].

'I do not detect any difference in principle behind these varying verbal formulations. It is clear that established, definite insolvency before the transaction or dealing in question is not a pre-requisite for a duty to consider the interests of creditors to arise.'

13.44 In *Bti 2014 Llc v Sequana SA*[111] Rose J said that she accepted what John Randall QC had said in *Re HLC Environmental Projects Ltd*.

13.45 The case-law on this issue, and other issues in this area, as we will see, is not clear. This is partly because the courts in England and around the Commonwealth have got themselves into a bit of a mess by making marginal distinctions between various states of financial difficulty. It has been said that 'it is extraordinarily difficult to slice the world into categories of solvency, insolvency, and the vicinity of insolvency'.[112] Other commentators have made the point that: 'the question of whether a company is, or is not, solvent requires detailed accounting analysis and is not one that directors can easily judge when making commercial decisions.[113] In *Bell Group Ltd (in liq) v Westpac Banking Corporation (No 9)*[114] Owen J acknowledged that there was some substance in the view that it is impractical for directors, while they are involved in the course of day-to-day activities, to form views as to whether the company's financial position has got to the point of indicating doubtful solvency.[115] But his Honour did say that businesspersons make decisions in light of their company's finance every day, and these can involve consideration of legal concepts, and he did not think that determining their company's financial state short of insolvency was impossible.[116]

13.46 As far as determining the trigger the following caveat has been sounded:

'if the duty is imposed at one extreme of the financial spectrum, namely insolvency, there is the significant danger that creditors will not benefit... If the duty was to apply at the other extreme, namely when the company is clearly solvent,[117] then it would have the effect of unreasonably interfering with the decision-making of directors, hamper the business of the company and would be likely to lead to directors being over-cautious.'[118]

---

[111] [2016] EWHC 1686.

[112] R Barondes et al 'Twilight in the Zone of Insolvency: Fiduciary Duty and Creditors of Troubled Companies – History & Background' (2007) 1 *Journal of Business & Technology Law* 229 at 239.

[113] A Hargovan and J Harris 'For Whom the Bell Tolls: Directors' Duties to Creditor After Bell' (2013) 35 *Sydney Law Review* 433 at 437.

[114] [2008] WASC 239.

[115] Ibid at [4447].

[116] Ibid at [4448]–[4449].

[117] The controversial dictum of Lord Templeman in *Winkworth v Edward Baron Development Ltd* [1986] 1 WLR 1512 at 1517, seems to provide that directors of companies which are solvent are under the duty. But, save for the decision in *Jeffree v NCSC* (1989) 7 ACLC 556 no court seems to have followed that view.

[118] A Keay *Company Directors' Responsibilities to Creditors* (Abingdon, Routledge-Cavendish, 2007) at 209.

So in deciding on a point when liability should arise, there must be a balance. On the one hand the courts must not place unreasonable limitations and burdens on directors, and must permit companies to be managed commercially.[119] Yet, on the other hand, the courts must ensure that they do not allow directors absolute freedom so that the position of the creditors is ignored. Limited liability is a privilege and it must not be forgotten that it can work to the disadvantage of creditors.[120] Hence, courts have the somewhat difficult task of reconciling the interests of the creditors on the one hand and the shareholders/directors on the other.

13.47 It has been submitted[121] that the point at which the duty is triggered should be where the circumstances of a company are such that its directors know, or can reasonably expect, that the action upon which they are going to embark could lead to the insolvency of the company.[122] The reason for suggesting this point is that companies that are not insolvent or even close to that state can slip into that state quickly in some situations, for all it takes is one risk that goes wrong for a company to find itself insolvent. A prime example is Barings Bank, which was once highly solvent, but which became insolvent as a consequence of huge losses on derivatives.[123] The trigger suggested seeks to encourage directors to address the likely risks of their decision-making. It is quite possible that directors might refrain from identifying all of the risks of what they propose when their company's financial state is not in a parlous position. Naturally, if this were the point at which the duty would arise, courts would have to take into account the circumstances of each company.

13.48 The suggested trigger above is not that revolutionary as it is not far from some of the existing judicial comments.[124] For instance, Cooke J in *Nicholson v Permakraft*,[125] provides some foundation for the trigger put forward here. He said that a duty to creditors existed where the company is insolvent, near insolvent, of doubtful solvency or 'if a contemplated payment or other course of action would jeopardise solvency'. His Honour went on to say that as a matter of business ethics it is proper that directors take into account whether any course of action will deleteriously affect their company's ability to discharge promptly debts owed to creditors.[126] Also, in obiter comments it was

---

[119] See the comments of Lockhart J in *Australian Innovation Ltd v Paul Andrew Petrovsky* (1996) 14 ACLC 1357 at 1361.

[120] See the comments of Cooke J in *Nicholson v Permakraft (NZ) Ltd* (1985) 3 ACLC 453 at 459.

[121] A Keay *Company Directors' Responsibilities to Creditors* (Abingdon, Routledge-Cavendish, 2007) at 215.

[122] See the comments of V Finch 'Directors' Duties: Insolvency and the Unsecured Creditor' in A Clarke (ed) *Current Issues in Insolvency Law* (London, Stevens, 1991) at 106.

[123] N Denton 'The Barings Crisis: Disaster, Just When Most Things Were Going Right' *The Financial Times*, 27 February 1995 at 3.

[124] A Keay *Company Directors' Responsibilities to Creditors* (Abingdon, Routledge-Cavendish, 2007) at 215–216.

[125] (1985) 3 ACLC 453 at 449.

[126] Ibid.

said in *Re Horsley & Weight Ltd*,[127] by Cumming-Bruce LJ, that the applicant liquidator failed in a case for misfeasance as, 'the evidence fell short of proof that the directors should at the time have appreciated that the payment was likely to cause loss to creditors.'[128] What can be deduced from this is that if directors had appreciated that what they were intending to do might cause creditor loss, they would be in breach.

13.49   Finally, it is to be noted that In making their decisions the courts will have to consider all relevant factors at the time of the director's decision and cases like *Nicholson v Permakraft*,[129] *Linton v Telnet*[130]and *Brady v Brady*[131] indicate that they have done so, and hence there is no great burden on the courts.

VI HOW SHOULD DIRECTORS ACT?

A Generally

13.50   We have considered the situations when directors have been held liable for failing to take into account the interests of creditors and what the trigger should be. Determining the trigger assists, but only to some degree. What is critical, especially for directors, is to know what they should do to ensure that they avoid a breach when s 172(3) applies. This is also important for creditors for it will mean, hopefully, that if directors function appropriately and do not breach their s 172(3) duty then creditors will not lose out, certainly to the extent that they would where there is a breach.

13.51   One potential problem for directors is that it is unlikely that the move from being subject to s 172(1) to being subject to s 172(3) is going to be seamless. Companies do not always spiral downhill financially out of control and keep going that way. They might well move in and out of states of financial difficulty depending on a myriad of circumstances, such as receiving or not receiving payments from their own debtors.

13.52   Section 172(3) provides some unwelcome uncertainty for both directors and those, likely most often to be either liquidators or administrators, who are contemplating whether to proceed against directors. Directors might well be confronted with making a decision at a board meeting at a time when they are unsure whether they should aim to fulfil s 172(1) or s 172(3). If there is doubt then it might well pay directors to act conservatively and make a decision that takes account of creditors' interests. While this could, possibly, precipitate a derivative action from shareholders for a breach of s 172(1), it is unlikely for a number of reasons. First, shareholders need to obtain the permission of the

---

[127]   [1982] 1 Ch 442.
[128]   Ibid at 455.
[129]   (1985) 3 ACLC 453.
[130]   (1999) 30 ACSR 465.
[131]   (1988) 3 BCC 535.

court to prosecute such an action, as is discussed in detail in the next chapter. Secondly, there will be costs and time elements for shareholders to consider. Thirdly, shareholders may well not be aware of the action taken by the directors, at least for an appreciable period of time, and by then the company might well be in administration or liquidation, or the company will have recovered, possibly justifying the action of the directors. Fourthly, even if the director did act in line with creditor interests, arguably they might still be regarded as adhering to s 172(1) on the basis that while the sub-section requires directors to have regard to several factors set out in s 172(1)(a)–(f), the provision clearly states that the factors in paragraphs (a)–(f) are not to be seen as exhaustive of the directors' consideration. Section 172(1) provides that the directors are 'to have regard to (*amongst other matters*)' (my emphasis) the factors in paragraphs (a)–(f). The legislation seems to allow directors to have regard to creditors' interests at any stage in the life of the company (provided that involves promoting the success of the company) and it might be thought to be prudent and proper that directors especially take creditors' interests into consideration when there are some doubts over the financial position and future of the company. If they do so then this might benefit the shareholders in the longer term in that the company survives and goes on to make profits. After saying all of that one must voice a word of caution. In the case of *Odyssey Entertainment Limited (in liquidation) v Ralph Kamp, Timeless Films Limited, Metropolis International Sales Limited*[132] a director, who recommended to his board that the company be wound down, and who disengaged from management of the company, was found to have given the board overly pessimistic advice and he was held liable, inter alia, under s 172(1).[133] The company had entered voluntary liquidation and had in fact been marginally solvent, and it was argued that its activities should not have been wound down and the company placed into liquidation. However, the judge held that the director had acted in bad faith and intentionally misled the board.[134] But, one could contend that provided that a director acts in good faith and beyond reproach, he or she can recommend caution and the taking into account of creditors' interests without incurring liability under s 172(1).

13.53 The problem for directors is that at present the case-law provides little, or no, indication as to what directors are to do when they are subject to the obligation to creditors without harming the interests of creditors, and when subject to s 172(3). In fact, as will be noted later, there is some unintentional divergence in the case-law. How does the obligation imposed on directors to take into account creditor interests fit in with the more traditional duties that directors have in relation to shareholders,[135] and particularly s 172(1). The difficulty is that the cases are very fact specific, and they have not developed a set of guidelines for the development of principles to cover the kind of situation

---

[132] [2012] EWHC 2316 (Ch).

[133] Ibid at [235], [269].

[134] Ibid at [24].

[135] This is the case in the United States also, where the position is still uncertain and developing: R Cieri, P Sullivan and H Lennox 'The Fiduciary Duties of Directors of Financially Troubled Companies' (1994) 3 *Journal of Bankruptcy Law and Practice* 405 at 405.

that we are examining. Generally speaking, the cases have been fairly unhelpful because they have merely said that directors must take into account the creditors' interests in making their decisions.[136] In *Gwyer v London Wharf (Limehouse) Ltd*,[137] Leslie Kosmin QC (sitting as a deputy judge of the High Court) was more helpful when he said that in considering the interests of creditors, directors are to take into account the impact of their decision on the ability of the creditors to recover the sums due to them from the company.[138] Perhaps a more helpful thing that the deputy judge said was that if directors fail to take into account creditor interests when they should have done so, then the test provided for in the case of *Charterbridge Corp Ltd v Lloyds Bank Ltd*[139] should be applied with the appropriate modifications for creditors. *Charterbridge Corp* was considered in **Chapter 6,** and we will come back to it in a moment. It will be remembered that the test as to whether a director has complied with the duty in s 172(1) is regarded as virtually the same as that which applied in relation to the duty that was the precursor of s 172(1), namely the duty to act in good faith in the best interests of the company.[140] In the classic case of *Re Smith & Fawcett Ltd*[141] the court said that directors were obliged to act 'bona fide in what they consider – not what a court may consider – is in the interests of the company...'[142] Section 172(1) in effect includes this formula and cases have said that the test applied in relation to the old duty applies to s 172(1).[143] As indicated above, Leslie Kosmin QC said in *Gwyer v London Wharf (Limehouse) Ltd*[144] that the same test that is used for s 172(1) will be applied with the appropriate modification for creditors when directors are subject to s 172(3).

13.54 In *Charterbridge Corp Ltd v Lloyds Bank Ltd*[145] Pennycuick J said, when dealing with a solvent company and the duty that is the precursor to s 172(1), that the subjective belief of the director is all-important. Did he or she believe that what was done was in the best interests of the company? But where the director against whom proceedings have been initiated had actually failed to consider whether the action that is the subject of complaint would be in the interests of the company, objective considerations came into play and the court had to ask whether an intelligent and honest man in the position of a director of the company involved, could, in the whole of the circumstances, have

---

[136] The same has been held in the Delaware courts in the United States: see *Credit Lyonnais Bank Nederland NV v Pathe Communications Corp* (1991) WL 277613; LEXIS 215; reported in (1992) 17 *Delaware Journal of Corporate Law* 1099 (Delaware Chancery Court).

[137] [2002] EWHC 2748 (Ch); [2003] 2 BCLC 153.

[138] Ibid at [81]; 181.

[139] [1970] Ch 62.

[140] See *Re West Coast Capital (LIOS) Ltd* [2008] CSOH 72; 2008 Scot (D) 16/5 (Outer House, Court of Sessions, Lord Glennie); *Cobden Investments Ltd v RWM Langport Ltd* [2008] EWHC 2810 (Ch).

[141] [1942] Ch 304.

[142] Ibid at 306 per Lord Greene MR.

[143] See, *Re West Coast Capital (LIOS) Ltd* [2008] CSOH 72; 2008 Scot (D) 16/5 (Outer House, Court of Sessions, Lord Glennie); *Cobden Investments Ltd v RWM Langport Ltd* [2008] EWHC 2810 (Ch).

[144] [2002] EWHC 2748 (Ch); [2003] 2 BCLC 153.

[145] [1970] Ch 62.

reasonably believed that the transaction was for the benefit of the company.[146] Hence, directors who are subject to the requirements of s 172(3) will be evaluated on the basis of: did they consider in good faith what they were doing or not doing would be in the interests of the creditors? If directors failed to consider creditor interests when the duty provided for in s 172(3) applies, then to ascertain whether they are liable the court is to ask whether an intelligent and honest person in the position of the directors, could, in the whole of the circumstances, have reasonably believed that the action that is impugned was for the benefit of the creditors. It was also said in *Charterbridge Corp Ltd v Lloyds Bank Ltd* that directors could be held liable if the judge hearing the case disbelieves the directors when they assert that they acted in the good faith belief that what they did was in the best interests of the company. So, in like fashion a judge could take the view that the directors who were subject to s 172(3) did not, as they testified, act in the good faith belief that they were taking into account the interests of the creditors in what they did or did not do. If a judge disbelieved the directors then they could be liable. This approach was approved of by John Randall QC (sitting as a deputy judge of the High Court) in the decision in *Re HLC Environmental Projects Ltd*,[147] when dealing with s 172(3). Interestingly, the deputy judge added that where a material interest is unreasonably overlooked by a director, such as the interests of a large creditor, in making his or her decisions, then an objective test should be applied.[148] In a recent decision, *Ross v Cosy Seal Insulation Ltd*,[149] HHJ Behrens accepted this approach and said:[150]

> 'Failing to take into account a material factor is something which goes to the validity of the director's decision making process. This is not the court substituting its own judgment on the relevant facts (with the inevitable element of hindsight) for that of the directors made at the time; rather it is the court making an (objective) judgment taking into account all the relevant facts known or which ought to have been known at the time, the directors not having made such a judgment in the first place.'

Furthermore, the deputy judge in *Re HLC Environmental Projects Ltd* suggested that directors cannot rely on the subjective test to exonerate themselves from failing to consider the interests of a major creditor because they did not think that the person was a creditor.[151] John Randall QC said that: 'if a particular debt...is of sufficient materiality that any reasonable director would have taken into account...then the law would then apply the objective

---

[146] *Charterbridge Corp Ltd v Lloyds Bank Ltd* [1970] Ch 62 at 74. The reasoning in this case has been approved of on many occasions by both English and Commonwealth courts. For example, see *Australian National Industries Ltd v Greater Pacific Investments Pty Ltd in Liq (No 3)* (1992) 7 ACSR 176; *Linton v Telnet Pty Ltd* [1999[NSWCA 33; (1999) 30 ACSR 465 at 471-473; *Extrasure Travel Insurances Ltd v Scattergood* [2003] 1 BCLC 598 at [91]; *Simtel Communications Ltd v Rebak* [2006] EWHC 572 (QB); [2006] 2 BCLC 571 at [104].
[147] [2013] EWHC 2876 (Ch) at [92].
[148] [2013] EWHC 2876 (Ch) at [92].
[149] [2016] EWHC 1255 (Ch).
[150] Ibid at [164].
[151] [2013] EWHC 2876 (Ch) at [93].

test ....'[152] Also this decision makes it clear that directors must do more than just assert that they acted in good faith. It is likely that they will need to be able to explain the actions that they took.

13.55 It should be mentioned that in the appellate decision of *Westpac Banking Corporation v Bell Group Ltd (in liq) (No 3)*,[153] Drummond AJA seemed to deviate from the approach in *Charterbridge Corp* for he advocated more of an objective assessment and he said that:

> 'This principle [to take into account the interests of creditors] is based on the duty that directors owe to their company to exercise their fiduciary powers for proper purposes. It cannot be grounded in the subjective duty to act bona fide in what the directors believe to be the interests of the company. If it were, as the cases applying the principle show, the interests of creditors would often receive scant recognition.'[154]

But it would appear that that approach has not met with the approbation of any English or other Australian judge thus far.

13.56 All of the above would seem to mean that if the application of s 172(3) is triggered then the directors must consider in good faith, when taking action or declining to take action, what are the interests of the creditors. If a director does not turn his or her mind to whether the action contemplated will affect creditors' interests or the director did not consider these interests in good faith, a court can apply an objective approach and ask whether an intelligent and honest person in the position of a director of the company involved, could, in the whole of the circumstances, have reasonably believed that the directors' actions would benefit the creditors.

13.57 But this still does not tell us exactly how directors should act. In *Nicholson v Permakraft (NZ) Ltd*,[155] Cooke J said that directors should consider whether what they are proposing to do will prejudice their companies' ability to discharge promptly the debts owed to creditors.[156] The learned judge said, what many might echo, namely, that if directors were to make a payment that prejudiced creditors when a likelihood of loss to them ought to have been known, then that is capable of making them liable for breach.[157]

13.58 The difficulty for the courts in this area is similar to that which they have found when considering the operation of the wrongful trading provision,

---

[152] [2013] EWHC 2876 (Ch) at [96].
[153] [2012] WASCA 157 at [2046]. An appeal was launched to the High Court of Australia and a hearing date was set in September 2013, but that date was subsequently vacated as the parties settled the matter beforehand. For those of us not party to the proceedings, this development was somewhat disappointing as it would have been interesting to see what the High Court had to say on the matter.
[154] Ibid at [2032].Also see [2056].
[155] (1985) 3 ACLC 453.
[156] Ibid at 459.
[157] Ibid at 460.

s 214 of the Insolvency Act 1986. The section prescribes the conditions for wrongful trading, but does not indicate how directors are to act to avoid it, except it provides that they are to take every step with a view to minimising losses to the creditors at a time when they knew or ought to have concluded that there was no reasonable prospect of the company avoiding insolvent liquidation. The courts have struggled with indicating when directors will be regarded as actually engaging in wrongful trading.[158]

B When the company is insolvent

13.59 Where a company is clearly insolvent there appears to be some divergence concerning how the directors are to approach the interests of the creditors. It might be possible to identify two approaches. First, the approach that potentially most strongly benefits creditors. There are a number of decisions, such as *Re Pantone 485 Ltd*,[159] *Gwyer v London Wharf (Limehouse) Ltd*,[160] *Re Capitol Films Ltd (in administration)*,[161] *Roberts v Frohlich*,[162] *Re HLC Environmental Projects Ltd*,[163] and most recently, *Re Pro4Sport Ltd; Hedger v Adams*,[164] where it has been stated that when a company is insolvent the creditors' interests are paramount. 'Paramount' means something that is more important than anything else,[165] so the creditors' interests are to be seen as preeminent. Thus, this would suggest that directors must put the interests of creditors before any other concern or interest. While not mentioning the paramountcy of creditors' interests on insolvency, Lesley Anderson QC (sitting as a deputy High Court judge) in *Re Idessa (UK) Ltd* (sub nom *Burke v Morrison*)[166] said that the interests of the creditors overrode those of the shareholders, and there probably is little difference between this and saying the interests of the creditors are paramount. The Irish Supreme Court in *Re Frederick Inns Ltd*[167] also seemed to require paramountcy when it said that:[168]

> '[b]ecause of the insolvency of the companies the shareholders no longer had any interest. The only parties with an interest were the creditors. The payments made could not have been lawful because they were made in total disregard of their interests.'

---

[158] See A Keay *Company Directors' Responsibilities to Creditors* (Abingdon, Routledge-Cavendish, 2007), Ch 8.
[159] [2002] 1 BCLC 266 at [69].
[160] [2002] EWHC 2748 (Ch); [2003] 2 BCLC 153 at [74].
[161] [2010] EWHC 2240 (Ch); [2011] 2 BCLC 359 at [49].
[162] [2011] EWHC 257 (Ch); [2012] BCC 407; [2011] 2 BCLC 625 at [85].
[163] [2013] EWHC 2876 (Ch) at [91], [92].
[164] [2015] EWHC 2540 (Ch); [2016] 1 BCLC 257.
[165] J Pearsall, *New Oxford Dictionary of English* (Oxford, OUP, 2001) at 1346.
[166] [2011] EWHC 804 (Ch); [2012] BCC 315 at [54].
[167] [1993] IESC 1 at [47].
[168] There is a divergence of opinion in the courts in the United States as to whether duties are still owed to shareholders when insolvency exists. See Millner, R 'What Does it Mean for Directors of Financially Troubled Corporations to Have Fiduciary Duties to Creditors?' (2000) 9 *Journal of Bankruptcy Law and Practice* 201 at 217.

13.60 Perhaps the pre-eminence of creditors' interests can be regarded as consistent with s 172(3) in that this provision trumps s 172(1) when the relevant circumstance exist as s 172(1) is subject to any rule of law requiring directors to consider or act in the interests of creditors.

13.61 Other courts do not appear to have put it quite as strongly as the cases mentioned above, but what they require directors to do seems very close to, if not the same as, the idea of paramountcy. In *Kinsela v Russell Kinsela Pty Ltd*,[169] a decision that has been widely approved and cited all around the Commonwealth, Street CJ said that if the company is insolvent the interests of the creditors intrude and the creditors become prospectively entitled to displace the power of the shareholders and directors to deal with the company's assets.[170] The general thrust of the sentiments expressed by Street CJ, while not using the word 'paramount', are not far from it as they appear to envisage the creditors supplanting the shareholders The foregoing statement of his Honour was contained in a quotation that was expressly approved of by the Court of Appeal in *Liquidator of West Mercia Safetywear Ltd v Dodd*.[171]

13.62 A second line appears to be represented by some Australian decisions. Included in this is the decision that really started this whole area developing, *Walker v Wimborne*.[172] Mason J said the directors of a company in discharging their duty to the company must take account of the interests of its shareholders *and* its creditors. But he did not say that the interests of creditors supplanted those of shareholders. This point was taken up and supported by Owen J at first instance in *Bell Group Ltd (in liq) v Westpac Banking Corporation (No 9)*.[173] His Honour then referred to the comments of Street CJ in *Kinsela* and the comments of the New Zealand Court of Appeal in *Nicholson v Permakraft (NZ) Ltd*,[174] but not to any English court commentary, and he said that:

> 'I do not read any of these statements [set out in the Australian cases] as demanding that the interests of creditors be treated as paramount. They emphasise the importance of treating the position of creditors with due deference and are a reminder to directors of the folly of a failure to do so... But it would be going too far to state, as a general and all-embracing principle, that when a company is in straitened financial circumstances, the directors must act in the interests of creditors, or they must treat the creditors' interests as paramount, to the exclusion of other interests.'[175]

13.63 So Owen J was clearly against any paramountcy requirement. When his decision went on appeal in *Westpac Banking Corporation v Bell Group Ltd (in*

---

[169] (1986) 4 ACLC 215; (1986) 10 ACLR 395.
[170] *Kinsela v Russell Kinsela Pty Ltd* (1986) 4 ACLC 215 at 221; (1986) 10 ACLR 395 at 401.
[171] (1988) 4 BCC 30 at 33.
[172] (1976) 137 CLR 1 at 7.
[173] [2008] WASC 239 at [4436].
[174] (1985) 3 ACLC 453.
[175] [2008] WASC 239 at [4438]–[4439].

liq) (No 3),[176] Drummond AJA did specifically agree with his Honour's comments, notwithstanding the fact that in other parts of his Honour's judgment it would seem that he favoured something close to paramountcy for creditor interests.

13.64 In *Bell* at first instance Owen J almost gets to the point of saying that when assessing creditors' interests directors had to engage in a balancing exercise where the risk to creditors could be included as one of several considerations to be taken by management. The greater the risk to creditors, the more directors and executive officers should take those considerations into account.[177] His Honour said that it might be that because of the particular circumstances, and not because a general principle has mandates it, that the treatment of the creditors' interests is paramount.[178] So, creditors' interests are not always paramount, according to Owen J, but they might be paramount in some circumstances.

13.65 Interestingly, in *Ultraframe (UK) Ltd v Fielding*[179] Lewison J (as he then was) took a similar approach to that adopted by the aforementioned Australian cases. His Lordship said that the duties which the directors owe to the company are extended so as to encompass the interests of the company's creditors as a whole, as well as those of the shareholders.[180] Yet this decision does appear to be the only English decision that takes this view.

13.66 Given the present state of the law it is likely that a High Court judge is going to follow the first approach, as judges have tended to take that view to date. It might be argued that this approach is envisaged by s 172(3) itself, as mentioned earlier. Perhaps it can be said that if the duty is subject to the obligation concerning creditors' interests then the interests of creditors are effectively paramount.

13.67 If creditors' interests are paramount, then the directors have to concentrate on the interests of the creditors to the exclusion of others, and particularly the interests of shareholders. The consequence is that the company's affairs are to be administered in such a way as to ensure that actions will enhance the wealth of creditors, that is, the creditors will be repaid more of the funds that are owed to them. Of course, what happens in practice is going to be very dependent on the situation facing the directors. There will be very obvious breaches of duty, such as where directors decide to enter into a transaction that could not possibly benefit the creditors, but many other actions or inactions of directors are not going to be as clear-cut.

---

[176] [2012] WASCA 157 at [2046].
[177] *Bell Group Ltd (in liq) v Westpac Banking Corporation (No 9)* [2008] WASC 239 at [1436]-[1439].
[178] Ibid at [4440].
[179] [2005] EWHC 1638 (Ch).
[180] Ibid at [1304].

13.68   But even if we can say that it is clear that when a company is insolvent the directors have to make creditors' interests paramount that still leaves directors with some difficulties. A company is likely to owe money to several different kinds of creditors who have different agenda, and who are dealt with in different ways by the law, particularly on winding up.[181] For example, there are likely to be significant differences between the interests of a bank with a charge over company assets compared with an unsecured trade creditor or with a creditor who has built its business around supplying the company that is in difficulty.[182] Do directors have to turn their minds to the various rights of creditors on a liquidation of the company? Obviously directors cannot be taken to be conversant with insolvency law and how they should deal with company affairs in light of it. And in fact Drummond AJA in *Westpac Banking Corporation v Bell Group Ltd (in liq) (No 3)*[183] said that the pari passu principle cannot provide any justification for any form of equal treatment of creditors prior to winding up even where a company is in an insolvency situation. A judge will not assess whether the action of the directors in considering the interests of creditors was what he or she or what an intelligent director would have done in the same position if the directors acted in good faith. But, as we have seen, directors are not able to simply assert that they acted in good faith and considered the interests of the creditors. Directors must do more than that. It is likely that they will need to be able to explain the actions that they took. In *Re HLC Environmental Projects Ltd*[184] John Randall QC (sitting as a deputy judge of the High Court) stated that a court could and should consider the validity of a director's decision-making process. Furthermore, as mentioned earlier, the deputy judge said specifically that the interests of a large creditor cannot be overlooked by the directors.[185] Does that mean that the interests of a large creditor take precedence? The deputy judge did not say so and I think that it would be going too far to read that conclusion into what he was saying and it would appear to fly in the fact of dicta in the case of *Re Pantone 485 Ltd*,[186] discussed in the next paragraph.

13.69   What the case-law seems to have done is to major on the fact that when the obligation to consider creditors' interests has been triggered, creditors should be treated as a class, and no creditors should be favoured over others. Although it does not resolve the problem that we are investigating, the decision in *Re Pantone 485 Ltd*[187] is noteworthy. In this case the liquidator of a company failed in a claim that the directors of the company in liquidation had disposed of company property without taking into account the interests of one of the creditors, an unsecured creditor entitled to priority in a distribution of

---

[181] This issue is dealt with in greater depth in A Keay *Company Directors' Responsibilities to Creditors* (Abingdon, Routledge-Cavendish, 2007) at 235–241.

[182] For an example of a case where there was conflicting interests amongst the creditors, see *Saltri III Limited v MD Mezzanine SA Sicar & Ors* [2012] EWHC 3025 (Comm); [2013] 2 BCLC 217.

[183] [2012] WASCA 157 at [2610].

[184] [2013] EWHC 2876 (Ch) at [92].

[185] [2013] EWHC 2876 (Ch) at [92].

[186] [2002] 1 BCLC 266.

[187] [2002] 1 BCLC 266.

the company's assets. The Court acknowledged that when a company was insolvent the directors had to have regard for the creditors' interests.[188] The claim failed because, according to the Court, the directors had a duty to make decisions, when their company was insolvent, while having regard for all of the general creditors, and not one, or a section, of the creditors. Thus, if directors are found, in their consideration of the interests of creditors, that they have favoured one or more groups, they will have failed to discharge their responsibility. However, there are dicta in the recent decision of *GHLM Trading Ltd v Maroo*[189] to suggest that if directors were to pay one creditor, but not other creditors, the directors might not be in breach of their duty.[190] Obviously such a payment might be avoided or adjusted as a preference under s 239 of the Insolvency Act 1986 if the company were to enter administration or liquidation. It would depend on whether all of the conditions for the avoidance of a preferential transfer were fulfilled.[191] If the payment could not be recovered as a preference, could the directors be held liable for it on the basis of a breach of duty? This occurred, it will be remembered, in *Liquidator of West Mercia Safetywear Ltd v Dodd*.[192] In *GHLM Trading Ltd v Maroo*,[193] Newey J stated that:

> 'It seems to me that a company seeking redress in respect of a "preference" to which section 239 does not apply is likely to need to show (a) that it has suffered loss, (b) that the director has profited (so that the "no profit" rule operates) or (c) that the transaction in question is not binding on the company.'[194]

13.70 In this statement Newey J introduces criteria that must exist before, in effect, a breach of duty can be established against a director. No other decision seems to have relied upon this criteria previously, and his Lordship does not cite authority for the three points he mentions.[195] Yet Newey J had said earlier in his judgment that where a company is insolvent then the directors' duty is to have regard to the interests of the creditors as a class. He said that: 'If a director acts to advance the interests of a particular creditor, without believing the action to be in the *interests of creditors as a class*, it seems to me that he will

---

[188] Ibid at [73].

[189] [2012] EWHC 61; [2012] 2 BCLC 369.

[190] For more discussion concerning this issue, see A Keay 'Directors' Duties and Creditors' Interests' (2014) LQR (forthcoming).

[191] For a discussion of the conditions for preferences and issues relating to them, see Walters 'Preferences' in J Armour and H Bennett (eds) *Vulnerable Transactions in Corporate Insolvency* (Oxford, Hart Publishing, 2003), Chapter 4; A Keay 'Preferences in Liquidation Law: A Time for a Change' (1998) 2 Cfi LR 198; A Keay 'The Recovery of Voidable Preferences: Aspects of Recovery' [2000] Cfi LR 1; R Parry et al, Transaction Avoidance in Insolvencies, 2nd edn (Oxford, Oxford University Press, 2011); A Keay, *McPherson's Law of Company Liquidation*, 3rd edn (Sweet and Maxwell, London, 2013) at 685–718.

[192] (1988) 4 BCC 30.

[193] [2012] EWHC 61; [2012] 2 BCLC 369.

[194] Ibid at [169].

[195] The approach was adopted and applied by Barma J of the Hong Kong Court of First Instance in *Moulin Global Eyecare Holdings Ltd v Lee* [2012] HKCFI 989; [2012] 4 HKLRD 263. The matter went on appeal ([2012] HKCA 537) and the Hong Kong Court of Appeal appeared to agree with Barma J (see [27]), although the Court of Final Appeal ([2014] HKFCA 63) was not so certain.

commit a breach of duty'[196] (my emphasis). The judge added that a director could be held liable even if all of the conditions for a preference under s 239 are not met.[197] It might be argued that any preference payment is going to prejudice the creditors in general as there will be less money available for distribution and should be prohibited. But, on the other hand a director might argue that a payment is necessary to keep the company's business going and that if the business continues the creditors might end up getting more of their debts repaid. This would then benefit all creditors. If this line of argument has merit, then it would seem that the nature and amount of the payment could be of critical importance. A director who does pay a creditor before others might seek to argue that the company suffers no loss as the company owes the amount that is paid.[198] Perhaps the riposte to that is that if the company is insolvent the company's interests are the creditors' interests as a class and if one creditor were paid then the others will lose out. In *Gwyer v London Wharf (Limehouse) Ltd*[199] Leslie Kosmin QC said that, in taking into account the interests of creditors, directors are to take into account the impact of their decision on the ability of the creditors to recover the sums due to them from the company.[200] In *Re HLC Environmental Projects Ltd*[201] John Randall QC said, when dealing with a situation where an insolvent company whose directors were subject to s 172(3) only paid some of its creditors, that the respondent director had breached his duty in choosing which creditors to pay and which to leave exposed to a real risk of not being paid.[202] This same approach was taken in *Re Micra Contracts Ltd*.[203] Perhaps whether directors will be liable or not if making payments to some creditors and not others will all depend on whether the directors, in advancing the interests of a particular creditor, can justify it on the basis that they were acting in good faith for the interests of the creditors as a class as the creditors as a class would be likely to benefit ultimately from the action of the paying of the creditor. In *Re Micra Contracts Ltd*[204] Registrar Barber said that not all payments of creditors which could constitute preferences give rise to a breach of duty.

13.71 But what if the creditors of a company that is insolvent are not all of the same class? For instance, it is likely to be the case most often there will be number of unsecured creditors and one or more secured creditors. This complicates things as it could be that a company is so insolvent that the company's property and funds is only enough to pay off the secured creditors.

---

[196] [2012] EWHC 61; [2012] 2 BCLC 369 at [168].
[197] Ibid.
[198] An argument accepted in *Moulin Global Eyecare Holdings Ltd v Lee* [2012] HKCFI 989; [2012] 4 HKLRD 263.
[199] [2002] EWHC 2748 (Ch); [2003] 2 BCLC 153 at [74].
[200] Ibid at [81].
[201] [2013] EWHC 2876 (Ch) at [106].
[202] Whilst it might be argued that all of the creditors paid were associated with the director making the payment or the payments benefitted the director either directly or indirectly, the deputy judge did not make any distinction between paying creditors that benefitted the director and paying creditors that did not provide any benefit.
[203] [2015] All ER (D) 24 (Aug) (13 July 2015) at [83], [112].
[204] Ibid at [112].

In such a situation it could be said that it is in the secured creditors' best interests if the company were to enter administration or liquidation as they are secured over property and will not lose out, save where the value of the property has fallen below the debt owed. Yet directors might argue that, provided that there is a reasonable chance that a restructuring strategy would work, that it is preferable to follow that strategy, because while it might well involve expending further funds, it could well benefit all creditors. If the company was turned around the secured creditors would profit from the fact that they would continue to be paid interest on the money they are owed and they would not be forced to find other places to lend the money that they recovered. Also, if the company was put into administration or liquidation the costs of, and payments in, administration or liquidation[205] could reduce the amounts received by secured creditors.

13.72 It would seem appropriate that courts will consider what efforts have been made in an attempt to save the company including any action taken to support a restructuring of a company's affairs, and it seems fair that directors not be penalised for bona fide attempts that are reasonable and do take into account the interests of the creditors. Naturally, it would not be good for overall business if directors eschewed any thoughts of restructuring for fear of being held liable for breach of duty.

C When the company is in a pre-insolvency position

13.73 So, where the company is in an insolvent position, the preponderance of English case-law seems to lead to a situation that is reasonably straightforward, as far as articulating in abstract terms what directors are to do broadly, namely to make the interests of creditors paramount in their thinking. But it is the period of time before insolvency occurs when the directors are obliged to take into account the interests of creditors that is more of a concern as far as determining in what manner directors are to function. Again, there appears to be some divergence in the case-law.

13.74 On one side are some cases that emit the view that the interests of creditors have to be regarded as paramount, even where the company is short of insolvency. This is well-illustrated by the decision of Leslie Kosmin QC in *Gwyer v London Wharf (Limehouse) Ltd.*[206] The learned deputy judge did not distinguish between insolvency and cases where the company is of doubtful solvency or on the verge of insolvency. In all of these instances the creditors' interests were to be seen as paramount.[207] Many subsequent cases have cited *Gwyer* with approval, but until relatively recently no cases approved of the point about the interests of creditors of a company that is short of insolvency being of paramount importance. But in the decisions of *Roberts v Frohlich,*[208]

---

[205] For instance, any payment that has to be paid under s 176A of the Insolvency Act 1986 out of the property that is covered by a floating charge (a so-called prescribed part payment).
[206] [2002] EWHC 2748 (Ch); [2003] 2 BCLC 153 at [74].
[207] At [74].
[208] [2011] EWHC 257 (Ch); [2011] 2 BCLC 625 at [85].

GHLM Trading Ltd v Maroo,[209] and *Re HLC Environmental Projects Ltd*,[210] Norris J, Newey J and John Randall QC, respectively approved of what Leslie Kosmin QC had said in so far as companies which are not necessarily insolvent but are of doubtful solvency or on the verge of insolvency. Also, in *City of London Group plc v Lothbury Financial Services Ltd*,[211] Proudman J said that directors must have concern for the interests of the company and the shareholders, but when a company is of doubtful solvency the interests of the company are those of the creditors. It may be recalled that in *Re Idessa (UK) Ltd* (sub nom *Burke v Morrison*)[212] Lesley Anderson QC (sitting as a deputy High Court judge) said that the interests of the creditors overrode those of the shareholders when the company was insolvent, but the learned deputy judge also said that interests of creditors overrode other interests when a company was in financial difficulties.[213] As mentioned earlier, this approach might in fact be envisaged by s 172(3) itself.

13.75   There are cases though which support the view that while directors must consider creditor interests, they are not obliged to focus solely on those interests. In *Re MDA Investment Management Ltd*[214] Park J indicated that when a company is in financial difficulties, but not insolvent, the directors' duties owed to the company are extended so as to *include* the interests of the company's creditors as a whole, *in addition to those of the shareholders*. This statement appeared to have been cited with approval in *Re Kudos Business Solutions Ltd*.[215] Lewison J *in Ultraframe (UK) Ltd v Fielding*[216] took the same approach and said that when a company is in financial difficulties the duties which the directors owe to the company are extended so as to encompass the interests of the company's creditors as a whole, as well as those of the shareholders.[217] In *Bell Group Ltd (in liq) v Westpac Banking Corporation (No 9)*[218] Owen J said that where the financial situation of a company is short of a winding up the shareholders retain their interest, as the creditors' interests do not supplant those of the shareholders.[219] In the New Zealand Court of Appeal in *Nicholson v Permakraft (NZ) Ltd*[220] a case where the company was

---

[209] [2012] EWHC 61; [2012] 2 BCLC 369 at [165].

[210] [2013] EWHC 2876 (Ch) at [92].

[211] [2012] EWHC 3148 (Ch) at [54].

[212] [2011] EWHC 804 (Ch); [2012] BCC 315 at [54].

[213] Many years ago, in *Australian Growth Resources Corp Pty Ltd v Van Reesema* ((1988) 13 ACLR 261 at 268) King CJ of the South Australian Supreme Court took a less creditor-oriented approach when he said (in a Full Court decision, and the other judges agreed with him) that if a 'company's financial position is precarious, the interests of the creditors *may* become the dominant factor in what constitutes "the benefits of the company as a whole."' (my emphasis).

[214] [2004] 1 BCLC 217 at 245; [2004] BPIR 75 at 102.

[215] [2011] EWHC 1436 (Ch); [2012] 2 BCLC 65 at [43].

[216] [2005] EWHC 1638 (Ch).

[217] Ibid at [1304].

[218] At [4436].

[219] At [4436].

[220] (1985) 3 ACLC 453.

said to be nearing insolvency[221] at the time of the alleged breach, Cooke J said that he did not think that the interests of the shareholders should be put aside.[222]

13.76 If the view taken is that directors are not to regard creditor interests as paramount when the company is in a state short of insolvency, but merely to take them into account, how are they to manage the affairs of their company? As one American court put it in relation to the law as it applied, at least in the State of Delaware: 'the extent to which directors of putatively insolvent corporations can continue to advance the interests of stockholders without violating their fiduciary duty to the corporate entity or to creditors remains hazy …'.[223] But how are they are to operate in considering these respective interests? Or, as Chris Riley has put it, 'Are the interests of the creditors merely one competing interest to be borne in mind by directors in their running of the company, and if so, how much prominence are they to be given?'[224] The question might be put in more economic terms as: how do directors fairly allocate company resources?

13.77 One matter that directors have to consider is what Leslie Kosmin QC said in *Gwyer v London Wharf (Limehouse) Ltd*,[225] namely, in taking into account the interests of creditors, directors are to take into account the impact of their decision on the ability of the creditors to recover the sums due to them from the company.[226] It cannot simply entail directors refraining from disposing of assets improperly or diverting property to insiders in the company, which is obvious, but it extends to all of the duties that are owed, and functions undertaken, by directors to companies.

13.78 One possible answer for directors is to provide that they are to balance the interests of creditors and shareholders. This has been supported by academic comment.[227] However, one might ask what does balancing actually mean as far as a director is concerned when he or she is trying to run the company's business?

13.79 As I have stated elsewhere:[228]

> 'The main problem is that balancing is a fairly nebulous idea unless there is a goal that has been set for the balancing exercise. To what end is the balancing to be directed? To be effective any balancing must be done in the context of achieving an aim.'

---

[221] (1985) 3 ACLC 453 at 459.

[222] (1985) 3 ACLC 453 at 460.

[223] *Jewel Recovery LP v Gordon* 196 BR 348 at 355 (1996).

[224] C Riley 'Directors' duties and the interests of creditors' (1989) 10 Co Law 87 at 89.

[225] [2002] EWHC 2748; [2003] 2 BCLC 153.

[226] Ibid at [81].

[227] R Barrett 'Directors' Duties to Creditors' (1977) 40 MLR 226 at 231(at [70]).

[228] A Keay 'Formulating a Framework for Directors' Duties to Creditors: An Entity Maximisation Approach' (2005) 64 *Cambridge Law Journal* 614 at 633.

13.80 Implementing the balancing of interests is difficult, as many have pointed out in relation to the use of stakeholder theory in corporate governance.[229] It is difficult for a director to know whether to favour shareholders or creditors in any particular situation. Yet, it is just not a matter of balancing shareholder interests as against creditor interests. There is likely to be more than one kind of creditor with claims against a company at any specific point of time. It would be onerous for directors to know what to do where different courses of action would favour different creditors. But, provided a director acts in demonstrable good faith and endeavours to take creditors' interests into account then, one would think, it would be difficult for a court to hold him or her liable. Many of the cases where directors have been held liable have involved directors clearly not acting in good faith because they engaged in excessive risks or entered into transactions of an improper nature, or, at least, transactions of highly questionable merit.[230]

13.81 Rather than trying to balance interests, it has been submitted that directors should invoke an entity maximisation approach,[231] which entails, essentially, the directors making decisions so as to maximise the general wealth of the company and enhance its sustainability. This involves directors taking actions that:

> 'value maximises the corporate entity so that the net present value to the company as a whole is enhanced (maximising the total financial value of the firm and taking into account the sum of the various financial claims that are made on the company) and not just its equity.' (footnotes omitted)[232]

13.82 In taking this approach the directors will seek to increase the market value of the firm in the long term.[233] The entity maximisation approach takes into account the interests of those who have claims on the company, including the creditors, so that the most efficient outcome can be achieved for the benefit of the entity.[234]

---

[229] For example, see W Leung 'The Inadequacy of Shareholder Primacy: A Proposed Corporate Regime that Recognizes Non-Shareholder Interests' (1997) 30 *Columbia Journal of Law and Social Problems* 589; E Sternberg 'The Defects of Stakeholder Theory' (1997) 5 *Corporate Governance* 3 at 6; A Sundram and A Inkpen 'The Corporate Objective Revisited' (2004) 15 *Organization Science* 350 at 353; A Keay 'Ascertaining the Corporate Objective: An Entity Maximisation and Sustainability Model' (2008) 71 MLR 663 at 677–678.

[230] Some of the problems in weighing up shareholder and creditor interests are discussed in A Keay *Company Directors' Responsibilities to Creditors* (Abingdon, Routledge-Cavendish, 2007) at 226–234.

[231] This approach is articulated in detail in A Keay 'Formulating a Framework for Directors' Duties to Creditors: An Entity Maximisation Approach' (2005) 64 *Cambridge Law Journal* 614 at 633-643; A Keay *Company Directors' Responsibilities to Creditors* (Abingdon, Routledge-Cavendish, 2007) at 241–250.

[232] A Keay *Company Directors' Responsibilities to Creditors* (Abingdon, Routledge-Cavendish, 2007) at 241–242.

[233] M Jensen 'Value Maximisation, Stakeholder Theory, and the Corporate Objective Function' (2001) 7 *European Financial Management* 297 at 299.

[234] W Leung 'The Inadequacy of Shareholder Primacy: A Proposed Corporate Regime that Recognizes Non-Shareholder Interests' (1997) 30 *Columbia Journal of Law and Social*

13.83 The advantage of this approach over balancing is that the directors do not have to engage in active balancing between the interests of particular groups or persons because their goal is to maximise entity wealth. Undoubtedly, the directors will inevitably have to undertake some balancing, for example, they have to decide what portion of profits to use to pay dividends and what portion should be used to purchase new equipment or stock etc. But in doing this they have a goal, namely to maximise entity wealth.[235]

13.84 Directors will have to assess the fairness and appropriateness of all investment opportunities when they are subject to the obligation to consider creditor interests. They would have to eschew wild risk-taking to the extent that they do not engage in what might be referred to as 'bet the firm' options.

13.85 The attractiveness of this maximisation approach is described below:[236]

'[I]t provides a happy medium between excessive risk and excessive caution. If the directors were only concerned for shareholder wealth maximisation they would, potentially, be inclined to indulge in excessive risk, while if they were focusing on creditor wealth maximisation, then directors would engage in excessively cautious activity, thereby perhaps leaving potential value unrealised. This should mean that when directors are under an obligation to consider creditor interests, they are not to react by acting too cautiously, causing the company to miss out on good deals, and, conversely, they must ensure that they re-consider such things as their operating strategy in light of creditor interests. In other words, the directors must undertake a balance so that creditors are protected and at the same time the company's ability to innovate and take some appropriate risks is not totally or unreasonably proscribed.' (footnotes omitted)

13.86 It has been argued that while directors must be permitted a wide discretion there are four broad elements that directors must address in implementing entity maximisation.[237] First, directors would have to have, taking into account the company's position, a real legitimate purpose of business in mind in taking any action. So, taking some action for an improper reason, such as transferring property for less than market value, would not be a legitimate purpose. Similarly, actions that are very risky from a financial point of view would not be legitimate.

13.87 Second, before acting the directors must ensure that they are adequately informed, and they are certainly to have regard for the company's financial position and, if they do not understand company accounts, then they are required to engage someone who can advise them appropriately.[238] Directors

---

Problems 589 at 605; L Mitchell 'A Theoretical and Practical Framework for Enforcing Corporate Constituency Statutes' (1992) 70 Texas L Rev 579 at 633.

[235] In this regard and in relation to companies that are solvent, see A Keay *The Corporate Objective* (Cheltenham, Edward Elgar, 2011), ch 8.
[236] A Keay *Company Directors' Responsibilities to Creditors* (Abingdon, Routledge-Cavendish, 2007) at 241 at 245–246.
[237] The following is based on ibid at 247–249.
[238] *Re Hitco 2000 Ltd* [1995] 2 BCLC 63.

should seek cash flow projections and re-assess the company's financial exposure at regular intervals, and the greater the financial straits encountered by the company the more regularly assessments should be undertaken. Directors should take into account the position of the company, the reasons for its financial difficulty and the future of the business. During this period when they are obliged to consider creditors, they should take into account the effect that their decisions will have on the creditors' ability to recover what they are owed.[239]

13.88   Third, any action taken by the directors must be taken in the good faith belief that it is reasonably likely to foster the long-term wealth of the company.[240] Fourth, a director must believe that a reasonable director in the position of the director with the relevant information he or she has, and with entity maximisation in mind, would agree to the action being considered.

13.89   One practical issue needs to be raised. What if there is dissent amongst the directors as to what action should be taken when arguably the directors are subject to the obligation to consider creditors' interests? What are those directors who are adopting a cautious approach to do? To what lengths must directors go to protect themselves? This issue is similar to the one encountered by directors who believe their company has no reasonable prospect of avoiding insolvent liquidation. If that is the situation the directors might be found liable under s 214 of the Insolvency Act 1986 for wrongful trading. A director has a defence to wrongful trading if he or she can establish that after the point when he or she first knew or ought to have concluded that there was no reasonable prospect that the company would avoid going into insolvent liquidation, the director took *every step* with a view to minimising the potential loss to the company's creditors as ought to have been taken (my emphasis).[241] It is very likely that many of the actions that can be suggested as constituting 'every step' in the context of s 214, are pertinent in deciding what a director should do where there is the dissension mentioned above. What might directors do? The following are suggestions with accompanying drawbacks:

- Take professional advice. This might not provide a way out for a director other than to demonstrate his or her concern.

- Insist that the minutes of the relevant board meeting indicate that they dissented from the proposed course of action that is believed to be in breach of the obligation to consider creditor interests. As we have seen earlier in the book, directors have a collective responsibility.

- Resign. If a majority decision is to take a particular course of action and resignation by a dissenter occurred prior to the actual taking of the action that turns out to prejudice creditors' interests, it might be argued that a

---

[239] *Gwyer v London Wharf (Limehouse) Ltd* [2002] EWHC 2748 (Ch); [2003] 2 BCLC 153 at [81].

[240] This element is consistent with what the Supreme Court of Canada in *Peoples' Department Stores v Wise* [2004] SCC 68; (2004) 244 DLR (4th) 564. The Court said that this was the proper action of directors when their company is in financial difficulty (at [46]).

[241] Insolvency Act 1986, s 214(3).

director who resigned was not a party to the actions that caused loss to creditors. However, perhaps it might be contended that because the director was under a duty at the time when the proposed action(s) was discussed, he or she should do more than merely resign. What he or she could do will obviously depend on the position that the director holds and the constitution of the board.

D Factors to consider[242]

13.90 Whether or not a company is insolvent there are a number of factors that emanate from what the courts have said in wrongful trading cases that might well be considered by courts hearing claims under s 172(3). For instance, directors might be held liable if they exhibited a cavalier attitude towards the creditors and their interests,[243] they continue to act in much the same way as they did before the company entered a position where the interests of creditors had to be taken into account by the directors,[244] they failed to face up to the fact that their company was in a precarious position,[245] they have a speculative hope that the action that they took might lead to everything being resolved,[246] or they 'bury their head' in the sand.[247]

13.91 Judges have tended to find directors not liable if they have acted responsibly and clearly made efforts to ascertain the problems of the business, engage in copious discussions concerning the financial problems that their company is suffering, and carefully assessed accounts.[248] In wrongful trading cases the judges have required directors: to have an understanding of basic accounting principles;[249] to ensure that they have a clear appreciation of the company's finances; to be in a position to participate in discussions concerning the company's accounts;[250] to have carefully reviewed the company's circumstances;[251] to have rational expectations as to the future of the company.[252] The courts have emphasised that just because a company is in financial difficulties or even insolvent directors should not be expected to place

---

[242] For further discussion, see A Keay 'Directors' Duties and Creditors' Interests' (2014) 130 *Law Quarterly Review* 443.

[243] *Re Kudos Business Solutions Ltd* [2011] EWHC 1436 (Ch); [2012] 2 BCLC 65 at [50].

[244] This approach was taken in relation to the wrongful trading claim in *Re Idessa (UK) Ltd* [2011] EWHC 804 (Ch); [2011] BPIR 957; [2012] BCC 315 at [120]. Also, see *Re Brian D Pierson (Contractors) Ltd* [1999] BCC 26 at 54.

[245] *Roberts v Frohlich* [2011] EWHC 257 (Ch); [2012] BCC 407; [2011] 2 BCLC 625 at [112]; *Re Brian D Pierson (Contractors) Ltd* [1999] BCC 26 at 54.

[246] *Singla v Hedman* [2010] EWHC 902 (Ch); [2010] BCC 684 at [106], [107].

[247] *Re Continental Assurance of London plc* [2001] BPIR 733 at [24].

[248] For example, see ibid, and especially at [24], [37], [109]. There was evidence in this case that one directors' meeting lasted for six hours (at 59]).

[249] Ibid, and especially at [258].

[250] Ibid.

[251] *Re Bangla Television Ltd (in liq)* [2009] EWHC 1632 (Ch); [2010] BCC 143 at [51]; *Re Marini Ltd* [2003] EWHC 334 (Ch); [2004] BCC 172 at [20].

[252] *Re Hawkes Hill Publishing Co Ltd* [2007] BCC 937 at [28]; *Re Langreen Ltd (in liq)* (unreported, but available on Lawtel) 21 October 2011, ChD, Registrar Derrett at [56].

their companies in administration or liquidation prematurely.[253] The courts have recognised that often directors face a difficult dilemma, that is, whether to go on or to cease trading.[254] Directors might need to arrange for special kinds of financial controls.[255] Whether or not directors have acted properly might depend on the strength of any assurances of financing or other support that they secure from other parties.[256] Directors have been criticised when they have placed too much on promised support, especially where that reliance is misplaced. Finally, the wrongful trading jurisprudence indicates that if directors act sensibly and take measures that involve sacrifices, such as foregoing salaries,[257] they are likely to escape liability, or at least this action will go to their credit in a judge's overall evaluation of the conduct of the director. Indeed, such action might well be sufficient to ensure that they are absolved from liability under s 172(3).

13.92 Whatever behaviour is expected of directors, whether the company is insolvent or short of insolvency, the decisions that directors make are usually going to be evaluated some years after the event. It has been indicated many times that hindsight is a wonderful thing,[258] and the effect that hindsight might have in any given situation has been recognised by the courts in dealing with cases in a number of areas of company law.[259] It was considered in **Chapter 8** in relation to the duty of care.[260] Courts have acknowledged that they must be careful in not engaging in hindsight lest they end up applying too severe a standard.[261] In *Re Sherborne Associates Ltd*[262] the judge expressed the view that there is always the danger of the courts taking the view, because of hindsight, that it can be assumed that 'what has in fact happened was always bound to happen and was apparent'.[263] Hence, the decisions of the director must be taken in the context of the material available to him or her and the situation that existed at the relevant time. Lesley Anderson QC said in *Re Idessa (UK) Ltd*[264] that: 'particular care should be taken not to invoke

---

[253] *Re Continental Assurance of London plc* [2001] BPIR 733 at [281]; *Re Langreen Ltd (in liq)* (unreported, but available on Lawtel) 21 October 2011, ChD, Registrar Derrett at [66].

[254] Particularly, see the judgments of Park J in *Re Continental Assurance of London plc* [2001] BPIR 733 and especially at [281], and Lewison J in *Re Hawkes Hill Publishing Co Ltd* [2007] BCC 937.

[255] *Re DKG Contractors Ltd* [1990] BCC 903 at 912.

[256] *Rubin v Gunner* [2004] EWHC 316 (Ch); [2004] BCC 684 at [87].

[257] *Re Marini Ltd* [2003] EWHC 334 (Ch); [2004] BCC 172 at [20].

[258] See *Linton v Telnet Pty Ltd* (1999) 30 ACSR 465.

[259] For example, see *Re Sherborne Associates Ltd* [1995] BCC 40 at 54; *Re Brian D Pierson (Contractors) Ltd* [1999] BCC 26 at 50; [2001] BCLC 275 at 303; *Secretary of State for Trade and Industry v Goldberg* ([2004] 1 BCLC 597 at 613; *Dryburgh v Scotts Media Tax Ltd* [2011] CSOH 147 at [114].

[260] See 8.111ff.

[261] See the comment of Cooke J in *Nicholson v Permakraft (NZ) Ltd* (1985) 3 ACLC 453 at 462. Also, see *Roberts v Frohlich* [2011] EWHC 257 (Ch); [2012] BCC 407; [2011] 2 BCLC 625 at [108].

[262] [1995] BCC 40.

[263] Ibid at 54 per HH Judge Jack QC.

[264] [2011] EWHC 804 (Ch); [2012] BCC 315 (sub nom *Burke v Morrison*).

hindsight and proper regard must be had to the difficult choices which often confront directors when deciding whether to continue to trade and on what basis.'[265]

13.93 It also should be pointed out that merely because a company is insolvent it is no reason for the directors to believe, necessarily, that the company is finished. The directors can still, in certain factual situations, take the view, legitimately, that the company's fortunes can be turned around either with or without some formal restructuring strategy. Clearly though if a company is insolvent that situation will often mean that the directors have to consider things differently than if the company was not insolvent. Of course, if the directors do not reasonably believe that the company can be restored to good health they are probably best advised to place the company into administration or liquidation for besides possibly being in breach of their duties if they continue on trading they could also be liable for wrongful trading.

VII IS THE OBLIGATION A DUTY TO CREDITORS?

13.94 Hitherto in this Chapter we have assumed that the directors owe a duty to the company to take into account creditor interests at certain points, that is, the duty owed to creditors is indirect; the duty is mediated through the company. The concept of imperfect obligation may be used to describe this concept.[266] It needs to be noted that there has been some significant debate over the years as to whether, first, the case-law can be read so as to impose a direct duty on directors to creditors, and, second, if it cannot, whether the law should do so. We are more concerned with the former issue than the latter, although we will consider some points pertaining to the latter issue.

13.95 Which of the two approaches, that is, whether a direct or indirect obligation is imposed, is correct can have several practical consequences. One important one relates to the identity of the person who has standing to take legal proceedings for a breach of the duty. It follows that while a direct duty would enable creditors to enforce any breach, if the indirect duty approach is adopted, the creditors cannot enforce a breach of the duty; that can only be done by the company itself, to whom the duty is owed, or an office-holder such as a liquidator, an administrator or an administrative receiver acting for the company. In fact, it would seem that nearly all of the UK, Irish and Commonwealth cases that have involved claims against directors for failing to consider creditor interests have been initiated by a liquidator.[267]

---

[265] Ibid at [113].

[266] *Re New World Alliance Pty Ltd; Sycotex Pty Ltd v Baseler* (1994) 51 FCR 425 at 444–445; (1994) 122 ALR 531 at 550 (Aust Fed Ct).

[267] A clear exception to this is the case of *Jeffree v NCSC* (1989) 7 ACLC 556 (WA S Ct (Full Ct)) where proceedings were taken by the Australian corporate regulator (then the National Companies and Securities Commission).

13.96 Prima facie there does not appear to be any indication from s 172(3) of the CA 2006 which approach is correct. The case that is usually seen as the genesis of the responsibility of directors to creditors, *Walker v Wimborne*,[268] has been relied on to support both a direct duty and an indirect duty. Mason J of the Australian High Court said that directors must take into account the interests of its shareholders and its creditors.[269] The comments of the learned judge have been taken by some as a basis for establishing the fact that directors owe a direct duty to creditors.[270] In contrast others have said that all that his Honour was saying was that directors must consider, as part of their duty to their company, creditor interests. Undoubtedly, this latter approach has attracted significant judicial and academic support in the UK and the Commonwealth,[271] although in the highly influential case of *Liquidator of West Mercia Safetywear Ltd v Dodd*,[272] the Court of Appeal did not, in its comments, indicate a preference for either view.

13.97 The highest courts in both Australia (the High Court) and Canada (the Supreme Court), have unequivocally rejected a direct duty. In *Spies v The Queen*,[273] the Australian High Court said, by way of dicta, that directors do not owe an independent duty to creditors. In *Peoples' Department Stores v Wise*[274] the Canadian Supreme Court adopted a similar view, saying that directors had a duty to act for the interests of their company and the interests of the company are not to be confused with the interests of the creditors or those of any other stakeholders.[275] The court stated that in determining whether directors have acted in the best interests of the company, it might be appropriate for the directors to take into account the interests of creditors; there is no duty owed to creditors, even where a company is in the vicinity of insolvency.[276]

13.98 There is case-law that arguably supports the view that directors owe a direct duty. Principally this comes from the judgment of Lord Templeman in

---

[268] (1976) 137 CLR 1; (1976) 3 ACLR 529.

[269] Ibid at 6–7; 531.

[270] For example, see R Sappideen 'Fiduciary Obligations to Corporate Creditors' [1991] JBL 365 at 366.

[271] *Re Horsley & Weight Ltd* (1982) Ch 442 at 454; *Nicholson v Permakraft (NZ) Ltd* (1985) 3 ACLC 453 at 459; *Kinsela v Russell Kinsela Pty Ltd* (1986) 4 ACLC 215 at 221; (1986) 10 ACLR 395 at 401; *Re New World Alliance Pty Ltd* (1994) 51 FCR 425 at 444–445; (1994) 122 ALR 531; *Yukong Lines Ltd of Korea v Rendsburg Investments Corporation* [1998] BCC 870 at 884; *Millgate Financial Corporation Ltd v BCED Holdings Ltd* (2003) CanLII 39497 at [89] (Ont SC); *Sojourner v Robb* [2006] 3 NZLR 808 (NZHC).

[272] (1988) 4 BCC 30.

[273] *Spies v The Queen* [2000] HCA 43; (2000) 201 CLR 603; (2000) 173 ALR 529 at [93]-[95].

[274] [2004] SCC 68; (2004) 244 DLR (4th) 564.

[275] Ibid at [43].

[276] Ibid at [46]. In a recent decision the Queensland Court of Appeal has rejected the notion that a creditor could bring an action against a director for breach of duty: *McCracken v Phoenix Constructions (Qld) Pty Ltd* [2012] QCA 129.

Winkworth v Edward Baron Development Co Ltd,[277] which was approved of by the other law Lords sitting on the appeal. Lord Templeman said:[278]

> '[A] company owes a duty to its creditors, present and future. The company is not bound to pay off every debt as soon as it is incurred and the company is not obliged to avoid all ventures which involve an element of risk, but the company owes a duty to its creditors to keep its property inviolate and available for the repayment of its debts ... A duty is owed by the directors to the company and to the creditors of the company to ensure that the affairs of the company are properly administered and that its property is not dissipated or exploited for the benefit of the directors themselves to the prejudice of the creditors.'

13.99   The comments can be read to suggest that directors can owe a duty to the company and to the creditors, and the general approach adopted by his Lordship was approved of by the Full Court of the Western Australian Supreme Court in *Jeffree v NCSC*.[279] Although it could be argued that this latter decision has not found support in any of the other Australian jurisdictions. McGuiness J in the Irish case of *Jones v Gunn*,[280] while not entering into a substantial consideration of whether a direct duty was owed, said that where a company is insolvent, at least, the directors owe a fiduciary duty to the creditors.[281]

13.100   Notwithstanding the fact that there is some judicial support for Lord Templeman's comments, generally speaking academic commentaries have been set against his Lordship's approach,[282] and cases have not cited his Lordship's comments with approval.

13.101   Certainly taking into account the decisions of the High Court in *Spies*, and the Supreme Court of Canada in *Peoples' Department Stores*, the direct duty argument does not appear to have sufficient support in Commonwealth jurisdictions, including the UK.

13.102   If this is correct, should a direct duty be owed to creditors? There are significant arguments against a direct duty, namely:[283]

- if there were a duty owed then any creditor could initiate proceedings and this could lead to a significant amount of litigation against the company;

- a duty to creditors could precipitate the situation where there is double recovery in that the creditors could sue individually and a liquidator could sue on behalf of the company if it is taken into liquidation, and, this would cause problems for the court in working out the respective rights of

---

[277] [1986] 1 WLR 1512.

[278] Ibid at 1516.

[279] (1989) 7 ACLC 556.

[280] [1997] 3 IR 1; [1997] 2 ILRM 245.

[281] Ibid at [48].

[282] For example, see L S Sealy 'Directors' Duties – An Unnecessary Gloss' [1988] CLJ 175.

[283] See A Keay *Company Directors' Responsibilities to Creditors* (Abingdon, Routledge-Cavendish, 2007) at 254–257.

the company and the creditors, so as to ensure that the directors do not pay damages twice over in relation to the one wrong;[284]

- if it is an indirect duty then one preserves the collective procedure of liquidation (ie creditors forfeit their respective individual rights to take action to enforce their claims and are given in exchange a right to prove in the liquidation);

- a direct duty could mean that many creditors could bring proceedings and if one or more were successful it might render the directors without funds to pay out other creditors who make claims later, thereby interfering with the operation of the pari passu principle, that is, there should be an equal and rateable distribution of an insolvent company's assets amongst its creditors.

VIII TO WHICH CREDITORS IS AN OBLIGATION OWED?

13.103 We have considered thus far that directors have some obligation to creditors where their company is in some form of financial difficulty. Does this obligation apply so that directors have to consider the interests of all creditors? If the obligation to creditors is triggered, do directors have to consider the interests of those who are not creditors at the time that the obligation arises? In relation to this issue, we are thinking of contingent, prospective and future creditors.

13.104 Most commentary that we have seen has been in relation to future creditors, although one must add that most of the cases that have been central to the development of the jurisprudence dealing with the obligation of directors to creditors have not addressed the issue of future creditors. Naturally, this could simply be because the courts did not consider the matter or was of the view that it was an issue that did not require consideration in the matters before them.

13.105 One kind of creditor that has excited some debate is the future tort claimant. To be sure directors will not be able generally to foresee whether their company will be liable in tort in the future, but it seems unfair to say that these creditors are not owed a duty merely because the company has not yet caused them injury or the tortious action is not complete, when the obligation to creditors arises. We are dealing here with creditors who have no say whatsoever in becoming creditors of the company. Obviously, there are some future creditors that cannot be known or foreseen by directors, such as future tort claimants, and save where the company is involved in risky activity that is likely to lead to tortious claims or where there are already indications that claims will be launched in the future, it is not possible for the directors to take into account such creditors. But it is different where there are creditors owed liquidated

---

[284] D Prentice 'Creditors' Interests and Directors' Duties' (1990) 10 OJLS 265 at 276.

sums, but which have not become due and payable.[285] The problem that does exist is that, for the most part, courts have not explained what they mean when referring to future creditors.

13.106 The clearest view that we have in relation to future creditors is that of Lord Templeman in *Winkworth v Edward Baron Development Co Ltd*.[286] His Lordship plainly said: '[A] company owes a duty to its creditors, present and future.'[287] Lord Templeman's approach was approved of in *Jeffree v NCSC*,[288] and Wallace J specifically recognised the fact that a duty was owed to present and future creditors.[289] Unless the duty could be extended to future creditors in that case, the director/defendant could not be held liable. In that case at the time when the director committed the alleged breach of duty, namely transferring the business of his company (W) to another company, the party (L) who allegedly suffered from the breach was not a creditor. L had had a dispute with W and arbitration proceedings were instituted. Evidence was led that the director feared an adverse award against W, and this precipitated the transfer of W's business. Obviously, if L succeeded in obtaining an award, and this would be after the transfer of the business, there would be no assets on which he could execute the award.[290]

13.107 In *Fulham Football Club Ltd v Cabra Estates plc*,[291] the Court of Appeal stated that: 'The duties owed by the directors are to the company and the company is more than just the sum total of its members. Creditors, both present and *potential*, are interested' (my emphasis). The use of the word 'potential' suggests that an obligation was owed to future creditors of the company, although it must be pointed out that the court was not addressing the typical situation considered in this chapter, where creditors lose out because of the actions of the directors, and the remark might be regarded very much as an aside. But more recently the majority of a bench of the Australian High Court in *Spies v The Queen*,[292] said that:

> 'It is true that there are statements in the authorities, beginning with that of Mason J in *Walker v Wimborne* which would suggest that because of the insolvency of Sterling Nicholas [the company], the appellant, as one of its directors, owed a duty to that company to consider the interests of creditors and *potential creditors* of the company ....' (my emphasis).

13.108 In *Nicholson v Permakraft (NZ) Ltd*,[293] Cooke J stated that it was proper that directors considered the payment of debts owed to current and

---

[285] See *Banner Lane Realisations Ltd (in liq) v Berisford plc* [1997] 1 BCLC 380 at 388.
[286] [1986] 1 WLR 1512; [1987] 1 All ER 114.
[287] Ibid at 1516; 118.
[288] (1989) 7 ACLC 556.
[289] Ibid at 560.
[290] It is probably possible to argue that the creditor in this case was a contingent creditor, rather than a future creditor.
[291] [1994] BCLC 363 at 379.
[292] [2000] HCA 43; (2000) 201 CLR 603; (2000) 173 ALR 529 at [93].
[293] (1985) 3 ACLC 453.

continuing trade creditors, but it would be much more difficult to 'make out a duty to future new creditors', on the basis that future creditors have to take a company as they find it when they decide to do business with it.[294] However, it might be said that Cooke J was in fact talking about creditors who were not in any relationship with the company at the time when the obligation is triggered, and was not contemplating future creditors whose debts simply have not become due and payable at the time of the triggering of the duty.

13.109 In the New South Wales Court of Appeal, Young CJ in Eq, in *Edwards A-G*.[295] seemed to imply that, at the moment, future creditors are not covered by the principle that has developed from *Walker v Wimborne*. But his Honour said that a court might extend the principles devised thus far in relation to directors' obligations to creditors, and hold that a company in a precarious financial position might not only owe duties to the shareholders and creditors but also to likely future creditors.

13.110 As far as academic commentary goes, there has been substantial criticism of any approach that has called for consideration of the interests of future creditors.[296] However, it is submitted that the cases indicate that one cannot assert that the courts are clearly against future creditors. The comments of Young CJ in Eq, referred to above in *Edwards*, among others, indicate that the jurisprudence has not developed to a point of complete certainty.

13.111 There are two other kinds of creditors that might be relevant to our consideration. First, prospective creditors, namely, those who are owed a sum of money not immediately payable,[297] and one who is owed a debt which will certainly become due in the future, either on some determined date or some date which will be determined by reference to future events.[298] While in *Jeffree v NCSC*[299] Brinsden J said that the duty owed was also owed to prospective creditors,[300] there appear to be no other judicial statements that pertain to this kind of creditor.

13.112 The second kind is contingent creditors. Such a creditor is, according to *Re William Hockley Ltd*,[301] to be taken to denote 'a person towards whom, under an existing obligation, the company may or will become subject to a

---

[294] Ibid at 459.

[295] [2004] NSWCA 272 at [153].

[296] For example, see L S Sealy 'Directors' Duties – An Unnecessary Gloss' [1988] CLJ 175; J Farrar 'The Responsibility of Directors and Shareholders for a Company's Debts' (1989) 4 Canta LR 12.

[297] R A K Wright and R Buchanan *Palmer's Company Precedents, Part 2: Winding Up Forms and Practice* (Stevens and Sons Ltd, London, 17th edn, 1960) at 41.

[298] *Stonegate Securities Ltd v Gregory* [1980] 1 Ch 576 at 579. An example of a prospective creditor is a person who has a claim, which is unable to be disputed, for unliquidated damages which remains to be quantified and will lead to a debt for more than a nominal amount (*Re Dollar Land Holdings Ltd* [1994] BCLC 404).

[299] (1989) 7 ACLC 556.

[300] Ibid at 565.

[301] [1962] 1 WLR 555. See *Winter v IRC* [1961] 3 All ER 855 at 864.

present liability on the happening of some future event or at some future date'.[302] This is broadly consistent with the view of Lord Reid in *Re Sutherland dec'd*,[303] where he said that a contingent liability was 'a liability which, by reason of something done by the person bound, would necessarily arise or come into being upon an event or events which might or might not happen'.[304] A prime example of contingent liability is the liability of a surety as a result of the failure of the principal debtor to pay what is owed.

13.113 There has been little UK or Commonwealth authority that has considered whether contingent creditors should be considered by directors, but in the New Zealand decision of *Sojourner v Robb*[305] the High Court said that directors do have to consider contingent creditors, especially if a contemplated course of conduct would endanger the company's solvency.

IX CONCLUSION

13.114 The obligation considered in this chapter appears to play an important role, and this is principally to supplement the wrongful trading action. There has not been a huge corpus of case-law that has developed in the past 30 years, but what we do have has made an important contribution. There are two main problems facing this area. First, there is the failure of the courts to say clearly what state of affairs will lead to the triggering of the duty. Second, the courts have not really told us what directors have to do when they are to consider the interests of creditors.

13.115 It is interesting that, notwithstanding the codification of duties, the Government has seen fit to permit the jurisprudence to continue to develop in relation to this obligation. Where there is an obligation to creditors then directors are freed from their duty to promote the success of the company for the ultimate benefit of the members, although it would appear that a court might say that shareholders' interests are still to be considered, save where the company is insolvent.

---

[302] [1962] 1 WLR 555 at 558.
[303] [1963] AC 235; [1961] 3 WLR 1062.
[304] Ibid at 249; 1069.
[305] [2006] 3 NZLR 808.

CHAPTER 14

DERIVATIVE PROCEEDINGS[1]

I INTRODUCTION

14.1 **Chapters 5–13** have considered duties that are imposed on directors. This chapter begins a series of chapters that are, in a sense, ancillary to those that have gone before. **Chapters 14–17** address matters that are related to consequences that flow from either the existence of the general duties or their breach.

14.2 If directors breach their duties to the company, English law has always held that the company was the correct complainant, and had to commence proceedings against the errant directors. This is known as the rule in *Foss v Harbottle*, deriving from the case of the same name.[2] In the far more recent case of *Prudential Assurance Co Ltd v Newman Industries Ltd (No 2)*[3] the Court of Appeal explained the effect of the rule when it stated that A is not able usually to take action against B in order to recover damages or other relief on behalf of C, where B has acted in such a way as to injure C. Sometimes this is known as 'the proper plaintiff rule'.[4] We know from s 170 of the CA 2006 that the general duties of directors are owed to the company, and not to the members, or anyone else, and so if there is any breach by a director it is logical that the company is the one who should take action for relief. The rule in *Foss v Harbottle* is also based on the notion of majority rule, and that the will of the majority is to be identified with the company's.[5]

---

[1] Parts of this chapter draw on: A Keay and J Loughrey 'Something Old, Something New, Something Borrowed: An Analysis of the New Derivative Action Under the Companies Act 2006' (2008) 124 LQR 469; A Keay and J Loughrey 'Derivative Proceedings in a Brave New World for Company Management and Shareholders' [2010] JBL 151; A Keay and J Loughrey 'An Assessment of the Present State of Statutory Derivative Proceedings' in J Loughrey (ed) *Directors' Duties and Shareholder Litigation in the Wake of the Financial Crisis* (Cheltenham, Edward Elgar, 2013), Chapter 7; A Keay 'Applications to Continue Derivative Proceedings on Behalf of Companies and the Hypothetical Director Test' (2015) 34 *Civil Justice Quarterly* 346; A Keay 'Assessing and Rethinking the Statutory Scheme for Derivative Actions Under the Companies Act 2006' (2016) 16 *Journal of Corporate Law Studies* 39. The last paper provides a detailed discussion of the possible flaws in the statutory scheme for derivative actions and the case-law that has interpreted the scheme as well as possible reform measures that could be implemented to address the flaws.

[2] (1843) 2 Hare 461; 67 ER 189.

[3] [1982] Ch 204 at 210.

[4] For example, see *Edwards v Halliwell* [1950] 2 All ER 1064; *Prudential Assurance Co Ltd v Newman Industries Ltd (No 2)* [1982] Ch 204 at 210.

[5] *Edwards v Halliwell* [1950] 2 All ER 1064.

14.3 The board of directors is usually charged with the management of the company, and the articles will usually invest the directors, as part of broad management powers, with the power to litigate and enforce the company's interests.[6] But they are not always the best people to decide whether one or more of their number should be sued.[7] Clearly, and not infrequently, boards have refrained from taking action for a number of reasons. One, of course, could be that the whole board or those who control the board are seen as the wrongdoers. Another might be that the board could be concerned that action against one or two directors could affect the whole board. Third, the board might be worried that any judgment obtained might not be able to be satisfied, and, therefore, costs expended in litigation might not be recovered. A fourth reason is that the board might refrain from taking any action against one or more of its number as the non-erring directors might feel that if they are tolerant of the miscreants those miscreants might show reciprocal tolerance if they commit any wrongdoing in the future. Fifth, and allied to the latter reason, is that boards are groups and are clearly affected by group dynamics. They have been described as 'elite and episodic decision-making groups,'[8] and there seems little doubt that boards are heavily dependent on social-psychological processes and they will be affected by social-psychological factors.[9] Therefore, directors may decide not to take action because they are influenced by: the fact that they have become friendly with the miscreant; other members of the board, and especially senior executives like the CEO,[10] might support the miscreant; issues of collegiality which might mean that directors find it difficult to question actions of colleagues.[11] Sixth, there is the cost of legal proceedings. Like any prospective litigant the company has to consider the likely costs that will be incurred. If the company were to take action and lose, then it is probable that costs would be awarded against it. Even if it were to succeed it might not be able to reclaim all of its costs from the other party. Seventh, again like anyone considering taking legal action, the board has to be convinced that the company would have a good chance of succeeding. The shareholders are not going to thank the board for spending money in taking action that was not supported by cogent evidence. Eighth, the board might be embarrassed by the breach. Board members might feel that they were, or could be perceived as, 'asleep on the job,' or that they put too much faith in the director, and this will affect their reputation. Finally, the board might take the view that it is better for business

---

[6] For example, the Companies (Tables A–F) Regulations 1985, Table A, reg 70. The Companies (Model Articles) Regulations 2008, SI 2008/3229, reg 2, Sch 1, art 5 (private companies); reg 4, Sch 3, art 5 (public companies).

[7] See R Nolan 'The Legal Control of Directors' Conflicts of Interest in the United Kingdom: Non-Executive Directors Following the Higgs Report' (2005) 6 *Theoretical Inquiries in Law* 413 at 424.

[8] D Forbes and F Milliken 'Cognition and Corporate Governance: Understanding Boards of Directors as Strategic Decision-making Groups' (1999) 24 *Academy of Management Review* 489 at 492.

[9] Ibid at 493.

[10] See, M O'Connor 'The Enron Board: The Perils of Groupthink' (2003) 71 *University of Cincinnati Law Review* 1233.

[11] J Macey *Corporate Governance: Promises Kept, Promises Broken* (Princeton University Press, Princeton, 2008) at 61.

that the breach is not publicised on the basis that it might bring either or both of the board and the company into disrepute. Liquidators have always been able to take action against errant directors, but it would be highly unfortunate if actions could not be brought until a company enters liquidation (or administration). There has to be some process that allows actions to be brought if the directors themselves refrain from taking action. At common law the courts developed some exceptions to the rule that no action could be brought to enforce a liability owed to the company, save by the company, in order to permit shareholders to commence proceedings. These proceedings came to be known as derivative proceedings, the description being used first in the UK by the Court of Appeal in *Wallersteiner v Moir (No 2)*.[12] The reason for the use of the description is that the right to bring the proceedings was derived from the right of the company.

14.4 There are objections to the concept of a derivative action. First, the action taken is not authorised by the appropriate company organ.[13] Second, the applicant is endeavouring to circumvent the majority rule principle.[14] Nevertheless, UK law has seen fit, first through the courts, and now through legislation, to permit such actions in limited situations.

14.5 The right to initiate derivative proceedings has been seen as a part of the arsenal of weapons that members have to control the directors. Some might say, with justification, that this arsenal is not that substantial or powerful.[15] The member brings derivative proceedings on behalf of all the members who are not made defendants.[16] Perhaps to make the weapon a little more powerful the CA 2006, following significant examination and debate, has done what several Commonwealth jurisdictions[17] have done, provides a statutory derivative action procedure. The scheme was put in force on 1 October 2007.[18]

14.6 The focus of the book is on directors' duties, but it would be remiss of the book if it did not address the issue of derivative proceedings in some depth as it has potentially great relevance to the enforcement of breaches against miscreant directors where the board fails to take action. However, the discussion must be limited in length and for further discussion readers might look to more detailed studies of the derivative action process that are provided elsewhere.[19]

---

[12] [1975] QB 373. The description was borrowed from American law.

[13] R Hollington *Shareholders' Rights* (London, Sweet and Maxwell, 5th edn, 2007) at 131.

[14] Ibid at 132.

[15] See A Keay 'Company Directors Behaving Poorly: Disciplinary Options for Shareholders' [2007] JBL 656.

[16] *Cooke v Cooke* [1997] 2 BCLC 28 at 31.

[17] For example, see Part 2F1A of the Corporations Act 2001 (Australia); Canada Business Corporations Act 1985, s 239 (Canada); Companies Act 1990, ss 216A and 216B (Singapore). Also, note that Hong Kong as introduced a legislative scheme. See Companies Ordinance, ss 2 and 168BC–168BG (HK). It became operative from 15 July 2005.

[18] Companies Act 2006 (Commencement No 3, Consequential Amendments, Transitional Provisions and Savings) Order 2007, SI 2007/2194, art 2(1)(e).

[19] For that, see, for example, A Reisberg *Derivative Actions and Corporate Governance* (OUP,

14.7 How important the procedure is, is a matter of some debate. It has been asserted that we live in a world where shareholder activism is becoming more widespread,[20] so this might mean a greater use of derivative actions. But Lord Goldsmith said, when taking part in the debates in the House of Lords on the Company Law Reform Bill 2005, that: '[On] the provision of new duties, we do not see why that should lead to increased litigation either.'[21] In fact there does not appear to have been an increase in litigation at all. In fact, as indicated shortly, there has been a relative paucity of cases brought before the courts. But notwithstanding that, clearly the action has potential importance and plays a critical role in the area covered by the book.

14.8 Before examining the provisions that allow for shareholders to initiate derivative actions, the Chapter discusses, somewhat briefly, the position at common law so as to provide some background to the statutory action. The Chapter also considers in some detail the criteria that any shareholder who wishes to bring a derivative action has to satisfy and the likely effect of the statutory scheme on litigation, as well as the position where causes of action occurred before the date on which the new scheme was put in force. The Chapter also examines whether a derivative action is possible where a company is in liquidation or is insolvent and whether a multiple-derivative claim is possible under UK law. I should note that while the new statutory derivative action has been in effect for over nine years we still do have, as indicated above, a relatively small corpus of case-law that addresses the new scheme. Since the scheme was put into law there have been, as at 1 April 2016, 24 derivative actions instituted[22] and this works out to be an average of 2.82 cases per year, which is actually less than that found in a study conducted in 2010.[23] The possible reasons for the paucity of cases has been the subject of a recent paper.[24]

14.9 The Chapter draws principles and insights not only from these cases, but also from the cases which dealt with the common law procedure (while the

---

2007) generally; R Hollington *Shareholders' Rights* (London, Sweet and Maxwell, 6th edn, 2012) ch 6; V Joffe et al *Minority Shareholders: Law, Practice and Procedure* (OUP, 4th edn, 2008) ch 3.

[20] G Milner-Moore and R Lewis *In the Line of Fire – Directors' Duties under the Companies Act 2006* Practical Law, available at http://corporate.practicallaw.com/9-205-9008 (last visited 9 October 2007).

[21] Lords Grand Committee, 6 February 2006, col 2.

[22] All of the cases dealt with permission hearings. This was from a search of Westlaw, Lawtel and Lexis databases. Cases, such as multiple-derivative actions, based on the common law procedure were not included. A 'multiple-derivative' action is a derivative action that is entitled to be brought by minority shareholders of a parent company for a breach of duty owed to a direct or indirect subsidiary, certainly where control of the subsidiary is not independent of the parent company's board. These applications are not brought under the statutory scheme but under the common law. See, *Re Fort Gilkicker Ltd* [2013] EWHC 348 (Ch); [2013] BCC 365. These kinds of proceedings are discussed later in the chapter.

[23] A Keay and J Loughrey 'Derivative Proceedings in a Brave New World for Company Management and Shareholders' [2010] JBL 151. This study found the number of cases per annum was 3.2.

[24] A Keay 'Assessing and Rethinking the Statutory Scheme for Derivative Actions Under the Companies Act 2006' (2016) 16 *Journal of Corporate Law Studies* 39.

common law process has been abolished by the CA 2006 as far as ordinary derivative claims are concerned[25] the principles in the case-law can be informative) and the jurisprudence from Commonwealth jurisdictions which have previously embraced a statutory derivative action scheme, and particularly Australia whose legislation is, perhaps, the closest of all Commonwealth countries to that of the UK's.

II THE COMMON LAW: SOME BACKGROUND

14.10 It is helpful to rehearse, briefly, the position at common law by way of background to the discussion of the statutory regime that now applies, and to enable us to have some context for the consideration of the cases which dealt with the common law position. These cases may well be relevant, to some extent, to the deliberations of courts hearing applications under the new statutory procedure. Also, it would seem that where there is a cause of action that could be the subject of a derivative action, and it occurred before 1 October 2007, shareholders can only obtain permission to bring proceedings if they meet the requirements at common law.[26] It is unlikely that any action would be brought in relation to the period before codification because of limitation of action issues. It is important to note at this point that, as discussed later in the Chapter, multiple-derivative actions will be subject to the common law as they do not come within the statutory scheme.

14.11 The derivative action developed at common law in order to provide a remedy for a company where the company had suffered a wrong but the wrongdoers were in control of the company, and they prevented it from taking legal proceedings in relation to that wrong. In such circumstances, and as already foreshadowed, the courts permitted individual shareholders to bring an action on the company's behalf, with the cause of action being derived from that belonging to the company. The court's decision constituted an exception to the rule that, where a wrong is done to the company, the company, as a separate legal entity, is the proper claimant in respect of that wrong. The decision of the courts to allow this exception was to do justice to the company, and they had a wide discretion in whether they considered that the exception should or should not be applied.

14.12 Notwithstanding the courts' decision to permit derivative proceedings, they were mindful of vexatious and disruptive litigation that could be taken by minority shareholders. Consequently, even if the company had a good claim against the alleged wrongdoers, an action brought on the company's behalf by a minority shareholder would not succeed unless the shareholder could establish standing to sue on the company's behalf. The rules on standing were restrictive. It was necessary for shareholders to bring themselves within the exception to

---

[25] *Re Fort Gilkicker Ltd* [2013] EWHC 348 (Ch); [2013] BCC 365.
[26] Companies Act 2006 (Commencement No 3, Consequential Amendments, Transitional Provisions and Savings) Order 2007, SI 2007/2194, art 20(2).

rule in the case of *Foss v Harbottle*,[27] and demonstrate that there was a prima facie case on the merits that there had been a 'fraud on the minority', which could not be ratified by the shareholders in general meeting,[28] and also that the company was under the control of the wrongdoer(s).[29] Usually a fraud on the minority would involve an abuse of power by directors in a fraudulent or negligent manner and so as to benefit them and hurt the company. Wrongdoer control might be constituted by the prevention of the bringing of a claim by the company. Wrongdoer control will exist if the persons who have acted wrongly have control of the majority of votes at a general meeting of the company, or the majority has approved a fraud on the minority, or the majority stifles legal action against the wrongdoer(s). If the wrongdoers are not in control of the company then the law's attitude was that the whole matter should be left to the company.[30] But the law has never demanded, before accepting that wrongdoer control exists, that a company meeting has been called and refused to institute proceedings against the wrongdoers. Wrongdoer control has been able to be demonstrated in other ways.[31] While the court in *Pavlides v Jensen*[32] seemed to regard wrongdoer control as being based on the majority being able to exercise their votes in order to have a decision in their favour, the Court of Appeal in *Prudential Assurance Co Ltd v Newman Industries Ltd (No 2)*[33] preferred a wider approach to control. The Court said that control could mean, at one extreme the wrongdoers could cast the majority of votes, and at the other extreme it could mean the situation where the majority of votes were in fact constituted by the wrongdoers together with those votes of people who were apathetic and/or those influenced by the wrongdoers.[34]

14.13   Perhaps a classic case that illustrates wrongdoer control, and which has been referred to in earlier Chapters, was *Cook v Deeks*.[35] Here three directors of a four-director company, X, negotiated on behalf of X to secure some contracts for the construction of a railway. During the course of their negotiations, the directors arranged for the contracts to be performed by them rather than X. The directors formed a new company especially to carry out the contracts. The fourth director of X learned of this, but the other three controlled the company and refrained from taking action against themselves on behalf of X. The fourth director brought derivative proceedings, successfully, as a minority shareholder to enforce the rights of X.

---

[27]   (1843) 2 Hare 461; 67 ER 189.

[28]   See **Chapter 15**, which deals with ratification.

[29]   *Prudential Assurance Co Ltd v Newman Industries Ltd* [1982] Ch 204 at 221–222. There have been statements to the effect that there were a number of exceptions to the rule (see *Edwards v Halliwell* [1950] 2 All ER 1064).

[30]   *Edwards v Halliwell* [1950] 2 All ER 1064 at 1067.

[31]   *Mason v Harris* (1879) LR 11 Ch D 97 at 108 (CA); *Alexander v Automatic Telephone Co* [1900] Ch 56 at 69 (CA).

[32]   [1956] Ch 565.

[33]   [1982] Ch 204.

[34]   Ibid at 219.

[35]   [1916] AC 554.

14.14 As a minority shareholder's ability to bring a derivative action was regarded by the courts 'as a matter of grace',[36] even if shareholders managed to satisfy the requirements concerning wrongdoer control, they would still be refused permission if the court took the view that permission should not be granted to the relevant shareholder because of attributes which were personal to him or her.[37] Courts would not permit the shareholder to pursue the action if it was not being brought bona fide, the member did not have a proper purpose, or there was another remedy available to the member.[38] Also, pursuant to something of a controversial development, in *Smith v Croft (No 2)*,[39] Knox J held that where an independent majority of the minority shareholders did not wish a derivative action to proceed, the action would not be permitted.[40]

14.15 The question of the shareholder's standing to sue in a derivative action was not dealt with in the substantive proceedings until the decision in *Prudential Assurance Co Ltd v Newman Industries Ltd*,[41] where it was established that the standing issue had to be settled as a preliminary matter.[42] Then, in 1994, the Rules of Court were amended to require shareholders to seek leave of the court to pursue a derivative action,[43] and it was the duty of the court to ascertain, as a preliminary issue, whether the shareholder should be allowed to sue derivatively.[44] At common law leave had to be applied for early on, after the plaintiff had issued the claim form and before taking any other step in the proceedings[45] The time limit within which the application had to be issued was within the time period for service of the claim form, being within four months of issue of the claim form for service within the jurisdiction and six months outside.[46] The courts said that it was critical that they maintained control, and the seeking of permission was not simply a technicality.[47]

14.16 Professor Paul Davies was of the opinion in 2003 that the balance at common law between the concept of a desire to see the collective nature of decision-making fostered, on the one hand, and the need for the enforcement of

---

[36] *Mumbray v Lapper* [2005] EWHC 1152 (Ch); [2005] BCC 990 at [121], citing L C B Gower *Modern Company Law* (London, Sweet and Maxwell, 4th edn, 1979) at 652.

[37] J Payne 'Clean Hands in Derivative Actions' (2002) 61 CLJ 76 at 81.

[38] *Barrett v Duckett* [1995] BCC 362.

[39] [1988] Ch 114 at 159.

[40] *Smith v Croft (No 2)* [1988] Ch 114 at 184–185. Professor Paul Davies was of the view that this decision would have a destructive effect if followed in other courts: P Davies *Gower and Davies' Principles of Company Law* (London, Sweet and Maxwell, 7th edn, 2003) at 463.

[41] *Prudential Assurance Co Ltd v Newman Industries Ltd* [1982] Ch 204.

[42] Ibid at 221.

[43] RSC Ord 15 r 12A.

[44] *Barrett v Duckett* [1995] 1 BCLC 243 at 250.

[45] RSC Ord 15, r 12A which required that the application had to be made within 21 days of intention to defend being given. This was superseded by CPR 19.9(3). The common law procedure is discussed in R Reed 'Derivative Claims: The Application for Permission to Continue' (2000) 21 Co Law 156.

[46] CPR 19.9(5); CPR 7.5.

[47] *Portfolios of Distinction Ltd v Laird* [2004] EWHC 2071 (Ch); [2005] BCC 216 at [60].

directors' duties, on the other, had been upset to the point that the former was advantaged over the latter, and so reform was warranted in a new Companies Act.[48]

III THE STATUTORY DERIVATIVE ACTION

A Introduction

14.17 The statutory derivative action, which came into operation on 1 October 2007, completely replaces the common law.[49] According to Lord Goldsmith, speaking for the Government in the debates in the House of Lords, the statutory process would provide greater clarity as to how a member might bring a derivative action.[50] The scheme does not include the concepts of fraud on the minority or wrongdoer control,[51] concepts that dominated derivative actions at common law.it should mentioned at this point that while the scheme might be said to have replaced the common law as far as the archetypal derivative action is concerned, it does not apply to multiple-derivative actions. This is, as mentioned above, discussed later in the Chapter.

14.18 We do have case-law on the procedure, but, as mentioned earlier, not, given the fact that we have had the statutory scheme in place for nine years, a great deal. So, as mentioned earlier, this Chapter relies for some assistance on the case-law prior to the statutory regime coming into force and Commonwealth case-law, and particularly the Australian regime.

14.19 There are two rationales that are often given for the existence of statutory derivative proceedings:[52] first, to ensure, if possible, that the company is compensated for the wrongdoing of its directors; second, it deters directors from acting improperly. Pearlie Koh has said[53] that:

> 'The introduction of the statutory derivative action is often premised on the view that an enhanced shareholder role not only complements existing regulatory regimes, and in the case of publicly held corporations, market and social forces, by deterring managerial wrongdoing, but is also effective in raising management's obligations and duties beyond a merely hortative level.'

---

[48] P Davies *Gower and Davies' Principles of Company Law* (London, Sweet and Maxwell, 7th edn, 2003) at 463.

[49] This is the same as in Australia, Canada and New Zealand, but compare the situation in Hong Kong where the two schemes sit side-by-side: *Waddington Ltd v Chan Chun Hoo Thomas* [2008] HKCFA 63; (2008) 11 HKCFAR 370; [2009] 4 HKC 381; [2009] 2 BCLC 82. Ribeiro PJ (at [29]-[32]) criticised this state of affairs.

[50] Lords Grand Committee, 27 February 2006, Hansard HL 679, col GC 4-5.

[51] Although some cases suggest that this might be of relevance. For example, see *Stimpson v Southern Landlords Association* [2009] EWHC 2072; [2010] BCC 387 at [46].

[52] See S Bottomley *The Constitutional Corporation* (Aldershot, Ashgate, 2007) at 157.

[53] P Koh 'Directors' Fiduciary Duties: Unthreading the Joints of Shareholder Ratification' (2005) 5 JCLS 363 at 376.

14.20   Under the CA 2006, as was the case at common law, permission has to be applied for by a member early on, just after the commencement of the derivative action. The procedure for permission that is set down in the CA 2006 is critical to the statutory scheme's operation.

14.21   We have already noted that at common law, following the decision in *Prudential Assurance Co Ltd v Newman Industries Ltd*,[54] standing had to be dealt with as a preliminary matter and since 1994 the Rules of Court were amended to require shareholders to seek leave of the court to pursue a derivative action. Consequently, the requirement in s 261(1) of the CA 2006 for permission to continue an action is not altogether new.

14.22   As mentioned above, an application may be brought only by a member,[55] and includes a person who is not a member but to whom shares in the company have been transferred or transmitted by operation of law.[56] It does not matter if the cause of action that is the subject of the claim occurred before he or she became a member.[57] In some other jurisdictions a former member may bring proceedings.[58]

14.23   While derivative actions are regularly and rightly associated with claims by minority shareholders, the legislation does not appear to exclude majority shareholders from bringing a claim. Practically it is not likely that a majority shareholder would want to, or, at least, to do so in only the most exceptional circumstances. This is reflected in *Cinematic Finance Ltd v Ryder*[59] where Roth J said that he would not say that it was never appropriate for a majority shareholder to be granted permission to bring a derivative claim, but it would only be in exceptional circumstances and he had difficulty in envisaging such exceptional circumstances.[60] In this case the majority shareholder/claimant could not establish exceptional circumstances.

B The elements for gaining permission

14.24   The elements for gaining permission are set out in ss 261 and 263 of the CA 2006 for England and Wales and Northern Ireland and ss 266 and 268 for Scotland, with the other sections of the relevant Chapter of Part 11 (Chapter 1 for England and Wales and Northern Ireland and Chapter 2 for Scotland) setting out the procedure for bringing the claim and what must be established for success.[61] The following will deal with the provisions that apply in England

---

[54]   *Prudential Assurance Co Ltd v Newman Industries Ltd* [1982] Ch 204.
[55]   Section 260(1).
[56]   Section 260(5).
[57]   Section 260(4).
[58]   For example, under the Australian Corporations Act 2001, s 236(1)(a)(i). In Canada applications by such persons have been denied on the basis that they did not have a sufficient interest. See, for instance, *Jacobs Farms Ltd v Jacobs* (1992) OJ No 813 (Ont Gen Div).
[59]   [2010] EWHC 3387 (Ch); [2012] BCC 797 at [22].
[60]   Ibid at [14].
[61]   For discussion of practical and procedural issues, see V Joffe et al *Minority Shareholders: Law, Practice and Procedure* (Oxford, OUP, 2008) ch 1.

and Wales and Northern Ireland but the Scottish provisions are very similar. In Scotland the claimant has to seek leave from the court to initiate derivative proceedings.

14.25 According to the statutory scheme, a derivative claim is one that is initiated by a member of the company in relation to a cause of action that is vested in the company, and relief is sought on behalf of the company.[62]

14.26 A claim may be brought where there is a cause of action arising from an actual or proposed action or omission involving negligence, default, breach of duty or breach of trust by a director of the company.[63] Clearly a derivative claim can be initiated where a director is in breach of the general duties, which are the subject of this work. As mentioned above, it does not matter if the cause of action arose before or after the applicant/claimant became a member of the company;[64] this preserves the common law position. The fact that the member may bring a claim in relation to happenings prior to his or her becoming a member makes sense as the claim relates to a wrong done to the company and not to the member. Effectively applicants are limited to members. This is the position with most jurisdictions around the world, but a number of other jurisdictions do allow for a wider range of applicants. For instance, s 238 of the Canada Business Corporations Act 1985 includes members, certain creditors, and directors, and also applications may be made by 'any other person who, in the discretion of a court, is a proper person to make an application'. Similarly, s 216A(1)(c) of the Singaporean Companies Act provides that the range of persons who can apply for a derivative action includes 'any other person who, in the discretion of the Court, is a proper person'.

14.27 Applicants now are able to instigate derivative claims in a broader range of circumstances than at common law, although the range is not sufficiently wide enough to cover any action against anyone under any cause of action that the company has, and where no action has been instigated by the board. Under the present scheme, the action must be one that arose as a result of the actions of the directors.[65]

14.28 For the purposes of Chapter 1 of Part 11, 'director' includes a former director, and a shadow director is treated as a director.[66] What about de facto directors? The fact that there is no legislative provision that defines the term might mean that there is no need to refer to the term. As a de facto director owes the same duties owed by a *de jure* director,[67] a member might be able to bring a claim against a de facto director if he or she is in breach of a duty. In

---

[62]   CA 2006, s 260(1).
[63]   CA 2006, s 260(3).
[64]   CA 2006, s 260(4).
[65]   Section 260(3) of the Act. See *Iesini v Westrip Holdings Ltd* [2009] EWHC 2526 (Ch); [2010] BCC 420, [75].
[66]   CA 2006, s 260(5)(a), (b).
[67]   *Re Canadian Land Reclaiming and Colonizing Co* (1880) 14 Ch D 660 at 670 (CA); *Mistmorn Pty Ltd (in liq) v Yasseen* (1996) 21 ACSR 173; (1996) 14 ACLC 1387; *Ultraframe UK Ltd v*

any event, s 260(3) of the CA 2006 does state that an action may be brought against a director or *another person*, thereby covering de facto directors. It is likely that the inclusion of the words 'another person' is essentially to cover cases where someone, not a director, has aided the director in the breach or received property as a result of the breach.[68] In the latter situation it would be critical for an order to be sought that property passed to a third party by a miscreant director could be recovered for the company.[69] Another case where action might be taken against a third party could be where a third party has been negligent and the company has a cause of action against that party, but the directors decided that they will not proceed against the third party. Perhaps the directors might be concerned that the third party might seek contribution from the directors on the basis that they were guilty of contributory negligence, which is what occurred in *AWA Ltd v Daniels*[70] when the company sued the company's auditors and the auditors joined the directors by way of third party notice (contribution notice) on the basis that they were liable because of contributory negligence.

14.29 Remedies for a successful derivative claim will be the same as they would for a claim brought by the company.

C The practice and procedure[71]

14.30 In England and Wales it is important to note that a derivative action is commenced and then the claimant/member must obtain the permission of the courts to continue it.[72] Rule 19.9(4) of the Civil Procedure Rules 1998 ('CPR') indicates that once a derivative proceeding has been commenced (and this is done by claim form) the claimant must not take any further action without obtaining the formal permission of the court. In some other jurisdictions around the world an application has to be made to the court for permission to commence an action.[73]

14.31 The application for permission must be constituted by an application notice under Part 23 of the CPR and it must be accompanied by written evidence to support it.[74] The company must not be made a respondent.[75]

Fielding [2004] RPC 24 at [39]; *Ultraframe UK Ltd v Fielding* [2005] EWHC 1638 (Ch); [2006] FSR 17 at [1257]; *Primlake Ltd v Matthews Associates* [2006] EWHC 1227 (Ch); [2007] 1 BCLC 686 at [284].

[68] Lord Goldsmith in the House of Lords made it clear that it was envisaged that there would only be a right against a third party where there had been a breach of duty by a director: Lord Goldsmith, Lords Grand Committee, 27 February 2006, Hansard HL, vol 679, col GC10.

[69] The substance of this is discussed in **Chapter 15**.

[70] (1992) 10 ACLC 933.

[71] This section of the Chapter draws on A Keay and J Loughrey 'Something Old, Something New, Something Borrowed: An Analysis of the New Derivative Action Under the Companies Act 2006' (2008) 124 LQR 469.

[72] Section 261(1). In Scotland the procedure is for permission to be sought to enable a claimant to commence derivative proceedings.

[73] The case in Scotland.

[74] CPR, r 19.9A(2).

14.32 Besides the provisions in the CA 2006, rr 19.9–19.9F of the CPR are very important from a practice point of view, and will be mentioned in various places in the Chapter. Also, it should be noted that a new Practice Direction was published in relation to derivative claims and in order to supplement rr 19.9-19.9F.[76]

14.33 The legislation provides in s 260 for a two-part process for obtaining permission.[77] The courts first have to determine, under s 261, if the claim discloses a prima facie case.[78] If the court comes to the conclusion that no prima facie case is established then the claim is dismissed. But if a case is made out, then the court may direct what evidence is to be provided by the company.[79]

14.34 Besides seeking permission to continue a derivative claim, a member is entitled, under s 262, to apply for permission to continue a company's existing claim as a derivative claim. This is where a company has brought a claim and the cause of action on which the claim is based could be prosecuted as a derivative claim. Section 262(2) provides that a member may apply for permission in this context on the ground that the way in which the company commenced or continued the claim constitutes an abuse of process of the court, the company has failed to pursue the claim diligently, and it is appropriate for the member to continue the claim as a derivative claim. What does pursuing a claim diligently involve? Probably that the company was taking action in a reasonable way, so if the company merely issued initiating process and did not file pleadings it might be said that it was not pursuing the claim diligently.[80] The type of case envisaged by the legislation is probably where the company has initiated proceedings against directors but has not proceeded with them or is going very slowly. As with applications under s 261, if the court comes to the conclusion that no prima facie case is established then the claim must be dismissed,[81] but if a case is made out, then the court may direct what evidence is to be provided by the company.[82] A member may also seek permission, under s 264, to continue an existing derivative claim. The two cases that the provision might be aimed at preventing is, first, where the directors have a member who is friendly to them in order to obtain permission to take derivative proceedings and, once gaining permission, does not prosecute them;[83] and, second, where a member obtains permission but is dilatory in taking the matter further. Section 264 applies in circumstances where a derivative claim has been brought,

---

[75]   CPR, r 19.9A(3).

[76]   *Practice Direction: Derivative Claims* [2007] BCC 840. For a discussion of the procedure and practice, see D Lightman 'The Role of the Company at the Permission Stage in the Statutory Derivative Claim' (2011) 30 CLQ 23.

[77]   Explanatory Notes to the CA 2006 at para 492.

[78]   CA 2006, s 261(2).

[79]   CA 2006, s 261(3)(a).

[80]   A Reisberg *Derivative Actions and Corporate Governance* (OUP, 2007) at 144.

[81]   CA 2006, s 262(3)(a).

[82]   CA 2006, s 262(4)(b).

[83]   P Davies *Gower and Davies' Principles of Company Law* (London, Sweet and Maxwell, 8th edn, 2008) at 621.

a member has continued as a derivative claim a claim brought by the company or has continued a derivative claim under s 264. In one of these cases another member is entitled to go to the court and seek permission to continue the claim because the manner in which the proceedings were commenced or continued by the claimant constitutes an abuse of the process of the court, the claimant has failed to pursue the claim diligently, and it is appropriate for the member to continue the claim as a derivative claim.[84] Again, as with applications under s 261, if the court comes to the conclusion that no prima facie case is established then the claim must be dismissed,[85] but if a case is made out, then the court may direct what evidence is to be provided by the company.[86]

14.35 It would seem that the courts are not overly strict when considering permission applications at the first stage. It has been asserted that there might be the danger of the courts letting the claim pass through the first stage, unless it is clearly a nonsense claim, because there might be something in the claim, possibly as a result of the uncertainty with directors' duties.[87]

14.36 Whether or not such a direction is given under either s 261 or 262 of the CA 2006, s 263(2) provides for a second stage to the permission application. It has two parts to it. First it requires a court, once it has determined that there is a prima facie case for permission, to refuse permission if it is satisfied that a person under a duty to promote the success of the company would not continue the action, or if the act forming the basis of the claim has been authorised[88] or ratified by the company.[89] If none of these apply then the court moves to the next step, the second part of the second stage, which involves the court considering a number of other elements. At this point the court has a discretion as to whether to allow the claim to proceed. The factors that are enumerated in s 263(3)–(4) will be taken into account by a court in exercising its discretion. They are: whether the shareholder is acting in good faith; the importance which a person operating under a duty to promote the success of the company would attach to continuing the action; whether the act could be ratified[90] or authorised; whether the company has decided not to bring a claim; the availability of an alternative remedy for the shareholder, which he or she can pursue in his or her own right; and the views of the independent members of the company in relation to the action. Independent members would be those with no personal interest in the matter that is the subject of a claim. While a

---

[84] CA 2006, s 264(2).

[85] CA 2006, s 264(3)(a).

[86] CA 2006, s 264(4)(a).

[87] S James 'The Curse of Uncertain Times' (2007) 7 JIBFL 447.

[88] This probably refers to the authorisation that the board can give under s 175(5).

[89] CA 2006, s 263(2). Not all breaches are necessarily ratifiable. See **Chapter 16**. At common law a company could always ratify an action before judgment and, if it did so, it would make a derivative action nugatory. Would the same be possible under the statutory scheme? There is nothing to suggest that the answer is other than in the positive.

[90] If an action was ratified then there is not a cause of action which a member could enforce.

court is required to consider these criteria when determining whether to grant permission, they are not exhaustive and, it would appear, the courts can take account of other relevant factors.[91]

14.37   In some respects the statutory criteria for the grant of permission have parallels in the common law. This is especially the case with the requirement in s 261(2) that: an applicant must, at the first stage of the process to gain permission, establish a prima facie case; the requirement at the second part of the second stage that the court must consider the applicant's good faith and consideration has to be given as to whether an alternative remedy is available to the applicant.[92] Also, while the common law had no equivalent to s 263(2)(a) or s 263(3)(b), which require courts to consider whether a person acting in accordance with s 172 (the duty to promote the success of the company) would continue with the claim, and the importance such a person would attach to it, it is notable that in a couple of decisions, delivered before the statutory scheme came into operation, the test for the grant of leave at common law has been seen as whether an independent board would sanction proceedings.[93] It has been asserted that it is at least arguable that there is sufficient similarity between these tests that the case-law on the latter test could potentially be used in interpreting the former,[94] although as the jurisprudence develops on the statutory scheme this may become less and less necessary.

14.38   A court will not make an order in relation to any part of a claimant's action that involves him or her making a personal claim. For instance, in *Hughes v Weiss*[95] the claimant included in the general claim, a small claim that was to be said to be owed by the company to the claimant. The judge refused to deal with it because it was a claim personal to the claimant and not brought on behalf of the company.[96]

14.39   The court has the power at a permission hearing to order the company to indemnify the successful shareholder in relation to his or her costs.[97] But, notwithstanding the fact that the Law Commission said that the inclusion of the power to provide for an indemnity was a significant incentive to shareholders to initiate proceedings,[98] in reality there is little incentive for shareholders because any relief that is ultimately ordered by a court will go

---

[91]   This follows from the wording of s 263(3) which states that the court must 'in particular' have regard to the listed factors. See also the Law Commission *Shareholder Remedies: Report on a Reference under section 3(1)(e) of the Law Commissions Act 1965* (Law Com No 246, Cm 3769) (London, Stationery Office, 1997) at para. 6.73.

[92]   CA 2006, s 263(3)(a) and (f).

[93]   *Mumbray v Lapper* [2005] EWHC 1152 (Ch); [2005] BCC 990; *Airey v Cordell* [2006] EWHC 2728 (Ch); [2007] Bus L R 391 at [56].

[94]   A Keay and J Loughrey 'Something Old, Something New, Something Borrowed: An Analysis of the New Derivative Action Under the Companies Act 2006' (2008) 124 LQR 469 at 478.

[95]   [2012] EWHC 2363 (Ch).

[96]   Ibid at [72]–[74].

[97]   CPR 19.9E.

[98]   *Shareholder Remedies*, Consultation Paper No 142, 1996, para 18.1.

wholly to the company itself.[99] The best that shareholders can hope for is that their costs will be covered, an issue that will be dealt with in detail later.

14.40 The final thing to mention is that a court might take the view that permission might only be granted up to a particular point in the litigation, such as to the time of disclosure. This occurred in *Kiani v Cooper*,[100] and *McAskill v Fulton*.[101] It was also something favoured by Roth J in *Stainer v Lee*[102] where a company had what appeared to be a very strong case of breach of duty, but it was unclear whether all the resulting loss had been repaid.

IV THE CRITERIA FOR DETERMINING WHETHER PERMISSION WILL BE GRANTED

14.41 When hearing an application for permission there are two possible problems for a judge; they both mirror those applying in applications for interim injunctions.[103] First, there is usually no oral evidence and no opportunity for cross-examination or disclosure; inspection of documents has not taken place, and sometimes no points of claim or points of defence have been drafted and/or served,[104] so that the judge does not have before him or her, in many instances, the full story or, at least, a tested full story. Second, a judge hearing an application for permission cannot devote the same time to it as the trial judge can, if and when the case is finally heard in full. It is critical that applications for permission are not overly-long, and that the substantive issues are not pre-judged, given the absence of evidence from the company and the uncontested nature of the first stage, because even if the judge directs the company to submit evidence, there is no suggestion that the company will argue the substantive points at this juncture. The company might not in fact wish to divulge its case at this point.

14.42 The Law Commission in its *Shareholder Remedies* report was most concerned that mini-trials were avoided at preliminary hearings.[105] The concern that it had was that a threshold test on the merits might well lead to fine

---

99   For instance, see I Ramsay 'Corporate Governance, Shareholder Litigation and the Prospects for a Statutory Derivative Action' (1992) 15 *University of New South Wales Law Journal* 149, 150 and 164.
100 [2010] EWHC 577 (Ch); [2010] BCC 463 at [14].
101 2014 WL 8106597.
102 [2010] EWHC1539 (Ch); [2011] BCC 134 at [37], [55].
103 The equivalent test in Australia is used in deciding interim injunction applications: *Charlton v Baber* [2003] NSWSC 745; (2003) 47 ACSR 31 at [55]; *Reale v Duncan Reale Pty Ltd* [2005] NSWSC 174 at [11].
104 D Bean *Injunctions* (5th edn, 1991) at 23.
105 Law Commission *Shareholder Remedies: Report on a Reference under section 3(1)(e) of the Law Commissions Act 1965* (Law Com No 246, Cm 3769) (London, Stationery Office, 1997) at para 6.71.

distinctions being drawn as to which side of the line a particular set of facts fell.[106] It favoured the development of a principled approach that was not tied to a particular rule.[107]

14.43   On the point of length, some of the cases for permission that have been heard under the statutory scheme have lasted several days,[108] and, consequently, led to the incurring of significant costs. So this is of some concern. David Donaldson QC (sitting as a deputy judge of the High Court) in *Langley Ward Ltd v Trevor* (sub nom *Re Seven Holdings Ltd*)[109] indicated his concern about permission hearings becoming time-consuming when he said:[110]

> 'In the present case, the court was presented with three lever-arch files of pleadings, statements and documents in addition to detailed skeleton arguments and extensive lists of authorities. The argument before me was contained within a day, but only as the result of extensive (and underestimated) pre-reading by the court and the submission and consideration of supplementary skeletons on an important point after the hearing.'

14.44   Generally cases will be decided on the documentary evidence presented to the court, as is the situation usually with interim injunction applications and the general practice of the Chancery Division, but, on occasions, in Australia, courts have permitted oral evidence to be given in leave applications, and they have permitted cross-examination of the applicant.[111] However, it must be noted that, in contrast to applications for interim injunctions, the proceedings for permission are not interlocutory, but final.[112] Having noted these problems we now move on to consider the criteria that is set down by the legislation for determining whether permission should be granted. Some warrant little comment while others demand detailed discussion.

A Specified criteria which courts must consider

1 Prima facie case

14.45   As mentioned earlier the Law Commission in its *Shareholder Remedies* report was most concerned to avoid mini-trials at preliminary hearings.[113] For this reason it was against the introduction of a threshold requirement. The

---

[106] Ibid at para. 6.72.

[107] Ibid at para. 6.72.

[108] For instance, *Iesini v Westrip Holdings Ltd* [2009] EWHC 2526 (Ch); [2010] BCC 420 at [79] lasted for five days.

[109] [2011] EWHC 1893 (Ch).

[110] Ibid at [61].

[111] For example, see *Talisman Technologies Inc v Qld Electronic Switching Pty Ltd* [2001] QSC 324 at [24].

[112] *Swansson v Pratt* [2002] NSWSC 583; (2002) 42 ACSR 313 at [24]; *Reale v Duncan Reale Pty Ltd* [2005] NSWSC 174 at [11]; *Ehsman v Nucetime International Pty Ltd* [2006] NSWSC 887 at [6].

[113] Law Commission *Shareholder Remedies: Report on a Reference under section 3(1)(e) of the Law Commissions Act 1965* (Law Com No 246, Cm 3769) (London, Stationery Office, 1997) at para 6.71.

concern that it had was that a threshold test on the merits might well lead to fine distinctions being drawn as to which side of the line a particular set of facts fell.[114] It favoured the development of a principled approach that was not tied to a particular rule.[115] Nevertheless the Act did include a threshold requirement as Parliament believed that it could prevent a plethora of proceedings being brought by every disenchanted individual in the country.[116] This is the first stage in getting permission. It involves a court being satisfied that the shareholder has a prima facie case that warrants the court granting permission to bring proceedings,[117] namely that there is a prima facie case that the company has a good cause of action and also that the cause of action arises out of a director's default, breach of duty etc.[118] It has been indicated that the aim of the first stage is to assess whether the company and the defendant should be put to the expense and inconvenience of considering and contesting the application for permission.[119] In *Langley Ward Ltd v Trevor* (sub nom *Re Seven Holdings Ltd)*[120] David Donaldson QC (sitting as a deputy judge of the High Court) said that to enable the court to do this it is incumbent on the applicant:

> 'to set out clearly and coherently the nature and basis of each claim together with the supporting evidence and legal basis. It must also draw the attention of the court squarely to any legal and evidential difficulties and to any fact at odds with its contentions. The same open, clear and frank approach must be adopted by the applicant as regards the factors which the court is required or may reasonably be expected to take into account in deciding whether it must, or ought to, refuse permission.'[121]

14.46 Persuading a court that he or she has a prima facie case is the first stage that an applicant/claimant has to address. The prima facie test is familiar to lawyers and was the primary test in applications for interim injunctions in most cases during the first three-quarters of the last century,[122] and is still invoked in some injunction hearings today. This was also a preliminary matter that has to be established in derivative proceedings at common law.[123]

---

[114] Ibid at para. 6.72.

[115] Ibid.

[116] HL Debate, 9 May 2006, vol 681, col 885, Lord Sharman.

[117] Companies Act 2006, s 261(2).

[118] *Iesini v Westrip Holdings Ltd* [2009] EWHC 2526 (Ch); [2010] BCC 420 at [78].

[119] *Langley Ward Ltd v Trevor* [2011] EWHC 1893 (Ch) at [62].

[120] Ibid.

[121] Ibid.

[122] For example, see *Hoffman-La Roche (F) & Co v Secretary of State for Trade & Industry* [1975] AC 295 at 338, 360; *Cavendish House (Cheltenham) Ltd v Cavendish-Woodhouse Ltd* [1970] RPC 234 (CA). The test was not applied across the board. In some cases the test was not employed as courts wanted to retain flexibility. See, *Hubbard v Vesper* [1972] 1 All ER 1023.

[123] *Prudential Assurance Co Ltd v Newman Industries Ltd (No 2)* [1982] Ch 204 at 221. For greater discussion of the position of decisions on the issue of the prima facie grounds for derivative actions at common law, see A Keay and J Loughrey 'Something Old, Something New, Something Borrowed: An Analysis of the New Derivative Action Under the Companies Act 2006' (2008) 124 LQR 469; A Keay and J Loughrey 'An assessment of the present state of statutory derivative proceedings' in J Loughrey (ed) *Directors' Duties and Shareholder*

14.47 Notwithstanding the familiarity of the prima facie case test, the meaning of the concept remains somewhat elusive.[124] Courts have not, either in applications for leave at common law or in injunction applications, discussed in detail the meaning of the term. Neither have the courts stated what exactly an applicant must do to establish a prima facie case.[125] The suggestion has been made that an applicant is required to demonstrate that a claim has a substantial chance of success in the final hearing.[126] This indicates that it is inevitable that there is some evaluation of the ultimate merits of the case. In injunction hearings, the use of the prima facie case test led to the court focusing on the relative strengths of the parties' cases and, often, involved a virtual trial within a trial. In order to establish a prima facie case an applicant in injunction applications had to establish a greater than 50 per cent chance of success.[127] But it would seem that the courts did not interpret the requirement strictly at common law and they continued this approach under the statutory regime, and, hence, it was not and is not a stiff test to pass, given the evidence we have from the case-law. The number of reported judgments on leave applications, and on derivative actions more generally, prior to the advent of the CA 2006, is small but, of these, there are few in which a shareholder has failed to establish a prima facie case. Where leave was granted, in three cases the applications were unopposed or the defendants conceded that there was a prima facie case,[128] in two the evidence against the defendant was strong enough to support an application for summary judgment, and therefore more than satisfied the threshold test of a prima facie case,[129] while in others, such as reports of trials of derivative actions, the grant of leave was referred to only in passing, if at all.[130]

14.48 Both before and after the introduction of the statutory scheme, in situations where leave has been refused, a prima facie case on the merits has often been established, but the application has failed because of other reasons,[131] or the failure to establish a prima facie case ended up not being the

---

Litigation in the Wake of the Financial Crisis (Cheltenham, Edward Elgar, 2013), Chapter 7; A Reisberg *Derivative Actions and Corporate Governance* (OUP, 2007).

[124] *American Cyanamid Co v Ethicon Ltd* [1975] AC 396 at 404.

[125] C Gray 'Interim Injunctions since American Cyanamid' (1981) 40 CLJ 307 at 307.

[126] J Heydon and P Loughlan *Cases and Materials on Equity and Trusts* (Butterworths, 5th edn, 1997) at 978.

[127] *American Cyanamid Co v Ethicon Ltd* [1975] AC 396 at 406–407.

[128] *Halle v Trax BW Ltd* [2000] BCC 1020 at 1023; *Fansa v Alsibahie* [2005] EWHC 299 (Ch); [2005] All ER (D) 80 (Jan); *Airey v Cordell* [2006] EWHC 2728 (Ch); [2007] Bus L R 391 at [68].

[129] *Fayers Legal Services Ltd v Day* [2001] All ER (D) 121 (Apr) at [4]; *Bracken Partners Ltd v Gutteridge* [2003] EWHC 1064 (Ch); [2003] 2 BCLC 84.

[130] *Knight v Frost* [1999] 1 BCLC 364; *Qayoumi v Oakhouse Property Holdings Plc* [2002] EWHC 2547 (Ch); [2003] 1 BCLC 352; *Gidman v Barron* [2003] EWHC 153 (Ch); *Fraser v Oystertec Plc* [2003] EWHC 2787 (Ch); [2004] BCC 233 at [20] (summary judgment application), though in a subsequent application to amend the company's claim, the court considered that permission should be withdrawn as there no longer appeared to be wrongdoer control and the company had succeeded on much of its claim: *Fraser v Oystertec Plc (Proposed Amendments)* [2004] EWHC 2225 (Ch); [2005] BPIR 389 at [32]–[33].

[131] *Barrett v Duckett* [1995] BCC 362, 364; *Portfolios of Distinction Ltd v Laird* [2004] EWHC

sole reason for the refusal of leave. One of the cases at common law was *Smith v Croft (No 2)* where Knox J was influenced by a report from the company's auditors, which had been commissioned by the board to investigate the shareholders' complaints, and which concluded that most of the complaints were unfounded.[132] Also, in *Harley Street Capital Ltd v Tchigirinski (No 2)*,[133] independent third party evidence that refuted the shareholder's allegations was led. The company, on the directions of the court, had commissioned a report by an independent firm of solicitors into the minority shareholder's allegations of wrongdoing. No evidence of wrongdoing was found and, furthermore, the shareholder was unable to advance evidence of any.[134] For these reasons, and because the shareholder lacked bona fides, the action was struck out as an abuse of process.[135]

14.49 Overall it would seem that courts have not expected a great deal from applicants and this is supported further by the fact that applicants for permission have been required to submit only fairly basic evidence in order to establish a prima facie case. Reed has argued[136] that under the common law system the claimant needed only to support the application for permission with written evidence, and meant that in practice this supporting evidence did little more than verify the facts on which the claim and the entitlement to sue on behalf of the company were founded. Under the CA 2006 the first stage is decided on the basis of the applicant's written evidence only,[137] (though the applicant can request an oral hearing if the application is initially unsuccessful),[138] and the courts have generally adopted a similarly undemanding approach to weighing that evidence and assessing whether there is a prima facie case.

14.50 In sum, at common law or under the statutory scheme the requirement to show a prima facie case on the merits appears not to have been a demanding obstacle for shareholders to negotiate. This is because, at the initial stage, the company plays no part, and the application is assessed on the basis of the shareholder's evidence alone. In so far as the need for the courts to give guidance on how to assess whether a shareholder has met this criterion, the cases under the statutory scheme have provided little assistance as they have not

---

2071 (Ch); [2005] BCC 216 at [64]; *Mumbray v Lapper* [2005] EWHC 1152 (Ch); [2005] BCC 990 at [21]-[24] and all cases after the introduction of the statutory scheme.

[132] *Smith v Croft (No 2)* (1988) Ch 114 at 150-154. *Jafari-Fini v Skillglass* [2005] EWCA Civ 356; [2005] BCC 842 may be another such case, though this was not the expressed reason for the refusal of leave.

[133] [2005] EWHC 2471 (Ch); [2006] BCC 209.

[134] Ibid at [116]-[118].

[135] Ibid at [141].

[136] R Reed 'Derivative Claims: The Application for Permission to Continue' (2000) 21 Co Law 156 at 156.

[137] Confirmed in *Langley Ward Ltd v Trevor* (sub nom *Re Seven Holdings Ltd*) [2011] EWHC 1893 (Ch); *Cinematic Finance Ltd v Ryder* [2010] EWHC 3387 (Ch); [2012] BCC 797 at [2] and envisaged by the CPR 1998, r 19.9A(9).

[138] CPR 19.9A(10).

given us a lot of reasoning. But the same could be said about the cases that were heard under the common law derivative action.

14.51 We now turn to considering what the case-law following the introduction of the statutory scheme has said. It is fair to say that the cases so far have not been clear or consistent regarding what exactly the first stage of the process requires. On appeal to the Inner House of the Court of Session in the Scottish case of *Wishart v Castlecroft Securities Ltd*,[139] the court seemed to require only a low threshold for the applicant to get over. The court said that 'the question is not whether the application and supporting evidence disclose a *prima facie* case against the defenders to the proposed derivative proceedings, but whether there is no prima facie case disclosed for granting the application for leave [permission in England].' Their Lordships went on to say that the applicant should not carry the burden of satisfying the court that he or she has a prima facie case, but rather there should be refusal if the court is satisfied that there is not a prima facie case, and it specified the matters which it thought must be taken into account.[140] It firstly dealt with some very formal elements with which the court must be satisfied, namely ensuring that the applicant is a member of the company involved, whether the application relates to derivative proceedings, and that the application specified the cause of action and facts on which the derivative proceedings are based.[141] But it also added that the courts should consider the factors that are set out in s 268(1)(2) and (3) (equivalent to s 263(2) and (3) for the rest of the UK) in order to determine whether the application should be granted. This means that the first stage might be seen as being more difficult to get through than the legislation seems to provide for, and more difficult than was the case at common law. This approach also appeared to be taken in *Stimpson v Southern Landlords Association*,[142] by HH Judge Pelling QC (sitting as a judge of the High Court). His Lordship said that:

> 'If the statute is followed strictly, the court is required to consider whether a prima facie case is established – see s 261(2). In considering that question the court is bound to have regard, not merely to the factors identified in s 263(3) and (4), but to any other relevant consideration since s 263(3) and (4) are not exhaustive.'[143]

14.52 In neither of the cases referred to in the previous paragraph was the court's ultimate decision on the application before it made on the basis of whether it was satisfied that the applicant had a prima facie case. But the comments that were made in each case do cause some concern in that they appear to set the bar far higher than would have been envisaged. With respect, there is nothing in the legislation either applying to England and Wales and Northern Ireland on the one hand and Scotland on the other, suggesting that the factors in s 263 (in England) must be addressed at the first stage. There is no

---

[139] [2009] CSIH 65; 2009 SLT 812 at [31]. See *Wishart, Petitioner* [2009] CSOH 20; 2009 SLT 376 for the decision at first instance. While the appeal court disagreed with the approach taken at first instance, it came to the same result.

[140] [2009] CSIH 65; 2009 SLT 812 at [31].

[141] The last requirement is peculiar to the provisions applying in Scotland. See s 266(2).

[142] [2009] EWHC 2072 (Ch); [2010] BCC 387.

[143] Ibid at [46].

connection in the legislation between s 261 on the one hand and s 263 on the other. Furthermore, the Law Commission only recommended one stage, which is the second stage provided for in the legislation. The Law Commission in fact expressed concern 'at the way [at common law] in which a member was required to prove standing to bring an action as a preliminary issue by evidence which shows a prima facie case on the merits.'[144] The main reason for the Law Commission not recommending a preliminary stage was that 'the inclusion of an express test would increase the risk of a detailed investigation into the merits of the case taking place at the leave stage, and that such a "mini-trial" would be time consuming and expensive.'[145] Obviously at the second stage where the company can appear and produce evidence, a court has to take into account the s 263 factors. But suggesting that they are relevant at the first stage makes the first stage far more substantial than it should be, particularly when one considers the position that existed prior to the enactment of the statutory derivative regime. No other cases have included reference to s 263 factors in the same breath as the prima facie criterion. Given consideration of the whole paragraph of HHJ Pelling QC's judgment in *Stimpson* and partly quoted above, it is questionable whether his Lordship was in fact intending to make the prima facie criterion a hard one to get over. But that still leaves us with the *Wishart* judgment. Generally speaking, the courts have let claims through the first stage without too much inquiry, it would seem, and have not employed a substantial bar to get over.

14.53 The regime seems to envisage that there will only be a substantial hearing at the second stage and not at the first, with the second being inter partes. But the *Wishart* judgment suggests two substantial hearings, and it causes one to ask what the difference is between the two stages, because the factors in s 263(2), (3) and (4) clearly have to be considered at the second stage. In fact, if there is a difference it would appear that the first stage is tougher than the second for a court must, at the first stage, consider the issue of 'prima facie case' besides those matters set out in s 263(2), (3) and (4), if the *Wishart* approach applies. But while the *Wishart* decision has been mentioned by several cases the approach the case seemed to put forward, and noted in **14.51**, has not been expressly adopted. It might be thought that with such an approach the reference to 'prima facie case' in s 261 is otiose for if a court takes the view that the applicant succeeds under the s 263 factors he or she clearly would have a prima facie case. It is worth noting that the first stage was added to the legislation late in the process, in the House of Lords, and this might be an indication that what the first stage actually involved was not thought through sufficiently.

---

[144] The Law Commission only recommended one stage: *Shareholder Remedies: Report on a Reference under section 3(1)(e) of the Law Commissions Act 1965* (Law Com. No 246, Cm 3769) (London: Stationery Office, 1997) at para 6.4.

[145] Law Commission, Shareholder Remedies: Report on a Reference under section 3(1)(e) of the Law Commissions Act 1965 (Law Com. No 246, Cm 3769) (London: Stationery Office, 1997) at para 6.71.

14.54   What is interesting is that several judges appear to have approved of the virtual telescoping of the two stages within the process if the parties are in agreement, with the result that there is just the one hearing.[146] This might well be sensible in some cases, but we must bear in mind the caveat sounded by David Donaldson QC (sitting as a deputy judge of the High Court) in *Langley Ward Ltd v Trevor*, some of which was mentioned earlier:[147]

> 'The inclusion in the Companies Act of an ex parte stage provides a hurdle and filter which in my view should not be dispensed with. As with any ex parte application the matter should be presented and explained transparently and fairly so that the court can make a properly informed decision whether it is right to put the company (and the potential defendant) to the expense and inconvenience of considering and contesting the application. This can only be achieved if the applicant sets out clearly and coherently the nature and basis of each claim together with the supporting evidence and legal basis. It must also draw the attention of the court squarely to any legal and evidential difficulties and to any fact at odds with its contentions. The same open, clear and frank approach must be adopted by the applicant as regards the factors which the court is required or may reasonably be expected to take into account in deciding whether it must, or ought to, refuse permission. All this is particularly important since the legislation contemplates that its preliminary examination will be done by the court solely on the papers.'[148]

14.55   In this case the structure of the statutory process was, in the words of the deputy judge, 'undermined',[149] as the matter did not pass through the ex parte stage; it was effectively bypassed. If it had been subject to the first stage, then, according to the deputy judge, a large number of the claims, and perhaps all of them, would have been eliminated at that point.[150] The case proceeded on the assumption that the judge was hearing the matter at the second stage. Clearly the danger with telescoping is the fact that a case could go on for much longer than it should, when it could have been either dismissed or the issues with which it was concerned, refined, at the first stage of the process.

14.56   The view of Roth J in *Stainer v Lee*[151] was that a court is able to revise its view as to a prima facie case at the second stage, once it has received evidence and argument from the respondents. If that is the case then it would seem that a court could decline to consider the factors that have to be considered at the second stage if the court believes, at the second stage, that in fact there is not a prima facie case after all.[152]

---

[146] *Wishart* [2009] CSIH 65; 2009 SLT 812 at [9]. For examples, see *Mission Capital Plc v Sinclair* [2008] EWHC 1339 (Ch); *Franbar Holdings Ltd v Patel* [2008] EWHC 1534 (Ch); [2008] BCC 885; *Stimpson v Southern Landlords Association* [2009] EWHC 2072 (Ch); [2010] BCC 387; *Parry v Bartlett* [2011] EWHC 3146 (Ch); [2012] BCC 700.

[147] [2011] EWHC 1893 (Ch).

[148] Ibid at [62].

[149] Ibid at [6].

[150] Ibid at [63].

[151] [2010] EWHC 1539 (Ch); [2011] BCC 134 at [29].

[152] Ibid.

14.57 It is submitted that the first stage should be limited to making sure that a claim has some substance to it, and should involve the court ensuring that the applicant is a member of the company and the application relates to derivative proceedings, as required by the court in *Wishart*. There might be a case in some situations for the delineation of the issues, as envisaged by David Donaldson QC in *Langley Ward Ltd v Trevor*.[153]

14.58 If the court is not satisfied that there is a prima facie case then the claim will be dismissed. If the shareholder succeeds, then the application for permission will proceed to the second stage when the court will direct the company to file evidence indicating why permission to proceed should be refused,[154] and the court has to decide whether the application should actually be granted.[155] As mentioned earlier, if a judge does not think, on the papers, that there is a prima facie case the applicant/claimant may ask, under CPR r 19.9A(10), for an oral hearing before the judge. The rule does not say to whom the request is made, but it might be assumed that it is to the judge who declined the application. One assumes that as the provision refers to 'asking' for a hearing, a judge may refuse to accede to the request if he or she thinks that it is not appropriate.

14.59 While there is merit, as highlighted by David Donaldson QC in *Langley Ward Ltd v Trevor*, in having a threshold requirement, one concern is that it might not deter the submission of long witness statements and large bundles as practitioners acting for the applicant/claimant might be concerned that if they do not include everything that they have there is always the chance that a judge will not let the application through to the second stage, especially given the fact that the burden of proof is not all that clear. Some have suggested that the approach of the courts is to allow claims to go to the second stage provided that there is something in the claim and they can always be knocked out at the second stage.[156] It might be thought that it is a waste of time and resources taking too much time on the first stage since the second stage could fulfil the purpose of the process of permission.[157] However, matters should not be let through to the second stage as a matter of course as that could mean a waste of time for the courts and a large costs bill for the parties.

14.60 Whatever way we look at the authorities it would seem that so far we can say that this first stage is one that is reasonably easy to traverse.

---

[153] [2011] EWHC 1893 (Ch) at [63].

[154] Companies Act 2006, s 261(3).

[155] *Wishart* [2009] CSIH 65; 2009 SLT 812 at [33].

[156] B Hannigan and D Prentice, *Hannigan and Prentice's The Companies Act 2006 – A Commentary* (Lexis Nexis, London, 2007) at para 4.46 and referred to in J Tang, 'Shareholder remedies: demise of the derivative claim?' (2012) 1 *UCL Journal of Law and Jurisprudence* 178 at 183.

[157] J Tang 'Shareholder remedies: demise of the derivative claim?' (2012) 1 *UCL Journal of Law and Jurisprudence* 178 at 184.

2 Elements as to which the court must be satisfied

14.61 If an applicant/claimant is adjudged to have a prima facie case, the court then has to move to the second stage of the permission process. The second stage begins with consideration of s 263(2) of the CA 2006. This subsection provides that a court *must* refuse permission if it is satisfied in relation to any one of the following three matters:

- a person acting in accordance with s 172 would not seek to continue the claim; or

- the claim relates to an act or omission that has not occurred as yet and it has been authorised by the company; or

- the claim relates to an act or omission that has occurred and it was authorised by the company before it occurred or it has been ratified since it occurred.

14.62 If any one or more of these apply then the application fails. There is no discretion given to the courts if any one of the criteria is fulfilled. If none of these apply then the court has a discretion under s 263(3) and (4) as to whether to allow the claim to proceed. More about this shortly.

14.63 It has been said that there was no particular standard of proof that has to be satisfied in relation to the elements in s 263(2).[158] In *Iesini v Westrip Holdings Ltd*[159] Lewison J (as he then was) held that something more than simply a prima facie case must be needed since that forms the first stage of the procedure; and that while it would be wrong to embark on a mini-trial the court must form a view on the strength of the claim, albeit on a provisional basis.

14.64 In *Stainer v Lee* the judge said that a court can grant permission even if it is not satisfied that there is a strong case, if the amount of potential recovery is very large.[160] While the merits of the claim will be relevant to whether permission should be given, they will not be decisive as there is no set threshold.[161] But obviously the merits will have a bearing on some matters, such as that found in s 263(2)(a), namely whether a director acting in accordance with s 172 would seek to continue the action.[162]

14.65 As far as the first element is concerned, located in s 263(2)(a),[163] a court is to refuse permission if it is satisfied that a person acting in accordance with s 172 would not seek to continue the claim. Section 172(1) provides that

---

[158] *Stainer v Lee* [2010] EWHC 1539 (Ch); [2011] BCC 134 at [29].

[159] [2009] EWHC 2526 (Ch); [2010] BCC 420.

[160] [2010] EWHC 1539 (Ch); [2011] BCC 134 at [29].

[161] *Kleanthous v Paphitis* [2011] EWHC 2287 (Ch); [2012] BCC 676 at [42].

[162] Ibid at [45].

[163] For greater discussion of this criterion, see A Keay 'Applications to Continue Derivative Proceedings on Behalf of Companies and the Hypothetical Director Test' (2015) 34 *Civil Justice Quarterly* 346.

directors have a duty to promote the success of the company. The meaning, operation and interpretation of s 172 were discussed extensively in **Chapter 6**. What the provision requires the directors to do is to do that which they consider, in good faith, is most likely to promote the success of the company for the benefit of the members as a whole, and in doing this they must have regard for several factors set out in s 172(1)(a)-(f). These factors are set out and discussed in **Chapter 6**. The operation of s 172 has not been considered in depth by any court and there remains uncertainty with the provision, as discussed in **Chapter 6**, but this does not seem to have impeded the courts in their consideration of this criterion. The judges in most of the permission hearing judgments have spent some time considering the criterion. For example, in *Franbar Holdings Ltd v Patel*[164] the judge took the view that he could not be satisfied that a director acting in accordance with s 172 would believe that the case did not warrant continuation.[165] So, the application could not be knocked out on this ground in that case. And in many cases this has been the criterion that has meant all the difference.

14.66 Decisions under the common law raised the possibility that the courts may require very clear evidence that a person under a duty to promote the success of the company would not pursue the action, or would not consider it sufficiently important to pursue, before refusing leave on this basis. In *Mumbray v Lapper*[166] the test for the grant of permission to bring derivative proceedings was said to be whether an independent board would sanction the pursuit of the proceedings.[167] This seems very similar to the requirement in s 263(3)(b) of the CA 2006. In the case itself the test was not explored further, and permission was refused because alternative remedies existed, as well as the fact that the shareholder had participated in wrongdoing.[168] However, in *Airey v Cordell*,[169] the test was applied in a manner which could have significant implications if it were to be adopted by courts interpreting the CA 2006.

14.67 In *Airey v Cordell* Warren J stated that 'there is a range of reasonable decisions' that a board might make, so that a reasonable board could take a decision either way.[170] He went on to say that shareholders would fail this test only if the court took the view that no board acting reasonably would sanction the action. Provided that the shareholder's decision was one which a reasonable board could take, the court should give permission to proceed even though another board could reasonably refuse to prosecute the action.[171] This was because it would not be 'right to shut out the minority shareholder on the basis

---

[164] [2008] EWHC 1534 (Ch); [2008] BCC 885.
[165] Ibid at [30].
[166] [2005] EWHC 1152 (Ch); [2005] BCC 990.
[167] Ibid at [5]. The test is drawn from earlier case-law dealing with whether the court should order the company to indemnify the shareholder's costs: see *Wallersteiner v Moir (No 2)* [1975] QB 373 at 404 (Buckley LJ); *Smith v Croft (No 1)* [1986] 1 WLR 580 at 590; *Jaybird Group Ltd v Greenwood* [1986] BCLC 319 at 321.
[168] [2005] EWHC 1152 (Ch); [2005] BCC 990 at [21]–[23].
[169] [2006] EWHC 2728 (Ch); [2007] Bus L R 391.
[170] Ibid at [69].
[171] Ibid at [75].

of the court's, perhaps inadequate, assessment of what it would do rather than a test which is easier to apply, which is whether any reasonable board could take that decision'.[172]

14.68 It has been noted that this approach is similar in many respects to the range of reasonable responses test in employment law.[173] In assessing a claim for unfair dismissal under s 98(4) of the Employment Rights Act 1996, the tribunal will not hold an employer liable if his or her actions fall within a range of responses which a reasonable employer might have taken, even though the dismissal could be seen as a harsh decision that is at the extreme end of a band of reasonable responses.[174] What is behind this is the fact that the courts are reluctant to second guess and set aside management decisions; however, it has been subject to criticism on the basis that employers' decisions will not be overturned unless they exhibit a standard of unreasonableness which equates to perversity.[175] Some might feel that such an approach would not be defensible in derivative action applications. While an interventionist approach in dismissal cases would lead to the courts interfering in management decisions, and so arguably justifies the range of reasonable responses test, this is not so in the case of derivative actions. Here it is the decision of a shareholder, not management, to sue that is scrutinised. Given that management has presumably opposed the action, allowing it to proceed would constitute interference with management's judgment, and the litigation itself could interfere with the running of the company's business. Some courts might be most reluctant to do so.

14.69 Nevertheless, it might be possible to argue that a reasonable responses test should be employed under the CA 2006. This is because it would apply to only one of the criteria that the courts have to take into account in determining whether to grant permission. Given that assessing whether a person under a duty to promote the success of the company would or would not seek to continue a claim does involve the courts attempting to form a view in relation to the commercial wisdom of the litigation, the test would relieve them of carrying out a task that lies outside of their normal role, and that they are not well equipped to carry out.[176] It would require them to refuse permission on

---

[172] Ibid.

[173] A Keay and J Loughrey 'Something Old, Something New, Something Borrowed: An Analysis of the New Derivative Action Under the Companies Act 2006' (2008) 124 LQR 469 at 494.

[174] Ibid and referring to *Iceland Frozen Foods v Jones* [1982] ICR 17; *Post Office v Liddiard* [2001] EWCA Civ 940; [2001] *Employment Law Review* 78. Although the EAT in *Beedell v West Ferry Printers Ltd* [2000] ICR 1263 at 1278-1279 stated that this was not a test of perversity equating it instead with the *Bolam* test (*Bolam v Friern Management Committee* [1957] 2 All ER 118), which is the standard of care test in professional negligence cases, this test has also been extensively criticised as causing courts to adopt an unduly non-interventionist approach, and resulting in very few findings of negligence against professionals.

[175] A Keay and J Loughrey 'Something Old, Something New, Something Borrowed: An Analysis of the New Derivative Action Under the Companies Act 2006' (2008) 124 LQR 469 at 494, and referring to A Freer 'The Range of Reasonable Responses Test-From Guidelines to Statute' (1998) 27 *Industrial Law Journal* 335 at 335–336.

[176] H C Hirt 'The Company's Decision to Litigate Against its Directors: Legal Strategies to Deal with the Board of Directors' Conflict of Interest' (2005) JBL 159, 165–166 and 195–196.

this basis only in the most obvious cases, where, for example, pursuing the action 'was wholly disproportionate and cost-ineffective'.[177] At the same time, applications could continue to be screened out applying the other permission criteria.

14.70 There is no particular standard of proof that has to be satisfied in relation to the elements in s 263(2)(a).[178] In *Hughes v Weiss*[179] HHJ Keyser QC (sitting as a judge of the High Court) said that there was no particular merits test that had to be satisfied before permission will be granted. Put somewhat differently, but conveying the same meaning, Newey J in *Kleanthous v Paphitis*[180] stated that the derivative actions statutory scheme does not require a specific threshold to be attained before a claim is to be allowed to continue.[181] This is consistent with the Law Commission's 1996 recommendation that there should be no threshold so as to avoid any risk of a detailed investigation of the merits of the claim at the permission stage.[182] In fact s 263(2)(a) seems to provide a fairly low threshold that has to be passed. The reason is that, according to the court in *Iesini v Westrip Holdings Ltd*[183] that just as with the approach taken by the court in *Airey v Cordell*[184] when dealing with the position applying at common law, a court should only refuse permission where *no* director would seek to continue the claim. In *Franbar Holdings Ltd v Patel*[185] William Trower QC (sitting as a deputy judge of the High Court) adopted a similar approach when assessing what a person under a duty to act in accordance with s 172 would do,[186] as did the appeal court in *Wishart*,[187] Roth J in *Stainer v Lee*,[188] HH Judge Keyser QC in *Hughes v Weiss*,[189] David Donaldson QC (sitting as a deputy High Court judge) in *Langley Ward Ltd v Trevor*[190] and HH Judge Hodge QC (sitting as a High Court judge) in *Singh v Singh*.[191] With this approach it is relatively easy for shareholders to demonstrate that the hypothetical decision-maker would sanction the action. It would be uncommon, one would think, that a derivative action was so obviously undesirable that no reasonable decision maker acting in the

---

[177] *Airey v Cordell* [2006] EWHC 2728 (Ch); [2007] Bus L R 391 at [69] per Warren J, though it should be noted that the judge was prepared to refuse leave if a suitable alternative remedy became available: at [83]–[86].

[178] For example, see *Wishart* [2009] CSIH 65; 2009 SLT 812; [2010] BCC 210 at [40]; *Kleanthous v Paphitis* [2011] EWHC 2287 (Ch); [2012] BCC 676 at [45].

[179] [2012] EWHC 2363 (Ch) at [33] and approved of by HHJ Hodge QC in *Singh v Singh* [2013] EWHC 2138 (Ch) at [17].

[180] [2011] EWHC 2287 (Ch) at [40].

[181] This was also indicated in *Wishart* [2009] CSIH 65; 2009 SLT 812 at [39], [40].

[182] Law Commission, *Shareholder Remedies: Report on a Reference under section 3(1)(e) of the Law Commissions Act 1965* (Law Com No 246, Cm 3769) (London: Stationery Office, 1997) at paras 6.71, 6.72.

[183] [2009] EWHC 2526 (Ch); [2010] BCC 420 at [86].

[184] [2007] BCC 785 at 800.

[185] [2008] EWHC 1534 (Ch).

[186] Ibid at [30].

[187] [2009] CSIH 65; 2009 SLT 812 at [32].

[188] [2010] EWHC1539 (Ch); [2011] BCC 134 at [28].

[189] [2012] EWHC 2363 (Ch) at [45].

[190] [2011] EWHC 1893 (Ch) at [9].

[191] [2013] EWHC 2138 (Ch) at [18].

company's interests would sanction it. However, there have been cases where courts have felt that the case of the applicant was so weak that no director would seek to continue the claim. A clear example is *Iesini*,[192] and this effectively was also the case in *Stimpson v Southern Landlords Association*.[193]

14.71 As indicated earlier, *Iesini* provided that something more than simply a prima facie case must be established and while this was not meant to create the need for there to be a mini-trial,[194] it is necessary that the court forms a view on the strength of the claim sought to be continued, albeit on a provisional basis.[195] Roth J acknowledged this in *Stainer v Lee* where he said that: 'The necessary evaluation, conducted on ... a provisional basis and at a very early stage of the proceedings, is therefore not mechanistic.'[196] In *Cullen Investments Ltd v Brown*[197] Norris J said that he had to form a provisional view of the merits whilst bearing in mind that the evidence was documentary only and had not been tested in cross-examination and there had not been disclosure of documents.[198] The making of a provisional view creates a potential problem for the courts, adverted to by Proudman J in *Kiani v Cooper*[199] when she noted the fact that where, as in the case before her, there are many factual disputes:[200]

> 'it is difficult to form a sensible provisional view as to the strength of the evidence on each side. The court is well aware that at trial with proper cross-examination a very different picture may well emerge from that appearing on documentary evidence alone.'

14.72 In *Iesini* the judge said that the kind of factors that a judge would consider in analyzing the application of this criteria are : the size of the claim; cost of proceedings; disruption to company activities, the company's ability to fund an action,[201] and any possible damage that might be done to the company's reputation if the claim was not successful.[202] In *Cullen Investments Ltd v Brown*[203] the fact the applicant shareholder was not seeking

---

[192] [2009] EWHC 2526 (Ch); [2010] BCC 420 at [79], [102].
[193] [2009] EWHC 2072; [2010] BCC 387.
[194] *Fanmailuk.com Ltd v Cooper* [2008] EWHC 2198 (Ch); [2008] BCC 877 at [2]. Also, see *Wishart* [2009] CSIH 65; 2009 SLT 812; [2010] BCC 210 at [39].
[195] *Iesini v Westrip Holdings Ltd* [2009] EWHC 2526 (Ch); [2010] BCC 420 at [79]. This was approved of specifically in *Kleanthous v Paphitis* [2011] EWHC 2287 (Ch); [2012] BCC 676 at [45].
[196] [2010] EWHC 1539 (Ch) at [29]. This was approved of in *Hughes v Weiss* [2012] EWHC 2363 (Ch).
[197] [2015] EWHC 473 (Ch); [2015] BCC 539.
[198] Ibid at [36].
[199] [2010] EWHC 577 (Ch); [2010] BCC 463.
[200] Ibid at [14].
[201] [2009] EWHC 2526 (Ch); [2010] BCC 420 at [85].
[202] Ibid. Also mentioned in *Franbar Holdings* [2008] EWHC 1534 (Ch); [2008] BCC 885 at [36] and *Langley Ward Ltd v Trevor* [2011] EWHC 1893 (Ch) at [12].
[203] [2015] EWHC 473 (Ch); [2015] BCC 539.

any indemnity against costs influenced the judge and he said that given this and other factors it is difficult to see why the hypothetical director would not seek to continue proceedings.[204]

14.73 Besides these frequently mentioned factors the courts have also addressed other less common factors. In *Langley Ward Ltd v Trevor David*[205] Donaldson QC thought the fact that there was a potential winding up of the company could be a significant factor in whether a director would attach importance to the pursuit of a claim. In this case the judge said that given the company's circumstances it was a natural candidate to be wound up on the just and equitable basis under s 122(1)(g) of the Insolvency Act 1986.[206] One would certainly expect this also to be a consideration where the company is in financial difficulties and there is clear creditor disquiet concerning the company's position, perhaps manifested by demands for payment or refusals to supply goods or services. But while the possibility of a winding up could tell against the continuation of proceedings, it might not always be the case. In some cases the fact that a company has extensive debts outstanding could be a reason for prosecuting an action as a recovery from it could discharge or go some way to discharging the company's debts. The riposte might be that recovery would take some time to achieve and the company's malaise might get worse. While this might indeed be true, except where the case is so strong that the shareholder could obtain summary judgment, creditors might be willing to wait for a resolution of the litigation before pursuing winding-up proceedings if they can be convinced of the likelihood of success of a derivative claim. It should be added that it has been held that permission should not be granted to a shareholder when a company is insolvent.[207] This is probably because the residual beneficiaries of the company are not the shareholder any longer, but the creditors in such circumstances.

14.74 In considering s 172 in the context of the criterion under discussion HH Judge Keyser QC said in *Hughes v Weiss*[208] that the notion of the success of the company mentioned in that provision, in the circumstances of the case before him, involved consideration of what would be a fair distribution of benefits to its members.

14.75 It would appear that another factor that might be considered by a court in the context of the issues under discussion is that the applicant/shareholder might be able to institute separate proceedings for unfair prejudice under s 994 of the Act.[209] This is a matter that is discussed in more detail later in the Chapter under the heading of 'Alternative remedy.'

---

[204] Ibid at [55].
[205] [2011] EWHC 1893 (Ch) at [14].
[206] Ibid at [15].
[207] *Cinematic Finance Ltd v Ryder* [2010] EWHC 3387 (Ch); [2012] BCC 797.
[208] [2012] EWHC 2363 (Ch) at [54].
[209] Something that might also be considered under s 263(3)(f).

14.76 It is perhaps worth noting that the approach taken in *Franbar Holdings* seems to mean that a court might take into account a factor mentioned in s 263(3) twice, once in the context of considering what view a hypothetical director might take in relation to continuing the proceedings, and then again separately as a standalone factor, and as required by the provisions of s 263(3). This might seem rather odd, but when deciding what a hypothetical director would do it is necessary for a judge to consider all of the possible issues that a director might well address and to consider the s 263(3) factors from the perspective of a director. When the judge considers them free from having to decide what a director would do he or she then might determine the matter from a more general perspective.

14.77 While there is no threshold test, the case-law predominantly suggests that the merits will have a bearing on a court deciding both whether a person acting in accordance with s 172 would seek to continue the action and the importance that would be attached to continuing it.[210] Notwithstanding the fact that the merits are important William Trower QC (sitting as a deputy judge of the High Court) in *Franbar Holdings Ltd v Patel*,[211] said that 'a director will often be in the position of having to make what is no more than a partially informed decision on continuation without any very clear idea of how the proceedings might turn out'.[212] The court in *Wishart* agreed with this latter view as it said that directors ordinarily have to take decisions concerning whether litigation should or should not be commenced 'on the basis of only partial information, without undertaking a lengthy investigation of the merits of the proposed case'.[213] If the judge is to stand in the shoes of a hypothetical director then it would seem that he or she might not delve into all issues in great detail. But this does not seem to be consistent with the fact that it was said in *Franbar Holdings*,[214] in addressing the importance to be attached to continuing the action under s 263(3)(b), that the court must find an *obvious* breach of duty.

14.78 While the merits of a case appear to have to be considered, it is inappropriate according to *Wishart*,[215] for the courts to express any detailed or conclusive view concerning the merits of the prospective action. Nevertheless, *Stimpson v Southern Landlords Association*[216] and *Kleanthous v Paphitis*[217] represent cases where the judge considered the merits of the case, against the potential respondents to a claim, in some depth, and appeared to come to a concluded view.[218] There is clearly some judicial uncertainty as to how far a judge can go in assessing a claim. This can make it difficult for applicants to

---

[210] *Kleanthous v Paphitis* [2011] EWHC 2287 (Ch); [2012] BCC 676 at [45].
[211] [2008] EWHC 1534 (Ch) at [37].
[212] Ibid at [36].
[213] [2009] CSIH 65; 2009 SLT 812 at [37].
[214] [2008] EWHC 1534 (Ch) at [37].
[215] [2009] CSIH 65; 2009 SLT 812 at [43].
[216] [2009] EWHC 2072; [2010] BCC 387.
[217] [2011] EWHC 2287 (Ch) at [45]–[68].
[218] Ibid at [29]–[33]. The judge looked at the likelihood of liability of the directors under ss 172, 175 and 176 of the Act.

know to what extent they are required to develop a case before seeking permission. While the courts have indicated, when considering s 263(3)(b), that they must take into account the fact that directors would not necessarily expect an 'iron-clad' case before instituting proceedings, the case-law does suggest that a shareholder has to demonstrate a case that is more convincing than that which is presented to a director when he or she comes to a decision concerning the institution of proceedings.

14.79 Generally when considering the issue of permission the focus is on s 172(1). But in addition to s 172(1), s 172(3) might be considered by a judge in the context of s 263(2)(a) and, for that matter, under s 263(3)(b). Section 172(3), and considered in the last chapter, provides that the duty set out in s 172(1) is subject to any enactment or rule of law requiring directors, in certain circumstances, to consider or act in the interests of creditors. Thus, in certain cases the obligation in s 172(3) trumps the duty in s 172(1).[219] This is when a company is insolvent or in financial difficulties.[220] From the evidence before the court in a permission hearing it might be argued that the company is in financial difficulties and thus it is subject to s 172(3). While an action might be seen as viable under s 172(1) it might not be under s 172(3). The board might legitimately be concerned that, in exercising its duty under s 172(3), an action is not in the best interests of the creditors because the costs involved could reduce the funds of the company to which the creditors are entitled. If the circumstances that require directors to act pursuant to s 172(3) exist, then why would shareholders be interested in pursuing a derivative action? If the company was in financial distress the shareholders might realise that their interest in the company was worthless or close to it, but if an action were successful, and it was a substantial claim, it might save the company and even produce dividends. Of course, in this type of situation a court might decide that a person acting in accordance with s 172 might not take action as the cost of it, together with the risk of failure, might reduce the amount of money that is available for creditors ultimately, and so an action would not be in the interests of the creditors. The issue was touched on in *McAskill v Fulton*[221] where Norris J felt said that the primary interests involved were those of the creditors.[222]

14.80 The second and third elements referred to above (s 263(2)(b) and (c)) might not, because of the facts, have to be considered in some cases.[223] If the act complained of has already occurred (and had been authorised), the second element, ratification, is of no relevance. The third, dealing with authorisation, may be of no relevance unless the company submits that authorisation occurred before the act was committed or ratification has occurred since it has been

---

[219] For a recent consideration of this, see A Keay 'Directors' Duties and Creditors' Interests' (2014) 130 LQR 443.

[220] See A Keay *Company Directors' Responsibilities to Creditors* (Abingdon, Routledge-Cavendish, 2007) at 199–220.

[221] 2014 WL 8106597.

[222] Ibid at [44].

[223] *Franbar Holdings Ltd v Patel* [2008] EWHC 1534 (Ch) at [27].

committed.[224] Of course, if there is authorisation or ratification the director has not committed a wrong and the company cannot challenge what the director did. This is subject to the issue of whether any actions cannot be ratified under s 239 of the CA 2006, a matter discussed in detail in **Chapter 16**. It should be remembered in the context of s 263(2)(c)(ii), where a ratification has occurred, that a court:[225]

> 'will need to determine whether the conditions for ratification are met and, in particular, where the purported ratification is by the general meeting, whether the shareholders were properly informed given that the wrongdoing directors are likely to conceal matters that might result in the shareholder vote going against them.'

14.81　In *Stainer v Lee* Roth J manifested concern that the shareholders in that case who voted by proxy in favour of the motion to ratify would not have actually given informed consent.[226] To enable a court to determine whether there is informed consent could lead to the submission of significant amounts of evidence and it could extend hearings substantially.[227] For a case where it was held that permission should be refused because the action complained of was either authorised beforehand or ratified ex post, see *Singh v Singh*.[228]

3 Other relevant factors

14.82　If an application is not knocked out by any of the factors in s 263(2) of the CA 2006, a court then considers six factors, which are a mixture of subjective and objective matters, and contained in s 263(3) and (4). These sub-sections do not prescribe a particular standard of proof that has to be satisfied but rather require consideration of a range of factors to reach an overall view.[229] These factors have to be weighed by the court.[230] Lord Goldsmith in the parliamentary debates expressed the view that all of the factors would be considered by the courts.[231] But one judgment has said that in any particular case not all of these factors may be relevant and need not be considered.[232] This is surprising given the fact that s 263(3) and (4) appear to make it mandatory for all of the factors to be taken into account. No factor is more important than another; it will all depend on the circumstances.[233] The

---

[224] For a case where permission was not given against one respondent because of ratification, see *Brannigan v Style* [2016] EWHC 512 (Ch).

[225] A Keay and J Loughrey 'An Assessment of the Present State of Statutory Derivative Proceedings' in J Loughrey (ed) *Directors' Duties and Shareholder Litigation in the Wake of the Financial Crisis* (Cheltenham, Edward Elgar, 2013), at n 90. Also, see *Stainer v Lee* [2011] EWHC 2287 (Ch); [2011] BCC 134 at [45]–[46].

[226] [2011] EWHC 2287 (Ch); [2011] BCC 134 at [46].

[227] J Tang 'Shareholder remedies: demise of the derivative claim?' (2012) 1 *UCL Journal of Law and Jurisprudence* 178 at 200.

[228] [2013] EWHC 2138 (Ch) at [39].

[229] *Stainer v Lee* [2010] EWHC 1539 (Ch); [2011] BCC 134 at [29]; *Hughes v Weiss* [2012] EWHC 2363 (Ch) at [33]; *Brannigan v Style* [2016] EWHC 512 (Ch) at [44].

[230] *Brannigan v Style* [2016] EWHC 512 (Ch) at [66].

[231] Lords Grand Committee, 27 February 2006, Hansard HL vol 679, col GC26.

[232] *Franbar Holdings Ltd v Patel* [2008] EWHC 1534 (Ch); [2008] BCC 885 at [31].

[233] Ibid.

factors that are enumerated in s 263(3) and (4) of the CA 2006 are not to be seen as exhaustive.[234] In *Franbar Holdings Ltd v Patel*[235] William Trower QC clearly accepted the fact that he could take into account factors not set out in the legislation.[236] The factors that are set out in s 263(3) and (4) and which must be taken into account are: whether the shareholder is acting in good faith; the importance which a person under a duty to promote the success of the company would attach to continuing the action; whether the wrong could be ratified or authorised; whether the company has decided not to bring a claim; the availability of an alternative remedy; and the views of the independent members of the company.[237]

4 Good faith

14.83 The first factor that courts must consider (s 263(3)(a)) is the requirement of good faith. This is a criterion that is found in most statutory derivative claim schemes around the common law world,[238] and it is used frequently in many areas of the law, not least of which is company law. The expression was discussed in **Chapter 6** in the context of s 172.

14.84 Professor Arad Reisberg points out that in Canada there have been a couple of approaches to the judicial view of good faith in the context of derivative claims. Courts have either taken an approach that involves considering each case on its own merits or seeing the good faith requirement as so serious that if there is a lack of good faith then leave would not be granted.[239] Certainly under the UK legislation the court must consider whether the applicant is acting in good faith and it would be entitled to refuse permission on the basis of a lack of good faith, but unlike the second approach in Canada it could only do so once it had considered all of the factors in s 263(3)–(4).

14.85 It has been held in Singapore[240] that the good faith element only relates to matters associated with the derivative proceedings, and not a wider scope, and while there is no case-law on the subject in the UK this is probably the position here as well.

14.86 The presence of the good faith factor has been criticised as a rhetorical device that is 'replete with uncertainty in conception and highly unworkable in

---

[234] In *Bamford v Harvey* [2012] EWHC 2858 (Ch) at [29] Roth J said that he did not see anything against a court taking into account in a permission hearing the potential for the company itself to commence proceedings.

[235] [2008] EWHC 1534 (Ch).

[236] Ibid at [31].

[237] Companies Act 2006, s 263(3) and (4).

[238] For example, Canada Business Corporations Act 1985, s 239(2)(b); Corporations Act 2001 (Australia), s 237(2)(b).

[239] A Reisberg *Derivative Actions and Corporate Governance* (Oxford, OUP, 2007) at 116 and referring to B R Cheffins 'Reforming the Derivative Action: The Canadian Experience and British Prospects' (1997) 2 CfiLR 227 at 249.

[240] *Fong Wai Lyn Carolyn v Airtrust Singapore Pte Ltd* [2011] SGHC 88.

practice'.[241] Nevertheless, the courts are likely to derive some guidance from cases that have addressed the requirement under the common law process for derivative actions.[242] Besides these cases, Professor Jenny Payne,[243] writing well before the drafting of the CA 2006, suggested that cases applying the 'clean hands' doctrine[244] could also be treated as relevant to interpreting good faith. Under the old system in the UK if a shareholder did not have clean hands applicants would be denied permission to bring a derivative claim on the grounds that it would be inequitable to allow them to succeed in the action.[245] Payne was of the opinion that it is likely that the same approach will be employed under a statutory derivative action, on the basis that the requirement that the applicant was acting in good faith would mean that any bad faith that the applicant exhibited would disqualify him or her.[246] So far we do not appear to have any specific comments from judges in post-CA 2006 cases. Of note is the fact that the courts have not disqualified applications under s 994 of the CA 2006 (or its precursor) on this basis,[247] and they might feel that they should not discriminate between how the provisions are interpreted. On the other hand, it might be argued that with small family companies there could be some justification for a continuation of the former approach of the UK courts, and, unless the concept is interpreted too broadly, it could be a useful factor to ensure that unjustified claims are not brought. Payne, however, argues that the application of the clean hands doctrine is misconceived – the fact that an applicant has not acted with all propriety should not end up penalising the company and protecting those against whom proceedings should be brought – and she maintains that the case-law which is relied upon as evidencing the application of the clean hands doctrine in derivative litigation can be explained on other grounds.[248]

14.87   The Canadian decision of *Abraham v Prosoccer*[249] makes it clear that if an applicant is only concerned about benefiting himself and not the interests of the company, then no leave will be granted.[250] If an applicant's self-interest coincides with the company's interests then the applicant would not be acting in bad faith in bringing the derivative proceedings.[251]

---

[241]   A Reisberg 'Theoretical Reflections on Derivative Actions in English Law: The Representative Problem' (2006) ECFR 69 at 101 and 103.

[242]   *Portfolios of Distinction Ltd v Laird* [2004] EWHC 2071 (Ch), [2005] BCC 216 at [30]-[31] and [63]; *Harley Street Capital Ltd v Tchigirinski (No 2)* [2005] EWHC 247 (Ch); [2006] BCC 209 at [134]–[141].

[243]   J Payne '"Clean Hands" in Derivative Actions' (2002) 61 CLJ 76.

[244]   This is a well-established equitable concept and means that a person has acted, in the eyes of equity, in such a way that it is unjust that a claim brought at his or her behest is successful. See *Nurcombe v Nurcombe* [1985] 1 WLR 370 (CA).

[245]   For example, *Towers v African Tug Co* [1904] 1 Ch 558; *Nurcombe v Nurcombe* [1985] 1 WLR 370 (CA).

[246]   J Payne '"Clean Hands" in Derivative Actions' (2002) 61 CLJ 76 at 80.

[247]   For example, see *Re London School of Electronics Ltd* [1986] Ch 211.

[248]   J Payne '"Clean Hands" in Derivative Actions' (2002) 61 CLJ 76 at 77, 80.

[249]   (1981) 119 DLR (3rd) 167.

[250]   Also, see *Vedova v Garden House Inn Ltd* (1985) 29 BLR 236 (Ont HC).

[251]   *Primex Investments Ltd v Northwest Sports Enterprises Ltd* (1995) CanLII 717 (BCSC); (1995) 13 BCLR (3d) 300 (SC).

14.88 It is clear in Australia (where good faith has been a critical issue in the obtaining of permission) and Canada that applicants will not be regarded as not acting in good faith merely because they stand to gain financially from a successful derivative action.[252] In fact in *Chahwan v Euphoric Pty Ltd*[253] the Court of Appeal of the New South Supreme Court said that if the applicant is a former member with nothing to gain directly by the success of the action the court will be very careful in examining the purpose behind the bringing of the application.

14.89 Some difficulty is caused by the decision in *Barrett v Duckett*.[254] In this case permission was denied by the court, in part because the shareholder had a collateral purpose in bringing the action, namely the litigation formed part of a personal vendetta. This is problematic because, as the judge at first instance noted, if ill-feeling disqualified a shareholder from bringing a derivative action, most derivative claims would be frustrated.[255] Such considerations have led the Australian courts to reject arguments that the good faith requirement will not be satisfied where the applicant is motivated by intense personal hostility or malice or where the applicant is a party to other legal proceedings that involve the persons who are to be the defendants in the derivative action.[256] As Palmer J stated in the New South Wales Supreme Court case of *Swansson v Pratt*,[257] 'it is not the law that only a plaintiff who feels goodwill towards a defendant is entitled to sue', though he did agree that where the sole purpose of the action was a private vendetta, good faith would not be present.[258] However, distinguishing between an action motivated by malice and one motivated by a personal vendetta is surely a difficult task. In other jurisdictions, such as Singapore, courts have recognised that the applicant might well not have a happy relationship with the board, but that does not constitute a lack of good faith,[259] and while the application was dismissed in *Seow Tiong Siew v Kwok, Fung & Winpac Paper Products Pte Ltd*,[260] the court indicated that the fact that there was acrimony between the applicant and the board did not of itself mean that the applicant was acting other than in good faith. This approach has been supported in Canada, and it has actually been said that proof of 'bad blood' between the parties did not alone justify the conclusion that the applicant was acting in bad faith.[261] But, in the recent decision in *Singh v Singh*[262] HH Judge Hodge QC (sitting as a High Court judge) said that he

---

[252] *Swansson v Pratt* [2002] NSWSC 583; (2002) 42 ACSR 313; *Magafas v Carantinos* [2006] NSWSC 1459; *Title v Harris* (1990) 67 DLR (4th) 619 (Ont HCJ); *L & B Electric v Oickle* (2006) 242 NSR (2d) 356; (2006) 267 DLR (4th) 263; (2006) 15 BLR (4th) 195 (Nova Scotia CA) at [63].
[253] [2008] NSWCA 52 at [70].
[254] [1995] BCC 362.
[255] *Barrett v Duckett* [1995] BCC 362 at 372.
[256] *Re The President's Club Pty Ltd* [2012] QSC 364.
[257] [2002] NSWSC 583; (2002) 42 ACSR 313.
[258] Ibid at [41]. See, also, *Lewis v Nortex Pty Ltd (in liq.)* [2006] NSWSC 768 at [3]–[6].
[259] For instance, see *Teo Gek Luang v Ng Ai Tong* [1999] 1 SLR 434 (Sing HC).
[260] [2000] 4 SLR 768.
[261] *Jabber v Ammache* [2011] ABQB 504.
[262] [2013] EWHC 2138 (Ch).

would refuse permission on the basis of the claimant's personal animosity to the defendant (his brother) that arose out of a family dispute.[263] His Lordship did add that he felt that the true motivation behind the claim was to strike at the respondent rather than to promote the best interests of the company.[264]

14.90 Perhaps an alternative interpretation of *Barrett v Duckett* is preferable. As the Australian courts have found, the issue of whether the shareholder is acting in good faith on the company's behalf is closely connected with whether the action is, in fact, in the interests of the company. Thus in *Barrett v Duckett* itself, the court's conclusion that the applicant was not litigating bona fide on the company's behalf was not based simply on evidence of her personal vendetta against the defendant. Rather, it was because she was conducting litigation in a manner that failed to advance or protect the company's interests. In particular she had failed to sue her daughter who was also involved in the wrongdoing, and she had initiated the litigation even though there was little hope of recovery for the company.[265] In the light of this, it is suggested that it is not necessary, nor is it desirable, for this case-law to be interpreted in a manner that would deny permission to a shareholder to bring an action simply because there was a high level of personal hostility between the parties. Rather, in such circumstances, the court should consider closely whether s 263(3)(b) is satisfied, that is whether a person under a duty to promote the success of the company would support the action. If this, and other, criteria are satisfied, then there appears no reason why litigation, which might otherwise be in the company's interests, should be prevented because it also serves the shareholder's private purposes.[266] When recommending the need for courts to consider the issue of good faith, the Law Commission also did not think that the fact that an applicant had some interest in the outcome of the derivative claim, would prevent him or her being granted leave.[267] On the other hand, where the shareholder's collateral purpose gives rise to a conflict of interest between the shareholder and the company, permission should be refused, either because the shareholder lacks good faith or because s 263(3)(b) is not satisfied. This approach would provide a barrier to actions pursued by a competitor of a

---

[263] Ibid at [44]. His Lordship did not simply rely on a lack of good faith, but would have refused permission on other grounds.

[264] Ibid.

[265] [1995] BCC 362 at 372–373. The court was also influenced by the fact that the applicant had failed to resort to her most obvious remedy being s 459 of the Companies Act 1985, and had only commenced the action after the defendant had attempted to put the company into liquidation: at 370. Furthermore, a preferable alternative remedy was available in the form of winding up: at 372. Reisberg also treats this case as one in which relief was denied as litigation was not in the company's interests: 'Theoretical Reflections on Derivative Actions in English Law: The Representative Problem' (2006) ECFR 69 at 105. Also, see J Payne '"Clean Hands" in Derivative Actions' (2002) 61 CLJ 76 at 82.

[266] See for example, the Australian case of *Lewis v Nortex Pty Ltd (in liq)* [2006] NSWSC 768 at [3]–[6].

[267] Law Commission *Shareholder Remedies: Report on a Reference under section 3(1)(e) of the Law Commissions Act 1965* (Law Com No 246, Cm 3769) (London, Stationery Office, 1997) at para 6.76.

company in order, for example, to gain access to confidential corporate information through the disclosure process, or to otherwise disrupt the company's business.[268]

14.91 The case-law under the statutory scheme seems to accept many of the points made by courts under the previous common law process or in other jurisdictions, particularly those made in Australia. The latest UK cases seem to indicate that an ulterior purpose will not automatically lead to a finding that good faith is absent, provided the claim can benefit the company. In *Franbar Holdings Ltd v Patel*,[269] William Trower QC (sitting as a deputy judge of the High Court), while not commenting on the issue at hand in any detail stated that if a member had an ulterior motive in seeking permission, it might mean that the member was not acting in good faith, but he refrained from saying that having an ulterior motive precluded him or her from acting in good faith within the section under consideration.[270] The deputy judge rejected the allegations that there was a lack of good faith demonstrated by the applicant. In other cases an ulterior purpose has not been fatal[271] and this has included cases where a third party has funded the proceedings in order that he or she might benefit.[272] In *Iesini* Lewison J made it clear that if the claim is brought to benefit the company then the fact that the claimant will benefit from the claim will not lead to permission being refused.[273] HH Judge Behrens (sitting as a judge of the High Court) took a similar approach in *Parry v Bartlett*,[274] as did HH Judge Keyser QC in *Hughes v Weiss*[275] when the latter said that a claim will not be regarded as being in bad faith merely because, besides the proper purposes of the litigation, the claimant is seeking to achieve a collateral purpose. The critical issue appears to be: is the claim in the interests of the company? This means that the issue of good faith can be tied to s 263(3)(b), which is going to require, as we have seen when considering the criterion in s 263(2)(a), examination of such an issue. Therefore, if the proceedings could benefit the company it is less likely that the court will find that good faith is lacking. But, if the action could not be in the company's interests the contrary conclusion is more likely to be drawn by a court. All of this seems to be consistent, in general, with the approach of the courts in Australia and Canada, as mentioned earlier.

---

[268] See *Harley Street Capital Ltd v Tchigirinski (No 2)* [2005] EWHC 2471 (Ch); [2006] BCC 209 at [68] and [5].

[269] [2008] EWHC 1534 (Ch).

[270] Ibid at [33].

[271] At first instance in *Wishart* ([2009] CSOH 20; 2009 SLT 376 at [33]) it was remarked that it was unclear why a claim which could benefit the company should not proceed simply because the shareholder had other motives in bringing it.

[272] See *Iesini v Westrip Holdings Ltd* [2009] EWHC 2526 (Ch); [2010] BCC 420 at [114] and [120].

[273] *Iesini v Westrip Holdings Ltd* [2009] EWHC 2526 (Ch); [2010] BCC 420 at [121].

[274] [2011] EWHC 3146 (Ch); [2012] BCC 700 at [86].

[275] [2012] EWHC 2363 (Ch) at [47].

14.92 Besides the issue of benefit for the company, in *Stainer v Lee* Roth J indicates that if the applicant seeks and obtains the support of other minority shareholders before proceeding with the action, that will constitute strong evidence of good faith.[276]

14.93 If it is found that the applicant's action is influenced by a hope that he or she will be awarded an indemnity as far as costs is concerned, when one would not be granted if the action were brought under s 994 on the basis of unfair prejudice, this does not mean of itself that the shareholder/applicant is not acting in good faith.[277]

14.94 As to what might constitute a failure to act in good faith, in *Wishart*[278] at first instance Lord Glennie acknowledged that there might be a lack of good faith where the applicant did not honestly believe that a cause of action existed or that it had a reasonable prospect of success. This accords broadly with what the Singaporean Court of Appeal said in *Ang Thiam Swee v Low Hian Chor*.[279] The Court said that whether the applicant honestly believed that a good cause of action existed is the key factor in determining whether an applicant acted in good faith. Where there is a lack of honest belief, it is probable that the good faith factor is not likely to be important as permission would not be granted in any event on the basis that a director would not attach importance to continuing the action (under s 263(3)(b)). Just on this issue the comments of Brereton J of the New South Wales Supreme Court in *Maher v Honeysett & Maher Electrical Contractors Pty Ltd*,[280] are relevant. His Honour was of the view that he did not think that it was necessary for a court to find any particular means by which the applicant's belief that a good cause of action exists and that reasonable prospects of success could be established, because applicants rarely will know whether a good cause of action does exist; they will ordinarily rely on the advice of lawyers in this respect.

14.95 It has been argued that when actions are pursued by a member who is in business as a competitor of the company, or where the claimant has purchased shares in the company after the wrong complained of has come to light and so the share price paid by the applicant reflects the company's loss, the courts should be more inclined to scrutinise the applicant's good faith, and swifter to bar a claim on grounds of lack of good faith.[281] Allegations of a lack of good faith have been made in a number of cases, but thus far a lack of good faith has only been established in two cases.[282]

---

[276] [2010] EWHC 1539 (Ch); [2011] BCC 134 at [49].

[277] *Bhullar v Bhullar* [2015] EWHC 1943 (Ch) at [45].

[278] [2009] CSOH 20; 2009 SLT 376.

[279] [2013] SGCA 11.

[280] [2005] NSWSC 859 at [33].

[281] A Keay and J Loughrey 'Something Old, Something New, Something Borrowed: An Analysis of the New Derivative Action Under the Companies Act 2006' (2008) 124 *LQR* 469 at 488 and 491.

[282] *Stimpson v Southern Landlords Association* [2009] EWHC 2072; [2010] BCC 387; *Singh v Singh* [2013] EWHC 2138 (Ch). In the latter case the finding of lack of good faith was not the

14.96 It is unclear whether the courts will interpret the good faith requirement in the CA 2006 to deny standing to a shareholder who falls within this category, but Payne's criticism of the unthinking application of 'clean hands' in these cases is convincing.[283] So, the UK courts, rather than following the common law on this point, might choose to follow the Australian approach, as adverted to earlier in this section of the chapter, where the courts have taken the view that they are not to examine whether the applicant has clean hands, nor are they to consider matters that are prejudicial to the credit of the applicant.[284]

14.97 The manner in which the Australian courts have considered the good faith requirement is helpful in other ways. Although they have allowed cross-examination of the applicant in order to determine whether he or she was acting in good faith,[285] it seems that good faith can be established on quite low evidence,[286] and in fact the indication from the New South Wales Supreme Court in *Braga v Braga Consolidated Pty Ltd*[287] was that the applicant will be regarded as acting in good faith, and the application will be allowed, if there is no reason to think, or an inference to be drawn, that the applicant is not acting in good faith.[288]

14.98 In Australia, in determining whether an applicant is or is not acting in good faith, it has been said that two questions have to be considered, namely: whether the applicant honestly believes that a good cause of action exists and has reasonable prospects of success; and, as we have seen, whether the applicant is seeking to act in a derivative capacity for such a collateral purpose as will amount to an abuse of process. Brereton J of the New South Wales Supreme Court in *Maher v Honeysett & Maher Electrical Contractors Pty Ltd*,[289] approved of the two questions. But, the Court of Appeal of the New South Wales Supreme Court emphasised that acting in good faith should not be limited to consideration of the two questions which were posed above.[290]

14.99 Again, in Australia, besides requiring the applicant to be acting in good faith, which is all about the subjective motivation of the applicant, applicants must also convince a court that the granting of leave is in the best interests of the company, an objective test.[291] Notwithstanding this difference in tests, it has been said that the outcome of the latter consideration might well assist in the

---

basis for the judge's decision. Judge Hodge based his decision on the fact that no director would take the action being sought to be taken by the applicant.

[283] J Payne '"Clean Hands" in Derivative Actions' (2002) 61 CLJ 76 at 83–85.

[284] *Magafas v Carantinos* [2006] NSWSC 1459 at [23].

[285] *Talisman Technologies Inc v Qld Electronic Switching Pty Ltd* [2001] QSC 324 at [24].

[286] For example, see *Lakshman v Law Image Pty Ltd* [2002] NSWSC 888 at [23].

[287] [2002] NSWSC 603 at [6].

[288] This appears to have been the general approach of the Australian courts. For example, see *BL & GY International Co Ltd v Hypec Electronics Pty Ltd* [2001] NSWSC 705; (2001) 164 FLR 268 at [89].

[289] [2005] NSWSC 859 at [33].

[290] *Chahwan v Euphoric Pty Ltd* [2008] NSWCA 52 at [82].

[291] *Talisman Technologies Inc v Qld Electronic Switching Pty Ltd* [2001] QSC 324 at [31].

determination of whether the applicant is acting in good faith.[292] So, it is not just a matter of the courts taking the assertion of applicants as to their belief as proof of good faith. For if no reasonable person in the circumstances would have held the belief that the applicant purports to hold, the applicant may well be disbelieved.[293] The courts take this view because in many cases the assertion of the applicant will be an unqualified opinion founded on hearsay and therefore has little weight or utility. Hence, the objective facts are more important.[294] It has been said that if there is no evidence to support the applicant's case the court will infer that there was no honest belief, and hence no good faith.[295] Thus far it does not appear that any UK court has permitted any inferences to be drawn from the conduct of applicants and general objective circumstances. It must be added that the Australian courts do not require applicants to depose to their belief, for all that is necessary is for the court to be satisfied concerning the applicant's good faith.[296]

14.100 Finally, the Australian case-law indicates that the onus of proof on the applicant varies, depending on his or her standing. In *Swansson v Pratt*[297] Palmer J indicated that where the applicant is a current shareholder with more than a token shareholding and the derivative claim is seeking recovery of property that will increase the value of the applicant's shares, good faith will be relatively easy to establish. For example, in *Magafas v Carantinos*,[298] where the applicant was a current shareholder in the company, holding 50 per cent of the shares, and the claim would enhance the value of the company's shares, the applicant was said to be acting in good faith.[299] The same goes for a director who is able to show a legitimate interest in ensuring that the company is well-managed and the action is to enhance the welfare of the company. A similar approach was taken at common law in the UK. In *Harley Street Capital v Tchigirinsky (No 2)*,[300] for example, the court found that a corporate shareholder lacked bona fides when it held less than 0.28 per cent of shares, which it had bought after the alleged wrongdoing had been made public, and where the shareholder had failed to explain who its funders were, who was providing instructions to its lawyers and why it, and those who stood behind it, were interested in bringing the litigation at all.[301] Given the common approach

---

[292] Ibid.

[293] *Swansson v Pratt* [2002] NSWSC 583; (2002) 42 ACSR 313 at [36]; *Magafas v Carantinos* [2006] NSWSC 1459 at [19]; *Ragless v IPA Holdings Pty Ltd (in liq)* [2008] SASC 90 at [28].

[294] *Magafas v Carantinos* [2006] NSWSC 1459 at [19]. It is to be noted that The Singaporean Court of Appeal in *Ang Thiam Swee v Low Hian Chor* [2013] SGCA 11 rejected the idea that the objective legal merits of a proposed action should be considered in determining the good faith of the applicant.

[295] *Carpenter v Pioneer Park Pty Ltd* [2004] NSWSC 973; (2004) 186 FLR 104; (2004) 211 ALR 457 at [23].

[296] *South Johnstone Mill Ltd v Dennis and Scales* [2007] FCA 1448 at [69].

[297] [2002] NSWSC 583; (2002) 42 ACSR 313 at [38]. Also, see *Magafas v Carantinos* [2006] NSWSC 1459 at [18].

[298] [2006] NSWSC 1459 at [20].

[299] Also, see *First Edmonton Place Ltd v 315888 Alberta Ltd.* (1988) Alta LR (2d) 60 (Ala QB) in this regard.

[300] [2005] EWHC 2471 (Ch); [2006] BCC 209.

[301] Ibid at [135]–[137]; 229.

of the Australian and UK courts (at common law) on this issue, it seems highly likely that, under the CA 2006, the courts will scrutinise the bona fides of a shareholder more carefully where the shareholder has no financial interest in the action either because, as in *Harley Street Capital,* the price at which the shareholder purchased the shares already reflected the market's response to the alleged wrongdoing or where, as in *Barrett v Duckett,* the company may be insolvent.[302] In such cases the courts are likely to require additional evidence as to bona fides.

14.101 In determining whether good faith exists, in Canada, where, as with Australia, good faith has been a critical issue, the courts will consider whether there was a genuine issue for trial in the derivative action and whether the proposed action was frivolous or vexatious.[303] But clearly, in each case good faith is ultimately a question of fact to be determined on all of the evidence and the particular circumstances of the case.[304] In Canada the judicial approach invoked is not to attempt to define good faith but rather to analyse each set of facts for the existence of bad faith on the part of the applicant. If bad faith is found, then the requirement of good faith has not been met.[305] The cases in this jurisdiction suggest that an applicant will be assisted in submitting that he or she is acting in good faith by tendering evidence of ongoing participation in corporate affairs,[306] and the courts will not be inclined to find good faith if applicants have delayed in bringing proceedings,[307] or have refused to look at information provided by those against whom proceedings are sought to be brought.[308]

14.102 The case-law does[309] place the burden of proving lack of good faith upon the defendants and it has been said that an allegation of bad faith would require 'precise averments and cogent evidence'.[310] This should deter speculative allegations of lack of good faith and so reduce the length of the proceedings.

---

[302] *Barrett v Duckett* [1995] 1 BCC 362 at 372. See, also, *Konamaneni v Rolls-Royce Industrial Power (India) Ltd* [2002] 1 WLR 1269 at 1292.

[303] *First Edmonton Place Ltd v 315888 Alberta Ltd* (1988) Alta LR (2d) 60 (Alta QB); *Winfield v Daniel* (2004) 352 AR 82; (2004) ABQB 40 (Alta QB); *Re Marc-Jay Investments Inc and Levy* (1974) 50 DLR (3d) 45 (Ont HC); *L & B Electric v Oickle* (2006) 242 NSR (2d) 356; (2006), 267 DLR (4th) 263; (2006) 15 BLR (4th) 195 (Nova Scotia CA) at [64].

[304] *Discovery Enterprises Inc v Ebco Industries Ltd* (1998) CanLII 7049 (BCCA); (1998) 50 BCLR (3d) 195 (BCCA); *L & B Electric v Oickle* (2006) 242 NSR (2d) 356; (2006), 267 DLR (4th) 263; (2006) 15 BLR (4th) 195 (Nova Scotia CA) at [59].

[305] *Winfield v Daniel* (2004) 352 AR 82; *L & B Electric v Oickle* (2006) 242 NSR (2d) 356; (2006), 267 DLR (4th) 263; (2006) 15 BLR (4th) 195 (Nova Scotia CA) at [60].

[306] *Appotive v Computrex Centres Ltd* (1981) 16 BLR 133 (BCSC); *Re Besenski* (1981) 15 Sask R 182 (Sask QB); *Johnson v Meyer* (1987) 62 Sask R 34 (Sask QB).

[307] *Churchill Pulpmill Ltd v Manitoba* [1977] 6 WWR 109 (Man CA); *LeDrew v LeDrew Lumber Co* (1988) 223 APR 71.

[308] *Benarroch v City Resources (Can) Ltd* (1991) 54 BCLR (2d) 373 (BCCA).

[309] For instance, *Franbar Holdings Ltd v Patel* [2008] EWHC 1534 (Ch); [2008] BCC 885 at [33]-[34]; *Wishart* [2009] CSOH 20; 2009 SLT 376 at [33].

[310] *Franbar Holdings Ltd v Patel* [2008] EWHC 1534 (Ch); [2008] BCC 885 at [33]–[34].

5 *Importance to a person acting in accordance with section 172*

14.103   This factor is set out in s 263(3)(b). The need to consider how a person would act in pursuing the duty found in s 172 was adverted to earlier. The criteria in s 263(2)(a) and s 263(3)(b) involve the same matters, but they undertake different roles. Also, while an applicant might be able to hurdle the s 263(2)(a) requirement as far as the s 172 duty is concerned, it would appear that he or she will encounter more difficulty when the duty is considered by the judge in terms of the s 263(3) factors.[311] In *Franbar Holdings Ltd v Patel*[312] William Trower QC said that the criterion in the latter provision is a difficult one to assess.[313] It would appear that while the use of it in s 263(2)(a) is to permit courts to refuse permission for claims that are not substantial, the use of it in s 263(3)(b) involves judges looking more closely at the kind of factors that would really determine where a director would indeed pursue the claim. Also, while in the former case it is considered on its own and on the basis that a court would refuse permission if the case was not one that a director would take on, in the latter case the criterion is assessed in conjunction with the other criteria that are adumbrated in s 263(3). William Trower QC indicated that a director who has to decide whether to take legal proceedings, and who was acting in accordance with s 172, would have concern for a number of considerations, namely: prospects of success; the likelihood of the company being able to recover property or money if successful; how disruptive it would be to the company's business in prosecuting proceedings; and any damage to the reputation and business of the company if proceedings turned out to be unsuccessful.[314] The appeal court in *Wishart*[315] added other matters, such as: the amount at stake;[316] and the prospects of getting a satisfactory result without litigation. These are probably wider in scope than those that the deputy judge laid down for consideration in *Franbar Holdings Ltd v Patel* when considering this criterion in the context of s 263(2)(a). This criterion has, in the majority of cases decided hitherto, consumed much of the court's time in arriving at its decision.

14.104   A difficulty that might exist for a member wanting to obtain permission is that in *Franbar Holdings* the deputy judge said that he felt that the applicant needed to do more work in formulating a claim for breaches.[317] Yet this comment was made after the judge had said earlier in his judgment that 'a director will often be in the position of having to make what is no more than

---

[311] See A Keay 'Applications to Continue Derivative Proceedings on Behalf of Companies and the Hypothetical Director Test' (2015) 34 *Civil Justice Quarterly* 346.

[312] [2008] EWHC 1534 (Ch).

[313] Ibid at [35].

[314] Ibid at [36].

[315] [2009] CSIH 65; 2009 SLT 812 at [37].

[316] Also mentioned in *Kiani v Cooper* [2010] EWHC 577 (Ch); [2010] BCC 463 at [44]. But in *Stainer v Lee* [2010] EWHC 1539 (Ch); [2011] BCC 134 at [29] Roth J appeared to downplay the fact that the amount of the recovery might be small where the applicant's case was strong as he felt that such a claim might stand a good chance of provoking an early settlement or leading to summary judgment.

[317] [2008] EWHC 1534 (Ch); [2008] BCC 885 at [54].

a partially informed decision on continuation without any very clear idea of how the proceedings might turn out'.[318] The court in *Wishart* agreed with this latter view as it said that directors ordinarily have to take decisions concerning whether litigation should or should not be commenced 'on the basis of only partial information, without undertaking a lengthy investigation of the merits of the proposed case.'[319] These comments appear to produce some uncertainty and it makes it difficult for an applicant to know how far he or she is required to develop a case before seeking permission. Clearly any case put before a court must indicate an arguable case in the applicant's favour,[320] but, as the respective courts above have indicated, when considering the factor in s 263(3)(b), they must take into account the fact that hypothetical directors would not necessarily expect an 'iron-clad' case before instituting proceedings. If the courts expect shareholders to make an application only when they have a substantial case then the ambit of the derivative claim will be severely circumscribed, particularly since much of the information needed to frame a detailed case will be in the hands of the directors, and will not be accessible to the shareholders until much later in the proceedings, perhaps at the disclosure stage of litigation.

14.105 This criteria is discussed further under the later heading 'Best interests of the company'.

6 Likelihood of authorisation or ratification[321]

14.106 According to s 263(3)(c) where the cause of action is the consequence of an act or omission yet to occur, the court must take account of the likelihood of it being authorised by the company before it occurs or ratified after it occurs. The following paragraph (s 263(3)(d)) provides that if the act or omission on which the cause of action is founded has occurred the court must consider the likelihood of it being ratified by the company. It is quite possible that the courts might, in taking into account this latter criterion, have to examine whether the act could be ratified legally or practically. Ratification is considered in detail in **Chapter 16.** The court has the power, under s 261(4), to adjourn a permission application, and it might do so and contemporaneously order a meeting of the members to see if a resolution to ratify succeeds. This criterion constitutes a 'tipping of the hat' to the age-old majority rule that has applied in company law for many years. Parliament does not want to be seen to be intervening in the democratic process in companies.

14.107 While the UK legislation talks about the likelihood of ratification, two other jurisdictions that have legislation closest to the UK's do not. In Canada ratification is not mentioned as a criterion to be considered in relation to

---

[318] Ibid at [36].

[319] [2009] CSIH 65; 2009 SLT 812 at [37].

[320] Ibid at [38].

[321] For greater discussion of this issue, see A Keay and J Loughrey 'An assessment of the present state of statutory derivative proceedings' in J Loughrey (ed) *Directors' Duties and Shareholder Litigation in the Wake of the Financial Crisis* (Cheltenham, Edward Elgar, 2013) at 202–207.

obtaining leave to bring a derivative claim.[322] In Australia s 239(1)(a) of the Corporations Act 2001 explicitly states that ratification does not prevent a person from bringing proceedings with leave or for applying for leave; but the next subsection does state that if ratification has occurred the court *may* take that into account in deciding what order to make.[323]

14.108 We must not forget that the ratification rules have been tightened somewhat by s 239 of the CA 2006, and this might mean that courts will not be so ready to assume, as they once might have been, that an act will be ratified. A court would need to consider in determining whether the action complained of would be ratified the nature of the votes of the shareholders, and who can be regarded as connected to the respondent/director, because connected persons would not be eligible to vote.[324] There might be some difficulty in convincing the court that a person is connected. In *Franbar Holdings Ltd v Patel*[325] William Trower QC considered this issue (an issue dealt with in more detail in **Chapter 16**). It was indicated to the court that it was likely that the action complained of would be ratified. In deciding whether to exercise its discretion in favour of granting leave the court therefore had to determine whether such ratification would be effective. The deputy judge was of the view that it was no more than a possibility that the alleged breaches of duty in relation to which the member wished to bring proceedings could be effectively ratified.[326]

14.109 It would seem that in this context the concept of wrongdoer control has made a re-appearance.[327] In *Parry v Bartlett* HH Judge Behrens (sitting as a High Court judge) found that the conduct complained of by the claimant was not ratifiable because the company was subject to wrongdoer control.[328] Perhaps consideration of wrongdoer control is necessary as a judge needs to get an idea of the way that persons are likely to vote. But it might be unhelpful to express it in this way. Potentially it could raise the issue of what amounts to wrongdoer control of the general meeting, an issue which gives rise to substantial difficulties, including the matter of ascertaining whether particular shareholders are connected or not. While it may be easy to show in small private companies that the alleged wrongdoers control the general meeting, in larger companies it would be difficult to identify on whose behalf shares are held.[329]

---

[322] Canada Business Corporations Act 1985, s 239.

[323] This issue is discussed in A Keay 'Assessing and Rethinking the Statutory Scheme for Derivative Actions Under the Companies Act 2006' (2016) 16 *Journal of Corporate Law Studies* 39.

[324] See s 239(3).

[325] [2008] EWHC 1534 (Ch).

[326] Ibid at [47].

[327] For a discussion of wrongdoer control, see A Keay and J Loughrey 'An assessment of the present state of statutory derivative proceedings' in J Loughrey (ed) *Directors' Duties and Shareholder Litigation in the Wake of the Financial Crisis* (Cheltenham, Edward Elgar, 2013) at 217.

[328] [2011] EWHC 3146 (Ch); [2012] BCC 700 at [81].

[329] Law Commission, *Shareholder Remedies: Consultation Paper* (Law Com, Consultation Paper No 142) (London, Stationery Office, 1997) at para 4.13.

14.110 There have always been two views as to when ratification would be effective or not, one turning on the nature of the wrong, and the other deeming an action not to be ratifiable because the wrongdoers were seeking to ratify their own default in order to oppress the minority.[330] The predominance of case-law and academic commentary has been in favour of the former view.[331] What Judge Behrens appeared to do in *Parry v Bartlett* was to employ the latter view. It has been submitted that it might be preferable for courts to focus on the former view and to categorise the alleged wrongs committed in order to ascertain if they are capable of being ratified.[332]

7 *The company has decided not to pursue the claim*

14.111 Section 263(3)(e) of the CA 2006 requires the court to take into account whether the company has decided not to pursue the claim. The fact that a company has decided not to pursue a claim could well be an important factor in the court's decision whether or not to give permission. But if the company has made this decision based on reasons that the courts do not find convincing or appropriate this might make the courts more ready to grant permission. Courts, it would appear, would need to investigate the circumstances and independence of decisions that have been made not to take action.[333]

8 *Alternative remedy*

14.112 The CA 2006 in s 263(3)(f) provides that the court must consider whether the act of omission in respect of which the derivative claim is brought gives rise to a cause of action that the member could pursue in his or her own right.[334] This was something that was also to be considered at common law. But, while the CA 2006 provides that the court must consider whether there is an alternative cause of action that the member could pursue in his or her own right,[335] the common law was broader, and all remedies were taken into account, including alternative avenues of redress for the company itself.[336] An

---

[330] A Keay and J Loughrey 'An Assessment of the Present State of Statutory Derivative Proceedings' in J Loghrey (ed) *Directors' Duties and Shareholder Litigation in the Wake of the Financial Crisis* (Cheltenham, Edward Elgar, 2013) at 205.

[331] K Wedderburn 'Shareholders Rights and the Rule in *Foss v Harbottle*' [1958] CLJ 93 at 96; J Payne 'A Re-Examination of Ratification' [1999] CLJ 604 at 614; H C Hirt 'Ratification of Breaches of Directors' Duties: the Implications of the Reform Proposal Regarding the Availability of Derivative Actions' (2004) 25 *Company Lawyer* 197 at 203.

[332] A Keay and J Loughrey 'An Assessment of the Present State of Statutory Derivative Proceedings' in J Loughrey (ed) *Directors' Duties and Shareholder Litigation in the Wake of the Financial Crisis* (Cheltenham, Edward Elgar, 2013) at 206.

[333] A Reisberg *Derivative Actions and Corporate Governance* (OUP, 2007) at 156.

[334] There has been some lack of clarity regarding the relevance of an alternative remedy: compare *Konamaneni v Rolls-Royce Industrial Power (India) Ltd* [2002] 1 WLR 1269 at 1279, where Lawrence Collins J stated that it was not an independent consideration, with *Mumbray v Lapper* [2005] EWHC 1152 (Ch); [2005] BCC 990 at [5] in which Robert Reid QC thought it could be an extremely important factor for the court to take into account.

[335] Companies Act 2006, s 263(3)(f).

[336] *Barrett v Duckett* [1995] BCC 362 at 372.

example of refusing permission where an alternative remedy was available occurred in *Cooke v Cooke*[337] where an application under the precursor of s 994 of the CA 2006 was viewed as being more appropriate. In *Mumbray v Lapper*[338] the judge said that whether an alternative remedy is available or not was a factor, and it may well be an extremely important factor; but it was not an absolute bar to permission being granted.[339]

14.113 In *Mumbray v Lapper* winding up on the just and equitable ground,[340] or a s 459 (now s 994) petition[341] were found to be preferable to a derivative action, and permission was refused. The petitioner had participated in the wrongdoing, the company was deadlocked and no longer trading and, if liquidation was pursued, the liquidator could determine whether to take proceedings in the company's name against the alleged wrongdoers.[342] It does not seem though that the fact that a quasi-partnership is deadlocked can, alone, lead to permission being refused on the basis that, for example, winding up is preferable. There are cases in which permission has been granted despite the fact that the only two members of a company that was a quasi-partnership can no longer work together.[343] In *Mumbray v Lapper*, however, it was significant that the applicant was also an alleged wrongdoer. It seems that the courts were more likely, at common law, to prefer alternative remedies where the applicant lacked good faith.[344]

14.114 In another case where permission was refused, *Jafari-Fini v Skillglass Ltd*,[345] the refusal was based on the fact that the shareholder had a personal cause of action arising out of the same facts as gave rise to the derivative claim and, if the shareholder succeeded in his personal claim he would retake control of the company and could then cause it to bring proceedings, whereas if he failed the company's claim also evaporated.[346] While this approach could have delayed any recovery to which the company was entitled, in this case the only asset that could have been recovered was worthless.[347] In the circumstances, therefore, the company had nothing to gain from litigation being brought on its behalf and it was not in its interests for

---

[337] [1997] 2 BCLC 28.

[338] [2005] EWHC 1152 (Ch); [2005] BCC 990.

[339] Ibid at [5].

[340] Under the Insolvency Act 1986, s 122(1)(g).

[341] Under the Companies Act 1985, and now superseded by s 994 of the Companies Act 2006.

[342] [2005] EWHC 1152 (Ch); [2005] BCC 990 at [23]; contrast the Australian case of *Kandt Stening Group Pty Ltd v Stening* [2006] NSWSC 307 at [33] (company dormant and had no assets save what was under dispute in the litigation, and leave was granted).

[343] *Halle v Trax BW Ltd* [2000] BCC 1020; *Qayoumi v Oakhouse Property Holdings Plc* [2002] EWHC 2547 (Ch); [2003] 1 BCLC 352; *Fansa v Alsibahie* [2005] EWHC 271 (Ch); [2005] All ER (D) 80 (Jan). With the exception of the company in *Halle v Trax*, however, it is not clear that the companies in question were deadlocked.

[344] *Barrett v Duckett* [1995] BCC 362; *Portfolios of Distinction Ltd v Laird* [2004] EWHC 2071 (Ch); [2005] BCC 216.

[345] [2005] EWCA Civ 356; [2005] BCC 842.

[346] Ibid at [47] and [52].

[347] Ibid at [25] and [52].

permission to be given.[348] This emphasises the fact that the derivative claim procedure is all about what is best for the company and not what is best for an individual shareholder.

14.115 A decision, *Airey v Cordell*,[349] made only shortly before the introduction of the new scheme, importantly gave a broad interpretation to the concept of an alternative remedy. The court held that it included a settlement of the dispute which adequately protected the shareholder's interests.[350] The problem with this is that it risks sanctioning 'green-mailing', the practice whereby shareholders bring derivative actions to pressurise company management to buy their shares at above the market price. It could deprive independent shareholders of a solvent company, and creditors of an insolvent one, of the benefit of recovery on the company's behalf. Again, if a shareholder were minded to accept a share purchase in settlement of the claim, the appropriate course would be to refuse permission on the basis that s 994 of the CA 2006 provided a preferable remedy. On the other hand, given the facts of *Airey v Cordell* itself, the approach may be defensible. The company was closely-held and solvent, so that the company's interests were comprised of the interests of the disputing shareholders, and the shareholder wished to remain in the company, and protect his interest in it.[351]

14.116 In *Franbar Holdings Ltd v Patel*[352] William Trower QC, who was dealing, it will be remembered, with the new law, was of the view that reference to an alternate cause of action should be seen as broad, and provided that another remedy was based on the same act or omission on which the derivative claim would be based, it would come within s 263(3)(f) of the CA 2006.[353] According to the deputy judge an alternate cause of action to be within the paragraph does not have to be one that is against the same people who would be the respondents in a derivative claim.[354] So, if the acts involved would enable the bringing of an action under s 994 for unfair prejudice, and in most cases this is the basis on which an alternate remedy will be available or at least that possibility will be considered by the court, the court will take this into account in deciding whether or not to grant permission to commence a derivative claim. In many cases there will be overlaps between a derivative claim and a claim under s 994 of the Act.[355] In *Franbar Holdings*, William Trower QC attached

---

[348] The Australian courts would probably adopt a similar approach. See, for example, *Swansson v Pratt* [2002] NSWSC 583 at [63]–[69]; *Promaco Conventions Pty Ltd v Dedline Printing Pty Ltd* [2007] FCA 586 at [46]–[52].

[349] [2006] EWHC 2728 (Ch); [2007] Bus L R 391.

[350] Ibid at [84]–[86].

[351] *Airey v Cordell* [2006] EWHC 2728 (Ch); [2007] Bus L R 391 at [48] and [84].

[352] [2008] EWHC 1534 (Ch).

[353] Ibid at [50].

[354] Ibid.

[355] For a discussion of this overlap, see, B Hannigan 'Drawing Boundaries Between Derivative Claims and Unfairly Prejudicial Petitions' (2009) 6 JBL 606. In *Langley Ward Ltd v Trevor* [2011] EWHC 1893 (Ch), the court held that a winding up petition on just and equitable grounds would have been a more suitable remedy than a derivative claim and permission would have been refused on this basis had it not already been refused on other grounds.

substantial weight to the fact that he thought that a s 994 action could bring the relief that the member sought and, thus taking into account other factors, he refused to grant permission to continue a derivative claim.[356] Earlier, Floyd J in *Mission Capital plc v Sinclair*[357] had taken the same view.[358] But in the more recent decision in *Bhullar v Bhullar*,[359] which involved a double derivative action that was not governed by the statutory scheme but by the common law, Morgan J did not deny the application for the continuation of a derivative claim when there was substantial argument put to support the view that a more appropriate way for the applicant to proceed was via a s 994 petition. The reasons why his Lordship appeared to take this view were that the issues in the derivative claim were relatively narrow and self-contained whereas the issues in a s 994 claim would be significantly wider and s 994 would be slow and expensive if the claim went all the way to a trial.[360] Also the judge might have been influenced by the applicant's argument that the derivative claim issues should be addressed first as that might precipitate the basis for a settlement of the overall dispute between the respective parties.[361] More importantly, in another recent case, *Hook v Summer*,[362] which did deal with the statutory scheme, the judge granted the application for the continuation of a derivative action even though there was evidence to suggest that the applicant could bring unfair prejudice proceedings. The court was influenced by the fact that the reason that the applicant did not present a s 994 petition was that he did not wish to be bought out and with successful s 994 petitions it was quite likely that a court might order that his shares be purchased. The judge, HH Judge Cook (sitting as a judge of the High Court) said that the applicant cannot be said to have acted unreasonably in preferring to bring a derivative action instead of instituting unfair prejudice proceedings.[363]

14.117 As at common law, the fact that a court takes the view that an alternative remedy is possible under the statute, it alone should not necessarily mean that permission should be refused. But the decisions in *Franbar Holdings*,[364] *Iesini*[365] and *Kleanthous v Paphitis*[366] seem to make the availability of an alternative remedy a compelling reason for withholding permission.[367] In *Kleanthous* Newey J considered that it was a 'powerful

---

[356]   Ibid at [54].

[357]   [2008] EWHC 1339 (Ch).

[358]   It is to be noted that David Donaldson QC in *Langley Ward Ltd v Trevor* [2011] EWHC 1893 (Ch) at [13], felt that a petition under s 994 did not fall easily within the expression 'cause of action' but he seemed to accept that s 994 could be an alternative remedy within the criterion.

[359]   [2015] EWHC 1943 (Ch).

[360]   Ibid at [44].

[361]   Ibid at [43], [44].

[362]   [2015] EWHC 3820 (Ch).

[363]   Ibid at [135].

[364]   [2008] EWHC 1534 (Ch); [2008] BCC 885 at [30].

[365]   [2009] EWHC 2526; [2010] BCC 420 at [86].

[366]   [2011] EWHC 2287 (Ch) at [81].

[367]   See the discussion in A Keay 'Assessing and Rethinking the Statutory Scheme for Derivative Actions under the Companies Act 2006' (2016) 16 *Journal of Corporate Law Studies* 39.

reason' to refuse permission.[368] This is notwithstanding that in *Iesini*, Lewison J said that the existence of an alternative remedy was not an absolute bar to permission being granted.[369] *Kiani v Cooper*[370] is an instance of a case where it was held that this factor was only one of several to consider and in that case the other factors outweighed it. In *Phillips v Fryer*[371] permission was granted even though the claimant had already presented a s 994 petition which involved relying on matters that overlapped with the derivative claim. The judge, Nicholas Strauss QC (sitting as a deputy judge of the High Court), did this because the derivative claim could be dealt with much more swiftly than the s 994 petition which was set down for six days, and also the derivative claim was apparently strong.

14.118 A court might take the view that if it sanctioned a derivative action where a member has also initiated s 994 proceedings, it would be seen as approving of 'green-mailing.' Also, a court could withhold permission on the basis that when hearing the s 994 petition it is able to make an order that the company institute proceedings against the directors or others.[372] The problem this view would create for the applicant is that there will be a long delay before the hearing of a claim against a director or others for damaging the company is actually heard. The applicant must wait for the s 994 petition to be heard, hope that the court orders the company to bring proceedings against the wrongdoer(s) and then wait for those proceedings to come to trial. The uncertainties and time delay inherent in this process could well see the wrongdoers escaping, for a number of reasons, not least being the fact that the member runs out of funds and/or energy.

14.119 The court may also take the view, as in *Kleanthous v Paphitis*,[373] that the shareholder is bringing a derivative action solely to obtain the benefit of a costs indemnity order, in which case the s 994 petition (where the shareholder bears his or her own costs until he or she succeeds and a court awards the shareholder costs[374]) would be more appropriate.[375] Yet in *Bhullar v Bhullar*[376] the deputy judge did not see a problem with the fact that the bringing of the applicant's derivative action was influenced by a hope that he would be awarded an indemnity as far as costs is concerned, when one would not be granted if his action were brought under s 994 on the basis of unfair prejudice. It must not be forgotten that a costs order in the shareholder's favour when permission is granted is discretionary.[377] Therefore, concern over costs need not deter the courts from granting permission if other factors point towards the

---

[368] Ibid.
[369] [2009] EWHC 2526; [2010] BCC 420 at [123].
[370] [2010[EWHC 577 (Ch); [2010] BCC 463.
[371] [2011] EWHC 1611 (Ch).
[372] See s 996(2)(c).
[373] [2011] EWHC 2287 (Ch).
[374] But even if this occurs all of the shareholders will not usually be paid by the respondent.
[375] [2011] EWHC 2287 at [81].
[376] [2015] EWHC 1943 (Ch) at [45].
[377] See the comments of HH Judge Keyser QC in *Hughes v Weiss* [2012] EWHC 2363 (Ch) at [55].

derivative claim being the appropriate remedy. What is important is the nature of the wrong alleged and the remedy sought.[378] In *Kleanthous* the wrong alleged was the diversion of a corporate opportunity.[379] This is misconduct which would properly form the basis of a derivative claim and would be most appropriately addressed by granting a remedy to the company. A further consideration is that directing these types of claims towards the unfair prejudice remedy and the grant of a personal remedy to the shareholder may prejudice the interests of creditors if the company is of doubtful solvency or in financial difficulties.[380]

14.120   It is likely that the usual alternative remedy that a court might find available to an applicant, as foreshadowed by our discussion thus far, is a s 994 petition. But in *Langley Ward Ltd v Trevor*[381] David Donaldson QC took the view that a petition to wind up, probably on the just and equitable ground (s 122(1)(g) of the Insolvency Act 1986), was more appropriate.[382]

14.121   While *Iesini* and *Kleanthous v Paphitis* regarded the availability of an alternative remedy as a compelling reason for refusing permission, other courts have not done so. The appeal court in *Wishart* did not consider it to be grounds for refusing permission because proceedings under s 994 would constitute an indirect means of achieving what could be achieved directly through the use of derivative action.[383] HH Judge Behrens reached a similar conclusion in *Parry v Bartlett*,[384] and he made the point that this criterion was only a factor that that had to be taken into account and did not operate as a complete bar to a derivative claim,[385] a view clearly taken at common law. Admittedly in these two latter cases the argument for derivative actions was probably stronger overall than any of the other cases heard thus far under the new scheme.

14.122   What is happening is that there are relatively few derivative actions being commenced and a proliferation of unfair prejudice proceedings.[386] The way that the jurisprudence has developed on this subject has led to a problem for litigants: on which basis should an action be initiated – a derivative basis or under s 994? The reason for this is that there has been a failure to distinguish between the wrongs that should be remedied by a derivative action and those

---

[378] *Stainer v Lee* [2010] EWHC 1539 (Ch); [2011] BCC 134 at [51] and citing Millett J *In Re Charnley Davies Ltd (No 2)* [1990] BCC 605 at 625.

[379] [2011] EWHC 2287 (Ch) at [32].

[380] B Hannigan 'Drawing Boundaries Between Derivative Claims and Unfairly Prejudicial Petitions' (2009) 6 *Journal of Business Law* 606 at 617–620. Hannigan argues that this problem could be addressed within the context of a s 994 petition by the court ordering both a buy out of the petitioner's shares and for the wrongdoers to compensate the company.

[381] [2011] EWHC 1893 (Ch).

[382] In *Singh v Singh* ([2013] EWHC 2138 at [45] (Ch)), HH Judge Hodge QC was of the opinion that either a s 994 petition or a petition on the just and equitable ground would constitute alternative remedies to a derivative claim.

[383] [2009] CSIH 65; 2009 SLT 812 at [46].

[384] [2011] EWHC 3146 (Ch); [2012] BCC 700 at [88]–[92].

[385] Ibid at [89], [91].

[386] See, A Keay 'Assessing and Rethinking the Statutory Scheme for Derivative Actions under the Companies Act 2006' (2016) 16 *Journal of Corporate Law Studies* 39.

by an unfair prejudice action, and this is due to the fact that the courts have not listed the personal rights of shareholders that will be protected by s 994.[387] This is a major issue and is outside the scope of this chapter and involves broader issues, so it is not intended to deal with it in any depth, but it has been discussed elsewhere.[388]

14.123 In dealing with whether a derivative action or an unfair prejudice was the correct way to proceed, Millett J (as he then was) said in *Re Charnley Davies Ltd (No 2)*[389] that the same facts could found either action, but the nature of the complaint and the appropriate relief will be different. His Lordship went on to say that if a shareholder's essential complaint was of the unlawfulness of a respondent's conduct, with the result that any order made would be for restitution, then a derivative action would have been appropriate and not an unfair prejudice petition. But if a respondent's unlawful conduct is alleged to be evidence of the manner in which he or she had conducted the company's affairs in disregard of the shareholder's interests and the latter wished to have their shares purchased, then an unfair prejudice was appropriate.[390] In a more recent derivative claim, *Stainer v Lee*,[391] Roth J referred approvingly to Millett J's judgment, and in *LPD Holdings (Aust) Pty Ltd v Phillips*[392] the Queensland Supreme Court recently took the same view as Millett J and said that in many cases conduct can have a dual character, namely actionable either as a derivative action or under the oppression provision (equivalent to the UK's s 994). In Canada it has been said that there is not a bright-line distinction between the claims that may be advanced under the derivative action section and those that may be brought under the oppression provision.[393] This is undoubtedly correct as far as the UK is concerned.

14.124 It would seem that there are several potential problems and concerns with permitting unfair prejudice petitions where the company has been wronged. For instance, the company does not benefit usually by relief granted in s 994 petitions, and hence, the other shareholders do not benefit indirectly; an order providing for a buy out of the shareholder is of no assistance to the company. Also, non-shareholder stakeholders do not benefit. The riposte to

---

[387] J Poole and P Roberts 'Shareholder Remedies – Corporate Wrongs and the Derivative Action' [1999] JBL 99 at 113-114.

[388] It is discussed in J Payne 'Sections 459-461 Companies Act 1985 in Flux: The Future of Shareholder Protection' (2005) 64 CLJ 647; R Cheung 'Corporate Wrongs Litigated in the Context of Unfair Prejudice Claims: Reforming the Unfair Prejudice Remedy for the Redress of Corporate Wrongs' (2008) 29 *Company Lawyer* 98; B Hannigan 'Drawing Boundaries Between Derivative Claims and Unfairly Prejudicial Petitions' [2009] JBL 606; A Gray 'The Statutory Derivative Claim: An Outmoded Superfluousness?' (2012) 33 *Company Lawyer* 295; A Keay 'Assessing and Rethinking the Statutory Scheme for Derivative Actions under the Companies Act 2006' (2016) 16 *Journal of Corporate Law Studies* 39.

[389] [1990] BCLC 760 at 783.

[390] Ibid.

[391] [2010] EWHC 1539 (Ch); [2011] BCC 134 at [51].

[392] [2013] QSC 225 at [40]–[42].

[393] *Malata Group (HK) Ltd v Jung* 2008 ONCA 11 per Armstrong JA. This view was also expressed by Basten JA in *Campbell v Back Office Investments Pty Ltd* [2008] NSWCA 95 at [214].

that might be that as far as shareholders are concerned it is up to them to take action themselves. But, of course, some shareholders might not have the resources. As far as other stakeholders, who might benefit indirectly from the company being awarded relief in a derivative action, are concerned, they simply do not have any right to bring proceedings. This might be a particularly important issue for creditors where the company is in financial distress.

14.125   It is submitted that the following cautionary words emitted by Brenda Hannigan need to be taken into account:[394]

> 'The important point is that issues as to the appropriateness of petitions or derivative claims are not solely matters of choice for the aggrieved shareholder, but matter of jurisdiction for the court, which in resolving the issue must be mindful of the fundamental principles underlying the rule in *Foss v Harbottle*, the derivative claim and the rule against recovery of reflective loss.
>
> It is time to develop a workable derivative claim and the courts should continue to be very cautious about allowing corporate relief to be sought and granted on an unfairly prejudicial petition.'

9 *Views of members with no personal interest in the matter*

14.126   The final factor, contained in s 263(4) of the CA 2006, that the courts must take into account is that they must consider any evidence before them as to the views of members of the company who have no personal interest in the matter. This was introduced to address the fact that it would not be either practical or desirable for large quoted companies to seek formal approval of the commercial decisions of the board from the shareholders.[395]

14.127   It might seem, at first blush, that the views of the members identified in the subsection are to be accorded special consideration given the fact that it says that the court is to give 'particular regard' to their views, but in fact the introductory words of s 263(3) also refer to the court taking into account 'in particular' the factors set out in the subsection. Thus the factors in s 263(3) and the one in s 263(4) are of equal strength.

14.128   There has not been a lot said in relation to the issue of independent shareholders. It is not clear to whom the subsection is actually directed.[396] As Lewison J said in *Iesini*,[397] the provision is not easy to understand as all members have an interest in any claim that is taken on behalf of the company because the value of their shares could rise or fall depending on the result of the

---

[394] B Hannigan 'Drawing Boundaries Between Derivative Claims and Unfairly Prejudicial Petitions' [2009] JBL 606 at 626.

[395] A Reisberg *Derivative Actions and Corporate Governance* (OUP, 2007) at 147.

[396] The Law Commission said that the position at common law was not clear: *Shareholder Remedies: Report on a Reference under section 3(1)(e) of the Law Commissions Act 1965* (Law Com, No 246, Cm 3769) (London, Stationery Office, 1997) at para 6.89.

[397] [2009] EWHC 2526; [2010] BCC 420 at [86].

claim.[398] After considering the provision's various interpretations Lewison J said that he was of the opinion that it was referring to those members who were 'not implicated in the alleged wrongdoing and who did not stand to benefit otherwise than in their capacity as members of the company.'[399] The potential problem is it might not always be possible to determine at the stage of the permission hearing whether members are able to benefit in a way that is out of the ordinary and in the way mentioned by his Lordship, but to be fair his Lordship's approach seems to be appropriate, sensible and as practicable as anything could be.

14.129 It is difficult to know what sort of emphasis a court will put on this criterion. HH Judge Pelling QC (sitting as a judge of the High Court) in *Stimpson* noted the views of some of the members[400] and they gave limited support to the applicant. The judge said that he would take this into account, but the upshot was that it made little difference to the judge's opinion. In *Bridge v Daley*[401] HH Judge Hodge QC (sitting as a judge of the High Court) held that disinterested members of the company, save for a few minority shareholders who supported the applicant, were against a continuation of the action. There is no indication from his Lordship the weight put on that finding, but it seemed to be significant along with the fact that he found that no reasonable director would support the continuation of the action in the circumstances.

14.130 In *Kleanthous v Paphitis*[402] there were three shareholders. These were the claimant, the main respondent (a director and majority shareholder of the company), and the third shareholder, C (a minority shareholder and director). Newey J examined the views of C when he came to consideration of s 263(4) even though he was a named respondent.[403] This appears to be somewhat contrary to what Lewison J said in *Iesini*. While Newey J had come to the conclusion that C, the 'independent' member, had not benefited from the actions about which the claimant was complaining, it was surely an issue that should be resolved at a final hearing. In any event, given both the fact that C was a director sitting on the company's board when it approved of the actions of the main respondent and majority shareholder, and the fact that C arguably appeared 'to be close' to the majority shareholder, it is difficult to see why he could be characterised as not having a personal interest, at least one that was indirect, in the outcome.

14.131 Clearly an issue that could well be considered when taking into account this criterion is whether the independent shareholders have been

---

[398] Ibid at [129].
[399] Ibid.
[400] [2009] EWHC 2072; [2010] BCC 387 at [42].
[401] [2015] EWHC 2121 (Ch).
[402] [2011] EWHC 2287 (Ch).
[403] Ibid at [83].

informed about the proceedings and the allegations made in them.[404] Where shareholders have not been properly informed this will reduce the weight that can be attached to their views.

B The best interests of the company

14.132 The Law Commission in its report on *Shareholder Remedies*[405] indicated that a court should take into account the interests of the company in deciding whether to permit a derivative claim to go ahead.[406] However, the legislation that was subsequently drafted did not refer expressly[407] to the need for the applicant to establish that the derivative claim would be in the best interests of the company. Nevertheless, the UK legislation does instruct the court, in s 263(2)(a), and s 263(3)(b) of the CA 2006 to consider the importance that a person acting in accordance with s 172 (duty to promote the success of the company) would attach to continuing the claim. The meaning of s 172 has been the subject of interesting commentary from academics and practitioners,[408] and it was discussed in detail in **Chapter 6**. Clearly the s 172 duty is tied up with the idea of acting in the best interests of the company, as made clear in *Re West Coast Capital (LIOS) Ltd*[409] and *Cobden Investments Ltd v RWM Langport Ltd*.[410] And it is unlikely that a UK court would grant permission unless it was convinced that the claim would be in the best interests of the company. Also, as ss 263 and 264 do not purport to state the only factors that a court may take into account, it would seem permissible for a court to consider whether an action was in the best interests of the company.

---

[404] See *Stainer v Lee* [2011] EWHC 2287 (Ch); [2011] BCC 134 at [45]–[46].

[405] Law Commission *Shareholder Remedies: Report on a Reference under section 3(1)(e) of the Law Commissions Act 1965* (Law Com No 246, Cm 3769) (London, Stationery Office, 1997) at paras 6.77–6.79.

[406] However, the Law Commission did not think that the fact that the derivative action was not in the interests of the company should mean that the court was bound to refuse leave: ibid at para. 6.80.

[407] This was the only criteria recommended by the Law Commission that was not adopted in the legislation.

[408] For instance, see A Keay 'Enlightened Shareholder Value, the Reform of the Duties of Company Directors and the Corporate Objective' [2006] LMCLQ 335; S Kiarie 'At Crossroads: Shareholder Value, Stakeholder Value and Enlightened Shareholder Value: Which Road Should the United Kingdom Take?' (2006) 17 *International Company and Commercial Law Review* 329; D Fisher 'The Enlightened Shareholder – Leaving Stakeholders in the Dark: Will Section 172(1) of the Companies Act 2006 Make Directors Consider the Impact of Their Decisions on Third Parties?' (2009) 20 *International Company and Commercial Law Review* 10; A Alcock 'An Accidental Change to Directors' Duties? (2009) 30 *Company Lawyer* 36; A Keay *Enlightened Shareholder Value Principle and Corporate Governance* (Abingdon, Routledge, 2013).

[409] [2008] CSOH 72 (Outer House, Court of Sessions, Lord Glennie) at [21].

[410] [2008] EWHC 2810 (Ch).

14.133 The Australian courts have discussed this concept frequently because the Australian legislation lays it down as a criterion, as does the Canadian legislation,[411] therefore the jurisprudence in these jurisdictions may be of some assistance.

14.134 The inclusion of best interests as a requirement is a recognition in Australia that a company might well have reasonable business reasons for not pursuing a cause of action.[412] The Australian courts, as well as those in Canada and New Zealand, have emphasised the fact that the requirement is that the claim *must be* in the best interests of the company, and an applicant cannot merely establish that the claim *appears to be* or is *likely to be* in the best interests of the company.[413] So the court is not invited to enter into some form of 'crystal ball gazing' – it must be satisfied on the facts that the action would be in the company's best interests. To establish this involves an applicant doing more than making out a prima facie case in this respect.[414] It has been held that the personal qualities of the applicant do not come into play in determining this condition,[415] for the focus is on the company. The applicant is required to adduce evidence in relation to:[416] the character of the company (is it a small or large company; is it a family company?); the business conducted by the company, in order to ascertain the effects of the proposed litigation on the proper conduct of the business; enabling a court to determine whether the substance of the relief that the applicant is seeking can be obtained without litigation; and the ability of the respondent to satisfy at least a substantial part of any order made in favour of the company in the proposed derivative action.

14.135 Whether or not the best interests of the company are fulfilled by permitting a derivative action is an objective test under the Australian provision.[417] Although neither the legislation nor the cases require it,[418] it has been argued that this assessment should involve a cost/benefit analysis.[419] The court might want the following kind of evidence to be adduced: how the proposed litigation will affect the proper conduct of the company's business; whether the substance of the relief sought is available by some other means; and the ability of the defendant to meet, at least, a substantial part of any judgment made in favour of the company.[420]

---

[411] Canada Business Corporations Act 1985, s 239(2)(c).

[412] Explanatory Memorandum to the Corporate Law Economic Reform Program Bill at para 6.38.

[413] For instance, see *Swansson v Pratt* [2002] NSWSC 583; (2002) 42 ACSR 313 at [55]–[56].

[414] *Re Bellman and Western Approaches Ltd* (1981) 130 DLR (3d) 193 at 201; *Vrij v Boyle* (1995) 3 NZLR 763 at 765; *Techflow (NZ) Ltd v Techflow Pty Ltd* (1996) 7 NZCLC 261, w138; *Swansson v Pratt* [2002] NSWSC 583; (2002) 42 ACSR 313 at [55]–[56].

[415] *Maher v Honeysett & Maher Electrical Contractors Pty Ltd* [2005] NSWSC 859 at [46]–[49].

[416] *Swansson v Pratt* [2002] NSWSC 583; (2002) 42 ACSR 313 at [57]–[60].

[417] *Talisman Technologies Inc v Qld Electronic Switching Pty Ltd* [2001] QSC 324 at [31].

[418] *Metyor Inc v Queensland Electronic Switching Pty Ltd* [2002] QCA 269; (2002) 42 ACSR 398 at [19].

[419] P Prince 'Australia's Statutory Derivative Action: Using the New Zealand Experience' (2000) 18 *Company and Securities Law Journal* 493 at 504.

[420] *Swansson v Pratt* [2002] NSWSC 583; (2002) 42 ACSR 313 at [58]–[60].

14.136 In Australia it has been said that where the company is insolvent, and even when it is in financial difficulties short of insolvency, the issue of the best interests of the company really involves deciding whether the claim would be in the interests of the creditors.[421] This is consistent with the fact that the common law in both the UK and Australia (and many parts of the Commonwealth) provides that directors, in discharging their duties to their company, have to take into account creditors' interests when their company is in financial difficulty.[422] This whole issue was discussed in detail in **Chapter 13**, and now involves some consideration of s 172(3) of CA 2006. UK courts might well consider creditor interests as part of their assessment, because of the fact that they are required to refuse permission to continue a derivative claim if a person acting in accordance with s 172 of the CA 2006 (duty to promote the success of the company) would not seek to continue the claim. Section 172 does provide in sub-s (3) that the duty imposed by s 172(1) has effect subject to any law that requires directors, in certain circumstances, to consider the interests of creditors.

C Costs

14.137 It is trite to say that the matter of costs is an issue in any litigation. It is perhaps the foremost obstacle for shareholders in initiating and pursuing a derivative action. In one empirical study it was concluded in Australia, which has a very similar statutory system to that in the UK, that the low numbers of derivative actions was due largely to the cost of taking proceedings.[423] A shareholder might have to secure litigation insurance or, like the shareholder in *Hughes v Weiss*,[424] come to an agreement with his or her solicitors that they act on a conditional fee basis as well as having insurance. In considering costs shareholders not only have to concern themselves with their own costs, they must accept that if the action fails the court might well order costs against them in line with the usual practice in the UK of costs following the result.

14.138 At common law the courts were able to order the company to indemnify a shareholder when granting permission to the shareholder to pursue a derivative action. This use of indemnification goes back to *Wallersteiner v*

---

[421] For example, see *Charlton v Baber* [2003] NSWSC 745; (2003) 47 ACSR 31 at [53]; *Chahwan v Euphoric Pty Ltd* [2006] NSWSC 1002 at [28]; *Promaco Conventions Pty Ltd v Dedline Printing Pty Ltd* [2007] FCA 586 at [41].

[422] *Liquidator of West Mercia Safetywear v Dodd* (1988) 4 BCC 30; *Facia Footwear Ltd (in administration) v Hinchliffe* [1998] 1 BCLC 218; *Re Pantone 485 Ltd* [2002] 1 BCLC 266; *Gwyer v London Wharf (Limehouse) Ltd* [2002] EWHC 2748 (Ch); [2003] 2 BCLC 153; *Re MDA Investment Management Ltd* [2003] EWHC 227 (Ch); [2004] BPIR 75; *Kinsela v Russell Kinsela Pty Ltd* (1986) 4 ACLC 215; (1986) 10 ACLR 395; *Jeffree v NCSC* (1989) 7 ACLC 556; (1989) 15 ACLR 217; *Spies v The Queen* [2000] HCA 43; (2000) 201 CLR 603; (2000) 173 ALR 529. See A Keay *Company Directors' Responsibilities to Creditors* (Abingdon, Routledge-Cavendish, 2007) at 153–220.

[423] R Tomasic 'Corporations Law Enforcement Strategies in Australia: The Influence of Professional, Corporate and Bureaucratic Cultures' (1993) 3 *Australian Journal of Corporate Law* 192 at 221.

[424] [2012] EWHC 2363 (Ch) at [55].

Moir (No 2).[425] The power to make such an order is now found in r 19.9E of the Civil Procedure Rules. It provides that a court *may* order the company to indemnify the shareholder bringing the derivative action against any costs incurred in relation to the permission application or the derivative action or both. This means that a court may indemnify a shareholder/applicant in relation to his or her own costs as well as an adverse order for costs made against the shareholder.[426]. If a costs order of this nature is to be made, it is normal to make it at the permission stage. It appears that the comments in a number of cases that considerable care should be taken by courts when deciding to order an indemnity[427] has turned into a general reluctance on the part of courts in the UK[428] to order any indemnity let alone an unrestricted indemnity. For example, in relation to the latter point indemnity orders have been made in two cases, *Kiani v Cooper*[429] and *Stainer v Lee*,[430] where permission to continue the derivative action was granted, but to a limited extent. In the former case Proudman J said that the indemnity order did not cover any adverse costs order made, and in the latter, Roth J placed an upper level of £40,000 but with liberty to apply for an extension of the order. In a case where a shareholder was successful in obtaining permission, *Parry v Bartlett*,[431] the court made no order concerning indemnity of costs. This could have been because there was no application for costs, but that is unlikely and we are not told in the judgment that that was the situation. The preliminary hearing to get permission is often robustly challenged and means that costs could be relatively high. All of this might well dissuade a shareholder from taking action.

14.139 If a court is minded to award an indemnity as to costs the impecuniosity of the claimants is not an issue.[432]

14.140 Some judgments given under the statutory scheme have provided, as did several cases decided at common law, some encouragement on the costs front to would-be applicants for permission. *Carlisle & Cumbria United Independent Supporters' Society Ltd v CUFC Holdings Ltd*[433] was a case which involved an appeal from a costs order made in relation to a claim relating to a breach of a director's duty, but which had been settled before the application to obtain permission to continue the claim as a derivative action was determined. Arden LJ said: 'As the action was a derivative action on behalf of the club, the trust [the applicant] had an expectation of receiving its proper costs from the

---

[425] [1975] QB 373.
[426] *Bhullar v Bhullar* [2015] EWHC 1943 (Ch) at [49].
[427] Ibid at [69].
[428] This is also the case in Australia. For example, see *Swansson v Pratt* (2002) 20 ACLC 1594; I Ramsay and B Saunders 'Litigation by Shareholders and Directors: An Empirical Study of the Statutory Derivative Action' (2006) 6 JCLS 397.
[429] [2010] EWHC 577 (Ch); [2010] BCC 463.
[430] [2010] EWHC1539 (Ch); [2011] BCC 134.
[431] [2011] EWHC 3146 (Ch).
[432] *Iesini v Westrip Holdings Ltd* [2009] EWHC 2526 (Ch); [2010] BCC 420 at [125].
[433] [2010] EWCA Civ 463; [2011] BCC 855.

companies on an indemnity basis if the action had gone forward ...'[434] In
Stainer v Lee[435] Roth J said that a shareholder who obtains the permission of
the court to proceed 'should *normally* be indemnified as to his reasonable costs
by the company'.[436] In *Bridge v Daley*,[437] while HH Judge Hodge QC did not
grant permission he did imply that if he had done so then the applicant would
be entitled to indemnification of costs.[438] This is consistent with comments
from judges in other Commonwealth jurisdictions. For instance, Barrett J of the
New South Wales Supreme Court in *Foyster v Foyster Holdings Pty Ltd*[439]
embraced the views of many commentators when he said that shareholders are
deserving of their costs because in legitimate cases they have been forced to
embrace the derivative action process in order to protect the company and as
their actions are necessary because the normal decision-makers of the company
have not been forthcoming, they should not be required to fund the
proceedings. But, as suggested earlier, other English judges, both when deciding
matters at common law[440] and under the statutory scheme, have tended to be
more cautious when it comes to ordering an award of costs in the context of
derivative actions, and the circumstances in which an order is to be made are
rather obscured.[441] Judges have emphasised the fact that the issue of costs is a
matter for the judge's discretion in each case.[442] The recent case-law clearly
demonstrates that the expectation referred to by Arden LJ in the previous
paragraph is not being fulfilled as the judges appeared to have taken their right
to use their discretion as tantamount to providing a basis for not granting a
costs order.

14.141 The cautious approach of the English courts[443] is manifested by the
fact that in only two of the nine cases[444] where the shareholder has been
successful under the statutory regime, from the time when the scheme was put
in force until 1 April 2016, has the court granted costs, and in these cases it
declined to grant costs without limit. For instance, as indicated earlier, in
Stainer v Lee[445] Roth J ordered an indemnity to a limit of £40,000. Therefore,
since the advent of the statutory scheme there is no English case that has
granted a successful applicant an unlimited indemnity for costs. In other
Commonwealth jurisdictions the courts have been more generous. In New
Zealand the courts have awarded costs in 37.5 per cent of cases where leave
was sought, and while this might not seem to be significant, one must

---

[434] Ibid, [8] and referring to *Wallersteiner v Moir (No 2)*.
[435] [2010] EWHC 1539 (Ch).
[436] Ibid, [56] (my emphasis).
[437] [2015] EWHC 2121 (Ch).
[438] Ibid at [86].
[439] [2003] NSWSC 135 at [13].
[440] For example, see *McDonald v Horn* [1995] 1 All ER 961 at 974.
[441] C Paul 'Derivative Actions under English and German Law' (2010) ECFR 81 at 96.
[442] For instance, see *Hook v Summer* [2015] EWHC (Ch) 3820 at [139].
[443] Also the position in Australia: I M Ramsay and B Saunders 'Litigation by Shareholders and
        Directors: An Empirical Study of the Statutory Derivative Action' (2006) 6 JCLS 397 at 432.
[444] But the applicant in one case where permission was given, *Cullen Investments Ltd v Brown*
        [2015] EWHC 473 (Ch); [2015] BCC 539 did not seek an order that the company fund the
        litigation.
[445] [2010] EWHC 1539 (Ch) at [56].

remember that courts have given permission in far more cases when compared with their UK counterparts, so we are dealing with larger numbers, and in 40 per cent of the cases where no order as to costs was made the applicant actually did not seek an order in relation to costs.[446]

14.142 In one recent decision, *Hook v Summer*,[447] where permission was granted, the judge, HH Judge Cook, said that he would not order the applicant/shareholder to be indemnified as that would give him an unfair advantage because the dispute was effectively one between the shareholders.[448] This is not an isolated approach. In *Bhullar v Bhullar*[449] Morgan J adopted a similar view. In both of these cases there was a recognition that the dispute that was subject to the application involved a dispute between shareholders and that unfair prejudice proceedings could either have been brought in lieu of the derivative action[450] or the derivative action was 'a stepping stone towards ... section 994 proceedings'.[451]

14.143 It does seem rather unfair and difficult to understand why a court would deny an indemnity for costs when an applicant for permission to continue derivative proceedings has jumped over all of the hurdles set for him or her in the two-stage process. It causes one to ask: what else must the applicant do? The problem is that there is nothing in the legislation or the rules of court that instructs the shareholder in this regard. The concern is that the shareholder is at the mercy of the court's discretion.[452] It has been suggested that to the extent that an applicant succeeds and costs are not ordered to be paid by the company, the company is unjustly enriched (and, possibly, so are other shareholders and non-shareholding stakeholders) as it gets the benefit from the efforts of the shareholder.[453] Further, if a court declines to award costs then a successful applicant might decide not to pursue the derivative action and this could mean that the ones who harmed the company get away scot free.

14.144 Other jurisdictions are far more generous to shareholders. In Germany if a shareholder's action is admitted then he or she will be indemnified.[454] The following position applies in New Zealand:[455]

---

[446] L Taylor 'The Derivative Action in the Companies Act 1993: An Empirical Study' (2006) 22 *New Zealand Universities Law Review* 337 at 355.

[447] [2015] EWHC 3820 (Ch).

[448] Ibid at [141].

[449] [2015] EWHC 1943 (Ch).

[450] *Hook v Summer* [2015] EWHC (Ch) 3820.

[451] *Bhullar v Bhullar* [2015] EWHC 1943 (Ch) at [70].

[452] L Thai 'How Popular are Statutory Derivative Actions in Australia? Comparisons with the United States, Canada and New Zealand' (2002) 30 *Australian Business Law Review* 118 at 136.

[453] J Wilson 'Attorney Fees and the Decision to Commence Litigation: Analysis, Comparison and an Application to the Shareholders' Derivative Action' (1985) 5 *Windsor Yearbook of Access to Justice* 142 at 177 and referred to in I M Ramsay 'Corporate Governance, Shareholder Litigation and Prospects for a Statutory Derivative Action' (1992) 15 *University of New South Wales Law Journal* 149 at 164.

[454] C Paul 'Derivative Actions under English and German Law' (2010) ECFR 81 at 113.

[455] Section 166.

'The court shall, on the application of the shareholder or director to whom leave was granted under section 165 to bring or intervene in the proceedings, order that the whole or part of the reasonable costs of bringing or intervening in the proceedings, including any costs relating to any settlement, compromise, or discontinuance approved under section 168, must be met by the company unless the court considers that it would be unjust or inequitable for the company to bear those costs.'

V FOLLOWING PERMISSION

14.145 If the court approves of the derivative claim, the litigation proceeds normally. The Civil Procedure Rules provide that the member is not able to discontinue, settle or compromise the claim without the permission of the court.[456] This requirement is an attempt to prohibit green-mailing, a practice which was discussed briefly earlier.[457]

14.146 The derivative claim will then be subject to all of the normal procedural matters that affect all litigation. Of course, if permission has been granted it might encourage the defendants to offer to settle the claim.

VI COMMON LAW PROCEEDINGS AND RETROSPECTIVE EFFECT

14.147 The right to issue derivative actions under the common law rules that existed prior to the enactment of the respective statutory derivative action scheme no longer apply, save where, as is discussed later, there is a multiple derivative action. Section 260(2) of the CA 2006 states that a derivative claim can now only be brought under Part 11 or in pursuance of an order of the court in unfair prejudice proceedings (now s 994 of the CA 2006).[458] The provisions were designed to codify common law rules.[459] The Australian regime is even more express than the UK's, for it is stated in s 236(3) of the Corporations Act 2001 that 'the right of a person at general law to bring, or intervene in, proceedings on behalf of a company is abolished'. This has been interpreted by the Australian courts as displacing the common law derivative action.[460] This is clearly the case where the cause of action on which the applicant relies occurred

---

[456] Part 19.9F

[457] See above at **14.115**.

[458] This is something recommended by the Law Commission in 1997 as it was of the view that it would make things confusing if actions could also be brought at common law: Law Commission *Shareholder Remedies: Report on a Reference under section 3(1)(e) of the Law Commissions Act 1965* (Law Com No 246, Cm 3769) (London, Stationery Office, 1997) at paras 6.51–6.55.

[459] A Alcock, J Birds and S Gale *Companies Act 2006: The New Law* (Bristol, Jordan Publishing, 2007) at 163.

[460] *Chapman v E-Sports Club Worldwide Ltd* [2000] VSC 403; (2000) 35 ACSR 462; *Karam v ANZ Banking Group Ltd* [2000] NSWSC 596; (2000) 34 ACSR 545; *Braga v Braga Consolidated Pty Ltd* [2002] NSWSC 603; *Metyor Inc v Queensland Electronic Switching Pty Ltd* [2002] QCA 269; (2002) 42 ACSR 398.

after the derivative claim provisions were put in force. But what about where the cause of action pre-dated the point when the provisions came into force, but no action had been taken? Given the time that the statutory scheme has been in place this is likely to be a relatively rare occurrence as any action is likely to be time barred, subject to some of the matters discussed earlier in **4.58–4.71**.If the cause of action did occur before the putting into force of the statutory regime should a derivative action be brought under the common law rules? The Australian case-law takes the view that the legislation will apply.[461] The reason given is that the statute was intended to be remedial, that is ameliorating the problems with the common law situation, and to deny this effect to those whose rights had accrued before the legislation became enforceable would be to frustrate the remedial purpose.[462] Furthermore, the Victorian Supreme Court made the point in *Advent Investors Pty Ltd v Goldhirsch*[463] that the intention of the legislature was to promote certainty concerning the nature of the derivative action and to avoid confusion because of divergence of common law principles vis à vis the statutory provisions.[464]

14.148 The Australian approach does seem to sit well with the fact the Law Commission's 1997 report recommended the complete replacement of the common law procedure with the statutory derivative action on the basis that if the former co-existed with a statutory scheme, there would be confusion,[465] as appears to be the case in Hong Kong where the two schemes both apply, sitting alongside each other. However, the UK sections were said by the Explanatory Notes to the CA 2006 not to formulate a substantive rule to replace the rule in *Foss v Harbottle*, but rather to reflect the recommendation of the Law Commission that there should be a 'new derivative procedure with more modern, flexible and accessible criteria for determining whether a shareholder can pursue an action'.[466] Arguably, though, the notes were merely pointing out that the statutory scheme introduced a new and all-encompassing approach to addressing derivative actions. Secondary legislation appears to support this latter interpretation of the Notes as art 20(3) of Sch 3 to the Companies Act 2006 (Commencement No 3, Consequential Amendments, Transitional Provisions and Savings) Order 2007[467] indicates, although not as clearly as one would like, that a derivative claim will only be allowed to proceed as a derivative claim, where the act complained of occurred before 1 October 2007

---

[461] *Karam v ANZ Banking Group Ltd* [2000] NSWSC 596; (2000) 34 ACSR 545; *Advent Investors Pty Ltd v Goldhirsch* [2001] VSC 59; (2001) 37 ACSR 529; *Roach v Winnote Pty Ltd* [2001] NSWSC 822; *Cadwallader v Bajco Pty Ltd* [2001] NSWSC 1193; *Swansson v Pratt* [2002] NSWSC 583; (2002) 42 ACSR 313.

[462] *Karam v ANZ Banking Group Ltd* [2000] NSWSC 596; (2000) 34 ACSR 545 at [27].

[463] [2001] VSC 59.

[464] The Australian courts are required by s 109H of the Corporations Act 2001 to have regard for any remedial purpose in interpreting the said Act.

[465] Law Commission *Shareholder Remedies: Report on a Reference under section 3(1)(e) of the Law Commissions Act 1965* (Law Com No 246, Cm 3769) (London, Stationery Office, 1997) at para 6.51–6.55.

[466] Ibid at para 6.15 and quoted by the Explanatory Notes to the Companies Act 2006 at para 491.

[467] SI 2007/2194. The Order came into force as far as this matter is concerned on 1 October 2007.

(the date of the commencement of Part 11), if it would have been able to do so under the law in force immediately before Part 11 was put in force. Hence, it would seem that where there is a cause of action that could be the subject of a derivative action, and it occurred before 1 October 2007, shareholders can only obtain permission to bring proceedings if they meet the requirements at common law.[468] The judgment of HH Judge Keyser QC in *Hughes v Weiss*[469] seems to support that although his Lordship did say that the court also must decide whether or not permission would be given under s 263. So, this means that the act complained of must be judged under both the statutory scheme and the common law. Where the act(s) complained of occurred partly before 1 October and partly after that then to the extent that the claim arises from acts or omissions that occurred before 1 October 2007 the law in force immediately before that date will apply.

VII COMPANIES IN LIQUIDATION OR INSOLVENT

14.149 When a company enters liquidation a liquidator will investigate the affairs of the company and he or she will consider, inter alia, whether the company has any legal rights that it can enforce against others with the aim of swelling the assets available for distribution to the creditors. As has been noted earlier in this book, a liquidator might well discover that directors have, in the past, breached their duties to the company. If that is the case then the liquidator might decide to take legal proceedings against the miscreant directors. But what if a liquidator decides not to, and this could be for a variety of reasons such as a belief that the risks of failing in a law suit are too high. Can a shareholder seek court permission to initiate derivative proceedings when the company is in liquidation and it is believed directors breached their duties? It is not intended to address the issue in any great depth as that has been done elsewhere,[470] but a few comments are perhaps apposite.

14.150 At common law the view seemed to be that no action could be brought by shareholders once a company had entered liquidation.[471] The rationale for this was that all claims relating to the company should be brought within the scope and control of the winding up, whether it is compulsory or voluntary.[472]

14.151 Since the statutory derivative action process was introduced into Australian law there have been a number of cases that have considered the issue at hand. Until recently it was probably possible to say that shareholders could seek permission to bring proceedings. The decisions that held this were all

---

[468] SI 2007/2194, art 20(2).

[469] [2012] EWHC 2363 (Ch).

[470] A Keay 'Can Derivative Proceedings be Commenced When a Company is in Liquidation?' (2008) 21 *Insolvency Intelligence* 49.

[471] For example, see *Cape Breton Company v Fenn* (1881) 17 Ch D 198; *Ferguson v Wallbridge* [1935] 3 DLR 66; *Scarel Pty Ltd v City Loan & Credit Corporation Pty Ltd* (1988) 12 ACLR 730; *Fargro Ltd v Godfroy* [1986] 1 WLR 1134.

[472] *Ferguson v Wallbridge* [1935] 3 DLR 66 at 84.

single judge decisions,[473] but they were large in number. The number of cases that were in favour of shareholders being entitled to seek permission led Barrett J of the New South Wales Supreme Court to say in *Carpenter v Pioneer Park Pty Ltd*[474] that the situation was such that the matter was now settled in Australia. However, two appellate decisions, one of the Victorian Court of Appeal in *Malhotra v Tiwari*[475] and the other of the New South Wales Court of Appeal in *Chahwan v Euphoric Pty Ltd t/as Clay & Michel*[476] have disturbed that notion. Although not having to decide the issue, the Victorian Court of Appeal said that 'ordinarily, it is inappropriate to allow derivative proceedings to be brought when a company is in liquidation because it would require the court to permit another to supplant the liquidator as the personification of the company for that purpose'.[477] The New South Wales court in *Chahwan v Euphoric Pty Ltd t/as Clay & Michel* was more forthright in clearly stating that the derivative proceedings regime should not be available in circumstances where the company the subject of the leave application is in liquidation.[478] The latter decision is not binding on courts in Australian jurisdictions, other than New South Wales, although it is highly persuasive and in a subsequent decision of the Federal Court of Australia, *Pearl Coast Divers Pty Ltd v Cossack Pearls Pty Ltd*,[479] Gilmour J followed *Chahwan*. To ensure consistency in the whole country it is likely that other courts will follow *Chahwan*.

14.152   The position taken by the court in *Chahwan v Euphoric Pty Ltd t/as Clay & Michel* appears to be in line with the position now in both New Zealand and Singapore. In *Hedley v Albany Power Centre Ltd (in liq)*,[480] Wild J if the New Zealand High Court concluded, albeit tentatively, that there was general support for the view that the statutory derivative jurisdiction was not available when the company the subject of proceedings was in liquidation; but that, even if it was, it ought not to be exercised.[481] In *Petroships Investment Pte Ltd v Wealthplus Pte Ltd*[482] the Singaporean Court of Appeal was quite clear in holding that when a company was in liquidation shareholders could not bring derivative proceedings.

---

[473]   For example, see, *Brightwell v RFB Holdings Pty Ltd* [2003] NSWSC 7; (2003) 44 ACSR 186 (NSW S Ct); *Charlton v Baber* [2003] NSWSC 745; (2003) 47 ACSR 31 (NSW S Ct); *William Kamper v Applied Soil Technology Pty Ltd* [2004] NSWSC 891 (NSW S Ct); *Mhanna v Sovereign Capital Ltd* [2004] FCA 1040 (Aust Fed Ct); *Carpenter v Pioneer Park Pty Ltd* [2004] NSWSC 1007; (2004) 186 FLR 104 (NSW S Ct); *Mhanna v Sovereign Capital Ltd* [2004] FCA 1252 (Aust Fed Ct); *Chahwan v Euphoric Pty Ltd* [2006] NSWSC (NSW S Ct); *Scuteri v Lofthouse* [2006] VSC 317; (2006) 202 FLR 1061 (Vic S Ct); *Promaco Conventions Pty Ltd v Dedline Printing Pty Ltd* [2007] FCA 586 (Aust Fed Ct), (in the last case mentioned, Siopis J indicated that he only took this view because of the of the fact that the preponderance of judicial opinion was in favour of leave being given in liquidations (at [38])).

[474]   [2004] NSWSC 1007; (2004) 186 FLR 104 at [8].

[475]   [2007] VSCA 101.

[476]   [2008] NSWCA 52.

[477]   [2007] VSCA 101 at [77].

[478]   [2008] NSWCA 52 at [124].

[479]   [2008] FCA 927.

[480]   [2005] 2 NZLR 196.

[481]   Ibid at [53].

[482]   [2016] SGCA 17.

14.153 In 2010 in *Cinematic Finance Ltd v Ryder*[483] Roth J said that derivative claims should not normally be brought on behalf of a company in liquidation (or administration). This suggests that an action would only able to be brought in exceptional circumstances.[484] This might leave some possibility of action although very rarely, whereas in Australia and Singapore (and possibly New Zealand) there seems to be no room whatsoever. Rather than looking at derivative actions shareholders might look at a different approach. The courts have an inherent power to sanction the bringing of proceedings by members in the name of the company when the company is in liquidation. In *Ragless v IPA Holdings Pty Ltd (in liq)*[485] the Full Court of the Supreme Court of South Australia referred to the inherent power. Debelle J, in giving the leading judgment, noted that this has been the situation in England for many years.[486] One assumes that the power has, as it has in Australia,[487] survived in the UK, and shareholders may seek to have courts exercise it. Another option might well be for the shareholder to seek, under s 167(3) or s 168(5) of the Insolvency Act 1986 in relation to companies subject to court winding up or under s 112 of the same statute for voluntary liquidation, to have the decision of the liquidator not to take action reviewed by a court.[488]

14.154 Of course, most companies that are in liquidation that is not a members' voluntary winding up will be insolvent. What about where a company is not in liquidation or administration, but is insolvent? It was held in *Cinematic Finance Ltd v Ryder*[489] that a member should not be granted permission when the company is insolvent, and this is probably because the creditors are the residual beneficiaries of the company's value and not the shareholders in such a situation. The problem with this is that if the company does not enter any formal insolvency regime, such as liquidation, there is no one who can bring proceedings on behalf of the company. Even if the company does enter a formal regime it could be some time before an office-holder will be able to institute proceedings and in all of this time the creditors are out of pocket.

---

[483] [2010] EWHC 3387 (Ch); [2012] BCC 797 at [22].

[484] R Tan, 'Leave to Commence Derivative Proceedings and the Threshold Issue of Liquidation' (2016) 37 Co Law 342.

[485] [2008] SASC 90.

[486] See, for example, *Cape Breton Co v Fenn* (1881) 17 Ch D 198 at 208; *Fargro Ltd v Godfroy* [1986] 1 WLR 1134 at 1136-1138.

[487] *BL & GY International Co Ltd v Hypec Electronics Pty Ltd.* [2001] NSWSC 705; (2001) 19 ACLC 1622; *Brightwell v RFB Holdings Pty Ltd* [2003] NSWSC 7; (2003) 44 ACSR 186; *Roach v Winnote Pty Ltd* [2001] NSWSC 82.

[488] For a discussion of this power, see A Keay *McPherson's Law of Company Liquidation* (London, Sweet and Maxwell, 3rd edn, 2013) at 603–607.

[489] [2010] EWHC 3387 (Ch); [2012] BCC 797.

VIII MULTIPLE DERIVATIVE ACTIONS

14.155 A 'multiple-derivative' action[490] is a derivative action that is entitled to be brought by minority shareholders of a parent company for a breach of duty owed to a direct or indirect subsidiary, certainly where control of the subsidiary is not independent of the parent company's board.[491] These actions are designed to prevent corporate wrongdoers being insulated from judicial intervention.[492]

14.156 Despite the fact that the Law Commission[493] was of the view that multiple-derivative claims will be rare, they have caused some debate in the common law world, and they might well not be as rare as the Law Commission suggested. They can occur where one has a simple or complicated corporate group situation with layers of companies. It is trite to say that corporate groups are a frequent part of the commercial landscape. And there have been at least three cases in the UK in recent times.

14.157 Prior to the advent of the UK's statutory regime it was clear that shareholders could bring a multiple-derivative action in the UK.[494] Since the introduction of the statutory regime there has been, until quite recently, uncertainty as to whether that remains the case. The reason for this uncertainty is that Parliament made it clear that the statutory regime in the CA 2006 entirely swept away the previous common law regime, because the statutory regime provided for a comprehensive scheme.[495]

14.158 Other jurisdictions have not been blighted by such uncertainty in recent times as they have had decisions making the position clear. In *Waddington Ltd v Chan Chun Hoo Thomas*[496] the Hong Kong Court of Appeal held that there was no objection to this kind of action. What was intended to be covered by this designation is that a shareholder in a holding company might bring a general law derivative action aimed at obtaining a remedy for a wholly owned subsidiary of that company for a wrong done to the subsidiary. The court said[497] that:

---

[490] Variations of it might be called 'double derivative claims' or 'triple derivative claims' depending on how many company layers are involved.

[491] R Hollington *Shareholders' Rights* (London, Sweet and Maxwell, 5th edn, 2007) at 146.

[492] *Waddington Ltd v Chan Chun Hoo Thomas* [2008] HKCFA 63; (2008) 11 HKCFAR 370; [2009] 4 HKC 381; [2009] 2 BCLC 82 at [66].

[493] Shareholder Remedies: Report on a Reference under section 3(1)(e) of the Law Commissions Act 1965 (Law Com No 246, Cm 3769) (London, Stationery Office, 1997) at para 6.109–6.110.

[494] See, *Wallersteiner v Moir (No.2)* [1975] QB 373; *Halle v Trax BW Ltd* [2000] BCC 1020; *Trumann Investment Group v Societe General SA* [2003] EWHC 1316 (Ch); *Airey v Cordell* [2006] EWHC 2728 (Ch); [2007] BCC 785.

[495] This was confirmed by Briggs J in *Re Fort Gilkicker Ltd* [2013] EWHC 348 (Ch); [2013] BCC 365 at [28].

[496] [2006] HKCA 196. This case involved what is sometimes called a 'double-derivative claim'.

[497] Ibid at [30] per Rogers VP.

'The circumstances of today, where large companies, particularly public companies, conduct their affairs with a multiplicity of subsidiary companies which are no more than assets wholly controlled and, in practice, virtually indistinguishable from the holding company, are very different from the days in which derivative actions were first devised. If it indeed be the case that a subsidiary company is no more than an asset which is controlled in much the same way as any other asset of a holding company, I cannot say that the law should deprive a shareholder of the holding company an opportunity to have a wrong righted, if that wrong was technically suffered by the subsidiary, but the effect of the wrong would resound to the holding company.'

14.159 An appeal to the Hong Kong Court of Final Appeal[498] on this point was dismissed. The Court noted that the application for permission was brought pursuant to the common law scheme (proceedings having been initiated before the advent of the statutory regime in 2005), but it accepted in dicta that a multiple derivative action was permitted under the Hong Kong derivative action scheme as the legislation did not abolish the common law process.[499]

14.160 In the New South Wales case of *Oates v Consolidated Capital Services Pty Ltd*[500] X was the holding company of Y and Y was the holding company of Z. The applicant, a former officer of X (under the Australian legislation officers and former officers are entitled to apply for leave to bring derivative actions[501]) sought to bring proceedings against the directors of Y and Z for breach of duties owed to Y and Z. The court said that a double derivative action (a type of multiple-derivative claim) was contemplated by the Australian legislation,[502] and the applicant would have been able to bring proceedings on behalf of Y in relation to breaches perpetrated against Y, if he had fulfilled the criteria set out in the legislation (which he did not, according to the judge). But the applicant was not entitled to bring a derivative action on behalf of Z as Y was the one who could apply for leave,[503] and the applicant could not cause Y to apply for leave.[504] The main reason why the judge would have permitted a double derivative claim[505] is that s 236(1)(a)(i) of the Australian legislation provides that a claim may be brought by a member of the company or of a related body corporate, and a subsidiary would come within that expression. The approach taken in *Waddington* and *Oates* indicates that the courts are prepared to take a realistic view of the fact that companies do operate in corporate groups.

14.161 But, the UK position is different from both Hong Kong and Australia. In relation to the former the common law remains in force and sits alongside

---

[498] *Waddington Ltd v Chan Chun Hoo Thomas* [2008] HKCFA 63; (2008) 11 HKCFAR 370; [2009] 4 HKC 381; [2009] 2 BCLC 82.
[499] See Companies Ordinance, sections 2 and 168BC to 168BG.
[500] [2008] NSWSC 464.
[501] Corporations Act 2001, s 236(1)(a)(ii). It is to be noted that New Zealand includes a similar provision of the Australian legislation. See Companies Act 1993, s 165(1)(a) (NZ).
[502] [2008] NSWSC 464 at [26], [34].
[503] Ibid at [35], [36].
[504] Ibid at [37].
[505] Ibid at [34].

the statutory regime. In the latter the legislation arguably provides specifically for multiple-derivative claims. Prima facie neither of these situations exists in the UK, that is, the common law derivative action does not exist any longer and the CA 2006 does not permit members of related corporate bodies to bring proceedings as does the Australian legislation.

14.162 Whether or not the UK courts will support multiple-derivative claims was not formally decided until the decision in *Re Fort Gilkicker Ltd*.[506] In that case Briggs J (as he then was) said that in determining what kind of effect the 2006 Act has wrought upon the common law derivative action is ultimately a question of construction of the legislation. And legislation is to be construed as only withdrawing common law rights if it does so expressly or by necessary implication.[507] His Lordship's conclusion was that the CA 2006 did not do away with the multiple-derivative claim.[508] His reasons were, first, there was before 2006 a common law procedural device which permitted claims in multiple-derivative situations.[509] Second, the CA 2006 provided a comprehensive statutory code in relation to derivative actions, and s 260 applied Ch 1 of Pt 11 only to that part of the old common law device that was labelled as derivative actions, leaving other instances of its application unaffected.[510] Third, Parliament did not expressly abolish the whole of the common law derivative action in relation to companies.[511] Fourth, the legislation could have easily have been drafted to indicate that it was intended to abolish all aspects of the common law processes, including multiple-derivative claims, and it did not.[512] Briggs J said that the court is, where necessary, prepared to permit derivative claims to be brought on behalf of companies in wrongdoer control by persons other than their immediate shareholders without regarding those cases as special, and in particular without thinking it necessary to distinguish between 'ordinary' and 'multiple' derivative actions.[513]

14.163 Subsequently David Richards J (as he then was) in *Abouraya v Sigmund*[514] applied the judgment in *Re Fort Gilkicker Ltd*. While not specifically applying the latter case, although referring to it, Morgan J in *Bhullar v Bhullar*[515] also agreed that a multiple derivative action was subject to the common law rules that survived the statutory regime's enactment.

14.164 In *Abouraya v Sigmund*[516] David Richards J did say that the approach of the law in England would not prevent a multiple derivative claim being brought by a person who was a shareholder of a foreign company.

---

[506] [2013] EWHC 348 (Ch); [2013] BCC 365.
[507] Ibid at [29].
[508] Ibid at [44].
[509] Ibid.
[510] Ibid at [45].
[511] Ibid at [46].
[512] Ibid at [47].
[513] Ibid at [24].
[514] [2014] EWHC 2777 (Ch).
[515] [2015] EWHC 1943 (Ch).
[516] [2014] EWHC 2777 (Ch).

14.165 Certainly the judgment of Briggs J in *Re Fort Gilkicker Ltd* might be seen to have produced a just result, and it is to be applauded for that. However, aspects of the reasoning might not satisfy all commentators. Also, while the judgment solves one problem, it creates another in that we now have a dual system, namely the statutory scheme applying to 'ordinary' derivative claims, and the common law applying to multiple-derivative claims. It would be best if Parliament amended the Act to provide clearly for multiple-derivative claims, perhaps in a way that is similar to the Australian scheme.

IX FOREIGN DERIVATIVE CLAIMS

14.166 An issue that was raised in the case of *Novatrust Ltd v Kea Investments Ltd*[517] was whether UK courts could still hear derivative claims that had been initiated in a foreign jurisdiction. In this case HHJ Pelling QC (sitting as a judge of the High Court) rejected the argument that the enactment of the statutory derivative regime meant that UK courts could only hear claims that were covered by the regime. The judge recognised that the regime did create a comprehensive code concerning the jurisdiction to entertain derivative claims, but he was of the opinion that this was only the case as far as claims to which it applied.[518] His Lordship went on to say that there was nothing in the regime that abrogated the common law rules that previously applied and as far as England and Wales were concerned the regime only applies to English and Welsh companies.[519] Thus the regime did not apply to foreign companies. This approach is consistent with the views expressed in *Re Fort Gilkicker Ltd*[520] and *Abouraya v Sigmund*,[521] both of which were mentioned above in the context of multiple-derivative actions, and means that the regime had not abolished the whole of the existing common law relating to derivative claims.

X APPEALS FROM DERIVATIVE CLAIM HEARINGS

14.167 If permission is sought and secured by a claimant and then the claimant does not succeed with his or her action at the final hearing, does the claimant have to obtain a further grant of permission in order to appeal or to seek leave to appeal? This has not been answered by a UK decision, but the Federal Court of Australia has held that permission must be secured, and the ordinary principles that apply to any consideration of a grant of permission to continue a derivative action will be taken into account and applied in the decision of the court.[522]

---

[517] [2014] EWHC 4061 (Ch).
[518] Ibid at [27].
[519] Ibid.
[520] [2013] EWHC 348 (Ch); [2013] BCC 365.
[521] [2014] EWHC 2777 (Ch).
[522] *Wood v Links Golf Tasmania Pty Ltd* [2013] FCA 143.

XI THE EFFECT OF THE NEW PROCEDURE

14.168 Joan Loughrey, Andrew Keay and Luca Cerioni[523] found in a study conducted before the derivative scheme took effect that lawyers believed that s 172 of the CA 2006 cannot be viewed in isolation from the new derivative action. Taken together these were described as likely to subject directors to a 'double whammy'.[524] It had been asserted that the new scheme would make it easier for activist shareholders and special interest groups to bring proceedings.[525] But, it would not appear that activist shareholders have, to date, availed themselves of the opportunity. Loughrey et al reported[526] that there was evidence before the new regime became operative of a widespread concern about derivative litigation amongst companies. In a survey undertaken by the law firm, Herbert Smith, 79 per cent of respondents believed that the CA 2006 would lead to an increased number of derivative actions. Although only 54 per cent were quite, or very, concerned about this, concern was mainly expressed by the smaller companies.[527] The concern over more litigation might have been based on the fact that shareholders might have more scope to bring proceedings compared with the situation that existed at common law. For example, at common law shareholders were not able, save where directors had benefited from their negligence, to initiate derivative actions against directors for negligence,[528] whereas under the new statutory derivative scheme in Part 11 of the CA 2006, shareholders are now able to bring proceedings where directors have been negligent, provided that permission can be secured from the court. Some lawyers suggested the fact that the new law allows actions to be launched against directors where they have been negligent, without any self-serving benefits for them, might permit activist shareholders to initiate a derivative action alleging that directors have negligently failed to have regard to one of the factors in s 172, or placed undue weight on other factors.[529] Also, some felt that there might well be more derivative actions because of the fact that it is arguably easier now to establish a breach of duties of care of directors. Not only was the likelihood of litigation mooted in client briefings, but, while the Bill, on which the CA 2006 is based, was passing through Parliament, there

---

[523] 'Legal Practitioners, Enlightened Shareholder Value and the Shaping of Corporate Governance' (2008) 8 *Journal of Corporate Law Studies* 79 at 96.

[524] A phrase first used by Lord Hodgson of Astley Abbots in the Grand Committee Stage of the Bill, 27 Feb 2006, Hansard HL Vol 679, col GC2, and subsequently adopted by Herbert Smith *In the Line of Fire – Directors Duties under the Companies Act 2006*, at 4 and Mills and Reeve *Briefing*, October 2006; Clifford Chance *The Companies Act 2006* (November 2006) at 3-4; Not all lawyers took this approach – see Ashurst *The Companies Act 2006* (November 2006) at 3.

[525] A Reisberg *Derivative Actions and Corporate Governance* (Oxford, OUP, 2007) at 146.

[526] 'Legal Practitioners, Enlightened Shareholder Value and the Shaping of Corporate Governance' (2008) 8 JCLS 79 at 97.

[527] G Milner Moore and R Lewis (Herbert Smith) *In the Line of Fire – Directors Duties under the Companies Act 2006*, at 4.

[528] *Daniels v Daniels* [1978] Ch 406.

[529] G Milner Moore and R Lewis (Herbert Smith) *In the Line of Fire – Directors Duties under the Companies Act 2006* at 3; Norton Rose *Shareholder Rights*; Freshfields Bruckhaus Deringer *Companies Act 2006: Directors Duties* (November 2006) at 11; Clifford Chance *The Companies Act 2006* (November 2006) at 4.

were very many high profile press stories, often based on lawyers' comments, to the effect that the new derivative action would increase litigation, and making the link between derivative litigation and s 172's predecessor clauses.[530] Loughrey et al found that lawyers were advising that while the risk of increased litigation is high, such litigation was unlikely to be successful.[531] The fact of the matter is that to date any concern that there would be an avalanche of proceedings has not been proved to be correct. As mentioned at various points in the Chapter, there have been relatively few claims made. This could be for a number of reasons. First, benefits of the process will go to the company, so that might be why shareholders are reluctant to commence proceedings. Admittedly, the member might secure some benefit from an action, but they might be somewhat discouraged by the fact that other members will get a free ride as far as any benefits going to members are concerned, while they who take action will bear most of the risks. Second, in *Langley Ward Ltd v Trevor* the court commented that permission applications were 'set fair to become another time-consuming and expensive staple in the industry of satellite litigation'.[532] And this is something that any prospective applicants have to bear in mind; the concern is that they might be deterred from instituting legitimate derivative actions. Third, and allied to the last point, the member who is contemplating taking action is always in danger of having to pay legal and other costs.

14.169 One commentator firmly stated in 2007 that the courts were likely to take as robust an approach with the statutory regime as they did under common law,[533] and therefore the amount of litigation may well not increase significantly, and that has proved to be correct.

14.170 We should not be surprised by the fact that there have not been a large number of applications for permission. This was and continues to be the experience in Australia. A wide-ranging Australian study in 2005 found that there had only been 31 cases initiated in the five years since the derivative claim process was put into a statutory form, and this was not much of an increase on the number commenced under the common law procedure in the five years before codification.[534]

XII CONCLUSION

14.171 As Reisberg has stated: 'Derivative claims provide an important mechanism by which shareholders can hold directors to account in exceptional

---

[530] See 'Directors on Guard Against Legal Action' *Financial Times*, 2 November 2005; 'Fears Weight of Law Will Fall on Directors' *Financial Times*, 3 May 2006; 'Bill leaves company's vulnerable on directors' duties' *Financial Times*, 8 May 2006; 'Company Law Reform' *Financial Times*, 9 May 2006; 'Threat to Directors Exaggerated, says Green Pressure Group' *Financial Times*, 12 May 2006.

[531] (2008) 8 JCLS 79 at 105.

[532] [2011] EWHC 1893 (Ch) at [61].

[533] D Ohrenstein 'Derivative Actions' (2007) 157 NLJ 1372.

[534] I M Ramsay and B Saunders 'Litigation by Shareholders and Directors: An Empirical Study of the Statutory Derivative Action' (2006) 6 JCLS 397 at 417.

and clearly defined circumstances.'[535] What we can conclude after nine years of the operation of the statutory scheme is that it is not providing a more accessible and more certain process. The fact is that the courts have kept a tight rein on the use of the derivative process.[536] Also, while one might argue that there has been a little more certainty introduced in the interpretation and application of the derivative action provisions in recent years, there remains some uncertainty concerning several criteria discussed in this Chapter.[537] The foregoing together with some of the issues raised earlier in the Chapter means that the following assertion appears to have merit:[538]

> 'While the reforms were never meant to make it materially easier for shareholders to litigate on the company's behalf, it was intended that the criteria should be clearer than what existed at common law, that the concept of wrongdoer control should be discarded, and that the procedure should become more efficient and less lengthy and costly. There is a real risk that these objectives will not be met.'

---

[535] *Derivative Actions and Corporate Governance* (Oxford, OUP, 2007) at 162.

[536] A Keay and J Loughrey 'An Assessment of the Present State of Statutory Derivative Proceedings' in J Loughrey (ed) *Directors' Duties and Shareholder Litigation in the Wake of the Financial Crisis* (Cheltenham, Edward Elgar, 2013), at 226.

[537] See, A Keay 'Assessing and Rethinking the Statutory Scheme for Derivative Actions Under the Companies Act 2006' (2016) 16 *Journal of Corporate Law Studies* 39 for a detailed discussion of the uncertainties and flaws in the scheme.

[538] A Keay and J Loughrey 'An assessment of the present state of statutory derivative proceedings' in J Loughrey (ed) *Directors' Duties and Shareholder Litigation in the Wake of the Financial Crisis* (Cheltenham, Edward Elgar, 2013), at 226 (footnote omitted).

CHAPTER 15

CONSEQUENCES OF BREACH

I INTRODUCTION

15.1 While at various points in the book there has been some consideration of the consequences which flow from a breach of duty, this chapter focuses solely on the issue and considers the consequences of breaches of the general duties in broad terms. The Chapter is essentially about relief that is available to the company where a breach is established. The Chapter is designed principally to be introductory as the issue of relief is a huge one and it is not possible to do it justice in one chapter of a book of this kind.

15.2 The new companies legislation adds little to the situation that existed before codification. The Parliament obviously decided that it would not seek to codify the remedies that are available where a breach of duty occurs, even though the CLRSG formulated a code of remedies in its Final Report.[1] It is notable that neither Australia nor New Zealand has at any time decided to codify remedies. Some might see the non-codification of remedies as a shame as the area tends to be confused and leads to some uncertainty.[2] But the task would be difficult as the ensuing discussion will demonstrate.

15.3 Section 178(1) of the CA 2006 states that the consequences of a breach are the same as would apply if the corresponding common law rule or equitable principle applied. The next subsection indicates that the general duties of directors, save for the duty of care, skill and diligence, are enforceable in the same manner as any other fiduciary duty owed to a company by its directors. While there is nothing in Chapter 2 of Part 10 that designates the duties as fiduciary the fact that s 178(2) provides that the duties in ss 171–173 and 175–177 are enforceable in the *same way as any other* fiduciary duty owed to the company indicates that they are fiduciary in nature.

15.4 It is at the point when one comes to considering remedies that the trustee analogy to which **Chapter 2** of the book adverted comes to the fore. It provides

---

[1]   *Modern Company Law for a Competitive Economy: Final Report* (London, DTI, 2001) vol 1 at para 15.28–15.30. Richard Nolan argued for it in 'Enacting Civil Remedies in Company Law' (2001) 1 JCLS 245.

[2]   P Davies *Gower and Davies' Principles of Company Law* (London, Sweet and Maxwell, 8th edn, 2008) at 479.

'a strong remedial structure'.[3] For instance, if, in breach of their duties, directors dispose of company property, they are regarded as acting in breach of trust.

15.5 The law provides a formidable array of equitable remedies that are available to a company that is the subject of a breach of fiduciary duty and it has been suggested[4] that a reason given for litigants in many Commonwealth jurisdictions, including the UK, attempting to establish a breach of fiduciary liability is to give them access to this great array. The remedies embrace both proprietary and personal means of redress, as we will see. There is a strong deterrent element in the imposition of liability for breach of fiduciary duty and this is evident in the consequences of a breach and the kind of liability that can be imposed.[5]

15.6 The Chapter is structured as follows. First, it considers the various forms of relief that may be available to a company in relation to a breach of duty when taking action against a miscreant director. This is then followed by a discussion of the relief that may be sought against any third parties who are involved in some way in the breach of duty.

15.7 It must be emphasised that the following does not purport to be a comprehensive discussion of the area. It is merely to be seen as an important companion to the earlier discussion in the book.

II THE RELIEF

15.8 The following presupposes the fact that a breach of duty by a director can be established. It examines the various kinds of relief that might or might not be available to a claimant.

15.9 The point should be made at the outset that remedies are discretionary and must be fashioned to fit the kind of case being mounted and actual facts.[6] The three primary remedies consequent upon a breach of a fiduciary obligation, according to *Nocton v Lord Ashburton*,[7] are dealt with first, namely compensation, accounts and restoration of property. All of the remedies discussed below are equitable except for damages, dismissal and recovery on the basis of money had and received.

---

[3] P Davies *Gower and Davies' Principles of Company Law* (London, Sweet and Maxwell, 7th edn, 2003) at 380.

[4] See, for example, D J Hayton and O R Marshall *Commentary and Cases On The Law Of Trusts And Equitable Remedies* (London, Sweet & Maxwell, 10th edn, 1996) at 33ff and referred to in J Lowry and R Edmunds 'The Corporate Opportunity Doctrine: the Shifting Boundaries of the Duty and its Remedies' (1998) 61 MLR 515 at 525.

[5] *Re Tobian Properties Ltd; Maidment v Attwood* [2012] EWCA Civ 998; [2012] BCC 98 at [23].

[6] *Warman International Ltd v Dwyer* (1995) 182 CLR 544 at 559.

[7] [1914] AC 932 at 956–957. Also, see *Warman International Ltd v Dwyer* (1995) 182 CLR 544.

15.10 Most breaches are likely to be of fiduciary duties and it should be noted at the outset that entitlement to a remedy in equity for breach of a fiduciary duty does not depend upon showing personal enrichment of the fiduciary, or of another, at the hands of the fiduciary. Such relief extends to conduct of the fiduciary that causes loss and detriment by reason of the breach of an essential obligation of the fiduciary relationship.[8]

15.11 Lord Toulson in the Supreme Court decision of *AIB Group (GB) v Redler*[9] has said that the essential right of a beneficiary (the company in our context) is to have the trust (the company's property and opportunities in the corporate context) duly administered in accordance with the provisions of the trust and the general law. He went on to say:[10]

> 'Where there has been a breach of that duty, the basic purpose of any remedy will be either to put the beneficiary in the same position as if the breach had not occurred or to vest in the beneficiary any profit which the trustee may have made by reason of the breach (and which ought therefore properly to be held on behalf of the beneficiary).'

A Damages or equitable compensation

15.12 A claim for this can occur where the company has suffered loss,[11] such as where there has been a breach of a fiduciary duty that leads to either a reduction in the funds or assets of the company, or causes the company to make expenditures. According to Mummery LJ in *Gwembe Valley Development Co Ltd (in receivership) v Koshy,*[12] 'the paradigm case is the application of the company's property, without authority, for a purpose which is in the interests of the directors, but is not in the interests of the company'.[13] Where there has been a breach of a fiduciary duty the claim will be for equitable compensation. The critical element here is that the company has suffered loss, and that the loss was caused by the breach, and would not have been incurred save for the breach.[14] Causation is required for liability to be established as liability is not unlimited,[15] but a breach of fiduciary duty is a wrong in itself,

---

[8]   *Westpac Banking v Bell Group* [2012] WASCA 157; (2012) 89 ACSR 1 at [883].

[9]   [2014] UKSC 58; [2015] AC 1503.

[10] Ibid at [64].

[11] *Bishopsgate Investment Management Ltd v Maxwell (No 2)* [1993] BCLC 1282 and affirmed on appeal at [1993] BCLC 814; *Gemstone Corporation of Australia Ltd v Grasso* (1993) 12 ACSR 47 (SA S Ct). In the former case the director was required to indemnify the company against all losses suffered by the company as a consequence of his default. Also, see *Dorchester Finance Co Ltd v Stebbing* [1989] BCLC 498; *J J Harrison (Properties) Ltd v Harrison* [2002] 1 BCLC 162 at 172 (CA).

[12] [2003] EWCA Civ 1048; [2004] 1 BCLC 131.

[13] Ibid at [142].

[14] *Target Holdings Ltd v Redferns* [1996] AC 421 at 432, 434 (HL); *Swindle v Harrison* [1997] 4 All ER 705 at 718, 733 (CA); *Hill v Rose* [1990] VR 129 (Vic S Ct); *Gemstone Corporation of Australia Ltd v Grasso* (1993) 12 ACSR 47 (SA S Ct).

[15] *AIB Group (GB) v Redler* [2014] UKSC 58; [2015] AC 1503 at [87].

regardless of whether a loss could be foreseen.[16] If more than one director is in breach they are liable jointly and severally.[17]

15.13 Equitable compensation is designed to achieve exactly what the word compensation suggests: to make good a loss in fact suffered by the company and which, using hindsight and common sense, can be seen to have been caused by the breach.[18]

15.14 Companies that have suffered at the hands of directors who breached their duty of care, skill and diligence (under s 174 of the CA 2006) are usually going to be limited to a claim for damages.[19] The company will seek damages to cover any loss that can be attributed to the breach.[20] As mentioned earlier, s 178(2) excepts a breach of the duty of care, skill and diligence from being enforceable in the same way as a breach of a fiduciary duty. The remedy structure for such a duty is not as complicated as it is for the breach of a fiduciary duty. Generally speaking a company will only be interested in seeking damages from the errant director(s), as would a claimant in a tort action alleging a breach of a duty of care. Where there is a breach of any duties owed under Chapter 2 of Part 10, other than that in s 174, equitable compensation may be requested. There has been debate over the years as to whether damages should be based on common law or equitable principles. It is likely that it is the former where there is a breach of s 174, as it is excluded by s 178(2).[21] Nothing really has to be said about damages for breach of s 174. It has been submitted that there is little to be had in distinguishing between relief at common law and in equity as the distinction has been blurred.[22] Nevertheless, equitable compensation is a more flexible concept than damages[23] as illustrated by the comment in *Maguire v Makaronis*[24] that: '[Equitable] remedies will be fashioned according to the exigencies of the particular case so as to do what is "practically just" as between the parties. The fiduciary must not be "robbed"; nor must the beneficiary be unjustly enriched.' Most of the following in this part of the Chapter relates to equitable compensation.

15.15 Sometimes it is said that companies can claim damages for breach of fiduciary duties. As suggested earlier, strictly speaking the claim would be for

---

[16] Ibid at [86].

[17] *Re Lands Allotment Co* [1894] 1 Ch 616 (CA).

[18] *Target Holdings Ltd v Redferns* [1996] AC 421 at 439.

[19] According to obiter comments of Millett LJ in *Bristol and West Building Society v Mothew* [1998] 1 Ch 1; [1996] 4 All ER 698 (CA), a company was entitled to obtain equitable compensation for breach of the duty of skill and care before the codification of duties.

[20] The company will have to demonstrate causation and that the damage sustained is not remote. See *Re HIH Insurance Ltd (in liq)* [2002] NSWSC 171; (2002) 41 ACSR 72 at [748].

[21] A view also taken by Professors Len Sealy and Sarah Worthington in *Cases and Materials in Company Law* (OUP, 8th edn, 2008) at 334.

[22] P Davies and S Worthington *Gower and Davies' Principles of Modern Company Law* (London, Sweet and Maxwell, 9th edn, 2012) at 615.

[23] *Sinclair Investments (UK) Ltd Versailles Trade Finance Ltd* [2011] EWCA Civ 347; [2011] 3 WLR 1153; [2011] 2 BCLC 501 at [47].

[24] (1997) 188 CLR 449 at 496.

equitable compensation.[25] Courts are able to make a monetary award in equity to a company where there has been a breach of an equitable duty.[26] The measure of compensation in respect of losses sustained by reason of breach of duty by a trustee or other fiduciary is determined by equitable principles and these do not necessarily reflect the rules for assessment of damages in tort or contract.[27] Equitable compensation is the remedy that is granted against trustees or other fiduciaries to require compensation for the loss experienced by the party to whom duties are owed, because of the breach. In addressing a claim for equitable compensation for breach of trust the court may have regard to what would have happened but for the breach.[28] The amount of compensation is based on the loss suffered by the company rather than the gain made by the director.[29] It is not altogether clear in English law whether a defendant can rely on contributory negligence. But in *Nationwide Building Society v Balmer Radmore*[30] Blackburne J said that an intentional breach of duty was analogous to an intentional tort and so contributory negligence could not be relied on. It has been suggested that the analogy is not a strong one.[31] Nevertheless, the Australian High Court has rejected the notion of contributing fault when considering the compensation to be awarded to the company.[32] All in all it is likely that it would be held that a company cannot have its right to compensation diminished for this reason.

15.16 There are two aspects to equitable compensation, namely the defendant's wrongful act caused loss to the claimant and the claimant would not have been placed in the position that he or she has, had not a wrong been perpetrated.[33] Indeed the object of equitable compensation is to restore persons who have suffered loss to the position in which they would have been but for the breach of the duty.[34] In *Target Holdings Ltd v Redferns*[35] Lord Browne Wilkinson said:[36]

---

[25] *Catt v Marac Australia Ltd* (1986) 9 NSWLR 639 at 659–60; *Yore Contractors Pty Ltd v Holcon Pty Ltd* (1990) 2 ASCR 663 at 669; *Coleman Taymar Ltd v Oakes* [2001] 2 BCLC 749 at 769.

[26] *Nocton v Lord Ashburton* [1914] AC 932 at 956.

[27] *Pilmer v Duke Group Ltd (in liq)* [2001] HCA 31; (2001) 207 CLR 165 at [85].

[28] *Murad v Al-Saraj* [2005] EWCA Civ 959 at [110].

[29] *Catt v Marac Australia Ltd* (1987) 9 NSWLR 639 at 659; *Yore Contractors Pty Ltd v Holcon Pty Ltd* (1990) 2 ASCR 663 at 669.

[30] [1999] Lloyds Rep PN 241.

[31] R Mulheron 'Contributory Negligence: Should Professional Fiduciaries Accept All the Blame?' (2003) 19 *Professional Negligence* 422.

[32] *Pilmer v Duke Group Ltd (in liq)* [2001] HCA 31; (2001) 207 CLR 165 at [86].

[33] *Target Holdings Ltd v Redferns* [1996] AC 421 at 432 per Lord Browne-Wilkinson.

[34] *Nocton v Lord Ashburton* [1914] AC 932 at 952 per Viscount Haldane LC; *Target Holdings Ltd v Redferns* [1996] AC 421 at 432 per Lord Browne-Wilkinson.

[35] [1996] 1 AC 421 at 439.

[36] This was accepted by Lord Millett in *Libertarian Investments Ltd v Hall* [2014] 1 HKC 368 at [168].

'Equitable compensation for breach of trust is designed to achieve exactly what the word compensation suggests: to make good a loss in fact suffered by the beneficiaries and which, using hindsight and commonsense, can be seen to have been caused by the breach.'

15.17 McLachlin J in the Canadian case of *Canson Enterprises Ltd v Boughton & Co*[37] stated:

'In summary, compensation is an equitable monetary remedy which is available when the equitable remedies of restitution and account are not appropriate. By analogy with restitution, it attempts to restore to the plaintiff what has been lost as a result of the breach, ie the plaintiff's lost opportunity. The plaintiff's actual loss as a consequence of the breach is to be assessed with the full benefit of hindsight. Foreseeability is not a concern in assessing compensation, but it is essential that the losses made good are only those which, on a common sense view of causation, were caused by the breach.'

15.18 A director may be held liable for the company's loss, even though he or she has not himself or herself received any of the company's misapplied property, if in breach of duties.[38]

15.19 A claim in equity for compensation against a director in respect of loss suffered will depend upon showing that there is an adequate or sufficient connection between the equitable compensation claimed and the breach of fiduciary duty.[39] Unlike in tort law the link required by equity involves no inquiry as to whether the loss was caused by or flowed from the breach but whether the loss would have happened if there had been no breach.[40] Once a breach of duty has been established and the loss sustained by the company, the director has the onus of establishing that the loss would have occurred notwithstanding the breach.[41]

15.20 According to the Court of Appeal in *Gwembe Valley Development Co Ltd (in receivership) v Koshy*[42] a director is not legally responsible for loss, which the company would probably have suffered even if the director had complied with the fiduciary-dealing rules on disclosure of interests.[43] A director is not entitled to argue against a finding that a breach occurred by demonstrating that the company would have approved or ratified the transaction if there had been disclosure.[44] In *Brickenden v London Loan & Savings Co*[45] Lord Thankerton in the Privy Council said that when a fiduciary:

---

[37] (1991) 85 DLR (4th) 129 at 163.
[38] *Gwembe Valley Development Co Ltd (in receivership) v Koshy* [2003] EWCA Civ 1048; [2004] 1 BCLC 131 at [142].
[39] *Maguire v Makaronis* [1997] HCA 23; (1997) 188 CLR 449 at 473; *AIB Group (GB) v Redler* [2014] UKSC 58; [2015] AC 1503.
[40] *Westpac Banking v Bell* [2012] WASCA 157; (2012) 89 ACSR 1 at [903].
[41] *Sojourner v Robb* [2006] 3 NZLR 808.
[42] [2003] EWCA Civ 1048; [2004] 1 BCLC 131.
[43] Ibid at [147].
[44] *Brickenden v London Loan & Savings Co* [1934] 3 DLR 465 at 469 (PC).
[45] Ibid.

'commits a breach of his duty by non-disclosure of material facts, which his constituent is entitled to know in connection with the transaction, he cannot be heard to maintain that disclosure would not have altered the decision to proceed with the transaction, because the constituent's action would be solely determined by some other factor, such as the valuation by another party of the property proposed to be mortgaged. Once the Court has determined that the non-disclosed facts were material, speculation as to what course the constituent, on disclosure would have taken is not relevant.'

15.21 According to Professor Matthew Conaglen[46] many have taken the view that equitable compensation was not available where there had been a breach of the no-conflict or no-profit rules as they were not duties, but disabilities;[47] equitable compensation could not be ordered, as disabilities were regarded as only justifying restitutionary relief and not compensatory relief. However, the learned commentator has argued that equitable compensation was available for a breach of the no-conflict or no-profit rules.[48] If that view were correct then a breach of s 175 or s 176 of the CA 2006 would permit a court to award equitable compensation. But even if it were not correct, because the no-conflict and no-profit rules have been effectively codified and made duties, compensation should be available.

15.22 It has been opined that to be able to claim equitable compensation a company must establish something more than mere breach, such as improper conduct or some form of wrongdoing.[49] The idea is that the director must have committed something that amounts to equitable fraud. Conaglen notes[50] that the approach that requires more than a mere breach seems to gain support from the speech of Lord Watson in *Cavendish Bentinck v Fenn*[51] and the judgment of Romer LJ in *Re Leeds and Hanley Theatres of Varieties Ltd,*[52] but he adds that allowing for equitable compensation where there is fraud demonstrates no more than 'a contingent connection between the two: fraud is clearly a sufficient connection for an award of equitable compensation, but the other judgments in these cases all suggest it is not a necessary condition'.[53]

15.23 Equitable compensation is a monetary remedy that is available when the equitable remedies of restitution and account are not appropriate.[54] When awarding equitable compensation, the court does not apply the common law

---

[46] 'Equitable Compensation for Breach of Fiduciary Rules' (2003) 119 LQR 246 at 247.

[47] See *Tito v Wadell (No 2)* [1977] Ch 106 at 248.

[48] Ibid at 262.

[49] 'Conflicts of Interest, Unjust Enrichment and Wrongdoing' in Cornish, Nolan, O'Sullivan and Virgo (eds) *Restitution: Past, Present and Future* (Hart Publishing, 1998) at 104 and cited in M Conaglen 'Equitable Compensation for Breach of Fiduciary Rules' (2003) 119 LQR 246 at 260.

[50] Conaglen, ibid, at 261.

[51] (1887) 12 App Cas 652 (HL).

[52] [1902] 2 Ch 809 (CA).

[53] M Conaglen 'Equitable Compensation for Breach of Fiduciary Rules' (2003) 119 LQR 246 at 261.

[54] *Canson Ltd v Boughton & Co* (1991) 85 DLR (4th) 129 at 163 per McLachlin J.

principles of remoteness of damage and causation.[55] But the authorities indicate that there must be some causal connection between the breach of trust and the loss to the estate for which compensation is recoverable.[56] The court must identify the criteria which supply an adequate or sufficient connection between the equitable compensation claim and the breach of fiduciary duty.[57] Even if the immediate cause of the loss is the dishonesty or failure of a third party, the director would be obliged to make good the loss of his or her company if, but for the breach, such loss would not have occurred.[58] The question for the courts to ask is: would there have been any loss if there were no breach?[59] Unlike with the common law, equity does not, when considering whether an adequate or sufficient connection exists, permit an examination of the relative importance of contributing causes.[60]

15.24 In *Gwembe Valley Development Co Ltd (in receivership) v Koshy*[61] Mummery LJ held that when determining whether any compensation, and, if so, how much compensation, should be paid for loss claimed to have been caused by actionable non-disclosure, the court is not precluded by authority or by principle from considering what would have happened if the material facts had been disclosed. If the commission of the wrong has not caused loss to the company, why should the company be entitled to elect to recover compensation, as distinct from rescinding the transaction and stripping the director of the unauthorised profits made by him?

15.25 In making an assessment of compensation the courts should have the full benefit of hindsight and commonsense in determining what loss has been caused by the breach.[62] The general rule is that assessment will be made at the date of judgment, and not based on an assessment at the date of the breach.[63] But, there is authority for the proposition that there might be unusual circumstances that justify assessing compensation at an earlier date.[64]

15.26 While the aim of the remedy is to make good the loss sustained by the company, the compensation might be assessed by reference to the gain made by the director or other defendant. This would be where the director has wrongly

---

[55] *Target Holdings Ltd v Redferns* [1996] 1 AC 421 at 434, 436; *Murad v Al-Saraj* [2005] EWCA Civ 959 at [59].

[56] *Target Holdings Ltd v Redferns* [1996] 1 AC 421 at 432, 434 (HL); *Swindle v Harrison* [1997] 4 All ER 705 at 718, 733 (CA); *Southern Real Estate Pty Ltd v Dellow and Arnold* [2003] SASC 318; (2003) 87 SASR 1 at [41]; *AIB Group (GB) v Redler* [2014] UKSC 58; [2015] AC 1503 at [87].

[57] *Maguire v Makaronis* [1997] HCA 23; (1987) 188 CLR 449 at 473.

[58] *Target Holdings Ltd v Redferns* [1996] 1 AC 421 at 434; *Bartlett v Barclays Trust Co (Nos 1 & 2)* [1980] Ch 515.

[59] *Youyang Pty Ltd v Minter Ellison Morris Fletcher* [2003] HCA 15; (2003) 212 CLR 484.

[60] *Barton v Armstrong* [1976] AC 104 at 118 (HL).

[61] [2003] EWCA Civ 1048; [2004] 1 BCLC 131 at [147].

[62] *Target Holdings Ltd v Redferns* [1996] 1 AC 421 at 439; *O'Halloran v R T Thomas & Family Pty Ltd* (1998) 29 ACSR 148 at 157–158.

[63] *Target Holdings Ltd v Redferns* [1996] 1 AC 421 at 437.

[64] *Southern Real Estate Pty Ltd v Dellow* [2003] SASC 318 at [52] (SA S Ct (Full Ct)).

appropriated and exploited a corporate opportunity which is the company's.[65] But, for the most part, in such a situation the company will seek an account.

15.27 Unlike the remedy of account there is little, if any, deterrent element with compensatory relief for all that the director risks is giving up the benefits of his or her wrongful activity. As Professor Sarah Worthington has pointed out, there may be little deterrence when a director's only punishment is disgorging the fruits of the wrongdoing as against the chance of taking substantial benefits.[66] The Supreme Court has said in *AIB Group (GB) v Redler*[67] that absent fraud, it would not be right to impose or maintain a rule that gave redress to a beneficiary for loss which would have been suffered even if the trustee had properly performed its duties.[68]

15.28 All of the directors who are parties to the breach will be liable jointly and severally, and any director(s) who are sued are at liberty to seek contribution under the Civil Liability (Contribution) Act 1978.

15.29 If a director is subject to a service contract and the company feels that he or she has breached duties which also involve a breach of the contract, the company must choose between claiming damages or an account for profits.[69] We come to the remedy of account next.

B Account of profits

15.30 The account of profits remedy is ancient and notoriously difficult to apply in practice.[70] It might be available where profits have been made by the director as a consequence of the breach of a fiduciary duty.[71] The idea is that the directors are liable to account for the profits stemming from the breach, such as where any company asset that has been misused provides gains to the director.[72] In *Bristol and West Building Society v Mothew*[73] Millett LJ described such relief as 'primarily restitutionary or restorative rather than compensatory'.[74]

15.31 An account might be a preferable remedy compared with equitable compensation as the actual profits secured by the director might be greater than

---

[65] *Dempster v Mallina Holdings Pty Ltd* (1994) 15 ACSR 1.
[66] 'Corporate Governance: Remedying and Ratifying Directors' Breaches' (2000) 116 LQR 638 at 639.
[67] [2014] UKSC 58; [2015] AC 1503.
[68] Ibid at [62].
[69] *Coleman Taymar Ltd v Oakes* [2001] 2 BCLC 749.
[70] See Kerly *An Historical Sketch of the Equitable Jurisdiction of the Court of Chancery* (1890) at 148-149; Meagher, Gummow and Lehane *Equity: Doctrines and Remedies* (Butterworths, 3rd edn, 1992) at 659-660; *Dart Industries Inc v Decor Corporation Pty. Ltd* [1993] HCA 54; (1993) 179 CLR 101 all sources referred to in *Warman International Ltd v Dwyer* (1995) 182 CLR 544 at [23].
[71] *Regentcrest plc v Cohen* [2002] 2 BCLC 80.
[72] *J J Harrison (Properties) Ltd v Harrison* [2002] 1 BCLC 162 (CA).
[73] [1998] Ch 1.
[74] Ibid at 18.

loss suffered by the company. As with the right to have property restored, there is no need for the company to establish loss[75] as the company is entitled to call on the director to account for any profits that are connected with his or her breach.[76] The purpose of the account is to strip a defaulting fiduciary of his or her profit,[77] and it is not to compensate the one to whom the fiduciary duty is owed.[78] The fact that no loss needs to be established by the company is a part of equity's aim of imposing stringent rules on fiduciaries in order to act as a deterrent against breach.[79] Importantly, the liability of a fiduciary to account does not depend on whether the one to whom the fiduciary duty was owed was unwilling, unlikely or unable to make the profits for which an account is taken or that the fiduciary acted honestly and reasonably.[80] Through this remedy companies are able to claim, in effect, windfall profits.

15.32 Once a breach is established the onus is on the fiduciary to prove that certain profits that have been made by the fiduciary are not for him or her to account.[81] In *Warman International Ltd v Dwyer*[82] the Australian High Court said, in a joint judgment, that:

> 'It is for the defendant to establish that it is inequitable to order an account of the entire profits. If the defendant does not establish that that would be so, then the defendant must bear the consequences of mingling the profits attributable to those earned by the defendant's efforts and investment, in the same way that a trustee of a mixed fund bears the onus of distinguishing what is his own.'[83]

15.33 But, a fiduciary is not able to mount a defence based on an argument that he or she would have made the profit even if there had been no breach of fiduciary duty.[84] Courts are disinclined to consider hypothetical situations.[85]

---

[75]   *Murad v Al-Saraj* [2005] EWCA Civ 959 at [58]; *Foster Bryant Surveying Ltd v Bryant* [2007] EWCA Civ 200; [2007] 2 BCLC 239 at [88], [101]; *Warman International Ltd v Dwyer* (1995) 182 CLR 544 at 557.

[76]   Ibid.

[77]   *United Pan–Europe Ltd v Deutsche Bank* AG [2000] 2 BCLC 461 at [47]; *Murad v Al-Saraj* [2005] EWCA Civ 959 at [56].

[78]   *United Pan–Europe Ltd v Deutsche Bank* AG [2000] 2 BCLC 461 at [47].

[79]   *Caffrey v Darby* (1801) 6 Ves 488; 31 ER 1159; *Murad v Al-Saraj* [2005] EWCA Civ 959 at [74]; *Re Tobian Properties Ltd; Maidment v Attwood* [2012] EWCA Civ 998; [2012] BCC 98 at [23].

[80]   *Furs Ltd v Tomkies* [1936] HCA 3; (1936) 54 CLR 583 at 592; *Regal (Hastings) Ltd v Gulliver* [1967] 2 AC 134 at 144-145; *Industrial Development Consultants Ltd. v Cooley* [1972] 1 WLR 443; *Warman International Ltd v Dwyer* (1995) 182 CLR 544 at 557; *Murad v Al-Saraj* [2005] EWCA Civ 959 at [59].

[81]   *Warman International Ltd v Dwyer* (1995) 182 CLR 544; *Murad v Al-Saraj* [2005] EWCA Civ 959 at [77].

[82]   (1995) 182 CLR 544.

[83]   Ibid at [34] and referring to *Hospital Products Ltd v United States Surgical Corporation* (1984) 156 CLR at 109-110; *Brady v Stapleton* [1952] HCA 62; (1952) 88 CLR 322 at 336.

[84]   *Gwembe Valley Development Co Ltd v Koshy* [2003] EWCA Civ 1048; [2004] 1 BCLC 131; *Murad v Al-Saraj* [2005] EWCA Civ 959 at [67].

[85]   *Murad v Al-Saraj* [2005] EWCA Civ 959 at [76].

15.34 A director is not liable to account for all of his or her profits – only those which relate to the breach.[86] For an account there is no requirement on the company to establish a causal link between breach and the profits.[87]

15.35 It has been held that an account is taken to establish what profits the company would have lost, and it is not a forfeiture of all profits,[88] thus the court has to be careful that the liability of the fiduciary does not lead to unjust enrichment for the company.[89] As the Australian High Court said in *Warman International Ltd v Dwyer*:[90]

> 'This is not to say that the liability of a fiduciary to account should be governed by the doctrine of unjust enrichment, though that doctrine may well have a useful part to play; the stringent rule requiring a fiduciary to account for profits can be carried to extremes and…in cases outside the realm of specific assets the liability of the fiduciary should not be transformed into a vehicle for the unjust enrichment to the plaintiff.'

15.36 So that the company is not unjustly enriched, the profits that can be claimed by the company may be limited to a portion of the profits made by the director, as they were in *Warman International* where the fiduciary was able to establish that some of the profits that had been made were due to his skill and effort. In this case the fiduciary was permitted to retain those latter profits. In such a case the director might be entitled to deduct from the profits that have been made and payable to the company, costs that relate to the making of the profits, such as expenses and overheads sustained.[91] Besides being entitled to claim expenses there is case-law to suggest that directors, like trustees, are permitted to claim remuneration for the work which they have done in making the profits.[92] This whole issue is discussed later in the Chapter.[93]

15.37 Ordinarily a director will be ordered to render an account of the profits made within the scope and ambit of his or her duty.[94] Of course, if the loss suffered by the company exceeds the profits made by the director, the company may elect to have a compensatory remedy against the director.[95] That election will bind the company.[96]

15.38 The assessment of the profit will often be extremely difficult in practice; accordingly it has been said that '(w)hat will be required on the inquiry … will

---

[86] *Bhullar v Bhullar* [2003] 2 BCLC 241; [2003] BCC 711 at 733-734; *Warman International Ltd v Dwyer* (1995) 182 CLR 544; *Murad v Al-Saraj* [2005] EWCA Civ 959 at [62].

[87] *Ultraframe (UK) Ltd v Fielding* [2005] EWHC 1638 (Ch) at [1588].

[88] *Murad v Al-Saraj* [2005] EWCA Civ 959 at [85].

[89] *Warman International Ltd v Dwyer* (1995) 182 CLR 544 at 561; *Ultraframe (UK) Ltd v Fielding* [2005] EWHC 1638 (Ch) at [1588].

[90] (1995) HCA 18 at [33]; (1995) 182 CLR 544 at 561.

[91] *CMS Dolphin Ltd v Simonet*; [2002] BCC 200 at [97].

[92] *Boardman v Phipps* [1967] 2 AC 46 (HL).

[93] Below at **15.67–15.71**.

[94] *Boardman v Phipps* [1967] 2 AC 46 at 127 per Lord Upjohn.

[95] *Warman International Ltd v Dwyer* (1995) 182 CLR 544 at 559.

[96] *Kendall v Marsters* (1860) 2 De [2001] 2 BCLC 704G F and J 200 (45 ER 598).

not be mathematical exactness but only a reasonable approximation'.[97] What is necessary however is to determine as accurately as possible the true measure of the profit or benefit obtained by the fiduciary in breach of his or her duty.[98] There is Australian authority for the proposition that a director is only to account for profits until the time when the company becomes aware that the director is improperly receiving benefits.[99]

15.39   The order of the court, once it accepts that an account is appropriate, depends on the facts. Lewison J (as he then was) said in *Ultraframe (UK) Ltd v Fielding*:[100]

> 'In some cases it will be appropriate to order an account limited in time; or limited to profits derived from particular assets or particular customers; or to order an account of all the profits of a business subject to all just allowances for the fiduciary's skill, labour and assumption of business risk. In some cases it may be appropriate to order the making of a payment representing the capital value of the advantage in question, either in place of or in addition to an account of profits.'[101]

15.40   Although an account of profits, like other equitable remedies, is said to be discretionary, it is granted or withheld according to settled principles. It will be defeated by equitable defences such as estoppel, laches, acquiescence and delay.[102] In *Ultraframe (UK) Ltd v Fielding*[103] Lewison J added another possible ground for withholding an account, namely that the taking of an account would be a disproportionate response to the gain that appears to have been made, or to the nature of that which has been misused.[104]

15.41   In *Kak Loui Chan v Zacharia*[105] Deane J said that:

> 'the liability to account for a personal benefit or gain obtained or received by use or by reason of fiduciary position, opportunity or knowledge will not arise in circumstances where it would be unconscientious to assert it or in which, for example, there is no possible conflict between personal interest and fiduciary duty and it is plainly in the interests of the person to whom the fiduciary duty is owed that the fiduciary obtain for himself rights or benefits.'

---

[97]   *My Kinda Town Ltd v Soll* [1982] FSR 147 at 159 per Slade J.
[98]   *Hospital Products v United States Surgical Corp* (1984) 156 CLR at 110. Also, see *Warman International Ltd v Dwyer* (1995) 182 CLR 544.
[99]   *Warman International Ltd v Dwyer* (1995) 182 CLR 544 at 559.
[100] [2005] EWHC 1638 (Ch) at [1576] (there was an appeal on costs – [2006] EWCA Civ 1660; [2007] 2 All ER 983).
[101] [2005] EWHC 1638 (Ch) at [1588].
[102] *Warman International Ltd v Dwyer* [1995] HCA 18 at [28]. See *Re Jarvis (decd)* (1958) 1 WLR 815 at 820–821.
[103] [2005] EWHC 1638 (Ch) at [1576].
[104] Ibid at [1580].
[105] (1984) 154 CLR 178 at 204–205.

15.42 The conduct of the company may be such as to make it inequitable to order an account. For a company is not entitled to stand by, aware of the breach, and permit the defendant to make profits and then claim entitlement to those profits.[106]

15.43 In *Warman International Ltd v Dwyer*[107] it was said that:

'In determining the proper basis for an account of profits, it is of first importance in this, as in other cases, to ascertain precisely what it was that was acquired in consequence of the fiduciary's breach of duty. And, in some situations, it may also be relevant to ascertain what was lost by the plaintiff.'

15.44 It has been held that it is not enough for a miscreant fiduciary to show that, if he or she had not been fraudulent, the fiduciary could have got the consent of the party to whom he or she owed the fiduciary duty to allow the retention of the profit. It is only actual consent which obviates the liability to account.[108]

15.45 If on an account a court finds that the director must pay a sum to his or her company, the court might also order that interest be paid on that sum by the director.[109]

C Restoration of the company's property

15.46 If there is a misappropriation of company property, that is property beneficially held by the company, and the property ends up being held by the director in such a way that it involves a breach of fiduciary duty, then he or she will be regarded as a constructive trustee of the property,[110] a position that is discussed later in the Chapter.[111] The director can be obliged to restore the property to the company, rather than pay the value of the property.[112] The company has a proprietary and not just a personal claim in such a case.[113] The advantage that the company has is that if the director is impecunious or is not insured then it does not have to line up with all of his or her creditors, but has priority in relation to the relevant property, for the property does not belong to

---

[106] *Re Jarvis (decd)* (1958) 1 WLR 815 at 820-821 citing *Clegg v Edmondson* (1857) 8 De G M and G 787 (44 ER 593); *Aquaculture Corp (No 3)* (1986) 1 NZIPR 677 at 690.

[107] (1995) HCA 18 at [40].

[108] *Murad v Al-Saraj* [2005] EWCA Civ 959 at [71].

[109] *Warman International Ltd v Dwyer* (1995) 182 CLR 544 at 570.

[110] *J J Harrison (Properties) Ltd v Harrison* [2001] EWCA Civ 1467; [2002] 1 BCLC 162 (CA) at [27]-[30]. For a discussion of constructive trustee, see for example, the judgments of Millett LJ in *Bristol and West Building Society v Mothew* [1998] 1 Ch 1; [1996] 4 All ER 698 (CA); *Paragon Finance plc v D B Thakerar & Co* [1999] 1 All ER 400; *Sinclair Investments (UK) Ltd Versailles Trade Finance Ltd* [2011] EWCA Civ 347; [2011] 3 WLR 1153; [2011] 2 BCLC 501; *Williams v Central Bank of Nigeria* [2014] UKSC 10; [2014] AC 1189.

[111] Below at **15.59-15.66.**

[112] *Yore Contractors Pty Ltd v Holcon Pty Ltd* (1990) 2 ACSR 663 (NSWSC).

[113] *Sinclair Investments (UK) Ltd Versailles Trade Finance Ltd* [2011] EWCA Civ 347; [2011] 3 WLR 1153; [2011] 2 BCLC 501.

the director. Ordinarily the company can trace the property, as far as it can be traced under equity, and recover it in rem.

15.47 If a director breaches his or her duty and receives company property but then transfers it to a third party, the third party remains liable to restore the property. But in such a case the claim of the company does not have priority over other unsecured creditors,[114] unless it were established that the third party knowingly assisted in a breach of duty, when the company would have both a personal and a proprietary remedy against that third party,[115] and this would provide priority. The breach would have to fit into the first two categories identified by Lord Neuberger MR in *Sinclair Investments (UK) Ltd Versailles Trade Finance Ltd*[116] and accepted in *FHR European Ventures LLP v Mankarious,*[117] namely (in a company/director context) that an asset or money was or had been beneficially the property of the company and was misappropriated by the director or the miscreant director acquired the asset or money by taking advantage of an opportunity or right that was properly that of the company.

15.48 The claim of the company might effectively be a claim for money representing the value of the property. In *Neptune (Vehicle Washing Equipment Ltd) v Fitzgerald,*[118] Lightman J ordered the director in that case who was in breach, to repay the sum of £100,000 which was paid to him as a result of the breach of his duty to act in good faith. Besides the property itself the company might be able to claim in equity any profits made in breach of the duty where the profits in fact emanated from use of the company property.

15.49 Unlike with a claim for damages or equitable compensation the company is not obliged to establish loss. Company property involves things that might not be regarded as property in the ordinary sense of the word, including an opportunity or a contract, as discussed in **Chapters 9** and **10**.

D Injunction and declaration

15.50 Injunctions and declarations are remedies that will usually be sought when a breach of duty is threatened or imminent, but has not occurred as yet. In *Key-TV Ltd v Ramsay*[119] an injunction was sought, and granted, to prevent the director dealing with an invention that was owned by the company. The remedies might also be sought by the company to prevent a director disclosing company information to others. Perhaps one of the most obvious cases is where a director threatens to commence a competing business and to use his or her company's records etc.[120] Of course, due to lack of information about what a

---

[114] *Bairstow v Queen's Moat Houses plc* [2001] 2 BCLC 531 (CA).
[115] *Clark v Cutland* [2004] 1 WLR 783; [2003] 2 BCLC 393 at [31].
[116] [2011] EWCA Civ 347; [2011] 3 WLR 1153; [2011] 2 BCLC 501 at [88].
[117] [2013] EWCA Civ 17; [2013] 3 All ER 29; [2013] 2 BCLC 1.
[118] [1995] 1 BCLC 352.
[119] [2008] All ER (D) 323 (Feb) at [45].
[120] For example, see *Pacifica Shipping Co Ltd v Andersen* [1986] 2 NZLR 328.

director and/or his or her associates are planning to do and when, it might not be possible to obtain these remedies before a breach occurs.

15.51 Claimants might well seek a declaration that the director holds property as trustee for the company.[121] If it does then it will usually require another order either awarding equitable compensation (where the property has reduced in value) or ordering the defendant to return the property to the company. The court might indeed order an account where the property has yielded benefits.[122] A declaration relating to the holding of property might occur where the director misappropriates company property or if the director receives a benefit from a third party in breach of his or her duties (such as under s 176 of the CA 2006). Where a declaration is made in relation to company property, the company has a proprietary interest and will have priority over other creditors of the person holding the property as trustee.

E Rescission

15.52 A company is entitled to rescind a contract where, for instance, the director failed to disclose an interest in a proposed transaction or arrangement with the company (in breach of s 177 of the CA 2006).[123] This right may be lost under the normal circumstances in equity, namely where restitutio in integrum is not possible,[124] the company affirms the contract,[125] the company delays in acting, or a third party acting bona fide has gained rights as a result of the contract. If the company is stopped from rescinding for some reason, then it cannot obtain a declaration that the holder of the property holds it as a constructive trustee. This was the case in *Pacifica Shipping Co Ltd v Andersen*[126] where the company could not restore fully what had passed to it under the contract with a third party.

15.53 Where the contract cannot be avoided, then the company is left to claim either an account or equitable compensation.[127]

F Money had and received

15.54 Where a company has paid money out to a director or third party under a contract, but following a breach of duty, it could reclaim it on the basis of a

---

[121] For example, see *Key-TV Ltd v Ramsay* [2008] All ER (D) 323 (Feb); *Paul A Davies (Aust) Pty Ltd v Davies (No 2)* (1982) 8 ACLR 1.

[122] *Boardman v Phipps* [1967] 2 AC 46.

[123] For example, see *Re Cape Breton Co* (1885) 29 Ch D 795 at 803 (CA); *Transvaal Lands Co v New Belgium (Transvaal) Land and Development Co* [1914] 2 Ch 488 at 505 (CA); *Armstrong v Jackson* [1917] 2 KB 822 at 824 (HC).

[124] Davies has questioned how relevant this ground is given the courts' broad powers to order financial adjustments when ordering rescission: P Davies *Gower and Davies' Principles of Company Law* (London, Sweet and Maxwell, 7th edn, 2003) at 427.

[125] For example in *Re Cape Breton Co* (1885) 29 Ch D 795.

[126] [1986] 2 NZLR 328.

[127] *Movitex Ltd v Bulfield* (1986) 2 BCC 99,403 at 99,440; *J J Harrison (Properties) Ltd v Harrison* [2001] EWCA Civ 1467; [2002] 1 BCLC 162 (CA) at [54].

common law remedy, namely money had and received, being money that was wrongly paid to the director or third party under the contract.[128] It would have to be demonstrated that the receipt of the money was affected by a recognised vitiating factor such as fraud, mistake etc. An example of this is found in *Guinness plc v Saunders*[129] where a payment to a director could be recovered on this basis because the sum was paid to the director where there was a total absence of consideration.

G Dismissal

15.55 As executive directors are employees, a company might dismiss them summarily for the breach which could be regarded as serious misconduct. Non-executives are not employees and cannot be dismissed. But they could be removed by a general meeting resolution under s 168 of the CA 2006.

H Proprietary relief

15.56 While actions involving claims of a personal nature tend to be more commonplace where there is a breach, companies will also have, as a result and in certain cases, proprietary relief enabling them to trace an interest in money or other property into the hands of persons other than the wrongdoer.[130] The company could actually claim the return of property *in specie* instead of a payment covering its value. The benefit of the proprietary claim is particularly important when the defendant(s) is impecunious or not insured, for if the company had only a personal claim then it would only be an unsecured creditor in the defendant's bankruptcy, but if it had a proprietary claim then it would gain priority, over other creditors, in that it could claim specific property. However, establishing the right to a proprietary remedy is more difficult than establishing a personal remedy.[131] It is clear law that where a director's breach entails the misappropriation of company assets the company has both a proprietary and a personal claim against the director. If the assets have been transferred to other parties, then the company might be able to trace it in the hands of the transferee and recover the assets. But there has been some divergence in the case-law as to whether a company has a proprietary claim in relation to a breach where a director does not misappropriate company assets but commits a breach such as accepting a secret commission or bribe and being, now, in breach of s 176. This issue was discussed in detail in Chapter 11 in relation to secret commissions and bribes.[132] The following summarises the

---

[128] *Primlake Ltd v Matthews Associates* [2006] EWHC 1227 (Ch); [2007] 1 BCLC 686 at [335] and referring to *Woolwich Equitable Building Society v Comrs of Inland Revenue* [1993] AC 70; *Westdeutsche Landesbank Girozentrale v Islington LBC* [1996] AC 669, 683 and 710; *Guinness Mahon & Co Ltd v Kensington and Chelsea RLBC* [1999] QB 215. Also, see *Schmierer v Taoutk* [2004] NSWSC 345; (2004) 207 ALR 301.

[129] [1996] 2 AC 663.

[130] For example, see *Clark v Cutland* [2004] 1 WLR 783 (CA).

[131] R Goode 'The Recovery of a Director's Improper Gains: Proprietary Remedies for Infringement of Non-Proprietary Rights' in E McKendrick (ed) *Commercial Aspects of Trusts and Fiduciary Obligations* (Oxford, Clarendon Press, 1992) at 140.

[132] At **11.38-11.39**.

state of the law. Originally in *Metropolitan Bank v Heiron*[133] and *Lister & Co v Stubbs*[134] the Court of Appeal took the view that in the acceptance of a secret commission kind of situation, the company had a personal claim to the benefit obtained by the director, but it had no proprietary claim. This view was approved of three times by the Court of Appeal.[135] But it was disapproved of by the Privy Council in 1994 in *A-G for Hong Kong v Reid*.[136] Subsequently, and quite recently, the Court of Appeal in both *Sinclair Investments (UK) Ltd Versailles Trade Finance Ltd*[137] and *FHR European Ventures LLP v Mankarious*[138] rejected the approach posited in *A-G for Hong Kong v Reid* and followed the line set out in the old Court of Appeal decisions.[139] In the former of these Court of Appeal cases Lord Neuberger MR said that it was the general rule for the Court to follow its own decisions and leave it to the Supreme Court to overrule them.[140] The Supreme Court did overrule it in the appeal to it in relation to *FHR European Ventures LLP v Mankarious* (*FHR European Ventures LLP v Cedar Capital Partners LLC*[141]). While the judgment of the Supreme Court recognised that if a principal was granted a proprietary right the agent's unsecured creditors could lose out, as the principal would have a priority right to the benefit given to the agent by way of a bribe or secret commission, and be able to trace the benefit into the hands of knowing receipts,[142] the Court was of the view that the preferable result was to grant to a principal a proprietary right, especially where the agent's benefit consisted of secret commissions or bribes.[143] The Court concluded that the courts took a wrong turn in *Lister* and it and the cases that followed its approach were overruled.

I Choice of relief

15.57 Where there was a breach of the no-profit rule it was arguable that a company was entitled to elect whether to claim damages or an account of

---

[133] (1880) 5 Ex D 319.

[134] (1890) 45 Ch D 1.

[135] *Archer's Case* [1892] 1 Ch 322; *Powell & Thomas v Evan Jones & Co* [1905] 1 KB 11; *A-G's Ref (No 1 of 1985)* [1986] 2 All ER 219; [1986] QB 491. See Lord Neuberger MR in *Sinclair Investments (UK) Ltd Versailles Trade Finance Ltd* [2011] EWCA Civ 347; [2011] 3 WLR 1153; [2011] 2 BCLC 501 at [71], [77].

[136] [1994] 1 AC 324 at 331; [1994] 1 All ER 1 at 4.

[137] [2011] EWCA Civ 347; [2011] 3 WLR 1153; [2011] 2 BCLC 501.

[138] [2013] EWCA Civ 17; [2013] 3 All ER 29; [2013] 2 BCLC 1.

[139] But this approach was not followed in Australia (see *Grimaldi v Chameleon Mining NL* [2012] FCFCA 6). The approach in *Attorney-General for Hong Kong v Reid* [1994] 1 AC 324 was favoured. This was also the case in the Singaporean High Court in *Sumitomo Bank Ltd v Kartika Ratna Thahir* [1993] 1 SLR 735 and in the Canadian court in *Insurance Corporation of British Columbia v Lo* (2006) 278 DLR (4th) 148.

[140] [2011] EWCA Civ 347; [2011] 3 WLR 1153; [2011] 2 BCLC 501 at [74].

[141] [2014] UKSC 45; [2015] AC 250; [2014] 3 WLR 535.

[142] Ibid at [43], [44].

[143] Ibid.

profits against a director for breach of his or her fiduciary duty.[144] This is likely
to be the case where there is a breach of either or both of ss 175 and 176 of the
CA 2006. The choice between these alternative and inconsistent remedies does
not have to be made until a company is able to make an informed choice,[145] but
must normally be made before judgment.[146] The company would be bound by
any election made,[147] although having said that, if there is an appeal from the
decision at first instance and that makes another award more advantageous the
company is relieved of the earlier choice that it made.[148] Where there is a profit,
the better choice is usually obvious because the potential reach of the remedy of
account can be considerable.[149]

15.58 Where the director who is in breach was an executive director, the
company cannot recover twice for the same wrongdoing merely because it
could claim that those acts were both a breach of the director's fiduciary duty
and a breach of his or her employment agreement.[150]

III CONSTRUCTIVE TRUSTEE

15.59 It has been said by one commentator that too often when a director
commits a breach of a fiduciary duty he or she is said to be liable as a
constructive trustee, that is the director is seen as holding property upon a trust
for the company, and this is not correct;[151] liability as a constructive trustee
must be seen more narrowly. Before tackling that issue, we might refer to the
judgment of Lord Sumption in *Williams v Central Bank of Nigeria*[152] where his
Lordship said that the notion of constructive trustee encompassed persons who
never assumed and never intended to assume that position of trustee, but they
were liable for equitable relief because of the fact that they had participated in
the unlawful misapplying of trust assets. That is, the person held to be a
constructive trustee has acted unconscionably. The narrowness of the notion of
a constructive trust is evident from what Lewison J (as he then was) said at first
instance in *Sinclair Investments (UK) Ltd Versailles Trade Finance Ltd*,[153]
namely that the phrase 'held by the fiduciary as constructive trustee' has caused
much trouble, and it has led to considerable confusion.[154] This is largely due to

---

[144] *Coleman Taymar Ltd v Oakes* [2001] 2 BCLC 749 at [79]; *CMS Dolphin Ltd v Simonet*
[2001] 2 BCLC 704 at [140]; *Southern Real Estate Pty Ltd v Dellow and Arnold* [2003] SASC
318; (2003) 87 SASR 1 at [40].

[145] *Island Records Ltd v Tring International Plc* [1996] 1 WLR 1256 at 1258–1259.

[146] See *Tang Man Sit (dec'd) v Capacious Investments Ltd* [1996] 2 WLR 192 (PC); *Warman
International Ltd v Dwyer* (1995) 182 CLR 544.

[147] *Kendall v Marsters* (1860) 2 De G F and J 200 (45 ER 598); *Neilson v Betts* (1871) LR 5 HL
1.

[148] *Pilmer v Duke Group Ltd (in liq)* [2001] HCA 31; (2001) 207 CLR 165 at [179].

[149] J Lowry and R Edmunds 'The Corporate Opportunity Doctrine: the Shifting Boundaries of the
Duty and its Remedies' (1998) 61 MLR 515 at 525.

[150] *Coleman Taymar Ltd v Oakes* [2001] 2 BCLC 749 at [84].

[151] B Hannigan *Company Law* (OUP, 3rd edn, 2012) at 277.

[152] [2014] UKSC 10; [2014] AC 1189.

[153] [2010] EWHC 1614 (Ch); [2011] 1 BCLC 202.

[154] Ibid at [30].

the lack of precision in the explanation of the constructive trust concept. Lord Sumption in *Williams v Central Bank of Nigeria*[155] said: 'there are few areas in which the law has been so completely obscured by confused categorisation and terminology as the law relating to constructive trustees'.[156]

15.60 As explained by Lord Sumption, the concept of constructive trustee has been applied to two different situations. First, and mentioned above, it covers persons who have lawfully assumed fiduciary obligations in relation to trust property, but they have not been formally appointed.[157] Lord Sumption gives the example of a trustee de son tort.[158] They are people who, without having been properly appointed, assume the administration of the trusts as if they had been appointed. It also refers to 'trustees under trusts implied from the common intention to be inferred from the conduct of the parties, but never formally created as such'.[159] His Lordship referred to them as de facto trustees or even true trustees.[160]

15.61 The second situation is where there are:[161]

'persons who never assumed and never intended to assume the status of a trustee, whether formally or informally, but have exposed themselves to equitable remedies by virtue of their participation in the unlawful misapplication of trust assets. Either they have dishonestly assisted in a misapplication of the funds by the trustee, or they have received trust assets knowing that the transfer to them was a breach of trust. In either case, they may be required by equity to account as if they were trustees or fiduciaries, although they are not.'

15.62 Earlier, Millett LJ (as he then was) in *Paragon Finance plc v D B Thakerar & Co*[162] had provided a similar approach. His Lordship said:[163]

'The first [situation] covers those cases already mentioned, where the defendant, though not expressly appointed as trustee, has assumed the duties of a trustee by a lawful transaction which was independent of and preceded the breach of trust and is not impeached by the plaintiff. The second covers those cases where the trust obligation arises as a direct consequence of the unlawful transaction which is impeached by the plaintiff. A constructive trust arises by operation of law whenever the circumstances are such that it would be unconscionable for the owner of property (usually but not necessarily the legal estate) to assert his own beneficial interest in the property and deny the beneficial interest of another. In the first class of case, however, the constructive trustee really is a trustee.'

---

[155] [2014] UKSC 10; [2014] AC 1189.
[156] Ibid at [7].
[157] Ibid at [9].
[158] Ibid.
[159] Ibid.
[160] Ibid.
[161] Ibid.
[162] [1999] 1 All ER 400.
[163] Ibid at 408–409.

15.63 His Lordship (whose exposition was quoted by Lord Sumption[164]), was saying that the second case is where the defendant is implicated in a fraud.[165]

15.64 The constructive trust is the response of equity to the consequences of fraud. It supplies, according to Lord Sumption[166] (and earlier by the court in *Gwembe Valley Development Co Ltd v Koshy*[167]) a remedial formula, or, in the words of Millett LJ, an equitable formula for relief.[168] Millett LJ explained in *Paragon Finance* that the people in the second case mentioned above are not strictly trustees, but they are ones who abuse the trust and confidence reposed in them to obtain their principal's property for themselves.[169] Stafford and Ritchie explain the distinction succinctly in these terms: 'there is a distinction between those who lawfully assumed fiduciary obligations prior to the acts complained of, and those who become liable in equity because of the acts of which complaint is made.'[170]

15.65 Lord Millett was so concerned that fiduciaries had wrongly been said to be constructive trustees in some cases that he said in *Dubai Aluminium Co Ltd v Salaam*[171] that, in the second class of case referred to by his Lordship earlier in *Paragon Finance* and referred to in the above quotation, namely when the defendant is implicated in a fraud, 'the expressions "constructive trust" and "constructive trustee" create a trap', that they are 'nothing more than a formula for equitable relief', and that 'we should now discard the words "accountable as constructive trustee" in this context and substitute the words "accountable in equity"'.[172]

15.66 In the Court of Appeal decision in *FHR European Ventures LLP v Mankarious*[173] Etherton C, in his judgment, pointed out that in *Sinclair Investments (UK) Ltd Versailles Trade Finance Ltd*[174] Lord Neuberger MR divided into three categories the situations in which a fiduciary obtains a benefit for a breach of fiduciary duty.[175] I will put these categories in a corporate context. First, where the benefit was an asset held beneficially by the company and the director gains the benefit by misappropriating the asset.[176] Second, where the director usurps a corporate opportunity that was properly

---

[164] [2014] UKSC 10; [2014] AC 1189 at [11].
[165] [1999] 1 All ER 400 at 409.
[166] Ibid at [9].
[167] [2003] EWCA Civ 1048; [2004] 1 BCLC 131 at [88].
[168] [1999] 1 All ER 400 at 409.
[169] Ibid at 408.
[170] *Fiduciary Duties* (Bristol, Jordan Publishing, 2nd edn, 2015) at 511.
[171] [2002] UKHL 48; [2003] 2 AC 366; [2003] 1 BCLC 32 at [142].
[172] Ibid.
[173] [2013] EWCA Civ 17; [2013] 3 All ER 29; [2013] 2 BCLC 1 at [83].
[174] [2011] EWCA Civ 347; [2011] 3 WLR 1153; [2011] 2 BCLC 501.
[175] Although *Sinclair* was overruled in *FHR European Ventures LLP and others v Cedar Capital Partners LLC* [2014] UKSC 45; [2015] AC 250 with Lord Neuberger giving the unanimous judgment of the Court, what his Lordship said above in the text was not challenged.
[176] See, *Paragon Finance plc v D B Thakerar & Co* [1999] 1 All ER 400 (CA); *CMS Dolphin Ltd v Simonet* [2001] 2 BCLC 704; *J J Harrison (Properties) Ltd v Harrison* [2001] EWCA Civ 1467; [2002] 1 BCLC 162 at [26], [27].

that of the company.[177] Third, all other cases of breach. According to Lord Neuberger the first two categories only gave rise to a constructive trust. A director is held to be a constructive trustee because the property is seen as the fruit of the abuse of his or her position.[178] This follows from the principle that directors who dispose of the company's property in breach of their fiduciary duties are treated as having committed a breach of trust and that where the director is, himself or herself, the recipient of the property, the director is in a position where he or she holds the property upon a trust for the company.

IV ALLOWANCE TO DIRECTORS

15.67 The obligation of a fiduciary to account is not diminished by the fact that the fiduciary made use of some special talent that he or she had.[179] Nevertheless, a fiduciary may be entitled to fair equitable compensation for any services that the fiduciary may have rendered in realising profits for which he or she must account to his or her company, and so the courts might also make an allowance in favour of the fiduciary.[180] This is particularly evident in trust law, where the trustee who is in breach had contributed anything to the property held by him or her on behalf of the trust. Yet it would appear that the courts are sometimes reluctant to grant an allowance.[181] An allowance will only be granted when the court believes that to do so would be to do justice between the parties, and where it would not have the effect of encouraging trustees to place themselves in a position where their interests and those of the company clash.[182]

15.68 In *Warman International*[183] the Australian High Court said that:

'In the case of a business it may well be inappropriate and inequitable to compel the errant fiduciary to account for the whole of the profit of his conduct of the business or his exploitation of the principal's goodwill over an indefinite period of time. In such a case, it may be appropriate to allow the fiduciary a proportion of the profits, depending on the particular circumstances. That may well be the case when it appears that a significant proportion of an increase in profits has been generated by the skill, efforts, property and resources of the fiduciary, the capital he has introduced and the risks he has taken, so long as they are not risks to which the principal's property has been exposed. Then it may be said that the relevant proportion of the increased profits is not the product or consequence of the plaintiff's property but the product of the fiduciary's skill, efforts, property and resources.'

---

[177] An example is *CMS Dolphin Ltd v Simonet* [2001] 2 BCLC 704.
[178] *CMS Dolphin Ltd v Simonet* [2001] 2 BCLC 704.
[179] *Boardman v Phipps* [1967] AC 46 (HL); *Natural Extracts Pty Ltd v Stotter* [1997] FCA 471; (1997) 24 ACSR 110 (Aust Fed Ct).
[180] *Boardman v Phipps* [1967] AC 46 (HL); *O'Sullivan v Management Agency and Music Ltd* [1985] QB 428.
[181] B Hannigan *Company Law* (OUP, 3rd edn, 2012) at 287.
[182] *Guinness plc v Saunders* [1990] 2 AC 663.
[183] (1995) HCA 18 at [33].

15.69 Nevertheless in *Guinness plc v Saunders*[184] the court applied a stricter approach in relation to directors. In that case the House of Lords was of the opinion that the discretion to make an allowance in favour of a fiduciary who is in breach might not be exercised in relation to directors. Their Lordships indicated that the effect of the power to make allowances is limited to cases where it cannot have the effect of encouraging directors in any way to place themselves in a position where there is a conflict.[185] In *Quarter Master UK Ltd v Pyke*[186] Paul Morgan QC (sitting as a deputy judge of the High Court) applied what he referred to as the fundamental rule and he denied the director any allowance.[187] The judge was not swayed by the fact that the company would not have received the benefits that emanated from the breach had the breach not occurred.[188] The judge noted that the case before him was not exceptional and the directors did not exercise special skills or take unusual risks, all of which might mean that if the case had been exceptional or the directors had exercised special skills or taken unusual risks, he might have awarded an allowance. There was no unequivocal statement that allowances are not to be made in favour of directors in all cases, although the judge did, as indicated above, refer to the fundamental rule which was encapsulated in the comments in *Guinness plc v Saunders*.[189] At first instance, in *FHR European Ventures LLP v Mankarious*[190] Lewison J did not think that it was appropriate to make an allowance for work done by the defendant/agent. Notwithstanding all of this, there is evidence, in some cases, of a more liberal approach, as far as directors are concerned. In *Condliffe v Sheingold*[191] the Court of Appeal said that once a court has decided that a director was liable to account, the director could raise any matter that might act as a claim to any deduction made from the profit received.[192] This approach followed the comments of the Court of Appeal in *Murad v Al Saraj*.[193] It is also notable that Peter Smith J in *Crown Dilmun v Sutton*[194] indicated sympathy for what might be referred to as a more liberal approach to the allowance issue.

15.70 The existence of a fraudulent intent will, however, be relevant to the question of the allowances to be made on the taking of the account.[195] In

---

[184] [1996] 2 AC 663 at 694.
[185] Ibid at 701.
[186] [2004] EWHC 1815 (Ch); [2005] 1 BCLC 245.
[187] Ibid at [77].
[188] Ibid.
[189] [1990] 2 AC 663 at 694.
[190] [2011] EWHC 2308.
[191] [2007] EWCA Civ 1043.
[192] Ibid at [23].
[193] [2005] EWCA Civ 959 at [77]–[79] and [96].
[194] [2004] EWHC 52 (Ch); [2004] 1 BCLC 468 at [211].
[195] *Murad v Al-Saraj* [2005] EWCA Civ 959 at [68].

United States Surgical Corp v Hospital Products International Pty Ltd,[196] the New South Wales Court of Appeal withheld any allowance as fraud had been perpetrated.[197]

15.71 In conflict cases courts will take into account the kind of interest acquired as a result of the breach.[198] In making an award, the courts will consider the skill and expenses of the director or any other defendant involved, and if the director has been honest, extremely skilful, or taken unusual risks a liberal allowance will be made.[199] The director has the onus of establishing that it would be inequitable to order him or her to disgorge all of the profits made without taking into account a fair allowance in relation to the director's contribution.[200]

V THIRD PARTIES

A Generally

15.72 It is possible that persons other than the directors themselves are involved in, or involved subsequent to, a breach of duty. This section of the Chapter considers what liability, if any, they might incur in relation to persons other than the errant director. The remedies that might be awarded against the third parties will often mirror the remedies that are awarded against the miscreant director.[201] As the third parties who may be liable are not usually going to be directors and will not be liable for a breach of a duty within the ambit of this book, it is not intended to provide a detailed discussion,[202] but some consideration is warranted as it is an issue sometimes related to breaches of duty.

15.73 It is noted that there is a limited amount of case-law in England as far as guidance about the rules that govern the possible liability of third parties who make profits, but who are not in a fiduciary relationship with the company (or

---

[196] [1983] 2 NSWLR 157. The overall decision was reversed on appeal to the High Court of Australia ((1984) 156 CLR 41) but the High Court did not impugn the view of the Court of Appeal on the fraud point.

[197] Also see, *Bailey v Namol Pty Ltd* (1994) 125 ALR 228 at 238; *Harris v Digital Pulse Pty Ltd* [2003] NSWCA 10; (2003) 197 ALR 626 at [336].

[198] *Warman International Ltd v Dwyer* (1995) 182 CLR 544 at 560.

[199] Ibid at 562; *Quarter Master UK Ltd v Pyke* [2004] EWHC 1815 (Ch); [2005] 1 BCLC 245 at [77].

[200] *Warman International Ltd v Dwyer* (1995) 182 CLR 544 at 561–562; *Condliffe v Sheingold* [2007] EWCA Civ 1043.

[201] See Elliott and Mitchell 'Remedies for Dishonest Assistance' (2004) 67 MLR 16 at 40–44.

[202] For a more detailed consideration, see A Stafford and S Ritchie *Fiduciary Duties* (Bristol, Jordan Publishing, 2nd edn, 2015) at 333-370.

other vulnerable party owed a fiduciary duty).[203] Nevertheless, it would appear that actions against third parties have been increasingly employed for some years now.[204]

15.74 Any liability for which third parties are liable is based on the wrong done by the director in breach of his or her duty. The third party has been involved either in the wrong or is related to the director/wrongdoer in some way. The liability that we are now addressing is sometimes referred to as accessory liability.

15.75 While directors would be liable for the breach, it might be worthwhile considering taking proceedings against third parties as directors might have taken flight and cannot be found, be impecunious, be uninsured or simply cannot pay all that is owed, as they might have dissipated any property or profits made from the breach. Considering a third party is particularly useful where the third party is a person or an institution of substance. Obviously taking action against a third party might not be so worthwhile if that party is insolvent or close to it.

15.76 It is clear enough that the obligation to account for profits may extend beyond the fiduciary directly to others who actually participated in any fraudulent conduct of the fiduciary.[205] Such persons are fixed with what was described at first instance by Wootten J of the Supreme Court of New South Wales in *Queensland Mines Ltd v Hudson*[206] as 'transmitted fiduciary obligations'.

15.77 The third party that is often the subject of proceedings instituted by the company is another company that the director has established in order either to run a business in competition with the company to which the director owes duties, or in order to exploit a business opportunity to which that company is entitled. The classic case is *Cook v Deeks*,[207] considered earlier on a couple of occasions in the book. Where a company has a good claim against a director for an account because of a breach he or she committed, but he or she has not received any profits, having incorporated a company to exploit the opportunity, some cases[208] have held the company to be accountable as a matter of course, while others have held the director liable on the basis that the corporate veil can be pierced and he or she is in control of the company.[209] In *Trustor AB v*

---

[203] *Crown Dilmun v Sutton* [2004] EWHC 52 (Ch); [2004] 1 BCLC 468 at [188].
[204] S Thomas '"Goodbye" Knowing Receipt. "Hello" Unconscious Receipt' (2001) 2 OJLS 239 at 239–240.
[205] *Barnes v Addy* (1874) 9 Ch App 244, 251-2; *Natural Extracts Pty Ltd v Stotter* (1997) 24 ACSR 110.
[206] (1975–76) ACLC 40-266 at 28, 709.
[207] [1916] AC 554. For a more modern case, see *CMS Dolphin Ltd v Simonet* [2001] 2 BCLC 704; [2002] BCC 200.
[208] For example, *Cook v Deeks* [1916] AC 554; *Canadian Aero Service Ltd v O'Malley* [1974] SCR592 at 607; (1973) 40 DLR (3d) 371; *CMS Dolphin Ltd v Simonet* [2001] 2 BCLC 704; [2002] BCC 200 at [103].
[209] For example, see *Gencor ACP Ltd v Dalby* [2000] 2 BCLC 734; *Green v Bestobell Industries*

Smallbone[210] and other cases the courts have pierced the veil where directors had misappropriated money from the claimant company and some of it had been paid to one of the director's own companies on the basis that the corporate veil was being used to avoid or conceal liability. In recent times the Supreme Court in *Prest v Petrodel Resources Limited & Others*[211] indicated that some of the instances where it has been said the piercing of the veil was allowed might not be possible any longer. In giving the leading judgment in *Prest* Lord Sumption said that it was a well-established principle that the court may be justified in piercing the corporate veil if a company's separate legal personality is being abused for the purpose of some relevant wrongdoing.[212] His Lordship said that the main problem was determining what was the relevant wrongdoing.[213] He said that there will be a piercing of the veil where there is evasion; that is where there is a legal right against the person in control of a company 'which exists independently of the company's involvement, and a company is interposed so that the separate legal personality of the company will defeat the right or frustrate its enforcement'.[214] The judge distinguished this from what he called the concealment principle, which does not involve piercing the corporate veil at all. This is where a company or perhaps several companies are interposed so as to conceal the identity of the real actors; will not deter the courts from identifying them, assuming that their identity is legally relevant. In these cases the court is not disregarding the 'façade', but only looking behind it to discover the facts which the corporate structure is concealing.[215] His Lordship was of the view that the facts in *Trustor* involved the concealment principle not in fact a situation involving a piercing of the veil.[216] HHJ Havelock-Allan QC in *Airbus Operations Ltd v Withey*[217] applied what Lord Sumption said in *Prest* and the Supreme Court said in *VTB Capital plc v Nutritek*[218] and opined that an example of concealment is where a company that is controlled by a wrongdoer is employed to act as a recipient of funds.[219] The judge continued and said that this involved:[220]

> 'treating the company as no more than the alter ego or nominee of the wrongdoer with no right to the money as against the wrongdoer, does not involve disregarding or piercing the corporate veil. It is an example of looking beyond the personality of the company in order to establish the true legal relationship between the parties.'

15.78 It is worthwhile setting out what Lord Sumption said in *Prest*:[221]

Pty Ltd [1984] WAR 32. In the first case the court indicated that there would be a piercing of the veil because the company was the defendant director's alter ego.

[210] [2001] 1 WLR 1177; [2001] 2 BCLC 436; [2002] BCC 200.
[211] [2013] UKSC 34; [2013] 2 AC 415; [2013] 3 WLR 1.
[212] Ibid at [27].
[213] Ibid at [28].
[214] Ibid.
[215] Ibid.
[216] Ibid at [32].
[217] [2014] EWHC 1126 (QB).
[218] [2013] UKSC 5; [2013] 2 AC 337.
[219] [2014] EWHC 1126 (QB) at [453].
[220] Ibid.
[221] [2013] UKSC 34; [2013] 2 AC 415; [2013] 3 WLR 1 at [34]-[35].

'the corporate veil may be pierced only to prevent the abuse of corporate legal personality. It may be an abuse of the separate legal personality of a company to use it to evade the law or to frustrate its enforcement. It is not an abuse to cause a legal liability to be incurred by the company in the first place. It is not an abuse to rely on the fact (if it is a fact) that a liability is not the controller's because it is the company's ... I conclude that there is a limited principle of English law which applies when a person is under an existing legal obligation or liability or subject to an existing legal restriction which he deliberately evades or whose enforcement he deliberately frustrates by interposing a company under his control. The court may then pierce the corporate veil for the purpose, and only for the purpose, of depriving the company or its controller of the advantage that they would otherwise have obtained by the company's separate legal personality. The principle is properly described as a limited one, because in almost every case where the test is satisfied, the facts will in practice disclose a legal relationship between the company and its controller which will make it unnecessary to pierce the corporate veil ... I consider that if it is not necessary to pierce the corporate veil, it is not appropriate to do so, because on that footing there is no public policy imperative which justifies that course ... the principle has been recognised far more often than it has been applied. But the recognition of a small residual category of cases where the abuse of the corporate veil to evade or frustrate the law can be addressed only by disregarding the legal personality of the company is, I believe, consistent with authority and with long-standing principles of legal policy.'

15.79   Even if a director has a controlling interest in a company that receives a benefit as a result of a breach, he or she is not personally accountable for the receipt of the benefit unless it is proper to pierce the corporate veil,[222] although the director is likely to be liable for breach of his or her duties anyway. Arguably there is no need for the courts to pierce the veil in many situations as the company and the director jointly participated in the breach of the duty, and so both are liable, jointly and severally.[223] This was the case, according to the judgment of Lawrence Collins J (as he then was) in *CMS Dolphin Ltd v Simonet*.[224] It is also an example of a judge not feeling it was necessary to pierce the veil where there was company involvement. His Lordship did not think that it mattered whether the corporate vehicle took the opportunity directly or whether it was first taken by the director and then transferred to a company.[225] In this case the judge made the point that a director who is the active agent in a breach of fiduciary duty cannot evade responsibility by transferring the benefit to a company.[226]

15.80   While the third party is often a company that a miscreant director has incorporated to take the benefits of a breach, shadow directors also can be regarded as third parties who are liable in relation to a breach of duty. After denying the fact that shadow directors owed duties to the company and could therefore be liable for a breach of them, Lewison J in *Ultraframe (UK) Ltd v*

---

[222]   *Ultraframe (UK) Ltd v Fielding* [2005] EWHC 1638 (Ch) at [1576].
[223]   *CMS Dolphin Ltd v Simonet* [2001] 2 BCLC 704; [2002] BCC 200 at [103].
[224]   Ibid at [104].
[225]   However, Lewison J in *Ultraframe (UK) Ltd v Fielding* [2005] EWHC 1638 (Ch) at [1574]–[1576] did not agree.
[226]   [2001] 2 BCLC 704; [2002] BCC 200 at [104].

Fielding[227] did think that the company might be able to take action against the shadow if he or she could be said to have knowingly assisted the breaching of duties by the directors of the company. Of course, as indicated in Chapter 4, the preponderance of the case-law now suggests that an action could be brought directly against a shadow director for a breach of fiduciary duty if the necessary elements can be established. It is likely that in some cases a claim against a shadow director will be in the alternative.

15.81 Courts will, just as they are when considering actions against miscreant directors, be concerned that companies are not unjustly enriched by a decision that is made against a third party.[228] For instance, where both a director and a third party are liable the courts will ensure that the claimant does not get double recovery.[229]

15.82 Most often claimants will rely on the old case of *Barnes v Addy*[230] (and cases applying it) which provides, in effect, that an action might be brought successfully against a third party where either the third party knowingly assisted in the breach of duty or knowingly received benefits from the breach for his or her own use. We will shortly consider these situations. Before doing so it is worth pointing out that it has been held[231] that a general tort of inducing breach of fiduciary duty exists, and that there are well-developed principles within equity itself covering accessory liability as we will now examine.

B Knowing assistance

15.83 It may well be the case that a director has been assisted by a third party in the commission of a breach.[232] A third party has been said to be potentially liable if he or she was acting dishonestly,[233] even if the third party received no benefit from the breach. Third parties are also liable even if they did not realise that what was done by the director was a breach of duty provided that they knew or suspected that their involvement in the activity was dishonest.[234] This has been known as 'knowing assistance' or 'dishonest assistance'.[235] Such liability can apply to assisting in the breach of a fiduciary duty, and even where

---

[227] [2005] EWHC 1638 (Ch) at [1280].

[228] *Crown Dilmun v Sutton* [2004] EWHC 52 (Ch); [2004] 1 BCLC 468 at [211].

[229] B Hannigan *Company Law* (OUP, 3rd edn, 2012) at 287.

[230] (1874) LR 9 Ch App 244.

[231] See *First Subsea Ltd v Balltec* [2014] EWHC 866 (Ch) at [353].

[232] The view taken in *CMS Dolphin Ltd v Simonet* [2001] 2 BCLC 704; [2002] BCC 200 at [103]-[104]. Also, see *Wrexham AFC Ltd v Crucialmove Ltd* [2006] EWCA Civ 237; [2007] BCC 139; [2008] 1 BCLC 508 at [37].

[233] *Royal Brunei Airlines Bhd v Tan* [1995] 2 AC 378 (PC). Courts in a number of US jurisdictions have held third parties liable for aiding and abetting a breach: see R de Rohan Barondes 'Fiduciary Duties in Distressed Corporations: Second Generation Issues' Working Paper No 2005-08, Contracting and Organisations Research Institute, University of Missouri, 17 November 2005 at p10 and accessible at http://ssrn.com/abstract=846964.

[234] *Agip (Africa) Ltd v Jackson* [1990] Ch 263 at 295; *Madoff Securities International Ltd (in liq) v Raven* [2013] EWHC 3147 (Comm).

[235] For instance, see *Novoship (UK) Ltd v Nikitin* [2014] EWCA Civ 908; [2015] QB 499 at [77].

there is no property being held on trust and none has been misapplied.[236] If a third party is liable then it exposes him or her to the full range of remedies in equity that can be obtained against a trustee or a director. A third party can be liable for knowing assistance even if that person has been defrauded and suffered loss.[237] The kinds of conduct that can constitute assistance for the purposes of this rule are potentially legion, and the kinds of assistance that would qualify are not closed. For instance, it would include action taken by someone to accommodate a director's breach of his or her duties. More specifically it would cover the situation where X decides that he will establish a business in competition with his company and he uses information from the company in establishing the business, and Y helps X to set up the new business (and this *might* include providing legal or accounting services and setting up an office for X).

15.84 The following discussion can only be relatively brief and does not purport to be exhaustive. The foundation for liability for knowing assistance is located, as mentioned above, in the classic case of *Barnes v Addy*.[238] While there has been debate over whether the liability is primary or secondary, it appears to be the latter. Certainly, the Court of Appeal in *Grupo Torras SA v Al-Sabah (No 5)*[239] favoured the latter. There are three matters which a claimant needs to establish, according to Rix LJ in *Abou-Ramah v Abacha*[240] (and the other judges appeared to have agreed) in order to succeed: (1) the defendant, the assister, had the required knowledge; (2) given the knowledge that the assister has he or she acts in such a way that it is contrary to normally acceptable standards of honest conduct; (3) the assister is held to be dishonest.[241] One might also add, even though it might seem obvious, that it must be established that the action complained of did constitute actual assistance of the breach of duty. The assistance can have occurred before, during or following the breach of duty.

15.85 As mentioned earlier, it is unnecessary for an assister to know or even suspect that the transaction that is impugned is a breach of a fiduciary duty or the circumstances that constitutes it involves a breach.[242] It suffices if the assister knows or suspects that the transaction is such that it makes his or her involvement in it dishonest.[243] The issue of dishonesty is often the main issue

---

[236] *JD Wetherspoon plc v Van de Berg & Co Ltd* [2009] EWHC 639 (Ch) at [518]; *Fiona Trust and Holding Corporation v Privalov* [2010] EWHC 3199 (Comm); *Goldtrail Travel Ltd v Aydin* [2014] EWHC 1587 (Ch) at [128] and affirmed on appeal [2016] EWCA Civ 371; *Novoship (UK) Ltd v Nikitin* [2014] EWCA Civ 908; [2015] QB 499 at [92].

[237] *Goldtrail Travel Ltd v Aydin* [2014] EWHC 1587 (Ch) and affirmed on appeal ([2016] EWCA Civ 371).

[238] (1874) 9 Ch App 244.

[239] [2001] 1 Lloyds Rep Bank. 36; [2001] CLC 221.

[240] [2006] EWCA Civ 1492; [2007] Bus L R 220; [2007] 1 Lloyd's Rep 115.

[241] Ibid at [16].

[242] *Agip (Africa) Ltd v Jackson* [1990] Ch 263 at 295.

[243] *Abou-Ramah v Abacha* [2006] EWCA Civ 1492; [2007] Bus L R 220; [2007] 1 Lloyd's Rep 115 at [39]; *Barlow Clowes International Ltd (In Liquidation) v Eurotrust International Ltd* [2005] UKPC 37, [2006] 1 All ER 333, [2006] 1 WLR 1476 at [28].

that is the subject of argument in a case,[244] and it is one that has been controversial and consequently it has frequently created problems, particularly as far as establishing that a party is guilty of actual dishonesty. As a result 'the law in relation to dishonest assistance has, in the past decade, gone through tortuous judicial revisions and clarifications'.[245]

15.86 Equity has visited liability on third parties who are accessories to a breach of trust as a way of giving the injured party an alternative means of securing some relief in case the primary wrongdoer is impecunious or has absconded, and as a way of deterring the involvement of third parties in breaches.[246] In cases where dishonesty is alleged the burden of proof is firmly on the party alleging dishonesty, and the ordinary civil burden applies.[247] What has been a vexed issue is: what test does one apply – a subjective or an objective test? There is assistance obtained from the case-law that has been delivered in relation to claims that defendants have been guilty of assisting a breach of trust, with breach of trust being regarded as analogous to breach of duty (both involve improper actions by fiduciaries). In one such case, *Twinsectra v Yardley*,[248] Lord Millett favoured an objective test as the issue related to civil liability.[249] However, this was not the position of the other judges in that case. Lord Hutton (with whom the other three Law Lords agreed, and therefore it was supported by a majority) said that there were three tests that could be applied in determining whether someone acted dishonestly or not. The first two tests were the standard subjective and objective tests. But his Lordship applied[250] the third test, which he called 'the combined test'. This is:

> 'a standard which combines an objective test and a subjective test, and which requires that before there can be a finding of dishonesty it must be established that the defendant's conduct was dishonest by the ordinary standards of reasonable and honest people and that he himself realised that by those standards his conduct was dishonest.'

15.87 In a similar manner, Lord Nicholls had said earlier in the Privy Council in *Royal Brunei Airlines Bhd v Tan*[251] (and this was approved of by a majority of the House of Lords in *Twinsectra*) that:

> 'Honesty has a connotation of subjectivity, as distinct from the objectivity of negligence. Honesty, indeed, does have a strong subjective element in that it is a description of a type of conduct assessed in the light of what a person actually knew at the time, as distinct from what a reasonable person would have known or appreciated. Further, honesty and its counterpart dishonesty are mostly concerned

---

[244] For a recent example, see *Breitenfeld UK Ltd v Harrison* [2015] EWHC 399 (Ch).

[245] R Lee 'Dishonesty and Bad Faith after Barlow Clowes: Abou-Rahmah v Abacha' [2007] JBL 209 at 209.

[246] *Royal Brunei Airlines Bhd v Tan* [1995] 2 AC 378 at 386–387 (PC).

[247] *Re H* [1996] AC 563 at 586; *Statek Corp v Alford* [2008] EWHC 32 (Ch) at [101].

[248] [2002] UKHL 12; [2002] 2 AC 164.

[249] Ibid at [127]. So, it appears, did the Australian High Court. See *Consul Development Pty Ltd v DPC Estates Pty Ltd* (1975) 132 CLR 373.

[250] [2002] UKHL 12 at [27]; [2002] 2 AC 164 at 171.

[251] [1995] 2 AC 378 at 379.

with advertent conduct, not inadvertent conduct. Carelessness is not dishonesty. Thus for the most part dishonesty is to be equated with conscious impropriety. However, these subjective characteristics of honesty do not mean that individuals are free to set their own standards of honesty in particular circumstances. The standard of what constitutes honest conduct is not subjective. Honesty is not an optional scale, with higher or lower values according to the moral standards of each individual. If a person knowingly appropriates another's property, he will not escape a finding of dishonesty simply because he sees nothing wrong in such behaviour.'

15.88 So both the Privy Council and the House of Lords (the Privy Council in *Barlow Clowes International Ltd (in Liquidation) v Eurotrust International Ltd*[252] was of the view that the House of Lords decision in *Twinsectra* was consistent with *Royal Brunei Airlines*[253]) indicated that in determining dishonesty one considers whether an honest person in the defendant's position would have done what the defendant had done.

15.89 The Privy Council addressed the issue of dishonesty, again in the context of a claim of assisting a breach of trust, in *Barlow Clowes International Ltd (In Liquidation) v Eurotrust International Ltd.* The Judicial Committee, whose advice was delivered by Lord Hoffmann, interpreted the test as objective in that it is not necessary for the defendant to realise that his or her conduct was dishonest according to the ordinary reasonable standards of honest people. It has been thought by some, such as Rix LJ in *Abou-Ramah v Abacha*,[254] that Lord Hoffmann in *Barlow Clowes* was taking an approach that was close to that advocated by Lord Millett in *Twinsectra*. In its advice the Judicial Committee in *Barlow Clowes* said, in interpreting *Twinsectra*, that the defendant, to be liable, had to have knowledge of the elements of the transaction which rendered his or her participation contrary to ordinary standards of honest behaviour (the knowledge part of the action), and the defendant's knowledge of the transaction that was impugned had to be such as to render his or her participation contrary to normally acceptable standards of honest conduct.[255] There was no need for the defendant to have had reflections about what those normally acceptable standards were.[256] In other words, defendants would be liable if they transgressed ordinary standards even if they did not turn their minds to what the standards were.[257] The opinion of the Judicial Committee was that a third party could be held to know or suspect that doing something will provide assistance in the misappropriation of property even if he or she is unaware that the property is held on trust. A subsequently constituted committee of the Privy Council, in *Central Bank of Ecuador v Conticorp SA*,[258] applied the approach in *Barlow Clowes*, and said that if objectively no honest person would have acted as he or she did it was

---

[252] [2005] UKPC 37; [2006] 1 WLR 1476.
[253] Ibid at [18].
[254] [2006] EWCA Civ 1492; [2007] Bus L R 220; [2007] 1 Lloyd's Rep 115.
[255] [2005] UKPC 37; [2006] 1 WLR 1476 at [16].
[256] Ibid at [15].
[257] Ibid at [16].
[258] [2015] UKPC 11.

unnecessary to demonstrate the fact that the person actually recognised that their actions were dishonest, for while a defendant had to be aware of the elements of the transaction which made his or her participation a transgression of ordinary standards of honest behaviour, it was not necessary to establish that he or she should have considered what those standards were.[259] The Board said *per curiam* that a person who dishonestly assists a breach of duty cannot argue that he or she was not assisting in the breach because at the same time he or she was taking action that person was acting in his or her capacity as an officer or agent of a company.[260]

15.90 In *Abou-Ramah v Abacha*[261] Arden LJ favoured following the approach in *Barlow Clowes International*, as far as its interpretation of *Twinsectra* was concerned even though the Court of Appeal was not bound to follow the Privy Council's view. The other judges declined to consider the impact of *Barlow Clowes International* on *Twinsectra*,[262] and the comments in *Abou-Ramah* on the impact of the former case on the latter are obiter. However, in *Mullarkey v Broad*,[263] Lewison J (as he then was) was of the opinion that Rix LJ in *Abou-Ramah* proceeded on the basis that the interpretation of *Twinsectra* in *Barlow Clowes* represented the state of the law in England, and Pill LJ agreed with the reasons of Arden LJ for her decision in *Abou-Ramah*. In the latter case Arden LJ was firmly of the view that the Privy Council in *Barlow Clowes* clarified the situation and interpreted *Twinsectra* in such a way that a court does not require the defendant to be conscious of his or her wrongdoing for liability to attach. Arden LJ was of the opinion that it was sufficient for liability to be imposed if the defendant was aware of the elements of the transaction which made it dishonest according to normally accepted standards of behaviour. Like Lord Hoffmann in *Barlow Clowes International*, her Ladyship favoured an approach where there was no need, in establishing dishonesty, for the claimant to prove that the defendant was conscious of his or her wrongdoing.[264] She added that it was unnecessary to consider the defendant's view as to the morality of what he or she had done when having regard to civil, as opposed to criminal, liability. Arden LJ concluded that the test is largely objective but with subjective considerations.[265] In *Mullarkey v Broad*,[266] Lewison J, following the approach of Arden LJ, applied *Twinsectra* as explained in *Barlow Clowes*. The Court of Appeal in *Starglade Properties Ltd v Nash*[267] confirmed that the relevant standard was the ordinary standard of honest behaviour. Etherton C said that the subjective understanding of the person concerned as to whether his or her conduct is dishonest is irrelevant.[268]

---

[259] Ibid at [9]. This approach had been approved of earlier by the New South Wales Court of Appeal in *Hasler v Singtel Optus Pty Ltd v Almad Pty Ltd* [2014] NSWCA 266.

[260] [2015] UKPC 11 at [50], [120].

[261] [2006] EWCA Civ 1492; [2007] Bus L R 220; [2007] 1 Lloyd's Rep 115.

[262] Ibid at [91].

[263] [2007] EWHC 3400 (Ch); [2008] 1 BCLC 638 at [36].

[264] [2006] EWCA Civ 1492; [2007] Bus L R 220; [2007] 1 Lloyd's Rep 115 at [59], [65].

[265] Ibid at [66].

[266] [2007] EWHC 3400 (Ch); [2008] 1 BCLC 638 at [36].

[267] [2010] EWCA Civ 1314.

[268] Ibid at [32].

His Lordship went on to say that it is also irrelevant that 'there may be a body of opinion which regards the ordinary standard of honest behaviour as being set too high. Ultimately, in civil proceedings, it is for the court to determine what that standard is and to apply it to the facts of the case'.[269] So, just because business people regard actions as not dishonest that did not prevent a court finding that the relevant actions were dishonest for the purposes of proceedings that are the subject of this part of the Chapter and other proceedings.

15.91 In *Abou-Ramah* Rix LJ stated[270] (and the other judges appeared to have agreed), by way of summary (some of which was mentioned earlier):

> 'It would seem that a claimant in this area needs to show three things: first, that a defendant has the requisite knowledge; secondly, that, given that knowledge, the defendant acts in a way which is contrary to normally acceptable standards of honest conduct (the objective test of honesty or dishonesty); and thirdly, possibly, that the defendant must in some sense be dishonest himself (a subjective test of dishonesty which might, on analysis, add little or nothing to knowledge of the facts which, objectively, would make his conduct dishonest).'

15.92 Importantly, *Abou-Rahmah v Abacha* held, and putting it into director/company terms, that a third party does not breach the standards of objective dishonesty if that person only has general suspicions of impropriety in providing assistance to a director who commits a breach.

15.93 In *Madoff Securities International Ltd (in liq) v Raven*[271] the judge affirmed the fact that there was a subjective and an objective element. The subjective related to the knowledge of the alleged assister, that is, what did the assister actually know, understand, believe or suspect at the time of his or her impugned conduct.[272] It was pointed out by Lewison J in *Ultraframe (UK) Ltd v Fielding*[273] that '[a]lthough it is not necessary for the dishonest assistant to know all the details of the whole design, he must, I think, know in broad terms what the design is'.[274] It has been asserted,[275] on the basis of comments in *Ultraframe (UK) Ltd v Fielding*,[276] that English courts will not support the notion of joint and several liability as far as a wrongdoer director and a knowing third party who assists a breach are concerned, in the situation where gains are made by directors.

15.94 The company does not have to demonstrate the contribution which the third party made to the breach, as long as it can be established that he or she

---

[269] Ibid.
[270] [2006] EWCA Civ 1492; [2007] Bus L R 220; [2007] 1 Lloyd's Rep 115 at [16].
[271] [2013] EWHC 3147 (Comm).
[272] Ibid at [353].
[273] [2005] EWHC 1638 (Ch).
[274] Ibid at [1506].
[275] P Ridge 'Justifying the Remedies for Dishonest Assistance' (2008) 124 LQR 445 at 460.
[276] [2005] EWHC 1638 (Ch); [2006] FSR 17 at [598], [600].

dishonestly provided some assistance to the perpetration of the breach.[277] But the company is not obliged to establish that the assistance caused the loss that has been suffered as a result of the breach, save, as we will see later, where the company is seeking an account of profits.[278]

15.95 If a court finds that a third party assisted a director in a breach and he or she received property as a result of the breach, it has been held that the third party could be held to be a constructive trustee,[279] but that view must be taken with the decision of *Paragon Finance plc v D B Thakerar & Co*[280] in mind and, as discussed earlier in the Chapter, the English appellate courts have warned about the incorrect use of the term 'constructive trustee'.[281]

15.96 Any claim against a third party will be compensatory and not restitutionary. Outside of compensating the company for any loss that it might have suffered, could the third party who assisted a breach be forced to disgorge any profit he or she had made from the breach? In *Fyffes Group Ltd v Templeman*,[282] a case not involving a breach of a director's duty, a third party was ordered to do so. In that case the benefit was a bribe. Lewison J in *Ultraframe (UK) Ltd v Fielding*[283] opined that the approach taken in *Fyffes* might be applied in a scenario involving a breach of duty to a company.[284]

15.97 Companies could, if it were established that the third party knowingly assisted in a breach of duty, have both a personal and a proprietary remedy against that third party.[285] The breach would have to fit into the first two categories identified by Lord Neuberger MR (as he then was) in *Sinclair Investments (UK) Ltd Versailles Trade Finance Ltd*[286] and accepted in *FHR European Ventures LLP v Mankarious*,[287] namely (in a company/director context)that an asset or money was or had been beneficially the property of the company and was misappropriated by the director or the miscreant director acquired the asset or money by taking advantage of an opportunity or right that was properly that of the company.

C Knowing receipt

15.98 A third party might not assist in the actual breach of duty but might receive the fruit of the breach, namely money or property, or profits made from

---

[277] S Baughen 'Accessory liability at common law and in equity – "The redundancy of knowing assistance" revisited' [2007] LMCLQ 545 at 553.

[278] See, *Novoship (UK) Ltd v Nikitin*. [2014] EWCA Civ 908; [2015] QB 499.

[279] *ASIC v AS Nominees Ltd* (1995) 18 ACSR 459.

[280] [1999] 1 All ER 400 at 409.

[281] For example, see *Dubai Aluminium Co Ltd v Salaam* [2002] UKHL 48; [2003] 2 AC 366; [2003] 1 BCLC 32 at [142].

[282] [2000] 2 Lloyd's Rep 643.

[283] [2005] EWHC 1638 (Ch) at [1309].

[284] Ibid at [1594].

[285] *Clark v Cutland* [2004] 1 WLR 783; [2003] 2 BCLC 393 at [31].

[286] [2011] EWCA Civ 347; [2011] 3 WLR 1153; [2011] 2 BCLC 501 at [88].

[287] [2013] EWCA Civ 17; [2013] 3 All ER 29; [2013] 2 BCLC 1.

the property. The essential requirements of knowing receipt were identified by Hoffmann LJ in *El Ajou v Dollar Land Holdings plc*:[288]

> 'For this purpose the plaintiff must show, first, a disposal of his assets in breach of fiduciary duty; secondly, the beneficial receipt by the defendant of assets which are traceable as representing the assets of the plaintiff; and thirdly, knowledge on the part of the defendant that the assets he received are traceable to a breach of fiduciary duty.'

15.99   Unlike with knowing assistance, there is no need to establish dishonesty for knowing receipt, even though dishonesty will often be present,[289] but there is need to establish that trust property was involved in the breach. That is, knowing assistance may well not relate to property that is controlled by the directors, but dealing with trust property is at the centre of the action. As noted in Chapter 10, there has been some uncertainty concerning the meaning of property of the company. Some items are clearly able to fall within the term. Examples are land, equipment and cars. But other items do cause some concern. Of particular concern are business opportunities and confidential information. Some dicta dealing in cases that have not involved knowing receipt have found these to be property, but in knowing receipt cases the indication is that they are not.[290] Of course, depending on the facts, the company might have a claim for knowing assistance against a third party.

15.100   Conversely and like knowing assistance, the foundation for liability for knowing receipt is located in the classic case of *Barnes v Addy*.[291] According to the Court of Appeal in *Grupo Torras SA v Al-Sabah (No 5)*:[292]

> 'The basis of liability in a case of knowing receipt is quite different from that in a case of dishonest assistance. One is a receipt-based liability which may on examination prove to be either a vindication of persistent property rights or a personal restitutionary claim based on unjust enrichment by subtraction; the other is a fault-based liability as an accessory to a breach of fiduciary duty.'[293]

15.101   The Court of Appeal, led by Nourse LJ, in *Bank of Credit and Commerce International (Overseas) Ltd v Akindele*[294] was of the opinion that as there was a single test for dishonesty in relation to knowing assistance, there should be a single test for knowing receipt. The test that the court fastened onto was one of unconscionability.[295] His Lordship thought that it would enable courts to be able to make more commonsense decisions in the commercial

---

[288] [1994] 2 All ER 685 at 700.
[289] *Bank of Credit and Commerce International (Overseas) Ltd v Akindele* [2001] Ch 437 at 450 (CA).
[290] See *Commonwealth Gas and Oil Co Ltd v Baxter* [2009] CSIH 75; 2009 SLT 1123.
[291] (1874) 9 Ch App 244.
[292] [2001] 1 Lloyds Rep Bank. 36; [2001] CLC 221.
[293] Ibid at [122].
[294] [2001] Ch 437.
[295] Ibid at 455.

context.[296] On this basis a person is liable if his or her state of knowledge would make it unconscionable for him or her to retain the benefit of the receipt.[297] It has been indicated that the test for knowledge in knowing receipt is lower than for knowing assistance.[298]

15.102 The unconscionability test is criticised on the basis that, while it might have the value of giving the courts flexibility[299] (the point made by Nourse LJ), the test of unconscionability provides no guidance to the courts,[300] and it might mean that the courts fail to apply the test consistently.[301] It has been pointed out that the test is subjective and context specific.[302] Professors Alan Dignam and John Lowry argue for a single test for knowing receipt and knowing assistance, and one that is consistent with that stated in *Twinsectra*.[303]

15.103 In trust law, where the circumstances are such that what is conveyed to the third party is not trust property, the company's claim against the third party is personal and not proprietary.[304] But, as Chadwick LJ stated in *J J Harrison (Properties) Ltd v Harrison:*[305]

> 'It follows from the principle that directors who dispose of the company's property in breach of their fiduciary duties are treated as having committed a breach of trust that a person who receives that property with knowledge of the breach of duty is treated as holding it upon trust for the company. He is said to be a constructive trustee of the property.'

15.104 In this context the comments in the Court of Appeal cases of *Paragon Finance plc v D B Thakerar & Co*[306] and *Sinclair Investments (UK) Ltd Versailles Trade Finance Ltd*[307] concerning the application of the over-use of the tag 'constructive trust' to every case involving a breach of duty, and mentioned earlier in the Chapter, must be considered.[308]

---

[296] Ibid.

[297] *Houghton v Fayers* [2000] 1 BCLC 511 (CA); *Bank of Credit and Commerce International (Overseas) Ltd v Akindele* [2001] Ch 437 (CA).

[298] *Otkritie International Investment Management Ltd v Urumov* [2014] EWHC 191 (Comm) at [81].

[299] S Thomas '"Goodbye" Knowing Receipt. "Hello" Unconscious Receipt' (2001) 2 OJLS 239 at 264.

[300] J Penner *The Law of Trusts* (OUP, 2008) at para 12.48 – 12.58 and referred to by A Dignam and J Lowry, *Company Law* (OUP, 5th edn, 2008) at 344.

[301] S Thomas '"Goodbye" Knowing Receipt. "Hello" Unconscious Receipt' (2001) 2 OJLS 239 at 241.

[302] Ibid.

[303] A Dignam and J Lowry, *Company Law* (OUP, 5th edn, 2008) at 344.

[304] *Paragon Finance plc v DB Thakerar & Co* [1999] 1 All ER 400 (CA); *Houghton v Fayers* [2000] 1 BCLC 511 (CA); *J J Harrison (Properties) Ltd v Harrison* [2001] EWCA Civ 1467; [2002] 1 BCLC 162.

[305] [2001] EWCA Civ 1467 at [26]; [2002] 1 BCLC 162 at 173. Also, see *Consul Development Pty Ltd v DPC Estates Pty Ltd* (1975) 132 CLR 373 (Aust HC).

[306] [1999] 1 All ER 400 at 409.

[307] [2011] EWCA Civ 347; [2011] 3 WLR 1153; [2011] 2 BCLC 501.

[308] See above at **15.59–15.66.**

15.105 As indicated earlier in this chapter and in Chapter 11, there are benefits of being able to have a proprietary claim, not least being the fact that there is recourse to the property in priority to other creditors if the recipient is insolvent.

15.106 What knowledge does a third party have to have if he or she is to be liable? The Court of Appeal in *Bank of Credit and Commerce International (Overseas) Ltd v Akindele*,[309] while acknowledging the fact that in Commonwealth courts constructive knowledge of a breach of duty is sufficient[310] to visit liability on a third party who is in receipt of benefits, declared that in the UK actual knowledge must be established.[311]

15.107 In establishing knowledge concerning the receipt of property obtained as a result of a breach of duty, it might be possible to attribute the knowledge of the miscreant director to the company, where he or she is involved, as is generally the case, with the third party company. This was the approach taken by Peter Smith J in *Crown Dilmun v Sutton*.[312] Where a director who is in breach forms a company for the purpose of perpetrating a breach and he or she is the principal shareholder, director and de facto mind and will of the company, the knowledge of the breach is attributed to the company.[313] Nevertheless, it is not sufficient to attribute knowledge, it must also be established that it is unconscionable for the third party to retain any benefits.[314]

15.108 Not uncommonly, as already mentioned, directors establish companies to take advantage of an opportunity that should have been that of the company to which they owed duties, and where it is the former company that gains any benefits, and not the director, it is clear that the company established by the director can be held liable for knowing receipt.[315] While, as indicated earlier, in *CMS Dolphin Ltd v Simonet*[316] Lawrence Collins J held that directors in such a situation can be jointly liable for the profit made by the company, the company could always seek to pierce the corporate veil as occurred in *Trustor AB v Smallbone (No 2)*.[317] In that case the company sought to make a director who breached his duty to his company, T, and organised payments from T to a company, I, that he established, jointly and severally liable with I on the ground that receipt by I was, in the circumstances, to be treated also as receipt by the

---

[309] [2001] Ch 437.
[310] For example, see *Westpac Banking Corp v Savin* [1985] 2 NZLR 41; *Equiticorp Industries Group Ltd v Hawkins* [1991] 3 NZLR 700.
[311] [2001] Ch 437 at 450–452. Constructive was sufficient according to some previous English cases, such as the Court of Appeal decision in *Rolled Steel Products (Holdings) Ltd v British Steel Corp* [1985] 3 All ER 52.
[312] [2004] EWHC 52 (Ch); [2004] 1 BCLC 468 at [203].
[313] *Re Rossfield Group Operations Pty Ltd* [1981] Qd R 372 at 377; (1981) 3 ACLR 237 (Qld S Ct); *Yore Contractors Pty Ltd v Holcon Pty Ltd* (1990) 2 ASCR 663 at 670.
[314] *Criterion Properties Plc v Stafford UK Properties LLC* [2002] EWCA Civ 1883; *Crown Dilmun v Sutton* [2004] EWHC 52 (Ch); [2004] 1 BCLC 468 at [200].
[315] *CMS Dolphin Ltd v Simonet* [2001] 2 BCLC 704; [2002] BCC 200.
[316] [2001] 1 WLR 1177; [2001] 2 BCLC 704; [2002] BCC 200 at [103]–[104].
[317] [2001] 1 WLR 1177.

director. The court pierced the corporate veil and held the director liable as I was used as a device or facade to conceal the true facts thereby avoiding or concealing any liability of that individual.[318] The court recognised the receipt of T's money by I as knowing receipt by the director. As discussed earlier, it might be that it is not necessary to pierce the corporate veil in this type of case. In *Prest v Petrodel Resources Limited & Others*[319] Lord Sumption in the Supreme Court said that it was a well-established principle that the court may be justified in piercing the corporate veil if a company's separate legal personality is being abused for the purpose of some relevant wrongdoing.[320] His Lordship said that there will be a piercing of the veil where there is evasion; that is where there is a legal right against the person in control of a company 'which exists independently of the company's involvement, and a company is interposed so that the separate legal personality of the company will defeat the right or frustrate its enforcement'.[321] This was to be distinguished from what Lord Sumption called the concealment principle, this is where the interposition of a company conceals the identity of the real actors. This is not to stop the courts from identifying them, assuming that their identity is legally relevant. In these cases the court is not disregarding the 'façade', but only looking behind it to discover the facts which the corporate structure is concealing.[322]

15.109 In *Ultraframe (UK) Ltd v Fielding*[323] Lewison J said that it appeared to him that just because a director has a substantial interest in a company that willingly receives trust property, does not make the director personally accountable for the receipt. But he felt that this was different where the company is a mere cloak or alter ego of the fiduciary, for in that type of situation it may be appropriate to pierce the corporate veil and treat the company's receipt as the fiduciary's receipt.[324] This, like in *Trustor AB v Smallbone*,[325] might in fact be an instance of a concealment.

15.110 Companies would, if it were established that the third party was a knowing recipient of company property, have both a personal and a proprietary remedy against the third party.[326]

D Relief

15.111 The Chapter has already discussed the major forms of relief that might follow a finding of breach of duty. Nevertheless, it is appropriate to say a few words about some specific aspects of relief that might be granted against third parties that are found to have been involved in knowing assistance or knowing receipt.

---

[318] Ibid at 1185. The Court applied *Gilford Motor Co Ltd v Horne* [1933] Ch 935 (CA).
[319] [2013] UKSC 34; [2013] 2 AC 415; [2013] 3 WLR 1.
[320] Ibid at [27].
[321] Ibid.
[322] Ibid.
[323] [2005] EWHC 1638 (Ch).
[324] Ibid at [1576].
[325] [2001] 1 WLR 1177; [2001] 2 BCLC 436; [2002] BCC 200.
[326] *Clark v Cutland* [2004] 1 WLR 783; [2003] 2 BCLC 393 at [31].

15.112 In deciding on relief the issue of causation can be an issue. Where a claimant is seeking compensation in relation to knowing assistance it is not necessary for the claimant to establish that the assistance caused the loss that the claimant has sustained. It suffices for the claimant to prove that he or she has suffered loss and that the loss was caused by the breach of fiduciary duty. But, as we will see shortly, this is not the case with an account of profits.

15.113 It has been stated on a number of occasions by courts at first instance that the court has the power to order an account of profits against a knowing assister, even where no corresponding loss has been suffered by the beneficiary.[327] The Court of Appeal in *Novoship (UK) Ltd v Nikitin*[328] said that the nature of the liability of the knowing recipient or knowing assister is the responsibility of an express trustee, and that that responsibility would include, in an appropriate case, a liability to account for profits.[329] The Court went on to say that where an equitable wrong is itself linked with a breach of fiduciary duty it saw no reason why a court of equity should not be able to order the wrongdoer to disgorge his or her profits in so far as they are derived from the wrongdoing.[330] Thus the Court concluded that a knowing assister can be liable for an account of profits even if the relevant breach does not involve a misapplication of trust property.[331] The liability of a fiduciary (like a director) to account is not dependent on causation at all, for it suffices if the profit that is received comes within the ambit of his or her duty of loyalty where a knowing assister is involved, but in the absence of a duty of loyalty to the beneficiary/company the common law rules of causation are to apply to determine the scope of the liability.[332] Thus a 'but for' test, which is less demanding than the causation rules at common law, is not applicable.[333]

15.114 The Court in *Novoship (UK) Ltd v Nikitin* was of the view that when a claim for an account of profits is made against someone who is not a fiduciary, and does not owe fiduciary duties then, as Lord Nicholls said in the *Attorney-General v Blake*,[334] the court has a discretion to grant or withhold the remedy. So, ordering an account in a non-fiduciary case is not automatic. The Court said that one ground on which the court may withhold the remedy is

---

[327] For instance, *Fyffes Group Ltd v Templeman* [2000] 2 Lloyd's Rep 643; *Ultraframe (UK) Ltd v Fielding* [2005] EWHC 1638 (Ch) at [1589]–[1594]; *Tajik Aluminium Plant v Ermatov (No 3)* [2006] EWHC 7 (Ch) at [23]; *OJSC Oil Co Yugraneft v Abramovich* [2008] EWHC 2613 (Comm) at [377], [392]; *Fiona Trust & Holding Corpn v Privalov* [2010] EWHC 3199 at [66]; *Otkritie International Investment Management Ltd v Urumov* [2014] EWHC 191 (Comm) at [79].

[328] [2014] EWCA Civ 908; [2015] QB 499.

[329] Ibid at [82].

[330] Ibid.

[331] Ibid at [93].

[332] For criticism of this conclusion, see P Devonshire 'Account of Profits for Dishonest Assistance' (2015) 74 CLJ 22 at 233.

[333] Ibid at [114].

[334] [2001] 1 AC 268.

where an account of profits would be regarded as disproportionate in relation to the particular form and extent of wrongdoing.[335]

E Summary

15.115 If a director commits a breach of duty and takes the profits from the breach then he or she can be ordered to account for the profits. If a third party is involved in knowing assistance or receives profits from a breach and it is held that that party was in knowing receipt then he or she can be required to account. Where profits are received by a company and it is not liable for knowing receipt then it will not be accountable for the profits even if the director has an interest in the company, unless the corporate veil can be pierced and it is on the basis that there was some form of evasion going on. A wrongdoing director and his or her company may both be jointly held to account for profits flowing from a breach where the director received the profits and then passed them on to the company, provided that the latter can be proved to be a knowing recipient.

---

[335] [2014] EWCA Civ 908; [2015] QB 499 at [119].

CHAPTER 16

AUTHORISATION AND RATIFICATION OF BREACHES OF DUTY

I INTRODUCTION

16.1 Although directors might have committed a breach of their duties, it is possible that they will not, for one reason or another, be held liable. Obviously one reason is that the company decides not to make any claim against the directors. If the company does not do so, then, as we saw in **Chapter 14**, a member might seek to take derivative proceedings against the director (and, possibly, others). There are other situations where a director might not be held liable. This chapter and the following one deal with the issue of directors who have committed breaches of their general duties being given absolution for what they have done by either the members of the company or the courts, before or after they committed the breach.

16.2 Historically, directors have always been able to go to the shareholders in general meeting and get the shareholders either to authorise what they are going to do[1] or, *ex post*, to seek their forgiveness in relation to any breaches of duty that they have committed. The shareholders are effectively regularising a voidable act. This is in accordance with the traditional principle that fiduciaries may be released from their legal responsibilities by those to whom duties are owed.

16.3 While the book has, on several occasions, mentioned the issue of ratification in the context of discussing the general duties, this chapter focuses squarely on the ratification issue, after some discussion of the *ex ante* authorisation of directorial actions. Shareholders have been entitled at common law, subject to some limitations, to ratify what the directors have done provided full disclosure is made. The CA 2006 introduced, for the first time, provisions that addressed the issue of ratification. but clearly the common law still has great importance, as the leading provision, s 239 of the Act only makes a relatively small, albeit significant, change to the common law. What is also clear

---

[1] The leading case on prospective consent is *New Zealand Netherlands Society Oranje Inc v Kuys* [1973] 1 WLR 1126.

is the fact that the law is not certain and it is not without a degree of unclearness.[2] It is muddled and that state of affairs is likely to continue to be so for the reasons mentioned below.

16.4 As indicated in the last paragraph, the Chapter considers authorisation and ratification, which both involve the shareholders sanctioning what is to be done, or has been done, by the directors. We must distinguish them from shareholders making a decision after the event not to take action against the directors for breach. Such a decision, unless formalised in a legal waiver, deed of release or binding contract, does not prevent the shareholders approving of an action later (within time limits).

16.5 I should note at the outset that the discussion of ratification in this chapter is limited, as far as legislation is concerned, to ratification of breaches of duty under the CA 2006. There is also discussion of the common law, which is still relevant and operational.

16.6 A classic instance of where ratification has been employed is where a director has been in a conflict situation, and the board, where it is empowered by the articles of association, has failed or refused to give consent for the conflict. Under the new legislation, director approval has, in certain circumstances, replaced the need for ratification from members. For instance, s 175(4)(b) of the CA 2006, replaces the rule that conflicts of interest must be authorised by the members of the company,[3] unless some alternative procedure is properly provided by permitting, in certain cases, authorisation by the directors. In the case of a private company, a conflict can be authorised by the directors of the board unless the company's constitution prevents this.[4] The position for public companies is that the constitution must expressly permit authorisation by the board.[5] Also, s 177 provides that directors must disclose interests which they have in relation to a proposed transaction or arrangement with the company, and the disclosure must be made to the board, and if this is done then the directors are not in breach.

16.7 In Part II of the chapter the statutory provision on consent, approval or authorisation by the members is considered. Part III covers ratification. First, the essence of ratification and the background to it are discussed. This is followed by the main element of the Chapter and that involves a discussion of the position that exists at common law. This is important as the codification of ratification does not, as indicated above, greatly affect the common law position. Next, the relevant part of s 239 is discussed. Then there is a brief

---

[2]   Law Commission *Shareholder Remedies: Report on a Reference under section 3(1)(e) of the Law Commissions Act 1965* (Law Com No 246, Cm 3769) (London, Stationery Office, 1997) at para 6.81.
[3]   *Crown Dilmun v Sutton* [2004] EWHC 52 (Ch); [2004] 1 BCLC 468.
[4]   CA 2006, s 175(5)(a).
[5]   CA 2006, s 175(5)(b).

consideration of breaches of statutory duty, and the final sections of the Chapter discuss exclusion from voting on a ratification vote and limits to the use of ratification.

II CONSENT, APPROVAL OR AUTHORISATION BY THE MEMBERS

16.8 Section 180 of the CA 2006 addresses the issue of member consent, to what the directors have done, in two ways. First, it deals with the case where a director is in a conflict situation and has complied with the law concerning obtaining directorial approval or has declared an interest which the director has in a transaction. Second, it indicates the relationship between the general duties in Chapter 2 of Part 10 and the provisions in Chapter 4 of Part 10 that require member approval. Chapter 4 deals, inter alia, with the obligations on directors where they are involved in transactions with their companies. It has largely taken over from Part X of the CA 1985.

16.9 Section 180(1) of the CA 2006 addresses the first matter identified in the previous paragraph. It deals with the issue of conflicts covered by ss 175 and 177. It may be recalled that s 175(5) (discussed in **Chapters 9** and **10**) provides that authorisation might be given to any conflict in which directors are involved (and the company is not), if, in private companies, there is no provision in the company's constitution invalidating such authorisation by the board of directors, and with public companies their constitution specifically provides that directors may give authorisation. Similarly, under s 177 (and discussed in **Chapter 11**) if a director has an interest in a proposed transaction that involves the company, he or she must declare the interest to the other directors and that absolves the director. Section 180(1) provides that where either of s 175 or s 177 is complied with, the relevant transaction is not liable to be set aside because of any common law rule or equitable principle requiring member consent. However, this does not apply if a provision in the constitution of the company requires consent or approval.

16.10 Section 180(2)–(5) of the CA 2006 address the second matter raised by the section. Section 180(2) provides that there is no effect on the application of Chapter 2 duties even if the circumstances involved bring the matter within Chapter 4 of Part 10 of the CA 2006, except that where Chapter 4 applies and approval is given pursuant to that Chapter or the matter is one as to which it is stated that approval is not required, there is no need to comply with s 175 or s 176. Section 180(3) indicates that merely complying with the general duties does not mean that there is no need for approval under Chapter 4, in the appropriate case. Obviously Chapter 4 adds additional obligations for the director.

16.11 Section 180(4) preserves any current ability of the members of a company to authorise conflicts that would otherwise be a breach of the general duties,[6] provided that where the company's constitution has a provision for addressing conflicts it is not infringed by anything done by the directors. Section 180(4)(a) preserves the approach that applies at common law. The GC100, a group of the general counsel and company secretaries of the FTSE 100 companies (Association of General Counsel and Company Secretaries of the FTSE 100 companies), has stated that there are two views taken in relation to s 180(4)(b). The first is that the articles need to indicate that a director will not be in breach of duty if, for instance, he or she withholds information from the company. The second view is that the articles should allow the board, when it authorises a conflict, to state that the director is not required to disclose information received from a conflict situation.[7] For authorisation to be valid, there must be full and frank disclosure of all material facts by the director who seeks it.[8] According to Simon J in *FHR European Ventures LLP v Ramsey Neil Mankarious*:[9] 'The materiality of what must be disclosed is to be assessed on the basis of whether it might have affected the principal's decision and not whether it would have done so.' It is interesting to note that, as we will see, s 239(4) provides that a resolution to ratify is only able to be passed if the majority can be achieved without the wrongdoing director or any of those who are connect with him or her, voting, s 180(4) places no such limits on a vote of authorisation.

16.12   Finally, s 180(5) of the CA 2006 provides that the general duties have effect notwithstanding any enactment or rule of law that exists, except where there is an express or implied exception to this rule. The example given by the Explanatory Notes to the CA 2006 is of s 247 which provides that directors may make provision for employees on the cessation or transfer of a company's business even if this would otherwise constitute a breach of the general duty to promote the success of the company.[10]

III RATIFICATION BY THE MEMBERS

A The essence of, and background to, ratification[11]

16.13   It has been suggested that ratification is a term that probably 'derives from the nineteenth century notion of directors being agents of the company',[12] while another commentator has linked it to trust law.[13] If the former is correct,

---

[6]   Explanatory Notes to the CA 2006, at para 340.
[7]   GC100, Companies Act (2006) – Directors' duties, 7 February 2007 at para 3.2.
[8]   *New Zealand Netherlands Society Oranje Inc v Kuys* [1973] 1 WLR 1126 at 1132.
[9]   [2011] EWHC 2308 (Ch) at [79].
[10] Explanatory Notes to the CA 2006, at para 320.
[11] For a discussion of the meaning of ratification, see P Koh 'Directors' Fiduciary Duties: Unthreading the Joints of Shareholder Ratification' (2005) 5 JCLS 363 at 366–378.
[12] R Cranston 'Limiting Directors' Liability: Ratification, Exemption and Indemnification' [1992] JBL 197 at 198.
[13] J Payne 'A re-examination of ratification' [1999] CLJ 604 at 606. See P Koh 'Directors' Fiduciary Duties: Unthreading the Joints of Shareholder Ratification' (2005) 5 JCLS 363 at 365, where the learned commentator challenges the view that ratification is based on the trust concept of release.

and it is probable that it is, it no longer has the same meaning as in the law of agency.[14] The Law Commission saw ratification as the action of curing a wrong such that there is no cause of action permitting the company to bring proceedings.[15] It may involve the shareholders agreeing to adopt a course of action and forgiving what a director has done, even though it is in breach of the director's duties, or it might simply involve exoneration of the director, depending on the nature of the breach and its consequences. If, for instance, a director arranges a contract for the company with another party, but fails to declare an interest in the contract, the company can decide to affirm what is in fact a voidable contract. Once this is done the contract can no longer be rescinded or, if completed, set aside. The forgiveness element comes in if the company agrees to overlook the fact that the director breached his or her duty in not disclosing the interest. An example of where only the forgiveness aspect is involved is where a director receives a secret commission from a third party, and the general meeting forgives him or her. It might even permit the director to retain it.

16.14 In *Bamford v Bamford*[16] it was said that ratification might be regarded as a whitewash process where there had been a breach, and that really covers the second of the two types of example which have just been given.[17] Harman LJ in *Bamford* talked about the directors being able to get absolution and forgiveness for their sins.[18] The upshot of ratification is that the action of the director binds the company and the company no longer has a cause of action against a director, and, consequently, the director has peace of mind that the company will not turn around and take proceedings against him or her at a later date for the action that is the subject of ratification. This security is particularly pertinent if the company is taken over and a new board installed or the company becomes subject to administration or liquidation.

16.15 Powers were given to members, under common law principles, to ratify directors' breaches of duties,[19] although this is restricted by constitutional conditions such as notice requirements and special majority voting demands.

16.16 At common law ratification has always been able to be obtained by way of an ordinary resolution of the members in general meeting;[20] a simple majority is sufficient. Thus, the mere fact that members knew of a breach is not

---

[14] R Partridge 'Ratification and the Release of Directors from Personal Liability' (1987) 46 CLJ 122 at 122.

[15] Law Commission *Shareholder Remedies: Report on a Reference under section 3(1)(e) of the Law Commissions Act 1965* (Law Com No 246, Cm 3769) (London, Stationery Office, 1997) at para 6.80.

[16] [1970] Ch 212.

[17] Ibid at 238.

[18] Ibid.

[19] *Bamford v Bamford* [1970] Ch 212.

[20] *North-West Transportation v Beatty* (1887) 12 App Cas 589 (PC); *Bamford v Bamford* [1970] Ch 212.

sufficient to absolve the director;[21] there must be a resolution. Any notice sent out calling a meeting to consider ratification of a director's conduct had to indicate in clear terms that its purpose was to approve of the director's conduct or else any resolution might be regarded as deficient,[22] certainly against those at the meeting who dissented from ratifying, and those members who were not present. Furthermore, to be effective a resolution must be passed when the general meeting is fully informed,[23] so that there is a full and frank explanation of the circumstances of the breach,[24] and the members must have fully understood what they were ratifying, although they do not need to know that it was a breach of duty.[25] The director who claims ratification against an action for breach of duty has the onus of establishing that the members were fully informed. Ratification would not be ineffective if something were not disclosed but only where disclosure would not have affected the decision of the members.[26] However, one would think that in many circumstances it might be difficult for a court to gauge whether the non-disclosure was or was not critical, and probably if there were any doubt the court would err on the side of nullifying any purported ratification.

16.17 One last point should be made before moving on to a detailed examination of the common law position. We know, according to s 170, that directors owe their duties to the company, but obviously the company, in ratifying a breach, can only act through human representatives. The shareholders take on this role in ratification. But, as Professor Jenny Payne states:[27]

> 'As a matter of policy, questions can be asked about the appropriateness of shareholders to represent the company. The shareholders, whilst being asked to act on behalf of the company in this regard, are in a peculiar position in relation to the company which may make it almost impossible for them to remain impassive or wholly independent when deciding whether or not to ratify a wrong done to the company.'

---

[21] See *Multinational Gas and Petrochemical Co v Multinational Gas and Petrochemical Services Ltd* [1983] Ch 258 at 281 per May LJ.

[22] *Kaye v Croydon Tramways Co* [1898] I Ch 358 (CA); *Northern Counties Securities Ltd v Jackson & Steeple Ltd* [1974] 1 WLR 1133 at 1143.

[23] Although the House of Lords in *New Zealand Netherlands Society Oranje Inc v Kuys* [1973] 1 WLR 1126 at 1135 commented that the process of ratification is not flawed where there is not disclosure of a particular matter if that matter would not have affected the ultimate decision.

[24] *Earle v Burland* [1902] AC 83 (PC); *Bamford v Bamford* [1972] Ch 212 at 239 (CA); *New Zealand Netherlands Society Oranje Inc v Kuys* (1973) (HL); *Queensland Mines Ltd v Hudson* [1978] 52 ALJR 399 (PC). It must be realised that in some cases it might not be best for members to be given all information as that might well make the matter difficult to understand and make an assessment. See *Buttonwood Nominees Pty Ltd v Sundowner Minerals NL* (1986) 10 ACLR 360.

[25] *Knight v Frost* [1999] 1 BCLC 364; [1999] BCC 819, where it was alleged that member acquiesced to a breach of duty.

[26] *New Zealand Netherlands Society Oranje Inc v Kuys* (1973).

[27] J Payne 'A re-examination of ratification' [1999] CLJ 604 at 609.

16.18 The fact that the shareholders are entitled to ratify ties up with s 172 of the CA 2006 in that the directors are to act in such a way as to promote the success of the company for the benefit of the members. If there has been a breach the shareholders have the ultimate say.

B Position at common law

1 What may be ratified?

16.19 As we have seen, the common law position is important, not only to provide a background to our consideration of s 239 of the CA 2006, but because much of the common law is still applicable after codification. Nevertheless, as we will see below, the common law position is not clear and may be regarded as somewhat confusing and difficult to get a handle on. What follows is a discussion of the case-law and an attempt to make some sense of it.

16.20 We have already noted that at common law shareholders were permitted to ratify actions of directors. But while 'it is an elementary principle of the law relating to joint stock companies that the court will not interfere with the internal management of companies acting within their powers',[28] courts will not permit ratification in certain cases. So, there are limits on what can be ratified and when. The reason for placing restrictions on the power to ratify is that no fiduciary duties are imposed on the members *qua* members; the members can act selfishly and vote in support of their own interests.[29] The big problem though is identifying the line between what may and what may not be ratified. Professor Paul Davies has said that finding a satisfactory answer while taking into account the case-law is difficult, and, perhaps, impossible.[30] This is of concern as there is a need for greater certainty.

16.21 Some wrongs are ratifiable, requiring only a majority vote. Other wrongs are not ratifiable, even with a unanimous vote of the members. It would appear that traditionally the factor that determines whether a breach can be ratified or not is the nature of the directorial wrong.[31] Absent anything in the company's constitution to the contrary, one would think that a company has the capacity to exculpate a director, but the issue is more probably whether to do so is proper.[32] The law, in an attempt to protect minority shareholders from

---

28 *Earle v Burland* [1902] AC 83 at 93.
29 *North-West Transportation v Beatty* (1887) 12 App Cas 589 (PC); *Burland v Earle* [1902] AC 83 (PC); *Northern Counties Securities Ltd v Jackson & Steeple Ltd* [1974] 1 WLR 1133.
30 P Davies *Gower and Davies' Principles of Company Law* (London, Sweet and Maxwell, 7th edn, 2003) at 439.
31 J Payne 'A re-examination of ratification' [1999] CLJ 604 at 614; S Worthington 'Corporate governance: remedying and ratifying directors' breaches' (2000) 116 LQR 638 at 672. This is known as the 'transaction-based' approach to ratification: H Hirt 'Ratification of Breaches of Directors' Duties: The Implications of the Reform Proposal Regarding the Availability of Derivative Actions (2004) 25 Co Law 197 at 201.
32 Worthington, ibid, at 673.

being oppressed by the majority, provides that some wrongs cannot be ratified.[33] But what will constitute activity that is not able to be ratified is not clear.

16.22   There appear to be two kinds of wrong that will not be able to be ratified, and they are expropriation of company property[34] (and breaches involving this category are broad), and where the breach entails dishonest actions.[35] In such cases the minority of members who might not support ratification are being protected. If there is a purported ratification a shareholder could bring a derivative action, which involves, in effect, a challenging of the ratification.[36]

16.23   It has been held many times that a majority of members are not entitled to ratify a fraud or expropriation to a director of the company's property as all shareholders have an interest in the company's property.[37] In *Earle v Burland*,[38] Lord Davey said that the cases where ratification is essentially not available is where the acts complained of are of a fraudulent character or beyond the powers of the company. He went on to observe that the classic example is where the majority are endeavouring, directly or indirectly, to appropriate to themselves money, property, or advantages which belong to the company, or in which the other shareholders are entitled to participate, as was alleged in the case of *Menier v Hooper's Telegraph Works*,[39] a case where the majority voted to expropriate the assets of the company to its favour. In *North-West Transportation v Beatty*[40] Sir Richard Baggallay, in giving the advice of the Privy Council, said[41] that:

> 'Any such dealing or engagement may, however, be affirmed or adopted by the company, provided such affirmance or adoption is not brought about by unfair or improper means, and is not illegal or fraudulent or oppressive towards those shareholders who oppose it.'

16.24   Perhaps the classic example of what Lord Davey was talking about can be seen in *Cook v Deeks*,[42] a case which we have considered before in the book on a couple of occasions. It might be remembered that three directors of a four-director company, X, negotiated on behalf of X to secure some contracts for the construction of a railway. During the course of their negotiations, the directors arranged for the contracts to be performed by them rather than X.

---

[33]   *Prudential Assurance Co Ltd v Newman Industries Ltd (No 2)* [1981] Ch 257 at 307.
[34]   *Cook v Deeks* [1916] AC 554; *Menier v Hooper's Telegraph Works* (1873-74) LR 9 Ch App 350 (CA).
[35]   (1867–68) LR 5 Eq 464; *Mason v Harris* (1879) 11 Ch D 97 (CA).
[36]   A classic example is *Cook v Deeks* [1916] AC 554.
[37]   *Re Halt Garage (1964) Ltd* [1982] 3 All ER 1016; *Aveling Barford Ltd v Perion Ltd* [1989] BCLC 626.
[38]   *Earle v Burland* [1902] AC 83 at 93.
[39]   (1873-74) LR 9 Ch App 350.
[40]   (1887) 12 App Cas 589 (PC).
[41]   Ibid at 593–594.
[42]   [1916] AC 554.

The directors formed a new company especially to carry out the contracts. The fourth director of X became aware of this, but the other three controlled the company and passed a resolution at a general meeting ratifying what had been done. They then resigned from the board of X. The fourth director brought proceedings as a minority shareholder to enforce the rights of X. The upshot was that the Privy Council held that the three directors were liable as they had profited from their roles as directors and they held the contract in trust for X; the ratification was not effective. It was said that the directors who hold a majority of votes are not allowed to make a present of the company's property to themselves. The board in this case adverted to the point made in the quotation above in *North-West Transportation v Beatty* and it indicated that the case before it fell into the last part of the judge's comment. There seems to be no reason why this approach may not be applied to the case where directors make a present of the company's property to others.[43] In *Atwool v Merryweather*[44] the court came to the same view as in *Cook v Deeks* on the basis that there was fraud on the part of the controlling shareholders. This view has been accepted by the Australian High Court in *Angas Law Services Pty Ltd (in liq) v Carabelas*[45] where it was indicated that a misappropriation of company property could not be effectively ratified by the members.[46]

16.25 To ensure that minor misappropriations are not covered by a blanket disallowance of ratification, Professor Ross Cranston (as he then was) suggested that it should cover only serious breaches.[47] Of course, it is always difficult to know where to draw the line and how far such qualifications to rules are to be applied.

16.26 Professors Davies and Worthington have said that while ratification of a misappropriation, such as in *Cook v Deeks*, or a misapplication of company funds, cannot be proper, it is possibly proper for the members to ratify actions of directors where they make an incidental profit.[48] An example of the latter might be the facts in *Regal (Hastings) Ltd v Gulliver*.[49] This distinction depends on assuming that the information available to the directors in the latter case was not company property, or else the directors would have been misappropriating company property.[50]

---

[43] P Davies *Gower and Davies' Principles of Company Law* (London, Sweet and Maxwell, 7th edn, 2003) at 439.

[44] (1867-68) LR 5 Eq 464.

[45] [2005] HCA 23; (2005) 215 ALR 110.

[46] Ibid at [24], [32]. Also, see *Forge v ASIC* (2004) 213 ALR 574, where the Court of Appeal of the New South Wales Supreme Court indicated that it is not possible to ratify the wrongful appropriation of the company's assets.

[47] R Cranston 'Limiting Directors' Liability: Ratification, Exemption and Indemnification' [1992] JBL 197 at 201.

[48] *Gower and Davies' Principles of Modern Company Law* (London, Sweet and Maxwell, 9th edn, 2012) at 625.

[49] [1967] 2 AC 134. Lord Russell commented that the directors could have sought protection by way of resolution of the general meeting to ratify their actions: at 150.

[50] E Ferran 'Shareholder Remedies: The Law Commission Report' (1998) 1 *Company Financial and Insolvency Law Review* 235 at 244.

16.27 There has been significant discussion in academic commentaries concerning the distinction between *Cook v Deeks* and *Regal (Hastings) Ltd v Gulliver*.[51] We considered the latter case in detail in **Chapter 9**[52] and I will not rehearse the facts again. As we have seen, in *Cook v Deeks* ratification was not effective, but in *Regal Hastings*, while the directors did not seek the approval of the members for their breach of duty, Lord Russell in obiter comments said that the directors could have protected themselves by getting their actions ratified. This leads us to ask why could the directors be able to do so in this case and not (legitimately) in *Cook v Deeks*? Davies has given one reason as set out above. Two other reasons are often given. First, in *Regal Hastings* the directors acted in good faith and in *Cook v Deeks* they were acting fraudulently. Second,[53] in *Regal Hastings* the miscreants did not have the majority of shares (and could not therefore control the shareholders' meeting), while the directors in *Cook v Deeks* did have control.[54] The good faith reason may be said to tie up with the decision in *North-West Transportation v Beatty*.[55] In that case it was said that directors could only vote at the members' meeting called to ratify the directors' actions, if the directors had acted in good faith. But using good faith as the reason for distinguishing between *Cook v Deeks* and *Regal Hastings* has been criticised by Pearlie Koh, on the basis, inter alia, that the directors in *Regal Hastings* were not the epitomes of good faith that everyone thinks they were.[56] To substantiate her point she refers to related litigation, *Luxor (Eastbourne) Ltd v Cooper*,[57] a case involving a claim by an estate agent appointed by the holding company for unpaid commission.[58] Nevertheless, there was no finding in the *Regal Hastings* case that the directors had acted other than in good faith.

16.28 It would appear that the courts have not consistently decided on ratification by considering that good faith was required. Clearly, the directors in *Cook v Deeks* did not act in good faith. But in *Bamford v Bamford*[59] the Court of Appeal said that even if the directors in the case before it had acted in bad faith and from an improper motive, what they had done could be ratified by a majority of the shareholders at the general meeting of the company.

16.29 The second reason for distinguishing between *Regal Hastings* and *Cook v Deeks* receives some support from the judgment of Vinelott J in *Prudential*

---

[51] [1967] 2 AC 134. Lord Russell commented that the directors could have sought protection by way of resolution of the general meeting to ratify their actions: at 150.

[52] Above at para **9.17**.

[53] See *Prudential Assurance Co Ltd v Newman Industries Ltd (No 2)* [1981] Ch 257 at 308.

[54] Koh asserts that neither reason holds up: 'Directors' Fiduciary Duties: Unthreading the Joints of Shareholder Ratification' (2005) 5 JCLS 363 at 392–393.

[55] (1887) 12 App Cas 589 (PC).

[56] P Koh 'Directors' Fiduciary Duties: Unthreading the Joints of Shareholder Ratification' (2005) 5 JCLS 363 at 392–393.

[57] [1941] AC 108.

[58] P Koh 'Directors' Fiduciary Duties: Unthreading the Joints of Shareholder Ratification' (2005) 5 JCLS 363 at 392.

[59] [1969] 1 Ch 212 at 242.

Assurance Co Ltd v Newman Industries Ltd (No 2)[60] when he said that while the editor's note in the report of *Regal Hastings*[61] that the resolution 'would have been a mere matter of form, since [the defendant directors] doubtless controlled the voting', he could see nothing in the report that supported this observation. His Lordship went on to say he interpreted the comments of Lord Russell in such a way that the latter appeared to contemplate that the defendant directors might have protected themselves by a resolution in general meeting precisely because they had *not* control of the majority of the votes.[62]

16.30   Vinelott J mused in *Prudential Assurance* that it may be that the cases where the minority can sue are limited to those where the act complained of is of a fraudulent character.[63] Bob Austin, Harold Ford and Ian Ramsay have suggested the difference between *Cook v Deeks* and *Regal Hastings* was that in the latter the directors believed that their actions would not harm the company and there was no misappropriation of existing company property.[64] With respect, that view seems to have strength to it.

16.31   Finally, as far as reconciling *Cook v Deeks* and *Regal Hastings*, one leading text suggests that while the directors expropriated company property in the former case, this did not occur in *Regal Hastings*.[65] However, it might be argued that the directors in *Regal Hastings* did in fact expropriate an opportunity for the company to make more profit, and that could be classified in broad terms as company property.

16.32   Another way of differentiating those wrongs that are able to ratified and those that are not, is to say that the latter covers situations where directors engage in self-serving or self-aggrandising activity.[66] But most activity will involve in some way benefits going to directors, so one queries whether that holds water.

16.33   Koh says that self-serving conduct would involve 'self-appropriative acts by which management seeks to take for itself property or potential that would otherwise belong to the corporation'.[67] Where does one draw the line with self-serving behaviour? It has been suggested that: 'It is ultimately an ethical judgment (as to the degree of directorial misbehaviour for which ratification is permissible) in the guise of legal principle.'[68] It has been asserted that the cases

---

[60]   [1981] Ch 257.

[61]   [1942] 1 All ER 378 at 379.

[62]   [1981] Ch 257 at 308.

[63]   [1981] Ch 257 (in the report it says the majority, but the judge must have meant minority).

[64]   R Austin, H Ford, I M Ramsay *Company Directors* (Sydney, LexisNexis Butterworths, 2005) at 397.

[65]   A Alcock (ed) *Gore-Browne on Companies* (Bristol, Jordan Publishing) at 17-4.

[66]   P Koh 'Directors' Fiduciary Duties: Unthreading the Joints of Shareholder Ratification' (2005) 5 JCLS 363 at 394.

[67]   V Brudney 'Revisiting the Import of Shareholder Consent for Corporate Fiduciary Loyalty Obligations' (2000) 25 Journal of Corporation Law 209 at 225 and quoted in Koh, ibid at 394.

[68]   A Boyle 'The Private Law Enforcement of Directors' Duties' in K Hopt and G Teubner (eds)

of *Pavlides v Jensen*[69] and *Daniels v Daniels*[70] (the former, before the introduction of the statutory derivative scheme, held that directors could not be sued in derivative actions for negligence and the latter qualified that by saying that directors can do so, where their negligence is self-serving) can be reconciled on the basis that in the latter the director was in a conflict situation that led to benefits of a serious kind.[71] Again, there is some difficulty in determining what is 'serious' in this context. Where does one draw the line?

16.34 The problem is that if members can ratify a benefit that a director has made, whether he or she acted in good faith, the upshot appears to be the same as a case like *Cook v Deeks* where a corporate opportunity has been taken in bad faith. In both cases the end result is that the company is giving away assets.

16.35 The above discussion illustrates the fact that there has traditionally been two views as to when ratification would be effective or not, one turning on the nature of the wrong, and the other deeming an action not to be ratifiable because the wrongdoers were seeking to ratify their own default in order to oppress the minority.[72] The first focuses on the wrong and the latter on control (and abuse?). In a case like *Cook v Deeks* ratification is not permitted under either of the two views, as the directors committed fraud and controlled the general meeting.

16.36 Is it possible to say that there should, therefore, be a unanimous vote for any breach where a director is exploiting company opportunities and/or information as that involves a potential loss of benefits in which all shareholders have an interest? Certainly in *Cook v Deeks* the Privy Council would not permit directors to get away with a majority vote when they had made 'a present to themselves' of company contracts.[73] Can you have unanimous consent to a fraud as in *Cook v Deeks*? There seems to be no reason why this approach may not be applied to the case where directors make a present to others. Against that, it might be argued that minority shareholders who do not gain at all from the action of the directors might be coerced or subject to duress and so their consent is not able to be regarded as valid.

16.37 As we will see later, if the company is in financial difficulties it would not be appropriate for the shareholders to ratify a breach.

Corporate Governance and Directors' Liabilities (1984) p 265 and quoted by Brenda Hannigan in *Company Law* (London, LexisNexis Butterworths, 2003) at 507.

[69] [1956] Ch 565.

[70] [1978] Ch 406.

[71] P Koh 'Directors' Fiduciary Duties: Unthreading the Joints of Shareholder Ratification' (2005) 5 JCLS 363 at 395.

[72] A Keay and J Loughrey 'An Assessment of the Present State of Statutory Derivative Proceedings' in J Loughrey (ed) *Directors' Duties and Shareholder Litigation in the Wake of the Financial Crisis* (Cheltenham, Edward Elgar, 2013) at 205.

[73] [1916] 1 AC 554 at 564.

2 *What about unanimous voting?*

16.38   There are occasional cases like *Canada Safeway Ltd v Thompson*,[74] a decision of Manson J of the British Columbia Supreme Court, which suggest that a unanimous vote is needed for all ratifications of directors' breaches, but this does not even appear to represent the law now in the UK, and s 239 of the CA 2006 clearly provides that a simple majority is sufficient for ratification. But can it be a means of ratifying that which cannot ordinarily be ratified by a majority? Some judicial support[75] can be gleaned for this, provided that what is being ratified is within the members' power. Professor Jennifer Payne[76] gives the example of May LJ in *Multinational Gas and Petrochemical Co v Multinational Gas and Petrochemical Services Ltd* where he said 'the unanimous decision of all the shareholders in a solvent company about anything that the company under its memorandum of association has power to do shall be the decision of the company',[77] a view which found support, albeit in obiter, in Lord Hoffmann's judgment in *Meridian Global Funds Management Asia Ltd v The Securities Commission*.[78] Other cases have held that a company is bound in relation to any matter intra vires by the unanimous agreement of its members, whether the act be mandated in advance or subsequently ratified.[79] And breaches of duty by directors can be so ratified provided that the members are fully informed, and directors have been absolved for acting negligently in carrying out their duties[80] and exercising their powers for an improper purpose.[81] The comment of Slade LJ in *Rolled Steel Products (Holdings) Ltd v British Steel Corp*[82] that 'the clear general principle is that any act which falls within the corporate capacity of a company will bind it if it is done with the unanimous consents of all the shareholders or is subsequently ratified by such consents' appears to indicate that unanimity can rectify a wrongdoing. It must be noted that his Lordship did go on to say that: 'This last-mentioned principle

---

[74]   [1951] 3 DLR 295 at 321 (and affirmed on appeal at [1952] 2 DLR 591).
[75]   *Salomon v A Salomon & Co. Ltd* [1897] AC 22 at 57 per Lord Davey; *Re Horsey & Weight Ltd* [1982] Ch 442 at 454 per Buckley LJ; *Rolled Steel Ltd v British Steel Corp* [1986] Ch 246 at 296 per Slade LJ; *Aveling Barford Ltd v Perion Ltd.* [1989] BCLC 626 at 630–631 per Hoffmann J.
[76]   J Payne 'A Re-examination of Ratification' [1999] CLJ 604 at 618–619.
[77]   [1983] Ch 258 at 280.
[78]   [1995] 3 All ER 918 at 923.
[79]   *Salomon v Salomon & Co. Ltd* [1897] AC 22 at 57, per Lord Davey; *Re Express Engineering Works Ltd* [1920] 1 Ch 466; *Parker & Cooper Ltd v Reading* [1926] Ch 975; *Multinational Gas and Petrochemical Co v Multinational Gas and Petrochemical Services Ltd* [1983] Ch 258 at 289-290; *Rolled Steel Products (Holdings) Ltd v British Steel Corp* [1986] Ch 246; *Re Horsley & Weight Ltd* [1982] Ch 442 at 454.
[80]   *Multinational Gas and Petrochemical Co v Multinational Gas and Petrochemical Services Ltd* [1983] Ch 258; *Re D'Jan of London Ltd* [1994] 1 BCLC 561.
[81]   *Winthrop Investments Ltd v Winns* [1975] 2 NSWLR 666; *Bamford v Bamford* [1969] 1 Ch 212; *Hogg v Cramphorn Ltd* [1966] 3 All ER 420.
[82]   *Rolled Steel Products (Holdings) Ltd v British Steel Corp* [1985] 3 All ER 52 at 86. See also *Re Halt Garage (1964) Ltd* [1982] 3 All ER 1016 at 1037; *Re Horsley & Weight Ltd* [1982] [1982] Ch 442.

certainly is not an unqualified one. In particular, it will not enable the shareholders of a company to bind the company itself to a transaction which constitutes a fraud on its creditors.'[83]

16.39 The argument in favour of permitting ratification of any breach by unanimous support would be that no one is harmed. However, is that necessarily the case? The problem with permitting unanimity to rectify a breach is that potentially the approval of actions of directors might, in some circumstances, have long standing effects and might prejudice future shareholders. Also, while the company might be solvent at the time of the ratification, it might be deleterious for the company in the long run, and may impact on creditors at some stage. Furthermore, there is the point made earlier that support could be secured sometimes through duress or undue influence.

16.40 Certainly it could be said that the judgment of Vinelott J in *Taylor v National Union of Mineworkers*[84] is against allowing unanimity to rectify a breach. His Lordship opined that a breach such as a misapplication of company funds cannot be ratified by any majority of members, however large, and one would think that that would include a unanimous vote.

3 Who is bound by ratification?

16.41 As Professor Brenda Hannigan has said: 'the majority in general meeting may use their voting power to ratify such breaches and this operates as a complete bar to any derivative action by a minority shareholder. Effective ratification ends the matter'[85] (footnote omitted). So, a minority shareholder at the time of the ratification vote cannot take any action. This is confirmed under the statutory derivative action scheme because if ratification has occurred a judge is unable to give permission to a shareholder to continue a derivative action.[86] But what is not clear is whether ratification only binds the shareholders at that time and whether it binds the company, that is, can a liquidator or a board appointed by new controllers initiate proceedings against a miscreant director whose actions have been ratified by the general meeting? Does the ratification only stop the present shareholders from brining a derivative action or does it extinguish the cause of action for any future shareholder? It was said in *North-West Transportation Co Ltd v Beatty*[87] that:

> '[u]nless some provision to the contrary is to be found in the charter or other instrument by which the company is incorporated, the resolution of the shareholders, duly convened, upon any question with which the company is legally competent to deal, is binding upon the minority, *and consequently upon the company*.' (my emphasis)

---

[83]　*Rolled Steel Products (Holdings) Ltd v British Steel Corp* [1985] 3 All ER 52 at 86.
[84]　[1985] BCLC 237 at 254.
[85]　'Limitations on a Shareholder's Right to Vote – Effective Ratification Revisited' [2000] JBL 493 at 504.
[86]　CA 2006, s 263(2)(c)(ii) (England and Wales and Northern Ireland); s 268(1)(c)(ii) (Scotland).
[87]　(1887) 12 App Cas 589 at 593 per Sir Richard Baggallay.

Does the last part of this quotation mean that the company as represented by a differently constituted board or a liquidator is bound? If it did not then it would seem to be strange, for as soon as one shareholder sold shares to a new shareholder the ratification would be otiose.

16.42   Cranston J when he was an academic asserted some time ago that following ratification for breach of duty, directors desiring full protection should insist on a formal release.[88] Santow J of the New South Wales Supreme Court in *Miller v Miller*[89] appeared to agree with that view.[90] His Honour said that ratification blocks minority shareholders from taking action against directors, but it leaves directors vulnerable to an action from new controllers of the company.[91]

16.43   Payne has argued that the valid ratification of a breach will usually constitute a decision not to sue by the company.[92] She feels that the better view is that ratification should be regarded as extinguishing the right to sue in the future, and cites several cases in support.[93] If that is correct, then would the same apply to where a liquidator brings proceedings for a breach that has been ratified? It might be argued that while the liquidator is bringing the proceedings in the name of the company, he or she is effectively acting on behalf of the creditors and the commencement of winding up divested the company of the beneficial interest in its property and the liquidator holds the property on statutory trust for the creditors.[94] A cause of action is property for the purposes of the liquidation and the liquidator can enforce it. While this has some attraction, it is submitted that the liquidator should not be able to claim provided that the ratification was valid and at the time it occurred the company was not in such financial difficulty that the directors were under an obligation to take into account the interests of creditors.[95] The fact that a liquidator or subsequent controller of the company should not be able to bring proceedings following ratification follows from the obiter comments of Lord Russell in *Regal Hastings* when his Lordship said that that the directors could have sought protection by way of resolution of the general meeting to ratify their

---

[88]   R Cranston 'Limiting Directors' Liability: Ratification, Exemption and Indemnification' [1992] JBL 197 at 200.

[89]   (1995) 16 ACSR 73.

[90]   Ibid at 87.

[91]   Ibid.

[92]   J Payne 'A Re-examination of Ratification' [1999] CLJ 604 at 616.

[93]   Ibid at 617. The cases are *Salomon v A Salomon & Co. Ltd* [1897] AC 22 at 57 per Lord Davey; *Re Horsley & Weight Ltd* [1982] Ch 442 at 454 per Buckley LJ; *Rolled Steel Ltd v British Steel Corp* [1986] Ch 246 at 296 per Slade LJ; *Aveling Barford Ltd v Perion Ltd* [1989] BCLC 626 at 630-631 per Hoffmann J; *Multinational Gas and Petrochemical Co v Multinational Gas and Petrochemical Services Ltd* [1983] Ch 258 at 280 per May LJ; *Meridian Global Funds Management Asia Ltd v The Securities Commission* [1995] 3 All ER 918 at 923 per Lord Hoffmann.

[94]   *Re Oriental Inland Steam Co* (1874) 9 Ch App 557 at 560; *Cambridge Gas Transport Corp v Official Committee of Unsecured Creditors of Navigator Holdings Plc* [2006] UKPC 26; *Financial Services Compensation Scheme Ltd v Larnell (Insurances) Ltd* [2005] EWCA Civ 1408; [2006] BCC 690; [2006] BPIR 1370 at 18.

[95]   See *Kinsela v Russell Kinsela Pty Ltd* (1986) 4 ACLC 215; (1986) 10 ACLR 395.

actions.[96] It will be recalled in that case directors had technically breached their duties and later they were sued at the behest of a new board appointed by new controllers of the company. Lord Russell was clearly envisaging the fact that the directors could have obtained exoneration from the members through ratification of their actions and that would have kept them safe from attack, because the cause of action would have been extinguished. The comment of Dillon LJ in *Multinational Gas* seems to support that conclusion. His Lordship said:[97]

> 'If the company is bound by what was done when it was a going concern, then the liquidator is in no better position...he [the liquidator] cannot sue the directors because the decisions which he seeks to impugn were made by, and with the full assent of, the members.'

16.44 This comment is effectively consistent with the decision of the Privy Council in *Attorney-General for Canada v Standard Trust Company of New York*[98] where the board said that the liquidator's position in representing the creditors cannot be higher than the title of the company through which the creditors claim.[99]

16.45 So, we may conclude from this that if an action is ratified properly no proceedings can be initiated in the future against the director(s) by a shareholder, a new board or a liquidator.

C The section

16.46 Section 239 of the CA 2006 is broad. It covers ratification of conduct by a director that involves negligence, default, breach of duty or breach of trust in relation to the company.[100] The provision does not specifically cover a breach of duty under Chapter 2 of Part 10, but a breach of duty is mentioned, so one would expect that it is able to be applied to a breach of one of the general duties discussed in this book.[101] The reference to a breach of trust does seem strange because misappropriation of company property is regarded as a breach of trust and it is unable to be ratified, certainly by way of an ordinary resolution.[102] Does that mean that a misappropriation is now able to be sanctioned? It would be odd if it could be, given the many comments about the impropriety of such an action, especially in cases like *Cook v Deeks*. But then, as we will see, ratification of the kind seen in *Cook v Deeks* could not usually occur for s 239 prevents interested directors voting their shares at a ratification meeting. So, perhaps the members can now ratify a misappropriation of property.

---

[96] *Regal (Hastings) Ltd v Gulliver* [1967] 2 AC 134 at 150.
[97] [1983] Ch 258 at 290.
[98] [1911] AC 498.
[99] Ibid at 504.
[100] CA 2006, s 239(1).
[101] The reasoning of Lord Hodge in *Eastford v Gillespie* [2009] CSOH 119 at [7]–[9] when addressing ratification by the board of a director's actions seems to support that conclusion.
[102] J Birds et al *Boyle and Birds' Company Law* (Bristol, Jordan Publishing, 6th edn, 2007) at 666.

16.47 Section 239(2) then provides that for ratification there must be a resolution of the members. The resolution may be a written resolution where there is no meeting, or a resolution passed at a meeting of members.[103] The resolution is an ordinary resolution, unless the company's articles require a greater majority or unanimity,[104] and an ordinary resolution merely requires a simple majority.[105] Written resolutions are only permitted in private companies.[106] Nothing less demanding than requiring an ordinary resolution for ratification can be provided for in the articles, but a more strict provision may be included and it will be enforced.

16.48 Both acts and omissions of directors can be the subject of a ratification resolution.[107] The reference to 'director' in s 239 includes both former and shadow directors.[108]

16.49 Under s 239, the relevant director(s) and any members connected to the director(s) are not eligible to vote.[109] Where a resolution is put at a meeting, it is only passed if the required majority is secured while disregarding the votes in favour of the resolution by the director(s) whose action is subject to possible ratification (assuming he or she is a member) as well as the votes of any persons connected with the director(s).[110]

16.50 Section 239(6)(a) does not affect the validity of a unanimous decision by the members. This, therefore, allows for the operation of the *Duomatic* principle,[111] a principle which enables companies to pass motions by way of informal unanimous assent.

16.51 The section does not affect the validity of the power of the directors to agree not to sue or settle a claim made by them,[112] but such action could itself constitute a breach of duty. If it does then it might be followed by a derivative claim.

16.52 Section 239 has had fairly little impact on the status quo. While in *Franbar Holdings Ltd v Patel*[113] counsel argued that under the new law a company can ratify any act provided that it was not ultra vires the company's powers,[114] William Trower QC (sitting as a deputy judge of the High Court) rejected that submission.[115] With respect, it is contended that the deputy judge

---

[103] CA 2006, s 281(1).
[104] CA 2006, s 281(3).
[105] CA 2006, s 282(1).
[106] CA 2006, s 282(2).
[107] See the definition of 'conduct' in CA 2006, s 239(5)(a).
[108] CA 2006, s 239(5)(b)(c).
[109] CA 2006, s 239(3).
[110] CA 2006, s 239(4).
[111] *Re Duomatic Ltd* [1969] 1 All ER 161.
[112] CA 2006, s 239(6)(b).
[113] [2008] EWHC 1534 (Ch).
[114] Ibid at [43].
[115] Ibid at [44].

was correct in his view. Section 239 provides in sub-s (7) that the provision does not affect any other enactment or rule of law imposing additional requirements to those found in s 239. Consequently, any rule of law that provides that a particular kind of breach is not able to be ratified still applies; s 239 provides for additional demands and does not subtract from the old law.[116] The problem is, as mentioned above, that it is not clear what breaches can and cannot be ratified. Also, as we have noted above, s 239 says nothing about the situation concerning the ratification of breaches of the duties in Chapter 2 of Part 10. What can we say about breaches of these duties and the issue of ratification? Under common law principles a breach of the no-conflict and no-profit rules could be ratified if the breach was committed in good faith, so it is likely that a breach, in good faith, of either s 175 or s 176 could be ratified. It would seem that ordinarily a breach of s 172 could not be ratified as it must involve the director not acting in good faith. But there could be cases, as there was under the old duty to act bona fide in the best interests of the company, where a director does not act in bad faith, but merely does not turn his or her mind to whether an action promotes the success of the company for the benefit of the members. Where directors do this they have been held liable under the common law unless an intelligent and honest man in the position of a director of the company involved, could, in the whole of the circumstances, have reasonably believed that the transaction was for the benefit of the company.[117] The primary case is *Charterbridge Corp Ltd v Lloyds Bank Ltd*.[118] So, if the director has not acted in bad faith, but failed to act as an intelligent and honest man in the position of the director would have, then possibly the director's action could be ratified. It is arguable that a breach of s 171(a), the duty to act in accordance with the constitution, is ratifiable, if the director was acting in good faith, such as where he or she genuinely believed that an act was in accordance with the constitution. The same might be said of the duty to exercise powers for proper purposes in s 171(b). We know from **Chapter 5** that a director can be liable for a breach of this duty even if he or she were acting in good faith.[119] We noted above that the negligent action of a director may be ratified at common law,[120] and hence it might well be that a breach of s 174 can likewise be ratified. Query, in light of *Daniels v Daniels*, whether ratification could occur where the negligence is self-serving. It is probable that the breaches of s 177 could be ratified provided that good faith can be established. It might be difficult for a director to establish good faith in some cases.

16.53 One last observation is that while at common law the rules on authorisation and ratification were the same, there is now a difference, which is perhaps unfortunate.

---

[116] Ibid.

[117] *Charterbridge Corp Ltd v Lloyds Bank Ltd* [1970] Ch 62 at 74; [1969] 3 All ER 1185 at 1194. Also, see *Shuttleworth v Cox Bros (Maidenhead) Ltd* [1927] 2 KB 9 at 23.

[118] [1970] Ch 62; [1969] 3 All ER 1185.

[119] For example, see *Hogg v Cramphorn* [1967] Ch 254; *Howard Smith Ltd v Ampol Petroleum Ltd* [1974] AC 821.

[120] For example, see *Pavlides v Jensen* [1956] Ch 565. But self-serving negligence could not be: *Daniels v Daniels* [1978] Ch 406. However, it must be noted that in the former case the directors did obtain an advantage.

D Ratification of breaches of statutory duties

16.54 The conduct for which directors will now seek to secure ratification will involve breaches of statutory duties. Has this changed anything? Are members able to ratify breaches of statutory duties? In *Miller v Miller*,[121] Santow J of the New South Wales Supreme Court was of the opinion that they could not.[122] It was followed later in the same court by Young J in *Gray Eisdell Timms Pty Ltd v Combined Auctions Pty Ltd*[123] However, Debelle J of the South Australian Supreme Court in *Pascoe Ltd (in liq) v Lucas*[124] took the opposite view. His Honour said that ratification was possible as the statutory duties reflect the duties at common law and in equity.[125] This is the situation in the UK now, as we have seen. Also, the Australian decisions on this question have to be considered in light of the fact that Australia has retained the non-statutory duties of directors that existed before introducing statutory ones. The case for ratification being able to apply to statutory breaches of duty is supported by the fact that s 239 does refer to breach of duty, and one would think that the general duties in Chapter 2 of Part 10 were in view when Parliament inserted this reference.

E Sole director/shareholders

16.55 An issue that is not readily clear is whether a sole director and shareholder of a company is able to ratify his or her own wrong? What is clear is that a wrong that is not ratifiable cannot be ratified by the director/shareholder.[126] But can a wrong that is ratifiable? There is no case-law directly on the point, for the only cases mentioning the issue deal with non-ratifiable wrongs.[127]

16.56 There cannot be ratification if the resolution to ratify is proposed as a written resolution because the director would not be an eligible member due to s 239(3)), and if there is a meeting then there can be no ratification resolution passed because a vote in favour by the director/shareholder must, according to s 239(4), be disregarded. Can the wrong be ratified by way of the application of the *Duomatic* principle and invoking s 239(6)(a)? In companies with two or more members and where ratification is sought for the wrongdoing of only one of them, and the parties are not connected, ratification by way of informal unanimous consent could occur. One might argue that a court is not likely to permit a sole director/shareholder to obtain a result through the application of the *Duomatic* principle when he or she could not obtain, because of s 239, the same result at a general meeting or through a written resolution. However,

---

[121] (1995) 16 ACSR 73.
[122] Ibid at 89.
[123] (1995) 17 ACSR 303 at 312–313.
[124] [1998] SASC 6660; (1998) 27 ACSR 737; (1998) 16 ACLC 1247.
[125] (1998) 27 ACSR 737 at 772; (1998) 16 ACLC 1247 at 1278. On appeal to the Full Court of the Supreme Court, no reference was made to this view.
[126] *Cook v Deeks* [1916] 1 AC 554; *Gold Travel Ltd v Aydin* [2014] EWHC 1587 (Ch).
[127] *Ultraframe (UK) Ltd v Fielding* [2005] EWHC 1638 (Ch) at [40]; *Goldtrail Travel Ltd v Aydin* [2014] EWHC 1587 (Ch) at [117].

support for the argument that the *Duomatic* principle would be applied gains some support from *Re Finch plc*,[128] in which the judge, while not referring to s 239, said that two shareholders could, through the application of the *Duomatic* principle, effectively ratify the wrong of one of them while acting as a director even where the shareholders were connected (husband and wife).[129] It could be argued from this case that if two connected shareholders can ratify what one of them has done, a sole director/shareholder should also be able to do so, because in both situations the shareholders concerned would be excluded from voting to ratify at a general meeting or as a written resolution.

16.57 Thus, while the answer to the question posed is not clear, as there is no authority that resolves the matter directly, the authority that most closely addresses the issue provides some support for the argument that a sole director/shareholder would be permitted, under the *Duomatic* principle, to ratify his or her own wrong.

16.58 The same reasoning could be employed where all the directors are the only shareholders of the company and they have all been involved in the commission of the wrong, although technically *Re Finch plc* could be distinguished as in that case one of the shareholders had not committed a wrong.

F Exclusions from voting

16.59 One major issue with ratification at common law has been if a miscreant director is a member of the company, may he or she vote on a resolution to ratify his or her actions? At common law the directors who committed a breach of duties were permitted, at the general meeting, to vote their own shares on a resolution to ratify provided that they had acted bona fide.[130] For example, in the leading case of *North-West Transportation v Beatty*[131] a director entered into a contract with his company, but because he did not make appropriate disclosure the contract was voidable, and ratification was sought. At the general meeting a resolution of ratification was passed, but with the director voting. The director had the majority of votes, but the Privy Council held that he was entitled to vote his shares as he had acted in good faith. This was approved of in the subsequent Privy Council decision of *Earle v Burland*.[132] Nevertheless, this does not smell right and is not consistent with stricter corporate governance approaches, as well as being contrary to cases such as *Cook v Deeks* and *Atwool v Merryweather*,[133] even though the distinguishing feature might be the good faith of the member.

---

[128] [2015] EWHC 2430, [2016] 1 BCLC 394.

[129] Ibid at [18].

[130] For example, see *North-West Transportation v Beatty* (1887) 12 App Cas 589 (PC); *Re Horsley & Weight Ltd* [1982] Ch 442; *Rolled Steel Products Ltd v British Steel Corp* [1986] Ch 246; *Northern Counties Securities Ltd v Jackson & Steeple Ltd* [1974] 1 WLR 1133.

[131] (1887) 12 App Cas 589 (PC).

[132] *Earle v Burland* [1902] AC 83 at 94.

[133] (1867-68) LR 5 Eq 464.

16.60   In *Prudential Assurance*[134] Vinelott J was not prepared to interpret *North-West Transportation v Beatty* widely. He said that what the case shows is that a contract between a company and a majority shareholder, which is ratified in general meeting, where the resolution being passed by the use of the controlling shareholder's votes, will not be set aside unless it is shown to have been an improper one.[135] His Lordship said that the case was not authority for the more general proposition that a controlling shareholder who is also a director can, by using his or her votes in general meeting, ratify an act that is not of a fraudulent nature, although a breach of his or her directorial duty, and thereby prevent the minority from bringing a derivative action.[136]

16.61   It is in the area of voting, that s 239 provides the major effect on the law. Directors who have committed a breach are excluded from voting for a ratification resolution in general meeting. Under s 239, which puts into effect the recommendation of the Company Law Review Steering Group,[137] if a resolution to ratify is proposed as a written resolution, the relevant director(s) and any members connected to the director(s) are not eligible to vote.[138] Where a resolution is put at a meeting, it is only passed if the required majority is secured while disregarding the votes in favour of the resolution by the director(s) whose action is subject to possible ratification (assuming he or she is a member) as well as the votes of any persons connected with the director(s).[139] But this requirement does not stop the director(s) or any member who is connected to the director(s) from attending, being counted towards the quorum and participating (short of voting) in the proceedings at the meeting at which the conduct of the director(s) is being considered.[140] In smaller companies, in particular, it might be argued that it is not appropriate for the director to be present and to have the opportunity to sway the views of members. Yet, on the other hand, it might be said that a director should be able to be present so that he or she can answer any questions and to put the argument for ratification, or at least a plea for mercy.

16.62   'Connected person' is defined in s 252 of the CA 2006. The definition is broad and includes members of the director's family.[141] Who constitutes family members is set out in s 253(2) and includes, as one would expect, the director's spouse, civil partner or children. Importantly, s 239(5)(d) excludes the application of s 252(3). This latter provision states that other directors are not regarded as persons connected with a director. The upshot is that a director's fellow directors can be counted as connected persons for the purposes of s 239. This would mean that where there is a breach by a number of directors, it would prevent resolutions being put for ratification of each director separately,

---

[134]   [1981] Ch 257.
[135]   Ibid at 309–310.
[136]   Ibid at 310.
[137]   Company Law Review *Modern Company Law for a Competitive Economy: Completing the Structure* (London, DTI, 2000) at para 5.85.
[138]   CA 2006, s 239(3).
[139]   CA 2006, s 239(4).
[140]   CA 2006, s 239(4).
[141]   CA 2006, s 252(2).

allowing other miscreant directors to vote in favour of ratification for their colleagues, thereby opening up the possibility of the directors ensuring that they are all absolved on the basis of all the errant directors supporting one another.

16.63 Mayson, French and Ryan point out that a director is excluded by s 239(4) from voting 'if a member'. It does not state that the director is prohibited from voting 'as a member'. The result is that a director would not be able to vote as a proxy if a member, but could do so if the director is not a member.[142]

16.64 Obviously the rationale behind the exclusion of directors from voting is to ensure that those with a personal interest in the motion before the meeting are not able to carry the day. Those without a personal interest can decide the issue and they are able to make a decision more objectively and so this rids the law of possible partiality. Of course, the new legislation does not stop those members who, whilst not connected with a director, are influenced by, or dependent on, him or her from taking the director's side. It would, of course, be virtually impossible to lay down any rules excluding persons from voting because of influence.

16.65 As was noted above, the section does not affect the validity of a unanimous decision by the members,[143] so the exclusions from voting do not apply when all members vote on an issue.

16.66 The fact that one or more directors are excluded from voting might lead to problems in small companies. The directors who are excluded from voting, together with their connected persons, might have a very large proportion of the shareholding and this might mean that a small minority gets to vote on ratification. Prima facie that might not seem to be a problem, but the small minority might be able to use this power to gain leverage over the directors,[144] they could engage in strategic voting, known as 'hold-out' tactics, namely voting strategically to seek to extract from a director(s) greater personal gains in exchange for the shareholders' consent.

G A limit on ratification

16.67 Earlier we considered what wrongs are ratifiable and what are not. We have seen that certain actions might well limit the operation of ratification. That discussion focused on the way that a director has acted and the nature of the wrong. But there are situations where ratification might not be permitted, even where this prohibition has nothing to do with the wrongdoing of the director. This section of the Chapter looks at this limitation.

---

[142] *Company Law* (OUP, 24th edn, 2007) at 488.
[143] CA 2006, s 239(6)(a). See *Re Duomatic Ltd* [1969] 2 Ch 365 on the principle of unanimous consent.
[144] L Sealy and S Worthington *Cases and Materials in Company Law* (OUP, 8th edn, 2008) at 349.

16.68 One of the significant limitations on shareholders releasing directors from their duties is that they are not entitled to do so, certainly when the company is insolvent,[145] and probably when the company is in financial strife short of insolvency.[146] This is because at this point the directors have to take into account the interests of creditors, and shareholders are not regarded at this time as the owners of the residual value of the firm, having been, in effect, supplanted by the creditors, whose rights are transformed into equity-like rights.[147] In a situation where creditors' interests intrude in the life of the company, and this is acknowledged by s 172(3) of the CA 2006, the shareholders cannot ratify any breach by directors,[148] as they can when creditors' interests do not have to be taken into account, for the shareholders are not the only group which is interested in the company's funds. Hence, the directors cannot be sure, just because they have secured the ratification of their actions by the shareholders that they are not going to be held liable at some time in the future. This was made clear in *Bowthorpe Ltd v Hills*[149] where it was said that ratification should not threaten the solvency of the company or prejudice creditors. Ratification could not apply if the company were insolvent as the interests of the creditors become paramount.[150] In *Kinsela v Russell Kinsela Pty Ltd*,[151] a case followed several times in the UK and elsewhere, the New South Wales Court of Appeal specifically held that a company could not ratify a breach when the company is insolvent. In that case Street CJ stated:[152]

'In a solvent company the proprietary interests of the shareholders entitle them as a general body to be regarded as the company when questions of the duty of directors arise. If, as a general body, they authorise or ratify a particular action of the directors, there can be no challenge to the validity of what the directors have done. But where a company is insolvent the interests of the creditors intrude. They become prospectively entitled, through the mechanism of liquidation, to displace the power of the shareholders and directors to deal with the company's assets .... Where ... the interests at risk are those of creditors I see no reason in law or logic to recognise that the shareholders can authorise the breach.'

16.69 But, as indicated above, the limit on the use of ratification is probably wider than just where a company is insolvent. *Bowthorpe Ltd v Hills*,[153]

---

[145] *Gold Travel Ltd v Aydin* [2014] EWHC 1587 (Ch).

[146] See *Kinsela v Russell Kinsela Pty Ltd* (1986) 4 ACLC 215; (1986) 10 ACLR 395.

[147] S Schwarcz in 'Rethinking a Corporation's Obligations to Creditors' (1996) 17 *Cardozo Law Review* 647 at 668. See D Baird 'The Initiation Problem in Bankruptcy' (1991) 11 *International Journal of Law and Economics* 223 at 228-229. For the view that several groups could be regarded as exposed to residual risk, see G Kelly and J Parkinson 'The Conceptual Foundations of the Company: A Pluralist Approach' (1998) 2 CfiLR 174.

[148] For instance, see *Re Horsley & Weight Ltd* [1982] Ch 442; *Kinsela v Russell Kinsela Pty Ltd* (1986) 4 ACLC 215; (1986) 10 ACLR 395; *Re DKG Contractors Ltd* [1990] BCC 903.

[149] [2002] EWHC 2331 (Ch); [2003] 1 BCLC 226.

[150] For example, see *Re Pantone 485 Ltd* [2002] 1 BCLC 266 at [69]; *Gwyer v London Wharf (Limehouse) Ltd* [2002] EWHC 2748 (Ch); [2003] 2 BCLC 153 at [74]; *Re HLC Environmental Projects Ltd* [2013] EWHC 2876 (Ch) at [91], [92].

[151] (1986) 4 ACLC 215; (1986) 10 ACLR 395.

[152] Ibid at 221; 401.

[153] [2002] EWHC 2331 (Ch), [2003] 1 BCLC 226, [2002] All ER (D) 112 (Nov).

Crown Dilmun v Sutton[154] and other older cases suggest that ratification is not possible when the company is in a position that is short of insolvency, such as where there is doubt over its solvency or it is simply in financial difficulty.[155] This issue was discussed in detail in **Chapter 13** and reference should be had to that chapter. The problem is, as pointed out in Chapter 13, that the point at which the creditors' interests intrude is not absolutely clear.

---

[154] [2004] EWHC 52 (Ch); [2004] 1 BCLC 468 at [114].
[155] For instance, see *Re Horsley & Weight Ltd* [1982] Ch 442; *Kinsela v Russell Kinsela Pty Ltd* (1986) 4 ACLC 215; (1986) 10 ACLR 395; *Re DKG Contractors Ltd* [1990] BCC 903.

CHAPTER 17

JUDICIAL EXCUSING OF BREACHES

I INTRODUCTION

17.1 This final Chapter tackles, like the previous chapter, a situation where the actions of directors are to be excused, even if they constitute a breach of their duties. Essentially the Chapter considers the section of the CA 2006, s 1157, that permit the courts, in their discretion, to excuse directors from liability. Interestingly, the judicial excusing of a director involves consideration of a statutory provision that is of significant longevity. This is unusual in the context of this book as most of the law that we are considering relates to common law with little consideration of statutory provisions other than the codified provisions dealing with duties. It should be noted that there is little authority to guide the construction of s 1157,[1] but is based largely on its precursor, s 727 of the Companies Act 1985, and includes the same essential elements.

17.2 After explaining the content of s 1157 the Chapter provides some background to the provision, then briefly explains both the procedure that relates to its use by directors and the rationale for the provision. The main parts of the Chapter deal with the provision's relevance in relation to the duty of care, the scope of the provision and conditions that are contained in s 1157, and which have been subject to a significant amount of case-law.

II THE PROVISION

17.3 The provision in the CA 2006 that permits judicial relief of those directors found liable for breach of their general duties (and other breaches and defaults), s 1157, was brought into force on 1 October 2008.[2] The section's immediate forebear was, as indicated above, s 727 of the CA 1985, and most of the cases considered in this chapter deal with s 727. This is not of any great consequence as the provisions, for our purposes, are virtually identical, although s 1157 is structured a little differently from s 727. Generally speaking when the Chapter deals with the provision it will refer to s 1157 as it constitutes the present law in force.

---

[1] *Northampton Regional Livestock Centre Co Ltd v Cowling* [2014] EWHC 30 (QB) at [160].
[2] Article 5(1)(d) of The Companies Act 2006 (Commencement No 5, Transitional Provisions and Savings) Order 2007, SI 2007/3495.

17.4 Section 1157 permits a court to excuse an officer from liability arising out of his or her negligence, breach of duty or breach of trust on the basis that he or she had acted honestly and reasonably, and, as a consequence of his or her actions, ought fairly to be excused from liability.[3] The term 'officer' is not defined in the CA 2006, save in the context of offences (in s 1121). Certainly s 1121(2)(a) includes directors within the definition of 'officer,' and directors have been generally regarded as officers of the company.[4] For example, in relation to s 1157's precursors, such as s 727 of the CA 1985, courts have quite happily applied the provision to directors. Also, when the original precursor of s 1157 was enacted,[5] it was directed only at directors. Section 1157(2) allows a director who has reason to apprehend that a claim will or might be made against him or her in relation to negligence, breach of duty or breach of trust, to apply to the court for relief without having to wait for the initiation of a claim.

17.5 The provision has been employed in the past by directors who have been found liable for breaching their duties as provided for under common law and equity. It is broad for it is obviously not limited to excusing directors who breach their general duties. In the past precursors of s 1157 have been considered, from time to time, in the context of the breach of provisions in the companies legislation. The New South Wales Court of Appeal opined in *Deputy Comr of Taxation v Dick*[6] that the original relieving provision enacted by the UK Parliament was not intended to apply to statutory obligations. That has not been the way that it has been construed in the UK, where applications have been entertained when directors have been in breach of statutory provisions. An example is s 270 of the Companies Act 1985 (improperly distributing dividends). So, there is no danger that the courts will not consider applications for relief where there are breaches of the duties of the kind found in Chapter 2 of Part 10,[7] just as they did when directors breached their duty at common law and in equity.

17.6 There are three elements[8] that have to be fulfilled if s 1157 is to apply, namely:

- the director acted honestly;
- the director acted reasonably; and
- the court must decide that having regard to all the circumstances the director ought, as a matter of fairness, be excused.

---

[3]   This is in the same terms as the Trustee Act 1925, s 61 that applies to trustees.

[4]   In Australia the term 'officer' has covered directors for many years. See, for example, s 9 of the Corporate Law Economic Reform Program Act 1999 (Cth).

[5]   Companies Act 1907, s 32.

[6]   [2007] NSWCA 190 at [35].

[7]   The Australian courts have entertained applications for relief in relation to statutory breaches. For example, see *Wall v Timbertown Community Enterprises Ltd (in liq)* (2002) 42 ACSR 1 (breach of the statutory duty of care).

[8]   *Dorchester Finance Co Ltd v Stebbing* [1989] BCLC 498 at 505; *Queensway Systems Ltd v Walker* [2006] EWHC 2496 (Ch); [2007] 2 BCLC 577 at [68].

17.7 The third element is a matter of judicial discretion, for s 1157 states that 'the court may relieve', while the first two elements are regarded as the trigger conditions for the exercise of that discretion.[9] Both of the first two elements must be satisfied before a court is to consider whether relief should be ordered.[10] But a director might be able to satisfy the two limbs but fall down because the court, as a matter of discretion, does not think that he or she ought to be fairly excused.[11] Clearly the first two factors can be established by evidence, but the last one is open-ended and purely a matter of judicial discretion. It would seem that the granting of the discretion gives licence to judges to consider and weigh up all or any of the elements of the company's affairs and the role of the director in those affairs.[12] These elements, and referred to as conditions, are discussed in detail later in the Chapter.

17.8 Section 1157 might be seen, in some ways, as a British equivalent of the business judgment rule, in that it may lighten the burden on directors. Yet the provision has not been applied frequently in reported cases, whilst the business judgment rule in the United States is regularly considered in breach of duty cases. Interestingly, Australia, which has adopted a business judgment rule,[13] retains an equivalent of s 1157.[14]

17.9 In the last paragraph it was mentioned that s 1157 has not been frequently applied, and in fact the judgments that we do have, manifest reluctance on the part of the judges to apply it.[15]

17.10 One other point to make is that the Chapter is essentially focused on whether directors are able to be excused for breach of the kinds of duty covered in Chapter 2 of Part 10 of the CA 2006. Some cases consider other issues and they will not be investigated in any detail except to the extent to which they pertain to breaches of the general duties.

III BACKGROUND

17.11 Section 1157 may be traced back to s 32 of the Companies Act 1907. The advent of the provision relates to the work of the Company Law

---

[9] *Bairstow v Queen Moat Houses plc* [2000] 1 BCLC 549 at 561 and affirmed by the Court of Appeal at [2001] EWCA Civ 712; [2001] 2 BCLC 531; [2002] BCC 91 at [58]; *Re Marini Ltd* [2003] EWHC 334 (Ch); [2004] BCC 172 at [57].

[10] *Bairstow v Queen Moat Houses plc* [2001] EWCA Civ 712; [2001] 2 BCLC 531; [2002] BCC 91 at [63].

[11] *Re J Franklin & Son Ltd* [1937] 2 All ER 32; *Bairstow v Queen Moat Houses plc* [2000] 1 BCLC 549 at 561.

[12] M Pasban, C Campbell and J Birds 'Section 1157 and the Business Judgment Rule: A Comparative Analysis of Company Directors' Duties and Liabilities in English and United States' Law' (1997) 6 *Journal of Transnational Law and Policy* 201 at 212.

[13] See **Chapter 8**.

[14] Corporations Act 2001, s 1318.

[15] See, for example, *Towers v Premier Waste Management Ltd* [2011] EWCA Civ 923; [2012] BCC 72.

Amendment Committee in 1906,[16] which was established to review the nation's company legislation. Section 32, based on s 3 of the Judicial Trustee Act 1896, gave courts the discretion to excuse a director from liability in negligence. It was enacted in order to provide a balance to the increase of liabilities of directors introduced in the Companies Act 1900,[17] because the perceived harshness of the 1900 Act's reforms had deterred appropriate people from taking on directorships, and there was a need to ensure that honest and prudent persons were not oppressed.[18] The section became s 279 of the Companies (Consolidation) Act 1908. Subsequently, in s 372 of the Companies Act 1929, the section developed further to encompass default, breach of duty or breach of trust and in s 448 of the Companies Act 1948 it was extended to apply to company officers and persons employed by the company as auditors. All in all, the present provision is not a lot different from the original provision.

17.12 Section 1157 has not attracted a great deal of academic commentary and the CLRSG did not devote a lot of time to it, considering it along with s 310 of the 1985 Act (now, for the most part, s 532 of the CA 2006). After saying that, the CLRSG did end up making suggestions for reform of s 1157. Perhaps the primary one was to delete the requirement for the director's action to be reasonable.[19] But this recommendation did not see light of day in the new legislation.

17.13 The CLRSG was of the view that s 1157 was not used much.[20] It is difficult to know whether the CLRSG meant that few applications were made under the provision or there are few instances of courts excusing directors. Certainly there do appear to be a number of reported cases where applications have been made by directors under the provision, although in many of them the director's application for relief failed. Notwithstanding its opinion, the CLRSG did think that the provision had value.

IV PROCEDURE AND EVIDENCE

17.14 A director is not required to plead before trial that he or she seeks relief under s 1157.[21] The director will usually apply for relief as part of the proceedings brought against him or her. The director has the burden of convincing the court that he or she is entitled to relief.[22] The burden is different

---

[16] Cd 3052, HMSO, London, 1906 and chaired by Lord Loreburn LC.
[17] Ibid at cl 24.
[18] Ibid at cl 16(3).
[19] Company Law Review *Modern Company Law for a Competitive Economy: Developing the Framework* (London, DTI, 2000) at para 3.77.
[20] Ibid.
[21] *Re Kirby Coaches Ltd* [1991] BCLC 414 at 416.
[22] *National Trustees Co of Australasia v General Finance Co of Australasia* [1905] AC 373; *Bairstow v Queens Moat Houses plc* [2000] 1 BCLC 549 at 572; *Gamble v Hoffman* (1997) 24 ASCR 369; *Re Loquitur Ltd, Inland Revenue Commissioners v Richmond* [2003] EWHC 999 (Ch); [2003] 2 BCLC 442; *Brocks Mount ltd v Beasant* (unreported, 2 April 2003, Sonia Proudman QC, Ch D).

when it comes to establishing reasonableness and fairness compared with honesty. Hoffmann J stated in *Re Kirby Coaches Ltd*[23] that a director is assumed to have acted honestly unless evidence indicates that that is not the case, while the director has to establish that he or she acted reasonably and ought fairly to be excused.[24] The courts have to consider the specific facts provided by the evidence, and determine if the director has acted reasonably.[25]

V RATIONALE FOR THE PROVISION

17.15 We saw earlier that the original provision was proposed by the Loreburn Committee in 1906 in the context of a concern to redress the balance that had seen people deterred from putting themselves forward to be directors because of the harshness of reforms in the Companies Act 1900. It has been asserted, adroitly it is respectfully submitted, there is little evidence to suggest that there is a lack of supply of directors for companies today, although this may well remain a concern of the Government.[26] So, what is the present rationale for the provision? There has been little said on the issue, perhaps suggesting that the original rationale still remains appropriate for later legislation. However, Peter Smith QC (sitting as a deputy judge of the High Court) (as he then was) in *Cohen v Selby*[27] did say that the reason for the provision is, inter alia, to achieve fairness between wrongdoers. In Australia Rogers CJ in Eq said in *AWA Ltd v Daniels*[28] that the Australian counterpart of s 1157 can be seen as an alternative to contributory negligence in circumstances where the claim is not accepted. But, of course, while it is a breach of the duty of care which often appears to precipitate an application under s 1157, the provision is wider than simply dealing with cases of negligence. Nevertheless, the provision is likely to be considered most often where directors are in breach of their duty of care. It is to that duty and the use of the provision to which we now turn.

VI THE PROVISION AND THE DUTY OF CARE

17.16 One of the prime concerns of the courts has been to determine whether s 1157 applies to breaches of directors' duties of care, skill and diligence? The question is important to ask as there is authority in the form of *Re Produce Marketing Consortium Ltd*[29] to the effect that it does not apply to claims for

[23] [1991] BCLC 414.
[24] Ibid at 415.
[25] *Re MDA Investment Management Ltd* [2004] EWHC 42 (Ch) at [25]; [2005] BCC 783 at 840.
[26] R Edmunds and J Lowry 'The Continuing Value of the Relief for Directors' Breach of Duty' (2003) 66 MLR 195 at 199.
[27] [2000] BCC 275 at 288. The decision of the judge was reversed on appeal ([2000] 1 BCLC 549), but this statement was not contradicted by the Court of Appeal.
[28] (1992) 7 ACSR 759.
[29] [1989] BCLC 513. Also see, *Re Brian D Pierson (Contractors) Ltd* [1999] BCC 26; [2001] BCLC 275. See the comments of Nelson J in *Bairstow v Queens Moat Houses plc* [2000] 1 BCLC 549.

directors' wrongful trading under s 214 of the Insolvency Act 1986, and we know from **Chapter 8** that the duty of care provision applicable in the UK is founded on s 214. The reason given for the non-application of the provision to wrongful trading is based on the idea that it is incompatible with the objective nature of the test found in s 214, namely that the action of the director could not be said to be reasonable. Having said that, HH Judge Weeks QC in *Re DKG Contractors Ltd*,[30] while he refused to apply s 1157 in the case before him, a wrongful trading case, indicated that the section could have been applied had the director acted reasonably, and in *Re Duckwari plc (No 2)*,[31] while not specifically disapproving of the view in *Re Produce Marketing Consortium Ltd*, the learned judge did indicate misgivings about limiting the scope of s 1157. Nevertheless, there is little indication that Parliament intended s 1157 to apply in wrongful trading situations.[32] Can it therefore apply to breaches of s 174? This questions is pertinent given the fact that if a person is found to be in breach of s 174 the court will have determined, inter alia, that the director did not act reasonably, and, of course, reasonableness is one of the components of s 1157.

17.17 Notwithstanding the decision in *Re Produce Marketing Consortium Ltd*, in *Re D'Jan of London Ltd*[33] where Hoffmann LJ (as he then was) held that the test in s 214(4) of the Insolvency Act 1986 was to be used in determining whether a director had breached his or her duty of care and skill, his Lordship said that a director found liable could be relieved under the s 1157's predecessor. In this case, the director signed an insurance form, which had been completed by his insurance broker, without first checking whether the contents of it were in fact accurate, and subsequently the insurance company repudiated liability in relation to an event covered by the insurance on the basis of the wrong answers provided on the insurance form by the director. In liquidation the liquidator of the director's company brought proceedings against the director based on the director's negligence.

17.18   Hoffmann LJ acknowledged that it might 'seem odd that a person found to have been guilty of negligence, which involves failing to take reasonable care, can ever satisfy a court that he acted reasonably'.[34] But, as his Lordship noted, s 1157 contemplates that a director may do so and 'it follows that conduct may be reasonable for the purposes of s 727 [s 1157] despite amounting to lack of reasonable care at common law'.[35] The defendant was held to be liable, but Hoffmann LJ decided that he should be excused under the precursor of s 1157 because the defendant's negligence was not gross and it was the kind of thing

---

[30]   [1990] BCC 903.
[31]   [1998] 2 BCLC 313 at 321 (CA).
[32]   M Pasban, C Campbell and J Birds 'Section 1157 and the Business Judgment Rule: A Comparative Analysis of Company Directors' Duties and Liabilities in English and United States' Law' (1997) 6 *Journal of Transnational Law and Policy* 201 at 205.
[33]   [1993] BCC 646.
[34]   [1993] BCC 646 at 649.
[35]   Ibid at 649.

that could happen to a busy director.[36] The learned judge accepted the evidence of the director that the company's insurance broker had completed the form and he, the director, simply signed it, having confidence in the broker, who had acted for the company for some five years. Hoffmann LJ went on to say that it was relevant that at the time of the signing of the form the company was solvent and the only interests that the defendant was putting at risk were those of himself and his wife, as they were the only shareholders of the company.[37] Hoffmann LJ said that: 'For the purposes of s 727 [s 1157] I think that he [the defendant] acted reasonably.'[38] All of this probably contributed to uncertainty as to the extent to which the provision allows relief for negligence.[39] The decision on the conduct of the director in this case can be contrasted with that concerning the main director in *Cohen v Selby*[40] where the judge decided not to apply s 1157 because he had engaged in gross negligence, and he was the prime cause of the company's loss.[41]

17.19 Hoffmann LJ is not the only judge to have passed comment about the fact that it seems odd that a director who has been found to be in breach of a duty of care can be excused on the basis of reasonableness. North P of the New Zealand Court of Appeal in *Dimond Manufacturing Co Ltd v Hamilton*[42] said that he found it 'difficult to understand how a negligent officer or auditor could nevertheless be held to have acted "reasonably"'. It appears that the comment led to the decision of the Australian legislature to omit any reference to reasonableness in the Australian equivalent.[43] More recently Evans-Lombe J in *Barings plc v Coopers & Lybrand*[44] applied what Hoffmann LJ said in *Re D'Jan*. Peter Smith QC (sitting as a deputy judge of the High Court) in *Cohen v Selby*[45] commented on the unusual situation produced by the section requiring a consideration of reasonableness when the defendant is liable for negligence.[46] Olsson J of the South Australian Supreme Court in *Maelor Jones Investments (Noarlunga) Pty Ltd v Heywood-Smith*[47] said, in a judgment pre-dating *Re D'Jan*, that the section was wider in scope, as well as in timeframe, than the law of negligence, therefore opening up the opportunity for judges to grant relief where directors had been negligent. In *Re Brian D Pierson (Contractors) Ltd* Hazel Williamson QC (sitting as a deputy judge of the High Court) concluded from *Re D'Jan* that reasonableness in the context of s 1157 is able to be satisfied by something less than adhering to the common law standard of care

---

[36] Ibid at 648, 649.
[37] Ibid at 649.
[38] Ibid.
[39] Company Law Review *Modern Company Law for a Competitive Economy: Developing the Framework* (London, DTI, 2000) at para 3.77.
[40] [2000] BCC 275.
[41] Ibid at 288.
[42] [1969] NZLR 609 at 645.
[43] Companies and Securities Law Review Committee, Discussion Paper No 9, at [114]–[115].
[44] [2003] EWHC 1319 (Ch) at [1133]–[1134].
[45] [2000] BCC 275.
[46] Ibid at 287.
[47] (1989) 7 ACLC 1232 at 1253.

in negligence.[48] This evidences a willingness on the part of the courts to dilute the objective nature of the reasonableness requirement.[49]

17.20 The cases suggest that courts may take into account the level of a director's culpability and his or her conduct. It would seem that provided that a director's negligence is not gross then he or she is eligible to be excused. This is illustrated by the case of *Cohen v Selby*[50] where a father and son (the latter was only 19 years old) were held liable in breach of their duty of care. The son was partially excused because he had not been responsible for the company's loss and had followed his father's instructions, but the father, who, as we have seen, had been grossly negligent, was not excused.

17.21 It would seem that we can extrapolate from the judgment in *Re D'Jan* that the concept of reasonableness in s 1157 is partly objective and partly subjective even though, of course, reasonableness is primarily objective in relation to liability for negligence.[51] This is an issue to which we will return later under the heading of 'Acting Reasonably.'

17.22 The way that the courts have interpreted s 1157 would suggest that courts will not, out of hand, dismiss any application for relief merely because the director has been negligent, and in *PNC Telecom plc v Thomas*[52] it was indicated that the provision assumes that one can have acted reasonably although one was negligent.[53] Courts have considered whether the director acted in the way in which one would expect a person, who handles her affairs with care and circumspection, to have acted.[54]

17.23 Section 1157 encompasses cases where a director has acted in breach of his or her duty of care, because what he or she did was not what one reasonably could expect from a person with his or her knowledge and experience, but the court is satisfied nevertheless that the director acted sufficiently reasonably.[55]

17.24 In *Bairstow v Queen Moat Houses plc*[56] Nelson J, when determining whether directors were liable for paying unlawful dividends, said[57] that:

[48] [1999] BCC 26; [2001] BCLC 275.
[49] A Dignam and J Lowry *Company Law* (Oxford, OUP, 5th edn, 2008) at 352.
[50] [2000] BCC 275 and reversed on appeal: [2002] BCC 82 (CA).
[51] M Pasban, C Campbell and J Birds 'Section 1157 and the Business Judgment Rule: A Comparative Analysis of Company Directors' Duties and Liabilities in English and United States' Law' (1997) 6 *Journal of Transnational Law and Policy* 201 at 209.
[52] [2007] EWHC 2157 (Ch).
[53] Ibid at [94].
[54] Ibid and referring to *Re Duomatic Ltd* [1969] 2 Ch 365 at 377.
[55] *Equitable Life Assurance Society v Bowley* [2003] EWHC 2263 (Comm); [2004] 1 BCLC 180 at [45].
[56] [2000] 1 BCLC 549.
[57] Ibid at 1034.

'[E]ven if under the rules of negligence a director ought to have known of the facts which rendered the payments unlawful, the court may nevertheless relieve him from liability if considering his personal situation it was reasonable that he did not in fact know. It is a matter of discretion for the court on the individual facts of the case as to whether the director should escape the normal consequences of his breach of duty and be excused liability for his negligence.'

17.25 The Court of Appeal[58] subsequently reversed his Lordship's decision to excuse the directors under s 1157 on the basis that, as the judge had found, the former directors were guilty of dishonestly preparing false accounts in order to deceive the market, and it was not open to the judge to find that they had acted honestly. However, the court did not impugn the judge's comments quoted above.

17.26 The CLRSG wanted to ensure that relief where the director was guilty of negligence was not controversial.[59] Whilst the CLRSG recommended that s 1157 is available where a director is found to have breached the duty of care, it recommended that that fact should be made clear in the companies legislation.[60] This recommendation was not taken up, although one could submit that the fact that the section does refer to both negligence and breach of duty would be sufficient to permit excusing from liability when there is a breach of a director's duty of care.

17.27 In completing this part of the Chapter, we should note that in *Equitable Life Assurance Society v Bowley*[61] Langley J said that he thought that it was possible for a court to make an order under s 1157 where there was a breach of the duty of care, but he indicated that it would be rather exceptional to do so on an application for summary judgment.

VII THE AMBIT OF THE PROVISION

17.28 Case-law on the trust equivalent of s 1157 has indicated that the wide words in the section are not to be narrowed.[62] It has in fact been said that the section is comprehensive and not to be restricted.[63] Astbury J adopted this type of view in the case of *Re Claridge's Patent Asphalte Co*,[64] when dealing with the actions of a director and he indicated that the discretion afforded to courts is broad.[65] Nevertheless, cases dealing with the corporate counterpart of the

---

[58] [2001] 2 BCLC 531.
[59] Company Law Review *Modern Company Law for a Competitive Economy: Final Report* (London, DTI, 2001) at para 6.4.
[60] Company Law Review *Modern Company Law for a Competitive Economy: Developing the Framework* (London, DTI, 2000) at para 3.77.
[61] [2003] EWHC 2263 (Comm); [2004] 1 BCLC 180 at [45].
[62] *Re Allsopp* [1914] 1 Ch 1 at 11.
[63] Ibid at 14.
[64] [1921] 1 Ch 543.
[65] Ibid at 548. Also, see *Circle Petroleum (Queensland) v Greensdale* (1998) 16 ACLC 1577 (Qld S Ct); *Reiffel v ACN 075 839 226 Ltd* [2003] FCA 194 at [65] (Aust Fed Ct); *ASIC v Vines* [2005] NSWSC 1349 at [45] (NSW S Ct).

trust provision have placed several limits on the application of the provision. In this part of the Chapter, we will seek to ascertain what parameters, if any, there are as to the application of s 1157.

17.29 The first major point to make is that the facts of each case are going to be critical in determining whether a director is able to avail himself or herself of the provision.

17.30 It has been held that a court will be less likely to make an order in favour of a person who is in receipt of a substantial amount of remuneration compared with someone who acts gratuitously or for a nominal sum.[66] It might be said, on the basis of *Cohen v Selby*,[67] that s 1157 relief might not be applied to anyone who is the prime cause of the loss to the company. It appears that no relief will be granted when directors have abused their positions so as to obtain personal gain. In *Neptune (Vehicle Washing Equipment) Ltd v Fitzgerald (No 2)*[68] the director was denied relief where he, a sole director, had passed resolutions to enable him to obtain a large sum on termination of his service contract. It was determined that he had not acted reasonably. In like manner the defendant director in *Guinness plc v Saunders*[69] also failed. There the director had retained £5.2m that had been paid to him on the basis, it was submitted, of being remuneration under a void contract. Australian authority has indicated that relief is unlikely to be granted where the director has benefited from the breach.[70] The decisions of the High Court of Australia in *PNC Telecom plc v Thomas*[71] and the New South Wales Supreme Court in the case of *ASIC v Vines*[72] seemed to take the same approach.

17.31 Interestingly in *Queensway Systems Ltd v Walker*[73] Paul Girolami QC (sitting as a deputy judge of the High Court) denied relief to the defendant on the basis that if he gave relief then he would be relieving the defendant from having to pay an amount to the company, and this would prejudice the creditors as the company was in insolvent liquidation.[74] This is similar to the view that was propounded in *Inn Spirit v Burns*[75] where Rimer J said that it was not appropriate that the directors be excused at the expense of the creditors.[76] The view of Rimer J seemed to meet with the approval of the Court

---

[66] *National Trustees Co of Australasia v General Finance Co of Australasia* [1905] AC 373 at 381 (PC).
[67] [2000] BCC 275 at 288.
[68] [1995] BCC 1000.
[69] [1988] 1 WLR 863 (CA), affirmed on other grounds on appeal ([1990] 2 AC 663 (HL)).
[70] *Re Lasscock's Nurseries Ltd (in liq)* [1940] SASR 251; *Re International Vending Machines Pty Ltd* [1962] NSWR 1408 at 1424; *Gamble v Hoffman* (1997) 24 ACSR 369 at 387.
[71] [2007] EWHC 2157 (Ch) at [105]. In this case the judge held that the defendant had not acted reasonably so he was not eligible for being excused.
[72] [2005] NSWSC 1349 at [84].
[73] [2006] EWHC 2496 (Ch); [2007] 2 BCLC 577.
[74] Ibid at [70].
[75] [2002] 2 BCLC 780.
[76] Ibid at [30].

of Appeal in *First Global Media Group Ltd v John Larkin*.[77] All of this causes one to ask whether the section will ever apply when a company is insolvent, for any relief of a director would normally mean that the creditors will be prejudiced as they are not, in an insolvent company, going to get all of their money back. Denying relief in this way would be consistent with the fact that it has been said that directors found liable under the wrongful trading provision could not be relieved by s 1157 on the basis that wrongful trading existed to protect the unsecured creditors from loss, and to compensate them if they do lose out. This might be regarded as a fair outcome, given the loss sustained by creditors, but it could mean a severe restriction on the application of the provision.

17.32 It is possible that relief is likely to be granted, at least in part, where the director is able to be regarded as vulnerable, particularly when compared with other directors, and perhaps constrained by family loyalty, as was the case in *Cohen v Selby*.[78] In this case the court partly relieved from liability the son because, inter alia, the son 'might feel reluctant to question his father's business acumen in an area where his father had many decades of business experience with apparently no difficulties at all and where he, the son, had no experience'.[79] This might mean that in the classic husband and wife company, where both spouses are directors and the latter is often a passive director (because even though the courts have spoken about directors must take a part in company affairs or else suffer the consequences), the wife might be able to avail herself of s 1157. But a court might not be willing to relieve the wife as other decisions have said that inactivity of directors is evidence of a failure to act reasonably.[80] Obviously the facts are going to be critical.

17.33 Section 1157 is only able to be relied on by a defaulting director when the claim is by the company, or someone standing in the shoes of the company, namely where the essential nature of the proceedings was to enforce an action for the benefit of the company. This would cover claims made by a liquidator or an administrator, but not claims by third parties, seeking to enforce third party rights.[81] In relation to the provision Patten J said in *Comrs of Inland Revenue v McEntaggart*[82] that it only applied:

> '[T]o a claim made by the company or somebody, in effect, standing in the shoes or representing the interests of the company, against a defaulting director. They have no application to a claim by a third party against a company director. In other words, they apply only where the essential nature of the proceedings, whether they

---

[77] [2003] EWCA Civ 1765 at [33].
[78] [2000] BCC 275 at 288.
[79] Ibid per Peter Smith J.
[80] *Lexi Holdings plc (In Administration) v Luqman* [2007] EWHC 2652 (Ch) at [224].
[81] *Customs and Excise Comrs v Hedon Alpha Ltd* [1981] 1 QB 818 (CA); *Comrs of Inland Revenue v McEntaggart* [2004] EWHC 3431 (Ch) at [46]; [2007] BCC 260 at 271; *First Independent Factors & Finance v Mountford* [2008] EWHC 835 (Ch); [2008] 2 BCLC 297 at [31]-[33].
[82] [2004] EWHC 3431 (Ch) at [46]; [2007] BCC 260 at 271.

be brought in equity or under the provisions of the companies legislation, is to enforce at the suit of or for the benefit of the company, the duties which the director owes to the company.'

17.34 But, of course, in a claim for breach of duties, the claimant would only be the company itself or someone taking action as the representative of the company.

17.35 While in England it has been held that the provision only applies to a director's liability to his or her company or where he or she is in breach of duties under the companies legislation, and is inapplicable to any claim by third parties,[83] in Australia there is authority to the effect that this view is too restrictive, and the provision could be used in relation to other liability.[84] In *Deputy Comr of Taxation v Dick*,[85] the New South Wales Court of Appeal was divided over the issue. The question in that case was whether the relevant director was able to be excused under the equivalent of s 1157 for breaches of the Income Tax Assessment Act 1936 (Cth). Spigelman CJ was of the opinion that the provision had no application to any obligation imposed by statute, other than under the Corporations Act 2001, the equivalent of the UK's Companies Act, while Santow JA said that the provision could apply provided that there was a requisite degree of corporate connection present and the relevant statute itself did not preclude the exercise of s 1157. The third judge on the appellate court did not seek to tackle the issue.

17.36 Where a director is liable for more than one breach of duty, it would seem, based on *Coleman Taymar Ltd v Oakes*,[86] that the judge will consider each of the breaches committed by the director on an individual basis, and the judge could determine that the director should be relieved from one breach and not from another.

17.37 In *Ultraframe (UK) Ltd v Fielding*[87] Lewison J was of the view[88] that the words:

> '"in all the circumstances of the case" in the section may, in my judgment, include a review of the director's stewardship of the company; but they do not involve a more wide-ranging inquiry into the director's character and behaviour. The circumstances of the case may also, in my judgment, include the behaviour of the company since the breach complained of.'

---

[83] *Customs and Excise Comrs v Hedon Alpha* [1981] QB 818 at 824, 826; *Comrs of Inland Revenue v McEntaggart* [2004] EWHC 3431 (Ch) at [46]; [2007] BCC 260 at 271.
[84] *Edwards v Attorney-General* [2004] NSWCA 272; (2004) 60 NSWLR 667 (NSWCA). Also, see *Daniels v AWA Ltd* (1995) 16 ACSR 607 at 685 (NSWCA).
[85] [2007] NSWCA 190.
[86] [2001] 2 BCLC 749.
[87] [2005] EWHC 1638 (Ch).
[88] Ibid at [1451].

17.38 It is worth noting that there is Australian authority in the form of *Pacific Acceptance Corporation Ltd v Forsyth*[89] that unreasonableness in post-contravention conduct as a director is relevant and able to be taken into account by a court in assessing whether the equivalent of s 1157 should apply, and this appears to be consistent with what was said in *Ultraframe (UK) Ltd v Fielding*. In *Ultraframe* all Lewison J appeared to be concerned about was that conduct outside of a director's directorial role should not be taken into account. The approach taken in relation to s 1157 is consistent with the way that the company directors' disqualification legislation is applied. Only the conduct of directors in relation to his or her role as a director is relevant in determining whether the director should or should not be disqualified.[90]

17.39 It was reasoned by Lewison J in *Ultraframe (UK)* that shadow directors are not able to avail themselves of s 1157. This view was taken on the basis that the provision covered 'officers' and this term means 'director, manager or secretary' (this is also the case under s 1173(1) of the CA 2006), and 'director' in s 741(1) of the CA 1985 (s 250(1) of the CA 2006) includes any person occupying the position of director, by whatever name called, but 'shadow director' is defined in a separate provision (s 741(2) (s 250(2) of the CA 2006)). So his Lordship said[91] that:

'Given that there is a specific statutory definition of 'officer of the company', it must, I think, follow that a shadow director cannot be relieved under s 727 [s 1157].'

17.40 Lewison J took the view in this case that shadow directors are not subject to the fiduciary duties. In **Chapters 2** and **4**[92] I discussed the fact that there are recent cases,[93] supporting the decision of Toulson J (as he then was) in *Yukong Line Ltd of Korea v Rendsburg Investments Corp of Liberia (No2)*,[94] that adopt the approach that shadow directors are subject to such duties. If these are correct, and it is respectfully submitted that they are, then it would seem unfair if shadows could not seek to avail themselves of s 1157 in an appropriate case, when both *de jure* and de facto directors can. Perhaps a way around this is to interpret 'officer of the company' in s 1157 to include a shadow director.

17.41 In relation to relief claimed by the claimant against a director, where a company had elected to claim an account of profits rather than damages against a director for breach of his or her fiduciary duty, s 1157 does not disentitle the director from asking the court for relief from liability merely because the relief

---

[89] (1970) 92 WN (NSW) 29 at 119.
[90] Company Directors' Disqualification Act 1986, s 6(3).
[91] [2005] EWHC 1638 (Ch) at [1452].
[92] Above at **2.29** and **4.45**.
[93] *Secretary of State for Business Innovation and Skills; Re UKLI Ltd* [2013] EWHC 680 (Ch); *Vivendi SA v Richards* [2013] EWHC 3006 (Ch).
[94] [1998] BCC 870.

sought was an account of profits rather than damages, since liability to account was just as much a liability as a liability to pay damages.[95]

17.42   One final point worth making in this section of the Chapter is that it has been accepted in cases that genuine reliance on professional advice might well render conduct which would otherwise be unreasonable as reasonable.[96] In *Murray v Leisureplay plc*[97] Stanley Brunton J said (and accepted by Bernard Liversey QC, sitting as a deputy judge of the High Court in *Re Ortega Associates Ltd (in liq); Green v Walkling*[98]) that if a director obtained and implemented legal advice, while not decisive, it is a relevant and important factor in considering whether relief should be granted under s 1157. But it can depend on whose advice a director has relied and in what circumstances. In *Coleman Taymar Ltd v Oakes*[99] the director had relied on the advice of a solicitor who was not a company lawyer, and he was not able to obtain relief.[100] Reliance on the advice of professionals was discussed in Chapter 8.

VIII THE CONDITIONS

17.43   We now turn to the conditions which s 1157 lays down as needing to be satisfied before relief can be granted.

17.44   As indicated earlier, there are three conditions which have to be satisfied. Just to recapitulate, the conditions are:

• the director acted honestly;
• the director acted reasonably; and
• the court must decide that having regard to all the circumstances the director ought, as a matter of fairness, be excused.

17.45   The first two are not matters for the judge's discretion, but the last is. Before any consideration of how fair it would be to provide relief the judge must be convinced that the director has acted honestly and reasonably.

17.46   It has been submitted that the courts have failed on occasions to see the conditions of reasonableness and honesty as separate and have conflated them.[101] However, the two conditions are clearly distinct and involve consideration of different matters. There is likely to be an overlap in some respects with reasonableness and fairness.

---

[95]   *Coleman Taymar Ltd v Oakes* [2001] 2 BCLC 749 at 770.
[96]   For example, see *Re Claridge's Patent Asphalte Co Ltd* [1921] 1 Ch 543.
[97]   [2004] EWHC 1927 at [121].
[98]   [2007] EWHC 2046 at [35]–[36].
[99]   [2001] 2 BCLC 749 at 770.
[100]   Ibid at [70]–[73].
[101]   R Edmunds and J Lowry 'The Continuing Value of the Relief for Directors' Breach of Duty' (2003) 66 MLR 195 at 202.

A Honesty

17.47 As mentioned earlier, it would seem that a director is assumed to have acted honestly unless there is evidence that suggests otherwise.[102] The honesty that is referred to in s 1157 is to honesty in relation to the conduct that is alleged to constitute the negligence, breach of duty etc.[103]

17.48 The difficulty is that there is a paucity of judicial consideration in judgments as to what constitutes honesty in the context of s 1157 and, in any event, honesty has tended to be a slippery concept, as mentioned in Chapters 6 and 15. Courts have not explained how actions are to be measured in terms of honesty. Two issues come to mind. Can a court only consider what a respondent says about his or her state of mind, or can any objective considerations be taken into account in determining whether the director was dishonest? Can courts infer what the director's state of mind was from the actions of the director and the circumstances surrounding the breach? Another related issue is: what standard of honesty is to be applied? Is it that of the director according to his or her testimony, namely what he or she regarded as honest conduct, or is it some other standard?

17.49 Professor Ross Parsons once asserted that a director could be considered honest if he or she did not seek to hide any aspect of his or her actions from the company.[104] That approach does not appear to have been taken on by the courts, which have tended to focus on whether the honesty concept should be seen from a subjective or an objective standpoint.

17.50 In *Bairstow v Queen Moat Houses plc*[105] the Court of Appeal questioned the view of the judge at first instance that honesty is essentially to be assessed from a subjective perspective.[106] The view was expressed by Robert Walker LJ (as he then was), with whom the other judges agreed, that an objective test was preferable. His Lordship relied on the statement by Lord Nicholls in *Royal Brunei Airlines Sdn Bhd v Tan*[107] when dealing with whether a person was liable for acting dishonestly as an accessory to a breach of trust. Lord Nicholls said that the standard for honest conduct was not subjective.[108] We will return to this case in a moment. Interestingly, while Park J in *Re MDA Investment Management Ltd*[109] agreed with Robert Walker LJ that the reasonableness of a director's conduct must be assessed objectively, his Lordship was of the view that the issue of subjectivity was relevant when assessing the honesty of a director.[110]

---

[102] *Re Kirby Coaches Ltd* [1991] BCLC 414.
[103] *Cook v Green*, unreported, Ch D, Manchester District Registry, His Honour Judge Pelling QC, 2 May 2008 at [45].
[104] 'The Director's Duty of Good Faith' (1967) 5 MULR 395 at 418.
[105] [2001] EWCA Civ 712; [2001] 2 BCLC 531.
[106] Ibid at [58].
[107] [1995] 2 AC 378.
[108] Ibid at 389.
[109] [2005] BCC 783.
[110] Ibid at 838.

17.51 Besides breach of trust cases, some of which were considered in **Chapter 15**, the issue of honesty has been considered regularly, of course, in some criminal cases and in relation to claims that directors and others have engaged in fraudulent trading, either in breach of s 213 of the Insolvency Act 1986 (with civil consequences), or in breach of what is now s 993 of the CA 2006 (with criminal consequences). Lord Lane CJ in the case of *R v Ghosh*,[111] which dealt with a prosecution for obtaining property by deception in breach of the Theft Act, said that defendants would be acting dishonestly where they act in ways that they know are considered by ordinary people to be dishonest, even if they assert that they believed that what they were doing was morally justified.[112] The Court of Appeal in *R v Lockwood*,[113] a fraudulent trading case, said that the definition[114] of dishonesty given in *Ghosh* was of general application. This is consistent with the approach sanctioned by both the Privy Council and the House of Lords in three cases that have addressed the concept of dishonesty in a civil setting. The cases, *Royal Brunei Airlines Snd Bhd v Tan*,[115] *Twinsectra Ltd v Yardley*[116] and *Barlow Clowes International Ltd (In Liquidation) v Eurotrust International Ltd*,[117] considered the issue of dishonesty in the context of a claim that the respondents were involved in dishonestly assisting a breach of trust, and the cases have been discussed in **Chapter 15**.[118] Some of it is worth repeating. In *Twinsectra v Yardley*, Lord Hutton (with whom three of the Law Lords agreed) said that there were three tests that could be applied to determining whether someone acted dishonestly or not. The first two tests were the standard subjective and objective tests. But his Lordship[119] applied the third test, which he called 'the combined test.' This is a:

> 'standard which combines an objective test and a subjective test, and which requires that before there can be a finding of dishonesty it must be established that the defendant's conduct was dishonest by the ordinary standards of reasonable and honest people and that he himself realised that by those standards his conduct was dishonest.'

17.52 In a similar manner, Lord Nicholls[120] had said earlier in *Royal Brunei Airlines* (and this was approved of by a majority of the House of Lords in *Twinsectra*) that:

---

[111] [1982] QB 1053 (CCA).

[112] Ibid at 1064.

[113] (1986) 2 BCC 99, 333 at 99, 340.

[114] One might quibble with the use of this word as courts have been at pains to say that they will not attempt to define dishonesty.

[115] [1995] 2 AC 378.

[116] [2002] UKHL 12; [2002] 2 AC 164. It is interesting that in this case, involving the issue of whether the respondent was liable for being an accessory to a breach of trust, Lord Millett, who dissented, favoured a totally objective test.

[117] [2005] UKPC 37.

[118] Above at **15.86–15.97**.

[119] [2002] UKHL 12 at [27]; [2002] 2 AC 164 at 171.

[120] [1995] 2 AC 378 at 389.

'Honesty has a connotation of subjectivity, as distinct from the objectivity of negligence. Honesty, indeed, does have a strong subjective element in that it is a description of a type of conduct assessed in the light of what a person actually knew at the time, as distinct from what a reasonable person would have known or appreciated. Further, honesty and its counterpart dishonesty are mostly concerned with advertent conduct, not inadvertent conduct. Carelessness is not dishonesty. Thus for the most part dishonesty is to be equated with conscious impropriety. However, these subjective characteristics of honesty do not mean that individuals are free to set their own standards of honesty in particular circumstances. The standard of what constitutes honest conduct is not subjective. Honesty is not an optional scale, with higher or lower values according to the moral standards of each individual. If a person knowingly appropriates another's property, he will not escape a finding of dishonesty simply because he sees nothing wrong in such behaviour.'

17.53 More recently the Privy Council addressed the issue of dishonesty, again in the context of a claim of assisting a breach of trust, in *Barlow Clowes International Ltd (In Liquidation) v Eurotrust International Ltd,*[121] and the Judicial Committee in its judgment made it clear in its interpretation of *Twinsectra*, that it was not necessary for a respondent to have thought about the standards of ordinary honest people in considering whether he or she had acted honestly. In other words, respondents would be liable if they transgressed ordinary standards even if they did not turn their minds to what the standards were.[122]

17.54 Certainly if a purely subjective test were applied in s 1157 applications, it is likely that the provision would be undermined.[123] There is nothing stated in any s 1157 cases that suggests the combined test of Lord Hutton is not appropriate. Lord Millett in his dissenting opinion in *Twinsectra v Yardley* said that an objective test should apply in the case before him. The test which his Lordship put forward was not in fact totally objective as the respondent had to have knowledge of the facts that constitute dishonesty, so there is a subjective element that has to be present. The approach of Lord Millett was employed by the Privy Council in *Barlow Clowes International Ltd (In Liquidation) v Eurotrust International Ltd,*[124] and subsequently by a later Privy Council decision in *Central Bank of Ecuador v Conticorp SA,*[125] and, perhaps more importantly for precedent purposes, by the Court of Appeal.[126]

17.55 It might be argued that while a combined approach is the most appropriate when it comes to cases with criminal consequences, an objective approach would be more appropriate in relation to s 1157. The Lord Millett

---

[121] [2005] UKPC 37.
[122] Ibid at [16]. It can be argued that the Court of Appeal in *Abou-Rahmah v Abacha* [2006] EWCA Civ 1492 seemed to accept that the opinions expressed in *Barlow Clowes International Ltd* represented the law in England and Wales.
[123] R Edmunds and J Lowry 'The Continuing Value of the Relief for Directors' Breach of Duty' (2003) 66 MLR 195 at 206.
[124] [2005] UKPC 37.
[125] [2015] UKPC 11.
[126] *Abou-Ramah v Abacha* [2006] EWCA Civ 1492.

approach, if applied in the context of s 1157, would mean that courts are to ignore whether or not a defendant realises that what he or she has done is dishonest.[127] Such an approach, focused on conduct rather than state of mind, has its attractions as it would be easier for a court to apply.[128] Rod Edmunds and John Lowry argue for the combined approach on the basis that directors will often have been held to be liable for a breach of a duty of care that is objectively dominated, and to have a too objectively orientated test would render the section's value nugatory.[129] There is undoubted merit in what the learned commentators say, but two things must not be forgotten. First, some breaches are dependent on subjective considerations, such as a breach of s 172 of the CA 2006 (the essential element is the good faith of the directors). Second, whether there has been a breach of duty of care under s 174 is dependent on both objective and subjective considerations.

17.56 Obviously each set of facts have to be considered on their merits when deciding whether the director acted honestly or not, but Austin J in *ASIC v Vines*[130] did give some idea as to what he thought would not come within the category of honesty for the purposes of the Australian equivalent of s 1157, when he said:[131]

> 'There was no finding that he obtained personal gain or benefit from his contraventions, or that any of his contraventions was 'flagrant', or that he engaged in impropriety or deceptiveness, or that he was conscious of impropriety on the part of others.'

17.57 Finally, it has been held that unless a director gives oral evidence then he or she cannot establish the honesty element of the section.[132]

B Acting reasonably

17.58 It is often the case, particularly with breaches of the duties of care, skill and diligence, that it is undisputed that the directors have acted honestly. In such cases much will then turn on whether the directors have acted reasonably. This is often going to be a difficult obstacle for directors to hurdle.

17.59 As mentioned earlier, according to the wrongful trading case of *Re Produce Marketing Consortium Ltd*,[133] an essentially subjective approach was required. In *Bairstow v Queen Moat Houses plc*[134] Nelson J agreed with that approach.[135] He went on to say that the test under the provision cannot be the

---

[127] [2002] UKHL 12; [2002] 2 AC 164 at [121].
[128] R Edmunds and J Lowry 'The Continuing Value of the Relief for Directors' Breach of Duty' (2003) 66 MLR 195 at 206.
[129] Ibid at 207.
[130] [2005] NSWSC 1349.
[131] Ibid at [84].
[132] *In a Flap Envelope Co Ltd, Re*[2003] EWHC 3047 (Ch); [2003] BCC 487 at [60].
[133] [1989] BCLC 513 at 518; [1989] 1 WLR 745 at 750.
[134] [2000] 1 BCLC 549.
[135] Ibid at 560.

same as that used for deciding whether the director is liable for breach of duty. If it were s 1157 would rarely, if ever, operate where a director had been found to have acted honestly but negligently.[136] His Lordship looked to *Re D'Jan of London Ltd*[137] where Hoffmann LJ, it will be remembered, noted that conduct may be reasonable for the purposes of s 1157 despite amounting to lack of reasonable care at common law.[138] Nelson J in *Bairstow* indicated that the court can take into account the degree of culpability of the director's conduct. So, provided the director's conduct was honest but he or she was nevertheless guilty of negligence, the director might still be relieved from liability if the negligence was not gross.[139] His Lordship indicated that a court can consider the concept of reasonableness in s 1157 from a subjective perspective. But in the appeal to the Court of Appeal in that case Robert Walker LJ, with whom the other judges agreed, indicated that a court cannot consider the concept of reasonableness in s 1157 from a subjective perspective;[140] it must be considered from an objective perspective. This view was subsequently adopted in *Re MDA Investment Management Ltd*[141] where Park J said that the reasonableness of a director's conduct must be assessed objectively, and the issue of subjectivity is only relevant when assessing the honesty of a director. This was also a point made in *Coleman Taymar Ltd v Oakes*.[142]

17.60 It has been asserted that the decision of Hoffmann LJ in *Re D'Jan* tended to dilute the objective nature of the concept of reasonableness.[143] But Park J in *Re MDA Investment Management Ltd*[144] did not think that Hoffmann LJ intended to provide a purely subjective test.[145] His Lordship in *Re MDA Investment* found against the director on the s 1157 point because he felt that the director's conduct was more blameworthy than that of the defendant in *Re D'Jan*. Nevertheless, there are other decisions, besides *Re D'Jan*, which might well point to a more subjective perspective. In *Re Gilt Edge Safety Glass Ltd*[146] two persons acted for two years as directors in breach of the Companies Act 1929 because they did not have the minimum qualifying shares. Crossman J said that the defendants were negligent in a way, and he took into account the fact that the directors had committed a breach of duty in continuing to act as directors without knowing it.[147] Subsequent to *Re D'Jan*, Peter Smith QC (sitting as a deputy judge of the High Court) in *Cohen v Selby*[148] relied on Hoffmann LJ's view on the concept of reasonableness. As it

---

[136] Ibid.
[137] [1993] BCC 646.
[138] Ibid at 649.
[139] *Bairstow v Queen Moat Houses plc* [2000] 1 BCLC 549 at 561.
[140] [2001] EWCA Civ 712; [2001] 2 BCLC 531; [2002] BCC 91 at [58].
[141] [2004] EWHC 42 (Ch) at [14]; [2005] BCC 783 at 838.
[142] [2001] 2 BCLC 749 at 770.
[143] R Edmunds and J Lowry 'The Continuing Value of the Relief for Directors' Breach of Duty' (2003) 66 MLR 195 at 207.
[144] [2004] EWHC 42 (Ch) at [15]; [2005] BCC 783 at 837.
[145] Ibid at [16]; 838.
[146] [1940] 1 Ch 495.
[147] Ibid at 503.
[148] [2000] BCC 275.

has been pointed out,[149] the successful applicant for relief, the 19-year-old director, had not acted as a reasonable director would have acted, but the learned deputy judge believed that his position was such that he warranted some relief. But, as discussed in relation to honesty, in *Bairstow* Robert Walker LJ took issue with the notion that reasonableness should be assessed, for the most part, from a subjective standpoint.[150] In like manner HH Judge Reid QC (sitting as a High Court judge) in *Coleman Taymar Ltd v Oakes*[151] played down the relevance of subjective considerations. In the view of the judge a subjective approach must be limited to the honesty element. The learned judge said that 'I do not see how the reasonableness requirement can be a subjective requirement. Any reasonableness test must by its very nature be objective.'[152] This received the full agreement of Patten J in *Re MDA Investment Management Ltd.*[153] Thus while we do not have a really clear view it would appear that the stronger view is that a court cannot consider the concept of reasonableness in s 1157 from a subjective perspective.

17.61   Leaving aside the issue of subjectivity, we now consider what the cases have specifically said about directors acting reasonably. In *Re Duomatic Ltd*[154] Buckley J held that the director involved was not entitled to take advantage of the precursor of s 1157 as he had not acted reasonably. His Lordship said, in words reminiscent of the approach taken historically in dealing with breach of duty cases involving directors,[155] and borrowed from the field of trusts,[156] that the director had not been acting: 'in the way in which a man of affairs dealing with his own affairs with reasonable care and circumspection could reasonably be expected to act in such a case.'[157] Specifically, Buckley J was critical of the fact that the director did not seek any legal advice at all but elected to deal with the matter himself without a proper exploration of the considerations which contribute, or ought to contribute, to a decision as to what should be done on the company's behalf.[158]

17.62   In *Coleman Taymar Ltd v Oakes*[159] the learned judge was of the opinion that objectively the director did not act reasonably in going behind the back of his company to negotiate personal leases with his company's landlords for another company for whom he was going to work after leaving the first company.[160]

---

[149] R Edmunds and J Lowry 'The Continuing Value of the Relief for Directors' Breach of Duty' (2003) 66 MLR 195 at 208–209.
[150] [2001] EWCA Civ 712; [2001] 2 BCLC 531 at [58].
[151] [2001] 2 BCLC 749.
[152] Ibid at [85].
[153] [2004] EWHC 42 (Ch) at [17]; [2005] BCC 783 at 838.
[154] [1969] 2 Ch 365.
[155] For example, see *Re Brazilian Rubber Plantations and Estates Ltd* [1911] 1 Ch 425 at 436.
[156] See *Speight v Gaunt* (1883) 22 Ch D 1157 at 739.
[157] [1969] 2 Ch 365 at 377.
[158] Ibid.
[159] [2001] 2 BCLC 749.
[160] Ibid at [95].

17.63 In *Re DKG Contractors Ltd*[161] the judge said that the directors had not acted reasonably in that they failed to obtain, as they should have, some professional advice before trading in the way that they had, and they had not taken up what advice they were offered.[162] The judge decided not to relieve the directors of liability under s 1157.[163]

17.64 In the case of *Dorchester Finance Co Ltd v Stebbing*[164] the defendant directors signed blank cheques and left the making of loans to another director, the chairman, who was not supervised, and this permitted the subsequent misapplication of company funds. The defendants were held liable for breach of their duty of care and were unsuccessful in their application for relief.[165]

17.65 In *Bishopsgate Investment Management Ltd (in liq) v Maxwell*[166] the Court of Appeal indicated in dicta that the defendant director, who was found to have used his powers improperly, would not have been entitled to relief under s 1157, if he had claimed it, since in fact he made no inquiry into the actions of other directors. Consequently, the director had not acted reasonably.

17.66 It has been held that complete inactivity is unreasonable conduct within the terms of s 1157.[167]

17.67 In determining that the director in *Re D'Jan of London Ltd*[168] was entitled to relief on the basis that he had acted reasonably, although he was negligent, Hoffmann LJ was influenced significantly by the fact that the director owned 99 per cent of the company's issued shares and was entitled to take risks with what was essentially his own property. Of course, it could be said that shareholders do not own company property, and Hoffmann LJ did acknowledge that the company was a separate entity from the director/shareholder. But his Lordship felt that the courts should look at the economic realities when exercising discretion.[169] What is of concern is that his Lordship did not take note of the fact that the company was insolvent. One would think that in such a situation the interests of creditors and the financial position of the company generally would be relevant considerations. If the company were insolvent the shareholders are no longer the owners of the residual value of the firm (the residual owners being those whose wealth directly rises or falls with changes in the value of the company[170]). The creditors may be seen as the major

---

[161] [1990] BCC 903.
[162] Ibid at 912.
[163] Ibid at 913.
[164] [1989] BCLC 498.
[165] Ibid at 506.
[166] [1993] BCC 120 at 140.
[167] *Lexi Holdings plc (In Administration) v Luqman* [2007] EWHC 2652 (Ch) at [224].
[168] [1993] BCC 646.
[169] Ibid at 649.
[170] D Baird 'The initiation problem in bankruptcy' (1991) 11 *International Review of Law and Economics* 223 at 228–229; S Gilson and M Vetsuypens 'Credit Control in Financially Distressed Firms: Empirical Evidence' (1994) 72 *Washington University Law Quarterly* 1005 at 1006. This seems to be what was being said in *Brady v Brady* [1989] AC 755, [1988]

stakeholders in the company.[171] In such a case perhaps the court needs to effect a balance between the conduct of the director and the creditors' losses. More will be said about this issue under 'Fairness.'

17.68   While one can refer to examples of unreasonable conduct that takes a director outside of s 1157 there is general uncertainty concerning the meaning of reasonableness that is to be applied. One way of possibly solving this would be to require reasonableness in terms of the assessment of reasonable care at common law, but it would eliminate the relief as a possibility for any director who is in breach of the duty of care, something with which I think Hoffmann LJ was concerned in his judgment in *Re D'Jan*. To prevent directors liable for a breach of the duty of care might be seen as unfair now that there appears to be much more likelihood of more actions against directors for breach of that duty. Edmunds and Lowry raise the issue of whether it would be more appropriate to interpret reasonableness in relation to breaches of duty of care differently from breaches of other duties.[172]

17.69   The CLRSG recommended that s 1157's precursor should be amended in order to delete the requirement for the director's action to be reasonable.[173] This was not implemented, although it is interesting to note that the Australian equivalent, s 1318 of the Corporations Act 2001, which was based on the original English provision, and is framed in a very similar fashion, does not now mention acting reasonably.[174] Section 1318(1) provides:

> 'if, in any civil proceeding against a person to whom this section applies for negligence, default, breach of trust or breach of duty in a capacity as such a person, it appears to the court before which the proceedings are taken that the person is or may be liable in respect of the negligence, default or breach but that the person has acted honestly and that, having regard to all the circumstances of the case, including those connected with the person's appointment, the person ought fairly to be excused for the negligence, default or breach, the court may relieve the person either wholly or partly from liability on such terms as the court thinks fit.'

17.70   But, notwithstanding the omission of the reasonableness factor, Australian case-law indicates that whether a director should be relieved or not,

---

2 All ER 617, [1988] 2 WLR 1308, (1988) 4 BCC 390, [1988] BCLC 579, [1988] 2 FTLR 181, (1988) PCC 316, 132 SJ 820, HL, reversing (1987) 3 BCC 535, [1988] BCLC 20, [1987] 2 FTLR 414, (1987) 137 NLJ 898, (1977) PCC 434, C. Mr Leslie Kosmin QC (sitting as a Deputy Judge of the Chancery Division in *Guyer v London Wharf (Limehouse) Ltd* [2003] 2 BCLC 153; [2002] EWHC 2748 (Ch) specifically stated that creditors' interests should be paramount at the time of insolvency (at [74]).

[171]   *Kinsela v Russell Kinsela Pty Ltd* (1986) 4 ACLC 215 at 221; (1986) 10 ACLR 395 at 401.

[172]   The learned authors almost rejected the idea on the basis that would be too cumbersome from a practical aspect: 'The Continuing Value of the Relief for Directors' Breach of Duty' (2003) 66 MLR 195 at 210.

[173]   Company Law Review *Modern Company Law for a Competitive Economy: Developing the Framework* (London, DTI, 2000) at para 3.77.

[174]   The abolition of the acting reasonably criterion dates back to the Companies Code 1982 that was applied on a national basis in Australia.

consideration will be given as to whether his or her conduct could be regarded as reasonable or not.[175] The courts have talked about the reasonableness of contravening conduct.[176]

C Fairness

17.71 Section 1157 states that a judge is to consider 'all the circumstances of the case' in determining whether or not it is fair to excuse the director. This does not refer to the litigation but primarily to the circumstances in which the breach took place.[177]

17.72 According to HH Judge Reid QC in *Coleman Taymar Ltd v Oakes*[178] it had to be noted that it does not follow that simply because a director has acted honestly and reasonably the court is required to excuse him or her. Clearly establishing that a director has acted honestly and reasonably are pre-conditions for the court's jurisdiction, and if they are proven then the court must consider whether in all the circumstances the director ought fairly to be excused, and if he or she ought to be excused, the judge may relieve him or her either absolutely or partly on the terms the court thinks fit.[179] This obviously involves the court using its discretion. The basis on which the court is to exercise its discretion is fairness.[180] There appear to be no guidelines in s 1157 to inform the court's discretion, which is consistent with the counterpart provision under the Trustee Act 1925 (s 61). Olsson J in *Maelor Jones Investments (Noarlunga) Pty Ltd v Heywood-Smith*[181] observed that the authorities make it most clear that it is extremely difficult to attempt to formulate general principles because, of necessity, each case will very much depend on its own circumstances.[182] However, the case-law does shine some light on the matters that will be taken into account by judges. In the trusts field the courts have taken the view that courts should be reluctant to excuse the liability of paid trustees save where they have undertaken all reasonable actions to rectify the breach of trust.[183] Yet, save for community and charitable companies, directors will always be remunerated, so it is perhaps not surprising that there are no company cases that have made this point. It is submitted that

---

[175] *Commonwealth Bank v Friedrich* (1991) 5 ACSR 115 at 196; *Circle Petroleum (Qld) Pty Ltd v Greenslade* (1998) 16 ACLC 1577 at 1598; *Kenna & Brown Pty Ltd (in liq) v Kenna* (1999) 32 ACSR 430; (1999) 17 ACLC 1183.

[176] For example, see *ASIC v Vines* [2005] NSWSC 1349 at [34].

[177] *Ultraframe (UK) Ltd v Fielding* [2005] EWHC 1638 (Ch) at [1451]; *Re Paycheck Services 3 Ltd* [2008] EWHC 2200 (Ch); [2008] 2 BCLC 613 at [221].

[178] [2001] 2 BCLC 749 at 770.

[179] Ibid at [86].

[180] *National Trustees Co of Australasia v General Finance Co of Australasia* [1905] AC 373 at 381; *Re Westlowe Storage and Distribution Ltd (in liq)* [2000] BCC 851 at 871; *Bairstow v Queen Moat Houses plc* [2000] 1 BCLC 549 at 561 and *Bairstow v Queen Moat Houses plc* [2001] EWCA Civ 712; [2001] 2 BCLC 531 at 552 (CA); *Coleman Taymar Ltd v Oakes* [2001] 2 BCLC 749 at 770.

[181] (1989) 7 ACLC 1232.

[182] Ibid at 1251.

[183] *National Trustees Co of Australasia v General Finance Co of Australasia* [1905] AC 373 at 381.

the case-law indicates the fact that directors are paid does not necessarily mean that they will be unable to be considered for relief, but if they are able to rectify their breach, at least in some way, or demonstrated that they have made some attempt to do so, that might go in their favour in an application under s 1157.

17.73 What appears to be relevant to the court's decision is whether the director sought professional legal advice before doing that which constitutes a breach of duty,[184] an issue considered in Chapter 8. But seeking professional advice is not a panacea. It depends on from whom advice was sought, the advice given and what the director did in response to the advice given. In *Coleman Taymar* the director took legal advice but it was from a lawyer who did not realise that the director was in a conflict situation and the lawyer was not a company lawyer. All of this meant that the director could not rely on his advice and the court ended up refusing relief.[185] Furthermore, in *Re Loquitar Ltd, IRC v Richmond*[186] Etherton J (as he then was) denied relief even though the directors had taken advice from senior counsel because, inter alia, of their actual knowledge of the state of the company's affairs and that they were experienced businessmen.

17.74 It has been said that the fact that the director had obtained the approval of the board to do what he or she did that is sought to be impugned may go towards finding that the director ought to be excused.[187] It has also been said that courts should take into account the economic realities when exercising discretion.[188]

17.75 The seriousness of the director's breach will be taken into account.[189] According to Austin J this has three components, namely: 'the importance of the provision contravened, in terms of public policy; the degree of flagrancy of the contravention; and the consequences of the contravention in terms of harm to others'.[190] In *Re Barry and Staines Linoleum Ltd*,[191] Maugham J said that the applicant for relief should be relieved as the negligence was not of a very serious character.[192] In a similar facts situation in *Re Gilt Edge Safety Glass Ltd*[193] the judge granted relief as the breach of the legislation involved was a pure accident that the directors became disqualified as directors and therefore were liable; it was accepted that the directors had no idea that they

---

[184] For example, see *Re Gilt Edge Safety Glass Ltd* [1940] Ch 495; *Re Paycheck Services 3 Ltd* [2008] EWHC 2200 (Ch); [2008] 2 BCLC 613 at [223].

[185] *Coleman Taymar Ltd v Oakes* [2001] 2 BCLC 749 at [73].

[186] [2003] 2 BCLC 442.

[187] *Northampton Regional Livestock Centre Co Ltd v Cowling* [2014] EWHC 30 (QB) at [166].

[188] Ibid at [168]. This was something that Hoffmann LJ had also mentioned in *Re D'Jan of London Ltd* [1993] BCC 646 at 649. In fact Hoffmann LJ gave more weight to the issue than the judge in the former case.

[189] *ASIC v Vines* [2005] NSWSC 1349 at [52] per Austin J.

[190] Ibid.

[191] [1934] Ch 227.

[192] Ibid at 234.

[193] [1940] Ch 495.

had ceased to be directors. The directors' breach was a technical wrong only.[194] The court was also influenced by the fact that there was no loss and the director had relied on professional advice. In *Coleman Taymar*, the judge said that he was willing to give relief to the director in relation to any liability that related to his competing with his company after he had left the company but when he technically remained a director (at that time no one regarded him as still a director of the company), as that was merely a technical breach.[195] In *Claridge's Patent Asphalte Co*[196] relief was sought in relation to a claim based on the fact that the directors had engaged in activity that was ultra vires the company's constitution. Astbury J, who excused the directors, was clearly influenced by the fact that: the transaction, the subject of complaint by the liquidator/plaintiff, did little harm and was not grossly improper; the directors took the best advice; the directors acted in the way complained of openly and for no benefit to themselves, but for the benefit of their company; the breach was a mere technicality.[197] In one of the most recent cases to consider the provision, *Northampton Regional Livestock Centre Co Ltd v Cowling*,[198] Green J said: 'In the exercise of discretion under s 1157 it is necessary to measure the severity of the breach as found as against broader tenets of honesty and reasonableness. It follows that if the primary finding can be categorised as "egregious" or "gross" then it is less likely to be forgivable ....'[199]

17.76 The problem, when it comes to fairness, is that in most cases that are brought they are commenced by liquidators and the company is in insolvent liquidation. That means, obviously, that the general unsecured creditors, at least, will lose out to various degrees. His Honour Judge Seymour QC (sitting as a judge of the High Court) in *Re Marini Ltd*,[200] broached the issue and he said:[201]

> 'I have the greatest difficulty in seeing that it is ever likely that "in all the circumstances of the case" it is going to be right that a defaulting director "ought fairly to be excused for the negligence, default, breach of duty or breach of trust", if the consequence of so doing will be to leave the director, at the expense of creditors, in enjoyment of benefits which he would never have received but for the default. However honestly the director acted, however much it may have appeared at the time of the act complained of that the only person who might be harmed by the act would be the director himself, it just is not fair, as it seems to me, that if it all goes wrong the guilty director benefits and the innocent creditors suffer.'

17.77 A similar approach was invoked in *Queensway Systems Ltd v Walker*[202] by Paul Girolami QC (sitting as a deputy judge of the High Court). The deputy

[194] Ibid at 507.
[195] *Coleman Taymar Ltd v Oakes* [2001] 2 BCLC 749 at [100].
[196] [1921] 1 Ch 543.
[197] Ibid at 549.
[198] [2014] EWHC 30 (QB).
[199] Ibid at [160].
[200] [2003] EWHC 334 (Ch); [2004] BCC 172.
[201] Ibid at [57].
[202] [2006] EWHC 2496 (Ch); [2007] 2 BCLC 577.

judge denied relief to the defendant on the basis that if he gave relief then he would be relieving the defendant from having to pay an amount to the company, and this would prejudice the creditors as the company was in insolvent liquidation.[203] As I indicated earlier in this chapter, if a company's insolvency is going to be a major factor, then the ambit of s 1157 could be significantly circumscribed. It is submitted that the courts should be able to take into account a company's financial position and the fact that creditors will be the ones to lose out if the director is excused, as factors in their decision as to whether it is fair for the director to be relieved, but they cannot be regarded as trumping all other factors.

17.78 It is likely that if a director has benefitted from the breach he or she will not have the discretion exercised in his or her favour. But in *Re Paycheck Services 3 Ltd*,[204] Mark Cawson QC (sitting as a deputy judge of the High Court) considered that the court does retain a discretion to relieve when the director has not directly benefited from the breach itself.[205]

17.79 Finally on this topic, we might be able to say, in accordance with the recommendation of the Greene Committee in 1926,[206] that the court, in exercising its power to grant relief, should have regard, not only to the conduct that led to liability, but also to certain matters that may justify the conduct of directors.

IX APPREHENDED LIABILITY

17.80 Section 1157(2) of the CA 2006 provides that a director is entitled to apply to the court for relief, if he or she has reason to apprehend that a claim will or might be made against him or her. What does the provision cover?

17.81 The courts in both *Re Tollemache*[207] and *Re Rosenthal*,[208] cases dealing with the equivalent provision under the trust legislation, rejected the notion that relief could be given for a future breach of trust by a trustee, but they were cases which were decided on legislation which did not contain any equivalent to what is found in s 1157(2).

17.82 In *Re Barry and Staines Linoleum Ltd*,[209] a case dealing with a director and in relation to the 1929 Companies Act,[210] Maugham J said that the provision equivalent to s 1157(2) says nothing about the parties who ought to be present when an application for relief under the subsection is made, or about

---

[203] Ibid at [70].

[204] [2008] EWHC 2200 (Ch); [2008] 2 BCLC 613 at [224].

[205] In the appeal against the deputy judge's decision Rimer LJ seemed to agree, *Re Paycheck Services 3 Ltd* [2009] 2 BCLC 309 at [81]–[85].

[206] Report of the Company Law Amendment Committee (1925-26) (Cmd 2657) at para 46, p 20.

[207] [1903] 1 Ch 457 at 465–466.

[208] [1972] 1 WLR 1273 at 1278.

[209] [1934] Ch 227.

[210] The relevant provision was s 372(2).

the circumstances in which a court may relieve an officer of a company from liability to the company. The judge said that if there is jurisdiction it ought to be exercised with great care.[211] Also, his Lordship added[212] a particular requirement to exercising the discretion in that:

'It does not seem to me that the Court ought to be willing to exercise its jurisdiction under sub-s 2, without clear evidence as to the opinions held on the subject by the persons concerned. If, for example, a director by reason of an incautious vote has made himself liable to pay moneys to a company by reason of a contract entered into it would not be right for the Court to render proceedings by the company or its liquidator abortive without information as to the views of the creditors [if insolvent] or shareholders [if solvent].'

17.83 In this case the director had unknowingly breached s 141 of the Companies Act 1929 that required him to hold a certain number of shares as a director. He sought relief from the penalty for his breach. Relief was granted. What was more contentious was whether the director was entitled to relief in relation to any liability incurred for the period during which he acted as a director although he had in fact ceased to be a *de jure* director because he did not have sufficient qualification shares. No relief was given in this regard as the judge was concerned that the shareholders were not represented before him. In the case of *Re Gilt Edge Safety Glass Ltd*[213] there was a similar facts situation to *Re Barry and Staines Linoleum Ltd*. Crossman J granted relief, but, unlike *Re Barry and Staines Linoleum Ltd*, in this case the shareholders were represented at the hearing. The shareholders did in fact oppose the relief but Crossman J said that their view was only one of the circumstances to be considered by the court.

17.84 The provision covers the situation where a director has breached a duty and he or she either does not know whether proceedings are to be issued against him or her or the director knows that proceedings will be issued, but wants to get in first. The court has the same power to relieve as if an actual claim had been brought.[214] But does the provision extend further and permit a director to seek relief for a future breach of duty? In both *Re Gilt Edge Safety Glass Ltd* and *Re Barry and Staines Linoleum Ltd* the action that might lead to liability had actually occurred and come to an end as the directors had obtained the necessary shares, so the cases do not address the issue which has just been raised. If Maugham J in *Re Barry and Staines Linoleum Ltd* is correct and those affected by any relief granted must be represented before the judge, then it is highly unlikely that relief could be granted as one would not know who should actually be in attendance in court. As it would be future liability one is not sure who would be affected by the relief.

---

[211] [1934] Ch 227 at 233.
[212] Ibid at 234.
[213] [1940] Ch 495.
[214] *Deputy Comr of Taxation v Dick* [2007] NSWCA 190 at [84].

17.85 Section 1318(2) of the Australian Corporations Act 2001 is in virtually identical language to s 1157(2) of the CA 2006. There has been some consideration in Australia as to whether a more 'expansive' use of s 1318(2) is permitted. In *Edwards v Attorney-General*,[215] it was concluded by the New South Wales Court of Appeal that courts have no jurisdiction to grant relief unless there has been a past or continuing breach, even though one member of the bench, Young CJ, expressed regret at coming to this conclusion and not being able to permit relief for future breaches.[216] It follows, therefore, that if there has been no breach at all but merely an anticipated breach, then no application can be heard.[217] In a more recent case, in *Deputy Comr of Taxation v Dick*[218] a differently constituted bench of the New South Wales Court of Appeal touched on the issue, and while some of its members wanted to be more proactive in interpreting the provision, the Court held it was regrettable, but it could not extend forgiveness to future breaches.[219]

17.86 There is one case in the United Kingdom where a court has granted relief in respect of any potential allegation of breach. This is the decision of Harman J in *Re Home Treat Ltd*.[220] In this case a company went into administration. It had been carrying on the business of running nursing homes, an activity which was held to be ultra vires the company. The administrator sought protection under s 1157. The administrator made it clear that he wanted not only protection for any breach relating to the past running of a business that was ultra vires, but also wished for relief in relation to any future breach because he wished to continue to run the business so that he could sell the business as a going concern. Interestingly, it appears that no party seemed to argue about jurisdiction to excuse future conduct. Harman J granted the sought-after protection, holding that administrators were officers for the purposes of the Companies Act.[221] His Lordship said that the administrator should be given a direction validating his conduct of the affairs of the company.[222] In this case Harman J was obviously influenced by the fact that there was an informal alteration of the memorandum to which all members of the company consented before the business was commenced,[223] and the breach might be thought to be a technical one.

17.87 While *Re Home Treat Ltd* concerned an administrator, that should not make any difference as the section only talks about officers of the company, a term within which directors fall, as we established earlier. Directors are simply those officers who have sought relief more often than others. However,

---

[215] [2004] NSWCA 272; (2004) 60 NSWLR 667.
[216] Ibid at [76]–[77].
[217] Ibid at [132]–[133].
[218] [2007] NSWCA 190 at [35].
[219] The discussion on this point was merely obiter as the essence of the case was whether s 1318 of the Corporations Act 2001 could apply to any breaches of the Income Tax Assessment Act 1936 (Cth).
[220] [1991] BCC 165; [1991] BCLC 705.
[221] His Lordship relied on the liquidation case of *Re X Co Ltd* [1907] 2 Ch 92.
[222] [1991] BCC 965 at 170; [1991] BCLC 705 at 711.
[223] Ibid.

according to the case-law, the relief most often sought by directors relates to a breach of duty which might be perceived as more serious than the breach of the ultra vires rule or the breaches in both *Re Gilt Edge Safety Glass Ltd* and *Re Barry and Staines Linoleum Ltd*.

X CONCLUSION

17.88 In commenting on s 1157's precursor Edmunds and Lowry asserted that the overlap of the terms used in the provision, together with 'judicial elision'[224] of the terms, led to the provision being regarded as 'arcane'.[225] Yet it would seem fair that directors ought to have the chance of convincing a court that they should be relieved from liability. In fact the provision itself was introduced so that it produces something of a balance in relation to the liability of directors in that it mitigate the harshness of the application of the rules on directors' duties. It might be said that the provision should continue to meet that need, especially given the more strict application of directors' duties, particularly the duty of care. The existence of a relief provision for cases where directors have only technically breached duties or where they are the real 'owners' of the company, might seem appropriate.[226] The big problem is where a company is insolvent. How does one balance the loss to creditors and the action of the director? Clearly, it can only be determined on a case-by-case basis. Section 1157 has been infrequently applied by judges, and where the company is insolvent it is likely that the provision will be applied even less frequently, meaning that the giving of relief to a director will be rare to very rare.

17.89 There are not a huge number of reported cases dealing with the provision and many which do, do so in passing with little of substance to say on the matter. Nevertheless, the retention and application of the provision has been secured by its inclusion in the new companies legislation.

---

[224] 'The Continuing Value of the Relief for Directors' Breach of Duty' (2003) 66 MLR 195 at 197.
[225] Ibid.
[226] For example, ibid at 222.

INDEX

References are to paragraph numbers.